OBJECTIVE BIOTECHNOLOGY

OBJECTIVE BIOTECHNOLOGY

B.K. PRASAD
Asstt. Prof.
Deptt. of Genetics & Plant Breeding
A.S. (P.G.) College, Lakhaoti
Bulandshahr-245407 (U.P.)

B.D. SINGH
Rector
Banaras Hindu University
Varanasi-221005 (U.P.)

SANJEEV KUMAR
Scientist
Division of Crop Improvement and Biotechnology
Indian Institute of Vegetable Research
Varanasi-221305 (U.P.)

LUDHIANA • NEW DELHI • NOIDA (U.P.) • HYDERABAD • CHENNAI
KOLKATA • CUTTACK • GUWAHATI • COCHIN • BANGALORE

KALYANI PUBLISHERS

Head Office

B-1/1292, Rajinder Nagar, **Ludhiana**-141 008

Administration Office

4779/23, Ansari Road, Daryaganj
New Delhi-110 002

Works

B-16, Sector-8, NOIDA (U.P.)

Branches

1, Mahalakshmi Street, T. Nagar, **Chennai**-600 017 • Ph : 044-24344684
110/111, Bharatia Towers, Badambadi, **Cuttack**-753 009 (Orissa) • Ph : 0671-2311391
3-5-1108, Narayanaguda, **Hyderabad**-500 029 • Ph : 040-24750368
10/2B, Ramanath Mazumdar Street, **Kolkata**-700 009 • Ph : 033-22416024
Koratti Parambil House, Convent Road, **Cochin**-682035 • Ph : 0484-2367189
Arunalaya, 1st Floor, Saraswati Road, Pan Bazar, **Guwahati**-781 001 • Ph : 0361-2731274
No. 24 & 25, 1st Floor, Hameed Shah Complex, Cubbonpet Main Road, **Bangalore**-560 002

KP-P-J-14612 1

Reprinted, 2014

978-81-272-6937-1

PRINTED IN INDIA

At B.B. Press, A-37, Sector-67, NOIDA-201301
and published by Mrs. Usha Raj Kumar for
Kalyani Publishers, New Delhi-110 002

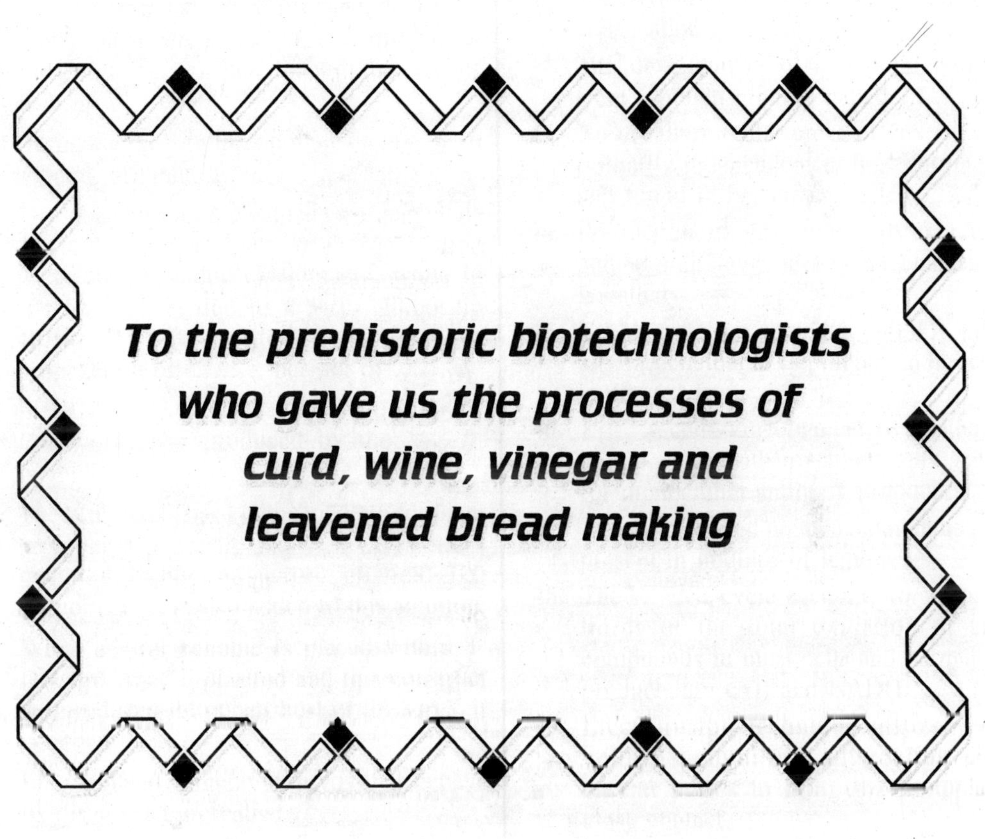

To the prehistoric biotechnologists who gave us the processes of curd, wine, vinegar and leavened bread making

PREFACE

A variety of developments during the last quarter of twentieth century have drastically changed our view of the living world. Emergence of biotechnology as a provider of novel products and services for human welfare is perhaps the most important development of this period, and biotechnology is regarded by many as the would be dominant field of activity during twenty first century.

India has been making determined efforts to promote research and development activities in biotechnology. It has also sponsored programmes to develop trained manpower with a view to support R&D efforts in this extremely promising area. Biotechnology become the subject of choice for students of biology, and postgraduate and undergraduate programmes have been launched by a majority of Indian universities.

One of us (BDS) had earlier developed two text books, 'Biotechnology' and 'Biotechnolgy : Expanding Horizons', which have been well patronized by the teachers and the students of this fast developing subject. We have also written two other books, 'Objective Plant Breeding' and 'Objective Genetics' which have also found favour with the readers. We now offer 'Objective Biotechnology' on the pattern of the earlier two books with a view to help students prepare for objective tests in the subjects.

We do recognise that many of the areas covered in this book are outside the area of our expertise. As a result, the extent and level of coverage of different areas may be markedly uneven, and even some errors may have been committed. We shall greatly appreciate every suggestion from readers.

One of us (BKP) highly appreciates the support from Dr. Bhoopal Singh (Principal), Dr. K.D. Verma, Dr. Shrikant and Dr. R.K. Singh of A.S. (P.G.) College, Lakhaoti for their suggestions and healthy discussions during the development of this book.

One of the authors (B.K. Prasad) expresses his gratitude to his wife Kiran Singh, daughter Khushi, son Ayush, niece Kavita and nephew Balvant for constant encouragement, affection and moral support during the successful completion of this project.

The second author (B.D. Singh) wishes to record his appreciation for the affectionate encouragement from his wife and sons, who have always shown immense understanding during such demanding projects.

We acknowledge the unqualified support from M/s. Kalyani Publishers, particularly, Sri S.P. Anand and his production team at New Delhi.

2011
Varanasi

B.K. PRASAD
B.D. SINGH
SANJEEV KUMAR

CONTENTS

SECTION I

DEFINITIONS

DEFINITIONS

A living modified organism. An organism whose genetic material has been modified by recombinant DNA technology.

Abiotic elicitor. An elicitor that is not of biological origin, *e.g.*, UV light, salts of heavy metals, etc.

Abscisic acid. A plant growth hormone involved in abscission; it induces seed/shoot bud dormancy; in plant tissue culture, it promotes somatic embryo (S.E.) maturation and makes SEs desiccation tolerant.

Absorption spectrum. A graph depicting the ability of a substance to absorb lights of various wavelengths.

Abzyme. An antibody with enzymatic action; it is produced in response to stable analog of the transition state of the substrate for the given enzyme action.

Acetosyringone. A phenolic compound produced by dicot plant cells at wound sites; acts as signal molecule for the expression of *vir* regulon of *Agrobacterium tumefaciens.*

Acid. Any compound that releases hydrogen ions when dissolved in water.

Acid break. In case of fermentation, a rapid conversion of acids into acetone and butanol leading to a fast decline in the acidity.

Acid-base and redox catalysis. A mode of enzyme action; electron transfer generally involves transition metals or coenzymes present as a component of such enzymes.

Acid precipitation. It includes acid rain, acid fog, acid snow and any other form of precipitation that is more acidic (less than pH 5.6) than normal. Excess acidity is derived from certain air pollutants, namely, sulphur dioxide and oxides of nitrogen.

Acoustic wave biosensor. These devices detect a change in the mass of the biological component of the biosensor.

Acquired immunity. It is initiated by the recognition of a foreign antigen, and leads to the production of a variety of cells and molecules, including antibodies, capable of specifically recognizing and selectively eliminating the foreign organism and macromolecule.

Acquired immunodeficiency. See, *Secondary immunodeficiency.*

Acquision of totipotency. Formation of proembryogenic cell masses in cultured cells/ tissues, usually in response to a high auxin concentration. Syn., *Induction of somatic embryo.*

Action spectrum. A graph relating the degree of physiological response caused by different wavelengths of light.

Activated sludge. The sediment from biologically treated sewage; it contains the microbes for anaerobic digestion of sewage.

Activated sludge process. It uses large aerated vessels for oxidation of liquid waste, which continuously flows into the vessels and treated water flows out of them at a predetermined rate to obtain optimal digestion of the dissolved organic matter.

Activation energy. The free energy needed to elevate a molecule from its stable ground state to the unstable transition state.

Activator. A protein that binds a specific sequence of an operon/a gene and thereby enables transcription initiation of that operon/gene.

Active immunity. The immunized individual produces antibodies against the concerned pathogen.

Active transport. Transport of solutes across a cellular membrane by mechanisms that use up metabolic energy; can lead to transport against an electrochemical potential gradient.

Adaptors. In recombinant DNA technology; short chemically synthesized DNA double-strands, which already have one or both sticky ends; used to join two DNA molecules having different cohesive ends; used in conjunction with other adaptors or linkers.

Adjuncts. Starch rich materials like wheat, rice, maize etc. that are added to barley malt during beer production.

Adjuvant. A non-antigenic preparation known to stimulate immune response.

Adsorption. Molecules adhere to the surface of carrier matrix due to a combination of hydrophobic effects and the formation of several salt links per molecule.

Adsorption chromatography. Separation of molecules due to their differential adsorption onto the solid matrix surface.

Adventitious shoot bud. A shoot bud that develops from a location other than leaf axil or shoot tip.

Adventive embryo. In case of polyembryony; embryo arising from any somatic cell of the ovule.

Aerobic fermentation. It requires an efficient air supply, usually by sparging and stirring; two types: stirred-tank and air-lift type.

Aerosols. Refers to microscopic liquid and solid particles originating from land and water surfaces and carried into the atmosphere.

Affinity biosensor. The biological material simply binds to the analyte molecules that leads to a change in its mass.

Affinity chromatography. Molecule separation based on their affinity to effector molecules immobilized on the matrix.

Affinity electrophoresis. It follows the principle as immuno-electrophoresis; but affinity electrophoresis employs interactions between various macromolecules, *e.g.*, lectin-glycoprotein, enzyme-substrate, and enzyme-inhibitor interactions, in the place of antigen-antibody interaction.

Agar. Polysaccharide derived from sea weed and used for gelling of medium.

Agarose. A polysaccharide obtained from red seaweed; dissolved in hot water.

Agarose gel. This gel prepared from agarose, has large pores and is used for analysis of molecules of over 10 nm diameter.

Agricultural biotechnology. Use of microorganisms, cells of animals and plants and their cellular components for stabilizing and/or enhancing agricultural production and/or produce quality. It consists of plant biotechnology and animal biotechnology.

Agrobacterium rhizogenes. A Gram-negative soil bacterium that produces hairy-root disease of plants due to its Ri (root inducing) plasmid; the natural genetic engineer.

Agrobacterium tumefaciens. A Gram-negative soil bacterium that produces crown gall in dicots by transferring the T-DNA of its Ti (tumour inducing) plasmid; the natural genetic engineer.

***Agrobacterium*-mediated gene transfer.** Transformation of plant cells using *Agrobacterium* as a vehicle; T-DNA (including the gene constructs) transferred into plant cells and integrated into plant genome.

Agroinfection. Introduction of a viral genome into plant cells using *Agrobacterium*; usually, a tandem dimer of viral genome is placed within the T-DNA of *Agrobacterium.*

Air pollution disaster. A short-term situation in industrial cities in which intense industrial smog brings about a significant increase in human mortality.

Air toxics. Refers to the category of air pollutants that includes radioactive materials and other toxic chemicals, which are present at low concentrations but are of concern because they often are carcinogenic.

Algal bloom. Sudden heavy growth of algae; generally occurs due to addition of nutrients, whose scarcity is normally limiting.

Alkaline. A substance that releases hydroxyl ions or uses up hydrogen ions.

Allele. Alternative form of the same gene; alleles are located at the same position in the homologous chromosomes.

Allele-specific ligation. Two short synthetic oligonucleotides that base-pair adjacent to each other on a DNA fragment, and are ligated by DNA ligase. If one of the alleles contains a mutation overlapped by the 3′-end of one oligonucleotide, ligation with the other oligonucleotide will be prevented.

Allele-specific PCR (AS-PCR). Amplification of specific alleles of a locus by designing one or both PCR primers so that they partially overlap the site of sequence difference between the amplified alleles; thus sequence information of the locus of interest is essential.

Allelic exclusion. A productive rearrangement in one allele of the gene encoding a light/heavy chain of an antibody, prevents the occurrence of productive rearrangement in its second allele.

Allograft. Graft obtained from genetically different individuals of the same species.

Allohaploid. A haploid obtained from an allopolyploid.

Alloplasmic line. A line having nucleus from one species and cytoplasm from a different species.

Alternate pathway. Of complement system; it is initiated by various cell surface constituents that are foreign to the host, *e.g.*, certain cell wall constituents of both Gram-negative and Gram-positive bacteria; a component of innate immunity.

Alternative splicing. Splicing of a single pre-mRNA transcript in two or more different ways but in well defined patterns; in each pattern, a defined set of exons is joined together to yield a functional (mature) RNA molecule.

Ambients standards. It is a air-quality standard, set by the Environmental Protection Agency (EPA) delimits cetain levels of pollutants that should not be exceeded in order to maintain environmental and human health.

Amniocentesis. Withdrawal of amniotic fluid with the help of a hypodermic syringe.

Amniotic Fluid. The fluid surrounding developing human embryo.

Amperometric biosensor. It measures the transfer of electrons to O_2 (present in analyte solution) or some other compound (present in the biosensor) due to redox reactions.

Amplicon. The DNA sequence/fragment that is amplified by PCR.

Amplification. An increase in the number of copies of a DNA segment, *e.g.*, during PCR.

Amplification refractive mutation system (ARMS) PCR. This PCR was devised to achieved sequence-specific amplification.

Amplified fragment length polymorphism (AFLP). The genomic DNA is digested with two restriction enzymes; the cut ends of the fragments are modified by ligating them with adaptors of 10-20 bp to make them blunt-ended. These fragments are now amplified using two AFLP primers, each of which has upto 3 additional selectional nucleotides at its 3′-end. The amplified products are resolved by denaturing polyacrylamide gel electrophoresis, and an AFLP marker is detected as a differential mobility of an amplified DNA fragment.

Amplified genomic library. Refers to the library which consists of recombinant phage lysates or bacterial clones of a genomic library.

Amplified ribosomal DNA restriction analysis (ARDRA). The amplification product of the gene encoding the 16S ribosomal RNA is subjected to restriction digestion to study the restriction fragment length polymorphism; this analysis is important for the bacterial identification/taxonomy.

Anabolism. Formation of macromolecules from smaller molecules; requires an input of energy.

Anaerobic digestor. A vessel or device used for anaerobic digestion of organic matter.

Anaerobic fermentation. Fermentation in the absence of O_2, *e.g.,* alcohol fermentation.

Anaerobic reactor. See, *Anaerobic digestor.*

Analyte. A compound, which is to be detected or assayed in a given sample.

Analytical breeding. In this strategy, dihaploids are isolated from autotetraploids, and breeding work is carried out at the dihaploid level; the chromosome number of the selected dihaploid lines is then doubled to obtain normal tetraploid lines.

Anatomic barriers. In case of innate immunity; these barriers include skin and surfaces of mucous membranes; they together prevent the entry of most micro-organisms.

Anchorage dependence. In all non-transformed cell cultures of animals, a cell must be attached to the substrate to be able to divide.

Anchored PCR. When sequence of only one end of a DNA segment is known, the primer specific to the known 3′-end is used to obtain copies of this strand; an oligo-G tail is then added at the 3′-ends of the single-strand copies, and oligo-

C is used as primer to obtain double-strand copies.

Anchored simple sequence repeats (ASSR). See, *SSR anchored PCR (SSR-A PCR).*

Androgenesis. Production of haploid plants from sperms (inside ovules) or pollen grain, (anther/pollen culture); ordinarily by anther/pollen culture.

Androgenic embryo. See, *Pollen embryo.*

Androgenic grains. Pollen grains, which exhibit androgenesis; believed to be s-grains.

Androgenic haploid. Haploid obtained from the activity of male gamete.

Anaerobic respiration. Respiration which occurs in the organisms in the absence of oxygen.

Aneuploid. A cell/an individual having chromosome number (complement) that is not exact multiple of the genome of the species.

Aneusomaty. Presence of aneuploid and euploid cells in the same tissue, especially *in vivo.*

Animal biotechnology. Use of animal cells, tissues, organs or their components to generate useful products or services; examples, monoclonal antibodies, cell culture-derived vaccines, transgenic animals, etc.

Animal cell culture. Culture of dispersed animal cells either as monolayer or as suspension of cells.

Animal cloning. The process of producing a group of complete normal animals from somatic cells of an adult animal; somatic cell is fused with eunucleate fertilized egg and the egg is implanted in the uterus of surrogate mother.

Animal organ culture. Whole embryogenic organs or small tissue fragments are cultured *in vitro* in such a manner that they retain their natural tissue architecture.

Animal testing. Procedures used to assess the toxicity of chemical substances using rats, mice and guinea pigs as surrogates for humans.

Animal tissue culture. Culture of aseptically isolated whole organs, tissue fragments as well as dispersed cells of animals in a suitable nutrient medium under controlled environments.

Annealing. See, *Renaturation;* pairing of a primer with the complementary sequence in a DNA molecule.

Annotation. In bioinformatics; identification of genes, including those that code for ribosomal RNA, tRNA and small nuclear RNAs, and their regulatory sequences, from genome sequence data.

Anonymous molecular marker. A cloned DNA fragment whose function or specific features are not known.

Anther. In androecium, the terminal portion of a stamen; produces and contains pollen grains (in pollen sacs).

Anther culture. *In vitro* culture of anthers/isolated pollen grains to obtain haploid plants (or callus).

Anther wall factors. Biochemicals/nutrients provided by anther wall to the developing pollen embryos during androgenesis; replaced by a mixture of glutamine, serine and *m*-inositol in *Datura*, and by only glutamine in tobacco.

Anthropogenic. Arising out of human actions.

Antiauxin. A compound that interferes with auxin action, *e.g.*, TIBA, $CoCl_2$, $AgNO_3$, PO_4^{3-}.

Antibiotic. A chemical produced by a microorganism, and capable of destroying or inhibiting the growth of other microorganisms; two types: biostatic and biocidal.

Anti-antibody. *See* Anti-immunoglobin.

Antibody. A special class of protein called immunoglobulin (Ig); produced in response to an antigen and specifically binds to the inducing antigen; consists of two identical light chains and two identical heavy chains held together by disulphide bridges.

Antibody engineering. Refers to the use of recombinant DNA technology to modify or design antibodies.

Antibody microarray. It consists of spots of different antibodies and is used to measure the abundance of thousands of different proteins in the samples.

Antibody producing effector cells. See, *Plasma cells.*

Anticaking agents. Substances which check powders such as milk powder from caking and sticking.

Antifoaming agents. Substances which reduce or prevent foaming in foods/fermenters.

Antigen. A molecule, which specifically interacts with an antibody.

Antigen presentation. The antigenic peptides bind within the cleft of MHC I (Major histocompatibility complex I) or MHC II molecules and are displayed on the surface of antigen processing cells (APCs).

Antigen presenting cells (APCs). These cells have on their surfaces class II MHC molecules, which bind to antigen-derived peptides and present them to a group of lymphocytes, which are then activated to mount the immune response.

Antigen processing. A foreign antigen is degraded into short peptides of 8 18 amino acids by antigen processing cells.

Antigen-antibody interaction. Highly specific binding of an antibody to an antigen epitope, which induced its production.

Antigen-binding domain. In antibodies, the area that binds to the antigen-epitope.

Antigenic determinant. See, *Epitope.*

Antigenic specificity. Ability of antibodies to differentiate between antigen molecules differing by a single amino acid.

Antigenically committed. The mature B cell is said to be antigenically committed since it is predetermined in its ability to recognize and respond to a specific antigen.

Antigenicity. Ability of an antigen to interact with an antibody, which is specific to it.

Anti-immunoglobulin. An antibody specific to another antibody; binds to the constant region of all antibodies of the class.

Antioxidants. Compounds that protect biological systems against potentially harmful effects of such reactions that can cause excessive oxidation.

Antisense gene construct. A gene construct in which the gene is located in antisense orientation so that the natural sense strand of the gene is now transcribed to produce antisense RNA; used in antisense RNA technology.

Antisense orientation. Reverse orientation of a gene in relation to its promoter; the promoter is now located at the 5′-end of the antisense strand so that the natural sense strand is now transcribed.

Antisense RNA. RNA produced by transcription of the sense strand; usually, in case of antisense gene constructs; complementary to antisense strand of the gene and to mRNA; pairs with mRNA.

Antisense RNA technology. An antisense construct of the target gene is integrated into the genome to suppress the concerned endogenous genes.

Antisense strand. The strand of a native gene, which is used by RNA polymerase as template to generate its complementary copy of RNA; this RNA ultimately functions as messenger RNA; the promoter sequence is, as a rule, located at the 3′-end of the antisense strand.

Apoenzyme. The protein component of an enzyme that has a coenzyme/cofactor.

Apoptosis. See, *Programmed cell death.*

Aqueous biphasic (two-phase) system. Both phases are aqueous, but they contain different polymers, which do not mix together.

Aqueous-organic biphasic (two-phase) systems. In these systems, the enzyme molecules are suspended in the organic solvent, while the second phase is aqueous, and is constituted by a thin layer of water surrounding each enzyme molecule.

Arabinogalactan protein (AGP). A group of glucoproteins; induce somatic embryogenesis in otherwise non-embryogenic cells, *e.g.*, of carrot (cultured *in vitro*).

ARS vector. A yeast vector having *ARS* (autonomously replicating sequence) module; it is quickly lost if selection pressure is absent.

Article 53(a). Article 53(a) of the European Patent Convention (EPC) excludes from patent protection such inventions that are contrary to the public order of morality.

Article 53(b). Article 53(b) of the European patent convention excludes from patent protection (1) plant and animal varieties and (2) essential biological processes for the production of plants and animals.

Artificial chromosome. A circular or linear vector that is stably maintained in, usually 1 to 2 copies per cell; several types; bacterial artificial chromosome (BAC), P1-derived artificial chromosome (PAC), yeast artificial chromosome (YAC), human artificial chromosome (MAC).

Artificial enzymes. See, *Synzymes.*

Artificial medium. *In plant tissue culture*; a chemically defined medium, having inorganic salts, vitamins, sucrose, agar and the required growth regulators. *In animal cell and tissue culture;* medium having various organic and inorganic nutrients; may or may not contain serum, etc.

Artificial seed. A somatic embryo/shoot bud encapsulated in a suitable gel (*e.g.,* calcium alginate) to ultimately recover whole plants; the gel contains necessary nutrients and growth regulators.

Asbestos fibres. These are crystals of asbestos, a natural mineral, that have the form of minute strands; asbestos is a serious health hazard in indoor spaces.

Aseptic. Free from contamination by microorganisms.

Assay culture. Microbial culture used for the assay of biological activities of microbial products.

Assimilation. Transformation of food into protoplasm.

Asthama. It is chronic disease of the respiratory system in which the air passages tighten and constrict, causing breathing difficulties; accute attacks may be life threatening.

Asymmetric gap LCR (AG-LCR). LCR using reverse transcriptase; specific for detection of RNA.

Asymmetric PCR. The two PCR primers are used in a 100 : 1 ratio so that one primer is finished ~10 cycles before the other; yields predominately single-strand copies that can be used for DNA sequencing.

Asymmetric somatic hybrid. A somatic hybrid that contains full chromosome complement of one fusion parent plus one or few chromosomes from the other fusion parent.

ATP. Adenosine triphosphate; a high energy organic phosphate that also participates in energy transfer in cellular reactions.

ATP synthase. A group of polypeptides that converts ADP and inorganic phosphate (Pi) to ATP and H_2O.

Attenuation. A drastic reduction in the virulence of a pathogen, usually due to a treatment like passage through a non-host animal/cultured cells, etc.; in case of most viral vaccines.

Augmentation gene therapy. The genetically modified cells contain both the defective (endogenous) as well as the functional (introduced) copies of the gene.

Autoantibodies. Antibodies specific to the antigens present in the cells and tissues of the animals that produce the antibodies in auto-immune diseases.

Autoantigens. Antigens present in the cells and tissues of the animal under reference.

Autoclavable. A substance, which does not deteriorate or undergo alteration due to autoclaving.

Autoclaving. Sterilization using moist heat at 15 psi (1.06 kg/cm^2) and 121°C for 5-40 min.; the duration of autoclaving depends on the nature of liquid and its volume; efficiency of sterilization depends on temperature and not directly on pressure.

Autograft. Graft obtained from the body of the recipient itself.

Autoimmune disease. A condition in which an animal produces antibodies against its own antigens.

Autoimmunity. See, *Autoimmune disease.*

Autonomously replicating sequence (ARS). In yeast chromosome; about 100 bp sequence serving as origin of DNA replication.

Autoradiography. Imaging a radioactive component onto an X-ray film; used to locate the presence of radioactive component within a tissue, cell or organelle.

Autotrophic phase of embryo development. In *ovulo*; embryo capable of synthesizing all the biochemicals it needs; the specific developmental stage varies with the species, *e.g.,* in *Capsella* late heart stage and later stages.

Auxin. In nature, IAA; promotes cell elongation, tropism, apical dominance, rooting, etc.; in tissue culture, natural and synthetic auxins used for inducing cell division, callus formation, root regeneration and somatic embryo induction.

Auxotrophic mutant. A mutant requiring a biochemical for its normal growth and development since it can not synthesize this biochemical due to mutation in a gene.

Avidity. The avidity of interaction of a ligand with its receptor is a function of density of the ligand × receptor density × affinity of the receptor for the ligand.

Avidity model. According to this model, a low avidity interaction between TCR of double positive (CD_4^+ CD_8^+) T-cells and antigen peptide-MHC complex/MHC molecule leads to positive selection; in contrast, negative selection is the consequence if this interaction is of a high avidity.

Axillary bud. Shoot buds present in leaf axil; generally, in dormant stage (due to apical dominance); proliferation induced, usually, by a cytokinin.

Azoospermia. A lack of motile sperms in the semen.

B cells. These are antibody producing lymphocytes; they differentiate into plasma cells and memory cells; mature within bone marrow.

B lymphocytes. See, *B cells.*

Back-bulb. In sympodial orchids; an old pseudobulb (often without leaves); alive and bears one or more buds behind the actively growing portion.

Back-bulb propagation. Procedure, which involves separation of the oldest pseudobulbil to force the development of its dormant bud.

Background selection. Selection for recurrent parent genotype in a backcross programme; also used in a pedigree selection scheme to ensure the recovery of a specified level of genome from the desired parent.

Bacteria. They are unicellular, prokaryotic organisms, which have no chlorophyll 'a' and, generally, reproduce by binary fission.

Bacterial artificial chromosome (BAC). It contains the origin of replication (*oriS*) of *E. coli. F* factor for a strict copy number control; low copy number helps in maintenance of DNA inserts without any change due to recombination; used for cloning of upto 300 kb DNA inserts.

Bacterial lawn. A continuous bacterial growth on an agar plate.

Bacteriophage. A virus, which attacks bacteria; most phages lyse the bacterial cells.

Bacteriostatic agent. An agent that has biostatic effect on bacteria.

Bacterization. Inoculation of plantlets with a suitable bacterial culture.

Bait. In yeast two-hybrid (Y2H) system, a protein (say, protein X) expressed as a fusion (a hybrid) protein with the DNA-binding domain of a transcription factor; used to find a protein that interacts with X.

Ballistic method. See, *Particle gun method.*

Barley malt. Barley seeds germinated at 17°C to a specific stage and dried at 65°C and, usually, powdered.

***barnase*.** A gene isolated from *Bacillus amyloliquefaciens* that encodes an RNase, which is cytotoxic to the cell expressing it; used to produce male sterility that is restored by *barstar.*

***barstar*.** A gene isolated from *Bacillus amyloliquefaciens* that encodes a specific inhibitor of *barnase* RNase; used for fertility restoration in *barnase* male sterile plants.

Basal medium. A growth regulator-free medium, *i.e.*, a medium containing inorganic salts, vitamins, sucrose and agar (where needed).

Base. Any compound that releases hydroxyl ions when dissolved in water.

Base collection. In conservation of germplasm, seeds containing 5±1 per cent moisture and stored at −18°C to −20°C for long periods of time; they are disturbed only for the purpose of regeneration.

Basic chromosome number. Gametic chromosome number of a diploid species or of the parental diploid species in case of a polyploid species.

Basic local alignment search tool (BLAST). A family of user-friendly sequence similarity search tools, designed to identify potential homologues for a given sequence; analyzes both nucleotide and protein sequences.

Batch bioreactor. In such a bioreactor, the medium and inoculum are loaded into the reactor in the beginning, and the cells are allowed to grow; there is no addition/replacement of medium, and the entire cell mass is harvested at the end of incubation period.

Batch culture. See, *Batch bioreactor*; growth in such cultures shows a typical sigmoid curve, and they require subculture/termination after a specific period of time.

Batch digestors. These are suited for digestion of solid wastes, where hydrolysis occurs in a solid bed, and the leachate is circulated through a methanogenic digestor and back over the solid waste bed.

Batch reactor. See, *Batch bioreactor*.

B-DNA. See, *DNA*.

Bead bed reactor. In animal cell culture; column packed with 3–5 mm glass beads, in which cells attach to the bead, surface, and medium is pumped up or down the column.

Beer. Undistilled beverage from barley malt fermented by yeast.

Beer wort. Filtered mash in beer making.

Behavioral resistance. The ability of an insect population to change its behaviour in order to avoid insecticides or other injurious factors.

Benign tumour. A tumour that is incapable of indefinite growth and invasion of healthy surrounding tissues.

Bergmann's cell plating technique. Cells are suspended in melted agar medium and spread in a 1 mm thick layer, usually in a Petri plate.

Bicellular pollen. See, *Binucleate pollen*.

Bifunctional enzyme. An enzyme, which can catalyze two reactions, encoded by a recombinant gene.

Binary vector. A Ti plasmid vector pair comprising one mini–Ti or micro-Ti (has T-DNA, but no *vir* region) and one helper Ti (has *vir* region but no T-DNA); both the vectors must be present in the same *Agrobacterium tumefaciens* cell.

Binucleate pollen. A pollen having two nuclei produced by the first pollen mitosis; most suitable stage for anther culture.

Bioaccumulation. See, *Biomagnification*.

Bioaugmentation. Inoculation with a suitable population of microbes having the necessary degradative capabilities for bioremediation.

Biobutanol. Butanol produced by microorganisms from biomass.

Biocatalyst. See, *Enzyme*.

Biochemical oxygen demand (BOD). Amount of O_2 used up after 120±1 hr incubation of 1 litre water at 20°C in complete dark.

Biochemical pesticides. These are naturally occurring substances that control pest by nontoxic means. These pesticides include natural insect growth regulators, *e.g.*, neem insecticide and insect pheromones that disrupt mating and reduce reproductive rates.

Biocidal agents. Agents that kill the susceptible microorganisms.

Biocontrol. See, *Biological control*.

Biocontrol agents. Microorganisms, *e.g.*, viruses, bacteria, fungi and protozoa employed for the control of insect pests, pathogens or weeds.

Bioconversion. See, *Biotransformation*.

Biodegradable. Any substance that is consumed/broken down by an organism.

Biodiesel. Diesel obtained from conversion of hydrocarbons accumulated by certain plants.

Biodiversity. See, *Biological diversity*.

Bioethanol. Ethanol produced from biomass by microorganisms.

Bioethics. The set of standards that may be used to regulate various activities based on their effect on the biological world.

Biofertilizer. Pollution-free, ecofriendly, less expensive microbial inoculant, which reduces the requirement of chemical nitrogen and/or phosphate fertilizer for realising optimum yield; it also improves soil structures, texture and cation exchange capacity and increases water holding capacity of soil.

Biofilm. In sewage water treatment; the layer of microorganisms present on filter particles.

Biofilter. A device to remove/breakdown/convert hazardous gases using biological agents maintained either in a solid support or immobilized on a membrane.

Biofortification. It is a method of breeding crops to increase their nutritional value; it can be achieved through conventional selective breeding or through genetic engineering.

Biofortified food. Refers to the food, obtained from those crop plants which have been developed through biofortification.

Biofuel. A fuel produced by using biological agents; usually, derived from biomass or a component of the biomass.

Biogas. A mixture of gases (mainly CH_4 and CO_2) produced by anaerobic digestion of organic matter by many bacteria.

Bioherbicides. Biological agents, mainly fungi and insects, used for control of weeds.

Biohydrogen. H_2 produced by biological agents.

Bioinformatics. Application of computer hardware and software for the analysis of large volumes of biological data sets; it consists of development of databases to store data, search- tools to find the desired data from databases, and statistical tools and algorithms to analyse and determine relationships between biological data sets, such as macromolecular sequences, structures, expression profiles and biochemical pathways.

Bioinsecticides. Use of biocontrol agents or their byproducts including plant extracts to control insect pests.

Biolistic method. See, *Particle gun.*

Biological agents. See, *Biocontrol agents.*

Biological containment. These strategies specially aim at making such genetic changes in genetically modified organisms that reduce the hazard from these organisms when they are accidently released into the environment or are accidently transported by the workers.

Biological containment for plants. In case of plants, biological containment procedures aim at minimizing the risk of dispersal of pollen and seeds of the plants, and of dissemination and establishment of plant-associated micro-organisms and insects.

Biological control. Use of biological agents to control insect pests, pathogens, or weeds.

Biological diversity. Biological diversity called biodiversity in short, refers to the diversity present among all living organisms found in natural world; this concept includes diversity among species, ecosystems and genetic diversity within a given species.

Biological indicators. Organisms, whose relative abundance/absence in river water serves as a good indicator of the level of pollution.

Biological information. Refers to the information present in the genome of an organism.

Biological invasion. When exotic species introduced in new areas and native species are subject to competition for food and space and the exotic species eliminate the native species.

Biological nutrient removal. A process employed in sewage treatment to remove nitrogen and phosphorous from the effluent coming from secondary treatment.

Biological oxygen demand. See, *Biochemical oxygen demand.*

Biological resistance. Ability of an insect population to develop enzymes that detoxify an insecticide or other injurious material before it can reach its site of action.

Biological treatment. See, *Secondary treatment of waste water.*

Biological wealth. The life sustaining combination of commercial, scientific and aesthethic values imparted to a region by its biota.

Biomagnification Progressive increase in the concentration of a lipid soluble xenobiotic compound as it passes through the food chain.

Biomass. It is the total cellular dry weight or organic material produced by an organism.

Biomass energy. Energy produced by burning plant related materials such as fire wood.

Biomethane. Methane produced by biological agents.

Biopesticides. Pesticides derived from animals, plants, microorganisms (viral particles, bacterial cells, fungal spores and their metabolites) and certain minerals, *e.g.*, canola oils and baking soda. EPA grouped biopesticides into three categories: microbial pesticides, botanical pesticides and biochemical pesticides.

Biopharmaceuticals. Biotechnology products having pharmaceutical applications.

Bipolar germination. In most angiosperms; development of roots and shoots from different poles of the embryo.

Bioreactor. Culture vessels of 1-1000 l or even larger; have facilities for aeration, stirring, contamination control, addition of fresh medium, removal of spent medium (with or without cells), and control of pH, temperature, etc.; used for large scale culture of the cell suspensions.

Bioremediation. Use of organisms, such as bacteria, fungi and plants, to reduce or eliminate toxic pollutants from contaminated sites by degradation, assimilation or transpiration in the atmosphere.

Biosensor. An analytical device based on a biological material that specifically interacts with the analyte and, ultimately, determines the analyte concentration.

Biosource. A patented technology that permits a rapid and effective elucidation of functions of unknown gene/DNA sequences.

Biosphere reserves. Natural areas set aside to protect genetic biodiversity.

Biostatic agents. They inhibit growth and multiplication of susceptible microorganisms.

Biota. The sum total of all living organisms of a region.

Biotechnology. It is the controlled use of various biological agents, such as microorganisms, animal/plant cells or cellular components like enzymes, toxins or processes to generate-products or services for human welfare.

Biotic elicitor. An elicitor of biological origin; usually, a component of cell wall, *e.g.*, pectin, pectic acid, chitin, chitosan.

Biotransformation. Modification of exogenous compounds by plant cells or other organisms into a more useful/valuable product by esterification, oxidation, hydroxylation and glycosylation; highly regio- and sterio-specific.

Biphase liquid system. It consists of two immiscible liquids in which the enzyme is able to function and remains fairly stable; two types: aqueous two-phase systems and aqueous-organic two-phase systems.

Biphasic (two phase) systems. See, *Biphase liquid system.*

Bispecific monoclonal antibody. A hybrid antibody specific for two different epitopes; usually, each epitope belong to a different antigen.

BLASTn. This programme is used to compare a nucleotide sequence with a nucleotide sequence database.

BLASTp. It compares the submitted protein sequence against a protein database.

BLASTx. This programme translates the submitted nucleotide sequence into amino acid sequence and compares the latter with a protein database.

Blotting. Transfer of nucleic acid (DNA/RNA) fragments or proteins from a gel onto a suitable solid support, *e.g.* nitrocellulose, nylon membrane, etc.

Blunt ends. When a restriction enzyme cuts both the strands of a DNA molecule at the same point, it produce blunt ends.

Bonus trait. When progeny from a somatic hybrid possess some novel feature not present in their fusion parents; such a feature is called bonus trait.

Botanical insecticides. An insecticides produced from a plant or plant product, *e.g.*, pyrethrum.

Breeder's exemption. Under plant breeder rights (PBR) regime; the use of a protected variety (the initial variety) for the development of new varieties is exempted from protection.

Broth. In fermentation; the medium containing both products and microorganism biomass.

Bud Pollination. Pollination of flower buds a couple of days before anthesis, before the stigmas are fully receptive; used to overcome both gametophytic and sporophytic self-incompatibility.

***Bulbosum* technique.** Production of haploids of wheat or barley by crossing them with *Hordeum bulbosum* ($2n = 4x = 28$); chromosomes of *H. bulbosum* are eliminated during embryo development, and embryo rescue is required specifically for haploid production.

Bulked segregant analysis (BSA). In this method, two bulked DNA samples are drawn from a segregating population originating from a single cross. Each bulk contains DNAs from individuals that are identical for a particular trait but arbitrary at all unliked regions. The bulks are screened for DNA polymorphisms; a marker that differs between the two bulks is expected to be linked to the particular trait for which the bulks were created.

Bulking agents. Substances like strach that are added in the food to increase the quantity of a food without affecting its nutritional value.

Button mushroom. Fruiting body of *Agaricus bisporus* grown on decomposed horse manure, etc.

Caliclone. A variant regenerated from a callus culture; *not in common use.*

Callus. Unorganised mass of cells produced on an agar medium containing an auxin (usually, 2, 4-D) and (in many cases) a cytokinin.

Cancer. Malignant tumours that can invade healthy tissues by a process called metastasis.

Cancer cells. Altered self-cells that do not need to normal growth regulating mechanisms; as a result, they continue to divide and produce a tumour and have the ability for metastasis.

Candied fruit. Fruit impregnated with sugar, drained and dried; it is not sticky, is plump, tender and exceedingly sweet with flavour.

Canning. Process of preserving food by the application of heat high enough for destroying essentially all microorganism present together with sealing the food in air-tight sterilized cans.

Cap site. In eukaryotes, the site of transcription initiation; represents the 5′-end of mRNA at which 5′ cap is added.

Capillary blotting. In this approach, gel is placed on top of a buffer-saturated filter paper, the blotting membrane is placed on top of the gel, and dry filter papers are placed on top of the membrane. The buffer moves from the bottom filter paper through the gel carrying macro-molecules alongwith it; the latter get trapped onto the blotting membrane.

Capillary electrophoresis. In this case, separation by electrophoresis is achieved in 20-30 cm long capillaries of fused silica having internal diameter of 50-100 μm.

Carbon source. Compound used by cells/tissues as the source of energy as well as carbon for their metabolic needs; usually, sucrose (2-5%).

Carcinogenic. Anything which has property of causing cancer at least in animals and, by implication, in humans.

Carrier DNA. In genetic transformation; unrelated DNA added to the solution of DNA used for transformation; enhances transformation frequency, rearrangements and multicopy integration.

Carrier matrix. Materials used for immobilization of cells/enzymes; usually inert polymers or inorganic materials.

Cartagena protocol. An international agreement governing trade in genetically modified organisms. This protocol was signed in January, 2000.

Casamino acids. See, *Casein hydrolysate.*

Casein hydrolysate. Hydrolysis products of milk protein; provides 20 amino acids.

Casing. Covering of mushroom mycelial growth with a 1.5-2 cm thick layer of sterilized mixture of sand and soil; essential for fruiting bodies to be produced.

Catabolism. Degradation of macromolecules to small molecules; often releases energy.

Catalysis by approximation. The substrate bound to an enzyme molecule is held close to another chemical group in the optimal orientation for the reaction to proceed.

Catalytic biosensor. Biological component of such a biosensor catalyzes the coversion of analyte into a new compound; this reaction produces a change in temperature, pH, etc.

Catalytic converter. A device used by U.S. automobile manufacturers to reduce the amount of CO and hydrocarbons in a car's exhaust. Converter contains a catalyst that oxidizes these compounds to CO_2 and water as they pass through the exhaust.

Caulogenesis. Regeneration of shoot buds from cells/tissues cultured *in vitro;* generally, cytokinins induce caulogenesis.

cDNA. It is the copy DNA or complementary DNA produced by using RNA (usually mRNA) as tempelate; produced by reverse transcriptase enzyme.

cDNA library. It is a preparation of bacterial transformants or phage lysates in which each mRNA isolated from an organism or tissue is represented as its cDNA insertion in a plasmid/ cosmid or a phage vector.

cDNA of satellite RNA-mediated virus resistance. cDNA copies of such a satellite RNA that reduces disease severity of an RNA virus is transferred into plants; expression of the satellite sequences reduces disease symptoms as well as virus accumulation.

Cell culture. *In vitro* culture of single or relatively small groups of cells, *e.g.,* suspension cultures; this term is often used for callus culture as well.

Cell density. Number of cells per unit volume; usually, expressed as cells/ml.

Cell doubling time. See, *Cell generation time.*

Cell generation time. The period, during which cell number in a culture becomes double of the initial number.

Cell line. In animal cell culture; when a primary culture is subcultured it becomes a cell line.

Cell selection. A suitable selection pressure exerted through selection agents, *e.g.,* toxins, antibiotics, herbicides, salts, etc., applied to cells cultured *in vitro;* this permits a preferential survival/ growth of the variant cells so that finally selection of cells having the desirable trait is achieved.

Cell synchronization. Induction of synchronous cell division in cell cultures; achieved through starvation (of a nutrient or a growth regulator; cells arrested in G_1/G_2, inhibition of DNA synthesis (by 5-aminouracil FUdR etc.), etc.

Cell-mediated immume response. It is based on cytotoxic T-cells, which are a type of lymphocyte.

Cellular oncogenes (*c-onc*). See, *Protooncogenes.*

Cellulase. A mixture of enzyme activities isolated, usually, from *Trichoderma viride;* digests cellulose component of the plant cell wall; generally, used in combination with pectinase to produce plant protoplasts.

Cellulose. Primary constituent of plant cell walls; composed of glucose subunits.

Cellulose acetate electrophoresis. Cellulose acetate membranes having large pores are used for separation of molecules entirely on the basis of their charge density; resolution and limit of detection is low.

CentiMorgan (cM). It is the distance, which allows 1% recombination between the concerned genes.

Central lymphoid organs. See, *Primary lymphoid organs.*

Character. An observable/estimable, *e.g.,* morphological, anatomical, biochemical, physiological or behavioural, etc. feature of an organism.

Chemical control of organ differentiation. Hypothesis due to Skoog and Miller (1957): organ differentiation depends on the relative (not absolute) concentrations of auxins and cytokinins; a high auxin to cytokinin ratio favours root regeneration, while the opposite promotes shoot regeneration; in fact, the exogenous need for the two GRs depends on their endogenous levels in the species/tissue.

Chemical energy. The potential energy that is contained in chemicals; most importantly, the energy contained in organic compounds, such as food and fuels, that may be released through respiration or burning.

Chemical oxygen demand (COD). Amount of oxygen required for chemical oxidation of the organic matter present in a water sample; provides an estimate of the total oxidizable organic matter.

Chemically defined medium. See, *Artificial medium.*

Chemoautotrophs. Organisms that derive their energy needs from oxidation of simple inorganic compounds and use CO_2 as carbon source.

Chemostat. An open continuous culture system in which a chosen nutrient is kept at such a concentration that it is depleted very rapidly to become growth limiting, while other nutrients are still in concentrations higher than required. Therefore, any addition of the growth limiting nutrient is reflected in cell growth.

Chemosynthesis. Process in which micro-organisms utilize the chemical energy contained in certain reduced inorganic molecule to produce organic materials.

Chemotherapy. Chemical treatment to eradicate viruses from plant cells/tissues; chemicals used : virazole, (ribavirin), actinomycin D, cycloheximide, etc.

Chlorinated hydrocarbons. These are synthetic organic molecules in which one or more hydrogen atoms have been replaced by chlorine atoms. These hydrocarbons are hazardous compounds because they tend to be non-biodegradable and therefore to bioaccumulate; many have been shown to be carcinogenic.

Chlorination. A disinfection process, in which chlorine is added to drinking water or sewage water to kill pathogenic microorganisms.

Chlorofluorocarbons (CFCs). Synthetic organic molecules that contain one or more of both chlorine and fluorine atoms and that are known to cause ozone destruction.

Chlorophyll. The green pigment in plants responsible for absorbing the light energy required for photosynthesis.

Chloroplast. Plastids containing chlorophyll; enclosed by two concentric membranes and contain typical stroma and grana organisation; contains DNA which contributes to cytoplasmic inheritance.

Chromosomal virulence genes. In *Agrobacterium;* chromosomal genes involved in infection; most of these genes are concerned with polysaccharide biosynthesis.

Chromosome jumping. Use of jumping and linking libraries to determine the correct order in a chromosome of the DNA fragments generated by the restriction enzyme used to prepared these libraries.

Chimaeric gene. A gene, which contains coding sequence from one organism and regulatory sequence from another organism; all prokaryotic genes expressed in eukaryotes have to be chimaeric, and *vice-versa.*

Chromosome walking. Use of restriction maps to identify overlapping DNA fragments in a small region of a chromosome.

Cisgenic plants. Refer to plants which have foreign gene(s) belong to the same species/a related species; risk of transfer of genes through pollen will not be a big issue in this case.

Classical pathway (of complement activation). Complement activation begins with soluble antigen-antibody complex (immune complex) formation or binding of antibody to an antigen present on a cell. IgM and certain subclasses of IgG activate the classical pathway.

Cleavage and differentiation stage (of embryo development). In morphogenetic terms, a zygote progresses through morphologically distinct stages of development, *viz.,* globular, heart, torpedo and finally differentiated cotyledonary stages; this is termed as cleavage and differentiation stage of embyro development.

Cleaved amplified polymorphic sequence (CAPS). Partial DNA sequence information for the locus of interest is used to create a set of PCR primers that are used to amplify the genome segment of interest. The amplification product is digested with the selected restriction enzyme, and digest is subjected to gel electrophoresis to detect polymorphism in the lengths of fragments so generated.

Clonal anergy. When extrathymic T-cells encounter antigens presented by such cells that lack the costimulatory molecules, they become nonresponsive; T-cell self-tolerance can also arise from clonal anergy.

Clonal deletion. B cells marked by negative selection die by apoptosis.

Clonal propagation. Multiplication of plants via asexual reproduction, *e.g.,* via micro-propagation, vegetative propagation, etc.

Clonal selection. Phenomenon of selective proliferation of lymphocytes, *e.g.,* B-cells, in response to their interaction with an antigen.

Clone. Progeny obtained from asexual reproduction of a single individual or cell.

Clone-by-clone sequencing. In this method, the fragments are first aligned into contigs, and each clone of the contig is then sequenced.

Cloning. *In biotechnology;* a technique of construction and introduction of recombinant DNA into a suitable host to, primarily, produce multiple copies of the recombinant DNA. *In plant breeding;* the process of obtaining/producing a group of cells or individuals (clone) from a single cell/individual through asexual reproduction.

Cloning vector. Vector used for propagation of DNA inserts in a suitable host.

Closed continuous culture. In this approach, a definite volume of culture is withdrawn regularly, cells are separated from the used medium and are added back to the culture so that cell biomass keeps on increasing.

CO_2 fertilization effect. The response of plants to elevated concentrations of CO_2.

CO_2 fixation. The enzymatic reaction in which CO_2 is attached to a receiver compound, such as ribulose-1,5-bisphosphate, thereby adding to the supply of organic carbon; occurs chiefly during photosynthesis.

Coat protein-mediated virus resistance. Transgenic plants expressing the coat protein gene of a virus exhibit resistance to the concerned and related viruses; resistance presumbly arises due to the inability of the viral genome to replicate and express.

Coconut milk. Liquid endosperm from immature nuts (before cellular endosperm formation has begun); boiled (to denature the proteins and enzymes), filtered and stored at –20°C.

Cocultivation. See, *Coculture.*

Coculture. Culture of plant cells/tissues of different species or even of different organisms (*e.g.*, plant cell with bacteria) together in the same culture vessel.

Coculture with *Agrobacterium*. Culture of plant cells/tissues with *Agrobacterium* cells, usually, to achieve genetic transformation.

Codominance. Both the alleles of a gene express themselves in heterozygotes.

Codon. A group of three bases of mRNA specifying an amino acid.

Codon bias. Preference for certain codons over the others from among the multiple codons specifying the same amino acid; each organism exhibits a different pattern of codon preference.

Coenzyme. In case of enzymes; a specialized molecule that mediates electron transfer during redox catalysis.

Cofactor. In case of enzymes; a transition metal that mediates electron transfer during redox catalysis.

Cohesive ends. See, *Sticky ends.*

Co-integrate Ti vector. A vector obtained by integration of an intermediate vector (IV) into the T-DNA region of a disarmed Ti plasmid; integration by homologous recombination; IV contains the DNA fragment/gene to be transferred into plants.

Col plasmids. These plasmids encode colicins, which are proteins that kill sensitive *E. coli* cells; they also carry genes that provide immunity to the particular colicins.

Colchicine. An alkaloid obtained from bulbs of autumn crocus (*Colchicum autumnale*); used for chromosome doubling as it prevents spindle formation.

Cold pre-treatment of anthers. Exposure of anthers to 5-9°C (tobacco) or 13-15°C (rice) for 3-14 days before culturing them at 22-25°C; enhances the frequency of androgenesis.

Colony hybridization. Colonies from a master plates are either lifted or replica-plated onto a nitrocellulose filter, cells are lysed, DNA is denatured and hybridized with radioactive probe to detect the colonies having DNA/RNA sequences complementary to the probe.

Colorimetric biosensor. It measures the heat released or absorbed during the reaction catalyzed by the biological component of the biosensor.

Colour retention agents. Agents that are used to preserve a food's existing colour.

Combustion. The practice of disposing of wastes by incineration in a special facility designed to handle large amounts of waste; modern combustion facilities also utilize some of the energy by generating electricity on the site.

Cometabolism. Degradation of xenobiotics depends on the presence and metabolism of a substrate.

Cometabolite. The substrate, which induces the enzymes necessary for degradation of a xenobiotic, and serves as a source of energy, carbon and reducing power.

Comparative genomics. Study of differences and similarities in genome structure and organization of different organisms.

Compatible trait transgenics. Those transgenics, which reduce the use of non-sustainable inputs without polluting the environment.

Competence for regeneration. Ability of plant cells to regenerate plants via shoot or somatic embryo regeneration; *same as totipotency.*

Competence for transformation. Ability of a cell to take up DNA and express the transgene.

Competent cell. A cell having the capacity to receive foreign DNA easily.

Complement. Initially, it was defined as "the activity of blood serum that completes the action of antibody"; it consists of over 30 soluble and cell bound proteins and glycoproteins that interact in a highly regulated cascade, following the initial activation and carry out a number of basic functions.

Complement system. See, *Complement.*

Complementary base pairing. The formation of hydrogen bonds between adenine and thymine, and between guanine and cytosine is known as complementary base pairing.

Complementary DNA. See, *cDNA*.

Complementary strand. In case of nucleic acids; a polynucleotide strand that has complementary bases at every position of another polynucleotide strand.

Complete digestion (of DNA). Complete digestion of DNA signifies that the restriction enzyme has cut the DNA at every recognition site for that enzyme present in the DNA.

Complex medium. In fermentation; it contain undefined constituents like soybean meal, molasses, cornsteep liquors, etc. and gives much higher yields of metabolites.

Complex organic additive. A nutritive mixture of undefined composition, *e.g.*, yeast extract, coconut milk, malt extract, tomato juice, etc.

Complex probes. The labelled mRNA used as probe; represents the total mRNA produced by the cell.

Compound. Any substance that is made up of two or more different kinds of atoms bonded together.

Composting. The process of letting organic wastes decompose in the presence of air; a nutrient-rich compost is the resulting product.

Computer. It is device that can accept data, perform certain functions on that data and present the results of those operations with accuracy.

Concatemer. End-to-end joined two or more molecules, *e.g.*, λ vector/DNA molecules used for transformation.

Conditioned medium. In case of plant tissue culture; a cell-free medium in which cells/tissues had been grown for some time; permits culture of cells at a much lower density than in fresh medium. In case of animal tissue culture; a medium in which homologous cells were grown for a period of time.

Conjugated enzyme. An enzyme made up of a protein part (apoenzyme) and a non-protein part.

Conjugative plasmid. Conjugative plasmids mediate DNA transfer through conjugation; as a result, they spread rapidly among the bacterial cells of a population, *e.g.*, F plasmids, many R plasmids and some Col. plasmids.

Consensus sequence. A base sequence occurring in majority of the DNA segments serving the same function.

Consequence analysis (in recombinant DNA research). Assessment of the consequences of GMOs producing adverse effects on the environment, including human health.

Conserved sequence. A base sequence present without any change in all DNA sequences having the same function.

Constant region. In case of antibodies; the non-variant regions of heavy and light chains; designated as C_H and C_L, respectively; C_H region determines the antibody class.

Constitutive genes. See, *House-keeping genes*

Constitutive promoter. A promoter, which does not require any specific stimulus for activity; always active in all cell types.

Contained use. Any operation undertaken within a facility, installation or other physical structure, which effectively limit the contact with and the impact on the external environment.

Containment. A combination of laboratory procedures, laboratory equipments and installations, and host-vector systems designed to minimize accidental release of organisms during laboratory operations, their dissemination and survival in the environment, and accidental infection of laboratory workers and of persons outside the laboratory; includes two types "physical and biological".

Contamination. Growth of an unwanted organism in a culture; chiefly due to fungi and bacteria.

Contig. A series of clones that contain overlapping pieces of DNA covering a specific region of chromosome or even the entire chromosome; *usually, constructed using YAC and cosmid clones.*

Continuous bioreactor. There is continuous inflow of fresh medium into the reactor, and outflow of used medium (with or without cells) during the entire incubation period; cell density can be maintained at a predetermined level; continuous source of biomass or inoculum.

Continuous cell line. In animal cell culture; a cell line that can be maintained indefinitely.

Continuous culture. In such a culture, the cell population is maintained in a steady state by regularly replacing a portion of the used medium by fresh medium. Such culture systems are of either closed or open type.

Continuous flow reactor. Substrate solution is continuously pumped into reactor, while product is continuously withdrawn; based on immobilized enzymes.

Continuous flow stirred tank digesters. These digesters are continuously fed as well as stirred to achieve a very high mixing; the spent substrate is also continuously removed; they are suited to treat medium to high strength (2-10% soilds) wastes; these are the most common type of digesters used for sewage and animal excreta treatment.

Continuous flow stirred tank reactor. Based on immobilized enzymes; substrate solution is continuously pumped in and product removed, and reaction mixture is continuously mixed by stirring.

Continuous free-flow zone electrophoresis. In this electrophoresis, a continuous stream of buffer flows perpendicular to the electrical field between two cooled glass plates kept 0.5 to 1.0 mm apart; it separates even such particles that have minimal differences in the surface charge; it separates even cells.

Continuous reactor. See, *Continuous bioreactor.*

Control of endophytic contamination. In this case, surface sterilization is ineffective; a suitable systemic fungicide and/or an antibiotic is usually added to the culture medium; preferably, explants are taken from green-house grown plants.

Convention on Trade in Endangered Species (CITES). An international treaty conveying some protection to endangered and threatened species by restricting trade in these species or their products.

Conventional crop variety. A crop variety whose genetic makeup is not modified by genetic engineering.

Conventional harvest. Economic yield harvested from a non-transgenic variety.

Conventional vaccine. A vaccine consisting of whole pathogenic organism, which may either be killed or attenuated.

Conversion adaptor. It is used to join a DNA fragment or insert cut with one restriction enzyme, say *Eco*RI, with a vector opened with another enzyme, *e.g.*, *Bam*HI.

Conversion of somatic embryo. Germination of an SE to yield a normal seedling.

Conservation. Refers to the management of a resource in such a way as to assure that it will continue to provide maximum benefit to humans in the long run; it includes various degrees of use or protection, depending on what is necessary to maintain the resource over a long period.

Co-operative death. Variant cells surrounded by non-growing/dying wild type cells exposed to a selection agent also die alongwith the latter mainly due to the cellular wastes liberated by the dying wild type cells.

Copicing. Production of young shoots, especially, after the main shoot has been cut off; the young shoots are juvenile.

Copy DNA. See, *cDNA.*

Copyright. It is a tool protecting the original literary works, *i.e.*, books, novels, lyrics, songs and computer software (programmes).

Corepressor. A low molecular weight compound that interacts with the inactive form of a regulator protein (the repressor) and makes it active, which then binds to operator to prevent transcription of a repressible operon.

Corn meal medium. It is prepared by grinding degermed (de-embryonated) corn to fine powder, and 8-10% of this corn meal is heated to gelatinize the starch.

Correct PCR product. At the second cycle of PCR, primers will anneal to the long product, *i.e.,* amplification product of first cycle much before its 3′-end where sequences complementary to them are located. Primer extension step in this cycle will produce a amplification product that will be much shorter than the long product; this is correct PCR product.

Correct reading frame. It is the longest frame uninterrupted by a stop codon; also called, *open reading frame.*

***cos* site.** The lambda genome is linear in the phage head, but within *E. coli* cells, its two cohesive ends anneal to form a circular molecule; the sealed cohesive ends form the *cos* site, which is the site of cleavage during packaging of the phage DNA into phage heads.

Cosmid. Essentially a plasmid vector containing a 250 bp of lambda phage DNA, which includes the *cos* and terminase binding and cleavage sites.

Cosuppression of gene. An over-expression of the sense RNA or mRNA of a gene leads to a drastic reduction in the level of expression of the concerned gene.

Co-transfection. The tendency of two different gene constructs that are mixed and used for transfection/transformation to be integrated together at the same site.

Cotyledonary stage of embryo. Distinct cotyledons are observable and the embryo continues to grow in size till it enters the maturation phase.

Covalent catalysis. The chemical groups, *e.g.,* amino groups, in the side chains of amino acids present in the active site of the enzyme become covalently bound to a group in the substrate molecule; another substrate may then react with the substrate bound to the enzyme to form the product.

CpG islands. Short stretches of CpG rich DNA often found associated with vertebrate genes.

Cre/lox system. This system is based on site-specific recombinase gene *Cre,* and the specific 34 bp sequence/site in DNA, called *loxP*, that is recognised by Cre recombinase; a DNA sequences flanked by *loxP* site is deleted due to recombination induced by Cre recombinase.

Critical level. In case of pollution, the level of one or more pollutants above which severe damage begins to occur and below which few, if any, ill-effects are noted.

Criteria pollutants. Certain pollutants whose levels are used as a gauge for the determination of air (or water) quality.

Crop characteristic modification strategies. These strategies are based on diverse group of techniques that change the floral biology or survival characteristics of the transgenic varieties in such a way that pollen transmission and, in some cases, volunteer survival is eliminated.

Cross contamination. Especially in animal cell cultures; presence of cells from other cell lines of the same species, or from some other species.

Cross-feeding. Cells of one species (or genotype) provide the biochemicals needed by cells of another species (or genotype); in coculture or feeder layer technique.

Cross reaction. In immunology; interaction of an antibody induced by one antigen with another antigen due to a similarity in their epitopes.

Crossing over. Exchange of homologous segments between homologous chromosomes.

Cross-protection. See, *Virus cross-protection.*

Cryobiology. The branch of science, which deals with preservation of cells, tissues, etc. in frozen state in liquid nitrogen.

Cryogenic injuries. Injuries to cells due to the procedure of cryopreservation; chiefly during freezing and, also, during thawing; may be physical (due to ice crystal formation, which may rupture cell organelles or even cells) or chemical (due to toxic solution effect and/or loss of vital solutes from cells through leakage during freezing/thawing).

Cryo-injuries. See, *Cryogenic injuries.*

Cryopreservation. See, *Freeze preservation.*

Cryoprotectant. A chemical added to the freezing mixture to protect cells/tissues from cryogenic injuries; usually, dissolved in the culture medium, *e.g.*, DMSO (5-8%), proline (10%), glycerol, etc.

Cryotherapy. Prolonged exposure (4 months or more) of plants to a low temperature (*e.g.*, 5°C), followed by shoot-tip culture for virus elimination; superior to thermotherapy.

Crystal protein. An insecticidal protein present as a crystalline inclusion in *Bacillus thuringiensis* spores; 17 distinct groups of 130 or 70 kDa proteins.

CTAB method. When CTAB (cetyltrimethyl-ammonium bromide) is added to the cell extracts, it forms an insoluble complex with nucleic acids, this precipitate is recovered through centrifugation and resuspended in 1 M NaCl; carbohydrates, proteins, etc., are discarded with supernatant. The nucleic acid solution is treated with RNase, and DNA is concentrated by ethanol precipitation.

Cultivar. Refers to the cultivated variety of a plant species. Genetically, all individuals of a cultivar are uniform.

Culture initiation. It consists of surface sterilization of explants and establishing them *in vitro.*

Culture medium. The medium on which cells, tissues and organs are cultured; contains inorganic salts, vitamins, a carbon source and growth regulators as per need.

Culture room. A room with controlled environment, *e.g.*, regulated temperature, light, etc., and used for culture of cells/tissues/organs/organisms.

Cutinization. Impregnation of cell wall with cutin; cutinization of the outer-most cell wall is essential for somatic embryo development.

Cybrid. A hybrid cell/individual derived from the fusion of a cytoplast from one parent and protoplast of the other parent; contains nucleus from one parent but cytoplasm from both the parents.

Cybridization. The process of cybrid production; usually, to transfer cytoplasm from one species into other.

Cytodifferentiation. Development of various cell types from the relatively undifferentiated meristematic cells.

Cytogenetic abnormalties. Changes in chromosome number and/or structure.

Cytogenetic instability. Origin of variation in chromosome number and/or structure; occurs in virtually all cell cultures.

Cytogenetic map. It depicts the locations of various genes in a chromosome relative to specific microscopically visible landmarks in the chromosomes; commonly used in eukaryotes since they have relatively large microscopically observable chromosomes.

Cytokines. Hormone like proteins that act by binding to specific receptors on cell surface; needed to activate B cells and T_C cells.

Cytokinin. In nature, involved in cell division, modification of apical dominance, shoot differentiation, etc.; in tissue culture: promotes cell division and shoot regeneration when used in small amounts; kinetin and zeatin are natural cytokinins.

Cytological map. See, *Cytogenetic map.*

Cytoplasmic hybrid. See, *Cybrid.*

Cytoplast. A protoplast without an active nucleus.

Dalton (Da). The mass of one hydrogen atom; this unit is used for representing molecular mass of proteins.

Database. It is an organized set of record on a subject; updated on a continual basis and available for national/regional application.

Database mining. Process of database utilization.

Database mining tools. Search engines and analysis tools needed for utilization of various databases.

DDT (Dichlorodiphenyl trichloroethane). This is the first and once most widely used synthetic organic pesticide; belongs to the chlorinated hydrocarbon class.

Decamer (oligonucleotide). An oligo-nucleotide 10 bases long; generally used in RAPD (randomly amplified polymorphic DNA) analysis.

Decapitation. Removal of the shoot-tip/shoot apex, usually of the main shoot; relieves apical dominance.

Dedifferentiation. Reversion of differentiated cell to the meristematic stage; induced by auxin and/or cytokinin.

Deep-well injection. Disposal of liquid chemical wastes by putting them into deep dry wells, where they permeate dry strata.

Defective viral genome-mediated resistance. In case of some viruses; a deleted version of their genomes, when integrated into host genome, leads to resistance to the concerned virus.

Defined molecular marker. A DNA fragment whose function or specific features are known.

Degenerate primer. A set of primers having the same sequence, except for one or more positions where variation occurs.

Degradative plasmids. These plasmids enable the host bacterium to metabolize unusual molecules like toluene and salicylic acid.

Delaney clause. A provision of the Federal Food, Drug and Cosmetic Act of 1958 that prohibits the use of any food additives that induces cancer in people or animals.

Deliberate introduction. See, *Planned introduction.*

Deliberate release. See, *Planned introduction.*

Demethylation. Removal of methyl ($-CH_3$) groups usually from methylated 'C' residues.

Denaturation. Dissociation of the two strands of a DNA molecule due to high temperature or alkaline pH.

Deoxyribonucleotide. A deoxyriboside having a phosphate residue at its 3′– or 5′– position; *in vivo*, 5′– phosphate is the rule.

Deoxyriboside. A compound obtained by a linkage between deoxyribose sugar and an organic base.

Deoxyribotide. See, *Deoxyribonucleotide.*

Desalinization. Refers to the process, which purifies seawater into high-quality drinking water via distillation or microfiltration.

Descriptor. A character used for evaluation and characterization of different accessions of germplasm.

Desiccated artificial seeds. Somatic embryos hardened by treatment with ABA and then coated with a suitable polymer to enable them to withstand desiccation; encapsulated in a suitable matrix and dried; afford easy handling and storage.

Designer crops. Crop varieties specially designed to meet certain specific consumer, industrial, etc. needs; they possess features that were specified before their development.

Development culture. A research culture producing a compound of sufficient commercial interest and used for developing large-scale fermentation procedures.

Developmental determination. During shoot regeneration; this phase follows morphogenic competence acquisition; during this phase, cells become irreversibly committed to a developmental path in response to the inductive condition.

Dhingri mushroom. Mushroom produced from *Pleurotus* sp. grown on chopped paddy or wheat straw, etc.

Dideoxynucleotide. A nucleotide in which oxygen is absent from the 2′ and 3′ positions of ribose; blocks further extension of a nucleotide chain beyond the point at which it incorporated into the chain.

Differentiation. Formation of various cell types and organs like root, shoot, etc. either *in vivo* or in cell cultures.

Digester. A low technology reactor used for anaerobic bacterial digestion.

Dihaploid. A haploid derived from a tetraploid.

Diplochromosome. A chromosome having 4 chromatids; produced by endoreduplication.

Diploid. A cell or an organism having two copies of single genome; represented by $2n = 2x$.

Direct gene transfer. Vector-independent gene transfer.

Direct selection. Cells resistant to the selection pressure survive and divide to form colonies, while the wild type cells are killed by the selection agent.

Direct somatic embryogenesis. Embryos develop directly from explant cells without any intervening callus phase; responding explant cells are themselves either embryogenic or quite/close to this state.

Directed sequencing of BAC contigs. See, *Clone-by-clone sequencing.*

Disarmed Ti plasmid. A Ti plasmid from which the three tumour inducing genes (genes *iaaM*, *iaaH* and *ipt* located in T-DNA) have been removed.

Disarming of Ti plasmid. Removal of the three tumour producing genes from T-DNA of a Ti-plasmid.

Disc electrophoresis. Acryonym of 'discontinuous electrophoresis,' which prevents aggregation and precipitation of proteins during sample entry into the gel matrix and promotes the formation of well defined bands, which are common problems in gels with small pores.

Discharge permit. A permit that allows a company to legally discharge certain amounts or levels of pollutants into air or water; technically called NPDES permit.

Disclosure. In case of patents; the inventor is required to describe the invention in sufficient detail so that a person of normal skill is able to reproduce it. In case of biological entities, already known organisms may be simply named. But if they have been genetically modified, the nature and the method of modification has to be described fully.

Discontinuity. The site in a DNA strand at which the phosphodiester bond between two adjacent nucleotides is broken.

Discovery. Isolation/identification of things which are already present in nature/universe; discoverer only indicates their presence.

Disinfectant. See, *Sterilizing agent.*

Disinfection. Killing of microorganisms in water or other media where they might otherwise pose a health threat, *e.g.*, chlorine is commonly used to disinfect water supplies. Inactivation of microorganisms present on the surface of explants, etc; also see, *Surface sterilization.*

Disomic. A cell/an individual having normal somatic chromosome complement of a species; each chromosome of the genome(s) is present in two copies.

Dispersed growth digesters. In such digesters, the microbial population is dispersed throughout the sewage being treated.

Dissolved oxygen (D.O.). Oxygen gas dissolved in water; concentration of D.O. is a measure of water quality.

Distant hybridization. Hybridization between distantly related taxa, *e.g.*, two different species, genera, etc.

Distinctiveness. In case of PBR; the new variety must be distinguishable from other varieties by one or more identifiable morphological, physiological or other characteristics.

DNA. A macromolecule in which deoxyribonucleotides are joined together by phosphodiester linkage; usually, double-stranded.

DNA, B form. Two strands of a DNA duplex molecule are coiled together in a right–handed helix having diameter of 19Å, and a pitch (= length of one turn of helix) of 34Å; it contains ~10 base pair per turn of the helix.

DNA array. A series of DNA sequences fixed as distinct spots on a suitable solid support, like a glass chip; basically two types: spotted DNA array and printed oligonucleotide chips.

DNA chips. Thin wafers of silicon that carry many different oligonucleotides directly synthesized on the chip at a density of 1 million/cm^2.

DNA cloning. See, *Cloning*.

DNA fingerprint. Molecular marker pattern of an individual obtained by using highly polymorphic markers; used for unequivocal identification of strains, individuals, criminals, etc.

DNA fingerprinting. Developing the DNA fingerprint of an individual.

DNA footprinting. It enables identification of the site on a DNA molecule to which a protein, such as RNA polymerase, binds.

DNA insert. The DNA segment to be cloned is called DNA insert.

DNA ligase. An enzyme that seals nicks in DNA strands by catalizing the formation of phosphodiester bond between the contiguous nucleotides.

DNA methylation. Addition of methyl ($-CH_3$) residues, chiefly to C residues, usually, located in CG or CNG (N means any one of the four DNA bases) sequences, after they are incorporated in DNA.

DNA microarray. An assembly of a very large number of small dots onto a solid support, each dot containing a short sequence of a different gene of the organism concerned.

DNA polymerase. The enzyme that catalyzes synthesis of DNA copies of template DNA; separate enzymes involved in DNA replication and DNA repair.

DNA profiling. See, *DNA fingerprinting*.

DNA sequencing. Determination of the base sequence of a DNA fragment.

DNA vaccine. It contains a gene encoding an immunogenic protein from the concerned pathogen.

Domain fusion method. See, *Rosetta stone method*.

Dominant allele. This allele expresses itself in the heterozygous state.

Donor plant. Plant from which explants are obtained for *in vitro* culture. Syn. *Mother plant.*

Dose. It is the mathematical product of the concentration of hazardous material and the length of exposure to it. The effects of any given material or radiation corresponds to the dose received.

Dot blot technique. In this technique, total DNA (or RNA) isolated from each of several test individuals/tissues are placed onto nitrocellulose filter as dots; DNA is denatured, fixed to the filter and hybridized with single-stranded DNA probe; hybridization is detected by autoradiography or fluorescence.

Double fertilization. In plants; fusion of one sperm with the egg cell and of the other sperm with the secondary nucleus (produces endosperm); both fusions must occur in the same embryo sac to ensure normal seed development.

Doubled haploid (DH). A disomic obtained by doubling the chromosome number (usually, by colchicine treatment) of a haploid; as a rule homozygous.

Downstream. The base sequences on the right side of the start point; the bases are sequentially represented as +1 (the first base on the right of the startpoint), +2, +3, and so on.

Downstream processing. The process of separation from biomass and purification of the desired product.

Driselase. An enzyme used for protoplast isolation; it has activities of cellulase, pectinase, laminarinase and xylanase; isolated from *Irpex lactes*.

Driver mRNA. The biotin-labelled mRNA from nonstressed cell is called driver mRNA.

Droplet method of cryopreservation. In this method, precultured and osmoprotected shoot-tips are placed singly in 2.5 μl droplets of PVS on aluminium foil pieces, which are frozen by immersing the foil packet into liquid nitrogen.

Dry heat sterilization. Sterilization by heating in an oven at 160–180°C for 3 hr.

Dry weight. Weight of cells/tissues after drying them at 60°C for 12 hr.

Early-region replacement vector. SV40 (mammalian) transducing vector; early region of virus is replaced by DNA insert.

Early replacement vector. See, *Early-region replacement vector.*

Economic threshold. The level of pest damage below which an application of pesticides to control the pest is more costly than the economic loss caused by the pest.

Ecosystem diversity. The differences among ecosystems including habitat diversity and ecological processes in an ecosystem.

Ectomycorrhiza. Mycorrhiza fungus located at the root surface.

Edible vaccine. An edible plant part in which an antigenic protein of a pathogen is produced and accumulated; feeding of this part generates immunity against the concerned pathogen.

Electrical polarity in embryogenesis. K^+ ions enter from the end that would later develop into plumule, while H^+ ions pass out of the would be redicular end; established much before the development of morphological bipolarity of embryos; redicular end exhibits a high concentration of calmodulin.

Electroblotting. A couple of sheets of filter paper soaked in anode buffer are placed on the anode plate, and blotting membrane is placed on top of these sheets. The gel is then laid on the top of the membrane and is covered with a couple of sheets of filter paper soaked in cathode buffer; the cathode plate is then placed on the top of these filter papers. The anions migrate from the gel onto the blotting membrane surface at the same speed; as a result, a regular transfer of molecule takes place.

Electrofusion. Fusion of, usually two, protoplasts induced by an exposure to a very short (few milliseconds) duration of a high voltage current.

Electrolysis. Refers to the use of electrical energy to split water molecules into hydrogen and oxygen atoms.

Electronic mail. See, *E mail.*

Electro-osmosis. A phenomenon of migration of water toward an electrode as a result of the supporting medium and/or the surface of the separation equipment, *e.g.*, of capillaries, also carrying charge.

Electrophoresis. Separation of charged molecules under the influence of an electrical field so that they migrate in the direction of electrode bearing the opposite charge; usually, proteins separate on the basis of charge/mass ratio.

Electrophoretic mobility. The speed of migration of a charged molecule under the influenced of an electric field; depends on the charge to mass ratio of the molecule.

Electroporation. Introduction of DNA into cells by a very brief exposure (few milliseconds to few microseconds) to a very high voltage (300–1,500 volts) electrical pulse that induces transient pores in the plasmalemma through which DNA enters into the cells.

Electroporator. A specially designed equipment used for protoplast fusion.

Element. *In genetics*; a sequence of DNA that serves as a protein binding site, *e.g.*, promoter, operator, etc.; it functions only in *cis* position. *In chemistry*; a substance made up of one and only one distinct kind of atom.

Elicitation. Use of an elicitor to enhance secondary metabolite production.

Elicitor. Compounds, which dramatically enhance the production of secondary metabolites; may be biotic or abiotic; the term was originally used for molecules of pathogen origin, which induced the expression of pathogenesis related proteins in resistant varieties of the host.

ELISA. Enzyme–linked immunosorbant assay; uses an enzyme conjugated to an antibody for detection of a specific antigen/antibody based on antigen-antibody interaction; the enzyme linked to the antibody produces detectable colour, which enables an easy and highly sensitive detection.

E-mail. The transmission, storage and distribution of text material in electronic form over communication networks.

Embryo. A very young individual (animal/plant) developing usually, from zygote.

Embryo culture. Culture of young embryos aseptically excised from developing seeds on suitable media to raise young seedlings.

Embryo-endosperm incompatibility. An interaction between embryo and endosperm tissues, which may lead to embryo degeneration.

Embryo-nurse endosperm technique. In embryo rescue; embryos are transplanted onto/into an, usually, immature endosperm cultured onto a suitable medium.

Embryo rescue. Recovery, by embryo culture, of seedlings by culturing such young embryos that would die due to endosperm abortion; usually, in cases of distant hybridization.

Embryo sac. Female gametophyte; derived from megaspore by, usually, 3 successive mitotic divisions yielding 8 haploid nuclei; 3 nuclei migrate to one pole and form 3 antipodal cells, 3 nuclei move to the opposite pole and form a central egg cell and two synergids, and two nuclei remain in the centre and fuse to produce the secondary nucleus.

Embryo splitting. Young animal embryos (4–8 cells) treated with trypsin to separate the individual cells; each such cell can develop into a separate embryo.

Embryo transfer. Transfer of a young embryo into a female in the suitable stage of oestrous cycle.

Embryo transplantation. Implantation of young embryos developed *in vitro* or obtained from the uterus of donor females into the womb of surrogate females.

Embryogenesis. Process of embryo development.

Embryogenic culture. A culture containing cells capable of producing SEs; usually, has embryogenic clumps and even globular stage SEs.

Embryoids. See, *Somatic embryo;* not in common use.

Embryonic clump. A localized group of meristematic and embryogenic cells, which are produced on somatic embryo induction medium; they give rise to somatic embryos when cultured on a suitable medium or proliferate and remain in embryogenic state on the induction medium.

Embryonic stem cells. Pluripotent cultured cells derived from early preimplantation embryos, *e.g.*, the inner cell mass of a blastocyst embryo; they can differentiate into a variety of cell lineages including germ cells.

Emulsifiers. Substances which allow water and oils to remain mixed together in form of an emulsion, *e.g.*, in ice cream, homogenized milk and mayonnaise.

Endangered species. A species whose total population is declining to relatively low levels such that if the trend continues, the species will most likely become exinct.

Endangered species act. The federal legislation than mandates the protection of species and their habitats which are determined to be in danger of extinction.

End filling. This method is used with those DNA molecules that have 5′-protruding ends; Klenow fragment is used to extent the recessed 3′–ends, thereby filling up the single-stranded ends.

Endemic species. The species which are confined to a particular country.

Endocytic and phagocytic barriers. These barriers operate by internalizing macromolecules (endocytosis), and particulate materials and cells (phagocytosis); the ingested materials are delivered into lysosomes, where they are digested; involved in innate immunity.

End-of-the-pipe technologies. The technologies used to clean up the pollution generated by other technologies.

Endogenous antigens. Antigens produced within host cell, *e.g.*, viral proteins, unique proteins produced by cancer cells, etc.

Endogenous elicitor. A class of biotic elicitors produced by cells, especially, of the same species.

Endogenous gene. A gene naturally present in an organism.

Endomycorrhiza. Mycorrhiza fungus located inside roots.

Endonuclease. An enzyme that produces internal cuts in a DNA molecule.

Endophyte. A microorganism living/present inside an organism; serious contamination source in cultures of explants obtained from field-grown plants, specially mature trees.

Endophytic contamination. Contamination of cultures caused by microorganisms, usually fungi (*e.g., Fusarium, Alternaria*) and bacteria, present inside the explant tissues.

Endopolyploidy. Occurrence of polyploid cells in differentiated tissues of most of the plants.

Endoreduplication. Two or more successive rounds of DNA replication take place in nuclei without attendant cell division.

Endosperm. The tissue surrounding young embryo and providing nutrition to the latter; in most (>81% of families) flowering plants, arises by fusion of two nuclei of female gametophyte (polar nuclei) with one sperm, hence triploid ($3n$).

Endosperm abortion. Failure of zygote to develop into a mature embryo and give rise to hybrid seedlings due to inability of the young endosperm to continue development and provide nutrition to the developing young embryo.

Endosperm culture. Culture of endosperm cells, usually, for obtaining triploid plants.

Energy crops. Crops that use solar energy efficiently to covert CO_2 into biomass.

Enhancer. A DNA sequence, which increases the expression of a gene by increasing the activity of its promoter, usually, in response to a specific stimulus; it may be located within or outside (on either side) of the concerned promoter.

Enhancer trapping. In this approach, a recombinant *P* element having *lacZ* reporter gene driven by a weak promoter is used to identify enhancer sequences present in *Drosophila* genome.

Entrapment culture. Cells are entrapped in an open matrix through which medium flows freely.

ENTREZ. It is one of the most popular search engines; searches bibliographic citations and biological data from a variety of databases.

Enucleate. A cell or protoplast without nucleus.

Environment. The combination of all the factors (biotic and abiotic) external to the individual or population of organisms in question.

Environmental biotechnology. Use of biological agents for the management of environmental problems.

Environmental impact. The effect on the natural environment caused by human actions; it includes indirect effects, for example, through pollution, as well as direct effects such as cutting down of trees.

Enzymatic procedure of DNA sequencing. Single–stranded DNA fragments are used for *in vitro* replication by Klenow fragment; replication is interrupted by each of the four 2′, 3′–dideoxynucleotides used in separate reaction mixtures; the partially synthesized chains are separated, subjected to electro-phoresis and subsequently to autoradiography.

Enzyme. Generally, a protein that catalyzes or speeds up a specific chemical reaction; biosynthetic or degradative function; usually, occur in living cells/living systems.

Enzyme engineering. Improvement in the activity and usefulness of an existing enzyme or creation of a new enzyme activity by making suitable changes in the amino acid sequence of concerned enzyme by recombinant DNA technology.

Enzyme immobilization. Confining the enzyme molecule to a distinct phase from the one in which the substrate and the products are present.

Enzyme-product complex. Enzyme molecule having the product molecule bound to its binding site.

Enzyme reactor. A vessel employed to carry out the desired conversion using an enzyme.

Enzyme-substrate complex. Enzyme molecule having the substrate molecules bound to its active/binding site; this state precedes catalysis.

Enzyme technology. Use of purified enzymes for generating useful products or services.

EPA (U.S. Environmental Protection Agency). The federal agency responsible for the control of all forms of pollution and other kinds of environmental degradation.

EPG fragments. Oligonucleotides produced from cell wall by endopolygalacturonase hydrolysis; affect morphogenic response of cell cultures; included under the general term *oligosaccharins.*

Epidermis. The outermost single (usually) layer of cells covering the entire plant body (primary body); forms a protective layer.

Epigenetic change. See, *Epigenetic variation.*

Epigenetic variation. When a variant trait shows stability during mitotic division in cell cultures, but disappears either during plantlet regeneration from them or during meiosis in the regenerated plants; may relate to up or down regulation of the promoter of the concerned gene.

Episome. A plasmid that becomes integrated into the bacterial chromosome.

Epitope. The part of antigen molecule involved in antigen-antibody interaction.

Equilibrium. A state, in which the forward and the reverse reactions proceed at identical rates and there is no *net* product formation.

Escape. A susceptible cell/individual being classified as resistant due to errors in evaluation/ classification.

Essential characteristic (of a plant variety). A heritable trait that contributes to the principal feature, performance or value of the plant variety.

Essential fatty acids. Mammals (including humans) can not synthesize linoleic (18:2) and linolenic (18:3) fatty acids; therefore, they must be supplied in their diet, and are called essential fatty acids.

Ethics. A set of standards by which a community decides to regulate its behaviour, and to determine what is legitimate in the persuit of particular aims; more technically, ethics can also refer to moral philosophy.

Ethylene (CH_2=CH_2). A plant hormone, which is involved in fruit ripening, leaf abscission, flower senescence, etc.

Eutrophication. Presence of organic materials and inorganic nutrients in river waters; contributed by waste water.

Excise. To remove a tissue or an organ, usually, by cutting with a scalpel, to obtain explants or during subculture, etc.

Exogenous antigens. Antigens produced outside host cell.

Exogenous elicitor. Elicitors produced by an organism, *e.g.,* a microorganism, other than the organism in question.

Exon. Expressed (= translated) sequences of an eukaryotic interrupted gene.

Exon shuffling. New combinations of exons produced by recombination within the intervening sequences; produces new genes that encode proteins with altered functions.

Exotic species. A species introduced into a geographical area to which it is not native.

Explant. Organ, tissue or cell obtained from a donor and used to initiate an *in vitro* culture.

Exponential phase. See, *Log phase.*

Expressed sequence tags (ESTs). These are 200–300 bp long cDNA sequences generated by picking thousands of random clones from cDNA libraries and using them for single-pass sequencing; represents a partial gene sequence; used in microarrays.

Expression casette. When an expression vector contains the promoter, ribosome binding site and transcription terminator sequences in a cluster, it is termed as an expression casette.

Expression library. A collection of recombinant clones that together contains all the available cDNAs from a cell type/tissue/organism; cDNAs are integrated in an expression vector so that they are able to generate their protein product.

Expression profiling. Determination of the cell types/tissues in which a gene is expressed as well as when, the given gene is expressed.

Expression proteomics. Quantitative study of protein expression between samples differing by some variable. The pattern of expression of the complete proteome or of its part (sub-proteome) between samples can be compared with the help of this approach; quite useful in identifying disease specific proteins.

Expression vector. A vector which is designed for the expression of, *i.e.,* production of, the protein specified by the DNA insert; contains the regulatory sequences like promoters, operators, ribosomal binding sites, etc., having optimum function in the chosen host.

***Ex situ* germplasm conservation.** Collection and conservation of germplasm away from the area of their origin as seed banks, field banks, shoot-tip banks, cells and tissue culture banks and DNA banks.

Extant variety. A notified variety or a farmers variety that is in public domain.

Extinction. Refers to the death of all the individuals of a species; it leads to loss of all the genes of that species.

Extraction. The process of recovering a compound or a group of compounds from a mixture or from cells into a solvent phase.

Extremozymes. Enzymes that function optimally under extreme conditions of temperature, pH, etc.

***Ex vitro* hardening.** Hardening of plantlets outside culture vessels.

***Ex-vitro* rooting.** See, *In vivo rooting.*

F plasmids. These plasmids carry *tra* genes that promote conjugation; 'F' from fertility.

F_1. First filial generation; produced by crossing two individuals, strains, populations, clones or species of dissimilar genotypes.

F_2. Second filial generation; produced by inter-mating or selfing of F_1 individuals.

Facultative parasites. Refer to those saprophytes which mostly feed on dead organic matter, but if they reach the living plants they also attack the same.

Facultative saprophytes. Refer to those parasites, which mostly feed on their living host plants but when living plants are not available, they feed on the dead residues of their hosts.

Farmer's privilege. PBR systems generally allow the farmers to use the material of a protected variety produced on their farm for planting of their new crop without any obligation to the PBR tittle holder. This exemption is known as farmer's privilege.

Farmer's rights. The right of farmers of developing countries, whose efforts are responsible for the conservation of a wide range of genetic variability in plants and animals, to derive economic benefits from the sale of modern high yielding varieties developed from these materials.

Farmer's variety. A variety that has been traditionally cultivated and evolved by farmers, or is a wild relative or land race in common knowledge of farmers.

Fed batch culture. A batch culture into which a predetermined volume of fresh medium is added at regular intervals, leading to an increase in the culture volume.

Feedback inhibition. Activity of an enzyme is inhibited by the end product of the biosynthetic pathway in which the enzyme participates.

Feeder cell layer techniques. Cells/protoplasts irradiated with 5 kR, washed 2–3 times, plated in soft agar at a density of 2.4×10^4 cells/ml form the feeder layer; non-irradiated protoplasts can be plated on the feeder layer at a density of 10–100 cells/ml.

Feeder layer. A layer of cells, treated to prevent their growth and to ultimately cause their death, that provides metabolites to the cloned cells.

Feminization. In feminization, the staminodes present in female flowers develop into fleshy carpels around the fruit leading to abnormal fruit development and partial to complete sterility.

Fermentation. A process mediated by or involving microorganisms in which a product of economic value is obtained.

Fermenter. See, *Bioreactor*.

Fertilization. Fusion of egg cell with a sperm leading to zygote production, which gives rise to embryo ($2n$).

Field collection. Maintenance of germplasm by growing different accessions in the field; ordinarily, in case of fruit and forest trees, tuber crops, etc.

Field strategies for transgene containment. These strategies are based on spatial isolation of the transgenic crops coupled with planting of continuous borders of a non-transgenic variety to serve as a pollen trap.

Field testing. See, *Planned introduction*.

Film reactors. These reactors contain a support for attachment of the bacterial cells to avoid their washout due to higher waste flow rates; support forms anaerobic filter through which the waste passes and is degraded; used to treat vegetable processing wastes of medium to high strength (1–10% solids), and animal wastes.

Filter paper bridge. A platform formed in a culture tube above the surface of liquid medium by inserting the two arms of a filter paper strip into the medium; explants are placed on the platform.

Filter paper raft-nurse tissue technique. Culture of single cells on a filter paper that was plated on an actively growing callus tissue several days before the culture of single cells; callus provides the nutrients needed by the single cells.

Filter sterilization. Thermolabile compounds are sterilized by passing their solutions through a membrane of 0.45 μ or lower pore size.

Finite cell lines. In animal cell culture; cell lines that die after several subcultures.

First-generation biosensors. These are the simplest amperometric biosensors; they use Clark oxygen electrode, which determines the reduction of O_2 present in the sample (analyte) solution; used to measure redox reactions.

First law of thermodynamics. The impirical observation, confirmed innumerable times, that energy is never created or destroyed but may be converted from one form to another, *e.g.*, electricity to light.

Fixed film digestors. In these digestors, the biological components or microorganisms are present in the form of a film on filter particles or large discs.

Flame sterilization. Instruments like forceps, scalpels, etc. are ordinarily sterilized by dipping them in 95% ethyl alcohol followed by flaming.

Flanking sequences. The sequences lying upstream and downstream of a given DNA sequence, *i.e.*, usually, on either side of the coding region of a gene.

Flash point. It is the temperature at which a substance catches fire.

Flavors. Additives that give a particular fragrance to the food; may be natural or artificial.

Flavor enhancers. Substances which enhance existing flavors of foods; may be natural or artificial.

Float culture of anthers. Anthers are floated on a liquid medium, where they dehisce to release pollen grains; anthers are often subcultured serially.

Floatation. Raising of microbial cells to the surface of medium by fine gas bubbles adsorbed to their surface.

Flocculation. Sticking together of bacterial and other cells induced by inorganic salts, mineral hydrocoloids, etc.

Flow-cytometry. A stream of cells/protoplasts suspended in liquid medium is passed through one/two light beams (usually from lasers), the light scattered or emitted by cell is collected and analyzed to evaluate upto 5000 cells/second; can assay cell size, pigmentation, staining with specific dyes, biochemical accumulation, cell cycle phase, etc.

Fluidized bed reactor. Contains 20–40 μm or larger particles having immobilized enzymes; the particles become suspended in the reaction mixture when substrate solution is pump in.

Fluorescein diacetate. A non-polar, non-fluorescent compound that is cleaved by esterase activity in living cells to release polar fluorescein, which fluoresces green with UV light.

Fluorescence-activated cell sorter (FACS). An automated system that separates cells on the basis of differential fluorescence of molecules displayed on their surface, *e.g.*, gene products arranged on the cell surface and available for binding of specific antibodies. It can be used for very fast (upto 1000 cells/sec.) sorting of transfected cells.

Fluorescence *in situ* hybridization (FISH). *In situ* hybridization uses fluorescent labelling in place of radioactive labelling.

Fluorescent molecule. A fluorescent molecule that aborbs light at a particular wavelength and then emits light at a longer wavelength.

Flush ends. See, *Blunt ends*.

Food enrichment. Restoration of the natural nutritive value of a food to the same level as that before it was processed.

Food security. Ability to meet the food needs of every citizen of a country providing freedom from hunger and malnutrition.

Foreground selection. In a backcross programme; selection for the gene/allele being transferred.

Forensic medicine. The knowledge and techniques of medical science applied to assist resolution of crimes, legal disputes, etc.

Fortification. Addition of vitamins or minerals to a food at levels higher than those it originally possessed.

Fortified Food. Refers to a food that has higher level of vitamins or mineral than was originally present in the food.

Forward reaction. The chemical reaction utilizes reactants A and B to yield the products C and D.

Fosmid. A useful derivative of BAC vector that contains λ phage *cos* sites to facilitate its packaging in heads of phage λ.

Fossil fuel. Fuel derived from coal or petroleum.

Framework region. In case of antibodies; the 4 invarient regions that separate the hyper-variable regions; denoted as FR1, FR2, FR3, and FR4.

Frankenfood. A scary name derived from the phrase 'Frankenstein's monster'; a nickname for GM food.

Free probe. Probe molecules that are not paired with the test nucleic acid sequence.

Free radicals. The chemical species with one or more unpaired electrons in their outermost orbit.

Freeze preservation. Preservation of cell suspensions, callus tissues, shoot-tips, and somatic and zygotic embryos for long periods of time in frozen state at –196°C in liquid nitrogen.

Freezing. In case of cryopreservation; lowering of the temperature of cells from 0°C to –196°C.

Fresh water. Refers to the water that has a salt content of less than 0.1% (1000 ppm).

Fresh weight. Weight of cells/tissues, cultures in their native state after removal of medium (by washing) and extra-cellular water (by partial vacuum).

Front-of-the-pipe technologies. Cleaner production technologies that generate less pollution than existing technologies.

Fuel biotechnology. Use of biological agents or their components to generate various energy-rich compounds from different substrates/ resources, which can be used as fuel.

Functional food. Any fresh or processed food claimed to have a health promoting and/or disease preventing property beyond the basic nutritional function of supplying nutrients is called functional food.

Functional genomics. The study of the patterns of expression of the genes present in the genome of organisms that leads to the growth and development of the organisms.

Functional proteomics. Use of proteomics techniques to analyze the characteristics of molecular protein networks involved in a living cell.

Fungi. They are numerous species of molds, mushrooms, brackens and other forms of non-photosynthetic plants; derive energy and nutrients by consuming organic material.

Fusogen. An agent that induces fusion of protoplast (or animal cells).

F-virosome. Sendai virus envelop that has only fusion glycoprotein (F-protein) and HN protein (but haemagglutin neuraminidase protein is removed), in which DNA is packaged; the F protein mediates the fusion of viral envelop with cell plasma membrane so that the DNA is delivered directly into the cytoplasm.

Gamete. A specialized cell involved in sexual reproduction; produced through meiosis in male and female animals/gametophytes of plants; has *n* chromosome complement.

Gametic chromosome number. The chromosome number (*i.e.,* complement) normally found in the gametes of the concerned species; denoted by *n*.

Gametoclonal variation. Genetic variation present among the haploid cells or plants regenerated from anther/pollen cultures; *not in common use.*

Gap ligase chain reaction (G-LCR). Ligase chain reaction using staggered probes; more efficient than LCR.

Gasohol. A blend of 90% gasoline and 10% alcohol that can be substituted for straight gasoline.

Gel electrophoresis. Electrophoresis, in which a variety of chemically inert gel matrices having adjustable and regular pore size are used as matrix.

Gel filteration chromatography. Matrix used is a gel of a neutral cross-linked carrier; molecules smaller than the pore size of the matrix are retained within the matrix and are later recovered.

Gel retardation analysis. A technique used to identify those DNA fragments to which a specific protein, such as DNA polymerase, binds.

Gelatinisation. Starch becomes dissolved to form a viscous suspension.

Gene. A segment of DNA (RNA in some viruses) that encodes a RNA and/or polypeptide and may, ultimately, lead to the development of a specific phenotype; it includes introns (in the case of eukaryotes) and 5′- and 3′-regulatory sequences.

Gene amplification. An increase in the number of copies of gene per genome of the organism in comparison to that naturally present.

Gene cloning. See, *Cloning.*

Gene cloning tools. See, *Genetic engineering tools.*

Gene desert. In human genome; gene-poor regions separating gene-rich regions.

Gene disruption. Integration of a DNA sequence within another gene so that the latter is inactivated; used to produce 'knockout' mice.

Gene expression. When a gene performs the specific function, which it is capable of, it is called gene expression; it begins with transcription of the gene and ends with the development of the specific phenotype; *ordinarily, it refers to transcription of the concerned gene.*

Gene farming. Production of proteins encoded by transgenes in animals/plants; the protein is recovered from milk, urine, blood (in animals), seeds, etc. (in plants).

Gene-flow. Introgression of genes from improved varieties of crop plants into their wild relatives.

Gene-knockout strategy. Homologous recombination is exploited to place a selectable marker gene within the gene of interest; this disrupts the target gene, *i.e.,* knocks out its function.

Gene machine. An automated microprocessor-controlled DNA synthesizer.

Gene pyramiding. Bringing two or more different genes conferring resistance to the same pathogen in the same line/variety.

Gene silencing. Suppression of transgene expression in later generations of transgenic plants; usually, due to transgene (including promoter) methylation; more common when the transgene is integrated in higher copy number.

Gene stacking. Many transgenes are transferred into a single variety through a single transformation event.

Gene tagging. Use of *Agrobacterium* T-DNA, transposons, etc. for identification and/or isolation of a gene by first integrating it into the concerned gene and isolating mutants so produced.

Gene targetting. See, *Targetted gene transfer.*

Gene therapy. Introduction of the normal functioning allele of the gene in the cells of a patient to correct a genetic or acquired disorder.

Genetic counselling. Educating perspective parents, either suffering from or suspected to be heterozygous for some genetic disease, on the risk of their children suffering from the same disease.

Genetic disease. A disease caused by a mutant gene; generally, due to the recessive allele.

Genetic diversity. The variability present within a species, between individuals of a population or different population groups of the same species for one or a group of traits.

Genetic engineering. Production of recombinant DNA and its transfer into a suitable host for multiplication/expression of the recombinant DNA. The recombinant DNA may or may not become integrated into the host genome.

Genetic engineering tools. The biological agents and biological products used for genetic engineering/gene cloning.

Genetic epidemiology. Analysis in large populations of the interactions of genes, genetic diseases and environment; this allows the discovery of new drug treatments, and to tailor them to individual genetic and life profiles.

Genetic immunization. Use of DNA for immunization.

Genetic instability. Origin of genetic variation in a relatively high frequency, usually, much higher than that ascribable to spontaneous mutations.

Genetic map. A schematic representation of various genes and molecular markers located in different chromosomes; different strategies are used to construct linkage maps, cytological or cytogenetic maps and physical maps.

Genetic marker. A specific location on a chromosome that is defined by naked eye polymorphism, protein or DNA sequence; the inheritance of a genetic marker can be followed in a mapping population.

Genetic material. The chemical that contains the genetic information, *i.e.,* of which genes are composed; in most of the organisms, DNA is the genetic material; in only some viruses, RNA serves this purpose.

Genetic resource. Sum total of all the genes and their alleles present in a species and its wild relatives.

Genetic transformation. Introduction of DNA or recombinant DNA into a suitable cell/organism.

Genetically engineered microbe. See, *Genetically engineered microorganism.*

Genetically engineered microorganism. Microorganism, which has one or more genetically engineered traits.

Genetically modified crops. A crop variety expressing a transgene; produced by genetic engineering.

Genetically modified food. Foods and additives obtained from genetically modified organisms.

Genetically modified organism. An organism with a unique gene combination that does not occur naturally, and is produced either by using genetic engineering or protoplast fusion.

Genetically modified plants. Plants with unique gene combinations that do not occur naturally and are produced either by using genetic engineering or protoplast fusion.

Genome. *In cytogenetics*; the complete haploid set of chromosomes of a diploid species; all the chromosomes of a genome are distinct from each other in gene content and often, in morphology. *In molecular biology*; the complete genetic information present in a cell/organism.

Genome analysis. It generally implies analysis of chromosome pairing relationships among genomes of different species.

Genome compaction. Reduction in genome size achieved by reducing sequences not involved in genetic functions.

Genome map. A detailed schematic description of the structural and functional organization of the complete genome of an organism.

Genome-wide mutant libraries. A collection of mutants that together represent mutation in (ideally) each gene of the genome. This is sometimes dubbed as *mutational genomics.*

Genomic library. A collection of plasmid clones or phage lysates containing recombinant DNA molecule so that the sum total of DNA inserts in this collection, ideally, represents the entire genome of the concerned organism.

Genomics. The science that deals with the determination of the structure (including DNA sequence) and function of the complete genome of an organism.

Geographical indications. A form of IPR protection; they cover such qualities, reputation or other characteristics of a product that can be essentially attributable to the geographical origin of the product, and that could be used to recognize that a product had originated from a particular terriority.

Germination. Emergence of roots and shoots from seeds due to cell division and expansion in mature embryos; regarded as extension of embryo development.

Germline gene therapy. Functional allele of the gene introduced and integrated into germ cells (ova or sperms) or even zygotes.

Germplasm conservation. The maintenance of germplasm of a species using one or more of the following approaches: *in situ* conservation, and *ex situ* conservation (field collection, seed banks, slow-growth cultures, cryopreservation and DNA banks).

Germplasm. See, *Genetic resource.*

Giant chromosome. See, *Polytene chromosome.*

Gibbrellin. A growth regulator that promotes cell elongation; in tissue culture, it is used for shoot elongation, somatic embryo germination, etc.; counteracts the effects of ABA.

Glass-house containment A. It is used when no plant pathogens are used, and where non-pathogenic vector systems and regeneration from single cells are used.

Glass-house containment B. It is recommended for experiments involving genetically manipulated plant pathogens, including plant viruses, and the growth of which still contain the pathogen.

Global climate change. Refers to the commulative effects of various impacts of rising levels of greenhouse gases on Earth's climate. These effects include global warming, weather changes and, a rising sea level.

Global expression profiling. Analysis of the expression pattern of (ideally) all the genes present in the genome at the same time; done either at the RNA level or at the protein level.

Global warming. The increase in global mean temperature presumably due to increased concentration of greenhouse gases in the atmosphere.

Globular embryo. A nearly spherical proembryo; the multicellular mass produced by repeated division of zygote (or some other cell); synthesizes its own auxin and gives rise to the heart shaped embryo.

Glucose syrup. It is produced from starch by the sequential process of gelatinisation, liquefaction and saccharification; contains 95–97% glucose; used to make high fructose syrup.

Gluten. A mixture of insoluble proteins present in wheat (and other cereal grains) giving wheat flour its distinctive character; a sticky sub-stance remaining after the starch has been extracted.

GM crops. See, *Genetically modified crops.*

GM Food. See, *Genetically modified food.*

Gobar gas. Biogas produced from cowdung.

Golden rice. A transgenic rice that accumulates β-carotene in its seeds; expected to combat vitamin A deficiency in areas where rice is the staple food.

Gradient gel electrophoresis. In this system, a gel having a pore gradient is employed.

Gratuitous metabolism. Enzymes necessary for degradation are induced by another compound, which is not needed as co-metabolite, and degradation of xenobiotic itself provides energy, carbon and reducing power to the microbes.

Gray water. Waste water, as from sinks and tubs, that does not contain human excreta. Such water can be reused without purification for some purpose.

Greenhouse effect. Traping of heat by earth's atmosphere due to greenhouse gases.

Greeenhouse gases. The atmospheric gases like CO_2, CH_4, CFCs and N_2O which absorb outgoing infra-red radiation from the earth.

Grit chamber. Part of preliminary treatment of waste water treatment plants; a swiming pool-like tank in which the velocity of the water is slowed enough to let sand and other gritty material settle.

Ground water remediation. Refers to the repurification of contaminated ground water.

Growth curve. A curve representing the increase in cell number or biomass; typically sigmoid (S shaped).

Growth hormone. A substance produced by an organism that drastically affects growth of that organism; acts in tissues other than the one that produces it.

Growth hormone autonomy. Ability of cells/tissues to grow on a growth regulator-free culture medium, *e.g.*, crown gall cells, habituated cells, etc.

Growth regulator. A substance that affects growth and development of an organism when it is used in very low concentrations, *e.g.*, in case of plants, auxins, cytokinins, GA, etc.

GST pull down. An alternative to Y2H (yeast two-hybrid) system is provided by the strategy called GST (glutathion-S-transferase) pull down.

Gynogenesis. Production of haploids from *in vitro* culture of unfertilized ovaries or ovules; two stages: induction and regeneration phases; haploid plants originate, usually, from egg cells, sometimes from synergids or even antipodals.

Gyratory shaker. See, *Orbital* shaker.

Habituation. The process of *in vitro* cultured plant cells becoming self-sufficient in their auxin and/or cytokinin needs; occurs occasionally.

Haemopoietic cells. Cells that produce blood cells.

Hairy root. Root covered with profuse and prominent hairs; regenerated from cells/tissues following their transformation by *Agrobacterium rhizogenes.*

Hairy root culture. Culture of hairy roots initiated by inoculation of 2–3 cm long 3–4 hairy roots (having root apical meristems), induced by *A. rhizogenes,* in liquid medium; growth rate comparable to that of suspension cultures; used for biochemical production.

Halogenated hydrocarbon. Refers to the synthetic organic compound containing one or more atoms of the halogen group, *e.g.*, chlorine, fluorine and bromine.

Haplome. Genomes of a haploid organism; *not in common use.*

Haplotype. The major histocompatibility complex (MHC) loci are closely linked; they are usually inherited as a complete set which is called haplotype.

Hapten. Small molecules that show antigenicity, but are unable to produce immune response on their own; when a hapten is linked to a large molecule, called carrier, it may, become immunogenic as well.

Hardening. Of *in vitro* raised plantlets; they are kept under high humidity and diffuse light for a few days; humidity is then gradually decreased and light intensity is increased over a period of 1–2 weeks to enable them to survive *ex vitro*.

Hardware. The physical components of computers, *e.g.*, keyboard, monitor, processing unit and printer.

Hard water. Water that contains relatively large amounts of calcium or certain other minerals that cause soap to precipitate.

HAT-medium. Used to select hybrid animal cells; contains hypoxanthine, aminopterin and thymidine; eliminates $HGPRT^-$ and/or TK^- cells.

Hazard. Any imaginable adverse effect that can be identified and measured. It may be cultural, biological, physical and chemical.

Hazard analysis (in recombinant DNA research). Analysis of the likelihood of GMOs having adverse effects on the environment, including human health, being realized.

Hazard assessment. Refers to the process of examining evidence linking a particular hazard to its harmful effects.

Hazardous material. Any material having one or more of the following attributes: ignitability, corrosivity, reactivity and toxicity.

Head space. The volume (20–25%) of reactor kept empty for aeration, splashing and foaming.

Heart-shaped embryo. A plant embryo in which morphological bipolarity is observable; a depression begins to develop at the site where plumule is to be formed; radicle forms at the opposite pole, *i.e.,* the suspensor end.

Heat labile. A chemical, which is destroyed on heating.

Heat pretreatment of anther. Exposure of anthers to high temperatures, *e.g.,* 35°C for *Brassica campestris*, for 1–2 days before culturing; it enhances frequency of androgenesis.

Heavy chain. About 450 amino acid long polypetide chains; 2 chains in each antibody molecule; determine the antibody class.

Heavy gravity beer. High calorie, high total solids beer produced by adding proteins to the wort.

Heavy metals. These are high-atomic-weight metals such as lead, cadium, mercury and zinc. They may be serious pollutants in water or soil because they are toxic in relatively low concentrations and they tend to bioaccumulate.

Helper plasmid. A conjugative plasmid, *e.g.,* pRK2013 used to mobilize the transfer of a non-conjugative plasmid; used for mobilization of intermediate vector from *E. coli* into *Agrobacterium*.

Helper Ti plasmid. A Ti plasmid having intact and functional *vir* region but lacking entire T-DNA; induces transfer of T-DNA (containing the desired gene construct) of a mini-Ti or Micro-Ti plasmid; one component of a binary vector system.

Helper virus. Late region replacement SV40 vector is used for infection of host cells in conjunction with another virus, called helper virus, which has the *VP1, VP2,* and *VP3* genes intact, but has a defective *large-T* gene.

Hemicellulase. An enzyme, which digests hemi-celluloses; used for production of protoplasts.

Hemizygous. An individual having a single copy of a gene/genes, *e.g.,* haploids are hemizygous for all their genes.

Heritable character. A character transmitted from one generation to the next; produced by a gene or a group of genes.

Heteroencapsidation. Encapsidation of genome of a virus into the capsid of another virus.

Heterogeneous. A mixture of different types; usually, different genotypes.

Heterogeneous reactor. In this system, circular glass or stainless steel plates mounted on a central shaft; cells attach to the plate surface, and medium flows through the reactor.

Heterokaryon. A cell having two nuclei of different genotypes.

Heterologous cells. Cells from different species.

Heterologous probe. A probe prepared from one species and used for the identification of recombinant clones/desired gene from another species; mainly due to sequence homology.

Heteroplasmic. When a cell contains a mix of wild type and mutant/transferred chloroplast/mitochondrial genomes, it is referred to as heteroplasmic; genetically unstable; two types: interplastidic and intraplastidic.

Heteroplasmy. See, *Heteroplasmic.*

Heteroplastomy. See, *Heteroplasmic*

Heteropolymeric protein. Multimeric protein in which polypeptide chains are non-identical; different polypeptides are encoded by different genes.

Heterotrophic phase of embryo development. In *ovulo*, embryo depends for at least some of its biochemical needs on endosperm and the surrounding maternal tissues; usually, upto globular stage and, in some cases, even upto early heart stage.

Heterozygous. An individual in which the two alleles of a gene are different, *e.g., Aa.*

High conversion syrup. Syrup produced from liquefied starch by the action of fungal α-amylase and glucoamylase; contain 30–37% maltose and 35–43% glucose; used for making soft candy.

High efficiency particulate air (HEPA) filter. It removes all particles larger than 0.3 μm; used in laminar air-flow cabinets and other devices for filter sterilization of air.

High fructose syrup. It is produced from glucose syrup by the action of immobilized glucose isomerase; may have 42% to 55% fructose.

High pH and high Ca^{2+} treatment. In protoplast fusion; exposure of protoplasts to a high pH (Ca. 10.5) solution having high Ca^{2+} ions (30 mmol/l $CaCl_2$) at 30°C for about 30 min; induces protoplast fusion.

High temperature enzymes. Enzymes having optimal temperatures for catalysis above 100°C; some have half-life of several days at the optimum temperature; ~30 enzymes isolated from hyperthermophile bacteria.

Highly active antiretroviral therapy (HART). A combination therapy based on, in most cases, two nucleoside analogues and one protease inhibitor.

Histocompatibility. Phenomenon of graft acceptance is called histocompatibility.

Hit-and-run method. This method was designed to recover those embryogenic stem cells in which a defective endogenous gene is replaced with a gene modified by site-directed mutagenesis.

Holoenzyme. The complex of an apoenzyme and the cofactor/coenzyme is called holoenzyme.

Homogeneous. Consisting of individuals of the same genotype or phenotype.

Homokaryon. A cell having two identical nuclei.

Homologous. Of DNA; DNA molecules having identical or very close to identical base sequence; of chromosomes; those having the same gene content.

Homologous cells. Cells from the same species.

Homologous recombination. Exchange of identical segments between two DNA molecules that have identical or almost identical sequences, the differences in their sequences being limited to allelic differences.

Homopolymeric proteins. Multimeric proteins in which all polypeptide chains are identical.

Homozygous. An individual in which the two alleles of a gene are identical, *e.g., aa* and *AA.*

Horizontal gene transfer. Genetic exchange between different evolutionary lineages.

Horizontal ultra-thin-layer electrophoresis. Ultrathin gels polymerized on support films are used as matrices.

Hormone. A substance produced in one part of a multicellular organism and transported to another part/other parts where it perform its function.

Host. An organism providing a suitable media for growth and multiplication of another organism; *in recombinant DNA technology*, a cell or an organism into which recombinant DNA is propagated.

Host non-specific toxin. The pattern of sensitivity of different strains of the host species to the toxin is not associated with their response to the concerned pathogen.

Host-specific toxin. See, *Specific toxin.*

Hotstart PCR. In case of hotstart PCR, a critical component like Mg^{2+} or *Taq* polymerase, is left out from the reaction mixture. Once the reaction mixture is heated to the denaturation temperature, this reagent is added to the PCR tubes by opening their tops; devised to prevent non-specific amplification.

House-keeping genes. Genes, which are continuously expressed in all the cells and tissues; believed to be essential for the survival of cells/tissues; Syn., *Constitutive genes.*

Hull factor. Unknown biochemicals provide by lemma and palea to the developing proembryos/young embryos of wheat, barley, etc.; essential for embryo development.

Human artificial chromosome vectors. See, *Mammalian artificial chromosome vectors.*

Human growth hormones. Somatostatin and somatotrophin act together to regulate human growth.

Humanised rodent antibodies. Antibodies having the variable region from a mouse antibody and the constant region of a human antibody.

Humoral immune response. Immune response based on antibodies; it can be conferred on non-immune individuals by administration of serum antibodies from an immune individual; binding of antibodies to a microorganism can activate the complement system which lyses the microorganism; antibodies bind to toxins and viral particles, and prevent their sub-sequent binding to host cells; involved in acquired immunity.

Humus sludge. The sattled down biofilm fragments and other solids from treated sewage.

Hybrid. Individual obtained by crossing/mating individuals/strains/varieties of dissimilar genotypes; produced by sexual or protoplast fusion routes.

Hybrid antibody. An antibody molecule designed or modified by recombinant DNA technology.

Hybrid cells (or protoplasts). Cells/protoplasts obtained by nuclear fusion in a heterokaryone; nuclear fusion during interphase does not yield viable hybrid cells, while nuclear fusion during mitosis produces hybrid cells capable of continuous division and further development.

Hybrid sorting. Anthers from F_1 hybrid from a selected cross are cultured to produce haploids, their chromosome number is then doubled to obtain homozygous doubled haploid (DH) lines, which represent, ideally, a random sample of homozygous lines extractable from the cross through continued selfing; the DH lines are subjected to selection.

Hybridization. *In genetics*, the process of producing hybrids, usually, by crossing; also by protoplast fusion. In case of *nucleic acids,* association of two complementary DNA sequence/RNA sequences or one RNA and one DNA sequence by complementary base pairing.

Hybridization probing. In hybridization probing, a labelled DNA/RNA probe is used for hybridization with the recombinant clones available in a cDNA/genomic library or obtained in an experiment.

Hybridoma. Production of hybrid cells through fusion of lymphocytes with tumour or tissue culture grown cells; these hybrid cells possess the ability to produce antibodies (from the lymphocytes) as well as the capacity for indefinite growth *in vitro* (from the tumour or tissue culture cell involved in the fusion).

Hybridoma technology. Production of monoclonal antibodies from hybridomes.

Hydrated artificial seeds. SEs/shoot-buds encapsulated in a hydrated gel, *e.g.*, calcium alginate; they are sticky, difficult to handle and store, and dry on exposure to air; beads may be coated with a waxy layer to overcome these difficulties.

Hydrocarbon emissions. Refer to the exhaust of various hydrocarbon compounds due to incomplete combustion of fuel. These are the major contribution of photochemical smog.

Hydrocarbons. *In chemistry,* natural or synthetic organic substances that are composed of carbon and hydrogen, *e.g.*, crude oil, fuels from crude oil, coal, animal fats and vegetable oils.

Hydrogen acceptor. A substance capable of accepting hydrogen atoms or electrons in the oxidation-reduction reactions.

Hydrolases. Enzymes, which catalyse hydrolytic reactions (and their reversals).

Hydrophobic chromatography. It uses hydrophobic carriers for purification of hydrophobic molecules.

Hydroxyl radical. The OH° group missing the electron; a natural cleansing agent of the atmosphere; highly reactive; readily oxidizes many pollutants upon contact and thus contributes to their removal from the air.

Hyperaccumulators. Plant species, which accumulate metal contaminants in considerable quantities; the biomass from such plants may be reduced in volume by thermal, microbial, physical or chemical means before disposal, or may be used for recovery of metals.

Hyperhydracity. During *in vitro* culture; leaves or even the whole shoot appears water-soaked and translucent, leads to reduced growth, multiplication rate, and survival.

Hyperpolymorphic probe. A probe that exhibits a very high degree of polymorphism; such probes are used for DNA fingerprinting.

Hyperthermophile organism. An organism, which grows at 90°C and above with optimum growth at 80°C or above.

Hypertonic solution. A solution having higher osmotic pressure than the cell/tissue in question.

Hypervariable dispersed repetitive sequence. VNTR sequences dispersed throughout the genome.

Hypervariable DNA. See, *Hypervariable region.*

Hypervariable region (of genome). Minisatellite and microsatellite DNAs together constitute the hypervariable region.

Hypervariable regions. The variable region of antibodies; each chain contains 3 highly variable regions, denoted as CDR1, CDR2 and CDR3 (CDR=complementarity-determining region).

Hypodiploid. A cell/an individual having less than diploid, but greater than haploid, chromosome number (complement).

Hypohaploid. A cell/an individual having less than the gametic chromosome number (complement) of the species.

Hypothetical protein. A protein that an orphan gene is expected to encode.

Hypotonic solution. A solution having a lower osmotic pressure than the cell/tissue in question.

Immobilization. Encapsulation of molecules, cells and cell masses in a suitable matrix or their confinement in a chamber made of a suitable membrane/stainless steel wire mesh; it may alter the physiology of cell.

Immobilized cell bioreactors. These bioreacters are based on cells entrapped either in gel to produce beads or in a membrane or metal (stainless steel) screen compartment, and the medium is circulated through the bioreactor; a portion of the medium may be regularly replaced for nutrient replenishment and/or recovery of cell products.

Immortalized cells. In animal tissue culture; cells that are capable of indefinite growth *in vitro.*

Immune interferon. See, *Interferon* γ.

Immune response. Production of antibodies by an animal exposed to a foreign antigen (foreign cell or molecule); the antibody is specific to the antigen and enables the elimination or neutralization of the antigens at this as well as subsequent exposures.

Immune system. The remarkably adaptive defence system of vertebrates that protects them from pathogenic microorganisms and cancer; generates enormous variety of cells and molecules that act together in a complex network to recognize and eliminate a virtually limitless variety of foreign invaders.

Immunity. The state of protection from infectious diseases; two types; innate or non-specific immunity and acquired or specific immunity.

Immunization. Introduction of a pathogen-derived antigen/vaccine into an individual/ animal; leads to the development of immunity in the vaccinated/immunized individuals to the concerned pathogen.

Immunodeficiency. Impairment of the immune system to various degrees so that it is unable to protect the affected individual from disease causing agents or malignant cells; affects either adaptive or innate immune functions, and it may be primary or secondary in nature.

Immunoelectrophoresis. The principle of this method is that a protein-antibody precipitate forms and becomes immobilized in the gel matrix when the protein and antibody concentration ratio is at the equivalence point; this method has three modification, *viz.,* counter-immunoelectrophoresis, rocket immuno-electrophoresis, and zone electrophoresis–immunodiffusion.

Immunofixation. The selected antibody is allowed to diffuse into the gel and form insoluble precipitates with the protein for which it is specific. Therefore, the non precipitated proteins are readily washed out, leaving in the gel only the concerned protein fraction.

Immunogen. A molecule, which induces the production of antibodies specific to itself when introduced into an animal, most antigens are immunogens as well.

Immunogenicity. Ability of an antigen to induce immune response.

Immunoglobulins (Igs). Antibodies; a special category of proteins that are ordinarily glycosylated; produced in animals in response to specific molecules called antigens.

Immunoglobulins class. Antibodies belonging to a class react to the same antibodies, *i.e.,* have the same constant region of the heavy chain; five classes: IgG, IgM, IgA, IgD and IgE.

Immunologic memory. Once the immune system has recognized and responded to an antigen, it is able to respond to this antigen more strongly on subsequent exposures; basis for long-term immunity to many pathogens.

Immunological screening. In this screening, an antibody specific to the protein encoded by the gene of interest is used to identify the desired recombinant clone.

Immunologically privileged sites. Lymphocytes can not enter certain body tissues, *e.g.,* brain, testis and the anterior chamber of eye, due to an effective barrier between blood and these tissues, therefore, these tissues are protected from the adaptive immune response, and are known as immunologically privileged sites.

Immunoprinting. In this case, an agarose gel or cellulose acetate membrane impregnated with antibodies is placed on top of the gel in which proteins were separated. The proteins diffuse from the gel towards the antibodies, and identification is done in the gel/cellulose acetate membrane containing the antibodies.

Immunopurification. Use of antibodies to purify specific antigens, *e.g.,* affinity chromatography.

Immuno-suppressive therapy. A drug administration regime that suppresses the immune response; used to prevent rejection of allografts.

Immunotoxin. A toxin polypeptide linked to an antibody, usually, specific to some tumour–specific antigen.

Immurement cultures. Cells are immobilized within a permeable barrier, *e.g.,* hollow-fibres.

Inbred. See, *Inbred line.*

Inbred line. In cross pollinated crops; a nearly homozygous line developed by continued inbreeding, usually, selfing accompanied by selection.

Inbreeding. Mating between individuals sharing a common parent in their ancestory.

Incompatibility group. In case of plasmids, two or more different plasmids belonging to the same incompatibility group, *i.e.,* they can not reside in the same host cell so that only one of them can be maintained in the cell; plasmids belonging to a single incompatibility group are believed to share the same mechanism of replication control.

Indel. It is the site where a segment of DNA has either been added into one sequence or deleted from the other sequence; indels are identified by comparing two almost identical/similar/related DNA sequences.

Indicator organism. An organism, the presence or absence of which indicates certain conditions, *e.g.,* presence of *E. coli* indicates that water is contaminated by faecal wastes and that pathogens may be present, the absence of *E. coli* indicates that water is free from pathogens.

Indicator plants. Plants of a species or variety, which is highly susceptible to a biological or abiological stress; used to detect the presence of the concerned stress.

Indirect selection. This selection strategy does not allow the desired mutants to divide, while wild type cells divide and thereby commit suicide taking up a negative selection agent, *e.g.,* 5–BUdR in their DNA.

Indirect somatic embryogenesis. Several mitotic cell divisions in explant cells produce unorganized mass of cells from which somatic embryos regenerate.

Induced embryogenic determined cells (IEDCs). Cells of an explant, which become embryogenic during *in vitro* culture.

Induced pollen grain. A pollen grain embarked on pollen embryo development in response to *in vitro* culture.

Induced protoplast fusion. Fusion brought about by a suitable fusogen or some fusion treatment, including a short high voltage pulse.

Induction medium. A medium which brings about dedifferentiation of explant cells to meristematic state; cells become capable of organogenesis.

Induction of androgenesis. Events occurring in pollen after anther culture and leading to the first cell division; represents dedifferentiation of pollen grains.

Induction of somatic embryo. See, *Acquision of totipotency.*

Inductive period. The period during which cultured explants undergo biochemical changes before they begin to divide; 6-12 days in anther culture.

Industrial alcohol. Ethanol used for industrial, laboratory and fuel purposes.

Industrial biotechnology. Use of biological agents, especially microorganisms/enzymes, in industrial processes to generate useful products and/or services for welfare of mankind.

Industrial microbiology. Use of microbes in industrial processes to obtain a product or service of economic value.

Industrial smog. The grayish mixture of moisture, soot, and sulphurous compounds that occurs in local areas in which industries are concentrated and coal is the primary energy source.

Infection. Establishment of the pathogen into the tissue.

Inflammatory response. This response is initiated by a variety of chemical mediators derived from invading microorganisms, damaged cells, various white blood cells, etc; the mechanism of initiation of inflammatory response is, however, not well understood.

Inhibitor-induced enzyme memory. When an enzyme is lyophilized in the presence of a competitive inhibitor, the enzyme molecules maintain their activated form in the organic solvent even after the inhibitor has been removed.

Innate immunity. It is the basic resistance to diseases that an individual has from the time of its birth; these mechanisms provide the first line of defence and eliminate most of the microorganisms encountered by a healthy individual; consists of four types of barriers, *viz.*, anatomic, physiologic, endocytic, and phagocytic and inflammatory components.

Inoculum. *In microbiology;* the cell, spore etc. used for inoculation. *In plant tissue culture;* the culture transferred into fresh medium during subculture; usually, 20% of the fresh medium volume.

Inoculum development. Preparation of a population of actively growing microorganisms, which is suitable for inoculation in the final production stage, from a dormant stock culture.

'In-out' strategy. See, *Hit*- and-run method; name based on the fact that the vector sequences are first integrated into the genome, and then they are removed out of the genome.

In ovulo. Within ovules.

***In planta* transformation.** Imbibition of *Arabidopsis* seeds or plants prior to flowering (under partial vacuum) in fresh cultures of *Agrobacterium* leads to stable transformation.

Insertion sequence. See, *IS element.*

Insertion vector. In case of λ vector, a large portion of the nonessential region is deleted and the two arms of λ genome are ligated. *In targeted gene transfer*; linearized vector that has at its two ends the sequences where recombination will occur to allow insertion of recombinant DNA at specific sites in the host genome.

Insertional inactivation. Inactivation of a gene by insertion of a DNA sequence within it.

Insertional mutagenesis. In this approach, a piece of DNA, *e.g.*, T-DNA of *Agrobacterium* or a transposable element, is randomly inserted into the genome causing disruption and loss of gene function. The inserted DNA sequence is used as a tag to isolate DNA sequences from the gene into which it is now located.

***In situ* germplasm conservation.** Conservation of germplasm in its natural location by protecting the area from human interference; applicable to germplasms of wild relatives only.

***In situ* hybridization.** Hybridization of radioactive probes with chromosomes, pathogens present within cells fixed on microscopic slides as sections/squashes, etc.; used for locating specific sequences in chromosomes, detecting viruses, etc. in cells/tissues.

***In situ* product recovery.** Continuous removal of the product during the period of fermentation; used in cases where product inhibits its own formation; achieved by vacuum, dialysis or two-phase systems.

Integrated waste management. An approach to municipal solid waste that provides several options for dealing with wastes, including recycling, composting, waste reduction, land-filling, and incineration.

Integrative transformation. Transgene integrated into host genome; stable and heritable, usually, shows typical Mendelian inheritance of transgene.

Intellectual property. It is an idea, a design, an invention, a manuscript, etc., which can ultimately give rise to useful product/application.

Intellectual property right (IPR). The right of an inventor to derive economic benefits from his invention, *i.e.,* intellectual property, and to exclude others from doing so.

Interest-sensitive speciesism. Acceptance of some animal suffering to serve the basic interest and welfare of mindkind.

Interferon. A protein produced by virus infected cells, which has the property of inhibiting other healthy cells from viral infection and cell prolification; can be used for the treatment of viral infection and cancer.

Interferon-α. A family of closely related proteins (interferons) produced by leucocytes in response to virus infection.

Interferon-β. A single protein species (interferons) produced by both leucocytes and fibroblasts in response to virus infection.

Interferon-γ. A single protein species produced by T-lymphocytes in response to antigen-activation.

Interferon-ω (omega). It is produced by virus infected cells.

Intermediate vector (IV). A modified *E.coli* plasmid containing a sequence of Ti or Ri T-DNA (without borders); integrated into the modified Ti to yield a cointegrate vector; used for cloning of genes in *E. coli.* prior to their transfer into plants.

Interplastidic. Wild type and transformed genomes are present in different chloroplasts.

Intersimple sequence repeats (ISSR). See, *Single primer amplification reaction (SPAR).*

Inter-SSR amplification (ISA). See, *Single primer amplification reaction (SPAR).*

Intra-ovarian pollination. Introduction of pollen grains directly into the ovary.

Intraplastidic. Two types of genomes (wild and transformed) are present within a single plastid.

Intron. In case of eukaryotic genes; the non-expressed sequences present in alternation with the expressed (exon) sequences; they are removed during mRNA processing and are absent from mature mRNA.

Invention. It is an intellectual creation by an inventor; before this creation, people would not know about it.

Inventiveness. The invention should not be obvious to persons skilled in the art and should represent an innovation.

Inverse PCR. Amplification of those DNA sequences, which are located on the outside of the primers used for amplification; it involves restriction digestion of sample DNA, ligation of the fragments, and opening of the circular DNA molecules before PCR.

Invert syrup. When 70% (w/v) cane sugar syrup is hydrolysed by invertase, it yield a mixture of glucose and fructose, which is called invert syrup; it is sweeter than sucrose syrup.

***In vitro*.** Literally, in glass; the process is carried out under sterile conditions outside the body of an organisms.

***In vitro* acclimatization.** See, *In vitro hardening.*

***In vitro* fertilization.** *In plants*, *in vitro* fusion between an isolated egg cell and a sperm. *In animals,* union between an oocyte and a sperm outside the body of female; the resulting embryo is transferred into the uterus of surrogate female.

***In vitro* grafting.** See, *Micrografting.*

***In vitro* hardening.** Tissue culture-raised plantlets are subjected to specific culture regimes aimed at making them capable of surviving the uncontrolled and harsher *ex vitro* environments.

***In vitro* ovular pollination.** Pollination of *in vitro* cultured ovules; pollen dusted directly onto the ovules.

***In vitro* pollination.** Application of pollen grains onto stigma of cultured pistils or onto cultured ovules.

***In vitro* techniques.** The techniques of cell, tissue and organ culture.

***In vitro* transformation.** See, *Transformation.*

***In vivo*.** Literally, in life; a process occurs inside the body of an organism.

***In vivo* rooting.** Shoots produced *in vitro* transferred directly into vermiculite or potting mix with or without treatment with an auxin; rooting occurs in the pots kept under high humidity and low light intensity.

Ion exchange chromatography. Separation of macromolecules based on their interaction with ionic groups present on the matrix.

Ionic osmoticum. It consists, usually, of salts, *e.g.*, 335 m mol/l KCl and 40 m mol/l $MgSO_4$; generally used with the ezyme solution during protoplast isolation; when used in protoplast culture medium, it interferes with cell wall development.

IS element. DNA segment of about 800–1400 bp, capable of integrating into, and dissociating from and moving to a new location in the chromosomes of prokaryotes and eukaryotes.

Isogenic lines. Lines identical in genotype at all loci, except one.

Isograft. Graft obtained from another individual that is genetically identical to the host.

Isomerases. A class of enzymes, which catalyse the formation of isomers of molecules.

Isoschizomers. When two different restriction enzymes recognize the some target sequence, but one of them is able to recognize both methylated as well as non-methylated target sequences, while the other enzyme can recognize only the non-methylated target sequence, such enzymes are known as isoschizomers.

Isotonic. A solution having the same osmotic pressure as the cell/tissue in question.

Isozyme. It is a variant of an enzyme or protein that shows a different mobility during electrophoresis; used as a genetic marker.

Jumping library. A clone of such a library contains sequences on one side each of two recognition sites of a rare cutting enzyme, *e.g.*, NotI for human genome.

Juvenile. In case of woody trees; young seedlings and saplings; juvenile shoots are easy to root and show easy shoot multiplication.

Kb. Kilobase; denotes the length of DNA in terms of nucleotide number.

Kinase. An enzyme that phosphorylates a substrate, *e.g.*, a protein kinase phosphorylates amino acids of a protein.

Kinetic energy. The energy inherent in motion or movement including molecular movement (heat) and the movement of waves.

Kinship analysis. Determination of whether two or more individuals are members of the same family.

Klenow fragment. DNA polymerase I of *E. coli* from which the fragment having $5' \rightarrow 3'$ exonuclease activity is deleted is called Klenow fragment; used in *in vitro* DNA replication.

Knockout mice. Mice strains in which specific genes have either been disrupted or replaced by other genes.

Koji. Solid substrate fermentation.

Kozak sequence. A sequence that flanks the AUG codon, *e.g.*, CCGCC***AUG***GGG; needed for optimal translation in eukaryotes.

Kozak's rules. For efficient translation in eukaryotes, the sequence around initiation codon should conform to Kozak's rules; of these, the most important is the presence of a purine at the –3 position and a G at the +4 position; the A of the AUG initiation codon is counted as +1, U as +2 and so on.

Kyoto Protocol. An International agreement among the developed countries to curb green house gas emissions. The Kyoto Protocol was formed in December, 1997.

Labelling. Tagging of a DNA molecule/protein, etc. by attaching to it an easily detectable, *viz.*, radioactive or nonradioactive, group

Lag phase. A brief period following subculture when there is no cell division/growth.

Lagging strand. The strand of a DNA duplex that is in $5' \rightarrow 3'$ orientation with respect to the origin of replication; it replicates in discontinuous manner and the site of replication follows at some distance from that of the leading strand.

Laminar air-flow cabinet. A cabinet or work station where sterile air flows through the cabinet at a velocity of about 27±3 m/min; used for aseptic handling of materials.

Land-fill site. A location at which a pit was filled with, usually, domestic refuse, covered with soil and, generally, landscaped.

Latent traits. Traits that are not expressed in wild species, but become expressed in the progeny derived from complex wild species hybrids.

Lateral gene transfer. See, *Horizontal gene transfer.*

Late-region replacement vector. SV40 (mammalian) transducing vector; the late region of SV40 virus genome that specifies VP1, VP2 and VP3 is replaced by DNA insert.

Late replacement vector. See, *Late-region replacement vector.*

Law of conservation of matter. This law states that in chemical reactions, atoms are neither created, nor changed nor destroyed; they are only rearranged.

Law of limiting factors. This law states that a system may be limited by the absence or minimum amount (in terms of that needed) of any required factor.

Leader sequence. The non-translated segment of an mRNA located at its 5′-end.

Leading strand. The DNA strand present in 5′ → 3′ orientation with respect to the origin of replication; its replication is continuous and proceeds ahead of the other strand.

Lectin pathway. It is initiated when MBL (mannose-binding lectin) is produced in inflammatory response; the lectin binds to a mannose residue on a glycoprotein or a carbohydrate.

Lectins. These are proteins that bind to a carbohydrate residue of a glycoprotein or a polysaccharide.

Library screening strategies. The various strategies used for identification of a single clone (from among the thousands obtained from a cloning experiment), which has the DNA insert of interest; they can be grouped into two broad categories: sequence-dependent screening and screening of the expressed product.

Liebig's law of minimums. See, *Law of limiting factors.*

Lifting the plasmid. The plasmid component of a phagemid vector contains the λ attachment (λ *attB*) site; as a result, the plasmid may integrate into the λ genome by the same site-specific recombination event that leads to the integration of λ genome into the bacterial chromosome; this event is called 'lifting the plasmid'.

Ligase chain reaction (LCR). A detection technique for target DNA sequences using a thermocycler, a thermostable DNA ligase and two probes representing contiguous sequences of the target pathogen genome.

Ligases. A class of enzymes, which catalyse the formation of covalent bonds between two molecules utilizing the energy obtained from hydrolysis of a nucleotide triphosphate like ATP, GTP, etc.

Lightbeer. Low calorie, low solids beer produced by hydrolysis of dextrins present in normal beer to glucose, which is converted to alcohol.

Light chain of antibodies. The 220 amino acid long chains; 2 chains present in each antibody molecule; two types: Lambda and Kappa.

Light response element (LRE). An enhancer sequence activated by light; it makes the activity of a promoter light-dependent.

Line. A group of individuals having common parents/ancestors.

Linkage. The tendency of two or more genes located on the same chromosome to be inherited together.

Linkage drag. Unintended transfer of undesirable characters linked to the character being transferred.

Linkage map. It depicts the order of genetic markers and the relative distances between them; measured by recombination frequency between the markers.

Linkers. These are short, chemically synthesized, double-stranded oligonucleotides, which contain within them one or more restriction endonuclease sites; joined to blunt-ended DNA fragments to produce suitable sticky protruding ends (after digestion with the appropriate restriction endonuclease).

Linking library. A clone of such a library has sequences present on either side of a single recognition site of a rare cutting enzyme like *Not I* for human genome.

Lipids. A class of natural organic molecules that includes animal fats, vegetable oils and phospholipids, the last being an integral part of the cellular membranes.

Lipofection. Delivery of DNA into cells using liposomes; the DNA is encapsulated within or adheres to the outside of liposomes; highly successful with animal cells.

Liposomes. Very small vesicles formed by lipids (neutral or cationic lipids); used for transformation, drug delivery, etc.

Liquefaction. Digestion of starch by α-amylase to produce soluble dextrin molecules.

Living skin equivalent (LSE). Reconstituted virtually complete skin (both epidermis and dermis) from epidermis produced *in vitro*; production technology employs a collagen matrix as a support for growth of the tissues.

Local alignment. It finds the optimal alignment between subregions or local regions of the submitted sequence and those in the database.

Locuslink. This search engine provides information about genes, including their official name; in addition, it also allows search for genes homologous to a given gene and to obtain information about these genes.

Locus. Fixed position of a gene in a chromosome; also used as synonomous of gene; ploural, loci

Lod score method. A statistical test used to detect linkage; pooled data from a large number of pedigrees or crosses are analysed to determine the probability that two markers exhibit a certain degree of linkage and also the probability that given data would have been obtained if two markers were unlinked; lod (logarithm of odds) score is the $\log_{10}$ of the ratio between these two values.

Log phase. The period of rapid increase in cell number (or biomass) in a batch culture; usually, 3-4 cell generation, (after this, growth begins to decline and stops completely).

Long product. During first cycle of amplification, extension of primer continues till the strands are separated during the denaturation step of the next PCR cycle. Therefore, amplification products of this extension step and indeed of every cycle based on the original template DNA, is of indefinite length; this PCR product is usually called long product.

Low technology digesters. These digesters are simple in design and consist of a digester, a tank for preparation of the substrate for feeding the digesters, an effluent transfer tank and a biogas storage tank, *e.g.*, gobar gas digester.

Luxury genes. Those genes, which are expressed either in specialized cells or in response to an specific stimuli.

Lyases. A class of enzymes involved in reactions resulting in the removal of a group of atoms from the substrate molecule.

Lymph. A clear watery fluid that is formed as a filtrate of blood; it contains white blood cells; collects in a series of special vessels and is returned to the blood stream.

Lymph nodes. These are enlargements in the lymph vessels; in these nodes, the lymphatic tissue is separated into compartments by fibrous partitions.

Lymphatic system. A system of fine thin-walled channels through which most of the tissue fluid flows.

Lymphocyte progenitor cells. Cells derived from lymphoid stem cells, and differentiate into B and T cells.

Lymphocytes. White blood cells, which possess antigen-binding cell-surface receptors and are responsible for the specificity, diversity, memory and self/non-self recognition by the immune system; two types: B and T lymphocytes.

Lymphoid stem cells. These cells differentiate into lymphocyte progenitor cells.

Lysogenic phage. A bacteriophage that either lyses the infected bacterial cells or it integrates into their chromosomes and replicates with them as prophage.

Lysozyme. This enzyme is present in egg white, tear and saliva; it digests the polymeric compounds that impart rigidity to the bacterial cell wall.

Lytic phage. A phage that always lyses the infected bacterial cells.

Macrocarrier. In case of particle gun; 2.5 cm diameter and 0.06 mm thick plastic membrane to which microprojectiles are attached; used only once.

Macerozyme. Pectinase activity; used for protoplast isolation; isolated from *Rhizopus* species; usual concentration, 0.1-0.5%.

Macroinjection. In genetic transformation of plants; DNA solution is injected into the lumen of developing inflorescence; DNA taken up by microspores, where it produces transformants; inconsistent results.

Macronutrients. Elements required by plants in concentrations greater than 0.5 mmol/l; six in number, *viz.,* N, P, K, S, Ca and Mg.

Macroprojectile. See, *Macrocarrier.*

Macrosatellite-primed PCR (MP-PCR). See, *Single primer amplification reaction (SPAR).*

Male sterility. Inability of a genotype to produce functional pollen; three types: cytoplasmic, genetic and cytoplasmic-genetic male sterility.

Malignant tumour. It has ability to grow indefinitely and invade the surrounding healthy tissues.

Malnutrition. Refers to the lack of essential nutrients, such as vitamins, minerals and amino acids.

Malt. See, *Barley malt.*

Maltose. A disaccharide, which yields two molecules of glucose on hydrolysis; in alfalfa tissue culture, improves the quality and quantity of somatic embryos and, at the same time, eliminates callus growth, concentration used, 7.5–300 mM.

Maltose syrup. It is produced from liquified starch by the action of fungal α-amylase; contains 45-60% maltose.

Mammalian artificial chromosome (MAC) vectors. These are linear vectors that contain telomeres, origin of replication, centromeric sequences and transcriptionally active chromosomal domains; these vectors resemble minichromosomes, are mitotically and cytogenetically stable in the absence of any selection, bind centromere proteins specific for active centromeres, *viz.,* CENP-B, CENP-C and CENP-E and are about 6-10 megabases ($6\text{-}10 \times 10^6$) in size.

Map unit. See, *CentiMorgan.*

Map-based cloning. A strategy in which a gene of interest is isolated and cloned, based on its mapped position on a chromosome, *i.e.,* close linkage to a known gene/genetic marker, *e.g.,* an RFLP locus, an STS or some other DNA marker.

Mapping population. A population that is studied for the preparation of genetic maps.

Marker-aided selection : *See Marker-assisted selection.*

Marker-assisted selection (MAS). DNA markers are used for indirect selection of those traits, which are difficult to select through visual observations based on phenotype.

Marker gene. See, *Reporter gene.*

Marker rescue approach. In this approach, a mutant strain of *E. coli* host is used for transformation. The cells are plated, following their transformation, under such a set of conditions in which function of mutant gene is essential for survival/multiplication of the cells. As a result, only those transformed cells will produce colonies that have this gene in their recombinant DNA and express the wild type allele of the mutant gene.

Marker. A morphological, biochemical or molecular trait used for selection/identification of organisms/cells exhibiting the marker.

Mash. See, *Mashing.*

Mashing. The malt is powdered and mixed with warm water at 70°C and pH 5.0.

Matrix. A biologically and chemically intert material generally used for immbolization of cells/tisues/enzymes, etc.

Maxam and Gilbert procedure of DNA sequencing. It is based on base specific chemical cleavage (at sites of G, C, G+A or C+T) of single end-labelled DNA stands.

Medical biotechnology. Refers to the development of various biochemicals for diagnosis/cure of various genetic/pathological diseases.

Medium. See, *Culture medium.*

Medium browning. In tissue cultures of woody species (usually), due to oxidation of phenolic compounds leached from explants; toxic to plant tissues; controlled by frequent subculture, culture in dark, using antioxidants like cysteine HCl (100 mg/l), ascorbic acid (50–100 mg/l) or citric acid (150 mg/l) or absorbents like activated charcoal or polyvinyl pyrrolidon (PVP).

Medium perfusion. Medium is continuously taken from culture vessel, passed through an oxygenation chamber and returned to the culture.

Melting temperature (Tm). In case of DNA; the temperature at which the two strands of the duplex dissociate, *i.e.,* denature.

Membrane confinement. Enzyme molecules, usually in an aqueous solution, may be confined within a semi-permeable membrane, which idealy allows a free movement in either direction to the substrates and products, but does not permit the enzyme molecules to escape.

Membrane (enzyme) reactor. Reactor vessel, having two chambers separated by a semipermeable membrane; one chamber contains enzymes, while the second chamber contains substrate and product; may be used in continuous or batch mode.

Memory cells. These cells differentiate from mature B cells after their interaction with an antigen; they do not secrete any antibody, and exhibit the sIg just as do the naive B cells.

Mericloning. Refers to micropropagation through meristem culture; *not in common use.*

Meristem culture. Culture of aseptically isolated axillary or apical meristems, particularly shoot apical meristems, to obtain shoots/plantlets.

Meristematic dome. See, *Shoot apical meristem.*

Meristematic region. The actively dividing zone in a plant.

Meristem-tip. See, *Shoot apex.*

Meristemoids. When explant/callus is cultured onto a medium favouring shoot regeneration, clusters of meristematic cells appear in the explant/callus; these are called meristemoids; considered to arise in areas that accumulate starch, which is believed to serve as an energy source for shoot bud differentiation; root regeneration also occurs.

Mesophyll. In case of leaf; parenchymatous cells between lower and upper epidermis (except vascular bundles); palisade and spongy tissues.

Metabolic cooperation. Cross-feeding among cells of a cell mass, so that wild type cells also survive alongwith variant cells; increases the frequency of escapes and chimeras.

Metabolic engineering. Introduction of transgenes affecting enzymatic, transport and regulatory functions to modify metabolic activities of an organism with a view to obtain a modified product, a new product, a better utilization of substrate, etc.

Metabolism. Chemical reactions that make life possible; two types: anabolism and catabolism.

Metabolite. A chemical that is a normal cell constituent capable of entering into bio-chemical transformations within living systems.

Metabolomics. Deals with the study of all metabolites.

Metastasis. A process in which small clusters of cancerous cells dislodge from a primary tumour, invade the blood or lymphatic vessels and are carried to other tissues where they continue to proliferate and give rise to secondary tumours.

Methane (CH_4). It is the primary constituent of natural gas and is also a product of fermentation by microbes; one of the green house gases.

Methylation. See, *DNA methylation.*

Metric traits. See, *Quantitative traits.*

Microarray. An assembly of a large number of small dots onto a solid support, each dot containing a short sequence of a different gene of the organism concerned or different antibodies.

Microbes. They are microscopic organisms, primarily bacteria, viruses or protozoa.

Microbial bioremediation. Bioremediation of organic contaminants based on either micro-organisms naturally present at the site or on microbial inoculants developed in the laboratory and introduced at the site.

Microbial ore leaching. Use of bacteria, mainly *Thiobacillus ferrooxidans,* to obtain leaching of metal sulphates from low grade ores containing insoluble metal sulphides.

Microbial pesticides. Refer to the pesticides which are formulated from microorganisms *viz.*, bacteria, fungi and viruses. *B. thuringiensis* is the most widely used microbial pesticides.

Microcarrier. See, *Microprojectile.*

Microcarrier culture. In this culture, 90-300 μm dia particles of dextran, etc. are used for cell attachment.

Microchromosome. A very small chromosome occurring naturally or produced by deletion of most of the chromatin of a chromosome.

Microelectrofusion. Protoplast pairs are individually transferred into microfusion chambers with the help of a micromanipulator setup, and are induced to fuse by a single or multiple negative DC-pulse of 800 to 1800 V/cm for 50 microseconds after mutual dielectrophoresis (1 MHz; 65-80 V/cm).

Microfiltration. It is a process for purifying water in which water is forced under very high pressure through a membrane that has fine enough pores to filter out ions and molecules in solution; used by small desalinization plants to filter out salt from seawater.

Micrografting. In this technique, *in vitro* derived virus-free shoots are grafted onto healthy root-stock seedlings grown *in vitro* to obtain virus-free plants.

Microinjection. Delivery of DNA directly into the cytoplasm/nucleus of cells/male pronucleus of fertilized egg/young embryos; micro-manipulators are used to hold the eggs and to microinject DNA.

Micronutrients. Elements required by plants in concentrations less than 0.5 mmole/l, *viz.*, Fe, Zn, Mn, Cu, B, Mo.

Microprojectile. In case of particle gun; 1-2 μm diameter tungsten/gold particles that are coated with DNA, and then attached to macrocarrier for delivery into cells.

Micropropagation. *In vitro* production of a large number of small plantlets from cultured cells/tissues; through axillary branching, adventitious shoot bud regeneration or somatic embryogensis.

Microprotoplast. It is a small protoplast; contains a micronucleus having a subdiploid chromosome complement.

Microsatellite DNAs. These are short DNA segments of less than 100 bp and are made up of tandem repeats of 2 to 7 bp.

Microscopic colony. A colony which is not visible to the naked eye so that it is not easily isolated and subcultured.

Microcosm study. In this approach, a piece of nature, *e.g.,* soil, river sediment, polluted river water, etc., is removed and brought to the laboratory; most environmental factors like temperature, humidity, day-night cycles, etc. are controlled and the survival of marked GEM strain is monitored over time.

Microspore. The haploid cell which matures into pollen and ultimately gives rise to the male gametophyte.

Microspore mother cell (MMC). In young anther; the cell which undergoes meiosis to produce pollen grains.

Micro-Ti plasmid. See *Mini-Ti plasmid.*

Midnight dumping. The illicit dumping of materials, particularly hazardous wastes, frequently under the cover of darkness.

Minamata disease. A disease named for fishing village in Japan where an epidemic first occurred. This disease was found to be the result of mercury poisoning.

Minichromosome vector. These yeast shuttle vectors behave like very small chromosomes in that they replicate only once during each cell division and are distributed to daughter cells like true chromosomes since they contain *ARS* and *CEN* sequences of yeast chromosomes.

Minimal medium. A medium containing only inorganic compounds and a simple carbon source.

Minisatellite DNAs. These are usually 0.2 to 2 kb long, and they consist of tandem repeats of 15-60 bp sequence.

Mini-Ti plasmid. An *E. coli* plasmid containing disarmed T-DNA (or at least the two borders of T-DNA); used for cloning of DNA inserts in *E. coli;* and then for transfer of DNA inserts into plant cells; one component of a binary vector system.

Mitotic index. The proportion of cells of a tissue that are in different stages of mitosis; thus MI (%) = (number of cells in mitosis/total number of cells).

Mixoploid. Tissue/cell mass containing cells of different ploidy levels.

Mobilization. When a non-conjugative plasmid is transferred alongwith a conjugative plasmid, which is residing in the same cell, this is called mobilization; depends on a sequence, *nic-bom site* (*bom,* basis for mobility), of the non-conjugative plasmid.

Mode of androgenesis. The pattern of initial few divisions in pollen grains during *in vitro* androgenesis; five distinct modes: pathways I, II, III, IV and V.

Model organism. An organism about which a large amount of scientific knowledge is already known/available.

Modern biotechnology. Application of *in vitro* nucleic acid techniques, including recombinant DNA techniques, and direct injection of nucleic acid into cells or organelles, or fusion of cells beyond the taxonomic family that overcomes natural physiological, reproductive or recombination barriers that are not the techniques of traditional breeding and selection.

Modified *cry* gene. A *cry* gene with changed base sequence, but unaltered amino acid sequence of the encoded protein; sequence modified to enhance expression in plants.

Modified droplet method of cryopreservation. The PVS-treated shoot-tips are placed singly in 7.5 μl droplets of the PVS onto pieces of heat-sterilized aluminium foil, and the foil packets are immersed in liquid nitrogen.

Module. A DNA segment/sequence performing a specific function, each module contains one or more genes. *Syn. Functional sequence.*

Molal solution. In this solution, one gram molecular weight of a substance is dissolve in one litre of water; final volume of the solution is generally greater than one litre.

Mole. Refers to molecular weight, *i.e.*, formula weight of a compound in grams; sum of the weights of the atoms in the chemical formula of a compound, *e.g.*, $C_6H_{12}O_6$; number of molecules per mole is constant for all compounds.

Mole/l. See, *Molar.*

Molar. It is the gram molecular weight of a compound present in one litre of solution; denoted by M; 1 molar = 1 gram molecular weight per litre = 1 mole per litre.

Molasses medium. It contains 6% sucrose (in form of molasses) to which are added ammonium sulphate, calcium carbonate, superphosphate and, sometimes, cornsteep liquor.

Molcular biology A branch of biology concerned with the study of molecular aspects of biological phenomena.

Molecular breeding. Plant breeding programmes that are supported by the use of DNA-based markers and recombinant DNA technology.

Molecular farming. See, *Gene farming.*

Molecular glue. See, *DNA ligase.*

Molecular marker. It is a genetic marker that is detected as differential mobility of a protein/DNA fragment or as differential amplification of a DNA sequence present in different individuals.

Molecular phylogeny. DNA and protein sequence data are used to investigate evolution of genes and their products.

Molecular scissor. See, *Restriction endonuclease.*

Monocistronic mRNA. An mRNA molecule that codes for a single polypeptide specified by a single cistron.

Monoclonal antibody. The antibody produced by a clone derived from a single hybrid cell (hybridome) obtained through the fusion of a single lymphocyte with either a tumour or tissue culture cell; it is specific to a single epitope of an antigen, and is highly pure as compared to those produced from the whole animals.

Monoploid. A cell/an individual having a single genome; haploid of a diploid species; represented by *x*.

Monopodial. The terminal bud of shoot continues to grow indefinitely and the lateral branches may or may not develop, *e.g.*, in orchids, *Vanda*, *Renanthera*, etc.

Monopolar germination. Development of both root and shoot from a single pole of the embryo, *e.g.*, from plumular pole in orchids and from radicular pole in parasitic members of Orobanchaceae.

Morality. The concept of certain things being right and certain other thing being wrong.

Morphogenesis. Development of a form or structure; in case of tissue culture, usually, the development of organs like shoot, root, somatic embryos, etc.

Morphogenic competence acquisition phase. During this phase of shoot induction; the explant cells acquire the capability to perceive the inductive stimuli and to respond to them; the cells remain flexible and can become committed to form either root or shoot.

Morphogenic potential. The ability of a cell/tissue to develop a form or structure; in case of tissue culture, usually, the ability of cells/cell masses to produce organs like shoot, root, somatic embryo, etc.

Morphological differentiation stage. During shoot regeneration; this stage follows shoot induction, and consists of repeated cell division leading to the specific pattern and organ formation.

Mosaic protein. Proteins composed of discrete domains, *e.g.*, serine proteases involved in blood coagulation.

Multicolour fluorescence *in situ* hybridization (McFISH). Different fluorochromes are used to identify the relative location of two or more genes by *in situ* hybridization.

Multilocus probe (MLP) analysis. Use of a probe that identifies several DNA fragments for DNA fingerprinting.

Multiplex PCR. In this PCR, a series of primers, each of which is specific for a separate STR locus, is used in a single reaction.

Multistage bioreactor. This culture system uses two or more bioreactors in a specified sequence each of which carries out a specific step of the total production process; used in batch or continuous mode.

Mushroom. Fruiting bodies of certain basidiomycetous fungi.

Mutagen. An agent, which has the ability to induce mutation; may be physical or chemical in nature.

Mutagenesis. Treatment of cells/tissues/organs, etc. with a mutagen for induction of mutations.

Mutant. A variant phenotype that is stable and heritable through sexual reproduction; only these can be used in crop improvment.

Mutant selection. Selection of mutant cells based on specific selection media and procedures, which allow selective survival and/or proliferation of mutant cells only.

Mutation. A sudden and heritable change in the character(s) of an organism; may be due to altered base sequence (addition, deletion or base substitution) of a gene, change in chromosome number/structure or in base sequence of a plasmagene.

Mycoplasma. A highly pleomorphic, plastic organisms that contain DNA, RNA and tRNA and are bounded by triple layered unit membrane (plasma membrane).

Mycorrhiza. Mycelia of certain fungi that grow symbiotically with the roots of some plants and provide additional nutrient uptake.

Myeloid stem cells. These cells produce various types of blood cells.

Myeloma. Tumour cells of the antibody-forming system, *e.g.*, from B-lymphocytes.

***n*.** Haploid or gametic chromosome number/complement; normally, found in the gametes of a species; half of the somatic chromosome number.

***2n*.** Sporophytic/somatic chromosome number; normally, found in the somatic cells of a species; see *also, Disomic*.

N'emec phenomenon. Production of pollen embryo sac (in nature).

NAD/NAD$^+$. Nicotinamide adenine dinucleotide; a coenzyme that can accept two electrons and a proton; an important electron/hydrogen carrier in catabolism.

NADP/NADP$^+$. Nicotinamide adenine dinucleotide phosphate; a coenzyme resembling NAD, but with an additional phosphate group; an important electron/hydrogen carrier in photosynthesis and anabolism.

NADPH. Reduced NADP.

Naive B Cells. Mature B lymphocytes that are yet to encounter an antigen.

Naive T Cells. Mature T lymphocytes that are yet to encounter an antigen.

Naked eye polymorphism. Those genetic markers whose inheritance can be followed with the naked eye, without any specialized biochemical or molecular technique.

***n*-Alkanes.** Saturated, straight-chain hydrocarbons; constitute 0-30% of crude oil.

National Ambient Air Quality Standard. Refers to the allowable levels of ambient air pollutants set by EPA regulation.

National Emission Standard for Hazardous Air Pollutants. The standards for allowable emissions of certain toxic substances.

National Pollution Discharge Elimination System. An EPA administered programme that addresses point-source water pollution through the issuance of permits that regulate pollution discharge.

Natural killer cells (NK cells). A type of lymphocytes identifiable as large granular lymphocytes.

Natural medium. In animal cell culture; biological fluid used as medium.

Near isogenic lines (NILs). The lines developed by breeders through repeated backcrosses over the years; it is expected that lines derived through backcrossing are approximately identical in genotype except for the gene in question and those linked to it.

Negative selection. In this case, wild type (non-mutant) cells divide normally and are killed by a counter-selection agent, *e.g.*, 5-BUdR or arsenate; the mutant cells do not divide and, as a result, escape the counter-selection agent.

Negative selection of T-cells. All the T-cells, whose TCRs interact with MHC I or MHC II molecule-self-antigen complex or with MHC molecules with a high affinity, are marked for elimination; this constitutes negative selection.

Neoplasm. See, *Tumour.*

Nested PCR. In this PCR, the target sequence is amplified using a pair of primers, and a portion of the amplification product is reamplified using another pair of primers complementary to regions located internal to the sites of the first pair of primers.

Network. In case of computers, two or more computers connected together by a cable so that they can exchange information.

New biotechnology. Refers to the use of recombinant DNA technology to generate novel capabilities in organisms for generating useful products/services.

Nick. Cut (due to breakage of diester bond) in any one of the two strands of a DNA duplex; each nick has a free 3′- OH group; sealed by DNA ligase.

Nick translation. The process of radioactive or non-radioactive labelling of double-stranded DNA molecules by first nicking them with DNase I, then subjecting them to *E.coli,* DNA polymerase I, which successively adds new labelled nucleotides to the free 3′-OH end and progressively digests the 5′-end at the nick.

Nitrification. Oxidation of NH_4^+ by joint action of *Nitrosomonas* ($NH_4^+ \rightarrow NO_2^-$) and *Nitrobacter* ($NO_2^- \rightarrow NO_3^-$) to NO_3^-.

Nitrogen fixation. The process by which N_2 is reduced to NH_4^+.

Nitrogen oxides (NO_x). It is a group of nitrogen-oxygen compounds formed when some of the nitrogen gas in air combines with oxygen during high temperature; a major category of air pollutants and, alongwith hydrocarbons are a primary factor in ozone destruction and other photochemical smog; major NO_x are nitric oxide (NO), nitrogen dioxide (NO_2), and nitrogen tetroxide (N_2O_4).

Nitrogenous base. See, *Organic base.*

Nitrous oxide (N_2O). It comes from biomass burning, fossil fuel burning and use of chemical fertilizers; it contributes to ozone destruction in the stratosphere.

Novelty. In case of patents; the invention must be new and should not be already known to the public. In case of PBR; a variety should not have been commercially exploited for more than one year before the grant of PBR protection.

Node. The part of a stem bearing a leaf and an axillary bud.

Non-conjugative plasmids. These plasmid do not mediate DNA transfer through conjugation, *e.g.*, most Col plasmids and many R plasmids.

Non-essential region of λ genome. The region containing most of the genes for lysogeny; whole or a part of this segment is deleted to create certain λ vectors.

Non-ionic osmoticum. It contains non-ionizable organic compunds, *e.g.*, sorbitol, mannitol, etc.; usually, supplemented with 50-100 mmol/l $CaCl_2$ for enhanced stability of plasma membranes of protoplasts.

Non-permissive temperature. The range of temperatures in which a temperature sensitive mutant is unable to perform similar to the wild type of the species.

Non-productive re-arrangement. Antibody gene rearrangement that generates a V-J-C and V-D-J-C combination that does not encode a functional antibody chain.

Non-professional APCs. These cells can be induced to express MHC II or a costimulatory singal and many of them function as APCs only for short periods of time during a sustained inflammatory response, *e.g.*, fibroblasts (skin), glial cells (brain), vascular endothelial cells, etc.

Non-radioactive labelling. Labelling by biotin, digoxigenin, a fluorescent tag, etc.; detection by cytochemical reaction (biotin), using an antibody linked with an enzyme (digoxigenin), fluorescence, etc.

Non-renewable resources. Resources such as ores of various metals, oil, coal, that exist as finite deposits and that can not be replenished by natural processes after they are mined.

Non-replicating vector. In animals; vectors unable to replicate in animal cells.

Non-restrictive gel. In this gel, the frictional resistance of gel is almost negligible; as a result, the elctrophoretic mobility of the molecules depends only on their net charge.

Non-sense codon. A codon specifying no amino acid; signals translation termination; three codons: UAG, UAA and UGA.

Non-specific immunity. See, *Innate immunity.*

Non-specific toxin. See, *Host non-specific toxin.*

Non-traditional enzymes. Organic molecules of biological origin other than traditional enzymes and having catalytic activity, *e.g.*, abzymes and ribozymes.

Non-transformed cells. In animal cell culture; normal cells, which show finite life span *in vitro.*

Normal cells. See, *Non-transformed cells.*

Northern blotting. It includes electrophoresis of RNA sample and transfer of RNA from the gel onto a nylon membrane.

Northern hybridization. RNA sample is subjected to gel electrophoresis, RNA transferred from the gel onto a nylon membrane, immobilized and hybridized with a single stranded radioactive probe; autoradiography reveals the RNA band hybridized to the probe; used for detection of transcription of transgenes.

Nucellus. In ovules; the vegetative tissue enclosed by the two integuments; it surrounds the germinal cell that ultimately gives rise to embryo sac.

Nuclear abnormalties. See, *Cytogenetic abnormalties.*

Nuclear fragmentation. A single nucleus breaks up into 2 or more nuclei of variable sizes; mechanism unknown, but does not involve regular division; observed in explants like *Vicia faba* cotyledons (having 2C-128C nuclei) cultured *in vitro;* expected to produce aneuploid nuclei.

Nuclear transplantation. In case of protoplasts; introduction of isolated nuclei into protoplasts; PEG induces nucleus uptake in upto 5% of the protoplasts.

Nucleic acid hybridization. See, *Hybridization.*

Nucleoside. A compound formed by a linkage between an organic base and a pentose sugar.

Nucleotide. A compound resulting from linkage between nucleoside and phosphate.

Nullisomic. A cell/an individual having one chromosome pair less than the normal disomic complement of the species; represented by $2n - 2$; survive only in polyploid species.

Nutraceutical. A food or a part of food that provides medical or health benefits, including treatment of a diseases; the food substances used as nutraceuticals contain antioxidants, probiotics, omega-3 fatty acid and certain photochemical fibres.

Nutrient medium. See, *Culture medium.*

Nutrification. Enriching or fortifying foods with nutrients.

Obligate parasites. The parasites which survive only on living host protoplasm.

Obligate saprophytes. Refer to the saprophytes which survive/feed only on dead organic matter.

Off-line. When computer is unable to access the network, then it is called off-line.

Oil quality. Types and proportions of different fatty acids present in the given oil, which together determine the uses to which this oil can be put to.

Oilzapper. A consortium of bacterial species has been developed in India to combat oil spills and oily sludge.

Okazaki fragments. Small (1,000-2,000 nucleotide long in *E. coli*) polynucleotide fragments produced due to discontinuous replication of the lagging strand.

Old biotechnology. Exploitation of the natural capabilities of microorganisms, animal and plant cells or their components for generating useful products/vaccines.

Oligogenes. Genes, which have major effect on the expression of the concerned traits.

Oligonucleotide. A DNA segment having a small number of bases.

Oligosaccharides in morphogenesis. See *Oligosaccharins.*

Oligosaccharins. Cell wall-derived oligosaccharides; usually, produced locally by insect feeding and pathogen attack; act as elicitors of defence response; affect morphogenesis of plant cell cultures; mechanism of action not clear.

Oligospermia. A low sperm count of the semen.

Oncogene. A gene involved in tumour development; in case of *Agrobacterium*, genes specifying auxin and cytokinin biosynthesis.

On-line. When a computer is turned on and is able to access the network, the computer is said to be on-line.

One unit (of restriction enzyme). One unit of restriction enzyme is that quantity of enzyme, which completely digests 1 μg of DNA in one hour.

Open continuous culture. In this system, a volume of culture medium alongwith cells is taken out regularly from the culture and is replaced with an equal volume of fresh medium so that the culture remains at submaximal growth indefi-nitely; two types: turbidostat and chemostat.

Open reading frame (ORF). An ORF has a series of codons that specify an amino acid sequence.

Operator. The region of an operon that acts as the binding site for regulator protein.

Opine. A nitrogeneous compound (amino acid derivative) produced by crown galls/hairy roots, cell cultures obtained from them and plants regenerated from such cultures; used by *Agrobacterium* cells as carbon and nitrogen sources.

Optical biosensor. It measures the light produced or observed during reaction catalyzed by the biological component of the biosensor.

Orbital shaker. Shaker platform moves in a 2-3 cm orbital motion, has interchangeable clips to hold culture flasks, and shaking speed is 30-200 rpm (usually).

ORFans. Newly discovered genes that have no known function, or have only presumed function assigned by analogy with known genes.

Organ culture. *In vitro* culture of an organ, *e.g.*, shoot-tip, root-tip, embryos.

Organic base. Heterocyclic compounds found in nucleic acids that contain nitrogen in their rings; two types: pyrimidines and purines.

Organized tissue. A tissue composed of regularly differentiated cells as found *in vivo* in various organs.

Organogenesis. See, *Regeneration.*

Origin of replication. Semi-conservative replication of a DNA molecule begins at a definite point called origin of replication.

Orphans. See, *ORFans;* Syn., *Orphan gene.*

Orthodox seed. Moisture content of such seeds can be reduced to 5% or lower without reducing their viability; suited for long term storage; seed banks are ordinarily based on them.

Orthologues. Homologous genes found in different organisms; they encode proteins having the same function; evolved by direct vertical descent, and have diverged by accumulating mutations.

Osmotic stabilizer. A solution of adequate osmotic concentration used to prevent bursting or excessive plasmolysis of protoplasts. Syn., *Osmoticum.*

Osmoticum. A solution used to provide the necessary osmotic pressure, *e.g.,* for stability of protoplasts.

Overlap extension PCR. Used to introduce desired mutations in the internal sites of genes; uses 4 primers, 2 specific for the 3′-ends of the gene, the other 2 specific for the site of mutation, and carrying the mutation to be introduced.

Ovule androgenesis. Embryos develop inside an ovule but from the sperm only; usually, detected in progeny from interspecific crosses; yields haploids.

Ovule culture. Culture of aseptically excised ovules, usually fertilized, on an artificial medium.

Oxidation. Loss of an electron from a molecule.

Oxidoreductases. A class of enzymes involved in redox (reduction-oxidation) reactions, *i.e.,* transfer of hydrogen or oxygen atoms between molecules.

Ozone (O_3). A gas and pollutant in the lower atmosphere, but it is necessary to screen out UV radiation in the upper atmosphere; used for disinfecting water.

Ozone shield. Refers to the layer of ozone gas in the upper atmosphere that screens out harmful of UV radiation from the sun.

P element vector. A shuttle vector for *Drosophila*; usually, it has 31 bp inverted border sequences from the P element and other sequences from an *E. coli* plasmid.

Packed bed reactor. This reactor is packed with 1-3 mm pellets containing immobilized enzymes; substrate solution flows in from the lower end and product flows out of the upper end of the reactor.

Packed cell volume. The volume of cells present in a suspension culture determined following centrifugation at 200× g for 5 min.; expressed as pellet volume in ml/l of suspension culture.

Paddy mushroom. Fruiting bodies of *Volvariella* sp. grown commonly on paddy straw at 30–35°C.

Palindrome. In a palindrome, the base sequence in the second half of a DNA strand is the mirror image of the sequence in its first half, *e.g.,* 5′–GAA↑AAG–3′;
3′–CTT↑TTC–5′.

Palindrome with rotational symmetry. In this case, the base sequence in the first-half of one strand of a DNA double helix is the mirror image of the second-half of its complementary strand, *e.g.,* 5′–GAA↑TTC–3′
3′–CTT↑AAG–5′.

PAN (Peroxyacetylnitrates). A group of compounds present in photochemical smog that are extremely toxic to plants, and irritating to the eyes, nose and throat membranes.

Parallel mapping. RFLP markers mapped in one species or genus are used to construct genetic maps in related species or genera.

Paralogues. These are homologous genes within the same organism; they encode proteins that have related, but non-identical functions; evolved by gene duplication followed by mutation accumulation, *e.g.,* genes of the globin family.

Parasexual hybrid. See, *Somatic hybrid.*

Parasexual hybridization. Production of hybrid cells/individuals without gametic fusion, *e.g.,* through protoplast fusion; also see, *Somatic hybridization.*

Parasite. Refers to the organism, which generally feeds on living protoplasm.

Parthenogenesis. Embryo development from unfertilized egg cell; produces haploids or normal diploids depending upon whether the egg cell was haploid or diploid (= unreduced).

Parthenogenetic embryo. Embryo arisen from unfertilized egg cell.

Partial digestion (of DNA). The selected restriction enzyme cleaves the DNA molecules only at some of the target sites present in the molecule; selection of cleavage site is random.

Particle gun. A device to accelerate 1-2 μm tungsten or gold particles coated with DNA to effect transformation of animal or plant cells/ tissues; acceleration achieved by firing a blank cartridge (not in use), pressurized helium (in common use) or exposing a droplet of water to high voltage (this releases electrostatic energy).

Passive immunity. Antibodies against the pathogen are introduced into an individual to generate immunity.

Passive transfecting vector. See, *Non-replicating vector.*

Pasteur effect. Differential growth and physiological processes of microorganisms leading to differential accumulation of product in response to the presence or absence of O_2.

Pasteur pipette. It has a bulb at one end, while the other end is usually thin and long-drawn; used to withdraw solutions/suspensions, *e.g.*, from protoplast preparations.

Patent. A patent is the right granted by a government to an inventor to exclude others from imitating, manufacturing, using or selling the invention in question for commercial use during the specified period.

Patentability. The subject matter of the patent must be patentable under the existing law and its current interpretation.

Pathogen. An organism producing disease; usually, fungi, bacteria, viruses, mycoplasma, and nematodes.

Pathogen-free plants. Plant tested and shown to be free from a specific pathogen, usually a virus; generally, obtained by shoot-tip culture with or without thermo-therapy and cryo-therapy.

Pathotoxin. A toxin produced by a pathogen; a poor term since many toxins are produced by both pathogenic and nonpathogenic organisms; preferred term, toxin.

Pathway I of androgenesis. The first division of pollen nucleus yields two equal cells, and both participate in pollen embryo development.

Pathway II of androgenesis. First division in pollen is unequal, producing a larger vegetative cell and a smaller generative cell; pollen embryo arises from the vegetative cell.

Pathway III of androgenesis. First division in pollen produces unequal cells, and pollen embryo arises from the generative cell.

Pathway IV of androgenesis. First division of pollen yields unequal cells and both vegetative and generative cells participate in pollen embryo development.

PCBs (Polychlorinated biphenyls). A group of widely used industrial chemicals of chlorinated hydrocarbon class; extremely resistant to breakdown and subject to bioaccumulation.

PCR efficiency. The number of copies of the target sequence generated after a given number of PCR cycles; influenced by a large number of factors.

Pectinase. An enzyme that digests pectin; leads to separation of cells and makes cell walls accessible to cellulase; used for protoplast isolation (in combination with cellulase).

Pectolyase. An enzyme with a strong pectinase activity; isolated from *Aspergillus japonicus;* used for protoplast isolation.

Pedigree. A record of all parent-offspring relationships going back to some common ancestor.

Pedigree analysis. A study of pedigrees to decipher the mode of inheritance of human traits, *e.g.*, genetic diseases.

Pellet. The solid mass, which sediments at the buttom following centrifugation of a suspension.

Peptide mass fingerprinting. The peptide fragments produced after digestion with enzymes are analyzed by mass spectrometry.

Perfusion cultures. At regular intervals, a constant volume of spent medium (without cells) is withdrawn and equal volume of fresh or replenished medium is added back. Syn., *Closed continuous cultures.*

Peripheral lymphoid tissues. See, *Secondary, lymphoid tissues.*

Permanent transfection. See, *Stable transformation.*

Permanent transformation. Integration of the introduced gene(s) into the host genome; it generally occurs through homologous recombination in yeast, but is ordinarily random in plants and animals.

Permissive temperature. The range of temperatures in which a temperature-sensitive mutant performs normally, *i.e.,* like the wild type.

Persistent organic pollutants. Refers to the class of organic pollutants that are resistant to biodegradation and are often toxic, *e.g.,* DDT, dioxin, PCBs.

Petrochemical. A chemical made from petroleum (crude oil) as a basic raw material; it includes plastics, synthetic fibres, synthetic rubber, etc.

pH memory. The phenomenon that charged groups on the enzyme molecules retain the same ionization state that prevailed in the aqueous solution from which they were freeze-dried.

Phage display technique. In this strategy, the proteins to be screened are expressed as fusion proteins in such a way that they are displayed on the surface of the bacteriophage particles.

Phagemid. A plasmid vector that contains origin of replication from a phage, in addition to that of the plasmid.

Pharmacogenomics. The field of study concerned with the effect of a genetic variation on disease susceptibility and drug response; expected to develop individualized treatments that will be safer as well as more effective.

Pharming. Cultivation of transgenic plants for recovery of pharmaceutical compounds (medicines).

Phasmid. A vector based on a shortened λ genome containing λ *cos* site, lytic and DNA replication modules and one or (usually) more copies of a plasmid in place of the deleted sequences.

Phloroglucinol. A phenolic compound in xylem sap of apple; promotive of shoot multiplication and/or rooting in rosaceous fruit species; effect may be genotype-specific; findings equivocal.

Phosphodiester bond. In a phosphodiester bond, the 5′C of the pentose residue of one nucleotide is linked with one –O– (ester bond) of the phosphate residue, while the 3′C of the pentose of the next nucleotide is linked with another –O– of the same phosphate residue; this generates a 5′C–O–P–O–C3′ linkage.

Phosphodiester linkage. See, *Phosphodiester bond.*

Phosphorylation. Addition of a phosphate group to a compound.

Photoautotroph. An organism that harvests energy from sunlight and uses CO_2 as carbon source.

Photochemical oxidants. A major category of secondary air pollutants, including ozone that are highly toxic and damaging, especially to plants and forests.

Photochemical smog. The brownish haze that frequently forms on otherwise clear sunny days over large cities with significant amounts of automobile traffic.

Phylogenetic footprinting. A comparative analysis of genome sequences of related species to detect orthologous DNA sequences.

Photolithography. In this process printed oligonucleotide chips are produced by a light-directed printing technology.

Photovoltaic cells. Devices that convert light energy into electrical current.

Physical containment. Use of special laboratory designs, containment equipment and special operational procedures to restrict the number of organisms accidently released during normal laboratory operations and to prevent the infection of laboratory workers.

Physical map. In this map, genes are depicted in order as they occur in chromosomes and the distances between them are shown as number of base pairs.

Physiological barriers. These barriers include temperature, pH, oxygen tension and various soluble factors like lysozyme, interferon and complement system; involved in innate immunity.

Phytochrome. A pigment found in higher green plants; associated with the control of development in response to light stimulus.

Phytohormone. A plant hormone, *e.g.,* IAA, kinetin, etc.

Phytoplankton. Many species of photosynthetic microorganisms that consist of single cells or small groups of cells that live and grow freely suspended near the surface in water bodies.

Phytoremediation. Use of green plants and their associated microorganisms, soil amendments, and agronomic practices to remove, contain or render harmless environmental contaminants.

Phytostabilization. Use of plants to sequester contaminants in cell wall lignins of root tissues, or to promote its binding to humus.

Phytotoxic. Toxic to plants/plant cells.

Phytotoxin. A compound toxic to plants/plant cells; a poor term since it may be toxic to other organisms as well; preferred term toxin.

Piezoelectric device. See, *Acoustic wave biosensor.*

Piezoelectric effect. Certain crystals contain positive and negative charges, which separate, when they are subjected to stress; this generates an electric field called piezoelectric field; such crystals can be used to assay the mass of analyte that binds to the biological component immobilized on the crystal surface.

Pigment. A substance that absorbs visible light.

Pistil culture. Culture of entire pistil (usually, alongwith the pedicel, calyx and corolla); usually for *in vitro* pollination or embryo rescue. Syn., *Ovary culture.*

Pistillate. A flower having only the female reproductive organ; also a plant having such flowers.

Plankton. It includes phytoplankton and zooplankton forms.

Planned introduction. The process of taking genetically modified organisms from contained use to the open environment.

Plant biotechnology. Refers to the generation of useful products or services from plant cells, tissues and often organs.

Plant breeder's rights. These are rights granted by the government to a plant breeder, originator or owner of a variety to exclude others from producing or commercializing the propagating material of that variety for a minimum period of 15–20 years.

Plant protoplast. A plant cell from which cell wall has been removed, usually, by enzymatic digestion.

Plantlet. A small rooted shoot or germinated embryo (usually, somatic); it is similar to seedling obtained from seed germination.

Plaque. A clear bacteria-free zone in a bacterial lawn; produced by a lytic phage.

Plaque hybridization. If a library is available in the form of chimaeric phage particles carrying the cloned segments, a bacterial lawn is infected with a mixture of chimaeric phage particles (*i.e.*, the libraray) and a large number of plaques develop overnight. These plaques can be treated just like the colonies in colony hybridi-zation to identify and isolate the chimaeric phage particle carrying the gene of interest.

Plasma cells. Antibody producing B-cells that are derived from differentiation of mature B-cells following their interaction with an antigen; a single plasma cell can secrete more than 2,000 antibody molecule/second.

Plasma lemma. Membrane enclosing the protoplasm of a cell; selectively permeable; integrity essential for cell function and viability.

Plasmid. A circular DNA molecule, other than bacterial chromosome, having capacity of independent replication and transmission; used for gene cloning; most common form of bacterial vectors.

Plasmid like vector. SV40 vector capable of replication; used for gene cloning.

Plasmodesmata. A channel, which connects cytoplasm of two neighbouring cells.

Plasmolysis. Loss of water from a cell leading to visible reduction in the volume of its cytoplasm, which shrinks and vacates a portion of the cell lumen.

Plasmolyticum. A solution, which causes plasmolysis.

Plating efficiency. The proportion of initially plated/cultured cells/protoplasts, which divide and form colonies.

Pleiotropy. A single gene influences the expression of more than one character.

Pleuricotyledony. Presence of more than two cytoledons in an embryo.

Ploidy. Refers to the number of genomes or the completeness of genomes of a cell/an organism.

Plug flow type of digesters. These are tubular digesters without any stirring device; mixing occurs due to the gas formation; full size tubular digesters have been used in South Africa and USA.

Plumule. The part/structure of an embryo, which gives rise to shoot; usually, has leaf primordia.

PM2 and PM10. A standard criterion for pollutant suspended particulate matter. PM10 refers to particle smaller than 10 micrometer in diameter, while PM2 indicates particle smaller than 2 micro meter; smaller particles are readily inhaled directly into lungs.

pOH. It is the negative logarithm of the concentration of hydroxyl (OH^-) ions. Like pH, pOH ranges from 0–14, with each unit representing a tenfold increase over the preceding one. Lower the pOH, the higher is the conc. of OH^- ions.

Point source. Specific points of origin of pollutants, such as factory drains or outlets from sewage treatment plants.

Poison sequence. The *nic-bom* region; it interferes with replication efficiency of extrachromosomal DNA in monkey cells.

Pollen. A haploid cell obtained by maturation of a microspore; produces male gametophyte, normally, on reaching stigma.

Pollen callus. Callus derived from pollen grains; in anther or pollen culture.

Pollen culture. See, *Anther culture*.

Pollen dimorphism. Occurence of two morphological types of pollen grains in an anther, *viz.*, large pollen grains filled with starch and small pollen grains (Ca. 1%), *i.e.*, *s*-grain, faintly stain with acetocarmine; the latter are believed to exhibit androgenesis.

Pollen embryo. An embryo obtained from repeated cell divisions in a pollen grain; obtained by anther/pollen culture.

Pollen mitosis. Mitotic division of pollen nucleus; two successive divisions; *first division* yields a vegetative or tube nucleus and a generative nucleus; the *second division* occurs in generative nucleus to yield two sperm nuclei.

Pollen trap. A non-transgenic variety used to trap any pollen from the transgenic crop that may travel beyond the isolation distance.

Pollination. Application of active/functional pollen grains onto a receptive stigma.

Pollutant. A waste that damages the environment; two types: primary and secondary pollutants.

Pollution. Contamination of air, water or soil with undesirable amounts of material or heat.

Polyacrylamide gel. It is obtained by copolymerization of acrylamide ($CH_2 = CH–CHONH_2$) monomers with a cross-linking agent (usually, N, N′–methylenebisacrylamide, bisacrylamide in short); the temperature during polymerization should be maintained above 20°C in order to prevent incomplete polymerization.

Polyamines. Low molecular weight, polycationic, aliphatic nitrogenous compounds present in all prokaryotes and eukaryotes, *e.g.*, putrescine, cadaverine, spermidine, and spermine; in low concentrations, they affect cell division, cell growth and differentiation; many regard them as growth regulator; *in tissue culture*, may promote SE/shoot bud regeneration.

Polycistronic mRNA. An mRNA molecule that codes for more than one polypeptides.

Polyclonal antibodies. A serum containing antibodies of more than one specificity; produced due to the presence of more than one distinct epitope in the antigen used for immunization.

Polyethylene glycol (PEG). An efficient fusogen of plant protoplasts, animal cells, etc., and even of plant protoplasts with animal cells; non-specific fusion occurs during PEG elution.

Polyfunctional enzyme. An enzyme, which can catalyze more than two reactions; encoded by a recombinant gene.

Polygenes. Genes, which have small and cumulative (additive) effect on the expression of a trait.

Polygenic traits. See, *Quantitative traits*.

Polymerase chain reaction (PCR). Amplification of a DNA segment achieved by using a thermostable DNA polymerase, two primers specific to the 3′–ends of the DNA segment, and a thermal cycler.

Polymorphic markers. Markers differing among individuals/strains of a species.

Polymorphic probe. A probe which produces different RFLP patterns with different strains/ species, *e.g.*, minisatellite and microsatellite sequences.

Polymorphic region (of genome). That region of genomic DNA the sequence of which is different in different individuals; polymorphism is studied as RFLP or by PCR amplification.

Polynucleotide. A long chain of nucleotides linked to each other by phosphodiester bonds.

Polypeptide. A polypeptide consists of several amino acids joined in a sequence by peptide bonds; generally lacks full protein activity.

Polyploid. A cell/an individual having more than one genome or more than two copies of a single genome.

Polyploidy. The condition of being polyploid.

Polyribosome. See, *Polysome.*

Polysomaty. Each chromosome has four or more (ordinarily in multiples of 2) chromatids; produced by endoreduplication.

Polysome. An mRNA molecule associated with more than one ribosome each of which is associated with a molecule of the polypeptide being synthesized.

Polysomic. An individual in which one or more chromosomes have more than two copies each.

Polytene chromosome. A giant chromosome made up of several (upto 1,024 or more) copies of itself produced by endoreduplication; usually, the homologues are paired as if during pachytene; in *Drosophila*, characteristic bands are present.

Polyvalent vaccines. Several antigen encoding genes, each from a different pathogen may be incorporated into a single vaccinia virus (VV) genome; such a recombinant VV vaccine will produce immunity to several diseases from a single inoculation.

Porous microcarriers. In case of animal cell cultures, there are small (170-6000 μm) beads of gelatin, collagen, glass or cellulose, having a network of inter-connected pores; used in stirred or fluidized bed reactors.

Position effect. In case of gene transfers; transgenes integrated at different sites in the host genome show different levels of expression due to the presence of regulatory sequences in region of integration, and general availability of the region for transcription.

Positional cloning. See, *Map-based cloning.*

Positive-negative selection. Use of two selectable markers, *e.g., neo* and *HSV-tk*, together; *neo* eliminates nontransfected cells, while *HSV-tk* enables killing of cells having random integration of the gene construct so that only cells having integration by homologous recombination survive; in the case of animal cells.

Positive selection. Selection pressure allows only mutant cells to survive or divide.

Positive selection of T-cells. All T-cells, whose TCR interacts with self-MMC molecules, are induced to proliferate; this is called positive selection.

Post-fertilization barriers. In distant hybridization; after fertilization/zygote formation, embryo development fails mainly due to endosperm abortion, and embryo-endosperm incompatibility.

Post-germinal development of embryo. The growth and development of an embryo after it begins to germinate and before it becomes an autotrophic plant.

Post-transcriptional gene silencing. Gene silencing in which transgene transcription is not affected; most likely due to RNA transcript degradation.

Post-zygotic barrier. See, *Post-fertilization barrier.*

Potentiometric biosensor. It measures the electrical potential generated due to a change in distribution of electrons.

Precocious germination. Germination of a plant embryo before it completes development; frequent in somatic embryos and cultured zygotic embryos.

Preculture. Culture of tissues/organs *in vitro* for 3-7 days before using them for some other purpose, *e.g.*, protoplast isolation, cryopreservation, etc.; usually, improves the responsiveness of tissues/organs.

Precursor cells. In case of animals; cells derived from stem cells, and committed to differentiation, but not yet differentiated; they retain the capacity of proliferation (cell division).

Pre-embryonic determined cells (PEDCs). Cells of explants already in or very close to embryogenic state; cells show direct somatic embryogenesis, *e.g.*, cells of a zygotic/somatic embryo.

Pre-fertilization barriers. In distant hybridization; the barriers, which occur before fertilization/zygote formation, *e.g.*, lack of pollen germination, slow growth of pollen tubes, etc.

Pre-freezing treatments. Treatments other than cryoprotection, given to cells/tissues/organs prior to freezing to enhance their survival during cryopreservation, *e.g.*, preculture of explants.

Pre-germinal development of embryo. The growth and develop of an embryo occurring till the time it begins to germinate; usually, a variable period of dormancy separates the pre- and post-germinal phases.

Pre-ignition. Ignition before the piston has reached the correct position during compres-sion cycle; it leads to power loss and damage to valve and piston.

Preliminary treatment of waste water. Removal of grit and heavy solids by settling, and of floating solids.

Preproinsulin. The extended single polypeptide chain, which is processed to yield both A and B chains of human insulin; it has an N′-terminal leader, B chain sequence, a C chain that links A and B chains, and the C-terminal A chain.

Pre-sequencing PCR. If the amount of tempelate DNA, to be used for sequencing, is low, it can be first amplified in a typical PCR.

Preservatives. Substances which prevent or inhibit spoilage of food due to contamination by fungi, bacteria, and other microoganisms.

Pretreatment. Exposure of cells/tissues to specific factors before they are used for culture.

Pretreatment for cryopreservation. Culture of cells/tissues/organs either at a low temperature or in the presence of certain compounds for a variable period of time to minimize cryoinjury.

Prey. Prey is a fusion protein generated by fusion of a different protein with the activation domain of the same transcription factor.

Pre-zygotic barriers. See, *Pre-fertilization barriers.*

Primary culture. In case of animals; a freshly initiated cell culture is called primary culture.

Primary energy sources. Fossil fuels, radioacive materials, and solar, wind, water and other energy sources that exist as natural resources and are subjected to exploitation.

Primary immune response. Immune response generated by the first exposure to a foreign antigen; it has a characteristic lag phase, during which naive B-cells proliferate and differentiate into plasma cells and memory cells.

Primary immunodeficiency. Immunodeficiencies arising from a genetic or developmental defect in the immune system.

Primary lymphoid organs. Bone marrow and thymus gland are called primary lymphoid organs; provide sites for lymphocyte differentiation.

Primary metabolism. The pathways concerned with the synthesis and utilization of such compounds that are of direct importance to the survival of organisms.

Primary physical containment. It is provided by laboratory practices and containment equipments.

Primary pollutants. The pollutants, which enter the atmosphere directly from various sources.

Primary recycling. It involves remaking the same material from the waste.

Primary screening. Selective procedures that permit the detection and isolation of micro-organisms producing the desired metabolite.

Primary somatic embryogenesis. Somatic embryo regenerated from the explant or callus.

Primary stock culture. Cultures kept in long-term storage; source of working stock cultures.

Primary treatment of waste water. Use of settling tanks of upward, horizontal or radial-flow type to allow 15–45 min residence time, during which about 70% of the suspended solids either settle to the bottom or float as scum on the top; the latter is removed by a scum baffle; if needed, a chemical coagulant may be added to promote settling.

Primer. An oligonucleotide sequence (about 20 bases long) used in PCR for the amplification of a DNA segment.

Primer extension. In PCR; synthesis of the complementary strands by utilizing the 3′–OH of the primers; the DNA segment lying between the two primers is copied; this is ensured by employing primers complementary to the 3′–ends of the segment to be amplified.

Primer walking. A strategy used to sequence longer DNA molecules; as the fragment is progressively sequenced from its 3′–end, new primers complementary to the 5′–ends of the sequenced segments are used to prime synthesis and sequencing of the remaining unsequenced segment.

Principle of microbial infallibility. Micro-organisms have the capability of degrading all naturally occurring compounds.

Prion. An infective proteinaceous agent, causing disease in animals, *e.g.*, Prp (a glycoprotein); produced by changed conformation of the protein molecules.

Proactive risk regulation. Development of regulatory mechanisms for potential hazards that are predicted in advance before there is any empirical evidence for such hazards.

Probe. These are 15–30 bases long labelled oligonucleotides (RNA or DNA) used for detection/identification/isolation of DNA segments having its complementary nucleotide sequence; used for disease diagnosis, etc.

Probiotics. The live microbial food supplements that beneficially affect an individual by improving intestinal microbial balance.

Process-based approach of risk regulation. In this approach, all GMOs, are considered to pose potential hazards, some of which may be unforeseable, to the environment; therefore, they should be regulated in a proactive manner so that any product that may give rise to hazards is excluded from further commercial development.

Process development. Determination of the optimum conditions for fermentation using a microbe producing a metabolite of interest.

Product-based risk regulation approach. In this approach, all GMOs are not recognized as a special category because they present no environmental hazards beyond those already identified for existing products; therefore, GMOs, can be regulated by the relative systems already in existence.

Production culture. A strain producing an economically attractive compound and used for commercial production.

Productive rearrangement. The rearrangement of antibody gene segments that results in a functional antibody chain production.

Proembryo. Embryo from 2-celled stage till the initiation of organ development; cell destinies become determined at the 8-celled stage of proembryo.

Proembryonic masses. See, *Embryogenic clumps.*

Professional APCs. Those cells that process and present antigens continually through a sustained inflammatory response; three types: dendritic cells, macrophages and B-cells.

Programme. A set of instructions designed to achieve a define result.

Programmed cell death. Death of cells in response to signals generated by their own genes.

Proinsulin. Preproinsulin folds spontaneously to yield proinsulin.

Proliferative embryogenesis. See, *Recurrent embryogenesis.*

PROMOT. This search tool can be used to match a sequence against the PROSITE database.

Promoter. A DNA sequence, generally located upstream of the coding region of a gene, to which RNA polymerase first binds during transcription; essential for transcription of any gene.

Propagule. Plant part used for propagation.

Property, physical. Estate wether in lands, goods or money.

PROSEARCH. This search tool searches SWISS-PROT and Tremble databases for a given motif.

PROSITE. It has a collection of functional sites and sequence patterns found in proteins; it also has search tools for matching patterns/motifs.

Prosthetic group. A non-protein organic molecule, usually, attached to the enzyme protein by covalent bonds; essential for catalytic activity.

Proteasome. A multifunctional protease complex that degrades protein-ubiquitin complex; present as a cylindrical particle with a central channel of 10–15 Å.

Protein. A functional molecule composed of one or more polypeptides of the same or different kinds.

Protein bodies. In storage cells in all kinds of seeds, the reserve proteins are deposited in membrane-bound structures called protein bodies.

Protein engineering. Modification of the properties of a protein by altering its amino acid sequence.

Protein-free medium. In animal cell culture; artificial medium free from any protein.

Proteome. The protein content of a cell; reflects the biochemical capability of the cell.

Proteomics. Determination of the complete set of proteins produced in a given tissue/organism; three types: functional, structural and expression proteomics.

Protoclone. Variant plants obtained from protoplast culture; *not in common use*.

Protocol. A standardized procedure that yields reproducible and predictable results.

Protocorm. In orchid seed germination; plumular pole of unorganized globose embryo forms a spherule-like tuberous structure called protocorm; it later produces shoot and root; also produced by cultured orchid embryos and shoot-tips.

Protoderm. The outermost tissue of root and shoot apex, which develops into epidermis.

Proto-oncogenes. Homologues of *v-onc* genes present in the host genome.

Protoplast adhesion. Aggregation of protoplasts together without membrane fusion.

Protoplast aggregation. See, *Protoplast adhesion*.

Protoplast fusion. Fusion of plasma membranes of two or more protoplasts.

Protozoa. A large group of eukaryotic microscopic organisms that consist of a single, relatively large complex cell or, in some cases a small group of cells; have some means of movement, *e.g.*, Amoeba, paramecia, etc.

Protruding ends. One strand of a DNA double helix extends some bases beyond the other.

Pseudobulb. A thickened portion of the stem of many orchids, that is used for vegetative propagation.

Pulsed-field gel electrophoresis (PFGE). In PFGE, DNA is driven through the gel using alternating pulses of electrical current that are at different angles to each other; it can achieve a good separation of DNA fragments that vary from 50 kb to 10 mb.

Pureline. Progeny of a single homozygous plant of a self-pollinated species.

Purified antigen vaccine. Purified antigen from a pathogen used as vaccine; highly safe.

Purine. A base, which consists of one six membered and a five membered ring; two purine bases: adenine and guanine.

Purity of DNA. The purity of DNA is inferred from the ratio of optical density (OD) of the solution at 260 nm to that at 280 nm (maximum absorption by proteins); a ratio of 1.8 signifies pure DNA solution, while a lower ratio indicates contamination by either protein or phenol.

Pyramiding. See, *Gene pyramiding*.

Pyrimidine. A six-membered pyrimidine ring, which is similar to the benzene ring, except that it contains nitrogen in the place of carbon at positions 1 and 3; three pyrimidine bases: thymine, cytosine and uracil.

Qualitative traits. Characters specified by oligogenes; they show distinct classes and are little affected by the environment.

Quantitative traits. Characters produced by polygens; they are markedly affected by the environment and show continuous variation.

Quantitative trait loci (QTL). Genes/gene blocks governing quantitative traits; a QTL may have one or more polygenes.

Quarantine. Inspection of plant materials for the presence of weeds, insect pests and pathogens.

Quasiquantitative traits. Traits that are governed by polygenes, but show discontinuous variation, *e.g.*, seeds/pod, tillers/plant, etc.

R plasmid. These plasmids carry genes for resistance to antibiotics, and make bacterial cells resistant to them; some of them have provided the antibiotic resistance marker genes used in cloning.

R_0 plants. Plantlets regenerated from cells/tissues cultured *in vitro* and transferred to soil.

R_1, R_2, ..., etc. plants. Selfed progeny of R_0, R_1 ... etc. plants, respectively.

Radicle. The part of an embryo that develops into a root.

Radioactive emissions. Various forms of radiation or particles that may be given off by unstable isotopes. Many such emissions have very high energy and can destroy biological tissues or cause mutations leading to cancer or birth defects.

Radioactive labelling. In case of probes, use of radioactive (^{32}P-labelled) nucleotides in probe structure; many methods of labelling, *e.g.*, nick-translation.

Radioactive materials. Substances that contain unstable isotopes and consequently, give off radioactive emissions.

Radioactive wastes. Waste materials that are contaminated with or contain radioactive substances. Many materials used in the nuclear industry become radioactive wastes due to contamination.

Radioisotope. An isotope of an element that is unstable and that gives off radioactive emissions.

Radioautographic technique. It consists of covering the squash preparation/tissue section with a special type of photofilm or photographic emulsion, storing the slides in dark and then developing the film; the areas having radioactivity would show silver grains on the photographic film.

Random amplified microsatellite polymorphism (RAMP). See, *Single primer amplification reaction (SPAR).*

Random amplified microsatellites (RAMs). See, *Single primer amplification reaction (SPAR).*

Random amplified polymorphic DNA (RAPD). It is defined by differences between individuals in terms of DNA regions either being or not being amplified in a polymerase chain reaction primed by random ~10 nucleotide long sequences.

Raw sludge. Untreated organic matter that is removed from sewage water by letting it settle; consists of organic particles from faeces, garbage, paper, and bacteria.

Reactant. Substances which participate in formation of product(s), usually, with the help of enzyme.

Reactive risk regulation. Regulation developed gradually in a piecemeal manner, and is designed to prevent the proven adverse effects shown by earlier products/activities.

Recalcitrant compounds. Xenobiotic compounds that resist biodegradation and thereby persist in the environment.

Recalcitrant seed. Reduction in moisture content of such seeds below 12-30% drastically reduces their survival, *e.g.*, seeds of citrus, tea, mango, coffee, etc.

Recalcitrant species. In tissue culture; plant species that show poor regeneration potential.

Receiving environment. The environment in which planned introduction is proposed.

Receptor. A molecule acting as a specific binding site for another molecule.

Recessive allele. The allele, which is unable to express itself in the heterozygous state.

Recognition sequences. See, *Recognition sites.*

Recognition sites. The sites/sequences recognised by restriction endonucleases for generating cleavage.

Recombinant antibody. See, *Hybrid antibody.*

Recombinant clone. A bacterial clone containing a recombinant DNA molecule.

Recombinant DNA. Literally, a DNA molecule created in the laboratory by ligation of two or more different pieces of DNA. *More specifically, refers to a vector containing a DNA insert.*

Recombinant DNA technology. All the techniques used to construct, study and use of recombinant DNA molecules.

Recombinant inbred lines (RILs). Inbred lines obtained from the F_1 population derived by crossing two inbred lines, ordinarily, differing for several traits.

Recombinant polypeptide vaccine. Produced by recombinant DNA technology; contains a single polypeptide or the immunogenic segment of a polypeptide.

Recombinant protein. Protein produced by a transgene.

Recombinant vaccine. Vaccine produced by recombinant DNA technology; contains a protein or a polypeptide, which is both immunogenic and critical to the pathogen function.

Recombination. Formation of new combinations of genes due independent assortment of unlinked genes, crossing over between linked genes and/or (even) intragenic crossing over.

Recoverable block of function (RBF) system. It consists of a function blocking sequence, *e.g.*, *barnase* gene, linked to the transgene of interest and a function recovering sequence, *e.g.*, *barstar* gene in this case; all the three genes are present in one transformable construct. The *barnase* gene may be driven by a germination-specific promoter, while the *barstar* gene would be under the control of a heat shock promoter. Under natural conditions, the *barstar* gene will not be expressed; as a result, expression of *barnase* in germinating seeds will kill the young seedlings.

Reculture. In cryopreservation; culture of thawed cells/tissues to induce them to resume growth and development.

Reculture of filter paper disc. In cryopreservation; thawed cells are cultured directly on a filter paper disc kept on an agar medium; the disc is transferred to a fresh medium after few hrs/days; ultimately, the cells are scraped off the filter paper and cultured directly on the medium.

Recurrent somatic embryogenesis. Regeneration of somatic embryos from young somatic embryos; either on the same medium or following subculture on another medium.

Recycling. Recovery of materials that would otherwise be buried in landfills or be combusted; two types: primary and secondary recycling.

Red data book (red list). Book/list containing a record of threatened species.

Redox reaction. A reaction in which electron is transferred between molecules; the term redox is derived from reduction and oxidation.

Reduction. Gain of an electron by a molecule.

Refuge crop. An insect susceptible nontransgenic variety of the crop, which is usually grown without insecticide application; it is presumed to serve as a breeding ground for Cry protein-susceptible biotypes of the pest, which will mate freely with those individuals that survive in the Bt-crop. This will tend to 'dilute' the Cry protein-resistance genes that may be selected for by the Bt-crops.

Regeneration. In tissue culture, development of organised structures like roots, shoots, and/or somatic embroys from cultured explants or callus/cell culture.

Regeneration medium. A medium that supports regeneration.

Regiospecificity. Ability to distinguish between similar parts of the substrate molecule.

Regulator gene. In prokaryotic gene regulation; a gene that encodes a regulator protein.

Regulator protein. A protein that either represses (= repressor protein) or activates (= activator protein) transcription of a transcription unit by binding to a DNA sequence in a highly specific manner.

Reinvigoration. Partial rejuvenation, *i.e.*, partial reversal of aging.

Rejuvenation. Production of juvenile shoots from mature adult trees, by suckering, copicing or a growth regulator treatment and, to some extent, by serial subculture *in vitro*; all tricks that improve propagation of mature trees.

Relaxed replication control. In this case, multicopy plasmids undergo more than one replication for each replication of their bacterial host genome.

Remediation. Refers to the return to an uncontami-nated state.

Renaturation. Reassociation of two complementary strands of a polynucleotide molecule, ordinarily, DNA, to yield a double-stranded molecule.

Renewable energy. Energy sources like those for solar, wind and geothermal energy, that will not be depleted by use.

Renewable resources. Refer to the biological resources like trees that may be renewed by reproduction and regrowth.

Repetitive embryogenesis. See, *Recurrent somatic embryogenesis.*

Replacement vector. *In case of λ vector*; insertion of DNA insert is accompanied with the deletion of all or the major part of the 'nonessential' region of λ genome. *In targetted gene transfer*; the linearized vector having the two halves of the target gene at its ends; recombination occurs in the two halves of the target gene so that the target gene becomes disrupted.

Replica plating. In this technique, a block of wood or cork, of suitable diameter is covered with velvet cloth, is sterilized and then lowered into the plate that is to be replica-plated till the velvet touches all the colonies. The block is then withdrawn and gently lowered onto the nitrocellulose filter kept on agar medium in a plate so that the bacterial cells sticking onto the velvet are transferred onto the filter where they form colonies.

Reporter gene. A gene, which allows either easy selection (selectable markers) or identification (scorable markers) of the cells/organisms in which it is present and expressed.

Representational difference analysis. When PCR is used to achieve substractive cloning, this is called representational difference analysis.

Repressor. A protein that binds to a specific operator and thereby prevents transcription of the operon concerned.

Rescue method (of selection). In this approach, the wild type cells are killed by the selection agent, while variant cells remain alive but, usually, do not divide; the selection agent is then removed, and the variant cells are recovered.

Research culture. A microbial strain discovered to produce a useful product, and used for studies on product recovery and identification, strain improvement, etc.

Reserves. The amount of a mineral resource, including oil, natural gas, and coal, remaining in the earth that can be exploited using current technologies at current prices.

Resources. Refer to the biotic and abiotic factors that are consumed by organisms.

Restitution nucleus. A nucleus formed following a regular division, but containing all the chromosomes present in the cell so that it contains twice as many chromosomes as the parent nucleus.

Restriction analysis. See, *Restriction mapping.*

Restriction endonuclease. An enzyme that cuts DNA at specific internal sites. Three types: Type I, Type II, and Type III.

Restriction enzyme. See, *Restriction endonuclease.*

Restriction fragment length polymorphism (RFLP). It is defined by differences between individuals in terms of the size of fragments generated by restriction enzyme digestion of genomic DNA and detected by hybridization with specific DNA sequences used as probes.

Restriction map. A linear map of a DNA molecule showing the relative positions of the recognition sites for a number of different restriction enzymes.

Restriction mapping. Preparation of a restriction map of a DNA molecule.

Restrictive agarose gel. Agarose gels above 1% concentration are cloudy, exhibit high electro-osmotic flow, and are used for the separation of very high molecular weight proteins or protein aggregates.

Restrictive gel. In these gels, size of the molecule has the major influence on the result of separation; bands are more distinctly separated and better resolved than those in the case of non-restrictive gels.

Retention time. It is the period of time, a given sample of waste/substrate stays in the digester/fermentor before it flows out.

Retroviral infection (method of transfection). Recombinant retroviruses produce virions, which are used to infect animal cells and mice embryos.

Revers osmosis. See, Microfiltration.

Reverse reaction. Formation of reactants A and B from their products C and D.

Reverse transcriptase. An RNA-dependent DNA polymerase; generally, obtained from Avian Myeloblastosis Virus (AMV); performs similar reactions as DNA polymerase, and has an absolute requirement for a primer with a free 3′–OH.

Reverse transcription PCR (RT-PCR). In this method, first of all a cDNA of the mRNA is produced using the enzyme reverse trans-criptase; the cDNA single-strand is then used for amplification to obtain cDNA duplexes.

Reversion. A mutant mutates back to its original phenotype.

RFLP map. The locations in the genome of different DNA sequences used as probes in detection of the RFLPs as determined by recombination.

***Rhizobium*.** Gram-negative bacteria capable of forming root nodules in host plants, *e.g.,* most leguminous plants; *Rhizobium* cells contain *nif* genes for nitrogen fixation on a megaplasmid.

Rhizosecretion. Secretion from roots; a transgene may be driven by a root specific promoter, and an appropriate signal sequence may be added to it to ensure the secretion of recombinant protein from the root.

Rhizosphere. The transition zone between soil and root; ordinarily, populated by microorganisms.

Ri plasmid. The plasmid native to *Agrobacterium rhizogenes*; it induces hairy root disease of several dicots and monocots.

Ribonucleoside. A compound produced by a linkage between ribose and an organic base.

Ribonucleotide. A ribonucleoside having a phosphate residue at the 3′- or 5′-position of the pentose residue; *in vivo* nucleosides have 5′-phosphate residues.

Riboprobe vector. A plasmid vector, *e.g., pB*luescript, that allows *in vitro* production of RNA copies of either strand of the DNA insert; the transcripts are labelled and used as RNA probes.

Ribosome inactivating protein (RIP). A protein that inactivates ribosomes; if it is expressed in a plant cell, protein synthesis can not take place and the cell dies.

Ribotide. See, *Ribonucleotide,*

Ribozyme approach. In this approach, a DNA sequence specifying an enzymatic RNA sequence is fused with a sequence of the gene against which the ribozyme is aimed; this gene sequence is, as a rule, in the antisense orientation; used for suppression of expression of the concerned endogeneous gene.

Ribozyme. A ribozyme is an RNA molecule, which has enzymatic activity, usually concerned with RNA degradation, *e.g.,* the satellite RNA of tobacco ringspot virus (TobRV) has sequences that have endoribonuclease activity; first described by Cech in 1986.

Risk. Undesirable consequences of an activity in relation to the likelihood of these con-sequences being realized.

Risk analysis. See, *Risk assessment.*

Risk assessment. It involves determination of the potential and anticipated adverse effects of an activity, *e.g.,* recombinant DNA research, to the concerned workers, and of the products of such research on human health and the environment consequent to their accidental or deliberate release (in case of living organisms) or as a result of their consumption.

Risk determination. It is the estimation of the overall risk posed by a GMO based on the evaluation of the likelihood and consequences of the identified adverse effects being realized.

Risk group 1 (RG1). Organisms belonging to this group are not associated with diseases in healthy humans.

Risk group 2 (RG2). Organisms belonging to this group are associated with such human diseases, which are rarely serious and for which preventive or therapeutic interventions are often available.

Risk group 3 (RG3). Organisms belonging to this group, are associated with such serious or lethal human diseases for which preventive or therapeutic interventions may be available.

Risk group 4 (RG4). Organism belonging to this group are likely to cause serious or lethal human diseases for which preventive or thera-peutic interventions are not usually available.

Risk management. The task of regulators to review risk data and make regulatory decisions based on the data with a view to minimise risk. The process often is influenced by consider-ations of costs and benefits as well as by public perceptions.

Risk perception. Non experts intuitive judgment about risks, which often are not in agreement with the level of risk as judged by experts.

Risk regulation. Development of practices/ procedures, assays/tests, biological agents, equipment and working design and structures to minimize the risk.

RNA interference (RNAi). See, *RNA mediated interference.*

RNA mediated interference. Silencing of homologous gene expression triggered by double-stranded RNA (dsRNA) is called RNA mediated interference.

RNA polymerase. The enzyme that transcribes DNA templates to generate their RNA copies; has high affinity for promoter sequences from where it initiates transcription.

RNA-dependent DNA polymerase. See, *Reverse transcriptase.*

Rocket immunoelectrophoresis. This electrophoresis uses an agarose gel that contains a uniform and definite concentration of the concerned antibody.

Root culture. Culture of roots *in vitro;* initiated from pieces of root containing root-tip; can be maintained indefinitely.

Rooting. Production of roots, usually, from shoots, induced, usually, by culture on an auxin containing medium.

Rosetta stone method. This method searches for functionally related proteins that are separate in some organisms, but are fused into a single protein (called Rosetta stone protein) in others.

Rotary shaker. Shaker platform kept in an inclined plane, and rotates on a shaft at 1-2 rpm; specially designed culture flask are used.

Rotating biological contactor. A device consisting of a set of discs of about 2-3 meter in diameter oriented vertically to the direction of waste water flow; the biofilm is adhered to disc surface, which keeps on rotating at the speed of 1-2 rpm.

Runway plasmid vector. Plasmid vectors that have temperature-dependent replication control so that they are maintained at a moderate copy number per cell at 30°C, but above 35°C the number of copies per cell keeps on increasing.

Salivary gland chromosome. See, *Polytene chromosome.*

Salvage pathway. It recycles the purine and pyrimidine nucleotides produced from degradation of nucleic acid.

'Sanitary sewer. Refers to the use of a separate drainage system to receive all the waste water from sinks, tubs and toilets.

Saprophytes. Organisms which generally feed on dead organic matter.

Scale up of the process. Utilization of the information gained from smaller fermenters to predict/determine the proper fermentation conditions for very large production fermenters.

Scaling up of cultures. Culture of cells/ tissues on increasingly larger scales; achieved by increasing the number or size (or both) of culture vessels.

Scorable marker. A gene that permits easy and rapid identification of the cell/organism in which it is present and expressed.

Screening. *In tissue culture*; evaluation of a large number of cells, clones or regenerated plants for identification and isolation of the desired cells, clones or regenerated plants. *In microbiology*; evaluation of several cells/individuals/clones/ species, etc. for one or more characteristics.

SDS-PAGE electrophoresis. The polyacrylamide gel contains 0.1% SDS, and the proteins are treated with an excess of SDS before being subjected to electrophoresis in restrictive polyacrylamide gels; there is a linear relationship between logarithm of the molecular weight and the relative distance of migration of the SDS-polypeptide molecule.

Sebum. The sebaceous glands associated with hair follicles secrete an oily substance, called sebum.

Second generation biosensors. These devices use mediators, *e.g.*, ferrocenes, which transfer the electrons generated by the reaction directly to the electrode rather than using them for reducing the O_2 dissolved in solution.

Secondary energy source. A form of energy such as electricity that must be produced from a primary energy source such as coal or radioactive material.

Secondary immune response. The immune response mounted by the animal following second or subsequent exposure to an antigen; much quicker and more intense than the primary response.

Secondary immunodeficiency. The loss of immune function as a result of exposure to various agents, such as, human immunodeficiency virus-1.

Secondary lymphoid organs. Spleen and lymph nodes constitute the secondary lymphoid tissues; sites for maturation of lymphocytes that migrate to these organs.

Secondary metabolism. Production of such compounds that are not of direct importance in survival, but help the organisms to function better in their environment.

Secondary metabolites. Chemical substances, which are found in cells, but are not necessary for their survival and are not the product of primary metabolism.

Secondary physical containment. Special laboratory designs that provide protection against accidental release of organisms into the environment; used where experiments of moderate to high potential hazard are performed.

Secondary pollutants. The pollutants, which are formed by chemical reaction between primary air pollutants and other atmospheric constituents.

Secondary recycling. In this recycling, waste materials are made into products that are different from those that gave rise to the waste.

Secondary screening. Screening of high producing cells of microorganisms subjected to mutagen treatment; follows primary screening.

Secondary somatic embryo. A somatic embryo regenerated from the cell/tissue of another somatic embryo or a part of a germinating somatic embryo.

Secondary somatic embryogenesis. See, *Recurrent somatic embryogenesis.*

Secondary treatment of waste water. Digestion of the organic matter dissolved/suspended in waste water by aerobic/anaerobic processes.

Secure landfill. A landfill with suitable barriers, leachate drainage and monitoring system such that it is deemed secure against contaminating groundwater with hazardous wastes.

Seed bank. A germplasm collection in the form of seeds stored at, usually, low temperature (cold storage) and low humidity.

Seed culture. A culture that serves as inoculum for a large scale culture.

Selectable marker. A gene, which permits easy and rapid selection for the cell/organism in which it is present and expressed.

Selection. Differential rates of reproduction of different genotypes.

Selection agent. An agent, *e.g.,* antibiotic, toxin, etc., that is used for selection of desired mutant cells.

Selection pressure. An environment, either chemical or physical, that allows differential survival and/or multiplication of cells/individuals.

Selective medium. A medium containing a selection agent; permits survival/poliferation of the desired mutant cells only.

Self-antigen. See, *Autoantigen.*

Selfish DNA. The repeated sequences with unknown function; these sequences may be maintained through non-phenotypic selection, and by a mechanism directed for self-preservation of these sequences.

Selfish genes. Genes, which propagate themselves despite being detrimental to the organisms that carry them.

Sense RNA. RNA produced by transcription of the antisense strand of a gene; in case of structural genes encoding proteins, it usually means mRNA.

Sense strand. The strand of a gene, which is not transcribed; it has the same base sequence as the mRNA (except for thymine in the place of uracil in the mRNA).

Septic system. An onsite method of treating sewage that is widely used in suburban and rural areas; requires a suitable amount of land and porous soil.

Sequence-dependent screening. This strategy uses nucleic acid hybridization in colony hybridization or chromosome walking/jumping or is based on PCR.

Sequence-tagged microsatellite sites (STMS). These microsatellite-based markers are analysed by PCR amplification using a pair of primers specific to the unique sequences flanking a SSR sequence; alleles differ for the number of repeats of the short repeating unit.

Sequence-tagged site (STS). When a pair of PCR primers amplifies only a single sequence within a haploid genome, the amplified region of the genome is called sequence tagged-site.

Serine-threonine kinase. It is a protein kinase that phosphorylates specific serine and threonine residues of the target proteins.

Serological test. Use of a specific antibody to detect the presence of an antigen, *e.g.*, for virus indexing.

Serum. It is the liquid exuded from coagulating blood.

Serum containing medium. In animal cell culture; artificial medium supplemented with 2-20% serum.

Serum-free medium. In animal cell culture, artificial medium lacking serum; however, growth factors, hormones, other proteins, etc. may be added as per need.

Settled sewage. The effluent from primary treatment is called settled sewage.

Sexual hybridization. Hybridization based on gametic fusion; one parent is used as female (its flowers are emasculated), and the other is used as male; pollen from male parent is placed onto the stigma of the female parent.

s-grain. The small proportion (~1%) of pollen grains that are smaller and stain faintly with acetocarmine; these are believed to respond during anther culture and produce pollen embryos/calli.

Shoot apex. The terminal portion of shoot; includes the shoot apical meristem plus two or three youngest leaf primordia.

Shoot apical meristem. The part of shoot-tip lying distal to the youngest leaf primordia; Ca. 100 μm in diameter and 250 μm in length. Syn., *Meristematic dome*.

Shoot bud differentiation. Development of shoot buds in cultured cells/tissues/explants.

Shoot bud induction. It consists of those molecular events that irreversibly commit cells of the explants to proceed on a particular developmental pathway; induction phase may consist of two distinct phases: morphogenic competence acquisition and development determination phase.

Shoot regeneration. Regeneration of shoots directly from explant cells or indirectly from callus; mainly two events occur during shoot generation: shoot bud induction, and shoot bud differentiation and development.

Shoot-tip. See, *Shoot apex.*

Short tandem repeats (STRs). See, *Microsatellite DNA.*

Short-term inbred. A partially homozygous line, which is isolated by few (usually 1-3) generations of selfing (inbreeding).

Shotgun approach of gene cloning. In this approach, partially digested genomic DNA is subjected to agarose gel electrophoresis or sucrose gradient centrifugation for separation from the mixture of fragments of appropriate size. These fragments are then inserted into a suitable vector for cloning.

Shotgun approach of sequencing. In this method, randomly selected clones are sequenced until all clones in the genomic library are analyzed; the sequences are aligned using computers.

Shuttle vector. A vector designed to replicate in two different host species; it contains two origins of replication (one for each host species) plus genes needed for replication and not provided by the host cells.

Signal transduction. It describes the process by which the function of a cell changes in response to small molecules that remain outside the cell and function by binding to specific receptors.

Signature-tagged mutagenesis. See, *Insertional mutagenesis*

Silencer. DNA sequences, which suppress promoter activity, usually, in response to a stimulus.

Simple sequence length polymorphism (SSLP). Polymorphism present in microsatellite DNA; also see, *Single primer-amplification reaction (SPAR)* and *microsatellite DNA.*

Simple sequence repeats (SSRs). See, *Microsatellite DNA.*

Single cell culture. Culture of isolated single cells to obtain callus and ultimately (usually) complete plants.

Single cell oil. Refers to the edible oil (triacylglycerol) produced by an extracted from microbial cells.

Single cell protein (SCP). Biomass produced by unicellular and multicellular microorganisms like bacteria, yeast, filamentous fungi and algae; processed and used as human food or animal feed supplement; rich in protein (Ca. 50% on dry weight basis).

Single locus probe (SLP) analysis. Use of a probe that identifies a single DNA fragment for fingerprinting.

Single nucleotide polymorphism (SNP). Occurrence of different nucleotides at a specific site in the genomes of different individuals of a species; human genome shows SNPs at about every 1,000 bp.

Single primer amplification reaction (SPAR). A DNA marker system that uses primers based on microsatellites and amplifies inter-SSR and DNA sequences; produces multiple fragments per reaction.

Single strand conformational polymerase (SSCP). This marker relies on secondary and tertiary structure difference between denatured and rapidly cooled amplified DNA fragments that differ slightly in their base sequences. Different SSCP alleles are resolved on non-denaturing acrylamide gel, usually at low temperatures.

Site-directed mutagenesis. Introduction of specified or desired changes at specific sites in the base sequences of genes.

Slow growth cultures. Cultures maintained under conditions like high osmoticum, low temperature, etc. that limit their growth rate; usually, shoot cultures; used for germplasm conservation.

Sludge. The particulate matter, *e.g.*, grit and fibres, that is present in liquid water, and is removed by sieving or settling down.

Sludge cake. Refers to the treated sewage sludge that has been dewatered to make a moist solid.

Sludge digester. Large tanks in which raw sludge (removed from sewage) is treated through anaerobic digestion by bacteria.

Smart genes. See, *Luxury genes.*

Smiling effect. In DNA sequencing, denaturation is achieved by electrophoresis at 50°C in the presence of urea, which may result in a higher temperature in the middle of the gel; as a consequence, the DNA bands at the end of the gel are progressively more advanced as one moves from two edges to the middle of the gel; this is commonly called smiling effect.

Smog. A product of smoke and fog; two types: industrial and photochemical.

SNP chips. DNA chips prepared for the detection of single nucleotide polymorphisms (SNPs).

Sodium dodecyl sulphate (SDS). A negatively charged ionic detergent that disrupts all hydrogen bonds, negates all hydrophobic interactions, prevents aggregation of the proteins, and masks individual charge differences; the polypeptides become unfolded and form ellipsoids with identical central axes.

Software. A group of programmes.

Soft water. Water with little or no calcium, magnesium, or other ions in solution that will cause soap to precipitate.

Solar cells. See, *Photovoltaic cells.*

Solid state fermentation. Microbial growth and product formation occur at the surface of solid substrates.

Solid waste. Total of materials discarded as trash and handled as solids.

Solvent engineering. Modification of enzyme properties simply by using appropriate organic solvents.

Somaclonal variation. The heritable variation for quantitative and qualitative traits present in the cells cultured *in vitro*, the plants regenerated from them, or progeny of such plants.

Somaclone. A variant cell/clone/plant obtained from plant cells cultured *in vitro*; generally, used for stable and heritable variants (*i.e*, mutants).

Somatic backcrossing. In case of somatic hybrids that are unable to flower or are sterile; the protoplast from the hybrids is fused with the protoplasts of one of the parental species; the somatic hybrids so produced may flower/set seeds.

Somatic back-hybridization. See, *Somatic backcrossing.*

Somatic chromosome number. Chromosome number normally found in somatic cells of a species.

Somatic chromosome pairing. Homologous chromosomes being located close to each other during mitosis.

Somatic embryo. Embryo produced from a somatic cell either *in vivo* or *in vitro.*

Somatic embryo, developmental phase of. Somatic embryo differentiation proceeds beyond the globular stage through heart-shaped and torpedo stage to the cotyledonary stage; in most species, occurs in a low auxin medium, in some others on a combination of auxin and cytokinin, in still some others induction medium itself supports development.

Somatic embryo, germination of. Development of root from radicles and shoot from plumules of SEs; promoted by GAs or even a cytokinin; in many species, basal (GR-free) medium is adequates.

Somatic embryo, induction of. Differentiated cells of explants dedifferentiate to become totipotent; embryogenic clumps and even globular SEs may be produced.

Somatic embryo, maturation of. Biochemical changes in fully developed SEs make them stress tolerant and enhance their conversion; promoted by culture on ABA, high sucrose concentration or partial desiccation.

Somatic embryogenesis. The process by which somatic cells develop through the stages of embryogeny to give rise to bipolar embryos that can ultimately develop into complete plants.

Somatic gene therapy. Introduction of the functional allele in the somatic cells of patients.

Somatic hybrid. A hybrid cell/plant derived from fusion of protoplasts of two plant strains or species.

Somatic hybridization. Production of hybrid plants via protoplast fusion; feasible in sexually incompatible combinations, in sterile/non-flowering species, etc.

Somatic incompatibility. Inability of somatic hybrid cells to regenerate shoots/SEs; cause is unknown.

Southern blotting. A procedure for transferring denatured DNA from an agarose gel onto a nitrocellulose filter to allow its hybridization with a probe.

Southern hybridization. Restriction digested DNA is subjected to gel electrophoresis, denatured, blotted onto a nitrocellulose/nylon membrane, fixed, hybridized with a single-stranded DNA/RNA probe, and hybridization of probe with DNA is detected by auto-radiography; used for detection of transgene integration into host genome, RFLP detection, DNA fingerprinting, etc.

South-western screening. A strategy that combines the principles of Southern and western blotting; used for isolation of clones encoding proteins.

Sparging. Bubbling of air through the medium.

Spawn. In case of mushrooms; spore and/or small pieces of the fruiting body used as inoculum.

Species diversity. The diversity present among different species in a defined geographical area, *i.e.,* species richness.

Specific immunity. See, *Acquired immunity.*

Specific toxin. The pattern of sensitivity of different host strains to such a toxin closely parallels their response to the concerned pathogen; plays the main role in disease development.

Spheroplast. A bacterial cell with cell wall degraded at numerous places, but with intact plasma membrane; produced by treatment of *E. coli* and related species cells with EDTA and lysozyme in the presence of sucrose.

Spin-filter bioreactors. A continuous stirred tank bioreactor having a central hollow shaft, which houses a spin filter (to filter out cells), a stirrer plate and a port for removal of only the spent medium.

Splicing. The removal of introns from pre-mRNA transcripts, and the linking together of all the exons in the correct order to yield a mature functional mRNA.

Spontaneous protoplast fusion. It occurs during protoplast isolation due to plasmodesmetal connections between cells; yields homokaryons only.

SSR-anchored PCR (SSR-A PCR). This is essentially single primer amplification reaction, except that the primer is either anchored at the 3′- or 5′-terminus with two to four arbitary nucelotides.

Stability. In case of PBR; the new variety must be stable in appearance and its clonal characteristics over successive generations over the specified environment.

Stable transfection. Introduced gene is retained and expressed in all the cells derived from the transfected/transformed cells; ordinarilly due to the integration of introduced gene into the host genome.

Stable transformation. See, *Stable transfection.*

Staggered cuts. The two strand of a DNA double helix are cleaved at different locations, *e.g.*,

5′–G¦AATTC–3′, generates protruding 3′ or
3′–CTTAA¦G–5′

5′ ends.

Starch gel. A gel prepared from hydrolysed potato starch; its handling is very difficult, and results are poorly reproducible.

Stationary phase (of cell cultures). The terminal phase of batch culture, when there is no culture growth mainly due to nutrient depletion; after a period in this phase, cells begin to die.

Stealth liposome. These are liposomes having monoclonal antibodies on their surface, and treated with polyethylene glycol; PEG treatment greatly increases the circulation time as well as the site-specific delivery of liposomes.

Stem cells. Undifferentiated cells capable of unlimited proliferation and differentiation into several types of cells.

Step-wise selection. The concentration/intensity of selection agent is increased, from a low level to a cytotoxic level, in a step-wise manner over several subcultures.

Sterilization. Inactivation of microbes present in/on vessels, instrument, culture medium, air, etc.

Sterilizing agent. A chemical used for surface sterilization of explants, etc.

Sticky ends. Protruding ends, which are complementary to each other.

Stimulus responsive gene. See, *Stimulus-specific gene.*

Stimulus-specific enhancer. An enhancer that makes the promoter activity stimulus specific.

Stimulus-specific gene. Gene expressed in response to only a specific stimulus.

Stimulus-specific promoter. A promoter that becomes active/inactive only in response to a specific stimulus; usually, due to enhancer/silencer sequences.

Stirred tank reactor. A simple tank containing a stirrer for mixing, fixed baffles, and temperature, pH, etc. control arrangements.

Stock culture. A culture used only as a source of inoculum.

Strain development. See, *Strain improvement.*

Strain improvement. Improving the productivity of a strain of a microorganism through genetic modification.

Streospecificity. Ability to distinguish between optical isomers of the substrate.

Stringent replication control. In such a case, the replication control of single copy plasmids is the same as that of the chromosome of their bacterial host cells so that they replicate and segregate with the host bacterial chromosome.

Structural gene. A gene, which encodes a diffusible product, *viz.*, protein or RNA.

Structural genomics. Determination of the genome maps and genome sequences, and the types of proteins produced by the tissues/organisms.

Structural proteomics. It is concern with mapping out the 3D structure and nature of protein complexes present in a particular cell/organelle.

Stuffer fragment. See, *Nonessential region.*

Subculture. Transfer of a portion of cell mass, organs, or tissues after a period of culture, to fresh media.

Subgenomic library. When a library represents only a part of the genome, it is called subgenomic library.

Substantial equivalence. This concept is designed to investigate if there are relevant differences, other than the intended changes, between the transgenic organism and its parent organism that is "generally regarded as safe" (GRAS).

Substitute mother. See, *Surrogate mother.*

Substrate saturation. The substrate concentration reaching the V_{max} value, beyond which there is no further increase in reaction rate due to an increase in substrate concentration.

Substrate. *In enzymology;* a compound or compounds on which enzymes act to makes them react together to yield certain products. *In industrial microbiology;* raw material(s) used to support production of biomass/biochemical. *In animal tissue culture;* the surface to which cultured cells attach as monolayer.

Substracted cDNA library. cDNA library generated by first removing those mRNA or cDNA sequences that are common to two sources; *e.g.,* two different cell types.

Subunit vaccine. See, *Recombinant vaccine.*

Suicide vector. A viral vector, which is unable to replicate after it delivers the gene it carries; used in gene therapy.

Sulphur dioxide. A major pollutants and toxic gas formed as a result of burning of sulphur; major sources are burning of coal that contains some sulphur and refining of metal ores (in smelters) that contain sulphur.

Sulphuric acid. A major constituent of acid precipitation; formed when sulphur dioxide emissions react with water vapour in the atmosphere.

Superovulation. Release of more than one ovum at the time of ovulation; usually, in response to a suitable hormone treatment regime.

Surface sterilization. Inactivation of microbes or their spores present on the surface of explants.

Surfactant. A compound, which reduces the surface tension of water, other liquids and aqueous and nonaqueous solutions.

Surrogate genetics. Genetic analysis of genes of one organism by expressing them into another organism.

Surrogate mother. A female into whose uterus an embryo is transplanted.

Suspension culture. A suspension of single cells and cell aggregates of various sizes produced in liquid medium; requires continuous agitation for mixing of medium and cells, breaking of cell clumps and aeration of the medium.

Suspensor. A short-lived structure found at the radicular end of zygotic proembryos; it begins to degenerate by early cotyledonary stage; provides GA_3 to young embryos.

Sustainable trait transgenics. Transgenics that are sustainable over time.

Sweetners. Substances, other than sugar, which are added to foods for enhancing sweet taste with increasing the food calories (energy); alternatively, they have beneficial effects for diabetes melitus, tooth decay and diarrhea.

Symmetric hybrid. A somatic hybrid that contains the full somatic complement of both the fusion parents.

Sympodium. The terminal bud of shoot tips growing, and the uppermost axillary bud begins to grow and takes over the functions of main stem, *e.g.,* in orchids *Cympidium, Cattleya, Dendrobium, Odontoglossum,* etc.

Synchronous culture. Ideally, all the cells in the culture progress together through the different stages of division; in practice, cultures are only partially synchronous.

Synfuels. See, *Synthetic fuels.*

Syntenic. When the gene order in a given region of the genome of two organisms is comparable, they are termed and the phenomena is called synteny.

Synthases. See, *Ligases.*

Synthetic fuels. Refers to fuels, which are similar or identical to those that come from crude oil or natural gas; produced from coal, oil shale or tar sands.

Synthetic genomics. Refers to synthesis of genome, *e.g., Mycoplasma geniculatum.*

Synthetic medium. See, *Artificial medium.*

Synthetic seed. See, *Artificial seed.*

Synthetic vaccine. A gene coding for an antigen may be isolated from the pathogen and cloned in, say, a bacterial host where it will produce the concerned protein. This protein (antigen) is then isolated and purified to be used as vaccine, which is called synthetic vaccine.

Synzymes. Synthetic polymers, including derivatised proteins, which have enzyme activity.

Systemic acquired resistance (SAR). Deliberately disarmed fungal pathogens can trigger the necessary response in susceptible (*i.e.,* slow responding) plants before the virulent pathogens arrive. This approach is known as systemic acquired resistance (SAR), which uses pathogen derived biocontrol agents to induce resistance in susceptible plants.

Tailing. Synthesis of protruding ends at the 3′–ends of blunt-ended fragments by the enzyme terminal deoxynucleotidyl transferase.

Tar sands. Refers to the sedimentary bitumen containing material that can be melted out using heat and then refined in the same way as crude oil.

Target cell. The cell that processes endogenous peptides and displays them on MHC I molecules; all nucleated cells can function as target cells.

Target gene. A gene, which is aimed to be modified.

Targetted gene transfer. The transgene integrates at the precise site of its allele present in the host genome by a process of homologous recombination so that the transgene replaces its allele in the genome.

Target-independent ligation. In ligase chain reaction (LCR); the blunt-ended probe duplexs, not paired to the target sequence, also become ligated at a low frequency.

Target sequence. The desired segment that is to be amplified by PCR.

TAXONOMY BROWSER. This search tool provides taxonomic information on various species.

tBLASTn. This programme is used to convert protein sequence into nucleotide sequence and to compare it with a nucleotide sequence database.

tBLASTx. This programme is used to translate the submitted nucleotide sequence as well as the nucleotide sequence database into amino acid sequence and search for homology between the two.

T-cells. These lymphocytes mature in the thymus gland; they act as helper/suppressor or cytotoxic cells; possess CD4 or CD8 antigens on their surface.

T-cell self tolerance. T-cells that survive negative selection have TCRs that have low affinity for self-antigens; this condition is called T-cell self tolerance.

T cytotoxic (T_c) cells. When T cells having CD8 on their surface interact with an antigen–MHC I complex (present on an APC), they proliferate under the influence of cytokines produced by activated T helper cells; these T_C cells differentiate into cytotoxic T lymphocytes (CTLs), which kill all such cells that display foreign antigen complexed with MHC I molecules.

T-DNA. Transfer DNA; a Ca. 23 kb segment of Ti/Ri plasmid that has 24 bp direct repeat border sequences and is transferred into the host plant genome during pathogenesis; has genes for auxin, cytokinin and opine biosynthesis.

Techno-foods. Foods and beverages that have been fortified in some way to confer health benefits beyonds the original nutritional value of the foods themselves.

Telomeric sequence. In yeast chromosomes, it is a 20–70 tandem repeat of the 6-base sequence 5′CCCCAA3′ (its complementary sequence, 5′TTGGGG3′, occurs in the other strand); there is a hairpin loop formation at the terminus, which makes the DNA duplex resistant to endonuclease action.

Temperate phage. See, *Lysogenic phage*.

Template. A molecule or structure that provides information for the production of another molecule or structure.

Template DNA. DNA molecule used for synthesis of complementary sequences either *in vivo* or in PCR.

Terminator technology. The technology designed to ensure that the seeds produced by a crop are non-viable; uses three genes that encode a regulator protein, a recombinase and a ribosome inactivating protein (or a toxin); expression of toxin encoding gene is controlled by *lea* promoter so that it is limited to late stage embryos; recombinase production is regulated by the regulator protein, which responds to a chemical, *e.g.*, tetracycline; designed to prevent transgene piracy and use of crop produce as seed.

Tertiary lymphoid tissues. These tissues normally contain fewer (~10%) lymphoid cells than secondary lymphoid organs, but they can import lymphoid cells during an inflammatory response; cutaneous-associated lymphoid tissues are the most prominent among such tissues.

Tertiary treatment. It aims to remove susupended matter so as to reduce BOD, and to remove specific materials, *e.g.*, phosphate, etc. from the biologically treated waste water.

Test tube baby. Baby produced by using *in vitro* fertilization followed by embryo transplantation.

Thawing. In cryopreservation; warming up of the frozen cells/tissues to 0°C by plunging ampoules into a waterbath maintained at 37–40°C for 90 seconds.

The U.S. Plant Patents Act (1930). This act covers varieties of asexually propagated crops, *e.g.*, ornamentals and fruit trees.

The U.S. Plant Variety Protection Act (1970). It is the U.S. version of the plant breeder's rights system followed by European Union and several other countries.

The Utility Patents Act (1985) of USA. This act was originally meant to cover man-made industrial inventions and processes. Non-obviousness is the main criterion of utility patents; patents for plant varieties are now being granted under the provisions of this act.

T-helper (T_H) cells. T-cells, which bind to the antigen epitope and interact with B-cells causing their proliferation and differentiation into plasma cells or memory cells; they have CD4 on their surface.

Thermal biosensor. See, *Colorimetric biosensor.*

Thermal cycle sequencing PCR. In this PCR, only one primer is used in combination with dideoxynucleotides; the primer is either radio or fluorescence labelled. The product of PCR reaction is subjected to PAGE for determining the base sequence of the template DNA.

Thermal cyclers. In automated PCR machines; the researcher has to only specify the number and duration of cycles, etc. after placing the complete reaction mixture for incubation, and the machine performs the entire programme of operations precisely.

Thermal pollution. Refers to the addition of abnormal and undesirable amounts of heat to air or water. It is most significant with respect to discharging waste heat from electricity generating plants, especially nuclear plants, into bodies of water.

Thermotheraphy. Exposure of plants (or cultured shoot-tips) to a high temperature (usually, 35–40°C) for a variable period of time to eliminate viruses; often combined with shoot-tip culture (shoot-tips excised from heat-treated plants).

Thickners. Substances that increase the viscosity of a mixture without substantially modifying its properties.

Thin cell layer (TCL) cultures. Cultures of thin layers of epidermal and cortical cells; used to study morphogenic influences of growth regulators and other factors; organogenesis takes place in subepidermal cells.

Thin layer electrophoresis. Separation of lipopolysaccharides and high molecular weight polysaccharides is achieved by thin layer silica gel electrophoresis.

Threatened species. A species whose population is declining precipitously due to direct or indirect human impacts.

Threshold level. Refers to the maximum degree of exposure to a pollutant, drug or some other factor that can be tolerated with no ill effects. It varies, depending on the species, the sensitivity of individual, length of exposure, and the presence of other factors that may produce synergistic effects.

Threshold model of cosuppression. Over-transcription of a gene leads to an accumulation of the RNA transcript beyond a threshold level; this somehow leads to a hyper-methylation of the sequences homologous to the degraded RNA transcripts; this drastically reduces the expression of the concerned gene.

Thymidine kinase. This enzyme belongs to the salvage pathway; it phosphorylates thymidine to yield thymidine monophosphate (dTMP), which is subsequently converted into thymidine triphosphate (dTTP).

Ti plasmid. Tumour inducing; a 150–250 kb (average 200 kb) conjugative plasmid responsible for the formation of crowngalls (tumours) in many dicot plants; vectors derived from it are used for gene transfer in plants.

TIBA. 2,3,5–Triidobenzoic acid; an anti-auxin; it blocks the polar transport of auxin from cells, which leads to an increase in its intracellular concentration.

Tissue culture. *In broad sense, in vitro* culture of aseptically isolated parts, *viz.*, cells, tissues as well as organs, on artificial/synthetic media under controlled environment; *in narrow sense, in vitro* culture of aseptically isolated cells in an unorganised state.

Tissue culture response genes. Genes controlling callus initiation and growth, and regeneration potential; both major and minor genes are known; even plasmagenes markedly affect regeneration.

Tissue engineering. Production of tissues, *e.g.*, human skin, using *in vitro* culture; used for transplantation in patients.

Tissue extract medium. In animal cell culture; extracts from embryos or other tissues used for, mainly, organ culture.

Tissue-specific enhancer. It makes the promoter activity tissue-specific.

Tissue-specific genes. Genes expressed only in specific tissues.

Tissue-specific promoter. A promoter that is active only in specific tissues; usually due to enhancer sequences.

T lymphocytes. See, *T-cells*.

Torpedo-shaped embryo. After heart-shaped stage; embryo elongates to assume the shape of a torpedo; before the cotyledons become distinct.

Total exposure assessment. Refers to the analysis of the impact of air pollutants on people based on the amount of time they spend in different spaces, specially in indoors.

Total maximum daily load programme. An EPA administered program to address non-point source water pollution that sets pollution limits according to the ability of a body of water to assimilate different pollutants.

Totipotency. In case of plants; the capacity of a cell to give rise to a complete plant particularly via somatic embryogenesis.

Touchdown PCR. The PCR is initiated at high annealing temperatures, which allows only perfectly matched primer-template DNA hybrid to form and support amplification. The annealing temperature is then dropped in a step-wise fasion with each cycle of PCR.

Toxic release inventory. An annual record of releases of toxic chemicals to the environment and the locations and quantities of toxic chemicals stored at all U.S. sites; required by the Emergency Planning and Community Right to Know Act (APCRA).

Toxic solution effect. During freezing; loss of water due to freezing enhances the concentration of cellular solutes to toxic levels; causes cryoinjury if it occurs before the protoplasm is frozen.

Toxic substances control act. Refers to a law requiring the assessment of the potential hazards of a chemical before the chemical is put on the market.

Toxicology. It is the study of the impacts of toxic substances on human health and the pathways by which such substances reach humans.

Toxoid. An exotoxin that has lost its toxicity, but retains immunogenicity; used as effective vaccines.

Trade secret. When the individual/organization owning an intellectual property does not disclose the property to any one and keeps it as a closely gaurded secret to promote his business interests, it is called trade secret.

Trademark. A logo, a symbol, word, phrase, picture, sound or even smell or a combination of all these which is used to distinguish one work/service from another; provides a distinct identity to a particular good/service and thus protect it from being copied.

Traditional enzymes. Specialized proteins serving the sole purpose of catalysis.

Trait. See, *Character*.

Transcription. Production of complementary RNA copy of a DNA strand; catalyzed by RNA polymerase.

Transcription unit. That segment of genome, which is transcribed into a single primary mRNA transcript; operon in case of prokaryotes, and one gene in eukaryotes.

Transcriptional fusion. Development of vectors permitting the synthesis of pure proteins encoded exclusively the DNA inserts.

Transcriptional gene silencing. See, *Transcriptional silencing*.

Transcriptional silencing. Denotes a suppression of transcription of the transgenes; it is the result of methylation of promoter region of transgenes.

Transcriptome. The full complement of RNA molecules produced by the genome.

Transducing vector. An SV40 (mammalian) vector; it produces virions on infection of monkey cells; contains SV40 origin, and genes for large-T, VP1, VP2 and VP3.

Transfection. *In prokaryotes;* introduction of viral recombinant DNA into the host bacterial cells by viral infection, *e.g.*, cosmid vector. *In case of animal cells/embryos;* introduction of DNA into the cells.

Transferases. A class of enzyme that catalyse transfer of an atom or group of atoms (like acyl-, alkyl- and glycosyl- groups) between two molecules.

Transformation. *In bacteria*; direct uptake of foreign isolated DNA by a cell; a portion of this DNA becomes integrated into the cell chromosome by a process of recombination. *In case of animals,* modification of cultured cells making them anchorage-independent and of contact inhibition.

Transformed cells. In case of animals; cells that have been phenotypically modified during *in vitro* culture to become anchorage-independent, and are able to grow in layers of several cell thick, as against monolayer growth of non-transformed cells.

Transforming virus. RNA virus that induce cancer; they are retroviruses, some of which carry 'oncogenes' or 'cancer genes'.

Transgene. A gene isolated from an organism and transferred into any organism through genetic engineering.

Transgene-flow. Transfer of genes from a transgenic variety to non-transgenic varieties, wild species and wild relatives through hybridization.

Transgene instability. Transgenes may become deleted or modified by recombination, following their integration into the host genome.

Transgene silencing. A decline in the level of transgene expression with the passage of generation of the transgenic line.

Transgenic. An organism, which contains a transgene.

Transgenic animal. An animal that contains in its genome a gene or genes introduced by recombinant DNA technology.

Transgenic plants. Plants in which a gene has been transferred through genetic engineering.

Transgenic volunteers. Volunteer plants from a transgenic variety.

Transient transfection. In animal cells; vectors that remain and replicate in extrachromosomal state are quickly lost in a few days even when selection conditions favouring their retention are imposed; this is called transient transfection.

Transition state theory. According to this theory; when the free energy levels of the molecules of two reactants are raised above a threshold level taking them to a very unstable, high energy state, called transition state, they react with each other.

Transitional trait transgenics. Transgenics that reduce environmental damage in the short term by substituting for an input.

Translation. Production of polypeptides with the help of mRNA, tRNA, ribosome and several other protein factors is called translation.

Translation initiation codon. AUG (ATG in DNA) codon, the codon first to be translated.

Translation termination codon. See, *Nonsense codon.*

Translational fusion. Refers to the construction of vectors, which allow the synthesis of fusion proteins comprising amino acids encoded by a sequence in the vector and those encoded by the DNA insert.

Transmissible plasmids. See, *Conjugative plasmids.*

Transplantation. It is the transfer of cells, tissues or organ, from one site to another.

Transporter associated with antigen processing (TAP). It is a heterodimeric (TAP1 and TAP2 subunits) transmembrane protein that uses energy from ATP hydrolysis to transport the antigenic peptide into rough endoplasmic reticulum.

Transposable elements. DNA sequences that move from one location in a chromosome to another location within the same chromosome or into another chromosome of the genome; repre-sented by insertion sequences (IS) and transposons (Tn).

Transposon. A >2000 bp long sequence that has insertion sequence-like elements repeated at its ends; codes for certain other proteins in addition to those needed for transposition.

Transverse thin cell layer (tTCL) cultures. Thin cell layer cultures initiated by using transverse sections.

Treated sludge. Refers to the solid organic material that has been removed from sewage and treated so that it is non-hazardous.

Trickling filter system. A system in which waste-water trickles over rocks or a framework coated with actively feeding microorganisms. The feeding action of the organisms in a well-aerated environment results in the decomposition of organic matter; used in secondary treatment of sewage.

Trinucleate pollen. A pollen having 3 nuclei produced by the two pollen mitoses.

Triple fusion. Fusion of a sperm with one secondary nucleus of an embryo sac to produce a triploid primary endosperm nucleus (3*n*).

Trypsinisation. A brief treatment of monolayers with cold trypsin to separate the cells from substrate and from each other.

Trisomic. A cell/an individual having one extra-chromosome in addition to the normal disomic complement of the species; extra-chromosome is member of its genome; represented by 2*n* + 1; survives in diploid species.

Truncated *cry* gene. A *cry* gene of shorter length having at least the sequence encoding the toxin fragment.

Tumour. An uncontrolled/abnormal growth in some part of the body/tissues.

Turbid. A cloudy liquid due to suspended particles.

Turbidostat. An open continuous culture; when the culture reaches a preselected turbidity, a predetermined volume of the culture is with-drawn and an equal volume of fresh medium is added back to the culture.

Two-dimentional electrophoresis. The protein extract is placed on a polyacrylamide gel and an electric charge is applied across the gel separating the proteins. When completed, the gel is rotated 90 degrees, and subjected to another round of electrophoresis so that the proteins are separated in a second dimension.

2 (Two) μm plasmid. Certain yeast strains contain a 6318 bp long plasmid called 2 μm plasmid.

Type I restriction endonucleases. These are complex endonucleases having recognition sequences of about 15 bp, they cleave the DNA about 1,000 bp away from the 5′–end of the sequence "TCA" located with the recognition site; *not used in gene cloning.*

Type II restriction endonucleases. These endonucleases are remarkably stable and cleave DNA either within (in most cases) or imme-diately outside their recognition sequences; require mg^{2+} ions for action; *used for restriction mapping and gene cloning.*

Type III restriction endonucleases. These are intermediate between the type I and type II enzymes; they cut DNA in the immediate vicinity of the recognition sites; *not used in gene cloning.*

Undernutrition. It is a form of hunger in which the individual lacks adequate food energy as measured in calories; starvation is the most severe form of undernutrition.

• **Uniformity.** In case of PBR; the new variety must be uniform in appearance under the specified environment of its adaptation.

Uninucleate pollen. A pollen having a single nucleus.

Unique DNA. In case of enkaryotes; the DNA sequences present in one copy per genome; most of the genes represent this class of DNA.

Unstable somaclonal variation. The variant trait disappears after a period of growth in the absence of selection pressure; chiefly due to temporary changes in gene expression, gene amplification, etc.

Unstable variant. See, *Unstable somaclonal variation.*

Upflow-anaerobic sludge blanket digesters. In this type of digester, liquid waste flows through a blanket of sludge consisting of the bacteria settled as granules of about 4 mm in diameter;

suited to treat low strength (Ca. 1% solids) soluble wastes.

Upstream. On the 5′ side of the cap of a gene; designated by a minus (–) sign, –10 means 10 base upstream of cap site.

Upstream production. Refers to the production of biomass (or the culture filterate for the externally secreted products) from which desired biochemical is to be purified.

Useful. In case of patenting of genes and DNA sequences, the term useful has been interpreted to mean practical utility.

Vaccination. See, *Immunization.*

Vaccine. It is a preparation containing a pathogen (disease producing organism) either in attenuated or inactivated (dead) state or an antigen derived from the pathogen.

Vacuum blotting. In this technique, a controlled low vacuum is used to hasten the movement of buffer (in case of protein) or NaOH solution (in case of DNA) through the gel and the blotting membrane.

Value-added product. Product whose value have been improved, by changing its quality, texure, colour, etc. at various stages of development/ manufacture.

Variable number of tandem repeats (VNTRs). Sequences consisting of a variable number of end-to-end tandem repeats of identical or nearly identical sequences of 2–80 bp each; two types: minisatellites and microsatellites.

Variable region. About 100 amino acid-long amino-terminal ends of both light and heavy chains of antibodies constitute their variable region, designated as V_L and V_H, respectively; the animo acid sequence of this region varies among antibodies specific to different antigens.

Variant. A cell/an individual exhibiting a different phenotype from the remaining population.

Variation. Individuals of a species or strain (or cells of a cell population) differ from each other for a character or a group of characters; it may arises due to genetic and/or environmental factors.

Variety. A strain of crop plant released for commercial cultivation by a competent authority.

Variety in common knowledge. Any variety for which an application for grant of PBR or for entering the variety in the official register of varieties has been filed in any convention country.

Vector. *In entomology,* an agent, such as insects (white fly) etc., that carries a parasite from one host to another. *In genetics*, a DNA molecule capable of autonomous replication in the host cell; contains several functional modules, *e.g.*, origin of replication, selectable markers, unique restriction sites at strategic locations, etc.; DNA/ gene to be cloned is integrated into the vector.

***vir* region.** Virulence region; it is essential for virulence of *Agrobacterium*; regulates T-DNA transfer by providing almost all the proteins involved in the process.

Viral oncogenes (*v-onc*). Oncogenes present in retroviruses.

Virosome. Viral envelopes, prepared from capsid proteins have been used to package the desired DNA in the form of particles called virosomes; used to transfect cells *in vitro.*

Virulence plasmids. These plasmids confer pathogenicity on their host bacteria , *e.g.*, Ti and Ri plasmids.

Virulence. Ability of a pathogen to produce disease in its host species.

Viruses. They are ultramicroscopic, obligate parasites that are highly infectious nucleoproteins, which behave as living *in vivo* (inside the host) and non-living *in vitro* (outside the host).

Virus bioassay test. In this test, sap from test plants is used to inoculate highly sensitive and healthy indicator plants.

Virus cross-protection. Plants infected with a mild strain of a virus resist development of symptoms upon infection by a more severe strain of the same virus.

Virus-free plant. A plant tested and shown to be free from a specific virus, usually obtained by shoot-tip culture with/without thermotherapy/ cryotherapy.

Virus indexing. Testing of plants or propagules for the presence of specific viruses by screening for symptoms, sap transmission to indicator strains, serological test, ELISA/DNA probes, etc.

Virus infectivity test. See, *Virus bioassay test.*

Virus-like vector. In animals; a replicating vector, the recombinant DNA of which produces virions.

Virus resistance. The ability of a strain/variety of a host species to limit the infection by a virus to a significantly lower level than that in the case of other strains/varieties of the same species, due to endogenous host genes/ transgenes.

Virus vector. A vector derived from plant/animal viral genomes.

Vitamin. A specific organic molecule that is required by the body in small amounts, but that can not be made by the body and therefore must be present in the diet.

Vitrification. See, *Hyperhydracity.*

Vitrification solution. In cryopreservation; a highly concentrated solutions of sucrose, glycerol, ethylene or propylene glycerol, DMSO, etc.; cells treated usually at 0°C for 5–10 min. before they are plunged into liquid nitrogen.

VNTR locus. Specific site at which a VNTR sequence is present constitutes a VNTR locus; different alleles of this locus consist of different numbers of the repeating unit of this VNTR sequence.

Volatile organic compounds. A category of major air pollutants present in vapour state; includes vapours of hydrocarbon fuel from incomplete combustion and evaporated organic com-pounds such as paint solvents, gasoline and cleaning solution; major factors in the formation of photochemical smog.

Volunteer plants. Those plants that are produced from seeds dropped or blown by wind during harvest, etc. or that are inadvertently planted.

Waste. A product, by-product or residue, which can not be profitably utilized.

Water quality. It is a set of chemical, physical and biological features of water, which determines its suitability for various uses.

Western blotting. Proteins are subjected to gel electrophoresis, transferred from gel onto a nylon membrane, and specific protein bands are identified by using labelled antibodies or lectins (for glycoproteins).

Whey. The liquid part of milk coagulum; waste from cheese production process.

Whole gene model. In this model, gene is a series of exons that are coordinately transcribed.

Wild forms. These are wild species from which crop species were directly derived; easy to cross with the concerned crop species.

Wild relatives. They include all other species, which are related to the crop species by descent during their evolution.

Working stock culture. Cultures kept in vigorous and uncontaminated state, and are used frequently as a source of inoculum for research, production, etc.

Wound response. Production of phenolic compounds, especially, acetosyringone and α-hydroxyacetosyringone, by wounded tissues of plants; exhibited by virtually all dicot species; these phenolics activate the *vir* regulon of *Agrobacterium;* essential for infection by *Agrobacterium.*

***x*.** Basic chromosome number; the chromosome number of a genome; gametic chromosome number of a diploid species or of the parental diploid species in case of a polyploid species.

Xenobiotic compound. A man-made compound, either not found in nature or found in a far lower concentration than that liberated by man.

Xenograft. Graft obtained from a different species.

Yeast artificial chromosome (YAC). Linear or circular shuttle vector; behaves in yeast like a chromosome, contains *ARS* sequence for replication, *CEN* sequence for centromeric function, telomeric sequences, one or two selectable markers, and the necessary sequences from *E. coli.* plasmid for propagation in *E. coli*; used for cloning upto 1,000 kb DNA

Yeast artificial chromosome vector. See, *Yeast artificial chromosome.*

Yeast episomal plasmid (YEP). A vector based on 2 μm yeast plasmid; most common vector used in expression systems.

Yeast integrative plasmid vector. It is essentially a bacterial plasmid that contains yeast gene, which functions as a selectable marker in a suitable yeast strain; lacks an origin of replication for yeast; therefore, it must be integrated into the yeast genome to be maintained in an yeast cell.

Yeast replicative plasmid vector. See, *ARS vector.*

Yeast two-hybrid (Y2H) system. It is an *in vivo* system for protein interaction studies and is currently the most amenable high throughput system; it uses 'bait' and 'prey' fusion proteins.

Yield drag. Reduced yield of a transgenic variety in comparison to the non-transgenic parent variety, when both are grown under optimum conditions.

Yield penalty. The reduction in yield as a consequence of the expression of a transgene transferred to achieve another objective is referred to as yield penalty.

Z-DNA. The two strands of a DNA molecule are coiled together in a left-handed helix having diameter of 18 Å, and the length of one turn of the helix is Ca. 69 Å; it contains 12 base pairs per turn in the helix.

Zone of thermotherapy. The range between the temperature at which the pathogen is inactivated and the temperature at which the host plant is killed; the wider this zone, the greater are the chances of success of thermo-therapy.

Zone-electrophoresis-immunodiffusion. In this method, proteins are first separated in the agarose gel by electrophoresis. Now the antibody is pipetted into trough cut on the sides parallel to the electrophoretic run. The proteins diffuse from the zones/bands formed by electrophoresis toward the antibodies and reaction bands are identified due to immunoprecipitation.

Zoo blot. A form of dot blot used to test the ability of a DNA probe from one species to hybridize with the genomic DNA from several other species.

Zooplankton. Animal groups, including protozoa, crustaceans, worms, molluscs, etc. that live suspended in water column and feed on phytoplankton and other zooplankton.

Zygote. Cell produced by the fusion of an egg cell (n) with a sperm (n); ordinarily, has $2n$ chromosome constitution; develops into an embryo.

Zygotic embryo. Embryo that develops from a zygote.

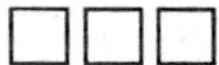

SECTION II

QUESTIONS

1
INTRODUCTION

1.1. MULTIPLE CHOICE QUESTIONS

1. Which of the following is concerned with computer-based analysis of large amounts of biological data sets ?
   (*a*) Molecular biology
   (*b*) Computer science
   (*c*) Information technology
   (*d*) Bioinformatics
2. GEM stands for which of the following ?
   (*a*) Genetically engineered metazoa
   (*b*) Genetically engineered microbes
   (*c*) Genetically engineered metabolism
   (*d*) Genetically engineered mustard
3. Hybridoma cells are developed by fusion of which of the following ?
   (*a*) T cells with myeloma cells
   (*b*) B cells with myeloma cells
   (*c*) T cells with B cells
   (*d*) B cells with APCs.
4. Which of the following molecular techniques can be used to characterize germplasm ?
   I. Techniques that simply desribe DNA polymorphism.
   II. Techniques based on DNA linked to a gene of interest.
   III. Techniques that characterize the gene of interest itself.

   Options :
   (*a*) I, II (*b*) I, III
   (*c*) I, II, III (*d*) II, III
5. The term 'transformation' is used to represent which of the following ?
   (*a*) Delivery of DNA into a bacterial cell by a virus.
   (*b*) Uptake of DNA by a cell.
   (*c*) Conversion of a normal vertebrate cell into a tumorigenic cell.
   (*d*) Both (*b*) and (*c*).
6. Which of the following is correct about bulbosum technique of haploid production ?
   I. The technique was developed with the cross *Hordeum bulbosum* × *H. vulgare*.
   II. It is based on the chromosome elimination during early embryo development.
   III. Generally embryo rescue is necessary.
   IV. This technique has been used with bread wheat.

   Options :
   (*a*) I, II, III, IV (*b*) I, II, III
   (*c*) II, III, IV (*d*) I, III, IV
7. Which of the following is correct about B cells ?
   (*a*) B cells develop and mature in bone marrow.
   (*b*) Mature B cells leave the bone marrow and migrate via blood stream to the secondary lymphoid organs or tissues, where they ultimately become plasma cells.
   (*c*) B cells play an important role in immune system of body.
   (*d*) All of the above.
8. Somaclonal variation may result from which of the following ?
   I. Gene amplification and de-amplification.
   II. Point mutation.

III. Chromosomal rearrangements.
IV. Non-reciprocal mitotic recombination.

Options :

(*a*) I, II, III, IV (*b*) I, II, III
(*c*) II, III, IV (*d*) I, III, IV

9. Which of the following is preferred for making artificial seeds ?
(*a*) Potassium alginate
(*b*) Sodium alginate
(*c*) Agar
(*d*) Gel-Rite.

10. Which of the following is called natural genetic engineer ?
(*a*) *Agrobacterium tumefaciens*
(*b*) *Escherichia coli*
(*c*) *Neurospora crassa*
(*d*) *Pseudomonas putida.*

11. Which of the following non-infectious diseases is associated with SCP industries ?
(*a*) Asthama
(*b*) Allergy
(*c*) Dermatitis
(*d*) All of the above.

12. Match the columns A and B carefully and select the correct option from those given below.

Column A	Column B
A. Proteomics	I. Single nucleotide polymorphism
B. DNA marker	II. mRNA content
C. Genomics	III. Proteins
D. Transcriptome	IV. DNA sequencing

Options :
(*a*) AII, BI, CIV, DIII
(*b*) AIV, BIII, CII, DI
(*c*) AIII, BI, CIV, DII
(*d*) AI, BII, CIII, DIV

13. Which of the following scientists is regarded as father of plant tissue culture ?
(*a*) P. Maheshwary
(*b*) G. Haberlandt
(*c*) P.R. White
(*d*) R.J. Gautheret

14. Which of the following enzymes is used for the production of glucose from starch ?
(*a*) Lipase (*b*) Glucoamylase
(*c*) α-amylase (*d*) Both (*b*) and (*c*)

15. Which of the following methods is used for building of phylogenetic trees ?
(*a*) Distance matrix methods
(*b*) Maximum parsimony methods
(*c*) Maximum likelihood methods
(*d*) All of the above.

16. Match the columns A and B and select the correct option from those listed below them.

Column A	Column B
A. Probe	I. Recombinant DNA technology
B. Transgene	II. Gene isolation
C. Embryo rescue	III. Cell fusion
D. Somatic hybridization	IV. Distant hybridization

Options :
(*a*) AII, BI, CIV, DIII
(*b*) AIII, BII, CIV, DI
(*c*) AIV, BIII, CII, DI
(*d*) AII, BIII, CI, DIV

17. Which of the following organisms was discovered by Fleming to produce the antibiotic penicellin ?
(*a*) *Aspergillus niger*
(*b*) *Penicillium notatum*
(*c*) *Penicillium griseofulvum*
(*d*) *Penicillium chrysogenum*

18. Bioinformatics can be used for which of the following ?
I. Genome mapping.
II. Identification of genes from gene sequences.
III. Determination of protein structure and simulation of protein interactions.
IV. Discovery of new therapeutic targets and designing of medicines aimed at specific target sites.

Options :
(*a*) I, II, III (*b*) II, III, IV
(*c*) I, II, III, IV (*d*) I, II

19. Which of following ***is not correct*** about abscisic acid ?
(*a*) It is a naturally occuring growth inhibitor.
(*b*) Precussor of ABA is maleic acid.
(*c*) It is synthesized in leaves.
(*d*) ABA counteracts the effect of GA and promotes dormancy in buds and seeds.

20. ***Assertion (A)*** : Using the concept of cross-protection, a number of transgenic lines against viruses have been developed.

Reason (R) : Genetically engineered cross-protection may occur due to inhibition of one or more events in the life cycle of virus.

Options :

(*a*) Both A and R are correct and R adequately explains A.
(*b*) Both A and R are correct, but R does not explain A.
(*c*) Only A is correct.
(*d*) Only R is correct.

21. Performance of a transgenic plant can be affected by which of the following events that can occur before it is field-tested ?

I. Site of transgene integration in the host genome.
II. Number of copies of the transgene that are integrated per genome.
III. Deletion and other rearrangments involving the transgene.
IV. Gene silencing.

Options :

(*a*) I, II, III (*b*) I, II, III, IV
(*c*) I, III, IV (*d*) II, III, IV

22. Physical containment relates to which of the following ?

(*a*) Laboratory design
(*b*) Containment equipment
(*c*) Special laboratory procedures
(*d*) All of the above

23. Totipotency is the property of which of the following ?

(*a*) Plant cells (*b*) Animal cells
(*c*) Cancer cells (*d*) Both (*a*) and (*b*)

24. Transfection is which of the following ?

(*a*) Transfer of host genes from one cell to another by a virus.
(*b*) Genetic transformation of animal cells.
(*c*) Conversion of a normal animal cell into a cancerous cell.
(*d*) A type of virus infection.

25. Which of the following is called stress hormone ?

(*a*) GA_3 (*b*) Ethylene
(*c*) ABA (*d*) Cytokinin

26. Which of following ministries established Department of Biotechnology in 1986 ?

(*a*) Ministry of Human Resource Development
(*b*) Ministry of Environment
(*c*) Ministry of Science and Technology
(*d*) Ministry of Agriculture.

27. Which of the following is considered as primary physical containment ?

(*a*) Containment equipment
(*b*) Special laboratory design
(*c*) Laboratory practices
(*d*) Both (*a*) and (*c*)

28. Consider the options in Q. 27 and pick the option that describes secondary containment.

29. Embryo therapy involves which of the following steps ?

I. *In vitro* fertilization of egg.
II. Production of several copies of the normal allele of defective gene.
III. Introduction of the normal allele into zygote, or in the cells of developing embryo.
IV. Integration of the normal allele (DNA), preferably in the place of the defective allele so that it may function normally.

Options :

(*a*) I, II, III, IV (*b*) I, III, IV
(*c*) II, III, IV (*d*) II, IV

30. Which of the following techniques can be used for the study of proteins ?

I. Mass spectrophotometry.
II. Two-dimensional gel electrophoresis.
III. Western blots.
IV. Chromatography.

Options :

(*a*) I, II, III (*b*) II, III, IV
(*c*) I, II, III, IV (*d*) I, II, IV

31. Success in germplasm storage is determined by which of the following ?

(*a*) Inherent longevity and physiological storage behaviour of the species.
(*b*) Initial quality (*e.g.*, moisture content) of the material stored.
(*c*) Storage methods and conditions used.
(*d*) All of the above.

32. An enzyme, aminoglycoside-3-phosphotransferase II, [APH(3)II] is commonly called which of the following ?

(*a*) β-glucuronidase
(*b*) Penicillinase
(*c*) Neomycin phosphotransferase II
(*d*) Streptomycin phosphotransferase

33. In terms of base sequence of genomic DNA, we are more than 98% similar to which of the following ?
(*a*) Lion (*b*) Chimpanzee
(*c*) Tiger (*d*) Monkey

34. Undesirable pleiotropic effect of a transgene on the transgenic plants may be corrected by which of the following ?
(*a*) Changing the genetic background of transgene through hybridization.
(*b*) Targetting of the transgene product into an appropriate cellular compartment.
(*c*) Mutagenesis in the transgene.
(*d*) Both (*a*) and (*b*).

35. International Centre for Genetic Engineering and Biotechnology is located at which of the following ?
(*a*) Trieste (*b*) New Delhi
(*c*) Bangalore (*d*) Both (*a*) and (*b*)

36. Synthetic vaccines have been developed for which of the following ?
(*a*) Typhoid and rabies
(*b*) Cancer (Feline leukaemia virus)
(*c*) Cholera, and foot and mouth disease of cattle
(*d*) All of the above.

37. Genetic engineering of industrially useful microorganisms aims at developing organisms that have which of the following features ?
I. Capacity to produce such compounds, which they are normally incapable of producing.
II. Ability to produce substances in quantities beyond their natural capabilities.
III. Elimination of their undesirable characteristics.

Options :
(*a*) I, II (*b*) II, III
(*c*) I, II, III (*d*) I, III

38. Strains of which of the following bacteria is used for the degradation of petroleum and management of oil spills ?
(*a*) *Pseudomonas putida*
(*b*) *Clostridium acetobutylicum*
(*c*) *Methylophilus methylotrophus*
(*d*) *Pseudomonas fluorescence*

39. Which of the following drugs is produced through biotechnology ?
(*a*) Erythropoeitin
(*b*) Fibroblast interferon
(*c*) Insulin
(*d*) All of the above

40. Which of the following strategies can be used to prevent interpopulation mating and the spread of transgenes ?
I. Introduction of male sterility in GM crop.
II. Removal of flowers from the transgenic plants before anthesis.
III. Removal of sexually compatible species from the area.
IV. Planting of a surrounding buffer crop of non-transgenic plants of the same species.

Options :
(*a*) I, II, III (*b*) II, III, IV
(*c*) I, II, III, IV (*d*) I, III, IV

41. In case of Q. 40, which strategy seems to be the most feasible ?
(*a*) IV (*b*) II
(*c*) III (*d*) I, IV

42. In case of Q. 40, which strategy seems to be the least feasible ?
(*a*) I, IV (*b*) I, II
(*c*) II, III (*d*) III, IV

43. Which of the following problems are faced by the conventional plant breeders ?
I. Limitation of utilizing genes from only such species that are sexually compatible with the concerned crop.
II. Inefficient selection/identification of superior genotypes, especially for metric traits, from segregating generations.
III. Many important traits can only be scored under specific environments.
IV. Lack of satisfactory system of genetic emasculation through male sterility in many crops.

Options :

(*a*) I, II, III (*b*) I, II, III, IV
(*c*) I, II, IV (*d*) I, III, IV

44. During World War II, technology for citric acid production was based on which of the following ?

(*a*) *Aspergillus niger*
(*b*) *Aspergillus oryzae*
(*c*) *Clostridium acetobutylicum*
(*d*) *Rhizobium* sp.

45. Department of Biotechnology promotes human resource development through which of the following ?

(*a*) Master's programmes
(*b*) Post-doctoral programmes
(*c*) Certificate/Diploma programmes
(*d*) All of the above

46. In India, which of the following overseas the large-scale commercial use of GMOs and recombinant DNA products.

(*a*) Department of Atomic Energy.
(*b*) Council of Scientific and Industrial Research.
(*c*) Ministry of Environment and Forests.
(*d*) Department of Biotechnology.

47. Consider the options listed in Q. 46 and pick the one that implements the research and development experiments utilizing GMOs and recombinant DNA.

48. Which of the following is correct about biosafety in laboratories ?

I. Strict adherence to standard laboratory practices is the basic requirement.
II. Special procedures, equipment and laboratory design provide physical barriers.
III. Specific hosts and vectors with impaired survival and dissemination are also used.
IV. They aim at reducing the risk to the laboratory workers.

Options :

(*a*) I, II, III (*b*) I, II, III, IV
(*c*) I, III, IV (*d*) II, III, IV

49. Which of the following is correct about polyhydroxy-butyrate (PHB) ?

I. PHB is used for the manufacture of biodegradable plastic.
II. At present, PHB is produced from bacterial fermentation as a result of which its cost is rather high.
III. It is hoped that PHB production from transgenic plants may reduce the cost.
IV. ICI, U.K. markets bacteria-derived PHB as 'Biopol'.

Options :

(*a*) I, III, IV (*b*) I, II, IV
(*c*) I, II, III, IV (*d*) II, III, IV

50. Many developed countries pay huge subsidies (*e.g.*, USA pays ~50 billion dollars per year) to their farmers for ***not growing*** which of the following ?

(*a*) Medicinal plants
(*b*) Food crops
(*c*) Horticultural crops
(*d*) All of the above

51. Which of the following is correct about bio-diesel ?

I. Govt. of India encourages farmers to grow more and more trees like *Jatropha,* karanj, neem and mahua.
II. The non-edible oil-bearing trees (*Jatropha,* neem, mahua and karanj) have potential of producing biofuel.
III. Biodiesel is vegetable oil processed to resemble diesel fuel.
IV. Biodiesel is chemically methyl or ethyl-ester of fatty-acids.

Options :

(*a*) I, II, III, IV (*b*) II, III, IV
(*c*) I, III, IV (*d*) III, IV

52. Terminator technology can be used for which of the following ?

I. To prevent the farmers from replanting/reusing of their own harvesting as seed.
II. To control the expression of male sterility.
III. To prevent expression of undesirable traits.
IV. To prevent the piracy of transgenes.

Options :

(*a*) I, II (*b*) II, III
(*c*) I, IV (*d*) I, II, III

53. Which of the following transgenic crops is being grown on commercial scale in India ?
(*a*) Bt-cotton (*b*) Bt-brinjal
(*c*) Bt-rice (*d*) Golden rice

54. Lipids are source of which of the following ?
(*a*) Vitamins
(*b*) Structural components of cell organization
(*c*) Energy
(*d*) All of the above.

55. Among the given macromolecules, which one is the richest source of energy ?
(*a*) Carbohydrates (*b*) Proteins
(*c*) Lipids (*d*) Nucleic acids

56. Among the options given in Q. 55, which one is the first to be used as a source of energy ?

57. In case of medicine, biotechnology can be used for which of the following ?
(*a*) Production of synthetic vaccines
(*b*) Diagnosis of diseases
(*c*) Production of rare drugs
(*d*) All of the above

58. Plants developed through a biotechnological activity should have which of the following ?
I. A useful feature.
II. Normal fertility
III. Good agronomic features
IV. Consumer acceptance

Options :
(*a*) I, II, III (*b*) I, II, III, IV
(*c*) II, III, IV (*d*) I, III, IV

59. Consider the following statements about biodiesel ?
I. It can be used as conventional diesel.
II. It contains no petroleum, but it can be blended with petroleum diesel to create a biodiesel blend or it can be used alone.
III. It requires no engine modification and increases engine life.
IV. It can provide the same payload capacity as diesel.

Options :
(*a*) I, III, IV (*b*) I, II, IV
(*c*) I, II, III (*d*) I, II, III, IV

60. Match the columns A and B and pick the correct option from those listed below ?

Column A	Column B
A. Sexual hybridization	I. mRNA content
B. Protoplast fusion	II. Transgenic organism
C. Recombinant DNA technology	III. Limited to closely related species
D. Transcriptome	IV. Difficult to predict outcome

Options :
(*a*) AIII, BII, CIV, DI
(*b*) AIII, BIV, CII, DI
(*c*) AIV, BI, CIII, DII
(*d*) AI, BII, CIV, DIII

61. Which of the following ***is not correct*** ?
(*a*) Fatty acid biosynthesis in plants is very similar to that in bacteria.
(*b*) In case of plants, fatty acids are synthesized in peroxysomes.
(*c*) High oleic acid oils are nutritionally more beneficial.
(*d*) Transgenic variety Laurical has high lauric acid content.

62. ***Assertion (A)*** : Consumption of oils containing high amount of oleic acid is beneficial for human beings.

Reason (R) : It has cholesterol lowering properties.

Options :
(*a*) Both A and R are correct and R is the correct explanation of A.
(*b*) Both A and R correct, but R does not explain A.
(*c*) Only A is correct.
(*d*) Only R is correct.

63. Genetic improvement of crop plants through biotechnology needs conventional breeding due to which of the following reasons ?
(*a*) The elite cultivars developed by plant breeding will be parents of the next generation of transgenics.
(*b*) Field testing across locations or cropping systems and over years will be needed to select the best transgenic event.

(*c*) Breeding may be required to minimise/ eliminate pleiotropic effects.
(*d*) All of the above.

64. Which of the following ***is not correct*** about gamma-linolenic acid (GLA) ?
(*a*) It is a non-essential fatty acid.
(*b*) It is the first intermediate in the conversion of linoleic acid to arachidonic acid.
(*c*) It is produced by desaturation of linoleic acid by the enzyme Δ^6 fatty acid desaturase.
(*d*) It is beneficial in alleviation of many physiological and pathological conditions such as hypercholesteremia, cancer and diabetes.

65. In case of phytoremediation, plants are used for which of the following ?
(*a*) To accumulate pollutants from soil.
(*b*) To control microbial attack on plants.
(*c*) To control microbial contamination of the water.
(*d*) All of the above.

66. Bioreactors are used for which of the following ?
(*a*) Production of enzymes
(*b*) Production of secondary metabolites
(*c*) Production of cell cultures
(*d*) All of the above

67. Consider the following statements.
I. Plant biotechnology only creates genetic variation.
II. The material generated by biotechnology must be subjected to atleast selection and evaluation before it can be released as a variety for commerical cultivation.
III. Biotechnology can assist in selection and rapid multiplication of desired genotypes through micropropagation.
IV. Stable transgene expression can be obtained by selection for stable expression in a breeding programme based on transgenic plants.

Which of the above statements is correct ?
(*a*) I, II, III (*b*) I, II, IV
(*c*) II, III, IV (*d*) I, II, III, IV

68. Which of the following organisms is used for production of single cell protein ?
(*a*) *Pseudomonas* (*b*) *Azospirillum*
(*c*) *Spirulina* (*d*) BGA

69. Immobilization of enzyme is done by which of the following ?
(*a*) Cross linking
(*b*) Entrapment
(*c*) Physical adsorption
(*d*) All of the above

70. Which of the following organisms ***is not used*** for preparation of biofertilizers ?
(*a*) *Azotobacter* (*b*) *Pseudomonas*
(*c*) *Azolla* (*d*) *Azospirillum*

71. Genetic modification of plants can be achieved by which of the following ?
(*a*) Somatic hybridization
(*b*) Genetic engineering
(*c*) Somaclonal variation
(*d*) All of the above

72. Consider the following statements:
I. The term biotechology has been derived through fusion of 'biology' with 'technology'.
II. At the 69th Session of Indian Science Congress held at Mysore in 1982, Indian Scientists focussed on the importance of gene technology.
III. On the recommendation of Science Advisory Committee to Parliament, Government of India formed the National Biotechnology Board under the Department of Science and Technology to promote biotechnological research in India.
IV. In the year 1986, a separate Department of Biotechnology was created in the Ministry of Science and Technology.

Which of these statements are correct ?
(*a*) I, II, III, IV (*b*) II, III, IV
(*c*) I, III, IV (*d*) I, II, III

73. Which of the following is associated with transgenic cotton varieties producing coloured cottons ?
(*a*) They would reduced pollution.
(*b*) They are attacked by large number of pests due to their colour.

(*c*) They require higher doses of inorganic fertilizers.
(*d*) They would have enhanced fibre strength.

74. Which of the following is correct about AIDS ?

I. AIDS is caused by an RNA virus called HIV.
II. The genome size of HIV is 9.7 kb.
III. HIV-1C is more common in India.
IV. Azidothymidine is used for the treatment of AIDS.

Options :
(*a*) II, III, IV (*b*) I, II, III, IV
(*c*) I, III, IV (*d*) I, II, III

75. Which of the following steps are involved in the production of transgenic mice ?

I. Transfer of desired gene into fertilized eggs through microinjection.
II. Transfected fertilized eggs are transplanted into surrogate mothers (female mice).
III. Development of mice in surrogate mothers and their identification after they are born.

Options :
(*a*) I, II (*b*) I, III
(*c*) I, II, III (*d*) II, III

76. Which of the following ***is not correct*** about somaclonal varieties ?

(*a*) A low neurotoxin somaclonal variety, Ratan, of khesari has been released for commercial cultivation in M.P.
(*b*) Pusa Jaikishan is a somaclonal variety of *B. juncea*.
(*c*) A somaclonal variety Bio-13 of *Citronella java* was developed by NBRI, Lucknow.
(*d*) Pusa Jaikishan was derived from Varuna.

77. Which of the following advantages are associated with biodiesel ?

I. It is biodegradable and nontoxic fuel.
II. The low-level blends (20% and less) of biodiesel with petroleum diesel fuels generally do not require any engine modification.
III. It has about 10% built in oxygen, which helps it to burn fully.
IV. Its higher octane number improves the ignition quality even when blended in the petroleum diesel.

Options :
(*a*) I, II, III (*b*) I, II, III, IV
(*c*) II, III, IV (*d*) I, III, IV

78. Which of the following is correct about map-based cloning ?

(*a*) A critical prerequisite is that the target gene must be localized definitely with respect to a molecular markers.
(*b*) It starts with an interesting phenotype observed at whole organism level and proceeds to clone the gene via genetic mapping and chromosome walking.
(*c*) Non-availability of tightly linked flanking markers to the gene of interest in a problem.
(*d*) All of the above.

79. Match the columns A and B carefully and pick the correct option from those listed below them.

Column A	Column B
A. Micropropagation	I. Haploid
B. Regeneration	II. Axillary bud break
C. Androgenesis	III. Interspecific hybrid
D. Embryo rescue	IV. Organogenesis and somatic embryo-genesis

Options :
(*a*) AIII, BIV, CII, DI
(*b*) AIV, BII, CIII, DI
(*c*) AI, BIII, CIV, DII
(*d*) AII, BIV, CI, DIII

80. Molecular probes can be used for which of the following ?

I. Diagnosis of diseases and DNA fingerprinting.
II. Screening of genomic and cDNA libraries.
III. Location of genes or DNA sequences on chromosomes.
IV. Identification of varieties of crop species.

Options :

(*a*) I, II, III, IV (*b*) I, III, IV
(*c*) II, III, IV (*d*) I

81. Many plant species are either asexually reproducing or produce recalcitrant seeds which are difficult to store. Germplasm of such species can be conserved by which of the following strategies ?

I. As field banks.
II. By cryopreservation.
III. As slow-growth cultures.
IV. As DNA clones.

Options :

(*a*) I, II, III (*b*) I, II, III, IV
(*c*) II, III, IV (*d*) I, III, IV

82. Which of the following advantages are offered by *p*UC series vectors over *p*BR322 ?

I. Each *E. coli* cell produces upto 700 copies without any treatment.
II. Cells containing recombinant DNA are selected in a single step.
III. The sites for DNA insert integration are confined to the polylinkers, which permits the use of two restriction enzymes to open the vector.
IV. They do not allow sequencing of the DNA insert.

Options :

(*a*) I, II, III, IV (*b*) I, III, IV
(*c*) I, II, III (*d*) II, III, IV

83. Intellectual property rights can be protected by which of the following ?

I. Patent.
II. trade secret.
III. Copyright
IV. Plant breeder's rights

Options :

(*a*) I, II, III (*b*) I, II, III, IV
(*c*) I, III, IV (*d*) II, III, IV

84. Which of the following is correct about HIV ?

I. HIV uses receptors, *viz.*, CD4 and CCR5, to infect T cells.
II. CD4 is essential for T cell function, but CCR5 appears to be dispensable.
III. Due to lack of CCR5 receptor in about 1% Caucasian population, such individuals naturally show immunity to AIDS.
IV. Inhibition of CCR5 expression through appropriate siRNA molecules reduces the infection of T cells by HIV.

Options :

(*a*) I, II, III (*b*) II, III, IV
(*c*) III, IV (*d*) I, II, III, IV

85. Which of the following is correct about PVY III ?

I. A new strain of potato virus Y (PVY) discovered in USA.
II. PVY III was highly necrotic to all American flue-cured germplasm.
III. Anther culture from a single plant of the flue-cured variety, McNair 944 yielded one plant resistant to PVY III; the doubled haploid from this plant was designated as NC602.
IV. The PVY III resistance of NC602 was governed by a single gene expressing additive effects (partial dominance).

Options :

(*a*) I, II, III, IV (*b*) I, II, III
(*c*) II, III, IV (*d*) I, III, IV

86. Consider the following statements about embryo culture ?

I. It is routinely used for the recovery of hybrid plants from distant crosses.
II. It is particularly useful where embryos fail to develop due to endosperm degeneration.
III. It has been used extensively in the extraction of haploid barley plants from *H. bulbosum* × *H. vulgare* crosses.
IV. Embryo culture is regularly used in orchid propagation and in breeding of those species that show dormancy, *e.g.*, *Iris*.

Which of these statements are correct ?

(*a*) I, II, IV (*b*) II, III, IV
(*c*) I, II, III (*d*) I, II, III, IV

87. Which of the following ***is not correct*** about Scarlet ?

(*a*) It is a somaclonal variety of potato.
(*b*) It was selected from shoot-tip culture-derived plants.
(*c*) This variety is comparable to the parent cultivar in yield and disease resistance.
(*d*) It shows darker and more stable skin colour, which is a desirable quality trait.

88. Which of the following ***is not correct*** about virus cross protection ?
(*a*) The phenomenon of cross protection was first observed by McKinney in 1929 in case of tobacco mosaic virus.
(*b*) Plants infected with a mild strain of virus resist the development of symptoms upon infection by a more severe strain of the same virus.
(*c*) A mild protecting strain effective for one region may be severe for another region.
(*d*) Selection of mild protecting strain is rather easy.

89. ***Problem (P)***: An inherent problem associated with the map-based cloning is the non-availablity of tightly linked flanking markers to the gene of interest:
Solution (S): Transposon tagging provides solution for the isolation of useful genes.
Options :
(*a*) Both P and S are correct and S roughly takes care of P.
(*b*) Both P and S are correct, but S does not take care of P.
(*c*) Only P is correct.
(*d*) Only S is correct.

90. Which of the following steps are involved in marker-assisted selection for disease resistance ?
I. Identification of tightly linked marker(s) with resistance gene(s).
II. Testing the validity of the linked markers in the breeding materials.
III. Marker-based indirect selection for disease resistant plants in segregating or non-segregating generation.
IV. Selection for disease resistance, followed by selection for the linked marker.
Options :
(*a*) I, II, IV (*b*) I, II, III
(*c*) I, III, IV (*d*) II, III, IV

91. DNA marker-based selection for disease resistance essentially requires which of the following conditions ?
I. The identified DNA marker(s) should co-segregate or be closely linked (1 cM or less) with the gene for resistance trait.
II. The availability of an efficient screening technique for DNA markers, which can practically enable to handle large populations.
III. The screening technique should be cost effective with high reproducibility.
Options :
(*a*) I, III (*b*) II, III
(*c*) I, II, III (*d*) I, II

92. The Marker-aided selection is useful for which of the following ?
I. To select for disease resistance QTLs.
II. To reduce linkage drag due to deleterious genes.
III. To accelerate the return to the genotype of the recurrent parent during back-crossing.
IV. As a substitute for disease screening.
Options :
(*a*) I, II, III, IV (*b*) I, II, III
(*c*) II, III, IV (*d*) I, III, IV

93. Which of the following programmes converts the submitted amino acid sequence into nucleotide sequence and compares it with nucleotide sequence database ?
(*a*) $BLAST_x$ (*b*) $BLAST_n$
(*c*) $tBLAST_n$ (*d*) $tBLAST_x$

94. ***Assertion (A)***: During preparation of embryo for culture, care should be taken to excise the young embryos with their suspensors intact.
Reason (R): Suspensor supplies GA_3 to young embryos.
Options :
(*a*) Both A and R are correct and R sufficiently explains A.
(*b*) Both A and R are correct, but R does not explain A.

(c) Only A is correct.
(d) Only R is correct.

95. *In vitro* techniques for germplasm storage are useful for which of the following ?
(a) Clonally propagated crops
(b) Crops producing recalcitrant seeds
(c) Crops producing orthodox seeds
(d) Both (a) and (b).

96. In which of the following cases, the *in vitro* strategies of germplasm storage are useful ?
I. When crop species are asexually propagated and/or at least some of their genotypes do not produce seed.
II. When crop species produce recalcitrant seeds.
III. When asexually propagated species are highly heterozygous.
IV. When materials developed by genetic transformation show instability.

Options :
(a) I, II, III (b) I, II, III, IV
(c) I, III, IV (d) II, III, IV

97. Which of the following statements is correct about thaumatin ?
(a) Gene encoding thaumatin is isolated from African shrub, *Thaumatococcus danielli.*
(b) It is a protein that is 100,000 times sweeter than sugar on a molecular basis and has a flavour enhancing effect at subsweetness levels.
(c) The gene producing thaumatin has been transferred and expressed in *E. coli* and yeast.
(d) All of the above.

98. Which of the following statements ***is not correct*** about cryopreservation ?
(a) It has proved to be the most reliable method for long-term preservation of cell cultures.
(b) It consists of choice of explants pre-culture and pretreatment, cryoprotection, freezing, storage, thawing and reculture.
(c) DMSO is rarely used.
(d) A general protocol applicable to all species and explants is not available.

99. Which of the following advantages is offered by *in vitro* technique of germplasm storage ?
(a) The material can be stored over long periods.
(b) They are ideal for germplasm exchange.
(c) The risk of errors in labelling are minimised.
(d) All of the above

100. ***Purpose (P)***: The gene encoding thaumatin has been transferred and expressed in *E. coli* and yeast with a view to obtain thaumatin at commercially accepted prices.
Hinderance (H): The cost of production remains unacceptably high due to rather low levels of expression.

Options :
(a) Both P and H are correct and H sufficiently explains P.
(b) Both P and H are correct, but H does not explain P.
(c) Only P is correct.
(d) Only H is correct.

101. Which of the following ***is not correct*** about protoplasts ?
(a) They may be cultured on a suitable medium in a variety of ways.
(b) They regenerate cell wall within 2-4 days of culture.
(c) The first division in protoplasts occurs generally after 2-7 days and multicellular colonies appears after 2-3 weeks.
(d) Protoplasts are cultured in light.

102. Which of the following advantage is offered by *in vitro* techniques of germplasm storage ?
(a) Require relatively very small space.
(b) Help in storage of germplasm free from diseases, insects, etc.
(c) Materials are clean source of nucleus seed.
(d) All of the above.

103. Which of the following ***is not correct*** about verminator technology ?
(a) Zeneca, U.K. has developed what it calls improved plant germplasm invention.

(*b*) Improved plant germplasm invention has been dubbed as verminator technology by RAFI, Canada.
(*c*) This technology uses a gene from the fat tissue of a goat, the product of which interferes with normal plant growth.
(*d*) If the transgenic crop is sprayed with a specific chemical, plants show normal growth.

104. Slow growth culture suffer from which of the following limitations ?
I. Relatively high cost inherent to the micropropagation.
II. Risk of contamination.
III. Risk of somaclonal variation.
IV. Selection pressure due to the growth restriction.

Options :
(*a*) I, II, III (*b*) I, II, III, IV
(*c*) II, III, IV (*d*) I, III, IV

105. ***Assertion (A)***: In case of elctrofusion technique, fusion of protoplasts is brought about by a short pluse of high voltage.
Reason (R): The high voltage creates transient disturbances in the organisation of plasma lemma.

Options :
(*a*) Both A and R are correct and R sufficiently explains A.
(*b*) Both A and R are correct, but R does not explain A.
(*c*) Only A is correct.
(*d*) Only R is correct.

106. Who said, "Environment today is à question of survival. Our rivers are dying, cities are choking, underground water tables are depleting, the air is not fit for breathing. Only a strong people's movement can bring a change in our present situation. Unless we have a green vote bank, the attitude of political parties towards the environment will not change" ?
(*a*) Rajendra Singh (*b*) M.C. Mehta
(*c*) R.T. Doshi (*d*) G.V.K. Mehta

107. Burning of plastic bags, emits toxic gasses leading to which of the following ?
(*a*) Bronchitis
(*b*) Lung infection
(*c*) Respiratory problems
(*d*) All of the above.

108. The first ever vaccination was against which of the following diseases ?
(*a*) Cholera (*b*) Rabies
(*c*) Small pox (*d*) Polio

109. 'Kwashiorkar' is concerned with which of the following ?
(*a*) Severe protein deficiency
(*b*) Food poisoning
(*c*) Flourine toxicity
(*d*) Nitrate toxicity

110. In Bt-cotton, expression of crystal protein occurs in which of the following ?
(*a*) Only in stem
(*b*) In leaves
(*c*) Systemic expression
(*d*) Both (*a*) and (*b*).

111. Which of the following is correct about reverse transcriptase ?
I. This enzyme was discovered by Temin and Baltimore.
II. It is generally obtained from avian myeloblastosis virus.
III. It is RNA dependent DNA polymerase.
IV. This enzyme performs similar functions as DNA polymerase and has an absolute requirement for a primer with a free 3′–OH.

Options :
(*a*) I, II, III (*b*) I, II, III, IV
(*c*) II, III, IV (*d*) I, III, IV

112. Biofertilizers can be used to achieve which of the following ?
(*a*) To fix atmospheric nitrogen.
(*b*) To solublize soil nutrients like phosphate
(*c*) To stimulate plant growth
(*d*) All of the above.

113. Which of the following is an example of a prokaryote ?
(*a*) Blue-green algae
(*b*) Sieve cell of phloem
(*c*) Fungi
(*d*) Yeast.

114. Which of the options given in Q. 113 ***does not contain*** nucleus ?

115. Which of the options given in Q. 113 may contain more than one nucleus per cell ?

116. Which of the following is correct about heavy metals ?

(*a*) Heavy metals refer to the metals which are present in the soil with a density greater than 5 or 6 g cm^{-3}.

(*b*) As, Cd, Cr, Hg, Cu, Ni, Pb are examples of heavy metals.

(*c*) They are harmful for humans as well as plants.

(*d*) All of the above.

117. Chromosome walking involves which of the following ?

I. Selection of a clone of interest from genomic library identified by a probe and subcloning of a small fragment from one end of the DNA insert from this clone.

II. The subcloned fragment of the selected clone is then hybridized with other clones in the library to identify a clone having DNA insert overlapping with that of the first one.

III. The restriction map of each selected clone is prepared and compared to know the region of overlapping.

IV. Identification of few overlapping restriction sites will amount to walking along the chromosome or along a long chromosome segment.

Options :

(*a*) I, II, III (*b*) I, II, III, IV
(*c*) I, III (*d*) I, II

118. Which of the following elements is extremely toxic in the soil under hyper accumulation ?

I. Cadium II. Mercury
III. Chromium IV. Calcium

Options :

(*a*) I, II, III (*b*) II, III, IV
(*c*) I, II, IV (*d*) I, III, IV

119. Usually which of the following RNA is used for production of cDNA ?

(*a*) rRNA (*b*) mRNA
(*c*) tRNA (*d*) siRNA

120. Which of the following statements is correct ?

(*a*) Earthworm (*Eisenia foetida*) has the ability to detoxify the toxic thermal power waste flyash.

(*b*) Uptake of high concentration of cadium cause itai-itai disease in humans.

(*c*) Excess of fluorine in drinking water causes dental and skeletal problems.

(*d*) All of the above.

121. How many microorganism are generally present per gram of biofertilizers ?

(*a*) 10^7–10^9 (*b*) 10^2–10^3
(*c*) 10^5–10^6 (*d*) 10^{12}–10^{15}

122. In order to move from a molecular marker to the linked gene of interest, which of the following approaches can be used ?

(*a*) Chromosome jumping
(*b*) Chromosome walking
(*c*) Colony hybridization
(*d*) Chromosome sorting

123. Which of the following elements show moderate toxicity in soil under hyper accumulation ?

I. Fluoride II. Nickel
III. Molybdenum IV. Lead

Options :

(*a*) I, II, III (*b*) I, II, III, IV
(*c*) II, III, IV (*d*) I, III, IV

124. Franken food is the 'nick name' of which of the following ?

(*a*) Fast food (*b*) Frozen food
(*c*) GM food (*d*) Fortified food

125. ***Problem (P)***: Deficiencies of various micronutrients including vitamnin A, zinc and iron in the diet are commonly found in the developing countries.

Consequence (C): Deficiencies of various micronutrients in the diet result higher incidence of blindness, weaker immune system, stunted growth and impaired cognitive development.

Options :
(*a*) Both P and C are correct and C is result of P.
(*b*) Both P and C are correct, but C is not result of P.
(*c*) Only P is correct.
(*d*) Only C is correct.

126. Due to which of the following reasons, algae have emerged as one of the most promising sources, especially for biodiesel production ?
(*a*) Algae can grow in places away from the farmlands and forests.
(*b*) The yields of oil from algae are orders of magnitude higher than those from traditional oilseeds.
(*c*) Algae can be grown in sewage(s) and next to power-plant smokestacks where they aid in pollution management.
(*d*) All of the above.

127. Which of following is correct about *Spirulina* ?
I. It is a filamentous cyanobacterium.
II. It is commercially cultivated as a source of human food.
III. The blue pigment from *Spirulina* is being used in eye shadow, eyeliner and lipsticks.
IV. A preparation of *Spirulina* chlorophyll in a mixture containing iron oxide and a higher alcohol was patented as a strong deodorant.

Options :
(*a*) I, II, III (*b*) I, II, III, IV
(*c*) II, III (*d*) I, III, IV

128. Carotenoids (carotene and xanthophyll) obtained from cyanobacteria are commercially used as which of the following ?
(*a*) Food colouring.
(*b*) Food additives to enhance flesh colour of salmon fish.
(*c*) To enhance colour of egg yolk.
(*d*) All of the above.

129. *Spirulina* has high nutritional value in terms of which of the following ?
I. High protein content
II. High vitamin content
III. Presence of unsaturated fatty acids, *e.g.*, γ-linoleic acid, which do not form cholesterol.
IV. Easy digestability due to absence of cellulosic cell wall.

Options :
(*a*) I, II, III (*b*) II, III, IV
(*c*) I, II, III, IV (*d*) I, III, IV

130. ***Problem (P)***: Deficiencies of micronutrients are common in the diet of developing world.
Solution (S): Deficiencies of micronutrients can be overcome by fortification/biofortification.

Options :
(*a*) Both P and S are correct and S adequately overcomes the P.
(*b*) Both P and S are correct, but S does not overcome the P.
(*c*) Only P is correct.
(*d*) Only S is correct.

131. Which of the following is correct about nutraceuticals.
(*a*) A combination of nutrition and pharmaceutical.
(*b*) It refers to extracts of foods claimed to have a medicinal effect on human health.
(*c*) It is usally contained in a medicinal format such as powder, tablet or capsule in a prescribed dose.
(*d*) All of the above.

132. Which of the following is used as a nutraceutical ?
(*a*) Soluble dietary fibre products such as *Psyllium* seed husk, broccoli (sulforaphane), soy or clover (isoflavonoids).
(*b*) Resveratrol from red grape products.
(*c*) Alpha-linolenic acid from flax seeds.
(*d*) All of the above.

133. Which of following is a soluble dietary fibre product, and is used as a nutraceutical to prevent cancer ?
(*a*) *Psyllium* seed husk
(*b*) Broccoli (Sulforaphane)
(*c*) Soy or clover products
(*d*) Resveratrol

134. Which of the options given in Q. 133 is used to reduce hypercholesteremia ?

135. Which of the options given in Q. 133 is used as antioxidant ?

136. Which of the options given in Q. 133 is used as antioxidant ?

137. Which of the following is correct ?

I. Functional foods are those foods which are being consumed as part of a usual diet but are demonstrated to have physiological benefits and/or reduce the risk of chronic disease beyond basic nutritional foods.

II. Enriching or fortying foods with nutrients is called nutrification.

III. Food enrichment is the restoration of natural nutritive value (*e.g.*, vitamins or minerals) of foods, which has been lost during processing.

IV. Food fortification is the public health policy of adding micronutrients (essential trace elements and vitamins) to foodstuffs to ensure that minimum dietary requirements are met.

Options :

(*a*) I, II, III, IV (*b*) II, III, IV
(*c*) I, III, IV (*d*) I, IV

138. Which of the following is an example of fortified food ?

(*a*) Addition of iodine to table salt (iodised salt).
(*b*) Addition of calcium to fruit juice.
(*c*) Addition of vitamin D to such foods as margarine.
(*d*) All of the above.

139. Which of the following is correct about dietary supplement ?

(*a*) It is also called nutritional or food supplement.
(*b*) It is a preparation intended to provide nutrients such as fatty acids, vitamins, minerals or amino acids that are missing or are not consumed in sufficient quantity in diet.
(*c*) The hormones DHEA, pregnenolone and pineal hormone melatonin are marketed as dietary supplements in the USA.
(*d*) All of the above.

140. Which of the following is correct about food additives ?

(*a*) These are substances added to food to preserve flavour or improve taste and appearance.
(*b*) They may be natural or artificial.
(*c*) To regulate these additives, and inform consumers, each additive is assigned a unique number; initially these were E numbers used in Europe for all approved additives.
(*d*) All of the above.

141. Which of the following is correct ?

(*a*) Convention on biological diversity (CBD) is concerned with conservation of whole biodiversity while PGR is concerned with conservation of plant diversity.
(*b*) SBBs stands for state biodiversity boards.
(*c*) BMCs stands for biodiversity management committees.
(*d*) All of the above.

142. Which of the following acids is commonly used in foods ?

(*a*) Fumaric and lactic acids
(*b*) Citric acid and vinegar
(*c*) Maleic acid and tartaric acid
(*d*) All of the above

143. When acids like vinegar (citric acid) are added in the foods, they act as which of the following ?

I. Improve taste II. Preservatives
III. Antioxidants IV. Colouring agents

Options :

(*a*) I, II, III, IV (*b*) II, III, IV
(*c*) I, II, III (*d*) I, III, IV

144. Which of the following can be produced from dead bodies of animals ?

(*a*) Calmodulin and aprotinin
(*b*) Myelin and ubiquitin
(*c*) Gelatin and protein kinase
(*d*) All of the above

145. Which of the following is correct about food stabilizers ?

I. Stabilisers, thickeners, and gelling agents like agar or pectin when used in jam gave a firmer texture.
II. They are not true emulsifiers.
III. They help to stabilize emulsions.

Options :
(*a*) I, II, III (*b*) II, III
(*c*) I, III (*d*) I, II

146. Which of the following is correct about biochemical oxygen demand (BOD) ?

(*a*) The amount of O_2 required by aerobic microorganisms to decompose the organic matter present in a sample of water.
(*b*) It is used to measure the degree of water pollution.
(*c*) It is also called biological oxygen demand.
(*d*) All of the above.

147. Which of the following is correct ?

(*a*) When available ESTs assembled in contiguous overlapping clusters are described as contigs.
(*b*) When ESTs appear as singles and which can not be assembled in contigs are described as singletons.
(*c*) Unigene set is a combined set of contigs and singletons.
(*d*) All of the above.

1.2. FILL IN THE BLANKS

1. Human genome project was officially completed in ....
2. The term 'bioinformatics' is derived by a combination of biology and ....
3. IRGSP stands for ....
4. .... is also called stress hormone.
5. Bands generated by RAPD, AP-PCR and DAF are .... markers.
6. The most common reason for post-zygotic failure of wide hybridization is embryo abortion due to poor .... development.
7. Terminator technology was patented by .... of USA.
8. Interferon was discovered by ....
9. ELISA test is based on............ interaction.
10. Recombinant human insulin is marketed as ....
11. L-sorbose is precursor of ....
12. β-Interferon is produced from ....
13. .... determined the amino acid sequence of insulin.
14. Kinetin was discovered by ....
15. The first transgenic animal to be patented was .... mouse.
16. Insulin controls the sugar concentration in ....
17. Ribozymes are composed of ....
18. First somatic hybrid through protoplast fusion was produced in the genus............
19. Pomato was produced by ....
20. The geranium variety called Velvet Rose, a somaclone of Rober's Lemon Rose, has .... the chromosome number of the parent variety.
21. Similar to ...., biodiesel can be used in diesel engines.
22. Lod score method of linkage detection was developed by ....
23. Northern blotting is an extension of ....
24. Plant biotechnology .... directly develop variety.
25. In plants, fatty acids are synthesized in ....
26. In case of RFLP, size of probes varies from .... bp.
27. The 35*S* promoter, the most extensively used constitutive promoter, was isolated from ....
28. Commercialization of many transgenic plants is restricted by .... due to which the level of transgene expression declines with the passage of time.

29. GLA is found in the oils of .... and ....
30. Ferretin gene from *Phaseolus* increases .... content in rice endosperm by a factor of 2.5.
31. The PVY III resistance of NC602 was found to be governed by a single gene expressing ....
32. For the preparation of high density linkage map, MAPMAKER package is commonly used, it was developed by a group of researchers working at the ....
33. *BKM* probe was developed by ....
34. MAHYCO, India collaborated with .... for exploiting the potential of *Bt* technology in cotton.
35. In wheat, callus growth and regeneration ability are governed by genes called ....
36. Rabies virus affects ....
37. Rice grain are .... in carotenoids.
38. .... is involved in diabetes.
39. Teichoic acid is present in the cell walls of .... bacteria.
40. Human genome contains about .... billion base pairs.
41. A plasmid used for providing the functions missing from another plasmid is called ....
42. Microbial cells devoid of cell wall ....
43. Enzyme produced by *nptII* gene inactivates kanamycin, G418 and neomycin by ....
44. Introduction of DNA into bacteria by viral infection is called ....
45. Golden rice is an example of ....

1.3. MARK TRUE OR FALSE

1. The aim of genetic engineering is to usually maintain all the desirable features of the target organism and introduce an additional phenotype produced by insertion of a transgene/few transgenes.
2. ELISA test is based on radioactivity.
3. IAA is a natural auxin.
4. Humulin is the first recombinant pharmaceutical product.
5. Milstein and Kohler got Nobel Prize for making monoclonal antibodies.
6. AIDS is transmitted through mosquito bite.
7. Polymerase chain reaction uses DNA ligase.
8. The term somaclonal variation includes epigenetic changes.
9. "Flavr Savr' is a transgenic variety of apple.
10. DAF stands for DNA amplification fingerprint.
11. Southern blots display differences in the length of restriction fragments.
12. Edward Jenner developed the first vaccine against small pox.
13. Commercial cellulase is obtained from *Bacillus licheniformis*.
14. Centre for Cellular and Molecular Biology is located at Hyderabad.
15. The so called 'Superbug' was developed by Dr. Anand Mohan Chakraborty.
16. National Research Centre on Plant Biotechnology is located at Pusa, Bihar.
17. Human genome contains about 3.2 billion base pairs.
18. Marker-assisted selection eliminates the confusing effects of the environment on selection and eliminates the need for creating specific environments required for assaying certain traits.
19. For the recovery of virus and other pathogen free stocks of clonal crops, meristem culture is rarely combined with thermotherapy/cryopreservation.
20. The largest area under transgenic varieties was in soyabean followed by maize, cotton and other crops.
21. Application of somatic hybridization is restricted mainly to solanaceous and cruciferous crops.

22. *In vitro* pollination can effectively overcome post-fertilization barriers in interspecific crosses.
23. GLA is important in alleviation of higher cholesteremia and certain other complications of heart.
24. Jatropha is an economically important oil-yielding crops as a biodiesel substitute.
25. In general, larger the shoot meristem explant, greater are the changes of survival, and of obtaining shoot development.
26. The pigments/dyes used for colouring plastic bags cause food contamination, kidney failure, etc.
27. Expression proteomics is quite useful in identifying disease specific proteins.
28. In a narrow sense, proteome describe the set of proteins expressed in a cell at a given time.
29. Amount of O_2 used up after 120±1 hr incubation of 1 litre water at 20°C in complete light is called biological oxygen demand.
30. Nucleopolyhedrosis virsus (NPV) is commercially used in U.S.A. for the control of cotton bollworm.
31. The term 'vaccine' is derived from Vaccinia (Virus).

2

RECOMBINANT DNA TECHNOLOGY

2.1. MULTIPLE CHOICE QUESTIONS

1. The process of indentification of genetic material began in 1928 with the experiments of which of the following ?
(*a*) Griffith
(*b*) Hershey and Chase
(*c*) Watson
(*d*) Avery and coworkers.

2. During 1957, Frankel-Conrat and Singer proved that RNA is the genetic material in which of the following organisms ?
(*a*) Cauliflower mosaic virus
(*b*) Tobacco mosaic virus
(*c*) Cucumber mosaic virus
(*d*) Tomato mosaic virus

3. Hershey and Chase used which of the following organisms for their experiments to show that DNA is the genetic material ?
(*a*) T_2 phage and *E. coli*
(*b*) T_4 phage and *E. coli*
(*c*) λ phase and *E. coli*
(*d*) T_7 phage and *E. coli*

4. Match the columns A and B and pick the correct option from those listed below them.

Column A	Column B
A. φX174 virus	I. Single-strand RNA
B. Rheovirus	II. Double-strand DNA
C. Plant wound and tumour virus	III. Double-strand RNA
D. Cauliflower mosaic virus	IV. Single-strand DNA

Options :
(*a*) AI, BII, CIII, DIV
(*b*) AII, BIII, CIV, DI
(*c*) AIV, BI, CIII, DII
(*d*) AIII, BIV, CII, DI

5. Eukaryotic chromosomes consist of which of the following ?
(*a*) Histone and non-histone proteins
(*b*) Nucleic acids
(*c*) DNA
(*d*) Nucleoproteins

6. Phosphodiester bond of DNA and RNA involves which of the following ?
(*a*) 2′C and 1′C (*b*) 5′C and 3′C
(*c*) 5′C and 2′C (*d*) 3′C and 1′C

7. Which of the following ***is not correct*** about DNA ?
(*a*) Double helix model of DNA was proposed by Watson and Crick.
(*b*) DNA molecules ordinarily consist of two polynucleotide chains/strands.
(*c*) DNA double helix is stablized by hydrogen bonds.
(*d*) Two strands of a DNA molecule are oriented antiparallel to each other.

8. Which of the following ***is not correct*** about RNA ?
(*a*) RNA molecules ordinarily consist of a single polyribonucleotide strand.
(*b*) RNA molecules contain uracil in the place of cytosine.
(*c*) Phosphodiester bonds are formed between ribonucleotides in the same manner as in the case of deoxyribonucleotides.
(*d*) RNA was, most likely, the first genetic material; it was much later replaced by DNA.

9. Which of the following ***is not correct*** about *E. coli* ?
(*a*) *E. coli* is rarely used for gene cloning.
(*b*) Single generation of *E. coli* is completed within 20-30 minutes, under optimum conditions.
(*c*) Chromosome length of *E. coli* is approximately 1 mm.
(*d*) Rate of chromosome replication is 30-40 μ per minute under optimum conditions.

10. Which of the following ***is not correct*** ?
(*a*) If the base sequence of one DNA strand is known, the base sequence of its other strand can be easily deduced.
(*b*) The formation of hydrogen bonds between adenine and thymine, and between guanine and cytosine is known as complementary base pairing.
(*c*) Usually, B-DNA molecule has right-handed coiling.
(*d*) Hydrophobic interactions are important in transcription.

11. Which of the following ***is not correct*** ?
(*a*) Double helix RNA generally follows the same rule of base-pairing as does DNA.
(*b*) The smallest RNA molecule is tRNA
(*c*) Antisense RNA is also called micRNA
(*d*) Ribosomal RNA is processed from larger primary transcripts.

12. Prokaryotic DNA polymerase I is known to function in which of the following ?
(*a*) DNA replication
(*b*) DNA repair
(*c*) Recombination
(*d*) Both (*a*) and (*b*)

13. Which of the following ***is not correct*** about DNA replication ?
(*a*) Mode of DNA replication is semi-conservative
(*b*) Mode of semi-conservative DNA replication was proposed by Watson and Crick.
(*c*) Evidence for semi-conservative replication of DNA was first reported by Meselson and Stahl in 1958.
(*d*) Semi-conservative mode of DNA replication was first demonstrated in T_2 phage of *E. coli*.

14. Which of the following ***is not correct*** about DNA replication ?
(*a*) The presence of replication fork in *E. coli* chromosome was first demonstrated by Cairns in 1963.
(*b*) DNA replication always proceeds in the $5' \rightarrow 3'$ direction.
(*c*) Both strands of DNA replicate continuously.
(*d*) DNA replication begins with the synthesis of a small RNA primer.

15. Among the given statements about B- and Z-DNA forms, which one ***is not common*** to both forms ?
(*a*) Double helix.
(*b*) Length of one full turn of helix is 34 Å.
(*c*) Two strands of double helix are antiparallel.
(*d*) Complementary base pairing.

16. Who proposed the concept of central dogma ?
(*a*) Crick (*b*) Watson
(*c*) Meselson (*d*) Cairns

17. Match the columns A and B carefully and select the correct option from those listed below them.

Column A	Column B
A. Taylor	I. Semi-discontinuous DNA replication
B. Kornberg	II. DNA polymerase I
C. Okazaki	III. Semi-conservative replication of eukaryotic chromosomes

Options :
(*a*) AI, BIII, CII (*b*) AIII, BI, CII
(*c*) AIII, BII, CI (*d*) AI, BII, CIII

18. DNA ligase is used for which of the following ?
(*a*) Joining of more than one fragment of DNA
(*b*) Synthesis of DNA
(*c*) Replication of DNA
(*d*) Cleavage of DNA

19. Direct repeat means which of the following ?
(*a*) Repetition of certain length of nucleotides in reverse order.
(*b*) Repetition of certain length of nucletoides in the same order.

(*c*) Repetition of certain length of nucleotides in either the same or the reverse order.
(*d*) Repetition of certain length of nucleotides to form a palindrome with rotational symmetry.

20. DNA polymerase III serves which of the following functions ?
(*a*) DNA repair
(*b*) DNA replication
(*c*) Initiation of DNA replication
(*d*) All of the above

21. In polymerase chain reaction, which of the following steps constitutes a single cycle ?
I. Denaturation of DNA at 90–98 (94)°C.
II. Annealing of the primers at 40–60°C.
III. Primer extension by the enzyme DNA polymerase at 72°C.
IV. Bringing the temperature down to 4°C.
Options :
(*a*) I, II, IV (*b*) I, II, III, IV
(*c*) I, III, IV (*d*) I, II, III

22. ***Assertion (A)***: PCR products can not be readily used for cloning.
Reason (R): PCR generates errors during DNA amplification.
Options :
(*a*) Both A and R are correct and R is the correct explanation of A.
(*b*) Both A and R are correct, but R does not explain A.
(*c*) Only A is correct
(*d*) Only R is correct.

23. Which of the following ***is not correct*** about *Taq* DNA polymerase ?
(*a*) It is isolated from *Thermus aquaticus.*
(*b*) It is stable at higher temperatures.
(*c*) It has proof-reading property.
(*d*) It is used in PCR for DNA amplification.

24. Multiple copies of a gene can be obtained by which of the following ?
(*a*) Gene cloning.
(*b*) Polymerase chain reaction.
(*c*) Combination of PCR with chemical synthesis.
(*d*) All of the above.

25. Recombinant DNA molecules are produced for which of the following ?
I. Obtaining a large number of copies of specific DNA segments.
II. Integrating the gene in question into the chromosome of a target organism where it expresses itself.
III. Recovery of large quantities of the protein encoded by the concerned gene.
Options :
(*a*) I, II (*b*) II, III
(*c*) I, II, III (*d*) I, III

26. Which of the following is called molecular glue ?
(*a*) DNA polymerase
(*b*) DNA ligase
(*c*) Exonuclease
(*d*) Endonuclease

27. Which of the following is correct about a clone ?
I. A group of individuals produced from a single individual through asexual reproduction.
II. All the individuals of a clone have the same genotype.
III. The individuals of a clone differ in genotype from their parent.
IV. Clone can be maintained through asexual reproduction and selection.
Options :
(*a*) I, II, IV (*b*) II, III, IV
(*c*) I, II, III, IV (*d*) I, II, III

28. Technique of Southern blotting was originally based on which of the following ?
(*a*) Capillary action
(*b*) Electromotive force
(*c*) Vacuum
(*d*) Both (*a*) and (*c*)

29. Which of the following is correct about PCR ?
I. It is also called people's choice reaction.
II. It was developed by Kary Mullis in 1985.
III. Kary Mullis got Nobel Prize in 1993 for development of PCR.
IV. PCR products are readily used for DNA cloning.

Options :
(*a*) I, II, III, IV (*b*) I, II, III
(*c*) I, III, IV (*d*) II, III

30. The phenomenon of transformation was discovered by which of the following ?
(*a*) N. Zinder (*b*) J. Lederberg
(*c*) E.L. Tatum (*d*) F. Griffith

31. Which of the following enzymes is called molecular scissor ?
(*a*) DNA ligase
(*b*) DNA gyrase
(*c*) Restriction enzyme
(*d*) Topoisomerase

32. Which of the following scientists got Nobel Prize in 1980 for the development of recombinant DNA technology ?
(*a*) W. Gilbert (*b*) F. Sanger
(*c*) D. Baltimore (*d*) P. Berg

33. Which of the following scientists developed *p*BR322 ?
(*a*) Boliver Rodriguez
(*b*) Berg Rosenberg
(*c*) Benfy Ris
(*d*) Bonner Riggs.

34. A class of enzymes, which cleaves DNA only within or near those sites that have specific base sequences is called which of the following ?
(*a*) Type I endonuclease
(*b*) Type III endonuclease
(*c*) Type II endonuclease
(*d*) Exonuclease

35. Match the columns A and B and select the correct option from among those listed below them.

Column A	**Column B**
A. Western blotting	I. DNA
B. Northern blotting	II. Protein
C. Southern blotting	III. RNA
D. Probe	IV. RFLP

Options :
(*a*) AII, BIII, CIV, DI
(*b*) AII, BIII, CI, DIV
(*c*) AIII, BI, CII, DIV
(*d*) AIV, BIII, CII, DI

36. Biotin labelled probes are generally prepared by which of the following ?
(*a*) Primer labelling
(*b*) Nick translation
(*c*) End labelling
(*d*) All of the above.

37. Which of following is correct about reverse transcriptase ?
I. It performs similar functions as DNA polymerase.
II. It is RNA dependent DNA polymerase.
III. It was discovered by Temin and Baltimore.
IV. It is generally obtained from Avian Myeloblastosis Virus.

Options :
(*a*) I, II, IV (*b*) II, III, IV
(*c*) II, III (*d*) I, II, III, IV

38. Which of the following is correct ?
I. Klenow fragment of *E. coli* DNA polymerase is used to make the protruding ends double-stranded.
II. Alkaline phosphatase is used for removing 3′-phosphate residues from DNA ends.
III. S1 nuclease is used for removal of single-stranded protrusions from ends.
IV. Terminal deoxynucleotidyl transferase is used for adding single-stranded sequences to 3′-ends of blunt-ended fragments.

Options :
(*a*) I, II, III, IV (*b*) I, III, IV
(*c*) II, III, IV (*d*) II, IV

39. The S1 nuclease is isolated from which of the following ?
(*a*) *Aspergillus oryzae*
(*b*) *Escherichia coli*
(*c*) *Neisseria lactamica*
(*d*) *Proteus vulgaris*

40. Which of the following scientists was awarded Nobel Prize in 1978 for the discovery of endonucleases ?
(*a*) Smith (*b*) Nathans
(*c*) Arber (*d*) All of the above.

41. Which of the following vectors has been constructed for use in two different hosts ?
(*a*) Shuttle vectors (*b*) Cosmids
(*c*) Phasmids (*d*) Phagemids

42. A good vector has which of the following characteristics ?

I. Ideally less than 10 kb in size.
II. Ability to replicate autonomously.
III. Easy to isolate and purify.
IV. Contains unique target sites for many restriction enzymes.

Options :

(*a*) I, III, IV (*b*) I, II, IV
(*c*) I, II, III, IV (*d*) I, IV

43. Length of lambda genome is which of the following ?

(*a*) 39 kb (*b*) 49 kb
(*c*) 59 kb (*d*) 29 kb

44. Which of the following is correct ?

I. When eukaryotic genes are isolated as cDNA, they can not be expressed in prokaryotes.
II. Any RNA molecule can be used to produce cDNA.
III. The identification and isolation of desired gene/DNA fragment is a critical step in recombinant DNA technology.
IV. When amino acid sequence/base sequence of a gene is known, it may be either chemically synthesized or amplified by using PCR.

Options :

(*a*) I, II, III, IV (*b*) II, III, IV
(*c*) I, III, IV (*d*) III, IV

45. Which of the following is an example of virulence plasmid ?

(*a*) Ti plasmid (*b*) Col plasmid
(*c*) Ri plasmid (*d*) Both (*a*) and (*c*)

46. Which of the following is a type II restriction endonuclease ?

(*a*) *Eco*PI (*b*) *Hinf*III
(*c*) *Eco*P15 (*d*) *Pst*I

47. For the identification of a desired gene, which of the following can be used for the preparation of a probe ?

I. Homologous gene from another organism.
II. mRNA of the gene.
III. cDNA derived from mRNA of the gene.
IV. A synthetic oligonucleotide representing the sequence of a part of the desired gene.

Options :

(*a*) I, II, III, IV (*b*) II, III, IV
(*c*) I, III, IV (*d*) I, IV

48. Which of the following ***is not correct*** ?

(*a*) A mixture of fragments of genomic DNA is used to produce a genomic library.
(*b*) Genomic library contains only those genes that are expressed in the concerned tissue/organism.
(*c*) cDNA obtained from mRNA may be cloned to give rise to a cDNA library.
(*d*) cDNA library contains DNA fragments that represent genes.

49. A good host has which of the following characterisitcs ?

I. Easy to transform.
II. Lacks active restriction enzymes.
III. Should not have methylase activity.
IV. It should support the replication of recombinant DNA.
V. It should be deficient in normal recombination.

Options :

(*a*) I, II, III, IV (*b*) II, III, IV, V
(*c*) I, III, V (*d*) I, II, III, IV, V

50. Which of following is correct about type II restriction endonucleases ?

I. The first enzyme to be isolated was *Hind*II.
II. They require Mg^{2+} ions for DNA cleavage.
III. Only this type of enzymes is used for gene cloning.

Options :

(*a*) I, II (*b*) I, III
(*c*) I, II, III (*d*) II, III

51. Which of the following nucleotide sequences is recognized by *Eco*RI ?

(*a*) G/AATT C
C TTAA/G

(*b*) T/CG A
A GC/T

(*c*) A/GATC T
T CGAG/A

(*d*) A/AGCT T
T TCGA/A

52. A good vector has which of the following characteristics ?

I. The vector should have suitable marker genes.

II. When the objective is gene transfer, it should have the ability to integrate either itself or the DNA insert it carries into the genome of host cell.

III. When expression of the DNA insert is desired, the vector should contain suitable control elements like promoter, operator, ribosome binding site, etc.

IV. It should be able to grow at least in two hosts.

Options :

(*a*) I, III, IV (*b*) I, II, IV
(*c*) I, II, III (*d*) II, III, IV

53. Theoretically, a recognition sequence of 6 bases, *e.g.*, 5′GAATTC3′ (for *Eco*RI), is expected to occur at, on an average, a distance of how many nucleotides ?

(*a*) 8188 bp (*b*) 1024 bp
(*c*) 4096 bp (*d*) 2048 bp

54. Most of the type II restriction endonucleases have recognition sites of how many of the following lengths ?

(*a*) 4 bp (*b*) 5 bp
(*c*) 6 bp (*d*) 4-6 bp

55. Which of the following is correct about blotting ?

I. It consists of transfer of macromolecules (DNA, RNA, protein) from gel onto the surface of a membrane.

II. It makes the macromolecules separated in the gel amenable to detection and analysis.

III. Free sites present on the membrane for binding of ligands are blocked by a suitable treatment.

IV. The substrate used for blocking may interfere with the macromolecule-ligand reaction.

Options :

(*a*) I, II, III (*b*) II, III, IV
(*c*) I, III, IV (*d*) I, II, IV

56. Dot blot technique ***does not*** involve which of the following ?

I. Digestion of DNA/RNA with a restriction enzyme.

II. Gel electrophoresis.

III. Transfer of DNA/RNA from gel to membrane.

Options :

(*a*) I, II (*b*) II, III
(*c*) I, II, III (*d*) I, III

57. An ideal plasmid vector must have which of the following features ?

I. Relaxed replication control.

II. At least two markers.

III. Unique restriction site for at least one restriction endonuclease.

IV. The unique restriction site must be located within one of the two markers.

Options :

(*a*) I, III, IV (*b*) I, II, III, IV
(*c*) II, III (*d*) III, IV

58. Which of the following restriction enzymes produces blunt ends ?

(*a*) *Bam*H1 (*b*) *Alu*I
(*c*) *Pst*I (*d*) *Hind*III

59. Probes can be used for which of the following ?

(*a*) To conform the integration of a DNA insert into the host genome.
(*b*) To prepare genome maps of eukaryotes.
(*c*) To identify the desired recombinant clone.
(*d*) All of the above.

60. Bacterial cells are usually multiply in which of the following ?

(*a*) Jensson medium
(*b*) Luria-Bertani (LB) medium
(*c*) YE medium
(*d*) Gamborg medium

61. Which of the following is an example of type I restriction endonuclease ?

(*a*) *Eco*K (*b*) *Hinf*III
(*c*) *Hind*II (*d*) *Bgl*II

62. Which of the following is the first bacterial artificial chromosome vector ?

(*a*) pBeloBAC11 (*b*) pBACe3.6
(*c*) pBAC108L (*d*) pBeloBAC1

63. A phagemid can be used as which of the following ?

(*a*) A sequencing vector
(*b*) An expression vector
(*c*) A cloning vector
(*d*) All of the above.

64. Which of the following is correct about *p*BR322 vector ?

I. It is the most widely used vector.
II. It has a single selectable marker.
III. It has origin of replication from plasmid pMB1.
IV. It is not a shuttle vector.

Options :

(*a*) I, II, III (*b*) I, III, IV
(*c*) I, II, IV (*d*) II, III, IV

65. Match the columns A and B carefully and select the correct option from among those listed below them.

Column A	**Column B**
A. Phagemid	I. λZAP
B. Cosmid	II. pBluescriptSK(+/–)
C. Phasmid	III. pJB8
D. Fosmid	IV. pFOS1

Options :

(*a*) AII, BIII, CI, DIV
(*b*) AII, BIV, CIII, DI
(*c*) AII, BIII, CIV, DI
(*d*) AIV, BI, CII, DIII

66. A bacterial artificial chromosome vector can be used to clone DNA inserts of upto which length ?

(*a*) 100 kb (*b*) 300 kb
(*c*) 800 kb (*d*) 600 kb

67. Find out the correct order of activities necessary for selection of a clone containing the DNA insert of interest ?

I. Identification and isolation of those clones that are transformed by the recombinant DNAs.
II. Eliminate the bulk of non-transformed bacterial cells.
III. Identification of the recombinant clone, which has the DNA insert of interest.

Options :

(*a*) I, II, III (*b*) II, III, I
(*c*) II, I, III (*d*) III, II, I

68. A good vector has at least how many marker genes ?

(*a*) One (*b*) Two
(*c*) Three (*d*) Four

69. Which of the following approaches is the most successful for chemical synthesis of DNA ?

(*a*) Phosphodiester
(*b*) Phosphite triester
(*c*) Phosphotriester
(*d*) Phosphite diester

70. Synthetic oligonucleotides can be used for which of the following purposes ?

I. Antisense oligonucleotides may be useful in treatment of disease.
II. Used as primer for cDNA preparation using reverse transcriptase.
III. Used as hybridization probes.
IV. Used as primers for PCR.

Options :

(*a*) I, II, III, IV (*b*) II, III, IV
(*c*) I, III, IV (*d*) II, III

71. Which of the following enzymes is used in PCR ?

(*a*) *Vent* polymerase (*b*) *Taq* polymerase
(*c*) *Pfu* polymerase (*d*) All of the above

72. Column A contains different heat stable DNA polymerases, while column B contains sources from which they are isolated. Match the two columns carefully and select the correct option from those listed below them

Column A	**Column B**
A. *Vent*	I. *Thermus acquaticus*
B. *Taq*	II. *Thermus litoralis*
C. *Pfu*	III. *Pyrococcus furiosus*

Options :

(*a*) AI, BII, CIII (*b*) AI, BIII, CII
(*c*) AII, BI, CIII (*d*) AII, BIII, CI

73. Which of the following is correct about colony/plaque screening with antibody ?

I. The antibody specific to the concerned protein product is spread uniformly over a solid support, which is placed in contact with an agar layer containing lyased bacterial colonies/phage plaques.

II. If any clone is producing the protein in question, it will bind to the antibody molecules present in the disc.
III. The disc is removed from agar and treated with a second radiolabelled antibody.
IV. The location of radioactivity on the disc is detemined by autoradiography.

Options :

(*a*) I, II, III, IV (*b*) I, III, IV
(*c*) II, III, IV (*d*) I, II, IV

74. Identification of protein using antibodies may be done by which of the following ?
(*a*) Enzyme-linked immunosorbant assay (ELISA).
(*b*) Western blotting.
(*c*) Precipitation and electrophoresis.
(*d*) All of the above.

75. Which of the following is correct about *p*UC8 ?
I. It has ampicillin resistance gene.
II. It has ColE1 origin of replication from *p*BR322.
III. Each transformed *E. coli* contains 500-700 copies of pUC8 plasmid without any treatment.
IV. The *E. coli* strains used as hosts have normal *lacZ* gene.

Options :

(*a*) I, II, III (*b*) II, III, IV
(*c*) I, II, III, IV (*d*) I, III, IV

76. Which of the following ***is not*** an example of insertion vector ?
(*a*) λgt10 (*b*) λEMBL4
(*c*) λgt11 (*d*) λZAP II

77. Southern hybridization can be used for which of the following ?
(*a*) Preparation of RFLP maps
(*b*) DNA fingerprinting
(*c*) Confirmation of transgene integration
(*d*) All of the above

78. Which of the following scientists isolated ribosomal RNA genes in 1965 ?
(*a*) Maxam and Gilbert
(*b*) Wallace and Birnstiel
(*c*) Sanger and Southern
(*d*) Brown and Gilbert

79. Which of the following is correct about phage M13 vectors.
I. Derived from the genome of *E. coli* filamentous bacteriophage M13.
II. This phage has a single-stranded linear DNA genome in phage particles.
III. Its genome remains double-stranded in progeny phage particles.
IV. M13 infects only F^+ *E. coli* cells.
V. Infected cells are ultimately lysed.

Options :

(*a*) I, II, IV (*b*) I, II, III, IV
(*c*) III, IV, V (*d*) II, III, IV, V

80. Which of the following is correct ?
I. *E. coli* cells are generally poorly accessible to DNA molecules.
II. $CaCl_2$ treatment promotes binding of DNA to *E. coli* cell wall.
III. DNA is taken up by the cells when they are subjected to heat shock.
IV. Each transformed bacterial cell takes up one DNA molecule.

Options :

(*a*) I, II, III, IV (*b*) II, III, IV
(*c*) I, II, IV (*d*) II, IV

81. Which of the following type of bacterial cells is obtained when recombinant DNA is used for transformation ?
I. Cells transformed with unaltered vector
II. Non-transformed cells
III. Cells transformed with recombinant DNA

Options :

(*a*) I, III (*b*) I, II
(*c*) I, II, III (*d*) II, III

82. Strategies based on which of the following can be used to select the clone of interest containing a specific DNA insert ?
I. Unique property of protein.
II. Hybridization probing.
III. Differential electrophoretic mobility of protein.
IV. Immunological screening.

Options :

(*a*) I, II, III (*b*) II, III, IV
(*c*) I, II, III, IV (*d*) I, II, III

83. Synthetic oligonucleotides can be used to fulfill which of the following purposes ?
(*a*) To produce a complete gene.
(*b*) As linkers and adaptors for gene cloning
(*c*) For enzymatic DNA sequencing
(*d*) All of the above.

84. *p*UC series vectors offer which of the following advantages over *p*BR322 ?
I. The unique restriction sites are clustered within a polylinker sequence.
II. Cells transformed with recombinant DNA are selected in a single step using a medium containing tetracycline.
III. Each *E. coli* cell normally produces 500-700 copies of the pUC recombinant DNA.

Options :
(*a*) I, II, III (*b*) II, III
(*c*) I, III (*d*) I

85. PCR utilizes which of the following ?
I. A DNA preparation containing the segment to be amplified.
II. Two nucleotide primers specific to the two 3′-borders of the desired segment.
III. The four deoxynucleotide triphosphates.
IV. A thermostable DNA ligase.

Options :
(*a*) I, II, III (*b*) II, III, IV
(*c*) I, II, III, IV (*d*) I, III, IV

86. The lambda genome contains which of the following ?
(*a*) Genes for head and tail proteins
(*b*) Origin of replication
(*c*) Proteins involved in lysogeny
(*d*) All of the above.

87. Replacement vector, λEMBL4 can be used to clone DNA of upto which size ?
(*a*) 10 kb (*b*) 20 kb
(*c*) 40 kb (*d*) 45 kb

88. If a DNA insert is isolated using one restriction enzyme, while the vector is opened with another restriction enzyme, which generate unmatched cohessive ends, which of the following approaches can be used to integrate the DNA insert into the vector ?
I. Use of adaptors.
II. The protruding ends converted into blund ends.
III. First, blunt ends are produce and then a linker can be attached to them.
IV. Blunt ends are produced, and they changed into protruding ends by 3′ tailing.

Options :
(*a*) I, II, III, IV (*b*) II, III, IV
(*c*) I, III, IV (*d*) III, IV

89. At the end of *n* cycles of PCR, how many copies of the amplified segment (amplicon) are ideally expected ?
(*a*) n^2 (*b*) 2^n
(*c*) $n^2/2$ (*d*) $2n$

90. Which of the following is the feature of cosmids ?
I. They can be used to clone DNA inserts of upto 40 kb.
II. These vectors are amplified and maintained in the same manner as the contributing plasmid.
III. Selection for recombinant DNA is based on the procedure applicable to the plasmid making up the cosmid.
IV. Cosmids can be packaged into empty T_4 particles, which infect host cell.

Options :
(*a*) I, II, III, IV (*b*) I, II, IV
(*c*) I, II, III (*d*) II, III, IV

91. If 8 bases long primer is used in the PCR, a sequence complementary to it may be expected to occur once every which of the following base pairs ?
(*a*) 8^4 bp (*b*) 4^8 bp
(*c*) 8^8 bp (*d*) 4^4 bp

92. Which of the following is done during northern hybridization ?
I. RNA bands are immobilized onto nylon membranes.
II. Hybridization with radioactive, single stranded DNA probes.
III. Bands showing hybridization detected by autoradiography.
IV. RNA is separated by gel electrophoresis.

Options :

(*a*) I, II, III, IV (*b*) I, II, IV
(*c*) I, III, IV (*d*) III, IV

93. In Q. 92, which of the following represents the proper order of the steps in northern hybridization ?

Options :

(*a*) I, II, III, IV (*b*) IV, I, III, II
(*c*) IV, I, II, III (*d*) IV, II, III, I

94. Cosmid vectors contain which of the following ?

I. Origin of replication from a plasmid.
II. A selectable marker from a plasmid.
III. *cos* site from λ phage DNA.
IV. Unique restriction sites from a plasmid.

Options :

(*a*) I, III, IV (*b*) II, III, IV
(*c*) III, IV (*d*) I, II, III, IV

95. Which of the following is correct ?

I. The frequency of transformed cells is 10^6-10^7 per μg of plasmid DNA.
II. M13 vectors produce white plaques on the lawn of an appropriate *E. coli* grown on medium containing X-gal plus IPTG, while recombinant DNA produces blue plaques.
III. Medium is so designed as to permit only the transformed cells to divide and produce colonies.

Options :

(*a*) I, III (*b*) II, III
(*c*) II (*d*) III

96. Which of the following ***is not*** a PCR-based molecular marker ?

(*a*) RAPD (*b*) RFLP
(*c*) STS (*d*) AFLP

97. PCR can be used for which of the following ?

(*a*) Study of DNA polymorphism
(*b*) Detection of presence of transgene in transformed cells
(*c*) Production of cDNA
(*d*) All of the above

98. A typical yeast minichromosome vector contains which of the following ?

I. The origin of replication from a bacterial plasmid.
II. *ARS* and *CEN* sequences from yeast.
III. A functional gene, *e.g.*, *LEU2*, from yeast.
IV. A selectable marker, *e.g.*, amp^r, from bacterial plasmid.

Options :

(*a*) I, II, III, IV (*b*) I, III, IV
(*c*) II, III, IV (*d*) II, III

99. The phage vectors offer which of the following advantages as compared to plasmid vectors.

I. The shelf-life is effectively infinite.
II. Transformation of bacterial cells is much easier.
III. Screening of phage plaques by molecular hybridization often gives clear results.
IV. Handling of phage particles is relatively more difficult.

Options :

(*a*) I, III, IV (*b*) I, II, III
(*c*) II, III, IV (*d*) I, II, III, IV

100. Which of the following features concerns vector λZAP ?

I. Suitable for cloning of cDNA.
II. The DNA insert is placed within the multiple cloning site located in the *lacZα* gene.
III. DNA insert can be expressed as fusion protein.
IV. RNA copies of the DNA insert can be generated.

Options :

(*a*) I, II, III (*b*) I, II, IV
(*c*) I, II, III, IV (*d*) II, IV

101. Phagemids contain which of the following modules ?

I. ColE1 origin of replication.
II. A multiple cloning site within *lacZα* gene.
III. *amp^R* gene for ampicillin resistance.
IV. Phage M13(f1) origin of replication.

Options :

(*a*) I, II, III, IV (*b*) II, III, IV
(*c*) I, III, IV (*d*) II, IV

102. If vector and DNA insert have both ends sticky and compatible, integreation of DNA insert into vector involves which of the following steps ?

I. The opened up vector and DNA inserts are mixed under annealing conditions.
II. The nicks are sealed by DNA ligase.
III. Growing *E. coli* cells are isolated and subjected to transformation.
IV. The transformed cells are suitably diluted and plated on a suitable medium.

Options :
(*a*) I, II, III (*b*) II, III, IV
(*c*) I, III, IV (*d*) I, II, III, IV

103. Enzymatic procedure of DNA sequencing was developed by which of the following ?
(*a*) Maxam and coworkers
(*b*) Gilbert and coworkers
(*c*) Sanger and coworkers
(*d*) Collins and coworkers

104. Melting temperature (Tm) of DNA can be calculated using which of the following formula ?
(*a*) [2(G + C)] + [4(A + T)]
(*b*) [4(G + C)] + [2(A + T)]
(*c*) [3(G + C)] + [2(A + T)]
(*d*) (4G + C) + (2A + T)

105. Which of the following ***is not correct*** about PCR ?
(*a*) Only intact genomic DNA can be used for PCR.
(*b*) PCR does not use radioactivity.
(*c*) Allele-specific primers can be used to detect specific alleles.
(*d*) PCR requires nanogram quantities of DNA

106. Which of the following is used for non-radioactive labelling of probes/nucleic acids ?
(*a*) Digoxigenin
(*b*) Fluorescent molecules
(*c*) Biotin
(*d*) All of the above

107. Which of following is correct about primer walking ?

I. First 600-800 bases from the 3′-end of one strand of the DNA duplex are sequenced using a primer, complementary to the 3′-end of one strand, *e.g.*, primer A1.
II. A new primer, *e.g.*, A2 is designed and used to sequence the next 600-800 bases.
III. The complementary strand is similarly sequenced and new primers are serially designed till the whole DNA duplex is sequenced.
IV. Primer walking is opposite to chromosome walking.

Options :
(*a*) I, II, III, IV (*b*) II, III, IV
(*c*) I, II, III (*d*) I, III, IV

108. Restrictive polyacrylamide gels are used for which of the following ?
(*a*) Viroid test
(*b*) Analysis of point mutations
(*c*) DNA sequencing
(*d*) All of the above.

109. PCR amplification is sensitive to which of the following ?
(*a*) Haem breakdown product
(*b*) Humic acid
(*c*) Phenolics
(*d*) All of the above

110. Which of the following advantages are offered by PCR ?

I. PCR procedure is relatively very simple in contrast to conventional gene cloning.
II. PCR allows detection of even a single copy of target DNA sequence present in the DNA sample.
III. The purity of DNA preparation is not critical in PCR.
IV. PCR requires DNA ligase.

Options :
(*a*) I, II, III (*b*) II, III, IV
(*c*) I, II, III, IV (*d*) I, III, IV

111. Which of the following is correct about PCR ?

I. The efficiency of PCR decreases with an increase in the amplicon size.
II. PCR can not be used to isolate an unknown gene.
III. The error rate of *Taq* polymerase has been estimated as 1 error per 9000 nucleotides, but after 30 cycles of PCR,

the rate becomes one error per 300 nucleotides.

IV. PCR amplification is sensitive to inhibitors that may be present in the DNA preparation.

Options :

(*a*) I, II, III (*b*) I, III, IV
(*c*) I, II, III, IV (*d*) II, III, IV

112. Vacuum blotting is a good substitute for capillary blotting because it has which of the following features ?

I. Saves time.
II. Saves expenses for solutions and papers.
III. Produces better resolution.
IV. Reduces mechanical stress on gel.

Options :

(*a*) I, II, III (*b*) I, II, III, IV
(*c*) II, III, IV (*d*) I, II, IV

113. In 1970, which of the following scientists synthesized the gene for alanine-tRNA of yeast ?

(*a*) Maxam and coworkers
(*b*) Sanger and coworkers
(*c*) Khorana and coworkers
(*d*) Smith and coworkers

114. Which of the following is correct about nitrocellulose membranes ?

I. The most commonly used membrane.
II. High affinity for double-stranded DNA.
III. It is used routinely in Southern blotting.
IV. It exhibits no affinity for RNA.

Options :

(*a*) I, II, III, IV (*b*) I, III, IV
(*c*) I, II, IV (*d*) II, III, IV

115. During DNA isolation, if bacterial cell extract has a heavy load of proteins, it is treated with which of the following ?

(*a*) Proteinase K (*b*) Trypsin
(*c*) Pronase (*d*) Both (*a*) and (*c*)

116. Efficiency of PCR may be influenced by which of the following ?

I. Primer length.
II. Annealing temperature.
III. Primer design
IV. Length of target sequence.

Options :

(*a*) I, II, III, IV (*b*) I, II, III
(*c*) II, III, IV (*d*) I, III, IV

117. Which of the following techniques can be used for radioactive labelling of probes ?

(*a*) Nick translation and direct labelling
(*b*) End labelling and primer extension
(*c*) Method based on RNA polymerase
(*d*) All of the above.

118. The techniques of Southern and northern hybridization show which of the following differences ?

I. In Southern blotting, DNA is separated by gel electrophoresis, while in northern blotting RNAs are separated.
II. In Southern hybridization, DNA has to be denatured, while this step is not needed in northern hybridization.
III. Nitrocellulose membrane is generally not used for northern hybridization, while it is often used for Southern hybridization.
IV. Hybridization with probe produces DNA : DNA hybrid molecules in Southern hybridization, but it generates RNA : DNA hybrid molecules in nothern hybridization.

Options :

(*a*) I, II, III (*b*) I, III, IV
(*c*) I, II, III, IV (*d*) II, III, IV

119. Which of the following is correct about polyvinylidenedifluoride (PVDF) membranes ?

I. They have affinity for proteins.
II. They are highly mechanically stable and can be used for direct protein sequencing.
III. They are made on teflon base.

Options :

(*a*) I, III (*b*) I, II
(*c*) II, III (*d*) I, II, III

120. Charge of a molecule is influenced by which of the following ?

I. Strength of the electrical field.
II. Type, concentration and pH of buffer.
III. The nature of support material used for electrophoresis.
IV. Temperature.

Options :

(*a*) I, II, III (*b*) I, II, III, IV
(*c*) II, III (*d*) I, III, IV

121. SDS PAGE offers which of the following advantages ?

I. Rapid separation.
II. Separation based on molecular weight.
III. SDS stabilizes all proteins.
IV. Charge differences between isozymes are cancelled by SDS.

Options :

(*a*) I, II, III, IV (*b*) II, III, IV
(*c*) I, II, III (*d*) I, II, IV

122. Which of the following PCR variants generates single-stranded products ?

(*a*) Asymmetric (*b*) Nested
(*c*) Anchored (*d*) Inverse

123. In which of the PCR variants given in Q. 122, two pairs of primers are used ?

124. In which of the PCR variants listed in Q. 122, target DNA cleavage and ligation is involved ?

125. In which of the PCR variants given in Q. 122, the concentration of one primer is much higher than that of the other ?

126. Which of the PCR variants listed in Q. 122, flanking regions of the target gene are amplified ?

127. In which of the PCR variants given in Q. 122, primers annealing to the 5′-ends of the target gene are used ?

128. Colony hybridization uses which of the following ?

I. Replica plating.
II. DNA immobilization.
III. Nucleic acid hybridization.
IV. PCR

Options :

(*a*) I, II, III, IV (*b*) II, III, IV
(*c*) I, II, III (*d*) I, II, IV

129. Complementation assay is based on which of the following ?

(*a*) Protein function
(*b*) DNA sequence homology
(*c*) Protein-protein interaction
(*d*) DNA-protein interaction.

130. Which of the options given in Q. 129 is the basis for colony hybridization ?

131. Which of the options given in Q. 129 is the basis of ELISA ?

132. Which of the options given in Q. 129 is the basis of Southern-Western assay ?

133. FACS uses which of the following ?

I. Antibody II. Enzyme
III. Probe IV. Fluorochrome

Options :

(*a*) I, II (*b*) I, IV
(*c*) III, IV (*d*) I, II, IV

134. Which of the options given in Q. 133 is used for ELISA ?

135. Which of the following is used in colony hybridization ?

(*a*) Antibody (*b*) Enzyme
(*c*) Probe (*d*) Substrate

136. In general, which of the following is used for initial cloning ?

(*a*) *B. subtilis* (*b*) *Agrobacterium*
(*c*) *E. coli* (*d*) *B. thuringiensis*

137. Which of the following enters *E. coli* cell in linear form ?

(*a*) A cosmid vector
(*b*) A λ phage vector
(*c*) *p*BR322
(*d*) Both (*a*) and (*b*)

138. Which of the following is the least likely to accumulate properly folded proteins encoded by an eukaryotic transgene ?

(*a*) Animal cells (*b*) *Saccharomyces*
(*c*) *E. coli* (*d*) *Pichia*

139. Which of the following affect the level of recombinant protein accumulation ?

(*a*) Promoter
(*b*) Context of AUG codon (initiator codon)
(*c*) Codon usage
(*d*) All of the above.

140. Transgene becomes integrated chiefly by homologous recombination in which of the following ?

(*a*) Yeast (*b*) Animals
(*c*) Plants (*d*) Both (*b*) and (*c*)

141. In which of the options given in Q. 140, transgene integration generally occurs at random sites ?

142. The term 'recombinant DNA' is specifically used to denote which of the following ?

(*a*) A DNA molecules having sequences from two or more sources.

(*b*) A vector into which a DNA insert is integrated.
(*c*) A transgene having sequences from two different organisms.
(*d*) A chromosome into which a transgene is integrated.

143. Use of an antibiotic resistance and the $lacZ_\alpha$ in a vector, eliminates the need for which of the following ?
(*a*) Plating on the antibiotic containing medium
(*b*) Replica plating
(*c*) Plating on a second selection medium
(*d*) Both (*b*) and (*c*)

144. When two selectable markers are used in a vector, where the DNA insert has to be integrated ?
(*a*) In one of the selectable markers
(*b*) In both the selectable markers
(*c*) Anywhere in the vector
(*d*) In either (*a*) and (*b*)

145. Use of two selectable markers in a vector can not achieve which of the following ?
(*a*) Selection of recombinant clones
(*b*) Selection of recombinant clones in a single step
(*c*) Elimination of non-transformed cell
(*d*) Both (*b*) and (*c*).

146. A plasmid vector can not achieve which of the following ?
(*a*) Gene expression
(*b*) Propagation of recombinant DNA
(*c*) Propagation in two different hosts
(*d*) Packaging in empty λ particles.

147. A cosmid vector can achieve which of the following that a plasmid vector ***can not*** achieve.
(*a*) Cloning of 40 kb DNA insert
(*b*) Packaging in empty λ phage heads
(*c*) Transfection of *E. coli* cells
(*d*) All of the above

148. A cosmid vector has which of the following ?
(*a*) A selectable marker
(*b*) λ phage *cos* site
(*c*) Terminase binding site
(*d*) All of the above

149. Which of the following restriction endonucleases ***is not used*** in gene cloning ?
(*a*) Type I (*b*) Type II
(*c*) Type III (*d*) Both (*a*) and (*c*)

150. Which of the following endonucleases introduces single-strand nicks in DNA ?
(*a*) DNase I (*b*) S1 nuclease
(*c*) *Eco*R1 (*d*) *Hin*dIII

151. Which of the options given in Q. 150 cleaves both the DNA strands at random sites ?

152. Which of the options given in Q. 150 has the recognition sequence 5′GAATTC3′ ?

153. Which of the following sequences forms a palindrome with rotational summary ?
(*a*) GAAAAG (*b*) GAAGAA
(*c*) GAATTC (*d*) Both (*a*) and (*b*)

154. Which of the options given in Q. 153 is a simple palindromic sequence ?

155. Which of the options given in Q. 153 is a tandem direct repeat sequence ?

156. Which of the options given in Q. 153 is a tandem inverted repeat sequence ?

157. Treatment with which of the following prevents vector circularization ?
(*a*) Polynucleotide kinase
(*b*) S1 nuclease
(*c*) Alkaline phosphatase
(*d*) λ exonuclease

158. Which of the following enzymes removes nucleotides from 3′-ends ?
(*a*) S1 nuclease
(*b*) Exonuclease *Bal*31
(*c*) *E. coli* exonuclease III
(*d*) λ exonuclease

159. Which of the options given in Q. 158 removes nucleotides from the 5′-ends ?

160. Which of the options given in Q. 158 is used to digest either the 3′- or the 5′-protruding ends from DNA fragments ?

161. Which of the options given in Q. 158 converts protruding ends into blunt ends ?

162. Which of the options given in Q. 158 is used to shorten DNA fragments ?

163. Which of the following enzymes is used for converting protruding ends into blunt ends ?
(*a*) Polynucleotide kinase
(*b*) S1 nuclease

(*c*) Klenow fragement of *E. coli* DNA polymerase I
(*d*) Both (*b*) and (*c*)

164. Which of the options given in Q. 163 is the preferred strategy for converting protruding ends into blunts ends.

165. Tailing uses which of the following enzymes ?
(*a*) Polynucleotide kinase
(*b*) Klenow fragement of *E. coli* DNA polymerase I
(*c*) Terminal deoxynucleotidyl transferase
(*d*) Both (*b*) and (*c*)

166. DNA fragments used for cloning can be generated by the following methods.
I. Restriction digestion of genomic DNA.
II. Polymerase chain reaction (PCR).
III. Mechanical shearing of genomic DNA
IV. Reverse transcription to produce cDNA.

Which of these methods yields fragments having blunt ends ?

Options :
(*a*) I (*b*) II, III, IV
(*c*) I, II, III, IV (*d*) I, II, III

167. Which of the options given in Q. 166 generates fragments with either blunt or cohesive ends ?

168. Which of the options given in Q. 166 yields DNA fragments with blunt ends only ?

169. Which of the options given in Q. 166 produces DNA fragments with cohesive ends ?

170. Which of the following features listed below are present in genomic libraries ?
I. Different library for different tissues of an organism.
II. Introns are present.
III. Sequence of a single gene represented in a single clone.
IV. Non-transcribed regions are represented.

Options :
(*a*) I, II (*b*) III, IV
(*c*) I, III (*d*) II, IV

171. Which of the options given in Q. 170 applies to cDNA libraries ?

172. The driver mRNA used for the preparation of a cDNA library enriched for genes expressed in salt-stressed yeast cells has which of the following features ?
I. It is isolated from salt-stressed yeast cells.
II. It is labelled with biotin.
III. It represents genes expressed in yeast cells grown under normal environment.
IV. It is not used for cDNA preparation.

Options :
(*a*) I, II, III (*b*) II, III, IV
(*c*) I, II, III, IV (*d*) III, IV

173. A subtracted cDNA library has which of the following features.
I. It does not represent cDNAs that are represented in the driver mRNA used for preparation of the library.
II. It permits isolation of cDNAs representing low abundance and rare mRNAs.
III. It is expected to contain only such mRNAs that are specifically expressed in the given tissue/under the given environment.

Options :
(*a*) I, II, III (*b*) I, II
(*c*) I, III (*d*) II, III

174. Which of the following ***is not correct*** about amplified genomic library ?
(*a*) Particular recombinant DNAs increase in frequency.
(*b*) Particular recombinant DNAs decrease in frequency.
(*c*) Some recombinant DNAs may be eliminated.
(*d*) Specified recombinant DNAs are amplified.

175. Which of the following is correct about subgenomic libraries ?
I. Prepared from single chromosomes, isolated by flow-cytometry.
II. Prepared from specific regions of isolated single chromosomes.
III. Prone to contamination by inappropriate DNA.
IV. Use of high capacity vectors like YACs has rendered them obsolete.

Options :
(*a*) I, II, III (*b*) II, III, IV
(*c*) I, II, III, IV (*d*) I, III, IV

176. Which of the following *E. coli* vectors yields single-stranded copies of cloned DNA ?
(*a*) pUC18/19
(*b*) λ phage vectors
(*c*) Phage M13 vectors
(*d*) Cosmid vectors

177. A phagemid vector has which of the following ?
(*a*) Phage origin of replication
(*b*) Plasmid origin of replication
(*c*) Both (*a*) and (*b*)
(*d*) *cos* sequence from λ phage

178. Which of the following vectors contains λ phage *cos* sequence ?
(*a*) Cosmid (*b*) Phagemid
(*c*) Phasmid (*d*) Both (*a*) and (*c*)

179. A probe for colony hybridization may be obtained from which of the following ?
(*a*) Sequence of the concerned gene.
(*b*) Amino acid sequence of the concerned protein product
(*c*) Same gene of another organism.
(*d*) All of the above.

180. DNA microarrays are high throughput version of which of the following ?
(*a*) Southern analysis
(*b*) Differential screening
(*c*) Gene tagging
(*d*) Colony hybridization

181. Translational fusion offers which of the following advantages ?
(*a*) Enhanced translation efficiency
(*b*) Protection of transgene product
(*c*) May facilitate purification
(*d*) All of the above

182. Which of the following versions of PCR is used for site-directed mutagenesis ?
(*a*) Overlap extension PCR
(*b*) Inverse PCR
(*c*) Touchdown PCR
(*d*) Anchored PCR

183. Which of the options given in Q. 182 aims at increasing the specificity of PCR without lowering the efficiency ?

184. Which of the options given in Q. 182 can be used when sequence of only one end of the desired segment is known ?

185. Which of the following variations of PCR aims to enhance specificity ?
(*a*) Anchored PCR
(*b*) Hotstart PCR
(*c*) Touchdown PCR
(*d*) Both (*b*) and (*c*)

186. ARMS PCR achieves which of the following ?
(*a*) High efficiency amplification
(*b*) Highly specific amplifcation
(*c*) Differential amplification of alleles
(*d*) Both (*a*) and (*b*)

187. ARMS PCR achieves differential amplification of alleles due to which of the following ?
(*a*) Primer sequence
(*b*) Annealing temperature
(*c*) Ion concentration
(*d*) Specific PCR protocol

188. Minisatellite variant PCR is an example of which of the following ?
(*a*) Hotstart PCR (*b*) Touchdown PCR
(*c*) Nested PCR (*d*) ARMS PCR

189. Most of the PCR products have which of the following type of ends ?
(*a*) Single nucelotide overhang
(*b*) Blunt
(*c*) Cohesive
(*d*) Either (*b*) or (*c*)

190. In most PCR products, a single nucleotide overhang is of which of the following types ?
(*a*) A at the 3′-end (*b*) A at the 5′-end
(*c*) T at the 3′-end (*d*) T at the 5′-end

191. The λ exonuclease digests from which of the following ends ?
(*a*) 3′-end having –OH
(*b*) 5′-end having P residue
(*c*) 5′-end having –OH
(*d*) Both (*b*) and (*c*)

192. Which of the following ***is not correct*** about PCR ?
(*a*) It does not use radioactivity
(*b*) It does not require specific skills
(*c*) DNA purity is not critical
(*d*) It always uses a pair of primers

2.2. FILL IN THE BLANKS

1. DNA polymerase I was, for the first time, isolated by ....
2. Nucleic acid was discovered by ....
3. Uracil is absent from ....
4. All the pyrimidines contain an H atom at position .... which is involved in their linkage with 1′C of pentose sugar.
5. DNA polymerase I is mainly involved in removing .... from Okazaki fragments and in filling in the gaps so created.
6. ELISA test used for the diagnosis of disease is based on .... and .... interaction.
7. Abbreviation PFGE stands for ....
8. Northern hybridization is useful in the identification and separation of ....
9. All the individuals of a clone have the same ....
10. Most commonly used bacterial vectors are derived from either .... or ....
11. Usually DNA ligase is prepared from *E. coli* cells infected with .... phage.
12. Usually methylation takes place in .... and .... residues.
13. The first letter of a restriction enzyme indicates the name of the .... of the source organism.
14. .... sequence of *p*BR322 has been deleted to yield pBR327.
15. Electrophoresis is usually done in .... gel, which effectively separates fragments ranging from 0.3 to 23 kb.
16. The λ phage has .... stranded DNA genome.
17. The F plasmids carry *tra* genes that promote ....
18. Cosmids are particularly attractive for construction of .... library.
19. A .... gene produces a phenotype, which permits either an easy selection or quick identification of the cells in which it is expressed.
20. In general, PCR is able to efficiently amplify DNA sequences upto 3 kb but ideally this length should be less than............
21. The restriction fragments of DNA present in agarose gel (after electrophoresis) are denatured by .... treatment.
22. DNA ligase is involved in formation of ....
23. The presence of restriction enzyme was postulated by .... during 1960, while the first true restriction enzyme, *Hind*II was isolated in 1970.
24. DNase I is normally obtained from cow ....
25. Each plasmid is maintained in the bacterial cell at a characteristic copy number mainly due to its ....
26. The letters UC in the abbreviation *p*UC stand for ....
27. *p*BR327 produces .... copies per *E. coli* cell as compared to 15 copies per cell by *p*BR322.
28. A marker gene that governs a feature, which enables only such cells that express it to survive under the selective conditions is called ....
29. *p*UC8 is a derivative of .... vector.
30. *Taq* polymerase, the most commonly used enzyme in PCR, appears to lack .... activity.
31. Horizontal polyacrylamide gels are preferred for .... analysis.
32. Polyacrylamide gels polymerised on ultra-thin films are used to separate .... molecular weight compounds.
33. T_4 polynucleotide kinase is used for addition of .... group to an end having a free 5′–OH.
34. The largest cloned insert size in a λ vector is just over .... kb, while that for plasmid vectors it is less than 15 kb.
35. .... markers produce distinct phenotypes, which allow an easy identification of

the cells having them from those that do not contain them.

36. The error rate of *taq* polymerase has been estimated as .... errors per 9,000 nucleotides.
37. The .... used in colony/plaque hybridization must share at least a part of gene/DNA sequence being searched.
38. Lambda exonuclease is used for removal of nucleotides from .... ends of DNA.
39. The abbreviation PAGE stands for ....
40. *E. coli* exonuclease III is used for removal of nucleotides from .... ends of DNA.
41. DNA molecules are .... charged.
42. Agarose gels with pulsed electric fields or field inversion are useful in separating DNA fragments of upto .... kb.
43. Reverse transcriptase is used to produce cDNA from ....
44. Linker and adaptor oligonucleotide sequences are used for modification of the .... of DNA fragment.
45. .... library contains only those genes that are expressed in the concerned tissue/ organism.

2.3. MARK TRUE OR FALSE

1. The nitrogen present at the ninth position of purines participates in a covalent linkage with the 1′C of the pentose sugar.
2. In deoxyribose sugar of DNA, an oxygen atom is missing from position 3′.
3. In most of the organisms, RNA performs non-genetic functions.
4. Most commonly used vectors are derived from either bacterial plasmids or bacterio-phage genomes.
5. Western blotting is used for the study of RNA.
6. DNA copy of an RNA molecule is produced by the enzyme reverse transcriptase.
7. Linkers are used for creation of sticky ends on blunt-ended DNA fragments.
8. Northern blotting hybridization is simply an extension of the Southern blotting technique.
9. Nick translation is the oldest method of nucleic acid labelling, but it is rarely used to label double stranded DNA molecules.
10. *In situ* hybridization has been used to establish the location of sat-DNA in chromosomes.
11. In western blotting, protein bands are separated by polyacrylamide gel electrophoresis.
12. Colony hybridization is also a form of *in situ* hybridization.
13. Horizontal agarose gels are used for separation of high molecular weight proteins and large fragments of DNA.
14. DNA ligase seals the gaps that remain in the recombinant DNA molecules.
15. The recognition sequences are the same for different restriction endonucleases.
16. Generally, mRNA is used for the production of cDNA.
17. Phagemid can be used as a riboprobe vector.
18. Expression vectors must contain weak promoters.
19. PCR can be used to generate single-stranded DNA.
20. Vent polymerase has proof-reading activity.
21. Thermal cycle sequencing is used extensively in automated DNA sequencing.
22. Nitrocellulose membrane is most commonly used for Southern blotting.
23. Diffusion blotting is mostly used with gels having small pores.
24. Polyacrylamide gel is used for separation of small fragments of DNA.
25. Colony hybridization is used to identify those bacterial colonies in a plate which contain a specific DNA sequence.
26. Type I restriction endonucleases have recognition sequences of about 25 bp.
27. Plasmids vary in size from about 1.0 kb to over 250 kb.

28. Functional mRNA molecules of eukaryotes have introns.
29. A YAC is a shuttle vector that is propagated in circular from in *E. coli* and is used for cloning in yeast in a linear form.
30. Integration of DNA insert into the vector can be achieved through site-specific recombination.
31. Colony/plaque screening with antibodies is analogous to colony hybridization.
32. Phage vectors are more efficient than plasmid vectors for cloning large DNA fragments.
33. PCR can not be used for DNA finger-printing.
34. All DNA polymerases commit errors during DNA replication, which they themselves correct by proof-reading.
35. Most of the restriction enzymes produce staggered cuts.
36. Most of the type II restriction endonucleases cleave DNA molecules immediately outside the target sequence.
37. Col plasmids code for colicins that kill sensitive *E. coli* cells.
38. The DNA of a cell is protected from its own endonucleases by methylation within their site.
39. The recognition sequences for type II endonucleases form palindromes with rotational symmetry.
40. The presence of restriction sites within the markers permits an easy selection for cells transformed with recombinant DNA of *p*BR322.

□□□

3

GENOME MAPS

3.1. MULTIPLE CHOICE QUESTIONS

1. Which of following is correct ?

(*a*) Genome is the basic set of chromosomes, which is equivalent to the gametic chromosome complement (number) of a doploid species.

(*b*) Genome map is the schematic depiction of structural and functional organization of all chromosomes in the genome of an organism.

(*c*) Genome project was started to develop genome maps, genome sequence and its annotation in man and other experimental organisms.

(*d*) All of the above.

2. Acronym IRGSP stands for which of the followings ?

(*a*) International Rice Genome Sequencing Project.

(*b*) International Rice and Groundnut Sequencing project.

(*c*) International Research on Groundnut, Sorghum and Pigeonpea.

(*d*) Indian Rice Genetic Resources Programme.

3. Match the columns A and B and select the correct option from those listed below them.

Column A	Column B
A. Genomics (functional)	I. Single nucleotide polymorphism
B. Marker	II. Proteins
C. Proteomics	III. Gene isolation
D. Probe	IV. Function of all genes

Options :

(*a*) AI, BII, CIII, DIV

(*b*) AII, BIII, CIV, DI

(*c*) AIV, BI, CII, DIII

(*d*) AIII, BIV, CI, DII

4. Which of the following is correct ?

I. First linkage/genetic map of *Drosophila melanogaster* was prepared by A.H. Sturtevant

II. Cytogenetic mapping is far more refined in organisms like *Drosophila* because of their polytene chromosomes.

III. A map unit is that distance, which allows 50% recombination between the concerned genes.

IV. In a physical map, distances between genes are shown as number of base pair separating the genes.

Options :

(*a*) I, II, III (*b*) I, II, IV

(*c*) II, III, IV (*d*) I, IV

5. DNA markers can be used for which of the followings purposes.

(*a*) Preparation of linkage map

(*b*) Map-based cloning of genes

(*c*) Mapping of quantitative trait loci (QTL)

(*d*) All of the above.

6. Cytogenetic mapping can be done by which of the following approaches ?

I. Somatic cell hybridization

II. Fluorescence *in situ* hybridization

III. Analysis of small changes in polytene chromosome structure.

Options :

(*a*) I, II (*b*) II, III
(*c*) I, II, III (*d*) I, III

7. Which of the following techniques can be used for isolation of individual chromosomes ?

I. Sephadex column chromatography
II. Pulsed-field gel electrophoresis
III. Fluorescence-activated cell sorting.

Options :

(*a*) I, II (*b*) II, III
(*c*) I, III (*d*) I, II, III

8. In case of linkage maps, the distance, between the markers are measured in terms of which of the following ?

(*a*) Recombination frequency
(*b*) Mutation frequency
(*c*) Angstroms
(*d*) Nucleotide number

9. Isozyme markers behave like which of the following ?

(*a*) Recessive (*b*) Dominant
(*c*) Codominant (*d*) Overdominant

10. Column A contains list of organisms and column B contains their estimated number of genes. Match the two columns carefully and select the correct option from those listed below them.

Column A	Column B
A. *Arabidopsis thaliana*	1. 20,000
B. *Drosophila melanogaster*	2. 6,000
C. *Caenorhabditis elegans*	3. 26,000
D. *Saccharomyces cerevisiae*	4. 16,000

Options ;

(*a*) A1, B2, C3, D4 (*b*) A2, B3, C4, D1
(*c*) A3, B4, C1, D2 (*d*) A4, B1, C3, D2

11. Which of the following conclusion is correct about genome maps/sequences ?

I. Most mutations occur in human males.
II. The genes are more densely distributed in G.C- rich regions.
III. Hundreds of human genes seem to have come directly by horizontal transfer from bacteria.
IV. Millions of single nucleotide ploymorphisms have been identified in the human genome.

Options :

(*a*) I, II, III, IV (*b*) I, II, III
(*c*) II, III, IV (*d*) I, III, IV

12. Which of the following scientists was appointed as the first Director of Human Genome Project.

(*a*) A.H. Paterson (*b*) P.M. Gresshoff
(*c*) K.E. Davis (*d*) J.D. Watson

13. Protein markers offer which of the following advantages over naked eye polymorphisms ?

I. Analysis of one marker usually does not interfere with the ability to assay other protein markers.
II. They reflect differences in gene sequences more directly than do naked eye polymorphisms.
III. Only a small amount of tissue is needed for their detection.
IV. They can often be detected when the plant is very young or even directly from seeds.

Options :

(*a*) I, II, III, IV (*b*) I, II, III
(*c*) II, III, IV (*d*) I, III, IV

14. Which of the following were the goals of human genome project ?

I. To sequence the entire human genome
II. To develop a genetic/linkage map of human genome.
III. To obtain physical map of human genome.
IV. To develop programmes focussed on understanding and addressing the ethical, legal, and social implications of the results obtained from the project.

Options :

(*a*) I, II, III (*b*) I, II, III, IV
(*c*) II, III, IV (*d*) I, II, IV

15. Which of the following populations are used for linkage mapping ?

(*a*) F_2 population
(*b*) Backcross population
(*c*) Recombinant inbred lines
(*d*) All of the above.

16. The basic strategy of the humane genome project may be grouped into which of the following stages.

I. Mapping
II. Sequencing
III. Functional analysis

Options :

(*a*) I, II (*b*) II, III
(*c*) I, II, III (*d*) I, III

17. Pulsed-field gel electrophoresis includes which of the following ?

I. Transverse alternating field electrophoresis
II. Field inversion gel electrophoresis
III. Contour-clamped homogeneous electric field.
IV. Polyacrylamide gel electrophoresis

Options :

(*a*) I, II, III, IV (*b*) I, II, III
(*c*) II, III, IV (*d*) II, III

18. Which of the following is correct about linkage analysis ?

I. Markers segregating in the population are tested pair-wise, *i.e.*, a two point test.
II. Once the linkage groups are identified by a two-point test cross, the markers within a group are ordered by three-point and multipoint linkage tests.
III. A fair degree of saturation is assumed when the maximum distance between any two adjacent markers is less than 10 cM.
IV. Among the crop plants, the rice genome map contains the maximum number of markers (2,275) and is considered to be the most saturated.

Options :

(*a*) I, II, III (*b*) I, II, III, IV
(*c*) I, III, IV (*d*) II, III, IV

19. RAPD is generated by using which of the following ?

(*a*) A single arbitrary primer
(*b*) Single-sequence-specific primer
(*c*) Two arbitrary primers
(*d*) A pair of sequence-specific primers

20. AFLP may arise due to which of the following ?

(*a*) A difference in restriction site.
(*b*) Deletions and insertions within the amplified restriction fragments.
(*c*) Mutations beyond the restriction sites that affect complementarity with the selection nucleotides of the AFLP primers.
(*d*) All of the above.

21. Lod score method was developed by which of the following ?

(*a*) Paterson (*b*) Morton
(*c*) Peltier (*d*) Rigby

22. Molecular maps have become increasingly useful in which of the following ?

(*a*) Genetic analysis of animals and plants.
(*b*) Location of functional genes within the genome.
(*c*) Physical mapping of eukaryotic genomes.
(*d*) All of the above.

23. Near-isogenic lines can be developed by which of the following method ?

(*a*) Single seed descent
(*b*) Mutagenesis
(*c*) Backcross method
(*d*) Continued inbreeding

24. Pulsed-field gel electrophoresis is able to separate chromosomes of which of the following ?

(*a*) Yeast (*b*) Bacteria
(*c*) Protozoa (*d*) All of the above.

25. DNA fingerprinting is used for which of the following ?

(*a*) Identification of varieties.
(*b*) Resolving disputed parentage.
(*c*) Identification of criminals
(*d*) All of the above.

26. Which of the followings ***is not correct*** about microsatellite DNAs.

(*a*) They are usually, larger than 2 kb long DNA fragments.
(*b*) They consist of repeats of 2-7 bp sequences.
(*c*) They are randomly and frequently distributed in all eukaryotic genomes, except yeast.
(*d*) They are almost ideal markers for genome mapping.

27. Which of the following ***is not correct*** about minisatellite DNAs.

(a) They are usually 200-2000 bp (0.2–2.0 kb) long DNA fragments.
(b) They consist of tandem repeats of 15-60 bp.
(c) In human genome, they are concentrated in the proterminal regions of chromosomes.
(d) They are a good marker system for human genome.

28. Which of the following has the smallest genome size ?
(a) *Mycoplasma genitalium*
(b) *Saccharomyces cerevisiae*
(c) *E. coli*
(d) *Caenorhabditis elegans*

29. Genome of which of the following organisms was the first to be sequenced ?
(a) *Pseudomonas putida*
(b) *Mycoplasma genitalium*
(c) *Saccharomyces cerevisiae*
(d) *Haemophilus influenzae*

30. How many alleles are possible at an SNP locus ?
(a) 1 (b) 2
(c) 4 (d) 3

31. An SNP locus may be located in which of the following regions of a genome ?
I. Promoters
II. Exons
III. Intergenic sequences
IV. Introns
Options :
(a) I, II, IV (b) I, II, III, IV
(c) II, III, IV (d) I, III, IV

32. Which of the following markers arises only due to a change in base sequence of a gene ?
I. Isozymes
II. Naked eye polymorphism
III. RFLPs
IV. AFLPs
Options :
(a) I, II, III (b) II, III, IV
(c) I, II (d) I, IV

33. Which of the following molecular markers is related to a change in restriction site ?
I. RAPD II. AFLP
III. SCAR IV. RFLP
V. STMS
Options :
(a) II, IV (b) II
(c) I, II, III (d) I

34. In Q. 33, which marker system is the least reproducible ?
Options :
(a) I, II, IV (b) I
(c) III, V (d) IV, V

35. In Q. 33, development of which marker system requires base sequence information ?
Options :
(a) II, III, IV (b) I, V
(c) III, IV (d) III, V

36. In Q. 33, which marker system detects the greatest amount of polymorphism ?
Options :
(a) I (b) III
(c) II (d) IV, V

37. In Q. 33, which marker systems are dominant ?
Options :
(a) I, II, III (b) I, II, III, V
(c) I, III, IV (d) II, III, IV, V

38. Which of the markers given in Q. 33 would normally generate a single band ?
Options :
(a) I, II (b) III, V
(c) IV, V (d) I, IV, V

39. Which of the molecular markers listed in Q. 33, ***may not work*** in more than one species ?
Options :
(a) I, III, IV, V (b) I, II, III
(c) II, III, V (d) I, III, IV

40. Which of the following have been involved in *Arabidopsis thaliana* genome evolution ?
(a) Polyploidization
(b) Genome reduction
(c) Single cycle of (a) followed by (b)
(d) More than one cycle of (a) followed by (b)

41. Human genome is estimated to contain about how many genes ?
(a) 35,000 (b) 25,000
(c) 50,000 (d) 40,000

42. Two-hybrid yeast system studies, which of the following ?
(*a*) Protein function
(*b*) Heterosis
(*c*) Protein-protein interaction
(*d*) Protein expression

43. In case of AFLP, selection nucleotides achieve, which of the following ?
I. Reduction in the number of amplified fragments.
II. Detection of polymorphism
III. Increased reproducibility.

Options :
(*a*) I, II (*b*) I, III
(*c*) I, II, III (*d*) II, III

44. Which of the following is correct about AFLP ?
I. It uses restriction enzyme
II. It is codominant
III. It detects a large amount of polymorphism.
IV. It is based on PCR.

Options :
(*a*) I, II, III, IV (*b*) I, III, IV
(*c*) II, III, IV (*d*) I, II, III

45. Initially, which of the following marker systems was used for human DNA fingerprinting ?
(*a*) RAPD (*b*) RFLP
(*c*) AFLP (*d*) STMS (STR loci)

46. Which of the marker systems listed in Q. 45 is currently used for human DNA fingerprinting ?

47. Selection nucleotides are used in which of the marker systems listed in Q. 45 ?

48. Which of the markers listed in Q. 45 uses PCR as well as restriction enzymes ?

49. Contigs can be created through which of the following ?
(*a*) Chromosome jumping
(*b*) Unique STSs
(*c*) Shotgun approach
(*d*) Both (*a*) and (*b*)

50. In which of the following, primers are specific to unique sequences ?
I. ISSR II. AFLP
III. STMS IV. SCAR

Options :
(*a*) I, III, IV (*b*) III, IV
(*c*) II, III, IV (*d*) I, II, III

51. In which of the marker systems listed in Q. 50, primers are specific to non-unique sequences ?

Options :
(*a*) I, II (*b*) II, III
(*c*) III, IV (*d*) I, IV

52. In which of the marker systems listed in Q. 50, primers are specific to SSR sequences ?

Options :
(*a*) I (*b*) II
(*c*) III (*d*) IV

53. The genome of which of the following plants was the first to be sequenced ?
(*a*) *Zea mays*
(*b*) *Oryza sativa*
(*c*) *Hordeum vulgare*
(*d*) *Arabidopsis thaliana*

54. Out of the options given in Q. 53, which has the smallest genome size ?

55. Out of the options given in Q. 53, which has the largest genome size ?

56. The genome of which of the following eukaryotes was first to be sequenced ?
(*a*) *Arabidopsis* (*b*) *Yeast*
(*c*) *Caenorhabditis* (*d*) *Drosophila*

57. Among the options given in Q. 56, which one has the smallest genome size ?

58. Among the options given in Q. 56, which one has the largest genome size ?

59. Among the options given in Q. 56, which one has the largest number of genes ?

60. Among the options given in Q. 56, which one has the smallest number of genes ?

61. Which of the following bacteria has at least two circular chromosomes in its genome ?
(*a*) *Bacillus*
(*b*) *Pseudomonas*
(*c*) *Vibrio cholerae*
(*d*) *Mycoplasma genitalium*

62. Contigs facilitate, which of the following ?
(*a*) Rapid sequencing
(*b*) Sequence alignment
(*c*) Sequence annotation
(*d*) Sequence interpretation

3.2. FILL IN THE BLANKS

1. Abbreviation DAF stands for ....
2. Resolution of cytogenetic mapping is much better in those species that have .... chromosomes.
3. 1 cM represents about .... kb of DNA in humans.
4. Chromosome jumping is used to create contigs of rather .... DNA fragments, while chromosome walking is applicable to much .... DNA fragments.
5. Abbreviation IHGSC stands for ....
6. AFLP behaves as .... marker.
7. If the lod score equals +3 or is greater, the two markers in question are considered to be ....
8. In mammals and plants, individual chromosomes can be isolated by the technique of ....
9. Abbreviation FACS stands for ....
10. The technique of chromosome jumping is used for the creation of ....
11. The term genome was introduced by ....
12. The Human Genane Project officially began on ....

3.3. MARK TRUE OR FALSE

1. Southern blots display differences in the length of restriction fragments.
2. Bands generated by RAPD, AP-PCR and DAF are dominant.
3. The rate of one recombination in 100 meioses gives one centiMorgan.
4. The ultimate aim of genome project is to decipher the sequence of entire human genome.
5. Physical mapping ultimately leads to complete sequencing of the whole genome.
6. RFLP markers result from a combination of a specific restriction endonuclease and a specific DNA sequence used as probe.
7. Sequence tagged sites are not useful in genome mapping and in DNA fingerprinting.
8. Chromosome walking is usually done with cosmid clones prepared from partial digests with one restriction enzyme or complete digests with two enzymes.
9. PFGE is used to separate large fragments of DNA and even small chromosomes.
10. A collection of contigs represents a physical map of a chromosome.
11. YAC cloning vectors are used to make contigs of prokaryotic chromosomes.
12. Man-mouse somatic hybrids have been used to map genes on particular human chromosomes.

4

GENOMICS AND BIOINFORMATICS

4.1. MULTIPLE CHOICE QUESTIONS

1. Which of the following is concerned with the development and application of computer hardware and software for acquisition, storage, analysis and visualization of biological information ?
(*a*) Computer science
(*b*) Biotechnology
(*c*) Bioinformatics
(*d*) Information technology

2. Match the columns A and B carefully and select the correct option from those listed below them.

Column A	Column B
A. Proteome	1. The complete set of genetic information
B. Genome	2. Genome structure and function
C. Genomics	3. Determination of the proteome
D. Proteomics	4. The complete set of proteins-encoded by genome

Options :
(*a*) A2, B4, C1, D3
(*b*) A4, B1, C2, D3
(*c*) A3, B2, C4, D1
(*d*) A4, B1, C3, D2

3. The term genomics was coined by which of the following ?
(*a*) Thomas H. Roderick
(*b*) H. Winkler
(*c*) A.H. Paterson
(*d*) Benzer

4. Which was the first prokaryotic genome to be sequenced ?
(*a*) *E. coli*
(*b*) *Agrobacterium tumefaciens*
(*c*) *Haemophilus influenzae*
(*d*) *Proteus vulgaris*

5. The rough draft of human genome was announced on which of the following dates ?
(*a*) June 26, 2000 (*b*) June 26, 2001
(*c*) June 26, 1999 (*d*) June 26, 2003

6. Shot-gun sequencing was conceptualized by which of the following ?
(*a*) Craig Venter
(*b*) Michelmore
(*c*) Giovannoni
(*d*) Young

7. The sequence of a human genome has how many nucelotide pairs ?
(*a*) 4.2×10^6 (*b*) 4.6×10^9
(*c*) 3.2×10^9 (*d*) 3.8×10^9

8. Which of the following eukaryotic genome was sequenced in 1999 ?
(*a*) *Caenorhabditis elegans* (worm)
(*b*) *Drosophila melanogaster*
(*c*) *Saccharomyces cerevisiae*
(*d*) Both (*a*) and (*c*).

9. The shot-gun sequencing approach would be the most suited for which of the following genomes ?
(*a*) *E. coli* (*b*) Yeast
(*c*) Humans (*d*) *Drosophila*

10. Bioinformatics can be used for which of the following ?
   I. Assessing the effects of virtual mutations on gene function.
   II. Determination of protein structure and simulate protein interactions.
   III. Identification of genes.
   IV. Genome mapping.

Options :
(*a*) I, II, III (*b*) I, II, III, IV
(*c*) II, III, IV (*d*) I, III, IV

11. Lateral gene transfer is also called which of the following ?
(*a*) Horizontal gene transfer
(*b*) Vertical gene transfer
(*c*) Parallel gene transfer
(*d*) Both (*b*) and (*c*).

12. In which of the following years, a proposal for sequencing of human genome was prepared ?
(*a*) 1984 (*b*) 1988
(*c*) 1986 (*d*) 1990

13. Bioinformatics includes which of the following activities ?
   I. Preparation of data-base.
   II. Compiling of genome sequence.
   III. Identification of genes.
   IV. Assigning functions to the identified genes.
   V. Development of computer hardware.

Options :
(*a*) I, II, III, IV (*b*) II, III, IV, V
(*c*) I, II, III (*d*) I, II, III, IV, V

14. One megabase pairs (Mb) is equal to how many base pairs ?
(*a*) 10^5 bp (*b*) 10^6 bp
(*c*) 10^8 bp (*d*) 10^9 bp

15. Which of the following conclusions were drawn from the human genome draft sequence ?
   I. Human genome was estimated to have about 35,000 genes.
   II. Only ~5% of the genome encodes proteins.
   III. It contains over 3.2 billions base pairs.
   IV. At least 50% of the genome is derived from transposable elements.
   V. Genome sequences of different individuals differ for over 2% of the base pairs.

Options :
(*a*) I, II, III, IV (*b*) I, II, III, V
(*c*) II, III, IV, V (*d*) I, II, III, IV, V

16. The amino acids were conventionally represented by three-letter symbols, while in bioinformatics, each of them is denoted by how many letters ?
(*a*) Single letter (*b*) Two letters
(*c*) Three letters (*d*) Four letters

17. Genomics includes which of the following activities ?
   I. Determination of complete set of proteins encoded by an organism.
   II. Functions of all the genes and metabolic pathways in an organism.
   III. Physical mapping and sequencing of the complete genome.

Options :
(*a*) I, II (*b*) II, III
(*c*) I, II, III (*d*) I, III

18. Which of the following benefits can be expected from human genome sequencing project ?
   I. Determination of the complete genetic information present in the genome.
   II. The relationships between genes.
   III. A better understanding of human genetic diseases.
   IV. An understanding of why different individuals respond differentially to the same drug.

Options :
(*a*) I, II, III, IV (*b*) I, III, IV
(*c*) II, III, IV (*d*) I, II

19. Which of the following procedures can be used for the identification/discovery of SNPs ?
(*a*) DNA chips.
(*b*) Microarrays.
(*c*) Analyzing the sequence data.
(*d*) All of the above.

20. Single nucleotide polymorphisms (SNPs) may be located in which of the following ?
(*a*) In the recognition sequence of an endonuclease.
(*b*) Within the concerned gene.
(*c*) Very close to the gene to show a tight linkage.
(*d*) All of the above.

21. Which of the following statements ***is not correct*** about prokaryotic genomes ?

(*a*) The genome size varies considerably.
(*b*) Pseudogenes do not occur in prokaryotic genomes.
(*c*) The frequency of paralogues increases with the genome size.
(*d*) The gene density is however, relatively constant at one gene per kilo base pairs.

22. Which of the following statement ***is not correct*** about eukaryotic genomes ?

(*a*) As the genome size increases, gene density decrease.
(*b*) A high percentage of proteins encoded by human genome have orthologs in other eukaryotic genomes.
(*c*) About 75% of repetitive DNA in human genome is due to LINEs and SINEs sequences.
(*d*) Intron sequences are as variable as exon sequences.

23. Which of the following features can be used to identify genes in bacterial genomes ?

(*a*) Protein-coding genes are composed of open reading frames.
(*b*) Coding region begins with an initiation codon (uaually ATG).
(*c*) Coding region ends with a termination codon (TAA, TAG or TGA).
(*d*) All of the above.

24. Which of following areas comes under proteomics ?

I. Protein mining and protein-protein interaction.
II. Expression proteomics.
III. Post-translational modification.
IV. Functional genomics.

Options :
(*a*) I, II, III (*b*) II, III, IV
(*c*) I, II, III, IV (*d*) II, IV

25. Which of the following is correct about structural proteomics ?

I. Mapping of 3-D structure and nature of protein complexes present specially in a particular cell/organelle.
II. To build a body of structural information that will help to predict the probable structure and potential function for almost any protein from a knowledge of its coding sequence.
III. It is quite useful in identification of disease-specific proteins.
IV. Assembling information about protein-protein interactions.

Options :
(*a*) I, II, III, IV (*b*) I, II, IV
(*c*) II, III, IV (*d*) II, IV

26. Which of the following phenomenon comes under post-translational modification ?

(*a*) Phosphorylation (*b*) Proteolysis
(*c*) Glycosylation (*d*) All of the above

27. Which of the following techniques is used in expression proteomics ?

I. Microarray.
II. Mass spectrometry.
III. Two dimensional gel elecrophoresis.
IV. Northern blotting.

Options :
(*a*) I, II, III (*b*) II, III, IV
(*c*) I, III, IV (*d*) I, II, III, IV

28. Which of the following concerns with determination of the function of a gene product ?

(*a*) Expression proteomics
(*b*) Structural genomics
(*c*) Functional genomics
(*d*) Structural proteomics

29. Which of the following scientists proposed that amino acid sequences of proteins may be used to study evolutionary relationships among organisms ?

(*a*) Zuckerland and Pauling
(*b*) Sensen and Buchler
(*c*) Dayhoff and Rashidi
(*d*) Tolin and Vidaver

30. The first comprehensive collection of amino acid sequences was compiled in the Atlas of Protein Sequence and Structure by which of the following ?

(*a*) European Bioinformatics Institute
(*b*) National Biomedical Research Foundation
(*c*) National Centre for Bioinformatics Information
(*d*) European Molecular Biology Laboratory

31. Functional genomics includes answers to which of the following questions ?
(*a*) How is a gene expressed ?
(*b*) How is a gene product related in sequence and structure to products of other genes of the same organisms ?
(*c*) How does a gene interacts with the proteins ?
(*d*) All of the above.

32. Column A contains a list of arrays, while column B contains applications of various arrays. Match the two columns and select the correct option from those listed below them.

Column A	Column B
A. Arrays of specific capture agents	1. Gene expression
B. Antigen arrays	2. Detection of specific proteins
C. Spotted DNA arrays	3. Detection of antibodies in solution
D. Protein chips	4. Binds to specific class of proteins.

Options :
(*a*) A1, B2, C3, D4 (*b*) A3, B4, C2, D1
(*c*) A2, B3, C1, D4 (*d*) A4, B1, C3, D2

33. Column A contains a list of arrays, while column B has the substances contained in the arrays. Match the two columns and select the correct option from those listed below them.

Column A	Column B
A. Spotted DNA arrays	1. dsDNA genomic or cDNA
B. Antibody chips	2. Antibodies specific to various proteins
C. Protein arrays	3. ssDNA syntheized on the solid support
D. Printed oligonucleotide chips	4. Proteins that recognize other proteins

Options :
(*a*) A1, B2, C4, D3 (*b*) A3, B4, C1, D2
(*c*) A4, B3, C2, D1 (*d*) A2, B1, C3, D4

34. Which of the following is correct about spotted DNA arrays ?
I. Each array has 10^6-10^9 double-stranded DNA molecules.
II. The functions of the DNA sequences used for spotting may be known, but this is not necessary.
III. Each spot or dot represents a distinct gene/DNA sequence.
IV. Spotting is done by robots.

Options :
(*a*) I, II, III (*b*) I, II, III, IV
(*c*) II, III, IV (*d*) I, III, IV

35. DNA sequences/molecules used for preparing spotted DNA arrays may be obtained from which of the following ?
(*a*) PCR amplification
(*b*) Genomic DNA
(*c*) cDNA clones
(*d*) All of the above

36. Which of the following ***is not correct*** about printed oligonucleotide chips ?
(*a*) These are produced by a light-directed printing technology.
(*b*) These chips have double-stranded oligonucleotides of 20-25 bases.
(*c*) Oligonucleotides are synthesized directly onto the chips.
(*d*) Each sequence is represented by a set of ~20 non-overlapping oligonucleotides to reduce false positive results.

37. Genome-wide mutant libraries have been developed in which of the following organisms ?
I. Plants II. Mammals
III. Bacteria IV. Yeast

Options :
(*a*) I, II, III, IV (*b*) II, III, IV
(*c*) I, III, IV (*d*) III, IV

38. Which of the following ***is not correct*** about homologous recombination ?
(*a*) Exchange of identical segments occurs between two heterologous DNA molecules/chromosomes.
(*b*) To achieve transgene integration by homologous recombination, the marker gene is flanked by appropriate sequences from or around the target gene.
(*c*) In prokaryotes, integration by homologous recombination may occur

upto 90% of the time when suitable targetting vectors are used.
(*d*) Mouse embryonic stem cells, may show upto 0.1% integration by homologous recombination.

39. Insertional mutagenesis has been reported in which of the following ?
(*a*) Mouse and *Drosophila melanogaster*
(*b*) Yeast and roundworm
(*c*) Zebrafish and *Arabidopsis*
(*d*) All of the above

40. Which of the following ***is not correct*** ?
(*a*) European Molecular Biology Laboratory endeavours to collect, organize and distribute nucelotide sequence data and related information.
(*b*) National Centre for Bioinformatics Institute was established in USA and serves as primary information databank and provider of information.
(*c*) RNA Data Bank was established by Japan.
(*d*) National Biomedical Research Foundation established the Protein Information System in 1984.

41. Which of the following ***is not correct*** about Gene trap vector ?
(*a*) In this vector, the insertion element contains a reporter gene, *e.g., lacZ* or *gusA,* downstream of a splice acceptor site.
(*b*) Reporter gene will be expressed only when the vector inserts within the transcribed region of a gene.
(*c*) It is used for detection and isolation of genes.
(*d*) This vector was isolated from *Bacillus thuringiensis.*

42. Which of the following is correct about the features of virus-induced gene silencing ?
I. A defence mechanism induced by dsRNA.
II. Sequence-specific in action.
III. The viral RNA genome has a transgene homologous to the target gene.

Options :
(*a*) I, II (*b*) II, III
(*c*) I, II, III (*d*) III

43. Which of the following ***is not correct*** ?
(*a*) In databases, base sequence of only one strand is listed.
(*b*) Base sequence runs from the 3′- to the 5′-directions.
(*c*) In single letter codes, R denotes guanine or adenine, while Y denotes thymine or cytosine.
(*d*) The nomenclature system adapted in bioinformatics is based on the recommendations of International Union of Pure and Applied Chemistry.

44. Databases on DNA sequences contain which of the following types of sequences ?
(*a*) EST and GST sequences
(*b*) Genomic DNA and cDNA sequences.
(*c*) Oganellar DNA sequences and sequences of other molecules such as tRNA, small RNAs.
(*d*) All of the above.

45. Which of the following is correct about EST sequences ?
I. These sequences are obtained by sequencing only a part of the cDNA.
II. These sequences are dubbed as tags.
III. The EST technique has generated enormous sequence data that permitted the construction of a preliminary transcript map of human genome.
IV. One of the problems with ESTs is duplication.

Options :
(*a*) I, II, III, IV (*b*) II, III, IV
(*c*) I, III, IV (*d*) I, II

46. Column A contains various databases while column B contains types of sequences contained in them. Match the two columns carefully and select the correct option from those listed below them.

Column A	Column B
A. Mito	1. Nucleotide sequence of immonologically important genes.
B. GenBank	2. Sequences of mitochondrial genomes.
C. Kabat	3. Nucleotide sequences of genomic DNA

D. IMGT 4. Nucleotide sequences that are of interest from immunological point of view.

Options :

(*a*) A1, B2, C3, D4 (*b*) A2, B3, C1, D4
(*c*) A2, B3, C4, D1 (*d*) A3, B4, C2, D1

47. Which of the following is an example of major nucleotide sequence database ?

(*a*) DNA Databank of Japan
(*b*) Nucleotide Sequence Database maintained by EMBL
(*c*) GenBank held by NCBI, USA
(*d*) All of the above

48. Which of the following is executed by BLAST programmes ?

I. The sequence submitted by researcher is compared base-per-base or amino acid-per-amino acid with the database sequences.
II. A substitution scoring matrix is used, in which each match is awarded a specific score, while each mismatch is penalized by a specified negative score.
III. The sequence alignment is assigned an overall score, which is the summation of scores assigned to each of its paired amino acids/nucelotides.
IV. Top scoring alignments are ranked according to set criteria. These criteria distinguish between a similarity due to ancestral relationship and that due to random chance.

Options :

(*a*) I, II, III, IV (*b*) II, III, IV
(*c*) I, III, IV (*d*) I, II, III

49. Which of the following databases is used by ENTREZ for bibliographic or citation search ?

(*a*) SWISS-PROT (*b*) PubMed
(*c*) TrEMBL (*d*) PDB

50. Column A contains various software, while column B contains various functions performed by them. Match these two columns carefully and select the correct options from those listed below them.

Column A	Column B
A. GeneScan	1. Detection of tRNA genes.
B. FASTA	2. Identification of functional domains/ motifs of proteins.
C. SMART	3. Detection of genes from genome sequence
D. tRNA ScanSE	4. Prediction of function of a new gene.

Options :

(*a*) A1, B2, C3, D4 (*b*) A2, B3, C4, D1
(*c*) A3, B4, C2, D1 (*d*) A4, B3, C2, D1

51. For access to BLAST server through web, which of the following steps a user needs to follow ?

I. The sequence for which homology is to be searched, is submitted into the "input sequence" box of the BLAST interface.
II. The appropriate BLAST programme is selected depending on the type of comparison to be made.
III. The appropriate database from which homologous sequences are to be searched has to be selected.
IV. The sequence is now submitted to the BLAST server.

Options :

(*a*) I, II, III (*b*) I, II, III, IV
(*c*) II, III, IV (*d*) I, III, IV

52. Which of the following software have been developed for the prediction/detection of genes from genome sequence of eukaryotes ?

I. HMM Gene and GRAIL
II. GeneFinder and GENESCAN
III. GENIE
IV. GENMARK

Options :

(*a*) I, II, III (*b*) II, III, IV
(*c*) I, II, III, IV (*d*) I, III, IV

53. Which of the following approaches have been used for the identification of genes ?

I. Northern blot II. CpG islands
III. Zoo blot IV. Exon trapping

Options :
(*a*) I, II, III (*b*) II, III, IV
(*c*) I, II, III, IV (*d*) I, II, IV

54. Which of the following programmes can be used for the identification/detection of genes from genome sequence of prokaryotes ?
(*a*) Glimmer (*b*) GENMARK
(*c*) GeneFinder (*d*) Both (*a*) and (*b*)

55. Which of the following bioinformatics tools can be used for the identification of protein motifs and protein domains ?
I. PRINTS II. tRNA ScanSE
III. BLOCKS IV. SMART
Options :
(*a*) I, II, III (*b*) II, III, IV
(*c*) I, III, IV (*d*) III, IV

56. Gene prediction programmes for eukaryotes search for which of the following gene-specific features ?
I. Polyadenylation sites
II. Promoter
III. Splice sites.
Options :
(*a*) I, II (*b*) I, II, III
(*c*) I, III (*d*) II

57. Which of the following is correct about genome annotation ?
(*a*) GAME is a programme for describing experimental evidence to support annotation.
(*b*) DAS is useful in indexing and visualization
(*c*) BioPerl 2001 is used for storing, manipulating and visualizing the genome annotation.
(*d*) All of the above

58. Which of the following approaches can be used for gene identification ?
(*a*) Exon trapping (*b*) cDNA capture
(*c*) cDNA selection (*d*) All of the above

59. Which of the following steps are involved in identification of the function of a new gene ?
I. The gene sequence is translated into the amino acid sequence of the protein it is expected to encode.
II. Protein sequence is then compared with a protein database.
III. If encoded protein is homologous to a protein in the database, it confirms the identification of this gene.
IV. Step III also suggests the functions of this gene.
Options :
(*a*) I, III, IV (*b*) II, III, IV
(*c*) I, II, III, IV (*d*) III, IV

60. Which of the following is used for comparing the submitted nucleotide sequence with nucleotide database ?
(*a*) BLASTn (*b*) BLASTx
(*c*) tBLASTx (*d*) tBLASTn

61. Which of the search tools given in Q. 60 is used for comparing the submitted nucleotide sequence with amino acid sequence database ?

62. Which of the search tools given in Q. 60 is used to compare submitted amino acid sequence with nucleotide sequence database ?

63. Which of the tools given in Q. 60 compares submitted amino acid sequence with amino acid database ?

64. Which of the following have been used for insertional mutagenesis in plants ?
I. Transposable elements
II. T-DNA
III. Viral vectors.
Options :
(*a*) I, III (*b*) I, II
(*c*) II, III (*d*) I

65. India has initiated genome sequencing project of which of the following ?
(*a*) Rice (*b*) Tomato
(*c*) Pigeonpea (*d*) Humans

66. India ***has not been*** involved in sequencing the genomes of which of the organisms listed in Q. 65.

67. Sequencing of the 24 human chromosomes was completed in which year ?
(*a*) 2001 (*b*) 2003
(*c*) 2006 (*d*) 2008

68. The *Mycoplasma genitalium* complete genome was chemically synthesized and assembled in which year ?

(*a*) 2001 (*b*) 2003
(*c*) 2006 (*d*) 2008

69. *E. coli* genome has about how many operons ?
(*a*) 200 (*b*) 600
(*c*) 1000 (*d*) 2000

70. In case of prokaryotes, which of the following represents the frequency of unique ORFs ?
(*a*) 50% (*b*) 100%
(*c*) 25% (*d*) 75%

71. Which of the following has operons similar to those of bacteria ?
(*a*) *C. elegans* (*b*) *Drosophila*
(*c*) *Arabidopsis* (*d*) Mouse

72. In which of the following is found the highest density of transposable elements ?
(*a*) *Arabidopsis* (*b*) *Drosophila*
(*c*) *C. elegans* (*d*) Humans

73. In Q. 72, which organism has the lowest density of transposable elements ?

74. Which of the following methods can be used for mRNA quantitation ?
I. Real-time PCR
II. *In situ* hybridization
IV. Northern hybridization
IV. Ribonuclease protection assays

Options :
(*a*) I, II (*b*) I, II, III, IV
(*c*) I (*d*) II, III, IV

75. Which of the options given in Q. 74 is the most sensitive method of mRNA quantitation ?

76. Which of the following PCR strategies monitors the fluorescence emitted during reaction to measure the amount of amplification product generated during the PCR cycles ?
(*a*) Anchored PCR (*b*) Touchdown PCR
(*c*) Real-time PCR (*d*) Nested PCR

77. Which of the following ***is not correct*** about TaqMan probes ?
(*a*) They are olignucleotides longer than the primers.
(*b*) They contain a fluorescent dye usually on the 5′-base, and a quenching dye typically on the 3′-base.
(*c*) When *Taq* polymerase replicates a tempelate to which a TaqMan probe is paired, its 5′-exonuclease activity cleaves the TaqMan probe.
(*d*) The fluorescence decreases proportionately to PCR amplification.

78. In case of Real-time PCR, which of the following methods can be used for the detection of amplification products ?
(*a*) Molecular beacons
(*b*) Scorpions
(*c*) TaqMan probes
(*d*) All of the above

79. Which of the following advantages is offered by Real-time PCR ?
(*a*) Multiplex PCR reactions can be used by employing molecular beacons/ TaqMan probes.
(*b*) It eliminates the post-PCR processing of PCR products needed for quantitative measurements of PCR products.
(*c*) Real-time PCR offers a much wider dyanamic range than conventional RT-PCR.
(*d*) All of the above

80. Which of the following ***is not correct*** about Real-time PCR ?
(*a*) Real-time PCR can detect the size of the amplicon.
(*b*) Design of primers, TaqMan probes and molecular beacons requires almost complete information of the target sequence.
(*c*) With SYBR green method, primer dimer artifact is a problem.
(*d*) The one-step RT-PCR can not be used for multiplex real-time RT-PCR.

81. Which of the following ***is not correct*** ?
(*a*) Both TaqMan probes and molecular beacons allow multiplex reactions, and thereby, detection of multiple DNA sequences in a single PCR reaction.
(*b*) In multiplexing, different probes/ beacons are labelled with different reporter dyes.
(*c*) Multiplexing does not allow amplification in a single PCR reaction

of both target and endogeneous control sequences.

(*d*) The use of probes/beacons avoids problems due to mispriming, primer-dimer artifacts, etc.

82. Which of the following ***is not correct*** about genomics ?

(*a*) In 1980, David Botstein and coworkers working at the Whitehead Institute of Biomedical Research, USA proposed that one could construct a genome map.

(*b*) In 1995, the first bacterial genome to be completely sequenced was that of *Haemophilus influenzae.*

(*c*) The sequencing of whole genome of first multicellular organism, round worm (*Caenorhabdits elegans*), was published in 1999.

(*d*) The sequencing of rice genome by International Rice Genome Sequencing Project was based on whole genome shot-gun approach.

83. Which of the following ***is not correct*** about genomics ?

(*a*) Sequencing, sequence assembly and annotation of the whole genome of an organism constitutes functional genomics.

(*b*) The first plant genome to be completely sequenced is that of the weed, *Arabidopsis thaliana.*

(*c*) *Arabidopsis thaliana* is a wild relative of mustards

(*d*) The *Arabidopsis* Genome Initiative followed the same method of sequencing as the Human Genome Project.

84. Which of the following ***is not correct*** ?

(*a*) The public funded Human Genome Project employed the clone-by-clone approach, while the private company Celera Genomics followed whole genome shot-gun approach.

(*b*) Clone-by-clone approach is based on contigs.

(*c*) In the whole genome shot-gun approach, genomic DNA is sheared to obtain 2 to 10 kb fragments, which are then cloned and sequenced from both the ends.

(*d*) Assigning biological functions to the DNA sequences using a variety of tools and techniques is described as structural genomics.

85. Which of following is correct about comparative genomics ?

I. It is the study of differences and similarity in the genome structure and organization of different organisms.

II. The objectives of comparative genomics to understand the process of evolution and to convert the DNA sequence data into proteins of known functions.

III. Genomes of Archaea have similarities with eukaryotic genomes.

IV. Some bacteria like *Vibrio cholerae* have two or more circular chromosomes in their genomes.

Options :

(*a*) I, III, IV (*b*) I, II, III, IV

(*c*) II, III, IV (*d*) III, IV

4.2. FILL IN THE BLANKS

1. The science, which deals with storage, analysis, interpretation and utilization of infomation about biological systems is called ....

2. The software TRNASCAN is commonly used to detect .... coding regions.

3. Abbreviation BTIS stands for ....

4. The buttom's up approach is popularly called ....

5. The Human Genome Project officially began on ....

6. *Arabidopsis thaliana* genome is estimated to have .... genes.

7. The largest gene in the human genome is the gene encoding ....

8. The European Bioinformatics Institute (EBI) is located at ....

9. It is estimated that human and chimpanzee genome sequences differ for only upto .... per cent of their base pairs.
10. SNPs are single base positions in genomic DNA at which different .... occur in different individuals of a population.
11. Based on effect of genes on survival of organisms, it has been estimated that living organisms require a minimum of .... to .... genes.
12. The minimum genome size for a unicellular eukaryote discovered so far is .... bp for the parasite *Encephalitozoan cuniculi.*
13. The smallest genome size for a vertebrate is that for the .... which has 4×10^8 bp DNA.
14. The animal and fungal mtDNAs are much .... than plant mtDNAs.
15. During evolution, *Mycoplasma leprae* has lost over .... genes.
16. Many human disease networks are highly conserved in ....
17. The eukaryotic mitochondrial genome strongly resembles the genome of ....
18. Complete set of proteins expressed during a cell's entire life time is called ....
19. If each human gene transcript was alternatively processed to yield an average of 3 different proteins, the estimated 35,000 human genes would code for .... different proteins.
20. Printed oligonucleotide chips are used for the detection of .... pattern.
21. DNA microarrays are used for studying .... pattern.
22. In case of spotted DNA arrays, DNA molecules are typically .... to .... bp long.
23. The DNA microarray is used for hybridization with labelled .... probes.
24. In case of printed oligonucleotide chips, the density of oligos is upto .... per cm^2, while 64,000 per cm^2 is quite common.
25. Creation of a genome-wide mutant library is dubbed as ....
26. The most popular strategy for random mutagenesis is ....
27. The abbreviation VIGS stands for ....
28. The functions of European Molecular Biology Laboratory are now performed by ....
29. Genomic DNA sequences represent the .... genome of the organism, irrespective of whether it is expressed or not.
30. Genome sequence tags are developed by sequencing the DNA fragments on either side of the cuts generated by ....
31. A vast collection of data pertaining to a specific topic in an electronic environment is known as ....
32. The radiation hybrid score vectors can be used to create chromosome maps that are an alternative to the ....
33. The BLAST server can be accessed through the web address ....
34. The clone that tests positive in zoo blot is expected to represent a ....
35. The first task in gene identification in a DNA sequence is the identification of the correct ....
36. The Human Genome Project was officially completed in ....
37. The pigeonpea genome sequencing has been initiated by ....

4.3. MARK TRUE OR FALSE

1. The first prokaryotic genome to be sequenced was that of *Haemophilus influenzae* in 1995.
2. The draft sequence of human genome was announced separately by Human Genome Sequencing Consortium and Celera Genomics.
3. A database is a vast collection of data pertaining to a specific topic, *e.g.*, nucleotide sequence, protein sequence, etc. in an electonic environment.
4. The science which deals with computer-based analysis of large biological data sets is called genomics.
5. About 85% of all differences in human DNAs are due to single nucleotide polymorphisms.

6. *Arabidopsis thaliana* has the smallest genome among higher plants.
7. Bioinformatics developed in the wake of generation of amino acid sequences of proteins and nucleotide sequences.
8. The shot-gun strategy works very well with eukaryotic genomes.
9. Hundreds of human genes seem to have been directly transferred from bacteria into the human genomes rather than having evolved from bacterial genes.
10. An SNP may be located within the concerned gene or very close to the gene to show a tight linkage.
11. Many human disease networks are highly conserved in *C. elegans*.
12. The rate of inversion is much higher in eukaryotes than in prokaryotes.
13. Phylogenetic footprinting allows the discovery of genes and regulatory elements.
14. The objective of genome analysis is to determine the functions of all the genes and to understand how these genes interact in the development and function of the organism.
15. Gene duplication has played a minor role in the evolution of eukaryotic genome.
16. Proteome discribes the set of proteins expressed in a cell at a given time.
17. Global expression profiling provides insights into complex biological phenomena.
18. In multicellular organisms, transcriptome obtained from one tissue is usually comparable to that obtained from another tissue.
19. In case of spotted DNA arrays, spots are rarely more than 5000 per cm^2.
20. DNA microarrays can be used for comparing gene expression patterns of two cell types.
21. The amino acid sequences in databases are listed from the *C–terminus* to the *N–terminus* of the polypeptide.
22. Protein function depends only on the primary structure rather than on the 3-D structure.
23. Protein structures are experimentally determined by X-ray crystallography and nuclear magnetic resonance spectroscopy.
24. To identify proteins, the mass of the peptides is compared with the masses predicted from data in genetic or protein databases.
25. The most important single development in genome annotation is the use of computers to predict genes from DNA sequences.

□□□

5

PLANT PHYSIOLOGY AND MOLECULAR BIOLOGY

5.1. MULTIPLE CHOICE QUESTIONS

1. Which of the following components are required for the process of photosynthesis ?

I. Chloroplast II. Carbon dioxide
III. Water IV. Sunlight

Options :

(*a*) I, II, III (*b*) I, II, III, IV
(*c*) II, III, IV (*d*) I, III, IV

2. Which of the following organisms form their food through photosynthesis ?

I. Plants
II. Algae
III. Fungi
IV. Photosynthetic bacteria

Options :

(*a*) I, II, III, IV (*b*) I, II, III
(*c*) I, II, IV (*d*) II, III, IV

3. Which of the following is correct about C_3 plants ?

(*a*) During photosynthesis, RuBP carboxylase enzyme plays a key role in the fixation of CO_2.
(*b*) 3-Phosphoglyceric acid (3-PGA) is the first stable product of photosynthesis.
(*c*) Carbohydrates are formed through Calvin cycle.
(*d*) All of the above

4. Which of the following is correct about photorespiration ?

I. It is a light-dependent process.
II. It occurs only in green chlorophyllous cells.
III. Site of photorespiration is chloroplast, peroxisome and mitochondria.
IV. Glycolic acid is the substrate for photorespiration.

Options :

(*a*) I, II, III, IV (*b*) I, III, IV
(*c*) II, III, IV (*d*) I, II, III

5. Which of following is correct about C_4 plants ?

(*a*) During photosynthesis, PEP carboxylase plays a key role in the fixation of CO_2.
(*b*) Malic acid is the first stable product of photosynthesis.
(*c*) Carbohydrates are formed through Hatch-Slack cycle.
(*d*) All of the above.

6. Which of the following plants bears intermediate features between C_3 and C_4 plants ?

(*a*) Maize
(*b*) *Moricandia arvensis*
(*c*) *Amaranthus*
(*d*) Both (*a*) and (*c*)

7. Which of the options given in Q. 6 is an example of C_4 plant ?

8. In which of the following plants stomata are closed in day time and open during night ?

(*a*) C_3 plants (*b*) C_4 plants
(*c*) CAM plants (*d*) All of the above

9. Which of the following have circular DNA ?
(*a*) Chloroplasts (*b*) Mitochondria
(*c*) Bacteria (*d*) All of the above

10. Dark reaction is also called which of the following ?
(*a*) Blackman reaction
(*b*) Hill reaction
(*c*) Cyclic reaction
(*d*) Both (*a*) and (*b*)

11. Which of the options given in Q. 10 is related to light reaction ?

12. Which of the following statements are correct ?
I. In case of C_3 plants, CO_2 acceptor is ribulose 1,5-bisphasphate, while phosphoenol pyruvate is the acceptor in case of C_4 plants.
II. C_4 plants have developed more efficient mechanism of CO_2 fixation than C_3 plants.
III. C_4 plants show negligible photorespiration, while C_3 plants show high rate of photorespiration.
IV. Optimum temeperature for photosynthesis in C_3 plants is 10–25°C while it is 30–45°C in case of C_4 plants.

Options :
(*a*) I, II, III, IV (*b*) II, III, IV
(*c*) I, III, IV (*d*) I, III, IV

13. Translocation of carbohydrates mostly takes place in the form of which of the following ?
(*a*) Maltose (*b*) Fructose
(*c*) Sucrose (*d*) Glucose

14. During photosynthesis, which of the following gases is evloved as byproduct ?
(*a*) CO_2 (*b*) H_2
(*c*) O_2 (*d*) Both (*b*) and (*c*)

15. The rate of photosynthesis, can be measured by which of the following ?
(*a*) Amount of carbohydrate accumulated
(*b*) The volume of CO_2 consumed
(*c*) The volume of oxygen librated
(*d*) All of the above.

16. During photosynthesis, light reaction occurs in which of the following ?
(*a*) Stroma (*b*) Thylakoids
(*c*) Oxysomes (*d*) Both (*a*) and (*b*)

17. Dark reaction occurs in which of the options given in Q. 16 ?

18. Which of the following occurs during light reaction ?
(*a*) Photolysis of water
(*b*) Photophosphorylation
(*c*) Fixation of CO_2
(*d*) Both (*a*) and (*b*)

19. Cosider the following statements about plastids :
1. They arise from small granular structures called proplastids.
2. Proplastids may differentiate into chloroplasts, chromoplasts and leucoplasts.
3. Chloroplasts of higher plants contain four different pigments like chlorophyll '*a*', chlorophyll '*b*', carotene and xanthophyll.
4. The chloroplast pigments occur mostly in the grana and are assciated with the thylakoid membranes.

Which of these statements is correct ?
(*a*) 1, 2, 3 (*b*) 2, 3 , 4
(*c*) 1, 2, 3, 4 (*d*) 1, 3, 4

20. Which of following ***is not an example*** of C_4 Plant.
(*a*) Sugarcane (*b*) Sorghum
(*c*) *Portulaca* (*d*) Wheat

21. During photosynthesis, oxgen is released from which of the following ?
(*a*) CO_2 (*b*) H_2O
(*c*) SO_2 (*d*) O_3

22. In case of C_4 plants, RuBISCO exists only in which of following ?
(*a*) Mesophyll cells (*b*) Bundle sheath
(*c*) Gaurd cells (*d*) All of the above

23. Nitrogenase consists of which of the following components ?
(*a*) Mo protein (*b*) Fe-protein
(*c*) MoFe-protein (*d*) Both (*b*) and (*c*)

24. *Cyanobacteria* protect nitrogenase from oxygen by which of the following ?
(*a*) Nodule formation
(*b*) Heterocyst formation
(*c*) Phycocyanin
(*d*) Leghaemoglobin

25. HMP pathway is also known by which of the following ?
(*a*) Pentose phosphate pathway
(*b*) Direct oxidative pathway
(*c*) EMP pathway
(*d*) Both (*a*) and (*b*)

26. Fe protein of nitrogenase is which of the following ?
(*a*) Homomeric dimer
(*b*) Heteromeric dimer
(*c*) Homomeric tetramer
(*d*) Heteromeric tetramer.

27. Glyoxysomes are invlove in breakdown of which of the following ?
(*a*) Sugar (*b*) Protein
(*c*) Fatty acids (*d*) All of the above

28. Site of oxidative election transport in cells is which of the following ?
(*a*) Golgi bodies (*b*) Mitochondria
(*c*) Nucleus (*d*) Chloroplasts

29. Which of the following elements is related to cytochrome ?
(*a*) P (*b*) Cu
(*c*) Fe (*d*) Zn

30. Acetylene reduction to ethylene is a measure of which of the following ?
(*a*) N_2 fixation
(*b*) Nitrate reduction
(*c*) Nitrite reduction
(*d*) CO_2 fixation.

31. Nitrate reductase is found in which of the following ?
(*a*) Vacuole (*b*) Mitochondria
(*c*) Cytoplasm (*d*) Chloroplasts

32. How many electrons are required for the reduction of one molecule of nitrogen to NH_4^-?
(*a*) 6 (*b*) 8
(*c*) 3 (*d*) 12

33. Reduction of nitrite to ammonium is catalyzed by nitrite reductase in which of the following ?
(*a*) Chloroplasts (*b*) Mitochondria
(*c*) Nucleus (*d*) Golgi body

34. Which of the following is correct about nitrogenase ?
I. MoFe protein of nitrogenase is made up of two subunits α and β polypeptides, encoded by *nif* D and *nif* K genes, respectively.
II. Fe protein of nitrogenase is a dimer of two identical polypeptides encoded by *nif* H gene.
III. MoFe protein requires a cofactor (FeMoCo) which is essential for N_2 binding and reduction.
IV. Electron transfer to nitrogenase in *Klebsiella pneumoniae* occurs from pyruvate to a pyruvate-flavodoxin oxidoreductase encoded by *nif* J and then to a flavodoxin encoded by *nif* F.

Options :
(*a*) I, II, III (*b*) II, III, IV
(*c*) III, IV (*d*) I, II, III, IV

35. Phosphorylation occurs in which of the following ?
(*a*) Mitochondria (*b*) Glyoxysomes
(*c*) Chloroplasts (*d*) Both (*a*) and (*c*)

36. The main function of leghaemoglobin in root nodules is concerned with which of the following ?
(*a*) N_2 supply (*b*) O_2 supply
(*c*) Mineral supply (*d*) CO_2 supply

37. Which of the following enzymes is invloved in conversion of ammonia to amino acid ?
(*a*) Alanine transferase
(*b*) Nitrate reductase
(*c*) Glutamine synthetase
(*d*) Nitrite reductase.

38. Which of the following enzymes is responsible for fixation of nitrogen ?
(*a*) Nitrite reductase (*b*) Nitrate reductase
(*c*) Carboxylase (*d*) Nitrogenase

39. Mature root nodules mostly consist of which of the following cells ?
(*a*) Diploid (*b*) Triploid
(*c*) Tetraploid (*d*) Pentaploid

40. During photosynthesis, water splits in which of the following ?
(*a*) PS I (*b*) PS II
(*c*) Cytoplasm (*d*) Stroma

41. Vernalization is related to which of the following ?
(*a*) Cold treatment
(*b*) Photoperiod

(*c*) Developmental buffering
(*d*) Male sterility

42. Which of the following contains DNA ?
(*a*) Peroxysomes (*b*) Mitochondria
(*c*) Centrosomes (*d*) Prions

43. In plants, respiration includes which of following ?
(*a*) Glycolysis
(*b*) Kreb's cycle
(*c*) Electron transport system
(*d*) All of the above.

44. Stomata plays a key role in which of the following ?
(*a*) Photoperiodism (*b*) Transpiration
(*c*) Respiration (*d*) Vernalization

45. Pyruvic acid is the end product of which of the following ?
(*a*) Hydrolysis of starch
(*b*) Citric acid cycle
(*c*) Photolysis
(*d*) Glycolysis

46. How many ATP molecules are produced in anaerobic respiration of one glucose molecule ?
(*a*) 2 (*b*) 4
(*c*) 8 (*d*) 6

47. In which of the following, electron transport leading to phosphorylation is a common reaction ?
(*a*) Chloroplasts
(*b*) Mitochondria
(*c*) Both (*a*) and (*b*)
(*d*) Golgi bodies

48. Most of the reactions of glyoxylate cycle occurs in which of the following ?
(*a*) Glyoxysomes (*b*) Cytosol
(*c*) Mitochondria (*d*) All of the above

49. Which of the following organelles is involved in ATP production by photophosphorylation ?
(*a*) Mitochondria (*b*) Chloroplasts
(*c*) Leucoplasts (*d*) Chromoplasts

50. Citric acid cycle occurs in which of the options given in Q. 49 ?

51. The electron transport system and oxidative phosphorylation are concerned with which of the options given in Q. 49 ?

52. Which of the options given in Q. 49 is an example of colourless plastid ?

53. The term carotenoid is related to which of the following ?
(*a*) Carotene (*b*) Chlorophyll
(*c*) Xanthophyll (*d*) Both (*a*) and (*c*)

54. Which of the following is the major pigment of chloroplasts ?
(*a*) Chlorophyll (*b*) Xanthophyll
(*c*) Carotene (*d*) All of the above.

55. Glycolysis uses, which of the following as substrate ?
(*a*) Glucose (*b*) Sucrose
(*c*) Lipids (*d*) Fatty acids

56. The enzymes for the oxidation of amino acids, fatty acids and Kerb's cycle are present in which of the following ?
(*a*) Lysosomes
(*b*) Stroma
(*c*) Grana
(*d*) Mitochondrial matrix

57. Which of the following is present in stroma ?
(*a*) DNA
(*b*) RNA
(*c*) Ribosomes
(*d*) All of the above.

58. Consider the following statements:
1. Grana and stroma lamellae are composed of several thousands of units called quantasomes.
2. A group of 3-8 quantasomes is capable of electron transport and photophosphorylation.
3. Enzymes concerned with dark reaction of photosynthesis are located in stroma.
4. Several copies of a ring-shaped DNA molecule are present in stroma of each chloroplast.

Of these statements, which are correct ?
(*a*) 1, 2, 3 (*b*) 1, 2, 3, 4
(*c*) 2, 3, 4 (*d*) 1, 3, 4

59. The main feature of light induced promoters of dicots is which of the following ?
(*a*) TATA box
(*b*) An upstream AG or AGGA box
(*c*) Both TATA and AG/AGGA boxes
(*d*) CAAT box

60. The alcohol dehydrogenase gene is induced by stress due to which of the following ?
(*a*) Heat
(*b*) Anaerobiosis
(*c*) Wound
(*d*) Pathogen invasion

61. Which of following is correct ?
I. In case of legume root nodules, enlarged nonmotile bacterium is referred to as a bacteroid.
II. A typical root nodule cell contains several thousand bacteroids.
III. The bacteriods usually occur in cytoplasm in groups.
IV. Nitrogen fixation in root nodules occurs directly within the bacteroids.

Options :
(*a*) I, II (*b*) II, III, IV
(*c*) I, III, IV (*d*) I, II, III, IV

62. Photoperiod is the most relevant for which of the following ?
(*a*) Abscission
(*b*) Flowering
(*c*) Shoot bud formation
(*d*) Root growth

63. In response to stress, which of the following amino acids is accumulated ?
(*a*) Proline (*b*) Glycine
(*c*) Lysine (*d*) Phenylalanine

64. RuBISCO has which of the following activities ?
(*a*) Carboxylase (*b*) Reductase
(*c*) Oxygenase (*d*) Both (*a*) and (*c*)

65. Which of the following are stress hormones ?
(*a*) Ethylene and IAA
(*b*) IAA and ABA
(*c*) ABA and ethylene
(*d*) ABA and IBA

66. Nitrite reductase contains which of the following prosthetic groups ?
(*a*) Siroheme (Fe_4–S_4) cluster
(*b*) FMN (Fe–S) cluster
(*c*) Mo cofactor (Fe–S) cluster
(*d*) All of the above.

67. *nifHDK* genes are organised in which of the following ways ?
(*a*) They are contigous
(*b*) *D* and *K* are separated by 11 kb DNA
(*c*) Separated by 91 kb DNA located between genes *D* and *K*
(*d*) Separated by 55 kb DNA between genes *D* and *K*.

68. *Azolla* contains an endosymbiont which fixes nitrogen; this organism belongs to which of the following genera ?
(*a*) *Aulosira* (*b*) *Azosprillum*
(*c*) *Nostoc* (*d*) *Anabaena*

69. In case of yeast mitochondria, mt-DNA encodes which of the following components of mitochondrial ATPase ?
(*a*) F_1 ATPase
(*b*) F_0 factor
(*c*) Both (*a*) and (*b*)
(*d*) Some subunits of both (*a*) and (*b*)

70. In case of plants, cpDNA encodes which of the following components of organellar ATPase listed in Q. 69 ?

71. A free living anaerobic bacterium capable of nitrogen fixation in the soil is which of the following ?
(*a*) *Azotobacter* (*b*) *Clostridium*
(*c*) *Rhizobium* (*d*) *Streptococcus*

72. Mitochondrial DNA ***does not code*** for which of the following ?
(*a*) tRNA
(*b*) Enzyme for DNA replication
(*c*) mRNA
(*d*) rRNA

73. Phytochrome is which of the following ?
(*a*) Monomer (*b*) Multimer
(*c*) Homodimer (*d*) Heterodimer

74. Cytochrome b6-f complex consists of how many polypeptides ?
(*a*) 1 (*b*) 2
(*c*) 4 (*d*) 10

75. Which of following is correct ?
I. The ratio of the volume of oxygen evolved to the volume of CO_2 taken in during photosynthesis is called photosynthetic ratio/photosynthetic quotient.
II. Chlorophyll 'a' has a methyl ($-CH_3$) group and chlorophyll 'b' an aldehyde

(–CHO) group attached to carbon number 3.

III. Stroma lamellae also called stroma thylakoids.

IV. Photosynthesis is an oxidation reduction process.

Options

(*a*) I, II, III, IV (*b*) II, III, IV
(*c*) I, II, IV (*d*) I, II, III

76. During cyclic photophosphorylation, which of the following is electron donor of PS II ?
(*a*) CO_2 (*b*) Water
(*c*) PS I (*d*) Cytochrome

77. The mitochondrial genome is the smallest in which of the following ?
(*a*) Mammals (*b*) Yeast
(*c*) *Arabidopsis* (*d*) Tomato

78. Which of the following is due to cpDNA alone ?
(*a*) Photosystem I
(*b*) Photosystem II
(*c*) Chloroplast RNA polymerase
(*d*) All of the above

79. Kranz type of leaf anatomy is found in which of the following ?
(*a*) Maize (*b*) *Amaranthus*
(*c*) Sorghum (*d*) All of the above

80. Apical dominance is the result of which of the following ?
(*a*) Auxin (*b*) Cytokinin
(*c*) Auxin and ABA (*d*) ABA

81. How many ATPs are produced (if we start with Acetyl CoA) in Kreb's cycle ?
(*a*) 18 (*b*) 30
(*c*) 24 (*d*) 38

82. Glycolysis occurs in which of the following?
(*a*) Cytoplasm (*b*) Mitochondria
(*c*) Nucleus (*d*) Golgi bodies

83. Electron transport system take place in which part of mitochondria ?
(*a*) Oxysome (*b*) Outer membrane
(*c*) Matrix (*d*) Both (*a*) and (*c*)

84. In which of following, PEP carboxylation takes place ?
(*a*) Mesophyll cells of C_4 plants
(*b*) Epidermal cells of C_4 plants
(*c*) Bundle sheath cells of C_4 plants
(*d*) Xylem cells of C_4 plants

85. In CAM plants, formation of malic acid takes place during which of the following ?
(*a*) Sunset (*b*) Morning
(*c*) Night (*d*) Afternoon.

86. Kreb's cycle is also known as which of the following ?
(*a*) Tricarboxylic acid cycle (TCA)
(*b*) Citric acid cycle
(*c*) Organic acid cycle
(*d*) All of the above

87. Crassulacean acid metabolism (CAM) occurs in which of the following ?
(*a*) *Agave* (*b*) Opuntia
(*c*) Pineapple (*d*) All of the above.

88. How many ATPs (gross ATP) are produced from complete oxidation of one molecule of glucose in respiration ?
(*a*) 36 (*b*) 38
(*c*) 30 (*d*) 24

89. In case of eukaryotes, which of the options given in Q. 88 indicates the net gain of ATP from the complete oxidation of one molecule of glucose in respiration ?

90. Kreb's cycle starts with entry of which of the following ?
(*a*) Acetyl-CoA (*b*) Oxaloacetate
(*c*) Both (*a*) and (*b*) (*d*) Pyruvic acid

91. Match the columns A and B and pick the correct option from those listed below them.

Column A	Column B
A. Chlorophyll	I. 3 ATP
B. $NADH_2$	II. Mg
C. $FADH_2$	III. 7.6 Kcal
D. ATP	IV. 2 ATP

Options :
(*a*) AI, BIV, CIII, DII
(*b*) AIV, BIII, CII, DI
(*c*) AIII, BII, CIV, DI
(*d*) AII, BI, CIV, DIII

92. Photosynthetic rate is the highest in which of the following plants ?
(*a*) C_3 Plants (*b*) C_4 plants
(*c*) CAM (*d*) Both (*b*) and (*c*)

93. ***Assertion (A)***: Plant species with C_4 pathway generally have higher photosynthetic rate than C_3 plant species, specially under high light intensity.

Reason (R): The main factor, which increases photosynthetic efficiency of C_4 plant species is the lack of measurable photorespiration in them.

Options :

(*a*) Both A and R are correct and R sufficiently explains A.
(*b*) Both A and R are correct, but R does not explain A.
(*c*) Only A is correct.
(*d*) Only R is correct.

94. Which of the following is correct about blue green alga, *Anabaena cylindrica* ?

I. It is a branched filamentous alga consisting of two type of cells, *viz.*, green photosynthetic cells and heterocysts.
II. Green photosynthetic cells fix atmospheric CO_2 and release O_2 during photosynthesis.
III. Heterocysts are slightly enlarged colourless cells, non-photosynthetic in nature, but can fix atmospheric nitrogen aerobically.
IV. It is associated with leaf cavities of the water fern, *Azolla* and coralloid roots of *Cycas*.

Options :

(*a*) I, II III (*b*) I, II, III, IV
(*c*) I, III, IV (*d*) I, II, IV

95. Which of following blue-green algae ***does not form*** heterocysts ?

(*a*) *Anabaena* (*b*) *Nostoc*
(*c*) *Gleotrichia* (*d*) *Scytonema*

96. Which of the following is correct about cyanobacteria ?

I. Nitrogen fixation occurs in heterocysts.
II. *nif* gene regulon is reorganised in heterocysts and is essential for N_2-fixation.
III. Heterocysts act as O_2–proof compartments, which protects nitrogenase from O_2 inactivation.
IV. Cyanobacteria accumlate biomass which improves the physical property of soil.

Options :

(*a*) I, II, III, IV (*b*) II, III
(*c*) I, III, IV (*d*) I, II, III

97. ***Problem (P)***: Nitrogenase is highly sensitive to O_2.

Solution (S): In root nodules of legumes, it is protected from O_2 by the pink pigment of leghaemoglobin.

Options :

(*a*) Only P is correct
(*b*) Only S is correct
(*c*) Both P and S are correct, but S does not solve P.
(*d*) Both P and S are correct and S adequately solves P.

98. In case of prokaryotes, net gain of ATPs from complete oxidation of one molecule of glucose in respiration is which of the following ?

(*a*) 40 (*b*) 38
(*c*) 36 (*d*) 30

99. How many cycles of Kreb's cycle is needed for complete oxidation of one glucose molecule ?

(*a*) 1 (*b*) 3
(*c*) 2 (*d*) 4

100. Which of the following is correct ?

I. Gene *RbcS* encodes the small subunit of RuBISCO.
II. A DNA sequence called light response element (LRE) located upstream from the amino acid coding sequences is necessary for the light regulated transcription of the gene.
III. LRE is an example of *cis*-acting genetic regulatory element.
IV. LRE controls the tissue-specific expression of the *RbcS* gene.

Options :

(*a*) I, II III (*b*) II, III
(*c*) II, III, IV (*d*) I, II, III, IV

101. Which of the following statements is correct ?

I. Starch is detectable only in areas of the leaf exposed to light.
II. Starch is the world's most abundant photosynthetic product formed by chloroplasts.
III. Usually proplastids are derived only from the unfertilized egg cells in most of the crop plants.

IV. Lycopene is found in chloroplasts and gives the red colour to tomato fruits.

Options :

(*a*) I, II III (*b*) I, II, III, IV
(*c*) II, III, IV (*d*) I, III, IV

102. Which of the following is correct ?

(*a*) Chloroplast DNA exists in 50 or more supercoiled double-stranded circles per plastid.
(*b*) Numerous plastid genes code for about 30 apparently all of the tRNA molecules and four rRNA molecules used by plastids for translation.
(*c*) About 85 other plastid genes code for proteins involved in transcription, translation and photosynthesis but most of the proteins needed in plastids are coded for by nuclear genes.
(*d*) All of the above.

103. Consider the following statements about PS II ?

1. It consists of a core complex of six integral polypeptides connected non-covalently to each other.
2. Six polypeptides of PS II are coded for by the chloroplast genome (DNA).
3. Out of the six polypeptides of PS II, two polypeptides with molecular weights near 33 kDa and 31 kDa are commonly called D_1 and D_2, directly bind reaction centre P680.
4. D_1 and D_2 contain quinones necessary for oxidation of water.

Out of these statements which are correct?

Options :

(*a*) 1, 2, 3 (*b*) 1, 2, 3, 4
(*c*) 1, 3, 4 (*d*) 2, 3, 4

104. Which of the following organelles mainly synthesize amino acids in the cells ?

(*a*) Mitochondria (*b*) Ribosomes
(*c*) Chloroplasts (*d*) Both (*a*) and (*b*)

105. Which of the following is correct about plastoquinones ?

(*a*) They are special quinones present in plastids.
(*b*) They carry two electrons from PS II toward PS I.
(*c*) They transport H^+ from stroma into the thylakoid lumen.
(*d*) All of the above.

106. Which of the following is correct ?

I. Pheophytin is a modified chlorophyll 'a' molecule in which two H atoms have replaced the central Mg^{2+}.
II. Most PS II is present only in the appressed regions of grana thylakoids.
III. Chlorophyll 'a', chlorophyll 'b' and xanthophylls are present in the PS II light harvesting complex.
IV. Probably all the proteins in PS II light harvesting complex (LHC II) are coded for by nuclear DNA.

Options :

(*a*) I, II III, IV (*b*) II, III, IV
(*c*) I, III, IV (*d*) I, II, III

107. Which of the following statements is correct ?

(*a*) PS I is located exclusively in stroma thylakoids and nonappressed region of grana that face the stroma.
(*b*) The PS I core complex from barley contains 11 different polypeptides varying in size.
(*c*) Out of the 11 polypeptide of PS I complex, six are coded for by nuclear genes.
(*d*) All of the above.

108. Calvin cycle includes which of the following steps ?

I. Carboxylation II. Reduction
III. Regeration

Options :

(*a*) I, II (*b*) II, III
(*c*) I, II, III (*d*) I, III

109. ***Assertion (A)***: In C_4 plants, photosynthesis is much less limited by CO_2 levels.

Reason (R): C_4 plants effectively pump CO_2 into bundle sheath cells where it is used in the Calvin cycle.

Options :

(*a*) Both A and R are correct and R adequately explains A.
(*b*) Both A and R are correct, but R does not explain A.

(c) Only A is correct.
(d) Only R is correct.

110. Which of following ***is not correct*** about starch ?
(a) It is stored in photosynthetically inactive organs like roots, modified shoots and seeds.
(b) The constituents of starch grains are amylose and amylopectin.
(c) Both amylose and amylopectin are made up of D-glucose units.
(d) Starch molecules have a definite molecular weight and are assembled into starch grains.

111. Properties of starch molecules are mainly determined by which of the following ?
(a) Degree of branching (including branch length).
(b) Types of bonds linking the glucose units.
(c) Chain length.
(d) All of the above.

112. Which of the following is correct ?
(a) Flower senescence is promoted by ethylene.
(b) Ethylene biosynthesis involves two enzymes, *viz.*, ACC synthase and ACC oxidase.
(c) ACC synthase enzyme is encoded by *acs* gene and ACC oxidase is encoded by *aco* gene.
(d) All of the above.

113. Which of the following is correct about starch biosynthesis ?
I. Starch biosynthesis uses ADP-glucose (adenosine diphosphate-glucose)as substrate.
II. ADP-glucose is produced from glucose-1-phosphate by the action of ADP-glucose pyrophosphorylase (AGPase).
III. ADP-glucose is used by starch synthases and starch branching enzymes (SBEs) to synthesize amylose and amylopectin.
IV. Branch length is modified by starch debranching enzymes (SDBEs).

Options :
(a) I, II III, IV (b) I, III, IV
(c) II, III, IV (d) I, II, III

114. Which of the following is correct ?
I. ADP-glucose is synthesized in the cytosol and is transported into plastids by ADP-glucose transporter protein.
II. Granule-bound starch synthase I (GBSS I) functions in polymerization of ADP glucose and is the main enzyme of amylose biosynthesis.
III. Soluble starch synthases (SSSs) function in polymerization of ADP-glucose into amylopectin.
IV. The major constituents of starch is amylopectin.

Options :
(a) I, II III (b) I, II, III, IV
(c) I, III, IV (d) I, II, III, IV

115. Which of the following is correct ?
I. Acetyl-CoA-ACP transacylase convert acetyl-CoA into acetyl-ACP.
II. β-Ketoacyl-ACP synthase I is involved in condensation of acyl-ACP with malonyl-CoA.
III. β-Ketoacyl-ACP synthase II is involved condensation of palmitic acid (16 : 0) into stearic acid (18 : 0).
IV. Stearoyl-ACP desaturase desaturates stearic acid (18 : 0) to oleic acid (18 : 1).

Options :
(a) I, II III (b) I, II, III, IV
(c) II, III, IV (d) I, IV

116. Which of the following is correct ?
I. During transcription, only one strand of a DNA molecule is transcribed, this strand is called antisense/template DNA, and the RNA produced is termed as sense RNA.
II. As a rule, orientation of the antisense strand is 3′→5′ in relation to the promoter of the gene.
III. RNA chain elongates in the 5′→3′ direction.
IV. Promoter is located at the beginning of the 3′–end of antisense strand.

Options :
(a) I, II III, IV (b) II, III, IV
(c) I, III, IV (d) I, II, III

117. Consider the following statements.

1. Promoter is that sequence of a transcription unit where RNA polymerase binds and initiates transcription.
2. Consensus sequence is a base sequence present in all the promoters (or other DNA segments having the same function) but with some variation.
3. Conserved sequence is a base sequence present without any change in all DNA segments having the same function.
4. Startpoint is the site within a promoter from which transcription begins.
5. The sequence located at the left of a startpoint is called downstream sequence.

Options :

(*a*) 1, 2, 3, 4, 5 (*b*) 1, 2, 3, 4
(*c*) 1, 3, 4, 5 (*d*) 1, 3, 4

118. Which of the following ***is not correct*** ?

(*a*) Startpoint is typically a single base within the promoter.
(*b*) The chief function of σ factor (of bacterial RNA polymerase) is to ensure that the holoenzyme binds stably at only promoter sequences.
(*c*) Transcription factors are essential part of RNA polymerases.
(*d*) Transcription factors can be divided into basal upstream and regulatory transcription factors.

119. A typical transcription unit contains which of the following ?

I. A promoter at its beginning (at the 3′– end of its antisense strand).
II. A startpoint.
III. A coding region.
IV. A terminator region
V. In almost all eukaryotes, transcription unit is the same as gene.

Options :

(*a*) I, II III, IV (*b*) I, II, III, IV, V
(*c*) I, III, IV (*d*) I, II, IV, V

120. Which of the following ***is not correct*** about transcription unit ?

(*a*) It is that sequence of a DNA molecule that is transcribed into a single RNA molecule.
(*b*) In case of all eukaryotes, each gene is a distinct transcription unit.
(*c*) In case of prokaryotes, each operon functions as a single transcription unit.
(*d*) Enhancer sequences are present within promoters.

121. Which of the following is correct about transcription factors ?

(*a*) These factors are required for transcription initiation at all the promoters of eukaryotes.
(*b*) They join RNA polymerase II to form a complex around the startpoint.
(*c*) They determine the site of transcription initiation.
(*d*) All of the above.

122. Which of the following functional sequence/module ***is not found*** in eukaryotic promoters ?

(*a*) TATA box (*b*) Pribnow box
(*c*) GC box (*d*) CAAT box

123. Which of the options given in Q. 122 is often present in several copies in a single promoter ?

124. Which of the options given in Q. 122 occupies a fixed position given in the promoter at –25 ?

125. Which of the options given in Q. 122 is usually surrounded by a GC rich sequence ?

126. Which of the following consensus sequences is recognized by more than one transcription factors ?

(*a*) –35 sequence
(*b*) CAAT box
(*c*) Octamer sequence
(*d*) GC box

127. Mitochondria and plastids present in eukaryotic cells contain RNA polymerases that are analogous to which of the following ?

(*a*) Eukaryotic polymerase
(*b*) Phage polymerases
(*c*) Bacterial polymerases
(*d*) Both (*b*) and (*c*)

128. Which of the following sequences constitutes generic eukaryotic promoter ?

I. Initiator (Inr) II. GC box
III. TATA box IV. CAAT box

Options :

(*a*) I, II, III (*b*) I, III
(*c*) II, III (*d*) I, IV

129. Which of the following is correct about RNA polymerase II ?
(*a*) It is present in nucleoplasm.
(*b*) It constitutes 20–40% of total activity.
(*c*) It transcribes all the genes that produce mRNA.
(*d*) All of the above.

130. Which of the following is correct about enhancers ?
I. Located on either side of the promoter upto several kilobase pairs away.
II. Can function in either orientation.
III. Have organization similar to that of promoters.
IV. Decrease the function of promoter lying in their vicinity.

Options :
(*a*) I, II III (*b*) I, II, III, IV
(*c*) II, III, IV (*d*) I, III, IV

131. The GC–AG rule ***does not apply*** to introns of which of the following ?
(*a*) Chloroplast introns
(*b*) Nuclear introns of yeast
(*c*) Mitochondrial introns
(*d*) All of the above

132. Which of the following is correct about RNA polymerase I ?
(*a*) It is present in nucleolus
(*b*) It constitues 50-70% of total activity.
(*c*) It transcribes genes for rRNA.
(*d*) All of the above

133. ***Assertion (A)***: Enhancer sequences increase the activity of a promoter lying in their vicinity.
Reason (R): Enhancers most likely function by increasing the concentration of transcription factors in the vicinity of promoters.

Options :
(*a*) Both A and R are correct and R adequately explains A.
(*b*) Both A and R are correct, but R does not explain A.
(*c*) Only A is correct.
(*d*) Only R is correct.

134. In case of eukaryotes, RNA processing is completed in which of the following ?
(*a*) Cytoplasm (*b*) Nucleolus
(*c*) Nucleus (*d*) Vacuole

135. Which of the following is correct about RNA polymerase III ?
(*a*) It occurs in nucleoplasm.
(*b*) It provides ~10% of total polymerase actitity.
(*c*) It transcribes tRNA and 5SRNA genes.
(*d*) All of the above

136. In eukaryotes, pre-mRNA is processed by which of the following to yield mature mRNAs ?
I. Deletion of introns.
II. Addition of poly-A tails.
III. 5′-capping.
IV. In some cases, RNA editing.

Options :
(*a*) I, III, IV (*b*) I, II, III, IV
(*c*) I, II, IV (*d*) II, III, IV

137. The process of translation requires which of the following components ?
I. mRNA
II. Ribosome.
III. tRNA.
IV. Translation factors.

Options :
(*a*) I, II III, IV (*b*) II, III
(*c*) I, II, III (*d*) II, III, IV

138. During RNA editing, a single base change occurs in which of the following ?
I. mRNA base sequences of measles virus.
II. mRNA base sequences of SV5.
III. mRNA base sequences of trypanosome mitochondria.
IV. Mammalian mRNA for apolipoprotein.

Options :
(*a*) I (*b*) III
(*c*) IV (*d*) II

139. Eukaryotic mRNAs have which of the following regions ?
I. A 5′–cap (serves as ribosome binding site) followed by an untranslated 5′–leader sequence of usually < 100 bases.
II. A single coding region, which begins with a translation initiation codon (AUG) and ends with a translation termination codon.
III. An untranslated 3′–trailer that may be upto 1000 bases.

IV. In ~70% of the total mRNAs, a poly-(A) tail of ~200 residues (bases) is added after transcription.

Options :

(*a*) I, III, IV (*b*) I, II, III, IV
(*c*) I, II, IV (*d*) II, III, IV

140. ***Assertion (A)***: In bulk of eukaryotic mRNAs, a poly-(A) tail is added at the 3′–end of primary transcripts or pre-mRNAs.

Reason (R): Addition of a poly-(A) tail at the 3′-end of primary transcript is essential for the processing of pre-mRNAs.

Options :

(*a*) Both A and R are correct and R adequately explains A.
(*b*) Both A and R are correct, but R does not explain A.
(*c*) Only A is correct.
(*d*) Only R is correct.

141. A gene is alternatively spliced, and its exon 1 joined to any one or more of exons produces a functional protein. How many different functional proteins will be produced if this gene has 3 exons ?

(*a*) 1 (*b*) 2
(*c*) 3 (*d*) 4

142. In case of Q. 141, how many functional proteins will be produced if this gene has 4 exons ?

(*a*) 4 (*b*) 6
(*c*) 8 (*d*) 7

143. In case of Q. 141, how may functional proteins will be produced if the gene had 5 exons ?

(*a*) 14 (*b*) 15
(*c*) 5 (*d*) 10

144. Guide RNA functions in which of the following ?

(*a*) RNA processing
(*b*) RNA editing
(*c*) RNA degradation
(*d*) Transcription regulation

145. Which of the following mRNAs lacks poly-(A) tail ?

(*a*) Histone mRNA (*b*) Globin mRNA
(*c*) Antibody mRNA (*d*) Vicilin mRNA

146. Splicing yields, which of the following ?

(*a*) rRNA (*b*) tRNA
(*c*) mRNA (*d*) All of the above

147. DNA replication in which of the following ***does not use*** a primer ?

(*a*) *E. coli*
(*b*) *Vicia faba*
(*c*) Production of replicative form of ϕX174 genome
(*d*) Replication of RF form of ϕX174 genome.

148. In eukaryotic DNA replication, primase action is due to which of the following ?

(*a*) PCNA (*b*) Pol α
(*c*) Pol δ (*d*) MF 1

149. In *E. coli*, DNA replication regulation is mostly likely based on which of the following ?

(*a*) Methylation of A in origin.
(*b*) Methylation of C in origin
(*c*) Licensing factor
(*d*) DNA polymerase synthesis

150. Which of the options given in Q. 149 is relevant for eukaryotes ?

151. Which of the following DNA polymerases functions in mitochondria ?

(*a*) Pol β (*b*) Pol ε
(*c*) Pol γ (*d*) Pol δ

152. Which of the following steps are involved in fatty acid biosynthesis ?

I. Fatty acids biosynthesis are started in chloroplast using acetyl coenzyme A (acetyl-CoA) as monomer.
II. The first step in fatty acids biosynthesis is the formation of malonyl-CoA from acetyl-CoA followed by the exchange of CoA residue for the acyl-carrier protein.
III. One molecule of acetyl-CoA is condensed with one molecule of malonyl-CoA and forms acetoacetyl-ACP.
IV. Acetoacetyl-ACP is ultimately converted into butyryl-ACP (4 : 0); the chain length is now extended by adding malonyl-ACP in a stepwise manner.

Options :

(*a*) I, II, III (*b*) I, II, III, IV
(*c*) II, III, IV (*d*) I, III, IV

153. Most of the 18:0 molecules (stearic acid) are desaturated to 18:1 molecules (oleic acid) in which of following organelles ?
(*a*) Plastids
(*b*) Mitochondria
(*c*) Endoplasmic reticulum
(*d*) Peroxysomes

154. Further desaturation of 18:1 molecule occurs in association with which of the options given in Q. 153 ?

155. Which of the following ***is not a constituents*** of protoplasm ?
(*a*) Cell wall (*b*) Cell membrane
(*c*) Vacuole (*d*) Both (*a*) and (*c*)

5.2. FILL IN THE BLANKS

1. The catalytic site for CO_2 fixation by RuBISCO is present on its ....

2. The pH of lumen of the thylakoid membrane is less than ....

3. The *nifB* gene product is used for the synthesis of ....

4. Glutamate dehydrogenase and glutamine synthetase enzymes are involved in the assimilation of .... produced by N_2 fixation.

5. In plants, the conversion of fatty acids to sugars by a series of reactions is called .... cycle.

6. Carbon fixation is catalyzed by the enzyme .... which is widely claimed to be most abundant protein on earth.

7. The .... accounts for about two-third of the total oxidation of carbon compounds in most cells and its major end products are CO_2 and NADH.

8. In plants .... is a large polymer of glucose that serves as a carbohydrate reserve.

9. The phenomenon where the terminal bud of a shoot suppresses the growth of axillary buds is called ....

10. Ferredoxin is a component of ....

11. Replication of chloroplast DNA is controlled by .... DNA.

12. Non-cyclic photophosphorylation involves .... and ....

13. In C_4 plants, ... ATP molecules are required to produce one molecule of glucose in photosynthesis.

14. Porometer is used for measuring .... pressure.

15. In C_3 plants, ... ATP molecules are required to synthesize one molecule of glucose in photosynthesis.

16. Cellulose is a polymer of ....

17. Four ATP molecules are formed in glycolysis but net gain is .... molecules.

18. The energy currency of cell is ....

19. Glycolysis is also known as ....

20. Energy content of one molecule of glucose is ....

21. Photorespiration occurs only in the presence of ....

22. *Azotobacter* is a .... bacterium capable of nitrogen fixation.

23. *Lyngbya* and *Oscillatoria* are the .... forms of blue-green algae.

24. Oxidation of pyruvic acid to Acetyl-CoA produces .... of ATP.

25. Plants that pump CO_2 in bundle sheath are called .... plants and others are called .... plants.

26. If plants or other ogranisms are exposed to elevated temperatures, they begin to express a special set of proteins called .... proteins.

27. *The RbcS* gene is specifically expressed in .... but not in roots.

28. In many grasses and some dicot plants, major product of photosynthesis is sucrose and fructose polymers which are collectively called ....

29. In all organisms (except some photosynthetic bacteria), Rubisco exists as a heteromer with .... identical large subunits of about 56 kDa each encoded by a chloroplast gene and eight small identical subunits of about 14 kDa each encoded by a nuclear gene making a total of 560 kDa for the whole molecule.

30. A total of............polypeptides exist in ATP synthase, some of which are coded for by chloroplast DNA and some by nuclear DNA.

31. The structure of chloroplast ATP synthase is very similar to those in .... and ....

32. Rubisco is functional in all photosynthetic organisms except few ....

33. An active site of Rubisco that binds the substrates RuBP and CO_2 and activator or Mg^{2+} exists on each .... unit.

34. Rubisco and PEP carboxylase are activated by ....

35. In ...., photosynthesis is often limited by atmospheric CO_2 levels.

5.3. MARK TRUE OR FALSE

1. Chloroplasts have extra membrane-bound compartments which are called grana.
2. Leghaemoglobin is synthesized exclusively in nitrogen fixing nodules.
3. Oxidation of water during non-cyclic photophosphorylation (during photosynthesis) involves PS I only.
4. Chelating agents are inorganic in nature.
5. Transpiration is measured by Lysimeter.
6. Electron transport system occurs in Golgi bodies.
7. Starch is the most common form of carbohydrates, and is stored in leucoplasts.
8. In case of C_4 plants, photosynthesis takes place in bundle sheath cells and mesophyll cells.
9. During respiration, O_2 molecules are released from the mitochondria.
10. Glycolysis is an anaerobic process.
11. One molecule of $NADH_2$ contains 52 Kcal energy.
12. The products of light reaction are $NADH_2$ and ATP.
13. In photosynthesis, radient energy is converted into chemical energy.
14. Cytochromes are the carriers of electrons and involved in the respiratory electron transport chain.
15. C_4 plant species use less energy than C_3 plant species to fix one CO_2 molecule.
16. DNA, RNA and ribosomes are present in stroma where both transcription and translation occur.
17. snRNA is involved in RNA editing.
18. Blue light is always less efficient, on an energy basis, in photosynthesis than red light.
19. Two H_2O molecules (four electrons) are required to reduce each molecule of CO_2.
20. Besides the function of carotenoids as light harvesting pigments, they also protect chlorophyll against oxidative destruction by O_2 when irradiance level are high.
21. Four Mn atoms are associated with each PS II core system, and all the fout atoms are essential for O_2 release.
22. The gene for the 2Fe-2S polypeptide of cytochrome b_6-cytochrome f complex (cyt b_6-f) is present in the cytoplasm whereas genes for other three in the nucleus.
23. Release of one molecule of O_2 requires oxidation of two molecules of H_2O.
24. Two light photons are required to oxidize each molecule of H_2O.
25. The cyt b_6-f complex exists in roughly equal concentrations in grana and stroma thylakoids.
26. Major function of cyt b_6-f complex is to pass electron from PS I to PS II.
27. The overall function of cyt b_6-f is to use light energy to reduce oxidized plastoquinon

(PQ) to its fully reduced form PQH_2 using electron from water.

28. Acyl carrier protein is essential for fatty acid biosynthesis and forms thioesters with acyl groups.
29. The first step in fatty acid biosynthesis is the carboxylation of acetyl-CoA to yield malonyl-CoA.
30. The activity of enzyme AGPase has been identified as the rate limiting step in starch biosynthesis.
31. Glucose is the basic carbohydrate from which more complex carbohydrates are built up in the plant body.
32. Carbohydrates are compounds of carbon, hydrogen and oxygen.
33. Linoleic acid (18 : 2) and Lionlenic acid (18 : 3) are an example of non-essential fatty acids.
34. Sucrose is of very wide occurrence in plants and is especially abundant in the root of sugarbeet and stem of sugarcane.
35. Starch and cellulose are more common polysaccharides.

6

PLANT TISSUE CULTURE

6.1. MULTIPLE CHOICE QUESTIONS

1. Use of diploids in breeding of crops like potato offers which of the following advantages ?

(*a*) Much easier hybridization with diploid wild species, which offers many genes of great value.

(*b*) Much simpler segregation ratios and, as a result, the need for smaller segregating populations.

(*c*) A greater efficiency of selection.

(*d*) All of the above.

2. Match the columns A and B and pick the correct option from those listed below them.

Column A	Column B
A. Sexual hybridization	I. Distant hybridization
B. Recombinant DNA technology	II. Parasexual hybrid
C. Embryo rescue	III. Transgene
D. Protoplast fusion	IV. Limited to closely related species

Options :

(*a*) AI, BII, CIII, DIV

(*b*) AII, BIII, CIV, DI

(*c*) AIV, BIII, CI, DII

(*d*) AIII, BIV, CI, DII

3. Gametoclonal variation may occur due to which of the following ?

(*a*) Residual heterozygosity

(*b*) Gene mutation

(*c*) Gene amplification

(*d*) All of the above.

4. Which of the following is correct about anther culture ?

I. In *Brassica campestris,* pretreatment of anthers at 30-45°C gives better induction.

II. Cold treatment of anthers kills weak or non-viable anthers and microspores, while arresting many of the microspores in the first mitosis, as starch production is blocked.

III. High concentration (6-12%) of sucrose is essential for androgenesis.

IV. Anthers are generally cultured in the dark at 20-30°C, but regenerated plantlets are transferred to light.

Options :

(*a*) I, II, III, IV (*b*) I, II, III

(*c*) II, III, IV (*d*) III, IV

5. Match the columns A and B and select the correct option from those listed below them.

Column A	Column B
A. Transgene	I. PEG
B. Meristem	II. Gene isolation
C. Probe	III. Transgenic
D. Fusogen	IV. Micropropagation

Options :

(*a*) AI, BIV, CIII, DII

(*b*) AIII, BIV, CII, DI

(*c*) AII, BIII, CI, DIV

(*d*) AIV, BII, CI, DIII

6. Match the columns A and B and select the correct option from those listed below them.

Column A	Column B
A. Auxin	1. Yabuta and Hayashi
B. Gibberellin	2. Wareing

C. Cytokinin 3. Went
D. Dormin 4. Letham

Options :

(*a*) A3, B1, C4, D2 (*b*) A2, B4, C3, D1
(*c*) A4, B2, C1, D3 (*d*) A1, B3, C2, D4

7. In 1922, Blakeslee and coworkers, for the first time, reported occurrence of haploids in *Datura* due to which of the following processes ?

(*a*) Androgenesis
(*b*) Gynogenesis
(*c*) Parthenogenesis
(*d*) Mutagenesis

8. Which of the following ***is not correct*** about haploid production ?

I. In 1964, Guha and Maheshwari reported *in vitro* production of haploids through anther culture.
II. Androgenic induction is only possible with immature anthers, containing immature pollen.
III. The early or mid-uninuleate stage of microspore development is the most responsive stage in most of the species.
IV. Bulbosum method of haploid production is the most successful in barley and wheat.

Options :

(*a*) I, II, III, IV (*b*) I, II, IV
(*c*) II, III, IV (*d*) II, III

9. During distant hybridization, problem of endosperm abortion can be overcome by which of the following ?

(*a*) Embryo culture (*b*) Ovary culture
(*c*) Ovule culture (*d*) All of the above

10. Which of the following are the characteristic of cytokinins ?

I. Initiate cell division.
II. Induce flowering in long-day plants.
III. Counteract apical dominance.
IV. Promote *in vitro* shoot regeneration.

Select the correct answer from given options.

(*a*) I, III, IV (*b*) I, IV
(*c*) II, III, IV (*d*) III, IV

11. In plant tissue cultures, ABA may effect which of the following ?

(*a*) Enhance shoot bud differentiation
(*b*) Promote somatic embryo maturation
(*c*) Induce somatic embryo coversion
(*d*) Both (*a*) and (*b*)

12. Plants with gametic chromosome number are termed as which of the following ?

(*a*) Diploid (*b*) Dihaploid
(*c*) Haploid (*d*) Monoploid

13. Micropropagation can be achieved through which of the following ?

(*a*) Enhanced axillary branching
(*b*) Somatic embryogenesis
(*c*) Production of adventitious shoot buds
(*d*) All of the above

14. How many types of synthetic seeds have been proposed ?

I. Uncoated, desiccated somatic embryos.
II. Coated, desiccated somatic embryos.
III. Encapsulated, hydrated somatic embryos.
IV. Hydrated somatic shoot buds within a gel.

Options :

(*a*) I, II, III, IV (*b*) I, II, III
(*c*) II, III, IV (*d*) II, IV

15. Which of the following are characteristics of an auxin ?

I. Prevents apical bud dominance.
II. Involved in differentiation of xylem.
III. Delayed abscission.
IV. Basipetal translocation.

Select the correct answer from given options.

(*a*) I, II (*b*) II, III, IV
(*c*) I, III (*d*) II, III

16. Match the columns A and B, and select the correct option from those listed below them.

Column A	Column B
A. Haploid	1. Secondary nucleus
B. Diploid	2. Antipodal cells
C. Triploid	3. Endosperm

Options :

(*a*) A2, B1, C3 (*b*) A2, B3, C1
(*c*) A3, B2, C1 (*d*) A1, B2, C3

17. Match the columns A and B, and select the correct option from those listed below them.

Column A	Column B
A. Auxin	1. Fruit ripening
B. ABA	2. Shoot elongation
C. Ethylene	3. Stress hormone
D. GA	4. Apical dominance

Options :
(*a*) A3, B2, C4, D1 (*b*) A4, B3, C1, D2
(*c*) A4, B1, C3, D2 (*d*) A4, B3, C2, D1

18. Somatic embryos can be used for which of the following ?
(*a*) Genetic transformation
(*b*) Production of uniform plant populations
(*c*) *In vitro* mutagenesis
(*d*) All of the above

19. Progress in haploid and dihaploid production is still slow due to which of the following bottlenecks ?
(*a*) High levels of albinism, especially in monocots.
(*b*) Low frequency of plantlet regeneration.
(*c*) Genetic instability.
(*d*) All of the above

20. Which of the following hydrogels have been used for encapsulation of hydrated somatic embryos ?
I. Sodium and potassium alginate.
II. Carageenan and Gel-Rite.
III. Sodium pectate and agar.
IV. Tragacanth and guar-gum.

Options :
(*a*) I, II, III, IV (*b*) I, III, IV
(*c*) II, III, IV (*d*) I, III

21. Somaclonal variation occurs due to which of the following ?
(*a*) Methylation and demethylation in the promoter region of genes.
(*b*) Activation of silent genes in multigene families.
(*c*) Non-reciprocal mitotic recombination and activation of transposable elements.
(*d*) All of the above.

22. Which of the following are characteristics of gibbrellic acid ?
I. Prevents genetic and physiological dwarfism.
II. In tissue culture, elongation of shoot.
III. Induces flowering in long-day plants.
IV. Induces bud dormancy.

Select the correct answer from given options.
(*a*) I, II, III (*b*) II, III, IV
(*c*) I, III, IV (*d*) I, IV

23. Among the given hydrogels, which one is the most preferred ?
(*a*) Agarose (*b*) Sodium alginate
(*c*) Agar (*d*) Gel-Rite

24. Which of the following is correct about bulbosum technique of hapoid production ?
I. This method was reported by Kasha and Kao in 1970.
II. It is based on chromosome elimination during early embryo development.
III. *Hordeum vulgare* is crossed with *H. bulbosum*.
IV. Embryo rescue/culture is essential for obtaining haploid plants from the crosses between *Triticum aestivum* and *H. bulbosum*.

Options :
(*a*) I, II, III, IV (*b*) I, II, III
(*c*) II, III, IV (*d*) III, IV

25. GA_3 is known to effect which of the following ?
(*a*) Suppress callus formation.
(*b*) Promote somatic embryo conversion.
(*c*) Promote shoot regeneration in some species.
(*d*) All of the above.

26. Survival of encapsulated somatic embryos has often been reported to be lower than that of the non-encapsulated ones probably due to which of the following ?
(*a*) Poor respiration under the almost anaerobic condition within the capsule.
(*b*) Poor photosynthesis
(*c*) Poor storage of food material
(*d*) All of the above.

27. Ethylene promotes which of the following ?
(*a*) Activity of cell wall destroying enzymes
(*b*) Ageing of leaves
(*c*) Activity of chlorophyllase
(*d*) All of the above

28. Guha and Maheshwari produced haploids from anther culture of which of the following.
(*a*) *Nicotiana* (*b*) *Datura*
(*c*) *Ginkgo* (*d*) *Hordeum*

29. Somaclonal variation generally serves the same purpose as which of the following ?
(*a*) Analytical breeding
(*b*) Mutation breeding
(*c*) Backcross breeding
(*d*) Hybrid sorting

30. Column A contains a list of GRs while column B contains their function in plants. Match the two columns carefully and select the correct option from those listed below them.

Column A	Column B
A. Ethylene	1. Abscission of leaves
B. ABA	2. Cell division
C. Auxin	3. Degreening of citrus and banana
D. Cytokinin	4. Parthenocarpy

Options :
(*a*) A3, B1, C4, D2 (*b*) A1, B2, C4, D3
(*c*) A4, B3, C2, D1 (*d*) A2, B1, C3, D4

31. Match the columns A and B carefully and select the correct option from those listed below them.

Column A	Column B
A. Natural auxin	1. Ethrel
B. Synthetic auxin	2. Dormin
C. Abscissic acid	3. IAA
D. Ethylene	4. IBA

Options :
(*a*) A2, B3, C1, D4 (*b*) A3, B4, C2, D1
(*c*) A4, B2, C3, D1 (*d*) A1, B2, C4, D3

32. Column A contains different hormones and column B contains a list of sources from which they are isolated. Match these two columns carefully and select the correct option from those listed below them.

Column A	Column B
A. Kinetin	1. Coconut milk
B. Abscisin II	2. Cotton boll
C. GA_3	3. *Gibberella fujikuroi*
D. Zeatin riboside	4. Herring sperm DNA

Options :
(*a*) A1, B2, C4, D3 (*b*) A2, B3, C1, D4
(*c*) A3, B4, C1, D2 (*d*) A4, B2, C3, D1

33. Which of the following ***is not correct*** about abscissic acid ?
(*a*) It is a naturally occuring growth inhibitor.
(*b*) It destroys the effect of GA and promotes dormancy in buds and seeds.
(*c*) It is synthesized in leaves.
(*d*) Precursor of ABA is malic acid.

34. Which of the following scientists first reported interspecific hybridization through protoplast fusion in two species of *Nicotiana* ?
(*a*) Powers and coworkers
(*b*) Carlson and coworkers
(*c*) Miller and coworkers
(*d*) Cocking and coworkers

35. Column A contains a list of some techniques/events and column B contains their applications. Match the two columns carefully and select the correct option from those listed below them.

Column A	Column B
A. Micropropagation	1. Virus eradication
B. Regeneration	2. Rapid clonal multiplication
C. Androgenesis	3. Haploid plants
D. Meristem culture	4. Organogenesis and somatic embryogenesis

Options :
(*a*) A2, B4, C3, D1 (*b*) A4, B3, C2, D1
(*c*) A1, B2, C3, D4 (*d*) A4, B2, C1, D3

36. ***Assertion (A)***: The *bulbosum* method is used for the production of haploids in wheat.
Mecahanism (M): This method is based on chromosome elimination during early embryo development.

Options :
(*a*) Only A is correct.
(*b*) Only M is correct.
(*c*) Both A and M are correct.
(*d*) Both A and M are correct and M is the correct explanation of A.

37. Which of the following is correct about ethylene ?
I. It is a natural product of ripening fruit.
II. Chemical name of ethrel is 2-chloroethylphosphonic acid.
III. It is phytogerontological hormone.
IV. Ethylene treatment increases the number of female flowers in cucumber.

Options :
(*a*) I, II, III, IV (*b*) I, II, III
(*c*) I, III, IV (*d*) II, III, IV

38. Use of which of the following minimizes the risk of variation during *in vitro* conservation of germplasm ?
(*a*) Shoot apices
(*b*) Zygotic embryos
(*c*) Somatic embryos
(*d*) Both (*a*) and (*b*)

39. Which of the following factors is responsible for the loss of plant genetic resources ?
I. Replacement of local genotypes with high yielding varieties including hybrids and transgenics.
II. Urbanization and industrilization.
III. Modern farming practices.
IV. Extension of farming into wild habitats.

Options :
(*a*) I, II, III (*b*) I, II, IV
(*c*) I, II, III, IV (*d*) I, IV

40. ***Assertion (A)***: Ethylene causes abscission of leaf.
Cause (C): Ethylene enhances the activity of cell wall destroying enzymes.

Options :
(*a*) Both A and C are correct and C correctly explains A.
(*b*) Both A and C are correct, but C does not explain A.
(*c*) Only A is correct.
(*d*) Only C is correct.

41. Success in germplasm storage is determined by which of the following factors ?
(*a*) Inherent longevity and physiological storage behaviour of the species.
(*b*) Initial quality (*e.g.*, moisture content) of material stored.
(*c*) Storage methods and conditions used.
(*d*) All of the above.

42. Pusa Jai Kisan (Bio-902) is a somaclonal variety of which of the following crops ?
(*a*) Rapeseed (*b*) Indian mustard
(*c*) Groundnut (*d*) Sunflower

43. Which of the following materials is conserved as germplasm ?
(*a*) Wild taxa related to crop species, weedy forms and land races.
(*b*) Obsolate varieties and advanced cultivars.
(*c*) Parents of hybrids, mutants and cytogenetic stocks.
(*d*) All of the above

44. Which of the following varieties was developed through somatic hybridization followed by backcross ?
(*a*) Delgold (*b*) Sigma
(*c*) A.C. Chang (*d*) Both (*a*) and (*c*)

45. Which of the options given in Q. 45 is a variety that was developed from somaclonal variants ?

46. Which of the following requirements must be fulfilled by any tissue culture technique that is used for conservation of germplasm ?
I. Genetic stability of the material to be preserved should be guaranteed.
II. A well-defined protocol which guarantees a high percentage of plant recovery from stored tissue.
III. Plant virus elimination from the stored tissues/organs.

Options :
(*a*) I, II, III (*b*) I, II
(*c*) II, III (*d*) I, III

47. Which of the following steps are involved in conservation of plant genetic resources ?
I. Exploration and collection of germplasm.
II. Conservation and evaluation of germplasm.
III. Data storage and retrieval.
IV. Utilization, training and global coordination.

Options :
(*a*) I, II, III, IV (*b*) I, II, III
(*c*) II, III, IV (*d*) I, III, IV

48. Why conservation of genetic resources is so important ?
(*a*) Due to piracy of genetic resource.
(*b*) Due to regular use in plant breeding.
(*c*) Due to genetic erosion and epidemics.
(*d*) All of the above.

49. The National Research Centre on Plant Biotechology is located at which of the following places ?
(*a*) New Delhi (*b*) Hyderabad
(*c*) Pune (*d*) Kolkata

50. Cryopreservation is based on which of the following ?
(*a*) Liquid CO_2 (*b*) Liquid helium
(*c*) Liquid nitrogen (*d*) Both (*a*) and (*c*)

51. Which of the following is thermolabile ?
(*a*) Zeatin (*b*) Pectinase
(*c*) ABA (*d*) All of the above

52. Which of the following scientists is regarded as father of plant tissue culture ?
(*a*) Herbert E. Street
(*b*) Gottlieb Haberlandt
(*c*) Jean P. Nitsch
(*d*) Philip R. White

53. Which of following is correct about alloplasmic lines ?
I. A line having nucleus of one species and cytoplasm of another species.
II. Produced by cybridization/repeated backcrossing.
III. Used for production of cytoplasmic male sterile lines.

Options :
(*a*) I, II, III (*b*) II, III
(*c*) I, III (*d*) II

54. The technique of embryo culture can be used to obtain which of the following ?
(*a*) Interspecific hybrids
(*b*) Propagation of orchids
(*c*) Overcoming dormancy and to shorten breeding cycle
(*d*) All of the above

55. For long-term storage of germplasm, which of the following is used ?
(*a*) Carbon dioxide (*b*) Liquid oxygen
(*c*) Liquid nitrogen (*d*) Mineral oil

56. Which of the following enzymes is used for obtaining protoplasts ?
(*a*) Maccrozyme (*b*) Cellulase
(*c*) Pectinase (*d*) All of the above

57. In general, callus cultures are subcultured after which of the following periods ?
(*a*) 4-6 days (*b*) 4-6 weeks
(*c*) 8-10 weeks (*d*) 2-3 months

58. Somatic embryo maturation ***is not*** promoted by which of the following ?
(*a*) Cytokinin
(*b*) High sucrose
(*c*) Partial desiccation
(*d*) Abscissic acid

59. The technique of cryopreservation involves which of the following ?
(*a*) Freezing and storage
(*b*) Thawing and reculture
(*c*) Freezing and reculture
(*d*) Both (*a*) and (*b*)

60. The term somaclonal variation was coined by which of the following scientists ?
(*a*) Vasil and Vasil
(*b*) Larkin and Scowcroft
(*c*) Skirvin and Karp
(*d*) Evans and Sharp

61. Protoplast fusion is induced by which of the following treatments ?
(*a*) High voltage electric pulse
(*b*) High pH (10.5) and high (50 m mol/l) Ca^{2+} concentration
(*c*) Polyethylene glycol (PEG)
(*d*) All of the above

62. In general, suspension cultures are sub-cultured after which of the following periods.
(*a*) 1-2 weeks (*b*) 10-15 days
(*c*) 3-10 days (*d*) 15-18 days

63. Among the given auxins, which one is the most frequently used in plant tissue culture ?
(*a*) 2, 4-D (*b*) IBA
(*c*) NAA (*d*) IAA

64. Pusa Jai Kisan (BIO-902) somaclone of Indian mustard was isolated from which of the following varieties ?
(*a*) Pusa Bold (*b*) Kranti
(*c*) Varuna (*d*) Karuna

65. Meristem culture can be used for which of the following purposes ?
I. Recovery of virus-free plants.
II. Clonal propagation.
III. Germplasm exchange and conservation.

Options :
(*a*) I, II, III (*b*) II, III
(*c*) I, III (*d*) I, II

66. Delgold and A.C. Chang, developed through somatic hybridization, are cultivars of which of the following ?
(*a*) *Nicotiana rustica*
(*b*) *Nicotiana tabacum*
(*c*) *Lycopersion esculentum*
(*d*) *Brassica napus*

67. Among the given compounds, which one is the most commonly used as cryoprotectant ?
(*a*) Proline (*b*) Sorbitol
(*c*) DMSO (*d*) Glycerol

68. In which of the following tree species, embryo culture is used to overcome dormancy ?
(*a*) *Taxus* (*b*) *Iris*
(*c*) *Prunus* (*d*) All of the above

69. Among the given varieties of tobacco, which one was developed through haploid phase ?
(*a*) F211 (*b*) DD413
(*c*) GSH3 (*d*) All of the above

70. Sugarcane somaclone Ono, isolated from the parental variety Pindar, is resistant to a disease caused by which of the following ?
(*a*) Fungus (*b*) Virus
(*c*) Mycoplasma (*d*) Bacterium

71. Scarlet is somaclone of which of the following ?
(*a*) Wheat (*b*) Sorghum
(*c*) Sweet potato (*d*) Potato

72. Among the given agents, which one is used as cryoprotectants ?
(*a*) DMSO, proline and valine
(*b*) DMSO, glycerol and proline
(*c*) DMSO, glycerol and acetic acid
(*d*) DMSO, arginine and acetic acid

73. Delgold is a variety of which of the following ?
(*a*) Cheroot tobacco
(*b*) Flue-cured tobacco
(*c*) Chewing tobacco
(*d*) Cigar and wrapper tobacco

74. The first plant from a mature plant cell was regenerated by which of the following.
(*a*) Braun (*b*) Haberlandt
(*c*) Cocking (*d*) White

75. During gynogenesis, haploid plants generally originate from which of the following ?
(*a*) Synergids (*b*) Antipodal cells
(*c*) Egg cell (*d*) Polar nuclei

76. In which of the following, somaclonal variation can occur ?
I. Direct somatic embryogenesis.
II. Direct adventitious shoot regeneration.
III. Axillary shoot proliferation.
IV. Suspension culture.
Options
(*a*) I, II, III (*b*) II, III, IV
(*c*) I, II, IV (*d*) I, II, III, IV

77. In question 76, which system is likely to show the least occurrence of somaclonal variation ?
(*a*) I, II (*b*) II, III
(*c*) III (*d*) I, IV

78. In question 76, which system is likely to yield the highest frequency of somaclones ?
(*a*) I, II (*b*) II, III
(*c*) I, II, IV (*d*) IV

79. Somatic hybridization has been the most successful in which of the following.
(*a*) Graminae
(*b*) Leguminosae
(*c*) Malvaceae
(*d*) Solanaceae and cruciferae

80. Among the given supplements/additives, which is an example of complex organic supplement/additive ?
(*a*) Coconut milk and tomato juice
(*b*) Corn milk and malt extract
(*c*) Yeast extract and casein hydrolysate
(*d*) All of the above

81. Tobacco cultivar A.C. Chang is resistant to which of the following ?
(*a*) Leaf curl (*b*) Black rot
(*c*) Damping off (*d*) TMV

82. Evergreen is a somaclone of which of the following ?
(*a*) Blackberry (*b*) Potato
(*c*) Cucumber (*d*) Carrot

83. Among the given surface sterilizing agents, which one gives the best result ?
(*a*) Silver nitrate
(*b*) Cetrimide
(*c*) Calcium or sodium hypochlorite
(*d*) Bromine water

84. Slow-growth shoot culture protocols have been developed for which of the following ?
(*a*) Coconut and citrus
(*b*) Sweet potato and garlic
(*c*) Ginger and banana
(*d*) Both (*b*) and (*c*)

85. Somaclone Scarlet has improvement in which of the following traits ?
(*a*) Skin colour
(*b*) Insect resistance
(*c*) Yield
(*d*) Disease resistance

86. Hyperhydracity of cultures ***may not be*** reduced by which of the following ?
(*a*) Agar hydrolysate
(*b*) Growth retardants
(*c*) Higher agar concentration
(*d*) Gibberellic acid

87. The cultivar A.C. Chang and Delgold were released for commercial cultivation in which of the following countries ?
(*a*) Japan (*b*) China
(*c*) Canada (*d*) Germany

88. Among the given varieties of rice, which one was developed through haploid phase ?
(*a*) IR36 (*b*) Shin Shu
(*c*) Pragati (*d*) IR8

89. Andro is a somaclone of which of the following ?
(*a*) Flax (*b*) Apple
(*c*) Maize (*d*) Cotton

90. Somaclone Adro represents improvement in which of the following traits ?
(*a*) Salt tolerance
(*b*) Oil quality
(*c*) Disease resistance
(*d*) Yield

91. In protoplast isolation and culture, ionic osmoticum ***is not preferred*** because of which of the following ?
(*a*) It reduces protoplast survival
(*b*) It reduces protoplast yield
(*c*) It reduces protoplast fusion
(*d*) It inhibits cell wall regeneration

92. For long-term *in vitro* storage of plant germplasm, which of the following is in practical use ?
(*a*) Cryopreservation
(*b*) Lyophilization
(*c*) Slow-growth cultures
(*d*) Both (*a*) and (*c*)

93. PEG-induced protoplast fusion is enhanced by which of the following ?
(*a*) High pH PEG treatment medium.
(*b*) High pH high Ca^{2+} washing medium
(*c*) High Ca^{2+} culture medium
(*d*) Low pH PEG treatment medium.

94. Distant crosses may fail due to which of the following ?
(*a*) Lack of pollen germination
(*b*) Failure of pollen tube growth
(*c*) Degeneration of endosperm
(*d*) All of the above

95. Among the given varieties of wheat, which one was developed through haploid phase ?
(*a*) Jinghua 1 (*b*) Janak
(*c*) Arjun (*d*) Pb543

96. Somaclone Andro has improvement in which of the following traits ?
(*a*) Rust immunity
(*b*) Powdery mildew resistance
(*c*) Wilt resistance
(*d*) Leaf spot resistance

97. Bio-13 is a somaclone of which of the following ?
(*a*) *Mentha arvensis* (*b*) *B. juncea*
(*c*) *Zea mays* (*d*) *Cironella java*

98. Intergeneric hybrids from which of the following crosses have been recovered through embryo culture ?
(*a*) *Hordeum vulgare* × *Triticum aestivum*
(*b*) *Triticum aestivum* × *Agropyron repens*
(*c*) *Hordeum vulgare* × *Secale cereale*
(*d*) All of the above

99. Which of the following options depicts the correct order of steps in somatic hybridization ?
I. Isolation of protoplasts
II. Selection of hybrid cells
III. Regeneration of hybrid plants
IV. Fusion of protoplasts

Options :
(*a*) I, II, IV, III (*b*) I, IV, II, III
(*c*) I, IV, III, II (*d*) I, III, IV, II

100. Which of the following steps are involved in cryopreservation ?
I. Freezing II. Storage
III. Thawing IV. Preculture

Options :
(*a*) I, II, III, IV (*b*) I, II, IV
(*c*) II, III, IV (*d*) I, IV

101. The positive cell selection approach may be classified into which of the following ?

I. Rescue method
II. Direct selection
III. Double selection
IV. Step-wise selection

Options :

(*a*) I, II, III (*b*) II, III, IV
(*c*) I, II, III, IV (*d*) III, IV

102. Anther culture ordinarily yields which of the following ?

(*a*) Haploid plants
(*b*) Disomic plants
(*c*) Polyploid plants
(*d*) Doubled haploid plants

103. Somaclonal variation arises due to which of the following ?

(*a*) Change in chromosome number
(*b*) Deletion/duplication
(*c*) Gene mutation/gene amplification
(*d*) All of the above

104. Sugarcane somaclone Ono was isolated from which variety listed below ?

(*a*) Co1148 (*b*) Pindar
(*c*) BO 54 (*d*) CoS771

105. Stirred tank reactors can be used as which of the following ?

I. Multistage bioreactors
II. Batch bioreactors
III. Immobilised cell bioreactors
IV. Continuous bioreactors

Options :

(*a*) I, II, III (*b*) I, II, IV
(*c*) I, II, III, IV (*d*) II, III, IV

106. 'New alleles' of known genes and even 'new mutations' of genes not known so far have been recovered through which of the following ?

(*a*) Embryo rescue
(*b*) Somaclonal variation
(*c*) Somatic hybridization
(*d*) Cybridization

107. Column A lists some compounds, while column B lists plant species from which these compounds are produced. Match both the columns carefully and select the correct option from those listed below them.

Column A	Column B
A. Quinine	I. *Taxus* species
B. Shikonin	II. *Lithospermum erythrorhizon*
C. Taxol	III. *Coptis japonica*
D. Berberine	IV. Cinchona

Options :

(*a*) AI, BIII, CIV, DII
(*b*) AIII, BI, CII, DIV
(*c*) AIV, BII, CI, DIII
(*d*) AII, BIV, CIII, DI

108. Column A contains some compounds, while column B contains their medicinal value. Match both the columns carefully and select the correct option from those listed below them.

Column A	Column B
A. Shikonin	I. Breast and ovarian cancer treatment
B. Taxol	II. Antimalarial
C. Quinine	III. Antiseptic
D. Berberine	IV. Anti-inflammatory

Options :

(*a*) AIII, BI, CII, DIV
(*b*) AIV, BIII, CI, DII
(*c*) AII, BIV, CIII, DI
(*d*) AI, BII, CIV, DIII

109. Column A contains some groups of biochemicals, while column B contains their examples. Match both the columns carefully and select the correct option from those listed below them.

Column A	Column B
A. Steroids	I. Anthraquinones
B. Terpenoids	II. Anthocyanins
C. Phenylpropanoids	III. Diosgenin
D. Quinones	IV. Menthol

Options :

(*a*) AI, BII, CIV, DIII
(*b*) AII, BI, CIII, DIV
(*c*) AIII, BIV, CII, DI
(*d*) AIV, BIII, CI, DII

110. Conventional *in vitro* environment used for micropropagation has which of the following features ?

I. Constant temperature and high relative humidity.

II. High sugar concentration and growth regulators.
III. Low photosynthetic photon flux density.
IV. Large differences in light and dark period CO_2 concentrations.

Options :

(*a*) I, II, III (*b*) I, II, III, IV
(*c*) I, II, IV (*d*) II, III, IV

111. Which of the following ***is not correct*** about micropropation ?
(*a*) Vitrification may be a problem in some species.
(*b*) Somaclonal variation may arise during *in vitro* culture.
(*c*) High production cost has limited the use of this technique to more valuable ornamental crops and some fruit trees.
(*d*) Suitable techniques of micro-propagation are available for all valuable species.

112. Which of the following ***is not correct*** about taxol ?
(*a*) It acts on spindle like colchicine.
(*b*) It promotes dissolution of microtubules into tubulin molecules.
(*c*) It is used for treatment of breast and ovarian cancer.
(*d*) It is obtained from *Trichosanthes* sp.

113. Secondary metabolites include which of the following compounds ?
(*a*) Terpenoids
(*b*) Alkaloids
(*c*) Phenylpropanoids
(*d*) All of the above

114. Biomass yields from cell cultures can generally be enhanced by which of the following approaches ?
(*a*) Use of larger inoculum size.
(*b*) Modification of nutrient medium.
(*c*) Selection of high producing cell clones.
(*d*) Both (*a*) and (*b*)

115. Biochemical production by cultured cells can be increased by using which of the following approaches ?
I. Development of high producing clones.
II. Optimization of medium and culture conditions.
III. Use of elicitors.
IV. Use of organ cultures and two-phase systems.

Options :

(*a*) I, II, III, IV (*b*) II, III, IV
(*c*) I, III, IV (*d*) I, II, IV

116. Which of the following ***is not an example*** of alkaloid ?
(*a*) Morphine (*b*) Codeine
(*c*) Camphor (*d*) Berberine

117. Somatic hybridization produces which of the following ?
(*a*) Cybrids
(*b*) Symmetric hybrids
(*c*) Asymmetric hybrids
(*d*) All of the above

118. Somatic hybrids are also called which of the following ?
(*a*) Parasexual hybrids
(*b*) Cytoplasmic hybrids
(*c*) Vybrids
(*d*) Both (*a*) and (*b*)

119. Which of the following ***is not correct*** about asymmetric hybrids ?
(*a*) Asymmetric hybrids provide an opportunity for introgression of few desirable genes from one fusion partner into the other.
(*b*) Degree of chromosome elimination does not appear to depend on the irradiation dose; it seems to depend mainly on the species combination used in the fusion.
(*c*) Asymmetric hybrids can be produced by fusion of cytoplasts of a species with irradiated protoplsts of another species.
(*d*) Several asymmetric hybrids have been produced in *Nicotiana, Brassica,* etc.

120. Which of the following ***is not correct*** about biotransformation ?
(*a*) Biotransformation reactions are catalyzed by enzymes present in cells.
(*b*) Products generated by biotransform ation are more useful or valuable than the precursors used.
(*c*) Low rate of biotransformation prevents commercial exploitation of the very large number of bioconversions known for plant cells.
(*d*) Arbutin is produced commercially by biotransformation.

121. Which of the following plant species, biotransforms hydroquinone into β-D-glucoside (Arbutin) ?
(*a*) *Rauwolfia serpentina*
(*b*) *Datura innoxia*
(*c*) *Catharanthus roseus*
(*d*) All of the above

122. A spin-filter bioreactor is a good example of which of the following ?
(*a*) Fluidized bed reactor
(*b*) Continuous-flow bioreactor
(*c*) Air lift bioreactor
(*d*) All of the above

123. Micropropagation of woody trees presents which of the following problems ?
(*a*) Difficulties in rooting
(*b*) Browning of medium
(*c*) Poor growth *in vitro*
(*d*) All of the above

124. Which of the following advantages is correct about micropropagation ?
I. Limited to a particular season.
II. Plants can be maintained *in vitro* in a pathogen-free state.
III. Extremely high multiplication rates.
IV. Plants of desired sex can be selectively multiplied.

Options :
(*a*) I, II, III, IV (*b*) II, III, IV
(*c*) I, III, IV (*d*) I, II, IV

125. Which of the following limitations is correct about somaclonal variation ?
I. Many variants may arise as a result of pleiotropic effects and may not be true variants.
II. The technique is applicable to those species cell cultures of which regenerate complete plants.
III. Selected cell lines often show reduced or no regeneration potential.
IV. Many selected clones show undesirable features like reduced fertility, growth and even overall performance.

Options :
(*a*) I, II, III, IV (*b*) II, III, IV
(*c*) I, II, III (*d*) I, II, IV

126. Symmetric hybrids produced through protoplast fusion provide which of the following opportunities in crop improvement programmes ?
I. Production of hybrids between non-flowering/sterile lines.
II. Creation of superior hybrids.
III. Widening of genetic base of an allopolyploid.
IV. Generation of novel materials for scientific studies.

Options :
(*a*) I, II, III (*b*) I, III, IV
(*c*) I, II, III, IV (*d*) I, II, IV

127. Protoplasts can be used for genetic transformation by which of the following techniques ?
(*a*) PEG-mediated DNA uptake
(*b*) Liposome-mediated delivery
(*c*) Electroporation
(*d*) All of the above.

128. Which of the following limitations is correct about somatic hybridization.
I. Techniques for protoplast isolation, culture or fusion may not be available.
II. Many somatic hybrids either do not regenerate or give rise to sterile regenerants.
III. Many somatic hybrids show genetic instability, which may be an inherent feature of some species combinations.
IV. In many cases, chromosome elimination occurs from somatic hybrids leading to asymmertic hybrid.

Options :
(*a*) I, II, III, IV (*b*) II, III, IV
(*c*) I, II, III (*d*) I, II, IV

129. Which of the following advantages is correct about *in vitro* techniques of germplasm storage ?
I. Germplasm can be stored for long periods.
II. Limited space is required for germplasm storage.
III. *In vitro* storage of germplasm increases the risk of error in labelling.
IV. Storage of germplasm free from diseases, insects and other pathogens is possible.

Options :
(*a*) I, II, III (*b*) I, II, III, IV
(*c*) I, II, IV (*d*) I, III, IV

130. *In vitro* conservation of germplasm of vegetatively reproducing plants or those producing recalcitrant seeds can be achieved by which of the following ?
I. Desiccated somatic embryos/artificial seeds.
II. DNA clones.
III. Freeze preservation of cells/tissues/ organs.
IV. Fast-growth cultures.
Options :
(*a*) I, II, III, IV (*b*) I, II, III
(*c*) I, III, IV (*d*) II, III, IV

131. Which of the following advantages is correct about somatic hybridization ?
I. Somatic hybrids can be produced between sexually incompatible species/ sterile parents/nonflowering strains.
II. Mitochondria of one species can be combined with chloroplasts of another species.
III. Cytoplasm can be transferred from one line/species into another in one year.
IV. Recombinant organelles can be produced by somatic hybridization.

Options :
(*a*) I, II, III (*b*) II, III, IV
(*c*) I, III, IV (*d*) I, II, III, IV

132. Which of the following limitations is correct about haploid production ?
I. Plants other than haploids are often recovered from anther cultures/inter-specific hybrids.
II. A non-random recovery of haploids may reduce the spectrum of variability recovered.
III. In some species like *Nicotiana* sp., anther culture may lead to reduced performance.
IV. In many crops, lack of a reliable haploid production protocol limits the use of this techniques ?

Options :
(*a*) I, II, III (*b*) II, III, IV
(*c*) I, III, IV (*d*) I, II, III, IV

133. Which of the following limitations is associated with biochemical production from cultured plant cells ?
(*a*) Often cultured plant cells do not produce compounds of high commercial value.
(*b*) High production cost is the major disadvantage.
(*c*) Due to lack of basic knowledge of the biosynthetic pathways, many systems are difficult to improve.
(*d*) All of the above.

134. Which of the following ***is not a feature*** of somaclonal variation ?
(*a*) A very effective selection can be practised at the cell level for several traits.
(*b*) Some new alleles or even 'new' mutations may be isolated, which were not available in the germplasm or through mutagenesis.
(*c*) Somaclonal variation occurs in very low frequency.
(*d*) Use of somaclonal variation may reduce the time required for the release of new variety as compared to mutation breeding.

135. Which of the following advantages are offered by haploids ?
I. Desirable mutants may be selected at the haploid level.
II. Their chromosome number may be doubled to obtain homozygous lines in a single generation.
III. Selection among doubled haploid lines is at least 6-8 times as efficient as that among segregating populations.
IV. Production of homozygous doubled haploid lines using haploids saves atleast 4 years in comparison to selfing/close inbreeding.

Options :
(*a*) I, II, III, IV (*b*) I, II, III
(*c*) II, III, IV (*d*) I, III, IV

136. Which of the following dis-advantages is correct about *in vitro* techniques of germplasm storage ?
I. In majority of plant species, preserved shoot-tip derived plants may show genetic instability.

II. Sophisticated facilities are required (particularly for freeze preservation and DNA cloning).
III. *In vitro* techniques demand a greater skill in handling and maintenance than do conventional techniques.
IV. Cells/tissues become damaged during cryopreservation.

Options :
(*a*) I, II, III (*b*) I, II, III, IV
(*c*) I, III, IV (*d*) II, III, IV

137. Which of the following limitations are associated with haploid production ?
I. High frequency of albinos are produced in anther cultures of monocots, especially cereals.
II. Occurrence of gametoclonal variations may limit the usefulness of pollen embryos for genetic transformation/gene transfer.
III. In many crops, large number of haploids can not be easily obtained.
IV. A sophisticated tissue culture laboratory and a dependable greenhouse are essential for success.

Options :
(*a*) I, II, IV (*b*) II, III, IV
(*c*) I, II, III, IV (*d*) I, III, IV

138. It is desirable to preserve which of the following tissues to minimise the risk of genetic instability ?
(*a*) Zygotic embryos
(*b*) Shoot-tips
(*c*) Suspension cultures
(*d*) Either (*a*) or (*b*)

139. Which of the following are the characteristic features of batch bioreactors ?
I. Constant level of cellular wastes.
II. Continuous change in the composition of cells.
III. Continuous depletion of nutrients.
IV. Alteration in growth rate.

Options :
(*a*) I, II, III, IV (*b*) I, III, IV
(*c*) II, III, IV (*d*) III, IV

140. Which of the following problems are correct about large scale culture of plant cells ?
I. The longer fermentation time increases the risk of contamination.
II. In case of biochemical production, generally, conditions favouring rapid growth may enhance biochemical formation and *vice-versa*.
III. Larger reactors and longer fermentation times are required.
IV. Characteristics of a cell population may change during culture, and prolonged continuous culture may be desirable.

Options :
(*a*) I, II, III (*b*) I, III, IV
(*c*) II, III, IV (*d*) I, II, III, IV

141. For rapid development of homozygous lines, haploids can be produced by which of the following approaches ?
(*a*) Anther culture
(*b*) Ovary culture
(*c*) Interspecific hybridization
(*d*) All of the above.

142. Which of the following elements ***is not essential*** for plant cell and tissue culture ?
(*a*) Ni (*b*) K
(*c*) Ca (*d*) P

143. Which of the following advantages are offered by biochemical production from cell cultures ?
I. In cases where plant material is limited in supply and/or the plants are slow growing, cell cultures offer a system of continuous supply.
II. It relieves pressure of over-exploitation/threat of extinction of natural populations of plant species.
III. Cultured cells produce higher levels of biochemical than do the differentiated plant tissues.
IV. Cells can be readily separated from the medium by simple filteration and stored at –30°C till the biochemicals are extracted.

Options :
(*a*) I, II, III, IV (*b*) II, III, IV
(*c*) I, III, IV (*d*) I, II, III

144. ***Assertion (A)***: Thermotherapy is usually effective against isometric and thread-like viruses.

Reason (R): Thermotherapy is based on the fact that most virsues are killed at temperatures much below those, which kill their host plants.

Options :

(*a*) Both A and R are correct and R roughly explains A.
(*b*) Both A and R are correct, but R does not explain A.
(*c*) Only A is correct.
(*d*) Only R is correct.

145. Somaclonal variations are preferable to induced mutations for which of the following reasons ?

I. Chimaerism is a major problem in the case of induced mutations, but not in the case of somaclonal variations.
II. Induced mutations are often associated with undesirable features like sterility.
III. Frequency of useful mutations is very low in the case of somaclonal variations.
IV. A highly effective selection can be applied *in vitro* for several economically important characters, which is virtually impossible in case of mutation breeding.

Options :

(*a*) I, III, IV (*b*) I, II, IV
(*c*) I, II, III, IV (*d*) I, II, III

146. Which of the following is used as growth retardant ?

(*a*) ABA and chlormequat (CCC)
(*b*) TIBA and paclobutrazole
(*c*) Daminozide
(*d*) All of the above

147. In case of slow-growth cultures, high osmotic concentrations are created by which of the following ?

(*a*) Mannitol (*b*) Sorbitol
(*c*) Sucrose (*d*) All of the above

148. Which of the following chemicals interferes with virus multiplication ?

(*a*) Cycloheximide
(*b*) Actinomycin D
(*c*) Virazole (ribavirin)
(*d*) All of the above.

149. ***Assertion (A)***: Characteristics of a cell population may change during culture and prolonged continuous cultures may not be desirable.

Reason (R): Cytogenetic, genetic and epigenetic variations arise during *in vitro* culture.

Options :

(*a*) Both A and R are correct, but R does not explain A.
(*b*) Both A and R are correct, and R sufficiently explains A.
(*c*) Only A is correct.
(*d*) Only R is correct.

150. Which of the following are the features of a spin-filter bioreactor ?

I. The central shaft of bioreactor houses a spinning filter.
II. A stirrer plate magnetically coupled to the central shaft provides continuous stirring.
III. The culture is aerated by a sparger.
IV. A port is provided for addition of fresh medium, while another port enables removal of the culture (used medium + cells) as per need.

Options :

(*a*) I, II, III, IV (*b*) II, III, IV
(*c*) I, III, IV (*d*) I, II, III

151. Cryoprotectants reduce cryoinjury by which of the following ?

(*a*) Reduction in cellular dehydraton.
(*b*) Reduced ice crystal formation.
(*c*) Reduced dislocation of structural water.
(*d*) All of the above

152. Cryoinjury results from which of the following ?

(*a*) Ice crystal formation
(*b*) Toxic solution effect
(*c*) Dislocation of structural water
(*d*) All of the above

153. Which of the following cryoprotectants acts through withdrawal of cellular water ?

I. DMSO II. Sorbitol
III. Glycerol IV. Proline

Options :

(*a*) I, III (*b*) II, III
(*c*) I, IV (*d*) II, IV

154. Which of the options given in Q. 153 acts by reducing cellular dehydration during freezing ?

155. Cryoprotection is done at which of the following temperatures ?
(*a*) 0°C (*b*) 5-10°C
(*c*) 24°C (*d*) 15-20°C

156. Vitrification/encapsulation eliminates the need for which of the following during cryopreservation ?
(*a*) Controlled freezing
(*b*) Cryoprotection
(*c*) LN refrigerator
(*d*) Both (*a*) and (*b*)

157. Partial desiccation step can be combined with cryopreservation of which of the following ?
(*a*) Somatic embryos
(*b*) Vitrified somatic embryos
(*c*) Encapsulated somatic embryos
(*d*) Both (*a*) and (*c*)

158. Which of the following ***is not correct*** about cryoprotectants ?
(*a*) DMSO is highly permeable.
(*b*) Sorbitol is nonpermeable.
(*c*) Sucrose is slowly permeable.
(*d*) Glycerol is highly permeable.

159. Which of the following ***is not correct*** ?
(*a*) Meristematic cells suffer from less cryoinjury than differentiated cells
(*b*) Dividing cells are more likely to survive cryopreservation than nondividing cells.
(*c*) Cryoprotectants minimise loss of structural water.
(*d*) Partial desiccation of tissues reduces cryoinjury.

160. Column A lists sterilization techniques and column B lists items for which they are used. Match the two columns and pick the correct option from those listed below.

Column A	Column B
A. Dry heat	1. Zeatin
B. Autoclaving	2. Scalpel
C. Filter sterilization	3. Explants
D. Surface sterilization	4. Culture media

Options :
(*a*) A2, B4, C3, D1 (*b*) A2, B4, C1, D3
(*c*) A2, B1, C4, D3 (*d*) A2, B3, C1, D4

161. Which of the following vitamins is essential for plant tissue cultures ?
(*a*) Thiamine (*b*) Pyridoxine
(*c*) m-Inositol (*d*) Nicotinic acid

162. Which of the following was the first to be achieved ?
(*a*) Embryo culture
(*b*) Anther culture
(*c*) Somatic hybridization
(*d*) Embryogenesis

163. Which of the options given in Q. 162 was the first to be applied to solve a practical problem ?

164. Which of the options given in Q. 162 was the last to be achieved ?

165. A batch culture has which of the following features ?
(*a*) Typical sigmoidal growth curve.
(*b*) Progressive nutrient depletion.
(*c*) Limited culture duration.
(*d*) All of the above.

166. Which of the following techniques used for cell cloning are used for protoplast culture as well ?
(*a*) Microchamber technique
(*b*) Filter paper raft-nurse tissue
(*c*) Microdrop method
(*d*) Bergman's plating technique

167. In case of shoot regeneration, GRs are required during which of the following ?
I. Morphological differentiation stage
II. Morphogenic competence acquisition phase.
III. Developmental determination phase.

Options :
(*a*) I, II, III (*b*) I, II
(*c*) II, III (*d*) I, III

168. A high auxin concentration is required during which of the following ?
(*a*) SE induction (*b*) SE development
(*c*) SE maturation (*d*) SE conversion

169. In case of which of the options given in Q. 168, GA_3 has a beneficial effect ?

170. In case of which of the options given in Q. 168, ABA is generally promotive ?

171. Rejuvenation may be brought about by which of the following ?
(*a*) Repeated sprays of a cytokining.
(*b*) Repeated grafting onto seedlings.
(*c*) Repeated subculture on cytokinin containing media.
(*d*) All of the above

172. GRs ***are not used*** during which of the following stages of micropropagation ?
(*a*) Preparation of mother plants
(*b*) Culture establishment
(*c*) Multiplication
(*d*) Rooting

173. In case of which of the options given in Q. 172, generally an auxin is used ?

174. Which of the following is the limitation of artificial seeds ?
I. Poor conversion in field.
II. High production cost.
III. Difficulties in storage.
IV. Difficult large scale production.

Options :
(*a*) I, II, III (*b*) II, III, IV
(*c*) I, III, IV (*d*) I, II, III, IV

175. In micropropagation, *in vitro* hardening is achieved by which of the following ?
(*a*) PEG in medium
(*b*) Use of a *Pseudomonas* culture
(*c*) Cooling of culture vessels at bottoms
(*d*) All of the above

176. Which of the following chemicals has been used to eliminate viruses fom plants ?
(*a*) Ribavirin (*b*) Actnomycin D
(*c*) Malachite green (*d*) All of the above

177. Virus-free plants produced by various *in vitro* techniques can be used for which of the following ?
(*a*) Breeding programmes
(*b*) For germplasm exchange
(*c*) Commercial cultivation
(*d*) Both (*a*) and (*b*)

178. 'Genetic erosion' is the consequence of which of the following ?
(*a*) Reduction in genetic variability among cultivated varieties.
(*b*) Reduction in genetic variability within cultivated varieties.
(*c*) Extinction of wild relatives of crop species.
(*d*) All of the above.

179. Which of the following is a sweetening agent ?
(*a*) Thaumatin (*b*) Shikonin
(*c*) Dioxgenin (*d*) Pyrethrin

180. Which of the options given in Q. 179 is a steroid ?

181. Which of the options given in Q. 179 has insecticidal activity ?

182. Shikonin production by cultured cells of *Lithospermum erythrorhizon* is suppressed by which of the following ?
I. NH_4^+ II. Cu^{2+}
III. 2, 4-D IV. Kinetin

Options
(*a*) I, II (*b*) I, III
(*c*) I, IV (*d*) II, IV

183. Which of the chemicals listed in Q. 182 promotes shikonin production by cultured cells of *L. erythrorhizon* ?
(*a*) I, II (*b*) II, III
(*c*) III, IV (*d*) II, IV

184. Biochemical accumulation by cultured plant cells is affected by which of the following ?
(*a*) Chemical composition of medium
(*b*) Light quality
(*c*) Inoculum size
(*d*) All of the above

185. Which of the following can serve as elicitors ?
(*a*) Chitosan
(*b*) Cell wall pectins
(*c*) Some glycoproteins
(*d*) All of the above

186. Certain biochemicals are produced by specialized cells present in organized structures. Which of the following culture systems will be useful for production of such compounds ?
(*a*) Immobilized cell cultures
(*b*) Organ cultures
(*c*) Callus cultures
(*d*) Suspension cultures

187. Two-phase culture systems offer which of the following advantages ?

I. Induce/enhance product release into the medium.

II. Remove and sequester the products from the medium.

III. Eliminate the risk of feedback inhibition.

IV. Reduce product loss due to evaporation.

Options :

(*a*) I, II, III (*b*) II, III, IV
(*c*) I, III, IV (*d*) I, II, III, IV

188. Arbutin is commercially produced from hydroquinone by which of the following processes ?

(*a*) Chemical reactions
(*b*) Biotransformation by *Digitalis* cells
(*c*) Biotransformation by *Datura* cells
(*d*) A combination of (*b*) and (*a*)

189. In which of the following, dihaploids are used for breeding, while tetraploids are used as commercial varieties ?

(*a*) Wheat (*b*) Potato
(*c*) Sugarcane (*d*) Tobacco

190. In which of the following plant species, YY males are used to produce all male populations ?

(*a*) *Silene latifolia* (*b*) *Coccinia*
(*c*) *Asparagus* (*d*) *Trichosanthes*

191. Which of the following breeding procedures is applicable to only autopolyploid crop species ?

(*a*) Hybrid sorting
(*b*) Analytical breeding
(*c*) Somaclonal breeding
(*d*) Both (*a*) and (*b*)

192. Which of the options given in Q. 191 involves haploid production ?

193. In most species, cells become committed to gametophytic development after which of the following stages ?

(*a*) Pollen mother cell
(*b*) Uninucleate pollen
(*c*) Binucleate pollen
(*d*) Trinucleate pollen

194. Which of the following stresses are known to promote androgenesis ?

I. Heat treatments

II. Cold treatment

III. Glutamine and sugar starvation

IV. ABA

Options :

(*a*) I, II, III (*b*) II, III, IV
(*c*) I, II, IV (*d*) I, II, III, IV

195. Which of the following have been shown to prevent precocious germination of cultured embryos ?

(*a*) High sucrose levels
(*b*) ABA
(*c*) Casein hydrolysate
(*d*) All of the above

196. Asymmetric hybrids can be produced by which of the following ?

(*a*) Spontaneous chromosome elimination
(*b*) Irradiation-incuded chromosome elimination
(*c*) Fusion of protoplasts of one species with microplasts of the other species.
(*d*) All of the above

197. Which of the following have been used as selection agents for cell selection to develop disease resistant somaclonal variants ?

I. Culture filterate

II. Pathogens

III. Toxins

IV. Proteolytic enzymes

Options :

(*a*) I, II, III, IV (*b*) I, II, III
(*c*) II, III, IV (*d*) I, III, IV

198. Somatic hybridization can be resorted to only when which of the following criteria are satisfied ?

(*a*) Isolation of protoplasts in large quantities.
(*b*) Totipotency of the isolated protoplasts.
(*c*) Availability of effective strategy for selection of hybrid cells.
(*d*) Both (*a*) and (*b*)

199. Cybrid/cytoplasmic hybrids are those cells or plants which contain nucleus of one species and cytoplasm of both the parental species. They are produced in variable frequencies in normal protoplast fusion experiments due to which of the following ?

I. Fusion of a normal protoplast of one species with an enucleated protoplast (cytoplast) of the other species.
II. Fusion of a normal protoplast of one species with a protoplast having an inactivated nucleus of the other species.
III. Elimination of the nucleus of one species from a normal heterokaryon.
IV. Gradual elimination of the chromosomes of one species from a hybrid cell during the subsequent mitotic divisions.

Options :

(*a*) I, II, III (*b*) I, II, III, IV
(*c*) I, III, IV (*d*) II, III, IV

200. Cybrids produced by cybridization provides which of the following opportunities ?

I. Transfer of plasmagenes of one species into the nuclear background/genome of another species.
II. Recovery of recombinants between the parental mitochondrial or chloroplast DNA.
III. Production of a wide variety of combinations of the parental and recombinant chloroplasts with the parental or recombinant mitochondria.
IV. Recovery of chromosome segment introgressions from the lost genome in combination with variations in the plasmon.
V. Mitochondria from one parental species may be combined with the chloroplasts of the other parental species.

Options :

(*a*) I, II, III, IV (*b*) I, II, IV, V
(*c*) I, II, III, IV, V (*d*) I, III, IV

6.2. FILL IN THE BLANKS

1. The most common reason for post-zygotic failure of wide hybridization is embryo abortion due to poor .... development.

2. Generally, auxin at low concentrations .... xylogenesis.

3. Cellulase is isolated from ....

4. A cell from which cell wall has been removed is called ....

5. Pomato was developed through .... between potato and tomato.

6. Enzyme polygalacturonase degrades ....

7. Reinert and Steward independently reported, for the first time, development of somatic embryos from .... tissue cultures.

8. Dry heat sterilization can be achieved by heating at a temperature between ...... and ...... °C for 3 hours.

9. A localized group of actively dividing cells is known as ....

10. Heritable variation present among cultured plant cells or among plants regenerated through tissue or cell cultures is termed as ....

11. In 1960, ... produced large quantities of protoplasts by using cell wall degrading enzymes.

12. Hairy roots are produced by transforming plant cells with ....

13. Vincristine is obtained from *Catharanthus roseus* and has medicinal value due to its .... activity.

14. Encapsulated somatic embryos, nodal explants, shoot-tips, etc. in a suitable matrix that give rise to complete plants are called ....

15. Most of the tetraploid and hexaploid wheats carry two dominant genes, *Kr1* and *Kr2*, which prevent seed development in crosses with ....

16. Cybrids are also called .... hybrids.

17. When low concentrations of elicitors are added to the culture medium, there is a dramatic increase in .... production.

18. Somaclonal variants are generally recovered in the .... of tissue culture regenerated plants.

19. A small rooted shoot or germinated embryo is called ....

20. In India, National Facility for Plant Tissue Culture Repository has been created in ...., New Delhi.

21. The abbreviation DMSO stands for ....

22. The thawing of cryopreserved materials has to be fast in order to avoid .... formation.

23. The main difference between a haploid and a monoploid is that the haploid has the gametic chromosome complement of any species, while the monoploid has the gametic complement of a .... species.

24. Liquid nitrogen has the temperature of .... °C.

25. Polima cytoplasmic male sterility was transferred from .... to *B. oleracea* var. *broccoli.*

26. Conventionally, viruses are eliminated by .... of whole plants.

27. Most of the modern tissue culture media have been derived from the work of .... and coworkers during 1950s and 1960s.

28. Meristem cultures have been extensively used for rapid .... propagation of a large number of plant species.

29. Conventionally, viruses are eliminated by exposure of the whole plants to temperatures between .... and .... °C for a few minutes to several weeks depending upon the host-virus combination.

30. Exposure of *Brassica campestris* anthers to 35°C for 24 hours markedly enhances the recovery of .... plants.

31. For micropropagation, generally, ... to .... mm shoot apices containing shoot apical meristem alongwith several leaf primordia are used for meristem culture.

32. Somaclone Bio-13 yields 37% more .... and 39% more citronellol than the parent strain.

33. Regeneration can occur via .... and ....

34. Gametoclonal variation appears to be more desirable than somaclonal variation because the mutant character is expressed in the .... generation.

35. Generally, chromosome instability of tissue cultures increases with the duration of *in vitro* culture, while their .... capacity decreases.

36. Generally, a mixture of .... at 0.1–1.0% and at 1-2% is appropriate for protoplast production in most plant materials.

37. The cryoprotectant DMSO is used at a concentration of ...... to ......% to protect tissues/cells from cryoinjury.

38. Somatic hybrids are denoted by a .... placed between names of the two fusion parents.

39. Somatic hybrids and .... can be used for transfer of plasmagenes.

40. Epigenetic variation is not transmitted through .... division.

41. Bio-13, a somaclone of *Citronella java* (a medicinal plant), was developed at ....

42. .... is the most commonly used fusogen as it induces high frequency fusion accompanied with low toxicity to most protoplasts.

43. In 1980, the first .... variety Mingo obtained through cross with *H. bulbosum* was licensed in Canada.

44. The osmotic concentration of enzyme solution for protoplast production should be between ...... and ...... m mol/l to prevent the protoplasts from ....

45. The *in vitro* techniques were developed initially to demonstrate .... of plant cell predicted by Haberlandt.

46. Lowering the temperature of cells/tissues to –196°C is termed as ....

47. Occurrence of polyploid cells in differentiated tissues is called ....

48. A chromosome having four chromatids and produced by endoreduplication is known as ....

49. The embryo that develops from a somatic cell is called ....

50. The two basic techniques used in plant biotechnology are .... and ....

51. Cultivation of plant cells under a defined environment was made possible by the brilliant contributions from .... in France and from .... in U.S.A.

52. .... is generally used as the carbon source in tissue culture media.

53. GR .... makes somatic embryos tolerant to desiccation.

54. High frequency .... protocol is a prerequisite for application of *in vitro* techniques for crop improvement.

55. .... method of cell selection has been used to recover low temperature and aluminium resistant variant cells.

56. A high concentration of an auxin is conducive to .... of somatic embryos.

57. Protoplasts can be isolated from all plant parts, but .... is the preferred source in most plant species.

58. A partial dehydration of the material before freezing has been found to .... the survival of cells/tissues.

59. It is believed that the s-grains present in anthers are ....

60. The occurrence of two or more successive rounds of DNA replication in a nucleus without intervening cell division is known as ....

61. A tissue/cell mass having cells of different ploidy levels is called...........

62. .... is the most commonly used auxin for cell cultures.

63. Laminar-flow clean air work stations provide .... conditions for explant transfer.

64. Generally, 2, 4-D is used at concentrations of .... to .... mg/l for cell/callus cultures.

65. Ribavirin and cycloheximide act as........... agents.

66. The term cytokinin was proposed by ....

67. The shoot-tips cultured for virus elimination, usually measure about ...... to ...... μm.

68. .... culture is widely used for successful elimination of even those viruses, which are not eliminated by thermotherapy.

69. When protoplasts are transferred to a culture medium, they, first of all, regenerate ....

70. Asymmetric hybrids can be produced by fusion between normal protoplasts of one parent with .... protoplasts of the other parent.

71. In 1985, the first wheat variety, named ...., based on androgenesis was licensed in France.

72. The frozen cells and tissues are stored in ....

73. During storage of cryopreserved cells/tissues, temperature of cells must not rise above ...., otherwise .... may form.

74. The protoplast mixture is treated with .... to .... % PEG for 15-30 minutes, followed by gradual washing of the protoplasts to remove PEG; protoplast fusion occurs during ....

75. Chemical substances produced by cells, but which are not necessary for their survival are called ....

76. Benzyl aminopurine and kinetin are the most commonly used ....

77. Hybrid sorting improves the effectiveness of selection, which is now based on .... genotypes only.

78. Treatment of protoplasts with high pH (10.5) and .... concentration of 50 mmol/l induces protoplast fusion.

79. An alfalfa, variety Sigma was developed through .... among selected somaclones.

80. Suspension cultures must be constantly agitated, generally, by a gyratory shaker at 50-250 rpm to facilitate .... and dissociation of cell clumps into smaller pieces.

81. A reliable protocol for .... of complete plant from single cells is a prerequisite for the production of transgenic plants.

82. ....approach provides an opportunity to combine the nuclear genome of one parent with the mitochondrial or chloroplast genome of the other parent.

83. A geranium variety, Velvet Rose is a .... of the variety Rober's Lemon Rose.

84. Regenerated plants often show variation in chromosome number due to the chromosomal .... of plant tissue cultures.

85. Homozygous diploid plants can be obtained by .... the chromosome number of haploid plants using .... treatment.

86. ....is the most common cell selection method and is used for the isolation of cells resistant to toxins, herbicides, elevated salt concentration, antibiotics, etc.

87. The optimum temperature for tissue cultures may vary from 18 to .... °C depending upon plant species and purpose of the culture.

88. *Iris* seeds may take two to several years to germinate; .... is used to effectively eliminate dormancy.

89. In case of tobacco, exposure of the excised flower buds to a low temperature, *e.g.*, 5°C for 72 hours, markedly increases the frequency of ....

90. In distant hybridization, when embryo fails to develop due to endosperm degeneration, ... is used to recover hybrid plants.

91. A plant cell without cell wall and nucleus is known as ....

92. Fusion of protoplasts of a somatic hybrid with that from one of its parents is called ....

93. A somatic hybrid that contains the full somatic complement of both fusion parents is termed as ....

94. A haploid obtained from a autotetraploid is called ....

95. Germplasm maintained by growing the various accessions in the field constitutes ....

96. Hybrid seeds from the cross *T. aestivum* × *H. vulgare* are not obtained, but hybrid seedlings from this cross can be obtained through ....

97. In case of cereals, the best stage for pollen culture appears to be the early or mid .... stage.

98. Stepwise selection often favours ...., which is unstable.

99. During anther culture, the walls of responsive anthers turn brown and after 3-8 weeks they burst open due to developing .... or ....

100. The frequency of stable .... clones may range from 8 to 62%, perhaps depending on the species and the selection agent employed.

101. In case of crop improvement, embryo culture technique is being used to recover .... hybrids.

102. In case of alfalfa (*Medicago sativa*), two cycles of recurrent selection improved .... capacity from 12 to 67 per cent.

103. Shoot apical meristems and some young tissues surrounding them are generally free from ....

104. When the objective is ...., the size of shoot-tip used for culture is not important.

105. When the objective is to free the stock from .... it is essential that the apical meristem should be excised alongwith the minimum of surrounding tissue.

106. Exposure of *Brassica campestris* anthers to 35°C for 24 hours markedly .... the recovery of haploid plants.

107. .... is the most commonly used cryoprotectant; it is added gradually over a period of 30-60 minutes and temperature of culture is maintained at around .... °C.

108. The dihaploid lines offer unique opportunity to improve the efficiency of selection for various traits since there is no .... variance in the population.

109. Somaclone Ono is resistant to ....

110. Barley varieties Mingo and Gwylan have been developed from haploid plants obtained through cross between...........and ....

111. In case of *Atropa belladona* and *Nicotiana sylvestris,* early .... stage is the most suitable for pollen culture.

112. In case of *Datura* and tobacco, the optimum stage of pollen for anther culture is just before or just after the .... mitosis.

113. The disease Southern leaf blight of corn is caused by ...., which produces a toxin that binds to .... membrane.

114. Carrot and tobacco cell lines resistant to the amino acid analogue 5-methyl tryptophan show a 10 to 27 fold increase in the level of free ....

115. Symmertic hybrids have been produced between sexually .... species.

116. In one study, upto 35% of .... clones developed through shoot-tip culture showed morphological variation.

117. In freeze preservation, cell and tissues are preserved at .... in ....

118. Embryo rescue is being routinely used in some crop improvement programmes to obtain ....

119. In Canada, two barely cultivars, Mingo and Gwylan, were produce using the .... route for haploid production.

120. .... was the first commercial biochemical obtained from cell cultures of ....

121. Ratan is a somaclonal variety of ....

122. Alloplasmic lines contain cytoplasm of one species and nucleus from .... species.

123. In case of alfalfa, ... treatment enhanced SE conversion to over 50% from 0-6% in the control.

124. For *ex vitro* rooting, the shoot of usually .... to .... cm are used for rooting.

6.3. MARK TRUE OR FALSE

1. A line that has nucleus of one species and cytoplasm from a different species is called alloplasmic line.
2. Pusa Jai Kishan is a gametoclonal variant from Varuna.
3. Endomitosis has been reported in barely and carrot tissue cultures.
4. Wildfire disease of tobacco is produced by *Pseudomonas tabaci.*
5. The first plant from a mature plant cell was regenerated by P.R. White.
6. The first embryo rescue, although crude, was done by Liabach to recover hybrid progeny from an interspecific cross in *Linum*.
7. The purpose of surface sterilization is to remove fungi and bacteria present within explants.
8. Generally, 10 per cent proline is used as a cryoprotectant to avoid cryoinjury.
9. The chief limitation of protoplast fusion technique is the selection of hybrid cells.
10. Tobacco cultivar AC Chang was released in Ontario, Canada for commerical cultivation.
11. Glucose is the most commonly used source of carbon in plant tissue cultures.
12. During micropropagation of banana, variants may arise at relatively high frequency.
13. Virazole was shown to eradicate potato virus X from shoot-tips of plants derived from tobacco protoplasts.
14. The ultimate aim of application of *in vitro* techniques to crop improvement is to obtain complete plantlets and to transfer them success-fully to soil.
15. Benzyl aminopurine is an auxin.
16. Sucrose (or a carbon source) is essential for anther culture.
17. Regeneration capacity appears to be epigenetically controlled.
18. An alfalfa variety called 'Sigma' is a homozygous somaclone.
19. In general, meristematic cells survive poorly during freeze preservation as compared to mature cells.
20. Cybrids can be produced by fusion of protoplasts from two diverse species.

21. The slow-growth of cultures may be achieved by maintaining plantlets on a medium having high osmotic concentration, *e.g.*, 20% sucrose or sorbitol.
22. Mitotic crossing over may lead to somaclonal variation.
23. Symmetric hybrids provide unique opportunities for synthesizing novel species.
24. Slow-growth of plantlets *in vitro* is a less attractive alternative to the freeze preservation of germplasm.
25. Gametoclonal variation appears to be less desirable than somaclonal variation.
26. A haploid has one copy of at least one genome but a monoploid has one copy of only one genome.
27. Negative selection approach is utilized for the selection of autotrophic mutants.
28. Proline is the most comonly used cryoprotectant.
29. The reasons for somatic incompatibility are well understood.
30. It may be pointed out that asymmetric hybrids are essentially cytoplasmic hybrids or cybrids, except for the introgressed genes or chromosomes.
31. The germplasm of those plants that produce long-lived seeds (orthodox seeds) are usually conserved in seed banks.
32. Generally, the thawed material is washed several times to remove the cryoprotectant before it is recultured. But it in case of sugarcane cell, this approach is not successful.
33. A doubled haploid strain may be released directly as a variety if it performs well in yield trials.
34. The pH of medium is generally adjusted, before autoclaving, to 5.5 using 0.1 N KOH or HCl.
35. The German botanist Gottlieb Haberlandt is regarded as father of plant tissue culture.
36. Axillary buds/nodal cuttings are occasionally used for micropropagation.
37. The organ and cell cultures are maintained under controlled environment, particularly temperature, and humidity.
38. Conventionally, viruses are eiiminated by thermotherapy of whole plants.
39. The *in vitro* techniques for germplasm storage hold promise for food crops.
40. The frequency of responding pollen grains during anther culture can be increased, over that of *s*-grains, by certain pre-treatments.
41. Double selection has been used for the selection of cells resistant to the herbicides amitrol and 2, 4-D to tobacco mosaic virus and aluminium.
42. In general, a suitable mutagenic treatment is applied to the cells for the recovery of somaclonal variants.
43. Thawing of the frozen material is achieved by plunging the vials into waterbath at 60°C for 90 seconds, the vials are then transferred into an ice-bath till the cells are recultured.
44. Hot water treatment is preferred to hot air treatment for thermotherapy.
45. Optimum concentration of an ionic osmoticum stabililizes protoplasts and promotes cell wall regeneration.
46. The application of plant tissue and cell culture to crop improvement is dependent primarily on the availability of techniques for regeneration of whole plants from cultured cells and tissues.
47. Most of the somaclonal variants are recovered in R_0 generation.
48. Maize cells resistant to the T toxin have been selected and plants regenerated from them were resistant to Southern leaf blight of corn.
49. Cell lines resistant to herbicide glyphosate have been developed.
50. A cryoprotectant prevents the formation of large ice crystals in cells and protects them from toxic solution effects.
51. Amino acid analogue resistant cells may be expected to show a relatively higher concentration of the concerned amino acid in their proteins.

52. In general, for protoplast isolation, fully expanded leaves are surface sterilized, their upper epidermis is peeled off with forceps and the peeled area is cut into small 1 mm^2 pieces for enzymes treatment.

53. One of the major problems of somaclonal variants isolated through cell selection appears to be the unstable nature of a large proportion of them.

54. A wider application of pollen culture in crop improvement depends primarily upon the development of techniques for production of large numbers of haploid plants.

55. Cell lines resistant to chilling have been isolated in chillies, and *Nicotiana sylvestris* using the direct selection approach.

56. Isolation of somaclonal variants is preferred to developing transgenic plants.

57. Production of hybrid cells/individuals without gametic fusion is called parasexual hybridization.

58. Electrofusion technique is a highly selective approach for protoplast fusion.

59. Virus elimination generally improves the yield of virus-free plants by ~20 per cent over the infected controls.

60. The culture vessels containing medium are autoclaved at 15 psi (pound per square inch) for 15-20 minutes to make them microbe free.

61. Sometimes, capacity of androgenic-haploid production improves with the age of donor plants.

62. The presence of one virus in a plants confers resistance to infection by other related viruses.

63. In some cases of somaclonal variation, herbicide resistance arises through gene amplification.

64. Meristem culture has been extensively used for vegetative propagation of food crops and fruit trees.

65. Surface sterilization is commonly achieved by treating the explants with 1-2 per cent solution of sodium or calcium hypochlorite or with 0.1% solution of mercuric chloride.

66. In some species, *e.g.*, wheat, a brief exposure of the anthers to a high temperature has a promotory effect on adrogenesis.

67. Seeds from virus infected plants, as a rule, do not contain the virus.

68. Seeds from virus-infected plants generally do not contain virus.

69. Unstable somaclonal variants may arise due to change in the promoter sequences and gene amplification.

70. Rice cells resistant to lysine analogue 5-(β-aminoethyl) cystein show much lower levels of lysine.

71. Haploid production is no longer the focus of plant biotechnology.

72. In case of cereals, the best stages of pollen culture appears to be the early or mid-uninucleate microspore stage.

73. Meristem culture involves the development of an already existing shoot apical meristem and the regeneration of adventitious roots. It does not involve the regeneration of new shoot meristem.

74. Thiman suggested to use the term phyto-hormone for hormones of plants.

75. The larger the size of shoot-tip explants, the lesser are the chances for elimination of viruses present in the mother plants.

76. Mutants for several traits can be more easily isolated from cell cultures than from whole plant populations. This is because a large number of cells, *i.e.*, 10^6-10^9, can be easily and effectively screened for mutant traits.

77. In order to eliminate viruses, in general, shoot-tips are subjected to thermotheraphy or cryotherapy.

78. The most appropriate application of haploid plants in crop improvement is to develop alien addition lines.

79. ABA promotes somatic embryo muturation and improves the rate of their conversion.

80. Cell number is the most infomative measure of culture growth.

81. Suspension cultures need to be subcultured about every 2-3 weeks.

82. Chemostats are ideal for determination of the effects of individuals nutrients on cell growth and metabolism.

83. *In vitro* haploid production was first reported by Guha and Maheshwari.

84. 2, 4-D, usually suppresses chemical production, but in some cases IAA may be promotory.

85. The chief objective of micropropagation is to produce progenies which have improved phenotype as compared to their parents.

86. Micropropagation is highly suited for rapid multiplication of rare genotypes and plants having low multiplication rates.

87. Prolonged exposure to a low temperature (say, 5°C) followed by shoot-tip culture has proved quite successful in virus elimination.

88. Practically, viability does not decline with duration of cryopreservation.

89. High cost of obtaining haploids and doubled haploids is still a major problem.

90. Most agronomic traits, *e.g.,* yield, quality, can be easily selected through *in vitro* cell selection techniques.

7

TRANSGENIC PLANTS

7.1. MULTIPLE CHOICE QUESTIONS

1. Which of the following is the correct definition of transgene ?
   (*a*) A gene from a related species.
   (*b*) A gene from an unrelated species.
   (*c*) A gene transferred into an organism using recombinant DNA technology.
   (*d*) A synthetic gene.
2. ***Assertion (A)***: Tomato transgenic, Endless Summer, has transgene for delayed ripening.
   Mechanism (M): Transgene blocks production of ethylene.

   Options :
   (*a*) Only A is correct
   (*b*) Only M is correct
   (*c*) Both A and M are correct, but M does not explain A.
   (*d*) Both A and M are correct and M is the correct explanation of A.
3. Which of the following are correct about virus cross-protection ?
   I. In 1929, the phenomenon of cross protection was first observed by McKinney in the case of Tobacco Mosaic Virus.
   II. Genetically engineered cross-protection is based on virus coat-protein gene.
   III. Plants infected with a mild strain of a virus resist development of symptoms upon infection by a more severe strain of the same virus.
   IV. Selection of mild protecting strain is a difficult task.

   Options :
   (*a*) I, II, III, IV (*b*) II, III, IV
   (*c*) I, III, IV (*d*) I, II, III
4. Transforming principle was discovered by which of the following ?
   (*a*) Hershey and Chase
   (*b*) Avery, MacLeod and McCarty
   (*c*) Zinder and Lederberg
   (*d*) Lederberg and Tatum
5. ***Assertion (A)***: Using the concept of cross-protection, a number of transgenic lines resistant to viruses have been developed.
   Reason (R): Genetically engineered cross-protection may occur due to inhibition of one or more events in the life cycle of virus.

   Options :
   (*a*) Both A and R are correct and R adequately explains A.
   (*b*) Both A and R are correct, but R does not explain A.
   (*c*) Only A is correct.
   (*d*) Only R is correct.
6. Genetic use restriction technology (GURT) is also called which of the following ?
   (*a*) Control of plant gene expression
   (*b*) Terminator technology
   (*c*) Antifarmer technology
   (*d*) All of the above.
7. Papaya transgenic Rainbow is resistant to which of the following ?
   (*a*) Papaya Mosaic Virus
   (*b*) Leaf Curl Virus
   (*c*) Papaya Ring Spot Virus
   (*d*) Distorted Ring Spot Virus

8. Nature Gard is a transgenic variety of which of the following ?

(*a*) Brinjal (*b*) Potato
(*c*) Cotton (*d*) Corn

9. Corn transgenic, KnockOut has been developed by which of the following ?

(*a*) Monsanto (*b*) Novartis
(*c*) DuPont (*d*) Aventis

10. Which of the following ***is not correct*** about *Agrobacterium tumefaciens* ?

(*a*) It is sometimes called natural genetic engineer.
(*b*) It is generally used for gene transfer in plants.
(*c*) It is a Gram positive soil bacterium.
(*d*) Optimum temperature for its growth is 28°C.

11. Consider the following terms:

Protein, DNA, RNA, trait

Select the correct option that depicts their biological relationship from among those given below ?

(*a*) DNA → RNA → Protein → Trait
(*b*) RNA → DNA → Protein → Trait
(*c*) Protein → RNA → DNA → Trait
(*d*) Protein → Trait → RNA → DNA

12. If a transgene has undesirable pleiotropic effect on the transgenic plants, it may be corrected by which of the following approaches ?

(*a*) Targetting the transgene product into the appropriate cellular compartment.
(*b*) Changing the genetic background of transgene through hybridization.
(*c*) Mutagenesis in the transgene.
(*d*) Both (*a*) and (*b*).

13. Performance of a transgenic plant can be affected by which of the following events during its development ?

I. Site of transgene integration in the host genome.
II. Number of copies of the transgene that are integrated.
III. Somaclonal variation arising during *in vitro* phase.
IV. Gene silencing.

Options :

(*a*) I, II, IV (*b*) II, III, IV
(*c*) I, II, III, IV (*d*) I, III

14. ***Assertion (A)***: Tomato transgenic Flavr Savr has transgene for reduced fruit softening.

Reason (R): The transgene prevents the production of softening related enzyme, polygalacturonase.

Options :

(*a*) Both A and R are correct and R correctly explains A.
(*b*) Both A and R are correct, but R does not explain A.
(*c*) Only A is correct.
(*d*) Only R is correct.

15. ***Assertion (A)***: Using coat protein genes of viruses, virus resistant transgenics have been developed in several crops.

Mechanism (M): Excess amounts of coat proteins encoded by the transgene accumulate in the cells and interfere with the virus replication.

Options :

(*a*) Only A is correct.
(*b*) Only M is correct.
(*c*) Both A and M are correct, but M does not expalin A.
(*d*) Both A and M are correct and M roughly explains A.

16. Enzyme aminoglycoside 3′-phosphotransferase II (APH (3′) II) is commonly called which of the following ?

(*a*) Luciferase.
(*b*) Neomycin phosphotransferase II
(*c*) β-glucuronidase
(*d*) Acyltransferase

17. Marker genes provide, which of the following advantages ?

I. They can be used to differentiate transgenic from non-transgenic plants.
II. Marker genes provide monitoring agencies with accurate, sensitive and non-molecular methods for monitoring value-added genes in genetically modified plants.
III. They are essential for the construction of genetically modified plants.

Options :
(*a*) I, II, III (*b*) II, III
(*c*) II, III (*d*) I, III

18. The concept of genetically engineered cross protection can be exploited using which of the following approaches.
(*a*) Expression of satellite RNA and replicase sequences.
(*b*) Expression of viral protease and movement proteins.
(*c*) Use of satellite RNA and antisense RNA.
(*d*) All of the above.

19. Stability/expression of transgenes in plants can be affected by which of the following ?
(*a*) Gene silencing
(*b*) Chromosomal rearrangements
(*c*) Pleiotropy
(*d*) All of the above

20. Which of the following strategies can be used to prevent interpopulation mating and the horizontal spread of engineered genes.
I. Introduction of male sterility in engineered crops.
II. Removal of flowers from the transgenic plants.
III. Removal of sexually compatible species from the vicinity.
IV. Planting of surrounding buffer crops of non-transgenic plants of the same species.

Options :
(*a*) I, III, IV (*b*) II, III, IV
(*c*) I, II, III, IV (*d*) I, IV

21. Neomycin phosphotransferase II (*nptII*) inactivates which of the following by phosphorylation.
(*a*) Kanamycin (*b*) Neomycin
(*c*) G418 (*d*) All of the above

22. ***Assertion (A)***: Two groups of workers have independently developed a transgenic scissor that cuts genes of interest.

Mechanism (M): The scissor is an enzyme which neatly snips out any DNA sequence located between a pair of identical 34 base pair sequences.

Options :
(*a*) Both A and M are correct and M correctly explains A.
(*b*) Both A and M are correct, but M does not explain A.
(*c*) Only A is correct.
(*d*) Only M is correct.

23. Which of the following ***is not correct*** about marker genes.
(*a*) Scorable markers provide valuable tools for identification of and tracking genetic modification in plants.
(*b*) They are not useful in quantifying both transformation efficiency and gene expression in transformants.
(*c*) They are particularly important where genetically modified plants can not be regenerated from single cells and direct selection is feasible or effective.
(*d*) They identify and tag transformed cells.

24. In 1983, the first transgenic plant was produced in which of the following ?
(*a*) Tobacco (*b*) Tomato
(*c*) Cotton (*d*) Maize.

25. Which of the following transgenic varieties was the first to reach the market ?
(*a*) Liberty Link (*b*) Endless Summer
(*c*) Flavr Savr (*d*) Bollgard

26. The first transgenic plant was produced in 1983, when a tobacco line expressing which of the following genes was produced ?
(*a*) Ampicillin resistance
(*b*) Kanamycin resistance
(*c*) Hygromycin resistance
(*d*) Phosphinothricin resistance.

27. ***Assertion (A)***: Potato transgenic New Leaf Y has transgenes for the control of insect pest (Colorado potato beetle) and for resistance to Potato Leaf Roll Virus.

Reason (R): Transgenes for the control of insect pest/Potato Leaf Roll Virus were isolated from a related species.

Options :
(*a*) Both A and R are correct and R adequately explains A.
(*b*) Both A and R are correct, but R does not explain A.

(*c*) Only A is correct.
(*d*) Only R is correct.

28. T-DNA is flanked on both the sides by direct repeat sequences of how many base-pairs ?
(*a*) 24 bp (*b*) 44 bp
(*c*) 34 bp (*d*) 14 bp

29. Crystal proteins from *B. thuringiensis* are solublized in the alkaline environment of insect midgut and then proteolytically processed to yield a toxic core fragment of which of the following sizes ?
(*a*) 50 kDa (*b*) 60 kDa
(*c*) 80 kDa (*d*) 70 kDa

30. Freedom II is a transgenic variety of which of the following ?
(*a*) Squash (*b*) Maize
(*c*) Cotton (*d*) Tobacco

31. Which of the following sequences has been used to produce a virus resistant variety of squash ?
(*a*) Defective virus genome
(*b*) Ribozyme sequence.
(*c*) cDNA of satellite RNA
(*d*) Virus coat protein gene

32. The *TA29* promoter sequence was isolated from which of the following ?
(*a*) Cotton (*b*) Tomato
(*c*) Tobacco (*d*) Cauliflower

33. The presence of transgene/DNA segment in plant cells can be detected by which of the following ?
(*a*) Dot blot assay
(*b*) PCR amplification
(*c*) Southern hybridization
(*d*) All of the above

34. CryI proteins are insecticidal to which of the following ?
(*a*) Coleoptera (*b*) Lepidoptera
(*c*) Orthoptera (*d*) Diptera

35. Transformation through electroporation has been reported in which of the following ?
(*a*) Rice (*b*) Tobacco
(*c*) Wheat (*d*) All of the above

36. The patent entitled 'Control of Plant Gene Expression' was granted in which country ?
(*a*) U.S.A. (*b*) Japan
(*c*) European Union (*d*) India

37. Gene *os* in T-DNA determines the synthesis of which of the following ?
(*a*) Cytokinin
(*b*) Indole acetic acid
(*c*) Opine
(*d*) Isopentenyl adenine

38. The cryIIB protein is specific to which of the following ?
(*a*) Coleoptera (*b*) Diptera
(*c*) Orthoptera (*d*) Lepidoptera

39. The term transformation is used to denote which of the following ?
(*a*) Delivery of DNA into bacterial/plant cell by a virus
(*b*) Uptake of DNA by a cell.
(*c*) Conversion of a normal verteberate cells into a tumourigenic cells.
(*d*) Both (*b*) and (*c*).

40. The *barnase* and *barstar* genes were isolated from which of the following ?
(*a*) *Bacillus thuringiensis*
(*b*) *Bacillus subtilis*
(*c*) *Agrobacterium rhizogenes*
(*d*) *Bacillus amyloliquefaciens*

41. 'Control of Plant Gene Expression' was dubbed as 'Terminator Technology' by which of the following ?
(*a*) Delta and Pine Land Company.
(*b*) United States Department of Agriculture, USA.
(*c*) Rural Advancement Foundation International, Canada.
(*d*) Department of Biotechnology, New Delhi

42. Potato transgenic variety New Leaf is resistant to which of the following ?
(*a*) Potato virus
(*b*) Colorado potato beetle
(*c*) Late blight
(*d*) Frost

43. *TA29* promoter has which of the following features ?
(*a*) Light-responsiveness
(*b*) Wound responsiveness
(*c*) Tissue specificity
(*d*) Development stage-specificity

44. Who said that we need to have a National Biodiversity Act, a Plant Variety Act, Farmers Right's Act, and a Geographic Appellation Act to deal with the problems created by terminator technology ?
(*a*) M.S. Swaminathan
(*b*) Suman Sahai
(*c*) R.B. Singh
(*d*) R.S. Paroda

45. Particle gun is suitable for transformation of which of the following ?
(*a*) Embryogenic calli
(*b*) Leaf discs
(*c*) Immature zygotic embryos
(*d*) All of the above

46. The *bar* gene conferring resistance to phosphinothricin was isolated from which of the following ?
(*a*) *Streptomyces* sp.
(*b*) *Azotobactor vinelandii*
(*c*) *Bacillus subtilis*
(*d*) *E. coli*

47. Among the given proteins, which has been evaluated for insect control ?
(*a*) Lectin and aprotinin
(*b*) Cowpea trypsin inhibitor and serine protease inhibitor
(*c*) Cystein protease inhibitor and proteinase inhibitor II
(*d*) All of the above

48. A gene can be obtained from which of the following ?
(*a*) Genomic library
(*b*) Chemical synthesis
(*c*) cDNA library
(*d*) All of the above

49. Among the given scorable markers, which one is generally used in plants ?
(*a*) Nopaline synthase (*nos*)
(*b*) β-glucuronidase (*gus*)
(*c*) Luciferase (*lux*)
(*d*) Octopine synthase (*ocs*).

50. Stable integration of T-DNA has been reported in which of the following ?
(*a*) Sunflower and *Brassica*
(*b*) Cotton and tomato
(*c*) Petunia and tobacco
(*d*) All of the above

51. The *barnase* gene was first used for producing male sterility in 1990 by which of the following ?
(*a*) Thorpe and coworkers
(*b*) Paterson and coworkers
(*c*) Mariani and coworkers
(*d*) Scowcroft and coworkers

52. Soybean transgenic variety Roundup Ready is resistant to which of the following ?
(*a*) Phosphinothricin (*b*) Atrazine
(*c*) Yellow mosaic (*d*) Glyphosate

53. *TA29* promoter is specific to which of the following ?
(*a*) Tapetum
(*b*) Pollen
(*c*) Ovule
(*d*) Pollen mother cells

54. The slow ripening transgenic tomato Flavr Savr was developed in USA using which of the following approaches/technologies ?
(*a*) Gene disruption
(*b*) Antisense RNA technology
(*c*) Ribozyme technology
(*d*) Cosupression apporach.

55. Gene *barnase* is expressed in which of the following tissues in order to produce male sterility ?
(*a*) Pollen mother cell
(*b*) Stamen
(*c*) Tapetum
(*d*) Pollen grain

56. Among the given selectable markers, which has been the most commonly used ?
I. Neomycin phosphotransferase, *nptII* (resistance to kanamycin).
II. Streptomycin phosphotransferase (resistance to streptomycin)
III. Gentamycin acetyltransferase (resistance to gentamycin)

Options :
(*a*) I (*b*) II
(*c*) III (*d*) II, III

57. Tomato transgenic variety 'Endless Summer' has which of the following features ?
(*a*) Delayed ripening
(*b*) Bacterial wilt resistance

(*c*) Delayed fruit softening
(*d*) Early ripening

58. Which of the following poses problems in gene transfer in plants through genetic engineering ?
(*a*) Low frequency of transformation
(*b*) Low level of transgene expression
(*c*) Gene silencing
(*d*) All of the above

59. Maximizer and Yield Gard are transgenic varieties of which of the following crops ?
(*a*) Cotton (*b*) Maize
(*c*) Wheat (*d*) Tobacco

60. Teminism refers to which of the following ?
(*a*) DNA–RNA hybridization
(*b*) DNA denaturation
(*c*) Reverse transcription
(*d*) Transcription

61. Which of the following aims at transformation of cells in the developing inflorescence cells ?
(*a*) Macroinjection
(*b*) Electroporation
(*c*) Microinjection
(*d*) Particle gun

62. Which of the following has been the most often used promoter for gene transfers in plants ?
(*a*) *Sh1* early promoter
(*b*) *nos* promoter
(*c*) *35S* promoter
(*d*) *Adh*1 promoter

63. Which of the following is the most commonly used vector for gene transfers in plants ?
(*a*) Ri plasmid vectors
(*b*) Ti plasmid vectors
(*c*) 2μ plasmid vectors
(*d*) Cauliflower mosaic virus

64. Which of the following is the most successful approach for gene transfer in plants ?
(*a*) Electroporation
(*b*) PEG induced DNA uptake
(*c*) Microinjection
(*d*) *Agrobacterium*-mediated transformation

65. Which of the following is the most difficult problem in case of *Agrobacterium*-mediated transformation ?
(*a*) Inability to transform apical meristems.
(*b*) Inability to transform monocot cells/ tissues.
(*c*) High frequency of transient transformations.
(*d*) Lack of 'wound response' in certain dicots as well.

66. Which of the following transformation techniques is the least likely to lead to rearrangements of the DNA inserts ?
I. *Agrobacterium*-mediated
II. Particle gun
III. Electroporation

Options :
(*a*) I, III (*b*) II, III
(*c*) I (*d*) II

67. In case of *Agrobacterium*-mediated genetic transformation, 'wound response' has a reference to which of the following ?
(*a*) Release of a signal molecule from plant wounds.
(*b*) Release of nutrients from plant wound sites.
(*c*) Release of antibiotic compounds from plant wounds.
(*d*) Both (*a*) and (*b*).

68. The terminator technology uses which of the following ?
(*a*) A *lea* promoter
(*b*) A recombinase gene
(*c*) A ribosome inactivating protein gene
(*d*) All of the above.

69. Protoplasts are required for which of the following methods of genetic transformation ?
I. Particle gun II. Electroporation
III. PEG-mediated IV. Microinjection

Options :
(*a*) I, II (*b*) II, III
(*c*) II, III, IV (*d*) I, III, IV

70. The controversial terminator technology seeks to provide which of the following ?
(*a*) Transgenic varieties that can be grown by farmers generation after generation.
(*b*) Protection from piracy of transgenes.

(*c*) Seeds fit for consumption but not for use as seed.
(*d*) Both (*b*) and (*c*).

71. The particle gun has been used to produce stable genetic transformations in which of the following ?

I. Soybean II. Tobacco
III. Maize IV. Wheat

Options :
(*a*) I, II, III, IV (*b*) II, III, IV
(*c*) I, III, IV (*d*) II, IV

72. Liposome-mediated DNA uptake has been reported in protoplasts of which of the following ?
(*a*) Petunia (*b*) Tobacco
(*c*) Carrot (*d*) All of the above

73. In general, development of transgenic plants involves which of the following steps ?

I. Introduction of a desirable gene into the cells of concerned plant species.
II. Integration of the transgene into the nuclear/organellar genome of the plant cells.
III. Expression of the transferred gene in the new genetic background.
IV. Regeneration of whole plants from transformed cells and finally transmission of the gene to the sexual progency of these plants.

Options :
(*a*) I, II, IV (*b*) I, III, IV
(*c*) I, II, III, IV (*d*) I, II, III

74. Which of the following techniques of transformation are based on special equipments ?

I. PEG-induced
II. Electroporation
III. Particle gene
IV. *Agrobacterium*-mediated

Options :
(*a*) II, III (*b*) II, III, IV
(*c*) I, II, III (*d*) I, III, IV

75. Which of the techniques given in Q. 74 is the least likely to yield multicopy insertions ?
(*a*) I (*b*) II, III
(*c*) IV (*d*) III, IV

76. Which of the techniques listed in Q. 74 is the most successful with organized meristems ?
(*a*) I (*b*) II
(*c*) III (*d*) IV

77. Which of the techniques listed in Q. 74 requires protoplasts ?
(*a*) I, II (*b*) II, III
(*c*) III, IV (*d*) I, II, IV

78. Which of the techniques listed in Q. 74 is dependant on the presence of acetosyringone ?
(*a*) I (*b*) II
(*c*) III (*d*) IV

79. Which of the following *Agrobacterium* proteins functions as a receptor ?
(*a*) VirA (*b*) VirG
(*c*) VirD1 (*d*) VirD2

80. Which of the options given in Q. 79 functions as transcription activator ?

81. Which of the options given in Q. 79 functions as an endonuclease ?

82. Which of the options given in Q. 79 has topoisomerase function ?

83. Which of the options given in Q. 79 undergoes dimerization in response to acetosyringone ?

84. Which of the proteins listed in Q. 79 guides the T-DNA into the plant cell nucleus ?

85. Which of the following *Agrobacterium* proteins are phosphorylated in response to acetosyringone ?
(*a*) VirA (*b*) VirB11
(*c*) VirG (*d*) Both (*a*) and (*c*)

86. Which of the proteins listed in Q. 85 has ATPase activity ?

87. Which of the following *Agrobacterium* proteins are most likely involved in the tube formation between bacterial and plant cells ?
(*a*) VirB (*b*) VirD4
(*c*) VirC (*d*) Both (*a*) and (*b*)

88. Which of the following *Agrobacterium* proteins are DNA binding protein ?
(*a*) VirG (*b*) VirD1
(*c*) VirE (*d*) All of the above.

89. Use of antibiotic resistance markers in production of transgenic plants may pose which of the following risks ?
(*a*) Toxicity
(*b*) Allergenicity
(*c*) Resistance in gut microflora
(*d*) All of the above.

90. Genes encoding which of the following can be used as a selectable marker when combined with a specific compound added to the medium ?
(*a*) β-glucuronidase
(*b*) Mannose-6-phosphate isomerase
(*c*) Xylose isomerase
(*d*) All of the above

91. Which of the options listed in Q. 90 ultimately yields a substitute for cytokinin in the medium ?

92. Which of the enzymes listed below enables substitution of the carbon source in the medium ?
(*a*) β-gluconidase
(*b*) Xylose isomerase
(*c*) Mannose-6-phosphate isomerase
(*d*) Both (*b*) and (*c*)

93. Which of the following promoters is seed-specific ?
(*a*) *Vicilin* (*b*) *Extensin*
(*c*) *35S* (*d*) *Adh1*

94. Which of the promoters given in Q. 93 has been the most widely used in dicots ?

95. Which of the promoters listed in Q. 93 specifies anaerobic expression ?

96. Which of the following promoters shows tissue-specific expression ?
I. RuBISCO small subunit
II. Sucrose synthase 1
III. Heat shock protein
IV. Lectin

Options :
(*a*) I, II, IV (*b*) I, II, III
(*c*) II, IV (*d*) II, II

97. Which of the promoters listed in Q. 96 shows expression in response to a specific stimulus ?
(*a*) I, II (*b*) I, III
(*c*) I, IV (*d*) I, IV

98. GFP fluoresces bright green when exposed to which of the following ?
(*a*) UV light (*b*) Blue light
(*c*) White light (*d*) Both (*a*) and (*b*)

99. Mutant forms of GFP show which of the following features ?
I. Fluoresces blue or yellow
II. Fluoresces at a specific pH
III. Fluoresces in white light
IV. 35 times more intense fluorescence

Options :
(*a*) I, II, III (*b*) I, II, IV
(*c*) I, III, IV (*d*) II, III, IV

100. The IV (intermediate vector) component of Ti plasmid cointegrate vector system ***does not have*** which of the following ?
(*a*) Origin for replication in *E. coli*
(*b*) Origin for replication in *Agrobacterium*
(*c*) T-DNA sequence lacking borders
(*d*) A selectable marker

101. In case of Ti vectors, which of the following has disarmed T-DNA with borders ?
I. Intermediate vector
II. Micro-Ti
III. Mini-Ti.
IV. Disarmed Ti
V. Helper Ti

Options :
(*a*) I, II, III (*b*) II, III, IV
(*c*) III, IV, V (*d*) I, III, V

102. Which of the plasmids listed in Q. 101 lacks T-DNA sequence ?
(*a*) I, II (*b*) III, IV
(*c*) V (*d*) IV, V

103. Which of the plasmids given in Q. 101 contains T-DNA sequence ?
(*a*) I, II, III (*b*) II, III, IV
(*c*) III, IV, V (*d*) I, II, III, IV

104. Which of the plasmids listed in Q. 101 contains T-DNA with borders ?

Options :
(*a*) I, II, III (*b*) II, III, IV
(*c*) III, IV, V (*d*) I, III, IV

105. Which of the plasmids given in Q. 101 is propagated in *E. coli* ?
(*a*) I, II, III (*b*) II, III, IV
(*c*) I, II, III, IV (*d*) II, III, IV, V

106. Which of the plasmids listed in Q. 101 has *vir* region ?
(*a*) I, II (*b*) II, III
(*c*) III, IV (*d*) IV, V

107. 'Agroinfection' acheives which of the following ?
(*a*) Genetic transformation
(*b*) Introduction of viral genome into plant cells
(*c*) Crown gall formatiom
(*d*) Both (*b*) and (*c*)

108. In a particle gun, acceleration of particles is achieved by which of the following ?
(*a*) Blank cartridges
(*b*) Pressurised helium
(*c*) Electrostatic energy
(*d*) All of the above

109. Which of the options given in Q. 108 is the most commonly used ?

110. Column A lists some genes, while column B lists the compounds to which they specify resistance. Match the two columns carefully and pick the correct option from those listed below.

Column A	Column B
A. *aroA*	1. Glufosinate
B. *bar*	2. Sulfonylureas
C. *bxn*	3. Glyphosate
D. *Hra* and *csr1-1*	4. Bromoxynil

Options :
(*a*) A3, B1, C2, D4 (*b*) A3, B2, C4, D1
(*c*) A3, B4, C1, D2 (*d*) A3, B1, C4, D2

111. Which of the following affects the level of expression of transgenes ?
I. Codon usage.
II. AAUAAA or AAUAAU sequence within transgenes.
III. AUUUA sequence within transgenes.
IV. Sequences resembling plant introns within transgenes.

Options :
(*a*) I, II, III (*b*) II, III, IV
(*c*) I, III, IV (*d*) I, II, III, IV

112. Which of the features given in Q. 112 affect mRNA stability ?
(*a*) I (*b*) II
(*c*) III (*d*) IV

113. Which of the options given in Q. 112 lead to mRNA processing ?

114. Which of the options given in Q. 112 affect the level of translation ?

115. *B. napus* transgenic variety 'Laurical' has a transgene that encodes which of the following ?
(*a*) Acyl-ACP desaturase
(*b*) Acyl-ACP thioesterase
(*c*) Acyl transferase
(*d*) Both (*a*) and (*c*)

116. In case of ribozyme approach of suppression of endogenous gene expression, the ribozyme encoding sequence is used as which of the following ?
(*a*) Independent of the target gene
(*b*) Fused with a sequence of the target gene in sense orientation.
(*c*) Fused with a sequence of the target gene in antisense orientation.
(*d*) Either (*b*) or (*c*)

117. Which of the following is used as processor for PHB synthesis ?
(*a*) Acetyl-CoA
(*b*) Aceto-acetyl-CoA
(*c*) Malonyl-CoA
(*d*) Butyryl-CoA

118. In case of fatty acid biosynthesis, which of the options given in Q. 117 is sequentially added during chain elongation ?

119. Which of the following ***is not correct*** about edible vaccines ?
(*a*) They are edible parts of transgenic plants.
(*b*) The transgene encodes an antigen from a pathogen.
(*c*) They are consumed in large quantities.
(*d*) They are in clinical trial stage.

120. Which of the following is correct about edible vaccines ?
(*a*) They can be used as regular component of food.
(*b*) Honey could be used as edible vaccine.
(*c*) Their production cost is comparable to that of conventional vaccines.
(*d*) They are useful only when the native antigen is orally inactive.

121. Which of the following can reduce transgene silencing ?

(*a*) Same orientation of the transgenes in the recombinant DNA.
(*b*) A.T composition of transgene similar to that of the host chromosome.
(*c*) Single copy integration of transgene.
(*d*) All of the above.

122. Which of the following constitutes gene silencing ?

(*a*) Low level of transgene expression in T_0.
(*b*) Low level of transgene expression in T_0 and subsequent generations.
(*c*) High level of transgene expression in T_0, but reduced levels of expression in subsequent generations.
(*d*) Both (*a*) and (*b*).

123. Gene silencing may cause which of the following difficulties ?

(*a*) Additional expenditure in evaluation.
(*b*) Delayed release of transgenics as varieties.
(*c*) Problems in registration of the transgenic varieties.
(*d*) All of the above.

124. Gene silencing leads to which of the following ?

(*a*) Reduced transgene expression
(*b*) Variable transgene expression
(*c*) Increased transgene expression
(*d*) Both (*a*) and (*b*)

125. Which of the following transgenic varieties ***could not be commercialized*** due to IPR probelms ?

(*a*) Endless Summer tomato
(*b*) Flavr Savr tomato
(*c*) Rainbow papaya
(*d*) Laurical *B. napus.*

126. Consider the following statements about golden rice.

1. It is a transgenic strain of *Oryza sativa.*
2. It was developed by transferring (through *Agrobacterium*) three beta carotene biosynthesis transgenes, *viz.*, *psy* (phytoene synthase), *lyc* (lycopene cyclase) and *crtI* into the nuclear genome of rice.
3. The resulting plants produce significant amounts of betacarotene in the endosperm.
4. Golden rice has been bred with local rice cultivars in philippines, Taiwan, etc.

Which of these statements is correct ?

(*a*) 2, 3, 4 (*b*) 1, 3, 4
(*c*) 1, 4 (*d*) 1, 2, 3, 4.

127. Consider the following statements about golden rice.

1. Nontransgenic rice grains synthesize and accumulate geranyl-geranyl pyrophosphate in the endosperm.
2. A plant gene *psy* (phytoene synthase) produces phytoene by condensation of two molecules of geranyl-geranyl pyrophosphate.
3. Phytoene desaturase converts phytoene into zeta-carotene and zeta-carotene desaturase converts zeta-carotene into lycopene; both activities were provided by the *Erwinia uredovora* phytoene desaturase encoded by gene *crtI*.
4. A plant gene *lyc* produces lycopene β-cyclase which converts lycopene into β-carotene, the cyclic C4O carotene, which is commonly called provitamin A.

Which of these statements is correct ?

(*a*) 1, 2, 3 (*b*) 1, 2, 3, 4
(*c*) 2, 3, 4 (*d*) 3, 4.

128. Which of the following ***is not correct*** about Golden Rice-2 ?

(*a*) During 2005, a team of researchers at biotechnology company Zeneca (now Syngenta) produced a variety of golden rice called Golden Rice-2.
(*b*) The team of researchers combined a phytoene synthase gene from maize with a *lyc* and *crtI* from the original golden rice.
(*c*) Golden rice-2 produces 23 times more betacarotene (37 micrograms per gram) than golden rice (1.6 micrograms per gram).
(*d*) Consumption of golden rice, helps in removal of diseases associated with deficiencies of vitamin A and iron.

129. Consider the following statements ?

1. In case of positive control, binding of the regulator protein to the operator is necessary for transcription to take place.
2. In case of negative control, binding of regulator protein to operator DNA prevents transcription.
3. Operons are regulated by specific proteins that bind DNA in the operator region.
4. Negative regulation is common in prokaryotes, and lower eukaryotes, while positive control predominantes in higher eukaryotes.

Which of these statements are correct ?

(*a*) 1, 2, 3 (*b*) 2, 3, 4
(*c*) 1, 2, 3, 4 (*d*) 1, 2, 4

130. Consider the following statements about inducible operons ?

1. Operons showing negative/positive control are divided into inducible and repressible operons.
2. The regulator genes of inducible operons produce active repressors that bind to the operator on their own.
3. Repressors are allosteric proteins that bind to operators of various operons and prevent their transcription.
4. As a rule, each repressor molecule has two distinct binding sites, *i.e.*, a DNA binding site that enables it to bind the operator, and an effector binding site, which allows it to interact with the effector.

Which of these statements are correct ?

(*a*) 2, 3, 4 (*b*) 1, 2, 3, 4
(*c*) 1, 2, 3 (*d*) 1, 3, 4

131. Which of the following are correct about repressible operons ?

I. The repressor encoded by the regulator gene is unable to bind operator; therefore, the operon is normally functional or derepressed.
II. When repressor interacts with the effector it becomes active and binds operator DNA, and represses the operon.
III. These operons generally encode enzymes that catalyze biosynthetic pathways.
IV. The *trp* operon of *E. coli* encodes the enzymes for tyrosine biosynthesis.

Options :

(*a*) I, II, III, IV (*b*) II, III, IV
(*c*) I, II, III (*d*) I, III

132. Consider the following statements:

1. Effectors are usually small molecules that interact specifically with regulator proteins.
2. In case of inducible operons, the repressor associated with the effector is unable to bind DNA.
3. In case of repressible operons, the repressor can bind DNA only when it is associated with the effector.
4. Binding of the effector at effector binding site changes the conformation of DNA binding site.

Which of these statements are correct ?

(*a*) 1, 2, 3 (*b*) 2, 3, 4
(*c*) 1, 3, 4 (*d*) 1, 2, 3, 4

133. Consider the following statements ?

1. Iron deficiency anaemia is the most common nutritional disorder in the world.
2. Rice grain has the lowest iron content among crops.
3. Rice grain has phytate, which reduces iron absorption in human intestine by upto 98%.
4. Phytate is used for phosphate storage in seeds, and it is used during seed germination.

Which of these statements are correct ?

(*a*) 1, 2, 4 (*b*) 1, 2, 3
(*c*) 2, 3, 4 (*d*) 1, 2, 3, 4

134. ***Assertion (A)***: Iron-deficiency anaemia is the most common nutritional disorder.

Reason (R): It is mainly caused by inadequate dietary iron intake.

Options :

(*a*) Only A is correct.
(*b*) Only R is correct.
(*c*) Both A and R are correct, but R does not explain A.
(*d*) Both A and R are correct and R adequately explains A.

135. Which of the following steps is involved in the development of high iron rice ?

I. Creation of a sink for iron in rice endosperm by expressing a ferritin gene.

II. Iron absorption from the rice grain is enhanced by increasing cystein content of the endosperm.

III. A metallothionin-like gene is expressed in rice endosperm to increase the cystein content.

IV. Iron absorption is improved by removing phytate by expressing phytase gene.

Options :

(*a*) I, II, III (*b*) I, II, III, IV
(*c*) I, III, IV (*d*) II, III, IV

136. Which of the following statements is correct ?

I. Ferritin gene from *Phaseolus* increased iron content of rice endosperm by a factor of 2.5.

II. Cystein-rich polypeptides are known to increase iron absorption by human intestine.

III. Enzyme encoded by a mutant *phytase* gene hydrolyses phytate into inorganic phosphate and myoinositol.

IV. The enzyme phytase is secreted into extracellular space so that it digests phytate only after the rice grains are cooked.

Options :

(*a*) I, II, III, IV (*b*) II, III, IV
(*c*) I, III, IV (*d*) I, II

137. Which of the following statement is correct ?

I. Nontransgenic rice grains accumulate geranyl-geranyl pyrophosphate, which can be converted to β-carotene.

II. In case of golden rice, conversion of phytoene to lycopene involves a total of four desaturation steps.

III. A 'high iron-high provitamin A' rice line was produced by crossing golden rice and high iron transgenic lines.

IV. A high β-carotene producing transgenic tomato has been developed by increasing its desaturation activity.

Options :

(*a*) I, II, III (*b*) II, III, IV
(*c*) I, III, IV (*d*) I, II, III, IV

138. In case of oilseeds, genetic engineering can be used for which of the following ?

I. Modification of fatty acid profile in storage oil.

II. Production of a new specialized macromolecules/biopolymers.

III. Improvement of oilseed quality.

IV. Development of transgenic resistance to biotic and abiotic stresses.

Options :

(*a*) I, II, III (*b*) II, III, IV
(*c*) I, II, III, IV (*d*) I, III, IV

139. Which of the following presents problems in gene transfer in plants ?

(*a*) Undesirable features of transgenic plants.

(*b*) Contamination by *Agrobacterium.*

(*c*) Low frequency of regeneration from transformed cells.

(*d*) All of the above.

140. Which of the following is correct about RNA interference (RNAi) ?

I. It is found in plants, vertebrates as well as mammals.

II. When long (> 400 bp) double stranded RNA (dsRNA) molecules introduced in the cells are cleaved by an RNase III enzyme, called Dicer, to generate small 21-23 nucleotide long dsRNA molecules called small interfering RNAs.

III. Successful completion of item II in the cells results in a sequence-specific degradation of complementary RNA sequences (homologous gene transcripts).

IV. RNAi is also called RNA-mediated interference.

Options :

(*a*) I, II, IV (*b*) I, II, III, IV
(*c*) II, III, IV (*d*) I, III, IV

141. Which of the following advantages are offered by cholorplast transformation ?

I. Ideal for prokaryotic gene expression.

II. Very high levels of transgene expression.

III. Elimination of the risk of transgene dispersal through pollen.
IV. Enhanced mortality of pest organisms.

Options :

(*a*) I, II, III, IV (*b*) II, III, IV
(*c*) I, II, III (*d*) I, III, IV

142. Which of the following is correct ?

I. Wheat germ agglutinin (WGA), the chitin-binding lectin from wheat germ, has been shown to be antimetabolic, antifeedant and insecticidal to the mustard aphid (*Lipaphis erysimi*, Katt).
II. Bioassays conducted in transgenic plants expressing WGA showed that feeding on transgenics induced high mortality and significantly reduced fecundity of aphids.
III. Hevein, a chitin-binding lectin from rubber plant has potent anti-fungal action.
IV. A cDNA encoding hevein has been transferred into Indian mustard for potential control of *Alternaria* blight caused by *Alternaria brassicae*.

Options :

(*a*) I, II, III (*b*) II, III, IV
(*c*) I, II IV (*d*) I, II, III, IV

143. Consider the following statements about transgenics.

1. Designer crops are designed to meet certain specified requirements.
2. Transitional trait transgenics reduce environmental damage in the short-term by substituting for an input.
3. Transgenics reducing the use of nonsustainable inputs without polluting the environment are described as compatible trait transgenics.
4. Transgenics that are sustainable over time are described as sustainable trait transgenics.

Which of these statements are correct ?

(*a*) 1, 2, 3, 4 (*b*) 1, 3, 4
(*c*) 1, 2, 3 (*c*) 2, 3

144. In many plants, certain traits related to quality can be improved by reducing or eliminating the expression of specific genes. The level of endogenous gene expression can be reduced by using which of the following approaches ?

(*a*) Small interfering RNA (siRNA)
(*b*) Antisense RNA
(*c*) Gene disruption
(*d*) Any of the above.

145. A DNA vector-based small interfering RNA (siRNA) production has an RNA polymerase III promoter, *e.g.*, U6 promoter, which drives the transcription of the DNA template that will yield siRNA; this DNA template consists of which of the following sequences ?

I. A 21 bases long sequence of the coding region of the target gene.
II. A 6 base long spacer sequence.
III. The same 21 bases long sequences as in item I, but in the reverse orientation.
IV. 5Ts (Thymines) to signal transcription termination.

Options :

(*a*) I, II, III, IV (*b*) II, III, IV
(*c*) I, II IV (*d*) I, III, IV

146. Which of the following ***is not correct*** about genetic transformation of chloroplasts ?

(*a*) The first successful chloroplast transformation in higher plants was achieved in 1989, when spectinomycin resistance was transferred into tobacco.
(*b*) *p*ZS148 vector can be used for plastid transformation.
(*c*) Particle gun is widely used and effective method of transforming chloroplasts.
(*d*) Transgenes integrated into the chloroplast genome generally show low levels of expression.

147. Which of the following ***is not correct*** ?

(*a*) Useful vectors are created by joining together segments performing specific functions.
(*b*) The uptake of foreign DNA by plant cells is called transfection.
(*c*) When viral genome is introduced into plant cells with the help of *Agrobacterium*, it is called agroinfection.
(*d*) A degenerate primer is a set of primers having the same sequence, except for one or more positions where variation occurs.

148. Which of following ***is not correct*** about small interfering RNA (siRNA) ?

(*a*) The two strands of an siRNA molecule are either synthesized chemically or they are produced *in vivo* by transcription.

(*b*) Chemically synthesized siRNA molecules have to be introduced into the cells, and they inhibit target gene expression for only 4-6 days.

(*c*) There are two common mechanisms, *viz.*, RNase H-dependent antisense mechanism, and siRNA mechanism by which short synthetic oligonucleotides can be used to modulate gene expression in mammalian cells.

(*d*) The siRNA and RNase H-dependent machanisms are not similar in any respect.

149. Which of the following is correct ?

I. The low expression level of native *cry* genes seems to be due to the presence in them of sequences not commonly found in plant coding regions.

II. Development of transgenic plants resistant to certain biodegradable herbicides was the first major achievement from genetic engineering.

III. Resistance to Cry proteins may be due to reduced binding of the toxin to midgut epithelium or incomplete degradation of Cry proteins.

IV. In 1986, the first transgenic plant resistance to TMV was produced in potato.

Options :

(*a*) I, II, IV (*b*) I, II, III, IV

(*c*) I, II III (*d*) I, III, IV

150. Which of the following strategies can be used for the introduction of chemically syntheized siRNA into animal cells ?

I. Electroporation.

II. Calcium phosphate precipitation

III. Defective genome can be used as vehicle for delivery of siRNA molecules.

IV. Lipofection using cationic lipids.

Options :

(*a*) I, II, IV (*b*) I, II, III, IV

(*c*) II, III IV (*d*) I, III, IV

151. RNA interference is used for which of the following purposes ?

I. Analysis of gene function in vertebrates, plants and animals.

II. Antiviral defence mechanism.

III. Suppression of endogenous genes at the desired stage of development and in the specified tissues.

IV. To produce low caffein coffee.

Options :

(*a*) I, II, III (*b*) II, III, IV

(*c*) I, II, III IV (*d*) I, III, IV

152. RNAi suffers from which of the following limitations ?

(*a*) Exogenous siRNAs must be delivered into the cells, which is not highly efficient.

(*b*) RNAi based on exogenous siRNA is rather short-lived, *e.g.*, for 4-6 days only.

(*c*) Longer dsRNA molecules trigger antiviral response and a general suppression of gene expression.

(*d*) All of the above.

153. Consider the following statements about transgene.

1. The transgene encoded protein product itself may be an important biomolecule of high value.
2. The transgene encoded protein itself may generate a valuable phenotype.
3. The transgene product may extend an existing pathway to produce modified product.
4. The transgene may trigger a pathway endogenous to the plant, the desirable phenotype being the consequence of this activation.
5. The transgene may create a novel pathway to give rise to a novel product.

Which of the above are the least likely to generate pleiotropic effects ?

(*a*) 1, 2, 3 (*b*) 3, 4, 5

(*c*) 1, 2 (*c*) 1, 3, 5

154. Which of the options given in Q. 153 is quite likely to generate pleiotropic effects ?

155. ***Assertion (A)***: The transgene either by itself or through its RNA/protein product blocks an endogenous pathway.

Effect (E): The transgene products may participate in the biochemistry and physiology of cell. Therefore, they are likely to generate pleiotropic effects.

Options :

(*a*) Only A is correct.
(*b*) Only E is correct.
(*c*) Both A and E are correct but E does not arise from A.
(*d*) Both A and E are correct and E is the result of A.

156. Which of the following ***is not correct*** ?

(*a*) MAHYCO collaborated with Ciba–Geigy, USA, for exploiting potential of Bt technology in cotton in India.
(*b*) The Bt transgenic cotton showed singificantly higher level of protection against *Helicoverpa armigera* with reduced number of insecticidal sprays.
(*c*) Based on the extended biosafety analysis and agronomic trials three hybrids, *viz.*, Bt MECH 12, Bt MECH 162 and Bt MECH 184 were approved for release.
(*d*) Cotton hybrids Bt MECH 12, Bt MECH 162 and Bt MECH 184 contain *cry1Ac* gene.

157. Which of the following ***is not correct*** ?

(*a*) MAHYCO developed Bt cotton hybrids by transferring Bt (*Cry1Ac*) gene from cotton transgenic variety Coker 312 into inbred lines.
(*b*) Cotton hybrids Bt MECH 12, Bt MECH 162 and Bt MECH 184 were approved by Genetic Engineering Approval Committee of the Ministry of Environment, Govt. of India, for commercial release.
(*c*) Till March 2005, a total of 20 Bt-transgenic cotton hybrids had been released for commercial cultivation in India.
(*d*) In 2004, of the 81.0 million hactares under transgenics, developing countries share was 53.4 mha (66%) as compared to 27.6 m ha (34%) in the industrial countries.

158. Which of the following countries has the largest area under cultivation of transgenic crops ?

(*a*) Canada (*b*) Brazil
(*c*) USA (*d*) Argentina

159. In Q. 158, which of the options contains the lowest area under cultivation of transgenic crops ?

160. Which of the following advantages ***is not offered*** by chloroplast transformation ?

(*a*) Reduced risk of evolution of resistance in insect pests.
(*b*) Ideal for eukaryotic gene expression.
(*c*) Very high levels of transgene expression.
(*d*) Elimination of the risk of transgene dispersal through pollen.

161. Which of the following Cry proteins is specific to Lepidoptera ?

(*a*) Cry I (*b*) Cry III
(*c*) Cry IV (*d*) Cry V

162. Which of the Cry proteins given in Q. 161 is specific to Coleoptera ?

163. Which of the Cry proteins listed in Q. 161 is specific to Diptera ?

164. Which of the following proteins is specific to nematodes ?

(*a*) Cry II (*b*) Cry V
(*c*) Cry VI (*d*) Both (*b*) and (*c*)

165. Which of the options given in Q. 164 is specific to both Lepidoptera and Diptera ?

166. 'Golden rice' has transgenes that provide which of the following enzyme activities ?

(*a*) Phytoene synthase
(*b*) Phytoene desaturase
(*c*) Lycopene β-cyclase
(*d*) All of the above

167. Consider the following base sequences of a gene.

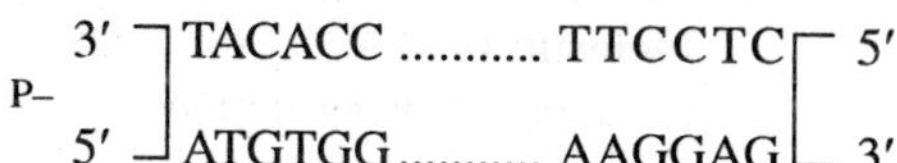

Select correct antisense construct from the options given below.

Options

(*a*) Pro. 3′ GAGGAA .... GGTGTA 5′
5′ CTCCTT .... CCACAT 3′

(*b*) Pro. 3′ TACACC .... AAGGAG 5′
5′ ATGTGG .... TTCCTC 3′

(*c*) Pro. 3′ ATGTGG .... TTCCTC 5′
5′ TACACC .... AAGGAG 3′

(*d*) Pro. 3′ TTCCTC .... TACACC 5′
5′ AAGGAG .... ATGTGG 3′

168. Which of the following is correct about toxic action of Cry proteins ?

I. When Cry proteins are ingested by insects, they are dissolved in the alkaline juice present in the midgut.

II. The midgut proteases process them hydrolytically to release the care toxic fragment.

III. The toxic fragments are believed to bind to specific high affinity receptors present in the brush border microvilli membranes of midgut epithelium.

IV. As a result of item III, the brush border microvilli membranes develop pores, permitting influx into epithelial cells of ions and water which causes their swelling and eventual lysis.

V. Presence of specific receptors in the midgut epithelium is most likely to be the chief reason for Cry toxin specificity.

Options :

(*a*) I, II, III, IV (*b*) I, III, IV, V
(*c*) I, II, III IV, V (*d*) II, III, IV, V

169. Which of the following approaches can be used to increase the toxicity of Cry proteins ?

(*a*) Increasing copy number of the *cry* genes.
(*b*) Site directed mutagenesis within the toxin encoding region.
(*c*) Production of hybrid *cry* genes by fusing selected toxin domains of two or more different *cry* genes.
(*d*) Both (*b*) and (*c*).

170. Which of the following is correct about toxic fragments of *Cry* proteins ?

(*a*) They have three domains, domain I functions in pore and ion channel formation, domain II is involved in binding of the receptor, and domain III is involved in receptor recognition.
(*b*) They are ~80,000 times more toxic to the target insects than organophosphate insecticides.
(*c*) They are highly selective in their action.
(*d*) All of the above.

171. Which of the following insects has developed resistance against Cry proteins under laboratory selection ?

I. *Plodia iterpunctella* and *Cadra cautella*

II. *Ephestia kuehniella* and *Plutella xylostella*

III. *Spodoptera exigua* and *Spodoptera littoralis*

IV. *Helicoverpa armigera* and *Helicoverpa virescens*

Options :

(*a*) I, II (*b*) I, II, III, IV
(*c*) I, II, IV (*d*) I, III, IV

172. In which of the following insects, a >250-fold (highest) increase in the resistance against Cry proteins was observed after 36 generations of laboratory selection ?

(*a*) *Helicoverpa virescence*
(*b*) *Cadra cautella*
(*c*) *Plodia interpunctella*
(*d*) *Plutella xylostella*

173. Which of the options given in Q. 172, shows a 7-fold (lowest) increase in resistance against Cry protein after 21 generations of laboratory selection ?

174. Which of the options given in Q. 172, shows resistance against *Bacillus thuringiensis* formulations ?

175. Which of the following is correct about development of insect resistance against Cry proteins ?

(*a*) Resistance to Cry proteins may be due to reduced binding of the toxin to midgut epithelium (*e.g.*, *P. xylostella*) or complete degradation of Cry proteins (*e.g.*, *S. frugiperda*).
(*b*) The inheritance of resistance to Cry proteins in insect populations is usually

recessive, and is governed by one or few major genes.

(*c*) It appears that insects may evolve resistance to some groups of toxins which faster than to others.

(*d*) All of the above.

176. Consider the following statements.

1. Production of value-added products like nutrition supplements, pharmaceuticals, fuels, etc. using transgenic crops is populary called molecular farming.
2. Edible vaccines are produced from transgenic plants in which an orally active antigen of the target pathogen is expressed and accumulated.
3. Hirudin is the first example of commercial production of a pharmaceutical product through transgenic plants.
4. Purification of the desired biochemical from the biomass or the culture medium is called upstream production.

Which of these statements are correct ?

(*a*) 1, 2, 3 (*b*) 2, 3, 4
(*c*) 1, 3 (*d*) 2, 3

177. Modification of flower colour intensity in petunia, rose, carnation has been achieved by which of the following ?

(*a*) Suppression of endogenous genes of chalcone synthase.

(*b*) Alteration of the cytokinin: auxin ratio by introducing and expressing specific transgenes.

(*c*) Over expression of the gene encoding phytochrome A.

(*d*) Gene disruption technology.

178. Which of the options given in Q. 177 can be used to modify size and shape of ornamental plants ?

179. Which of the options given in Q. 177 has been used in chrysanthemum and pelargonium to make these plants dwarf, delayed their leaf senescence and increased chlorophyll pigmentation.

180. Glyphosate resistance in plants can be generated by expressing in them transgenes that serve which of the following purpose ?

(*a*) Produce an enzyme that inactivates glyphosate.

(*b*) Over-production of EPSPS enzyme.

(*c*) Encode an EPSPS enzyme that is tolerant to glyphosate.

(*d*) Any of the above.

181. In case of bacterial and fungal pathogens, resistance has been sought by expression of which of the following transgenes ?

I. Expression of heterologous phytoalexins.
II. Ectopic expression of chitinases.
III. Expression of heterologous thionins.
IV. Genes encoding ribosome inactivating proteins.

Options :

(*a*) I, II, III (*b*) II, III, IV
(*c*) I, II, III, IV (*d*) I, II

182. The problem of development of insect resistance against Cry proteins may be managed by which of the following ?

I. Inducing *cry* gene expression only when the insect starts feeding.
II. Reducing the selection pressure on insects by limiting *cry* gene expression to only the economically important plant parts.
III. Combining two or more kinds of these proteins.
IV. Alternating two or more kinds of these proteins.

Options :

(*a*) I, III, IV (*b*) I, II, III, IV
(*c*) I, II, III (*d*) II, III, IV

183. The strategies for insect resistance management would depend on which of the following ?

I. Number of genes.
II. Nature of gene action
III. Insect behaviour.
IV. Insect × host genotype × environment interaction

Options :

(*a*) I, II, III, IV (*b*) I, II, III
(*c*) I, III, IV (*d*) I, II, IV

184. Sometimes *cry* gene may fail to provide adequate pest control in the field due to which of the following ?

I. Inadequate *cry* gene expression.

II. Reduced *cry* gene expression due to the environmental factors.
III. Presence of local Cry protein resistance insect populations.
IV. Development of resistance in the insect pest due to inadequate management.

Options :
(*a*) I, II, III (*b*) II, III, IV
(*c*) I, II, III IV (*d*) I, III, IV

185. In case of bacterial and fungal pathogens, resistance has been sought by expression of which of the following ?
I. Genes specifying artificially programmed cell death.
II. Genes encoding insensitive target enzymes.
III. Ectopic expression of pathogenesis related proteins.
IV. Genes specifying toxin inactivation.

Options :
(*a*) I, II, III (*b*) I, II, IV
(*c*) I, III, IV (*d*) I, II, III, IV

186. Which of the following ***is not correct*** about lectins ?
(*a*) Lectin gene was isolated from snowdrop (*Galanthus nivalis*).
(*b*) Lectins are plant glycoproteins which act against piercing and sucking insects like aphids.
(*c*) They are effective only when ingested in microgram quantities.
(*d*) As a result of item 'c', it has strong insecticidal effectiveness in transgenic plants to be of practical usefulness.

187. Which of the following transgenes shows protection from salt stress in tobacco ?
(*a*) *mtlID*
(*b*) *betA*
(*c*) *P5CS*
(*d*) Any of the above

188. Which of the following transgenes shows protection against drought in tobacco ?
(*a*) *sacB* (*b*) *hsf*
(*c*) *betB* (*d*) *ala3*

189. Which of the options given in Q. 188 provides protection against osmotic stress in tobacco ?

190. Which of the options given in Q. 188 generates protection against freeze stress in tobacco ?

191. Which of the options given in Q. 188, leads to protection against heat stress in tobacco ?

192. The designer crops may have which of the following features that make them more useful to mankind ?
I. A specified protein, fat or starch quality.
II. May produce a specific novel biochemical of pharmaceutical/industrial value.
III. Nutritional feature like vitamin content, elimination of an antinutritional factor.
IV. Colour, flavour, taste, etc. of fruit/grain.

Options :
(*a*) I, II, III (*b*) I, II, III, IV
(*c*) II, III (*d*) I, III, IV

193. Which of the following strategies can be used to modify fatty acids ?
I. Introduction of a novel enzyme, *e.g.*, an acyl transferase, or an acyl-ACP thioesterase.
II. Suppression of an enzyme activity, *e.g.*, α acyl-ACP desaturase.
III. Site-directed mutagenesis to alter the specificity of an enzyme.
IV. Creation of hybrid genes to generate novel enzyme activity.

Options :
(*a*) I, II, IV (*b*) II, III
(*c*) I, II, III, IV (*d*) I, IV

194. Column A lists some fatty acids and column B lists their functions/role. Match the two columns carefully and select the correct option from those given below them.

Column A	Column B
A. Oleic acid	I. Lowers cholesterol
B. Linolenic acid	II. Cooking and industrial uses
C. γ-Linolenic acid	III. Precursor of erucic acid, and of hormones like prostaglandins
D. Eicosenoic acid	IV. Alleviation of high cholesterol and several heart diseases

Options :
(*a*) AII, BI, CIV, DIII
(*b*) AII, BI, CIII, DIV
(*c*) AIV, BII, CI, DIII
(*d*) AIII, BIV, CI, DII

195. Which of the following ***is not correct*** ?
(*a*) Introduction of a transgene encoding AGPase may increase the activity of this enzyme and starch yield.
(*b*) Lauric acid occurs naturally in *Brassica* species.
(*c*) The rate limiting step in fatty acid biosynthesis is the carboxylation of acetyl-CoA to malonyl-CoA.
(*d*) Most successful example of fatty acid modification is the increased lauric acid content of *B. napus* transgenic, Laurical.

196. Which of the following ***is not correct*** ?
(*a*) Granule-bound starch synthase I (GBSS I) is the main enzyme of amylose biosynthesis.
(*b*) Suppression of GBSS I activity in potato (by antisense RNA technology) yielded an amylose-free or waxy starch potato.
(*c*) Production of waxy starch in potato is the first successful genetic modification of starch.
(*d*) All of the above.

197. Which of the following products is being produced in transgenic plants at commercial scale ?
(*a*) Avidin
(*b*) Hirudin
(*c*) β-glucuronidase (GUS) enzyme
(*d*) All of the above.

198. Production of recombinant proteins and other value-added products in plants offers which of the following advantages ?
I. Plants are easy to transform.
II. Transgenic plants can be multiplied very rapidly.
III. The upstream production costs are rather high.
IV. Plants provide a safe method of delivery of recombinant proteins for therapeutic use, and easy storage and distribution.

Options :
(*a*) I, III, IV (*b*) I, II, III, IV
(*c*) I, II, IV (*d*) II, III, IV

199. Which of the following transgenes can be used for development of insect resistant transgenics ?
(*a*) *Lectin* gene
(*b*) Cowpea trypsin inhibitor
(*c*) Serine protease inhibitor
(*d*) All of the above.

200. Which of the following is correct about vegetative insecticidal proteins (VIP) of *B. thuringiensis* ?
I. Some strains of *B. thuringiensis* produce VIP, *e.g.*, Vip3A, during vegetative phase of growth and secrete them into culture medium.
II. Vip3A is active against lepidoptern insect larvae.
III. These proteins are similar to Cry proteins.
IV. Efforts are being made to use *vip3A* gene for production of insect resistant crop varieties.

Options :
(*a*) I, II, IV (*b*) I, II, III, IV
(*c*) II, III (*d*) I, III, IV

201. Drastic reduction in ethylene production can be achieved by which of the following ?
(*a*) Expression of antisense constructs of ACC synthase or ACC oxidase.
(*b*) Cosuppression of either of these genes.
(*c*) Expression of such enzymes that metabolize S-adenosyl methionine (SAM), *e.g.*, SAM hydrolase gene from bacteriophage.
(*d*) All of the above.

202. Which of the following statements is correct ?
I. A reduced ethylene production results in delayed petal senescence in carnation and slow ripening of tomato fruits.
II. A carnation variety with longer vase-life has its ACC synthase gene co-suppressed.
III. A male sterile petunia has been produced by suppressing the expression of CHS gene.

IV. Gene, *gox* encodes the enzyme glyphosate oxido-reductase and detoxifies glyphosate by oxidizing it into amino ethylphosphonic acid and glyoxylate.

Options :

(*a*) I, II, III (*b*) I, II, III, IV

(*c*) II, IV (*d*) I, III, IV

203. Which of the following states of India, has the highest area under cultivation of transgenic cotton varieties ?

(*a*) Andhra Pradesh (*b*) Maharashtra

(*c*) Madhya Pradesh (*d*) Gujarat

204. Which of the options given in Q. 203 has lowest area under cultivation of transgenic cotton varieties ?

7.2. FILL IN THE BLANKS

1. Methylation of a promoter .... its activity.

2. Reporter genes help in the selection of .... cells

3. Two genes, ... and ...., present in T-DNA govern the synthesis of indole acetic acid.

4. Particle gun delivers DNA coated onto 1-2 µm .... or .... particles.

5. The *vir* operons are activated by ....

6. Ti plasmid is found in ...., which produces .... disease in dicot plant species.

7. Hairy root disease is caused by ....

8. Generally, selectable marker .... is used in dicot plants.

9. *Bacillus thuringiensis* strains are usually classified on the basis of...........

10. In tomato, enzyme polygalacturonase degrades ....

11. The Cry IV proteins are specific to ....

12. The *bar* gene isolated from *Streptomyces hygroscopicus*, confers resistance to the herbicide ....

13. The enzyme reverse transcriptase is generally obtained from ....

14. The term agroinfection is used for delivery of .... into plant cells.

15. The tomato transgenic variety Flavr Savr utilizes .... technology.

16. The technology patented as 'Control of Plant Gene Expression' was dubbed as............

17. A technology developed by Zeneca of UK, supresses .... rather than kill the seed, and has been dubbed as .... by RAFI.

18. Cotton transgenic Bollgard is resistant to .... and ....

19. T-DNA is expanded as ....

20. Gene *barnase* encodes an ...., which is cytotoxic and kills the cells in which it is expressed.

21. T-DNA has four important genes, *viz., iaaM, iaaH,* .... and *os.*

22. The border sequences of T-DNA are the sites where an endonuclease, encoded by .... operon, nicks the T-DNA.

23. Gene *ipt*, present in T-DNA, determines the production of ....

24. Electroporation creates .... pores in the .... through which DNA molecules enter protoplasts.

25. The *cry* genes are isolated from ....

26. The desired gene/DNA segment to be transferred into plant genome must be integrated within the .... of Ti plasmid.

27. Vicilin is the major seed storage protein of ...., and it contains 7% lysine but no .... amino acids.

28. Gene *barnase* has been successfully transferred in maize and rapeseed for producing ....

29. The patent for Control of Plant Gene Expression was issued in USA jointly to........... and ....

30. RAFI stands for ....

31. The Ri plasmid is involved in the .... disease of .... plant species.

32. Rural Advancement Foundation International is a non-government organisation located in ....

33. The cotton transgenic BXN is resistant to ....

34. The *vir* region has .... operons and is essential for the transfer of .... into the host plant genome.

35. The Cry (crystal) proteins have been grouped into several distinct classes, which either code for ~ 130 kDa or .... proteins.

36. The crystal proteins are solublized in the alkaline environment of the insect .... lumen.

37. Initially, macrocarrier acceleration in particle gun was achieved by using ....

38. Most of the *cry* genes are located on large conjugative plasmids, and many of the genes are bordered by........... like elements.

39. The male sterility induced by *barnase* is restored by ....

40. .... is a key enzyme of flavonoid biosynthesis.

41. Caulimo viruses infect many species of the family ....

42. The toxic fragments of Cry proteins are believed to be highly specific to high-affinity receptors present in the .... membranes of insect .... epithelium.

43. Integration of T-DNA into host genome occurs at .... sites and leads to stable transformation.

44. Sunup is a transgenic variety of ....

45. The CryIIA proteins are active against .... and .... insects.

46. The first report of engineered insect resistance was on the response of transgenic .... plants producing a Cry protein to the insects *Manduca sexta* and *Heliothis virescence*.

47. When two Cry protein toxin fragments interact with receptors, the .... of brush border develop pores, most likely .... in nature.

48. Binding of the Cry protein toxin fragments to the receptors leads to ion and water .... into the epithelial cells of midgut, which ultimatley leads to their...........

49. Wheat Dwarf Virus (a gemini virus) infects several members of the family...........

50. A sunflower seed storage protein, called sunflower albumin 8 (SFA 8), contains 23% .... plus cystein.

51. Genetic transformation through direct DNA uptake by protoplasts was first reported in the case of ....

52. The transgenic tobacco plants expressing .... protein at about 0.004% of their total leaf protein killed all *M. sexta* larvae within six days.

53. Rice .... gene encodes the major rice seed protein.

54. The first coat protein-mediated virus resistant transgenic plants were produced in tobacco; these contained the coat protein gene of .... strain U_1.

55. In most successful cases, the virus resistance in transgenic plants is produced by .... gene.

56. Most probably, virus resistance due to coat protein gene is generated due to the interference with the process of .... of virus particles, which is necessary for viral genome .... as well as its expression.

57. Isolated DNA directly enters a cell and a portion of this DNA becomes integrated into the cell chromosmes by a process of recombination; this is called ....

58. A phenolic compound, called ...., is produced by dicot plant cells at wound sites, and it acts as a signal molecule for the expression of *vir* operons of Ti plasmid.

59. All the genes present in T-DNA contain .... regulatory sequences.

60. Initially, golden rice developed in the background of Japonica rice variety...........

7.3. MARK TRUE OR FALSE

1. In case of wheat somaclones, variation for seed storage proteins occurs possibly due to a change in the methylation pattern of DNA.
2. The cotton transgenic Roundup Ready is resistant to the herbicide bromoxynil.
3. A technology, recently developed by Zeneca of United Kingdom and dubbed as 'Verminator' by RAFI, is an alternative to terminator technology.
4. *Agrobacterium* is a Gram-positive soil bacterium.
5. The desired gene/DNA segment to be transferred into plant genome can be integrated in the *vir* region of Ti plasmid.
6. Luciferase is generally used as selectable marker.
7. Ti plasmid is found in *Agrobacterium tumefaciens*.
8. Particle gun technique is equally applicable in dicot as well as monocot species.
9. The CryIII proteins are active against coleoptera.
10. Ri plasmid is found in *Bacillus thuringiensis*.
11. *Agrobacterium*-mediated gene transfer is successful with monocot species as well.
12. Electroporation enables the uptake of rather large DNA molecules and circular DNA is usually more easily taken up than is linear DNA.
13. Genes *iaaM*, *iaaH*, and *ipt* are involved in crown gall development.
14. The border sequences of T-DNA are not essential for the excision of T-DNA.
15. The expansion of *vir* is virulence.
16. *Agrobacterium*-mediated gene transfer is effective with monocot species provided exogenous acetosyringone during coculture.
17. DuPont (USA) scientists have synthesized and patented a gene encoding a protein containing 35% lysine and 22% methionine.
18. The *vir*D1 operon codes for an endonuclease, which cleaves the T-DNA at the direct repeat sequences bordering the T-region.
19. CytA protein also shows insecticidal activity.
20. DNA is taken up directly by plant cells, protoplasts, pollen grains, mature embryos and even whole seeds; in many cases, transient expression of foreign genes has been reported.
21. Genes produce their phenotypic effects by specifying the amino acid sequences of specific proteins.
22. Transgene *barnase* has been used to induce male sterility, which shows dominant behaviour.
23. Commercially grown insect resistant transgenic varieties contain either a gene from the bacterium *Bacillus thuringiensis* or cowpea trypsin inhibitor gene.
24. The *cry* gene of *B. thuringiensis* produces a protein, which forms crystalline inclusions in the vegetative cells.
25. Most probably the virus resistance generated by coat protein is due to a blocking of the process of uncoating of virus particles.
26. Flavonoids are essential for normal pollen development and funtion, but flavonoid deficiency does not affect pollen maturation.
27. The Flavr Savr transgenic tomato shows a drastically reduced expression of ploygalacturonase and markedly slower fruit softening.
28. The crystal proteins of *B. thuringiensis* are solubilized in the alkaline environment of insect midgut and are then proteolytically processed to yield a 40 kD (kilo Dalton) toxic core fragment.
29. The toxin function of Cry proteins is localized in the N-terminal half of the 130 kD cry proteins.
30. Tobacco plants expressing the satellite RNA of cucumber mosaic virus showed reduced disease symptoms when infected with cucumber mosaic virus or with related tomato aspermy virus.
31. The specificity of crystal proteins for their target insect species is primarily due to the proteolytic processing of Cry proteins, which may be cleaved differentially in different insect species.

32. Microinjection gives a very high rate of transformation, *e.g.*, 14–16% in case of alfalfa and tobacco protoplasts.
33. The specificity of Cry toxic fragments seems to be lost upon reduction of the cysteine residues of the protoxin, but can be restored by reoxidation of these residues.
34. A reporter gene and the desired gene to be transferred are integrated in the disarmed T-DNA region of Ti plasmid and the recombinant DNA is propagated in *Agrobacterium tumefaciens*.
35. The rapeseed/canola transgenic variety Laurical has lower lauric acid than the parent variety.
36. The aims of a genetic engineer is to usually maintain all the desirable properties of the target plant genotype and include an additional phenotype produced by the transgenes.
37. Transfection of *E. coli* is the same as transformation, except for the introduction of phage DNA in place of plasmid/other DNA.
38. Chloroplast targetting has been used to develop glyphosate resistant transgenic tomato and tobacco.
39. Insect, *Chrysomella scripta* and Leptinotarsa decemlineata show resistance against Cry proteins.
40. Out of eight *vir* operons, only four operons (*viz., virA, virB, virD* and *virG*) are essential for virulence.
41. Transfection of mammalian cells with small interfering RNAs (21-23 nucleotides long dsRNA molecules) results in sequence-specific degradation of complementary RNA sequences.
42. VirD2 induced nick at right border of T-DNA.
43. VirC involved in unwinding of T-DNA.
44. T-DNA enters plant cells in double-stranded form.

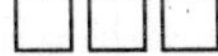

8

MOLECULAR MARKERS AND MARKER-ASSISTED SELECTION

8.1. MULTIPLE CHOICE QUESTIONS

1. ***Problem (P)***: Selection for complex characters governed by multiple genes with additive effects (quantitative trait loci) is difficult to achieve with conventional breeding strategies.
   Reason (R): The expression of genes controlling complex characters is greatly influenced by the environment.
   Options :
   (*a*) Only P is correct.
   (*b*) Only R is correct.
   (*c*) Both P and R are correct, but R does not explain P.
   (*d*) Both P and R are correct, and R adequately explains P.

2. Which of the following ***is not correct*** about marker-assisted selection ?
   (*a*) Use of linked molecular markers would allow selection for desirable traits in early segregating generations at the seedling stage independent of environmental influences.
   (*b*) Marker-assisted selection saves time and other resources needed for raising large segregating populations for several generations.
   (*c*) Indirect selection is expected to be less effective than the direct selection due to the absence of confounding effects of the environment in the case of latter.
   (*d*) Indirect selection allows pyramiding (accumulation) of genes for characters like disease resistance, which is difficult through the use of conventional methods of plant breeding.

3. Consider the following statements, and pick the option that contains the correct statement.
   1. RFLPs are dominant markers.
   2. RFLPs are generated by combinations of restriction enzymes and probes.
   3. RFLPs were the first DNA markers applied to genome mapping.
   4. RFLPs are very reliable markers in linkage analysis and breeding.

   Options
   (*a*) 1, 2, 3, 4 (*b*) 2, 3, 4
   (*c*) 1, 3, 4 (*d*) 1, 2, 3

4. Consider the following statements, and pick the option that contains the correct ones. Development of RFLP markers and their application is time consuming and expensive because:
   1. only one out of several markers provides polymorphism. This problem is serious, especially in crosses between closely related cultivated breeding lines.
   2. for every polymorphic locus tested in a cross, a separate experiment has to be performed, which is a formidable task with saturated maps such as those of tomato or maize where each linkage group has hundreds or more markers.

3. RFLP requires large amounts of DNA; as a result, the material from F_2 is soon exhausted and this limits the number of markers that can be tested.

Options :

(*a*) 1, 2, 3 (*b*) 2, 3
(*c*) 1, 3 (*d*) 1, 2

5. Consider the following statements and pick the option containing the correct ones.

1. Variation in DNA markers does not necessarily reflect in the phenotype.
2. Each molecular marker might be nothing more than a single nucleotide difference in a gene or a piece of repetitive DNA.
3. DNA markers are far more numerous than morphological markers.
4. DNA markers can be reliably detected.

Options :

(*a*) 1, 2, 3 (*b*) 1, 2, 4
(*c*) 2, 3, 4 (*d*) 1, 2, 3, 4

6. Which of following statements are correct about RFLPs ?

I. Restriction endonucleases are used for cleavage of genomic DNA.
II. The number of fragments generated by an endonculease depends on the number of recognition sequences in a given genome.
III. If a recognition sequence is present at a distinct genomic location in one individual but not in the other, the enzyme generates restriction fragments differing in size at this locus.
IV. This length polymorphorism can be detected only by a radioactively labelled probe, called complementary DNA probe, derived from this locus of the same species.

Options :

(*a*) I, II, III (*b*) II, III, IV
(*c*) I, II, III, IV (*d*) I, III, IV

7. The suitability of RFLP for elucidation of QTLs has been shown in which of following ?

(*a*) Tomato (*b*) Maize
(*c*) Potato (*d*) All of the above

8. Consider the following statements:

1. RAPD markers based on the LCR are much faster and cheaper than RFLP analyses.
2. Randomly generated synthetic oligonucleotides of 9 to 12 bases are used for RAPD analyses.
3. RAPD approach produces one to 10 fragments from a single primer PCR reaction.
4. The fragments generated in random primer-based PCR reaction are highly polymorphic.

Of these statements, which one is correct?

(*a*) 1, 2, 3, 4 (*b*) 2, 3, 4
(*c*) 1, 2, 3 (*d*) 1, 2, 4

9. Which of the following problems is associated with RAPD process ?

(*a*) It produces difficulties in reproducing RAPD patterns in different laboratories.
(*b*) RAPD patterns are not reproducible due to impurities in DNA preparation.
(*c*) RAPD patterns are not reproducible due to the use of small amount of DNA.
(*d*) Both (*a*) and (*b*)

10. Consider the following statements:

1. RAPD approach has several modifications.
2. RAPD marker can be readily converted into SCAR.
3. RAPD markers can be integrated with STMS marker-based maps.
4. RAPD can be used for characterization of germplasm.

Which of these statements is correct ?

(*a*) 1, 2, 3, 4 (*b*) 2, 3, 4
(*c*) 3, 4 (*d*) 1, 4

11. Which of the following steps are involved in DNA amplification fingerprinting (DAF) ?

I. DAF uses only one 8-10 nucleotide long primer.
II. Usually a single primer is used at the same concentration as that in RAPD.
III. Temperature cycling in the presence of a thermosensitive DNA polymerase produces a range of short amplified products of different lengths.
IV. Fragments can be adequately resolved and visualized by polyacrylamide gel

electrophoresis combined with silver staining.

Options :

(*a*) I, II, IV (*b*) I, II, III, IV
(*c*) I, III, IV (*d*) II, III, IV

12. Consider the following statements about DAF.

1. It is a dominant marker.
2. Temperature variation in the thermocycler block is not as crucial in the case of DAF as it is with conventional PCR.
3. DAF is amenable to automation.
4. It uses less stringent conditions for DNA hybridization and enzymatic reactions than does PCR.

Which of these statements are correct ?

(*a*) 1, 2, 3, 4 (*b*) 1, 2, 4
(*c*) 1, 2, 3 (*d*) 2, 3, 4

13. Primer designing for sequence-tagged sites (STS) is based on which of the following ?

(*a*) Random genomic DNA.
(*b*) Ends of large genomic DNA fragments.
(*c*) Sequences of cDNA (expressed sequence tags).
(*d*) All of the above.

14. Which of the following steps are involved in AFLP ?

I. The genomic DNA is digested with two restriction enzymes.
II. The cut ends of fragments are modified by ligating them with appropriate adaptors of 12-20 bp; this makes the fragments blunt ended.
III. The blunt ended fragments are amplified using two AFLP primers.
IV. The amplified products are resolved by denaturing polyacrylamide gel electrophoresis.

Options :

(*a*) I, II, III, IV (*b*) II, III, IV
(*c*) I, III, IV (*d*) II, III, IV

15. Consider the following statements about SCARs.

1. SCARs are similar to RFLP in application.
2. DNA sequence differences are manifested by the presence or absence of a single unique band.
3. SCARs are more reproducible than RAPDs and can be developed into plus/minus array where electrophoresis is not needed.
4. Some SCARs can theoretically be converted into codominant markers by digestion with 4 bp recognition sequence restriction endonuclease.

Of these statements, which ones are correct ?

(*a*) 1, 2, 3 (*b*) 2, 3, 4
(*c*) 1, 4 (*d*) 3, 4

16. Consider the following statements about AFLP.

1. It uses restriction enzyme-digested genomic DNA as template for PCR amplification.
2. The genomic DNA is digested with two restriction enzymes.
3. The fragments generated by restriction enzymes are modified and amplified using two AFLP primers.
4. AFLP is faster, less labour intensive and provide more information than RFLP.

Of these statements which ones are correct ?

(*a*) 1, 2, 3, 4 (*b*) 2, 3, 4
(*c*) 1, 3, 4 (*d*) 1, 2, 3

17. Consider the following statements about micro- or minisatellites or simple tandem repeats (STR).

1. Their sequence organization resembles the tandem arrangement of classical satellite DNA.
2. These sequences are dispersed in the eukaryotic genome in many copies of varying repeat unit number.
3. They were first found in human DNA but are present in nearly all genomes of higher eukaryotes including plants.
4. Due to the varying repeat numbers at a given locus, the elements frequently change their length due to slipped-strand mispairing and other less understood processes.

Which of these statements are correct ?

(*a*) 1, 2, 3, 4 (*b*) 2, 3, 4
(*c*) 1, 3, 4 (*d*) 1, 2, 3

18. How many loci can be detected from a single cross through AFLPs ?

(*a*) > 25 (*b*) > 400
(*c*) > 70 (*d*) > 1,000

19. The single primer amplification reaction (SPAR) is also called which of the following ?
(*a*) MP-PCR (*b*) RAMP
(*c*) SSLP (*d*) All of the above

20. Which of the following statements are correct about microsatellite repeats ?
I. Microsatellite repeats, particularly the dinucleotide repeats, have recently been shown to be abundant and highly polymorphic in eukaryotic genomes.
II. Plant genomes contain large numbers of simple sequence repeats (SSRs) of less than 6 bp.
III. These SSRs are tandemly repeated and widely scattered at many hundreds of loci throughout the plant genomes.
IV. SSRs are highly polymorphic and AG repeats are more numerous than AT repeats, atleast among the DNA sequences in genome database.

Options :
(*a*) I, II, III, IV (*b*) I, II, III
(*c*) II, III, IV (*d*) I, III, IV

21. Which of the following ***is not correct*** about sequence tagged microsatellite sites (STMS) ?
(*a*) STMS markers are dominant.
(*b*) These markers are extremely polymorphic and highly informative.
(*c*) The most important uses of STMS markers are tagging genes for economic traits and for the study of genetic diversity.
(*d*) STMS describes such microsatellite-based markers that are analysed by PCR amplification of a short genomic region containing the repeated sequence.

22. Which of the following ***is not correct*** about cleaved amplified polymorphic sequences (CAPS) ?
(*a*) This marker captures some of the adavantages of RFLP assay.
(*b*) It avoids the disadvantages of Southern blot analysis.
(*c*) CAPS was initially developed for use in pea.
(*d*) CAPS detects DNA sequence variation in terms of the lengths of DNA fragments generated by the restriction digestion of PCR products.

23. Consider the following statements about single primer amplification reaction (SPAR).
1. This DNA marker system uses primers based on microsatellites or simple sequence repeats and amplifies inter-SSR DNA sequences.
2. Of the di-, tri-, tetra- and penta-nucleotide SSRs, tetranucleotide repeats are the most effective in producing polymorphic multiband patterns.
3. The level of polymorphism is related to the genomic diversity within a given species.
4. Most SSR-SPARs are dominat markers, codominant markers can also be detected.

Which of these statements are correct ?
(*a*) 1, 3, 4 (*b*) 1, 2, 3
(*c*) 2, 3, 4 (*d*) 1, 2, 3, 4

24. Sequence tagged microsatellite sites (STMS) can be used as markers for which of following purposes ?
(*a*) Identification of germplasm and analysis of gene pool variation.
(*b*) Cultivar identification and determination of hybrid purity.
(*c*) Linkage mapping and diagnostic markers for traits of economic value.
(*d*) All of the above.

25. Consider the following statements.
1. The SSR-SPAR marker system may have broad applications across a range of plant species.
2. CAPS is a dominant marker.
3. Single strand conformation polymorphism could be useful as genetic marker.
4. DAF is amenable to automation, and use for fluorescence-labelled primers permits an early and easy determination of amplification products.

Which of these statements are correct ?
(*a*) 1, 2, 3 (*b*) 1, 3, 4
(*c*) 2, 3, 4 (*d*) 2, 3

26. Selection of a DNA marker system for plant breeding depends on which of the following ?

I. Objective of the research project.
II. Population structure.
III. Genomic diversity of the species under investigation.
IV. Availability of marker systems.

Options :
(*a*) I, II, IV (*b*) I, III, IV
(*c*) I, II, III, IV (*d*) II, III, IV

27. Which of the following points are considered during selection of a marker system ?
I. Potential utility in a given species.
II. The range of polymorphism detected by the marker system.
III. Reproducibility of results.

Options :
(*a*) I, II, III (*b*) II, III
(*c*) I, III (*d*) I, II

28. Consider the following statements.
1. In self-pollinated species, RFLPs are quite useful for detecting polymorphism.
2. RFLP loci mapped in one species can serve as heterologous probes for other species.
3. In case of ISSRs, polymorphic primers identified in one species are generally useful in other species.
4. SSR marker systems possess all the advantages of a PCR-based system, *i.e.*, small DNA sample requirement, high throughput and early detection.

Which of these statements are correct ?
(*a*) 1, 2, 3 (*b*) 2, 3, 4
(*c*) 1, 2, 4 (*d*) 1, 3, 4

29. Codominant markers, such as RFLPs, are useful for which of the following purposes ?
(*a*) Marker-assisted selection
(*b*) Evolutionary studies
(*c*) Linkage mapping
(*d*) All of the above

30. Once an RAPD marker linked to a trait of interest is found, it can be converted into a more reproducible PCR type assay by use of which of the following ?
(*a*) Allele-specific ligation
(*b*) Allele-specific PCR (AS-PCR)
(*c*) Sequence characterized amplified region (SCAR) assay
(*d*) All of the above.

31. Which of the following sampling strategies has been proposed for achieving a rapid foreground as well as background selection ?
I. Selection of the individuals carrying the marker linked to the gene under transfer.
II. Selection of individuals from among those given in item I, which are homozygous for the recurrent parent genotype at loci flanking the target locus.
III. Selection of individuals (from among those given in item II), which are homozygous for the recurrent parent genotype for the remaining loci of the chromosome having the target gene.
IV. Selection of at least one individual (from those given in item III) which is homozygous for the recurrent parent genotype at the maximum number of loci.

Options :
(*a*) I, III, IV (*b*) II, III, IV
(*c*) I, II, III, IV (*d*) II, IV

32. In Q. 31, which of the options represents background selection ?

33. Which of the following ***is not correct*** about application of molecular markers ?
(*a*) Molecular markers are very useful in unequivocal identification of plant varieties.
(*b*) Molecular markers can not be used for elimination of undesirable genes from segregating populations.
(*c*) Molecular markers are used for mapping of QTLs.
(*d*) They allow construction of high density linkage maps since the number of markers available per cross is very large.

34. Molecular breeding requires which of the following technology ?
(*a*) Genetic maps and molecular markers linked to agronomic traits.
(*b*) Automated and high throughput diagnostic techniques.
(*c*) A modification in breeding practice that takes full advantage of the information provided by such diagnostic assays.
(*d*) All of the above.

35. Which of the following mapping populations is used for linkage mapping of molecular markers ?
(*a*) Near-isogenic lines (NILs)
(*b*) Recombinant inbred lines (RILs)
(*c*) Backcross progeny
(*d*) Any of the above.

36. The predictive value of molecular markers used in marker-assisted selection depends on which of the following ?
(*a*) Their inherent repeatability.
(*b*) Map position.
(*c*) Linkage with economically important traits.
(*d*) All of the above.

37. Which of the options given in Q. 36 is the most critical in marker-assisted selection (MAS).

38. Which of the following statements are correct about MAS ?
I. Perhaps the most optimistic prospect for MAS is in disease resistance breeding, especially where several genes control resistance with complex interactions and where pyramiding of genes is desirable.
II. MAS may have potential in population and inbred line development.
III. When QTLs and single genes are adequately mapped, they can be isolated by map-based cloning strategies.
IV. The effectiveness of MAS will depend on the accuracy of genotypic classification of the trait in question.

Options :
(*a*) I, II, III, IV (*b*) II, III, IV
(*c*) I, II, III (*d*) I, III, IV

39. Which of the following ***is not correct*** about applications of molecular markers ?
(*a*) Molecular markers do not permit the identification of putative resistant plants in the absence of disease test.
(*b*) In resistance breeding, molecular markers can be very useful in gene pyramiding.
(*c*) Molecular markers may be useful in identifying heterotic combinations.
(*d*) MAS can be successfully used to select for such traits whose phenotypic evaluation is either problematic or costly.

40. Saturated molecular linkage maps have been developed in which of the following crops ?
(*a*) Potato (*b*) Tomato
(*c*) Maize (*d*) All of the above

41. Which of the following ***is not correct*** about recombinant inbred lines (RILs) ?
(*a*) RILs are also called inbred-derived lines.
(*b*) RILs are homozygous lines derived from a suitable cross.
(*c*) RILs are created by single seed descent (SSD) through at least five generations of continued selfing.
(*d*) At the end of SSD, seeds from each plant are harvested separately to obtain as many RILs as there are individual plants.

42. The saturated molecular linkage maps initially developed in tomato, potato and maize used which of the following molecular marker systems ?
(*a*) AFLP (*b*) RFLP
(*c*) SNP (*d*) DAF

43. Which of the following ***is not correct*** about the applications of molecular markers ?
(*a*) The molecular markers that are uniformly distributed throughout the genome can be used to estimate the genetic contribution of each parent to each individual of a segregating population.
(*b*) MAS can not be used to improve complex traits like yield.
(*c*) Molecular markers would enable an effective selection for horizontal resistance even in the presence of vertical resistance genes.
(*d*) Two rice varieties '*Angke*' and '*Conde*', developed by MAS for bacterial leaf blight resistance, have been released in Indonesia.

44. In case of breeding for disease resistance, MAS is potentially useful for which of the following ?
I. Selection of QTLs responsible for horizontal resistance even in the presence of vertical resistance.
II. As a substitute for a disease test.
III. Accelerated recovery of the genotype of disease susceptible recurrent parent.
IV. For reducing linkage drag.

Options :
(*a*) I, II, IV (*b*) II, IV
(*c*) I, II, III, IV (*d*) I, IV

45. Which of following ***is not correct*** about RILs ?
(*a*) RILs are created by SSD through at least five generations of continued selfing.
(*b*) Continued selfing yields a set of lines each of which contains a different combination of linkage blocks from the original parents.
(*c*) The different linkage blocks in RILs provide a basis for linkage analysis.
(*d*) RILs are, theoretically, mortal.

46. Dominant markers supply as much information as codominant markers in which of the following ?
(*a*) Doubled haploids.
(*b*) One of the two backcross populations in coupling phase.
(*c*) RILs
(*d*) All of the above.

47. Information obtained from dominant markers can be maximised by using RILs because of which of the following ?
1. All loci are homozygous, or nearly so.
2. Under conditions of tight linkage, dominant and codominant markers evaluated in a RIL population provide more information per individual than either marker type in a backcross population
3. Backcross populations are more informative (at low marker saturation) as compared to RILs where the distance between linked loci increases, *i.e.*, >15% recombination.
4. Increased recombination can be beneficial for resolution of tight linkages, but may be undesirable in the construction of maps with low marker saturation.

Options :
(*a*) 1, 2, 3, 4 (*b*) 1, 3, 4
(*c*) 1, 2, 3 (*d*) 2, 4

48. Which of the following are correct about RILs ?
I. They have been used for mapping of a number of useful genes.
II. They can be used to derive a map.
III. They are especially powerful for analysing quantitative traits.

Options :
(*a*) I, II, III (*b*) I, II
(*c*) II, III (*d*) I, III

49. The first strategy used for molecular mapping was based on which of the following ?
(*a*) Recombinant inbred lines
(*b*) Bulked segregant analysis
(*c*) Near-isogenic lines
(*d*) F_2 populations

50. Mapping of disease resistance genes has been based on which of the following markers ?
(*a*) ISSR (*b*) RAPD
(*c*) Microsatellite (*d*) All of the above

51. In 1923, the theory of QTL mapping was described by which of the following ?
(*a*) Stern (*b*) Sax
(*c*) Mather (*d*) Galton

52. Which of the following is correct ?
I. Polygenes are those genes that have small but cumulative effect on the concerned trait.
II. Several polygenes affect a single trait.
III. A quantitative trait locus (QTL) is a position in a chromosome that contains one or more polygenes involved in the determination of a quantitative trait.
IV. Quantitative trait expression is independent of the environment.

Options :
(*a*) I, III, IV (*b*) II, III, IV
(*c*) I, II, III (*d*) I, II, III, IV

53. Which of the following steps are involved in QTL mapping ?
I. Testing of DNA markers throughout the genome for likelihood that they are assiociated with a QTL.
II. Individuals in a suitable mapping population are analysed in terms of DNA marker genotypes and the phenotype of interest.
III. For each DNA marker, the individuals are split into classes according to marker genotype.

IV. Mean and variance parameters for the phenotype of interest are calculated and compared among the marker genotype classes.
V. A significant difference between the DNA marker and the trait of interest indicates a linkage between the DNA marker and the trait of interest.

Options :
(*a*) I, II, III (*b*) I, II, IV
(*c*) II, III, IV (*d*) I, II, III, IV, V

54. Which of the following varieties is the first variety in India developed by MAS ?
(*a*) Pusa Basmati 1
(*b*) Pusa 1401
(*c*) Pusa 1121
(*d*) Improved Pusa Basmati 1

55. Improved Pusa Basmati 1 (Pusa 1460), the first variety in India developed through MAS, has been improved by transferring which of the following ?
(*a*) Vitamin A content
(*b*) QTLs for grain size
(*c*) Disease resistance
(*d*) Cooking quality

56. Pusa 1460 has resistance for which of the following ?
(*a*) Bacterial leaf blight
(*b*) Blast
(*c*) Tungro
(*d*) Grassy stunt

57. Pusa 1460 has which of the following genes transferred through MAS ?
(*a*) *Xa21* (*b*) *xa*13
(*c*) Both (*a*) and (*b*) (*d*) *Xa*14

58. Which of the following markers systems has been used for developing Pusa 1460 ?
(*a*) RFLP (*b*) STMS
(*c*) ISSR (*d*) SCAR

59. Foreground selection achieves which of the following objectives ?
I. Selection for the gene under transfer.
II. Elimination of linkage drag.
III. Selection for the genotype of recurrent parent.
IV. Selection against the genotype of non-recurrent parent (except for the gene under transfer).

Options :
(*a*) I (*b*) I, II
(*c*) II, III, IV (*d*) I, IV

60. Background selection achieves which of the objectives given in Q. 59 ?
(*a*) I, II (*b*) I, II, III
(*c*) II, III (*d*) II, III, IV

61. During a backcross programme for disease resistance, MAS achieves which of the following ?
I. Reduction in number of backcrosses.
II. Reduction in number of plants required in each backcross generation.
III. Selection for resistance without disease test.
IV. Gene pyramiding.

Options :
(*a*) I, II, III (*b*) I, III, IV
(*c*) I, II, III, IV (*d*) II, III, IV

62. Which of the objectives given in Q. 61 constitutes foreground selction ?

Options :
(*a*) I, II (*b*) III, IV
(*c*) II, III (*d*) II, IV

63. During a backcross programme for disease resistance specified by a recessive gene, use of MAS achieves which of the following ?
I. Eliminates the need of growing BCF_2 generation.
II. Eliminates the need for disease test.
III. Reduced number of backcrosses.
IV. Gene pyramiding.

Options :
(*a*) I, II, III, IV (*b*) I, II, III
(*c*) II, III, IV (*d*) I, III, IV

64. Use of MAS-based foreground and back-ground selections during backcross programme for transfer of disease resistance offers which of the following advantages ?
I. Eliminates the need for disease test during the programme.
II. Selection for recurrent parent phenotype not required.
III. Field test of the variety so developed is not needed.
IV. Marker-based identification of the variety is feasible.

Options :
(*a*) I, II, III (*b*) I, II, IV
(*c*) I, III, IV (*d*) I, II, III, IV

65. Which of the advantages listed in Q. 64 are obtained from MAS-based foreground selection ?
Options :
(*a*) I (*b*) I, II
(*c*) I, III (*d*) I, IV

66. Which of the advantages listed in Q. 64 are available from MAS-based background selection ?
Options :
(*a*) I (*b*) II
(*c*) III (*d*) IV

67. A substantial reduction in the number of backcross generations needed for gene transfer is achieved by the use of MAS-based background and foreground selections due to which of the following ?
I. Accurate genotyping at the concerned diseases resistance locus.
II. Accurate gentotyping at the other loci.
III. Use of larger backcross populations.
IV. Highly efficient phenotype-based selection.
Options :
(*a*) I, II, III (*b*) II, III, IV
(*c*) III, IV (*d*) I, II

68. Which of the following mapping populations is immortal ?
I. Backcross II. F_2
III. RILs IV. NILs
Options :
(*a*) I, II (*b*) II, III
(*c*) III, IV (*d*) I, IV

69. Which of the populations listed in Q. 68 are derived by backcrossing ?
Options :
(*a*) I, II (*b*) II, IV
(*c*) I, IV (*d*) II, III

70. Which of the populations listed in Q. 68 are derived by continued backcrossing ?
Options :
(*a*) I (*b*) II
(*c*) III (*d*) IV

71. Which of the options given in Q. 68 lists populations that are derived by selfing ?

72. Which of the options given in Q. 70 lists a population that is derived by continued selfing ?

73. Development of which of the following populations requires the greatest effort ?
(*a*) F_2 (*b*) Backcross
(*c*) RILs (*d*) NILs

74. Development of which of the populations listed in Q. 73 requires the least amount of effort ?

75. The segregation ratios for dominant and codominant markers will differ in which of the following mapping populations ?
(*a*) F_2 (*b*) Backcross
(*c*) RILs (*d*) Both (*a*) and (*b*)

76. Which of the following populations may contain released varieties as well ?
(*a*) F_2 (*b*) RILs
(*c*) NILs (*d*) Backcross

77. The first case of linkage between a quantitative trait and a qualitative character was reported in *Phaseolus vulgaris* between which of the following traits ?
(*a*) Seed size and seed colour
(*b*) Seed size and flower colour
(*c*) Seed size and pod colour
(*d*) Seed yield and seed colour

78. Which of the following ***is not correct*** about molecular markers ?
(*a*) The sequence tagged sites (STS) marker system has all the advantages of PCR technique.
(*b*) RFLP is the first molecular marker that was developed in 1980s.
(*c*) RFLP markers are highly reproducible.
(*d*) A major limitation of RAPD markers is their non-reproducibility due to low annealing temperature.

79. Which of the following approaches can be used for the mapping of genes for monogenic traits in crop plants ?
(*a*) Bulked-segregant analysis of F_2 population.
(*b*) Use of near isogenic lines.
(*c*) Bulked segregant analysis of RILs.
(*d*) All of the above.

8.2. FILL IN THE BLANKS

1. The number of polymorphic .... markers is limited, especially in intervarietal/ intraspecific crosses and their expression is influenced by the ....
2. Unlike isozymes, number of DNA marker loci is nearly ...., their expression is not necessary for their detection and all loci can be detected with a single technique.
3. Ideal RFLP probes are .... that detect only one defined genomic fragment each, although, multilocus probes, such as repetitive DNA or cDNA, that detect several fragments at a time, are also used.
4. DAF uses .... stringent conditions for DNA hybridization and enzymatic reactions than does PCR.
5. AFLP shares some features of .... and ....
6. SCARs are similar to .... in construction and application.
7. AFLPs are .... markers, detect a very large number of markers per cross and are randomly distributed throughout the genome.
8. The abbreviation SSCP stands for ....
9. In case of ...., the fragments produced by restriction enzymes are modified and amplified using two primers, one primer has the sequence of the adaptor for one restriction enyme, while the other is specific to the adaptor for the second enzyme used for digestion of the genomic DNA.
10. Allele-specific associated primers give rise to the .... type of polymorphism.
11. For analysis of ISSR, tri- and tetra-nucleotide motifs gain more and more attention compared with mono- and di-nucelotide repeats because they present a clear banding pattern after ....
12. STMS is a .... marker.
13. Abbreviation RAHM stands for ....
14. CAPS was initially developed for use in ....
15. Abbreviation REMAP stands for ....
16. The presence of .... between qualitative trait and a molecular marker may be useful in marker-assisted selection.
17. The effectiveness of MAS will depend on the accuracy of the phenotypic classification of trait expression and the degree of .... between the marker and trait of interest.
18. Molecular markers permit identification of putative resistant plants in the absence of ....
19. During developent of RILs, SSD procedure is used for atleast .... generations..
20. The recombinant inbred lines are also called .... derived lines.
21. A breeding strategy in which selection for a gene is based on molecular markers closely linked to the gene of interest, and the markers are used to monitor the incorporation of the desirable allele from the donor source are called ....
22. Lines which are identical in their genotype, except for one gene (and the DNA region flanking this gene) are known as ....
23. Breeders have used typically 5 or 6 .... to generate most of the currently available NILs.
24. Perhaps, the most serious potential limitation in the near-isogenic gene mapping is the extent of molecular diversity between the genomes of the .... and .... parents.
25. 'RAPDs' is often pronounced as ....
26. In QTL mapping, ... and .... have a marked impact on the results; as a result, some QTLs may be detectable in some but not in other environments.
27. The maize variety, ... is developed through MAS.
28. .... can be used to select/improve those characters which have low heritability.
29. HHB-67-2 developed through MAS is a variety of ....
30. MAS is based on assumption that DNA marker can reliably predict the ....

8.3. MARK TRUE OR FALSE

1. Molecular markers can accelerate the generation of new varieties and allow connection of phenotypic characters with the genomic loci responsible for them.
2. At the beginning of genetics, it was already obvious that phenotypic differences between parents were often co-inherited but did not cosegregate in every case, depending on the markers concerned.
3. RAPD markers use a large amount of DNA.
4. DAF uses a small amount (25-200 ng/reaction) of DNA.
5. Microsatellite repeats are also known as simple sequence repeats.
6. AFLPs are as reproducible as RAPDs.
7. Allele-specific associated primers approach was developed to decrease the time for DNA extraction and increase the reliability of PCR for large-scale screening.
8. Like RFLPs, single strand conformational polymorphisms were found to be allelic variants of true Mendelian traits.
9. Abbrevation SAMPL stands for selective amplification of microsatellite polymorphic loci.
10. CAPS detects DNA sequence variation in terms of the length of DNA fragments generated by the restriction digestion of the PCR products; therefore, it is sometimes termed as PCR-RFLP.
11. Often the high cost of developing an RFLP marker system for a new species or inefficiency of MAS due to large quantity of DNA required and slow screening process forces a decision in favour of a PCR-based marker system.
12. Selection for multiple quantitative trait loci (QTLs) using molecular markers can not be effective if a significant association is found between a quantitative trait and a molecular marker.
13. In all cases of MAS, foreground selection is the primary interest of the breeder.
14. Linkage mapping of molecular markers is based on suitable mapping populations.
15. If two or more genetic maps possess a minimal number of common markers, they can be merged to create a more informative map.
16. Bulked segregant analysis has been extensively used in mapping of molecular markers.
17. The genome of any given near-isogenic line will most likely contain donor parent derived alleles at several of its loci, which accounts for the use of the term near-isogenic to describe such lines.
18. NILs have been rarely used to find molecular markers linked to such traits as disease resistance.
19. Individual polygenes can be mapped using conventional approaches.
20. The mapping population must be relatively large in order to detect QTLs having minor effects, and the biological relevance of uncovered QTLs depends on the cut-off chosen for statistical significance.
21. BSA has been extensively used in mapping of molecular markers.
22. DNA fingerprints can be prepared by using as probes simple sequence oligonucleotides.
23. In crops like tomato, cultivars may show infrequent polymorphism preventing the use of RFLPs for varietal identification.
24. RAPDs have similar applicaton as RFLPs.

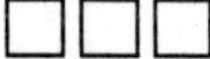

9

ANIMAL TISSUE CULTURE AND HYBRIDOMA TECHNOLOGY

9.1. MULTIPLE CHOICE QUESTIONS

1. Which of the following scientists showed that leucocytes can divide outside the body ?
(*a*) Meyers (*b*) Walker
(*c*) Arnold (*d*) Adams

2. Which of the following cell cultures is an example of continuous cell lines ?
(*a*) HeLa cell line
(*b*) *MDCK* dog kidney
(*c*) 3T3 fibroblasts
(*d*) All of the above

3. Which of the following ***is not correct*** about animal organ cultures ?
(*a*) The first attempt was made by Loeb in 1887.
(*b*) Loeb maintained adult rabbit liver, kidney, thyroid and ovary on small plasma clots in test tubes.
(*c*) Loeb noted that cultured organs retained their histological features for 13 days.
(*d*) In 1919, Loeb and Fleischer reported that culture tubes must be filled with O_2 to prevent central necrosis of explants.

4. Which of the following techniques are used for animal organ culture ?
I. Agar gel
II. Grid method
III. Maximow's single slide technique
IV. Watchglass method

Options :
(*a*) I, II, III, IV (*b*) II, III, IV
(*c*) I, III, IV (*d*) III, IV

5. Which of the following is an example of natural medium ?
(*a*) Tissue extract (*b*) Plasma clot
(*c*) Biological fluids (*d*) All of the above

6. Organ cultures can be used for which of the following purposes ?
I. Production of tissues for implantation in patients.
II. Regeneration of whole organisms.
III. Studies on the pattern of growth, differentiation and development of organ rudiments (foetal organs).
IV. Studies of action of drugs, carcinogenic agents on the animal organs.

Options :
(*a*) I, II, III, IV (*b*) I, III, IV
(*c*) II, III, IV (*d*) I, II, III

7. The technique of cyclic exposure to medium and gas phase is successful in long-term cultures of which of the following human adult tissues ?
(*a*) Mammary epithelium
(*b*) Oesophagus
(*c*) Uterine endocervix
(*d*) All of the above

8. The surface available for the attachment of cultured cells is called which of the following ?
(*a*) Surface attachment site
(*b*) Platform
(*c*) Substrate
(*d*) Both (*a*) and (*b*)

9. Which of the following ***is not correct*** about artificial skin ?
(*a*) The skin explants used for obtaining artificial skin may be either obtained from the patient concerned or from the foreskin of newborn babies.
(*b*) Skin cells of newborns grow as fast as those from adult skin.
(*c*) Use of PGA (a synthetic polymer) allows the newborn skin to grow without scars.
(*d*) Artificial skin from newborn skin explants is used to cover the wound till artificial skin is obtained from patient's own skin.

10. Cell cultures contain which of the following type of cells ?
I. Precursor cells.
II. Stem cells.
III. Differentiated cells.
IV. Dedifferentiated cells.
Options :
(*a*) I, II, III (*b*) I, II, III, IV
(*c*) II, III, IV (*d*) I, III, IV

11. Which of the following are examples of artificial animal tissue/cell culture medium ?
I. Chemically defined media
II. Serum containing media
III. Serum-free media
IV. Protein-free media
Options :
(*a*) I, II, III (*b*) II, III, IV
(*c*) I, II, III, IV (*d*) I, III, IV

12. In animal cell cultures, differentiation and cell proliferation (cell division) are affected by which of the following ?
(*a*) Cell density and serum
(*b*) Ca^{2+} ions and hormones
(*c*) Cell to cell interactions
(*d*) All of the above

13. Generally, cell proliferation is promoted by which of the following ?
(*a*) Low Ca^{2+} ions
(*b*) High growth factor levels
(*c*) Low cell density
(*d*) All of the above.

14. Which of the following statements are correct about substrates (culture vessels) ?
I. Glass is the most comonly used substrate in the form of slides, flasks, test tubes.
II. Glass and metal surfaces are naturally negatively charged.
III. Organic surfaces, *e.g.*, plastics, must be made wettable and negatively charged.
IV. In some cases, the substrate surface is made positively charged by coating with collagen, gelatin or polylysine.
Options :
(*a*) I, II, III, IV (*b*) II, III, IV
(*c*) I, III, IV (*d*) I, IV

15. Differentiation in animal cell cultures is promoted by which of the following ?
I. Cortisone growth factor
II. Low cell density
III. High Ca^{2+} ions
IV. Nerve growth factors.
Options :
(*a*) I, II, III (*b*) II, III, IV
(*c*) I, III, IV (*d*) I, II, III, IV

16. Which of the following ***is not correct*** about plastic substrates ?
(*a*) Most plasticware are nonautoclavable, and are supplied sterile for a single use.
(*b*) Polystyrene is the most commonly used, but polyethylene, perspex, PVC, polycarbonate, teflon, cellophane and cellulose acetate are all suitable substrates.
(*c*) All the organic substrates must be suitably treated to make them wettable and positively charged.
(*d*) Thin teflon films are available as Petri dishes or as membranes to be used as rafts; these films are permeable to O_2 and CO_2.

17. Which of the following ***is not correct*** about suspension cultures ?
(*a*) Cells of certain type are grown in liquid media as suspension cultures.
(*b*) Cells harvested from late log phase cultures are inoculated into fresh liquid medium maintained at 20°C.
(*c*) The initial cell density is usually between 5×10^4 to 2×10^5 cells/ml.
(*d*) The cultures are stirred at 200-350 rpm.

18. During suspension culture, which of the following factors affect cell yield ?

I. pH of the medium
II. Nutrient limitation
III. Accumulation of toxic products
IV. O_2 limitation.

Options :

(*a*) I, II, III, IV (*b*) II, III, IV
(*c*) I, III, IV (*d*) III, IV

19. Hybrid cells are useful for which of the following ?

I. Production of monoclonal antibodies.
II. Investigation of malignant transformations.
III. Gene or chromosome mapping.
IV. Study of the control of cell divison and gene expression.

Options :

(*a*) I, III, IV (*b*) II, III, IV
(*c*) I, II, III, IV (*d*) III, IV

20. Which of the following is the reason for production of antibodies of a single specificity by a hybridoma clone ?

(*a*) Fusion with a single B cell.
(*b*) Production of antibodies of a single specificity by a single B cell.
(*c*) Production of no antibodies by the other fusion partner of the hybridoma clone.
(*d*) All of the above.

21. Cell fusion is enhanced by which of the following ?

(*a*) Polyethylene glycol
(*b*) Ultraviolet inactivated Sendai Virus
(*c*) Colchicine
(*d*) Both (*a*) and (*b*)

22. Among the given biological fluids used as culture medium, which one is the most commonly used in animal cell cultures ?

(*a*) Serum
(*b*) Amniotic fluid
(*c*) Insect haemolymph
(*d*) Aqueous humour from eye

23. Among the given tissue extracts, which one is the most commonly used as culture medium ?

(*a*) Liver extract
(*b*) Chick embryo extract
(*c*) Plasma
(*d*) Bone morrow

24. Serum can be obtained from which of the following ?

(*a*) Placental cord blood
(*b*) Adult human blood
(*c*) Horse blood
(*d*) All of the above

25. Among the given serums, which one is the most commonly used in animal cell culture media ?

(*a*) Young calf serum
(*b*) Cattle serum
(*c*) Foetal calf serum
(*d*) Horse serum

26. Which of the following is commonly used for promoting cell growth in animal cell cultures ?

(*a*) Ethanolamine (*b*) Insulin
(*c*) Transferrin (*d*) All of the above

27. Which of the following ***is not provided*** by serum ?

(*a*) Carbohydrates and lipids
(*b*) Plasma proteins
(*c*) Alkaloids
(*d*) Some enzymes

28. Which of the following ***is not*** heat labile ?

(*a*) Growth factors and serum
(*b*) Trypsin and proteins
(*c*) Peptone and salts
(*d*) Both (*a*) and (*b*)

29. Serum-free media provide, which of the following advantages over serum containing media ?

I. Selective culture of differentiated and producing cell types.
II. Easier downstream processing.
III. Toxic effects of serum are avoided
IV. There is no danger of degradation of sensitive proteins by proteases.

Options :

(*a*) I, II, III, IV (*b*) II, III, IV
(*c*) I, III, IV (*d*) II, IV

30. Which of the following functions are performed by serum ?

I. It provides nutrients for cells.
II. It provides several hormones essential for growth of nearly all cells.

III. It provides proteins, *e.g.*, fibronectin, which promote attachment of cells to the substrate.
IV. It provides several binding proteins, which carry other molecules into the cells.

Options :
(*a*) I, II, III (*b*) I, II, III, IV
(*c*) II, III, IV (*d*) III, IV

31. Serum contains which of the following growth factors ?
(*a*) Epidermal and fibroblast growth factors.
(*b*) Transforming growth factor β.
(*c*) Endothelial and platelet-derived growth factors.
(*d*) All of the above.

32. Serum-free media suffer from which of the following disadvantages ?
I. Most serum-free media are specific to one cell type.
II. Growth rate and the maximum cell density attained are lower than those with serum containing media.
III. Cells tend to become fragile during prolonged agitated culture unless biopolymers or synthetic polymers are added.
IV. Control of pH, temperature is not necessary.

Options :
(*a*) I, II, III (*b*) II, III, IV
(*c*) I, II, III, IV (*d*) I, IV

33. Column A contains different media, while column B contains different cell types for which they are suited. Match these two columns carefully and select the correct option from those listed below them.

Column A	Column B
A. MEM	I. Non-transformed cells
B. CMRL 1066	II. Permanent cell lines
C. MCDB 301	III. Permanent cell lines in monolayers
D. MCDB 401	IV. Clonal growth of permanent cell lines

Options :
(*a*) AI, BIV, CIII, DII
(*b*) AII, BIII, CIV, DI
(*c*) AIII, BII, CI, DIV
(*d*) AIV, BI, CII, DIII

34. Albumin carries which of the following molecules into cells ?
(*a*) Vitamins (*b*) Hormones
(*c*) Lipids (*d*) All of the above.

35. Which of the following disadvantages are associated with serum when used in culture media ?
I. It interferes with downstream processing.
II. It may inhibit growth of some cell types, *e.g.*, epidermal keratinocytes.
III. Some growth factors may be inadequate for specific cell types.
IV. It may contain some cytotoxic or potentially cytotoxic constituents.

Options :
(*a*) I, II, III, IV (*b*) II, III, IV
(*c*) I, III, IV (*d*) III, IV

36. Development of serum-free formulations of culture media are based on which of the following approaches ?
(*a*) Limiting factor (*b*) Analytical
(*c*) Synthetic (*d*) All of the above

37. Which of the following enzymes is the most commonly used for disaggregation of explants.
(*a*) Elastase and pappain
(*b*) Mucase and elastase
(*c*) Trypsin and collagenase
(*d*) Both (*b*) and (*c*)

38. Cell lines having specific cell types may be obtained by which of the following methods ?
(*a*) Selective culture
(*b*) Cloning
(*c*) Physical cell separation
(*d*) All of the above

39. Contamination may be checked by looking for which of the following ?
I. Granular appearances outside the cells.
II. A rapid change in pH.
III. Cloudiness of the medium.
IV. Unidentified material floating in the medium.

Options :
(*a*) I, II, III, IV (*b*) II, III, IV
(*c*) I, III, IV (*d*) III, IV

40. *In vitro* transformation of animal cells may occur due to which of the following ?
(*a*) Spontaneously
(*b*) Chemically induced
(*c*) Induced by virus
(*d*) All of the above

41. Most of the cell lines will grow for a period of about how many weeks ?
(*a*) 5 (*b*) 12
(*c*) 3 (*d*) 18

42. Continuous cell lines provide which of the following advantages ?
(*a*) Lower serum requirement
(*b*) Ability to grow in suspension
(*c*) Faster rate of growth
(*d*) All of the above

43. Which of the following normal cells ***do not give rise*** to continuous cell lines ?
(*a*) Human glia cells
(*b*) Human fibroblast cells
(*c*) Chick fibroblasts
(*d*) All of the above

44. Which of the following statements are correct ?
I. Freeze preservation of animal cells is now routine.
II. A cryoprotective agent like glycerol or DMSO is generally added to minimise injury to cells during freezing and thawing.
III. Frozen ampoules are generally stored in liquid nitrogen.

Options :
(*a*) I, II (*b*) II, IV
(*c*) I, II, III (*d*) I, III

45. Cell cultures are used for obtaining which of the following ?
(*a*) Interleukins and interferons.
(*b*) Hormones, enzymes and antibodies.
(*c*) Viral vaccines.
(*d*) All of the above.

46. Which of the following are the common feature of continuous cell lines ?
I. Increased cloning efficiency
II. Reduced serum dependence
III. Decreased growth rate
IV. Increased malignancy

Options :
(*a*) I, II, III (*b*) I, II, IV
(*c*) I, II, III, IV (*d*) I, IV

47. Cell cultures are used for obtaining which of the following viral vaccines ?
(*a*) Foot and mouth
(*b*) Polio and mumps
(*c*) Measles and rabies
(*d*) All of the above

48. In animal cell suspension cultures, damage to cells can be reduced by which of the following ?
I. Lower gassing rates
II. Larger bubbles
III. Adding non-nutritional supplements like Pluronic F-68 and sodium carboxymethyl cellulose.

Options :
(*a*) I, II, III (*b*) I, II
(*c*) II, III (*d*) I, III

49. Culture systems based on immobilized cells offer which of the following advantages ?
I. Lower cell densities.
II. Suitability for both suspension and monolayer culture.
III. Stability and longevity of culture.
IV. Protection of cells from shear forces due to medium flow.

Options :
(*a*) I, II, III (*b*) I, II, III, IV
(*c*) II, III, IV (*d*) I, IV

50. Which of the following are common features of continuous cell lines ?
I. Ability to grow upto higher cell densities.
II. Reduced dependence on substrate adhesion.
III. Aneuploid (between $2n$ and $4n$) chromosome numbers.
IV. Smaller, more rounded cells with a higher nucleus/cytoplasm ratio.

Options :
(*a*) I, II, III, IV (*b*) I, II, III
(*c*) II, III, IV (*d*) I, III, IV

51. Cell cloning is used for which of the following purposes ?
(*a*) To obtain homogeneous cell lines from heterogeneous cell cultures.
(*b*) To develop hybridoma clones.

(*c*) To isolate biochemical mutants and cell strains with marker chromosomes.
(*d*) All of the above.

52. Which of the following approaches can be used to enhance the plating efficiency of cell lines ?
I. Use of conditioned medium.
II. Providing intermediate metabolites like keto-acids, nucleosides, etc.
III. Use of a chemically defined medium.
IV. Use of feeder layers.

Options :
(*a*) I, II, III, IV (*b*) II, III, IV
(*c*) I, II, IV (*d*) I, III, IV

53. Which of the following ***is not correct*** ?
(*a*) Cells derived from a single cell through meiosis constitute a clone.
(*b*) Plating efficiency of continuous cell lines is generally 10% or higher.
(*c*) A feeder layer is a layer of cells, which has been treated to prevent their growth.
(*d*) During colony isolation, desired colony may be shielded and the remaining colonies irradiated by a lethal dose of X-rays.

54. Which of the following features ***is not correct*** about animal organ cultures ?
(*a*) They can be maintained only for few months.
(*b*) Hormone-dependent organs remain hormone-dependent.
(*c*) Results from them are comparable to those from whole animals.
(*d*) The development of foetal organs *in vitro* is comparable to that *in vivo*.

55. Which of the following statements ***is not correct*** about production of artificial skin ?
(*a*) Intact skin explant is cultured on a suitable medium.
(*b*) Cell divison occurs in keratinocytes.
(*c*) Corneocytes present in the explant do not contribute to the artificial skin.
(*d*) Irradiated 3T3 fibroblast cells are used as feeder layer.

56. Which of the following cell types present in heterogeneous animal cell cultures are the least likely to divide ?
(*a*) Precursor cells
(*b*) Stem cells
(*c*) Differentiated cells
(*d*) Both (*a*) and (*c*)

57. Which of the options given in Q. 56 is essential for maintenance of heterogeneous animal cell cultures ?

58. Plasticware can be made wettable and negatively charged by which of the following treatments ?
(*a*) Oxidizing agents
(*b*) UV irradiation
(*c*) Strong acids
(*d*) All of the above

59. In which of the following culture systems, there is no change in culture volume during the culture period ?
I. Continuous-flow cultures
II. Fed-batch cultures
III. Batch cultures
IV. Perfusion cultures

Options :
(*a*) I, II, III (*b*) II, III, IV
(*c*) I, III, IV (*d*) I, II, IV

60. In which of the culture systems given in Q. 59, spent medium alongwith cells is withdrawn ?

Options :
(*a*) I (*b*) II
(*c*) IV (*d*) III

61. In which of the culture systems given in Q. 59, spent medium with or without cells is withdrawn ?

Options :
(*a*) I, II (*b*) I, III
(*c*) II, III (*d*) I, IV

62. In which of the culture systems given in Q. 59, cells are maintained in a steady state of growth ?

Options :
(*a*) I (*b*) II
(*c*) III (*d*) IV

63. Which of the following is the preferred enzyme for disaggregation of animal tissues ?

(*a*) Collagenase (*b*) Trypsin
(*c*) Elastase (*d*) Mucase

64. Trypsin is preferred over other enzymes for tissue disaggregation because of which of the following ?
(*a*) Effective for many tissues
(*b*) Tolerated by most cells
(*c*) Neutralized by serum
(*d*) All of the above

65. EDTA readily disaggregates which of the following tissues ?
(*a*) Fibrous tissues (*b*) Epithelium
(*c*) Skin (*d*) Muscle

66. Animal cell cultures may be contaminated by which of the following ?
(*a*) Viruses (*b*) Other cell lines
(*c*) Bacteria (*d*) All of the above

67. Which of the following culture vessels are used for large-scale culture of anchorage-dependent cells ?
I. Opticell culture system.
II. Hollow fibre cartridge.
III. Heli-cell vessels
IV. Microcarrier cultures.
Options :
(*a*) I, II, III (*b*) I, II, III, IV
(*c*) I, III, IV (*d*) II, III, IV

68. Which of the culture systems listed in Q. 67 is based on a ceramic cartridge ?
Options :
(*a*) I (*b*) II
(*c*) III (*d*) IV

69. Which of the options given in Q. 68 can be used for both suspension and monolayer cell cultures ?

70. Which of the options given in Q. 68 allows monolayers to be grown as suspension cultures ?

71. Which of the culture systems listed in Q. 67 is an example of cell immobilization ?
Options :
(*a*) I, II (*b*) II, III
(*c*) III, IV (*d*) I, IV

72. Which of the options listed in Q. 68 is an example of cell immbolization by entrapment ?

73. Which of the options listed in Q. 68 is an example of immurement cultures ?

74. Cell fusion leads to the production of which of the following ?
(*a*) Homokaryons (*b*) Heterokaryons
(*c*) Hybrid cells (*d*) All of the above

75. A hybrid cell obtained by cell fusion has which of the following ?
(*a*) Two genetically different nuclei.
(*b*) A single nucleus obtained by fusion of two genetically different nuclei.
(*c*) Cytoplasm derived from the two fusion partners.
(*d*) Both (*b*) and (*c*)

76. Which of the following techniques was used for development of 'Dolly' ?
(*a*) Nucleus removal (*b*) Cell culture
(*c*) Cell fusion (*d*) All of the above

77. Which of the following event(s) occurs during inflammatory response ?
(*a*) An increase in blood vessel diameter.
(*b*) An increase in capillary permeability.
(*c*) Influx of phagocytes from the capillaries into the tissues.
(*d*) All of the above.

78. Which of the following enzymes is loaded in lysosomes ?
I. Protease II. Dehydrogenase
III. Lipase IV. Nuclease
Options :
(*a*) I, II, III, IV (*b*) I, III, IV
(*c*) II, III, IV (*d*) I, II, III

79. Which of the following is correct about B- and T-cells ?
I. B cells mature in bone marrow, while T-cells mature in thymus gland.
II. B cell express unique membrane-bound antibodies (sIgs), while T cells express on their surface unique antigen-binding receptors, called T-cell receptors.
III. Antibodies produced by B cells are the effector molecules of the humoral branch of acquired immunity, while T cells function as helper or cytotoxic cells.
IV. Both T and B cells are types of lymphocytes.

Options :
(*a*) I, II, III, IV (*b*) II, III, IV
(*c*) II, IV (*d*) I, II, III

80. Which of the following is correct about T helper cells ?

I. When a T helper cell interacts with an antigen-MHC II molecule present on an APC, it becomes activated and begins to secrete cytokines.
II. Cytokines activate B cells, T cytoxic cells and various phagocytic cells.
III. Activated phagocytic cells are able to kill microorganisms like bacteria and protozoa.
IV. Recognition of an antigen-MHC complex by a specific mature T lymphocyte, induces its proliferation and differentiation into T helper cells and cytotoxic T lymphocytes, and into memory cells.

Options :
(*a*) I, II, III (*b*) II, III, IV
(*c*) I, II, III, IV (*d*) I, III, IV

81. Lymph nodes are located abundantly in which of the following ?
(*a*) Groin (*b*) Arm pit
(*c*) Neck (*d*) All of the above

82. Which of the following is correct about lymph ?

I. It is described as filtered blood plasma, but it has lower protein content than plasma.
II. It is clear, watery fluid, flowing through lymphatic vessels.
III. It is a link between blood and tissue fluid.
IV. Its lymphocytes destroy harmful pathogens.

Options :
(*a*) I, II, III (*b*) I, II, III, IV
(*c*) II, III, IV (*d*) I, II, IV

83. Which of the following functions is related to lymph nodes ?

I. Synthesis of certain antibodies.
II. They filter out cell debris and other injurious substances.
III. Production of lymphocytes and monocytes.
IV. Phagocytosis and destruction of bacteria and other pathogens.

Options :
(*a*) I, II, III, IV (*b*) II, III, IV
(*c*) I, II, IV (*d*) I, III, IV

84. Which of the following is correct about B cells ?

I. B lymphocytes originate from multipotent stem cells present in bone marrow.
II. Each mature B cell produces antibodies specific to a single antigen molecule.
III. The mature B cell is called a naive B cell so long as it has not interacted with an antigen.
IV. The naive B cells secrete antibodies only when they differentiate into plasma cells, following an interaction with the specific antigens.

Options :
(*a*) I, II, III (*b*) II, III, IV
(*c*) I, III, IV (*d*) I, II, III, IV

85. Which of the following ***is not correct*** about T cells ?
(*a*) T lymphocytes originate from myeloid stem cells.
(*b*) Lymphoid stem cells that migrate into thymus ultimately mature into T cells.
(*c*) During T cell maturation, rearrangement of the genes encoding T cell receptor (TCR) takes place.
(*d*) T cells are primarily of two types, *viz.*, T helper cells and T cytotoxic cells.

86. The lymphocytes protect from which of the following ?
(*a*) Viral pathogens
(*b*) Bacterial pathogens
(*c*) Cancer
(*d*) All of the above

87. Antibodies fight against which of the following ?
(*a*) Starvation (*b*) Ageing
(*c*) Infection (*d*) All of the above

88. Which of the following work is performed by lymph nodes ?
(*a*) Preparation of blood
(*b*) Elimination of CO_2
(*c*) Destruction of bacteria
(*d*) All of the above

89. Lymphoid stem cells give rise to which of the following cells ?
(*a*) Lymphocyte progenitor cells
(*b*) Pro-B and Pro-T cells
(*c*) Pre-B and Pre-T cells
(*d*) All of the above

90. Embryo transfer technology suffers from which of the following limitations ?
(*a*) The donor females are removed from production for the period they are used as donor of young embryos.
(*b*) A high degree of expertise is required for an efficient and successful operation.
(*c*) The cost of producing each progeny is several-fold higher than that from natural events.
(*d*) All of the above.

91. Which of the following techniques is used for the separation of X- and Y-chromosome bearing sperms ?
(*a*) Gel electrophoresis
(*b*) Sephadex gel column
(*c*) Zoobloting
(*d*) Both (*a*) and (*b*)

92. Which of the following statements are correct about B cells ?
I. As a B cell matures, its antibody genes undergo rearrangement to yield functional genes.
II. In each B cell, at first a single allele of the gene encoding the heavy chain of antibody and a single allele of the gene encoding antibody light chain is rearranged.
III. Mature B cell is said to be antigenically committed.
IV. Random rearrangements of antibody genes generate a tremendous diversity.

Options :
(*a*) I, II, III, IV (*b*) II, III, IV
(*c*) I, III, IV (*d*) II, IV

93. Which of the following ***is not correct*** about T cells ?
(*a*) During T cell maturation, rearrangement of genes encoding T cell receptor (TCR) takes place.
(*b*) Each TCR molecule is a heteromer consisting of an α and a β chain or a γ and a δ chain.
(*c*) Each T cell expresses TCR of a single antigenic specificity.
(*d*) TCR gene rearrangements follow the same general scheme as that for antibody genes.

94. Animal cloning allows which of the following ?
I. Indefinite multiplication of an elite desirable genotype without the risk of segregation and recombination.
II. The technique holds a great promise in genetic research, specially in understanding ageing and curing of genetic diseases.
III. This technique should make it feasible to target transgenes in livestock by nuclear transfer from transgentic cell populations developed *in vitro* into enucleated oocytes to recover non-chimaeric transgenic animals.

Options :
(*a*) I, II (*b*) II, III
(*c*) I, II, III (*d*) I, III

95. Which of the following is correct about chromosome walking ?
I. This technique is used for characterizing small, say few Kb, regions of chromosomes.
II. Generally, a cosmid library is used for chromosome walking.
III. In this technique, one can begin with a DNA fragment that contains a known gene/genetic marker.
IV. The sequence located at one end of this fragment is used to identify a clone that has such a DNA insert, which partly overlaps the first fragment; now the other (non-overlapping) end of this new DNA is used as probe.

Options :
(*a*) I, II, III, IV (*b*) II, III, IV
(*c*) II, IV (*d*) I, III, IV

96. An embryo transfer technology offers which of the following advantages ?
I. Rapid rate of multiplication of animals of selected superior genotypes.

II. Each young embryo can be split into 2-4 parts, each of which would develop into a separate progeny.
III. The young embryos can be frozen and stored in liquid nitrogen for upto 10 years or more and used at a subsequent date.
IV. Superior cows that are unfit to carry the foetus for full term, can serve as donors of the young embryos.

Options :
(*a*) I, II, III, IV (*b*) II, III, IV
(*c*) I, III, IV (*d*) I, II, IV

97. Conventional linkage maps suffer from which of the following ?
(*a*) The number of genes producing distinct morphological effects is rather limited.
(*b*) Their mapping is tedious and time-taking.
(*c*) Genes governing quantitative traits can not be mapped.
(*d*) All of the above.

98. Which of the following ***is not correct*** ?
(*a*) Proteins produced by genes transferred by genetic engineering into selected hosts are called recombinant proteins.
(*b*) In general, antigens are immunogenic.
(*c*) Antibodies belong to a special category of proteins, called immunoglobulins.
(*d*) Monoclonal antibodies are produced from hybrid cells obtained by fusing a memory B cell with a myeloma cell.

99. Peripheral lymphoid organs include which of the following ?
I. Lymphoid nodules in the gut and blood.
II. Spleen and numerous lymph nodes in various parts of body.
III. Tonsils and appendix.

Options :
(*a*) I, II (*b*) II, III
(*c*) I, III (*d*) I, II, III

100. Which of the following statements are correct ?
I. The random rearrangements of antibody and TCR genes generates more than 10^8 and $\sim 10^{15}$ different antigenic specificities during maturation of B and T cells, respectively.
II. An animal does not ordinarily produce antibodies against self-antigens.
III. Most T cells express αβ TCR2, while ~5% of T cells in adult mice express γδ TCR.
IV. T cells mature in bone marrow.

Options :
(*a*) I, II, III, IV (*b*) I, II, III
(*c*) I, III, IV (*d*) II, III, IV

101. Memory cells lack which of the following ?
(*a*) IgD (*b*) IgG
(*c*) IgM (*d*) IgA

102. Which of the following statements are correct about abzymes ?
I. These are antibodies with enzymatic action.
II. They are produced in response to stable analogues of the transition states of substrates for the given reaction.
III. It should be possible to generate such abzymes that catalyze reactions for which no natural enzymes exists.
IV. It may be possible to develop such abzymes that cleave proteins and carbohydrates at specific residues.

Options :
(*a*) I, II, III (*b*) I, II, III, IV
(*c*) II, III, IV (*d*) I, III, IV

103. In humans, which of the following steps are involved in *in vitro* fertilization and embryo transfer ?
I. Collection of sperms
II. Collection of oocytes
III. *In vitro* fertilization
IV. Implantation of the resulting zygotes in the uterus of would be mother.

Options :
(*a*) I, II, IV (*b*) I, II, III
(*c*) I, II, III, IV (*d*) II, III, IV

104. Which of the following statements are correct ?
I. Genes *RAG1* and *RAG2* are involved in somatic recombination of antibody genes.
II. Interferons reduce the cytotoxic activity of natural killer cells.

III. B and T cells exhibit clonal selection in response to the specific antigens.
IV. Intracellular antigens are most effectively eliminated by cytotoxic T lymphocytes.

Options :
(*a*) I, II, III, IV (*b*) I, III, IV
(*c*) II, III, IV (*d*) I, II, IV

105. An antibody molecule consists of which of the following ?
(*a*) Two identical light chains
(*b*) Two identical heavy chains
(*c*) Two α and 2δ chains
(*d*) Both (*a*) and (*b*)

106. Light chain of antibody consists of about how many amino acids ?
(*a*) 440 (*b*) 220
(*c*) 320 (*d*) 360

107. Which of the following ***is not correct*** ?
(*a*) A prolonged administration of human menopausal gonadotrophin (hMG) for stimulation of ovulation produces some side effects like abdominal discomfort and pleural effusion.
(*b*) Human chorionic gonadotrophin (hCG) is administered to prevent the inhibition of LH (luteinising hormone) surge by hMG.
(*c*) Laproscopy is usually done after ovulation.
(*d*) The time of natural ovulation is determined by monitoring the rise in the level of LH either in urine or in blood.

108. In humans, the time of ovulation is estimated on the basis of which of the following ?
1. Level of luteinising hormone in blood or urine.
2. Temperature chart of donor females.
3. Change in cervical mucous score.
4. Oestrogen level in blood or urine.

Options :
(*a*) 1, 2, 3, 4 (*b*) 1, 3
(*c*) 2, 3, 4 (*d*) 2, 4

109. Which of the following applications of monoclonal antibodies are concerned with diagnostics ?
I. Accurate detection of specific chromosomes of a given species.
II. Unequivocal classification of blood groups, *e.g.*, ABO, Rh, etc.
III. Clear and decisive detection of pathogens involved in diseases.
IV. Early detection of metastasis.

Options :
(*a*) I, II, III. IV (*b*) II, III
(*c*) I, III (*d*) I, II

110. Monoclonal antibodies produced for carcinoembryonic antigen and some tumour associated antigens can be used in histochemical assays that permit the identification of which of the following ?
(*a*) Tumour cell type.
(*b*) Benign and malignant nature of tumours.
(*c*) Early cases of metastasis.
(*d*) All of the above.

111. RFLPs provide which of the following advantages ?
I. Fewer individuals (25-50 individuals per F_2 population) need to be studied.
II. The number of RFLP loci is very large so that even very small segments of the chromosomes can be mapped.
III. Mapping does not necessarily depend on gene function.
IV. Quantitative trait loci (QTLs) can be mapped.

Options :
(*a*) I, II, III, IV (*b*) I, III, IV
(*c*) I, II, III (*d*) II, III, IV

112. Which of the following steps is involved in antibody engineering ?
1. Development of the antibody design to serve the specific purpose.
2. Bringing together the DNA sequences that would generate this antibody molecule into a suitable expression vector.
3. Introducing this recombinant DNA into a myeloma cell line.
4. Mass culture of the transfected clones of myeloma cell line.
5. Harvest of the recombinant antibodies so produced.

Options :
(*a*) 1, 2, 3, 4 (*b*) 1, 2, 3, 4, 5
(*c*) 2, 4, 5 (*d*) 1, 3, 5

113. Which of the following statements are correct about ricin ?

I. Ricin is a natural toxin found in the endosperm of linseed.

II. It has two polypeptides called A (toxin peptide) and B (a cell binding polypeptide, lectin).

III. Ricin A polypeptide enzymatically and irreversibly modifies the larger subunit of ribosomes making them incapable of protein synthesis.

IV. Ricin A is effective against both dividing and non-dividing cells as it inhibits protein synthesis.

Options :

(*a*) I, II, III, IV (*b*) II, III, IV
(*c*) I, III, IV (*d*) I, II, IV

114. Which of the following media can be used for oocyte incubation, *in vitro* fertilization and subsequent culture of the zygote ?

I. Earl's solution.

II. Modified Whitten's medium.

III. Modification of Ham's F10 medium.

IV. Whittinghams's T6 medium.

Options :

(*a*) I, II, III, IV (*b*) I, II, IV
(*c*) I, III, IV (*d*) II, III, IV

115. Which of the following statements are correct about interferons ?

I. Interferon was discovered by Issacs and Lindemann.

II. They are proteins produced by a cell infected by a virus.

III. They provide protection to healthy cells from pathogens.

IV. They are mainly classified into interferon-α, inerferon-β and interferon-γ.

Options :

(*a*) I, II, III, IV (*b*) II, III, IV
(*c*) I, II, IV (*d*) I, III, IV

116. Column A contains a list of interferons, while column B lists the cells by which they are produced. Match the two columns carefully and select the correct option from those given below them.

Column A	**Column B**
A. IFN-β	1. Human leucocytes
B. IFN-α	2. Stimulated T-lymphocyte cells
C. IFN-γ	3. Fibroblasts

Options :

(*a*) A1, B3, C2 (*b*) A3, B1, C2
(*c*) A3, B2, C1 (*d*) A2, B3, C1

117. Large-scale *in vitro* culture of hybridoma cells has been done in which of the following ?

(*a*) In vessels based on immobilized cells.
(*b*) Stirred bioreactors.
(*c*) Airlift fermentors.
(*d*) All of the above.

118. Which of the following advantages are associated with the use of animal cell lines for recombinant protein production ?

1. The signals for synthesis, processing and secretion of the concerned proteins are better recognized.
2. Protein products are readily secreted into the medium, which makes their recovery much easier.
3. Multimeric proteins are also assembled correctly.
4. The patterns of folding and disulphide bridge formation are similar to those of the natural proteins.

Options :

(*a*) 1, 2, 3 (*b*) 2, 3, 4
(*c*) 1, 2, 3, 4 (*d*) 1, 2

119. Which of the following ***is not correct*** about interferon ?

(*a*) Interferons induce in the cells production of 2, 5-adenosine polymerase.
(*b*) Interferons enhance the cytotoxic activity of natural killer cells.
(*c*) Interferons are known to enhance growth of some types of tumours.
(*d*) Large-scale (1000 l to 10,000 l) cell cultures are infected with Sendai Virus, and incubated for 24 hours, after which the supernatant is collected, centrifuged, and used for isolation of interferon.

120. Which of the following vaccine was the first to be produced from cell cultures ?

(*a*) Polio (*b*) Rabies
(*c*) Measles (*d*) Hepatitis-B

121. Column A lists some viral vaccines and cloumn B lists the cell lines from which these vaccines are produced. Match the two columns carefully and select the correct option from those given below them.

Column A	Column B
A. Foot and mouth disease (FMD)	1. Human diploid cells
B. Influenza	2. Cow kidney
C. Polio	3. Chick embryo
D. Rubella	4. Primate kidney

Options :
(*a*) A2, B4, C1, D3 (*b*) A2, B3, C4, D1
(*c*) A4, B2, C3, D1 (*d*) A3, B1, C2, D4

122. The medium used for *in vitro* culure of hybridoma cells must serve which of the following purposes ?
(*a*) Support adequate cell proliferation
(*b*) Give high antibody yield
(*c*) Both (*a*) and (*b*)
(*d*) Promote cell differentiation

123. Kappa light chain gene has which of the following ?
(*a*) 300 different V (variable) segments
(*b*) Five different J (joining) segments
(*c*) A single C (constant) segment
(*d*) All of the above

124. ***Assertion (A)***: The antigen-antibody interaction is highly specific, but some cases of cross-reaction (interaction of an antibody induced by one antigen with another antigen) are also known.
Reason (R): Cross reaction occurs possibly due to a similarity between the epitopes of the concerned antigens.
Options :
(*a*) Both A and R are correct, and R roughly explains A.
(*b*) Both A and R are correct, but R does not explain A.
(*c*) Only A is correct.
(*d*) Only R is correct.

125. Activation of B-lymphocytes leading to their proliferation and differentiation into antibody producting plasma cells is achieved by which of the following ?
I. B-cells are activated when an antigen binds to their sIg receptor.
II. T_H (T-helper) cells are usually involved in this activation.
III. T_H cells produce cytokines, which induces proliferation and differentiation of activated B-cells.
IV. Each B-cell divides to produce a clone of indentical cells.
Options :
(*a*) I, II, III (*b*) II, III, IV
(*c*) I, II, III, IV (*d*) I, II, IV

126. Attenuation can be achieved by which of the following ?
I. Selection of less virulent strains of pathogens.
II. Culturing pathogens under unfavourable conditions like high temperature.
III. Treatment of the pathogen with certain chemicals.
IV. Several passages through cultured cells of host or of a different species.
Options :
(*a*) I, II, III (*b*) I, II, III, IV
(*c*) II, III, IV (*d*) I, III, IV

127. ***Assertion (A)***: Introduction of a vaccine in an individual leads to the development of immunity in the vaccinated individuals to the concerned pathogen.
Reason (R): Immunity is induced by the antigens of pathogen origin and present in the vaccine.
Options :
(*a*) Both A and R are correct and R is the correct explanation of A.
(*b*) Both A and R is correct, but R does not explain A.
(*c*) Only A is correct.
(*d*) Only R is correct.

128. Which of the following statements are correct.
I. When an individual is vaccinated, the antigens of pathogen origin stimulate antibody production against them selves.
II. The antibody producing plasma cells die in due course so that the level of antibody production declines, but a population of memory cells remains alive.
III. When the same pathogen later enters into the system of the immunised animal, the memory cells respond quickly and produce a very high level of antibodies specific to the pathogen.
IV. The antibodies inactivate the pathogen, and thereby protect the animal against the disease.
Options :
(*a*) I, II, III, IV (*b*) II, III, IV
(*c*) I, III, IV (*d*) I, II, IV

129. Which of the following statements are correct about vaccination ?

I. The first case of vaccination was against rabies, and it was carried out by Louis Pasteur in case of a young boy bitten by a mad dog.

II. Pasteur used the fluid from the spinal cord of another mad dog for vaccination.

III. Vaccination offers the cheapest and most effective protection against diseases.

IV. For some diseases, *e.g.*, AIDS, it is the only means of protection.

Options :

(*a*) I, II, III (*b*) II, III, IV
(*c*) I, II, III, IV (*d*) I, III, IV

130. Cytotoxic T lymphocytes eliminate which of following ?

(*a*) Tumour cells
(*b*) Cells of tissue grafts
(*c*) Virus infected cells
(*d*) All of the above

131. Which of the following steps is involved in virus vaccine production using cell cultures ?

I. Cells to be used as host are inoculated in culture vessels and, later, the cultures are infected with the virus concerned and incubated.

II. After an appropriate period of virus multiplication and release, the culture medium containing virus particles is collected and suitably processed.

III. In case of killed-virus vaccines, the vaccine is usually subjected to a concentration step after virus inactivation.

IV. Suitable stabilizers are added to prevent loss of potency.

Options :

(*a*) I, II, III, IV (*b*) I, III, IV
(*c*) II, III, IV (*d*) I, II, IV

132. Complement system carries out which of the following basic functions ?

I. Lysis of cell, bacteria and viruses.

II. Opsonisation, which promotes phagocytosis of particulate antigens.

III. Suppression of immune response.

IV. Removal of immune complexes.

Options :

(*a*) I, II, III (*b*) I, II, III, IV
(*c*) I, II, IV (*d*) II, III, IV

133. Complement system activation can occur in which of the following ways ?

(*a*) Lectin pathway
(*b*) Alternate pathway
(*c*) Classical pathway
(*d*) All of the above.

134. Animal cell cultures are used to produce which of the following ?

(*a*) Enzymes and hormones
(*b*) Interferons and monoclonal antibodies
(*c*) Virus vaccines and hybrid antibodies
(*d*) All of the above

135. Column A contains a list of recombinant proteins, while column B lists their applications. Match both the columns carefully and select the correct option from those given below them.

Column A	Column B
A. Erythropoeitin	1. Haemophilia
B. Blood clotting factor VIII	2. Thrombolysis
C. Human growth hormone (hGH)	3. Anaemia
D. Tissue plasminogen activator (tPA)	4. Dwarfism

Options :

(*a*) A3, B4, C1, D2 (*b*) A3, B1, C4, D2
(*c*) A3, B1, C2, D4 (*d*) A3, B2, C4, D1

136. Which of the following host cells are used for large-scale production of recombinant proteins ?

I. Mammalian cell lines.

II. Chinese hamster ovary line.

III. Mouse mammary tumour line C127.

IV. Mouse myeloma cell lines.

Options :

(*a*) I, II, III, IV (*b*) II, III, IV
(*c*) I, II, III (*d*) I, III, IV

137. Which of the following ***is not correct*** about human blood clotting factor VIII ?

(*a*) Recombinant factor VIII is inferior to natural factor VIII.
(*b*) The complete cDNA has been driven by the promoter of whey acidic protein gene of pig.
(*c*) Factor VIII is now produced in pig mammary gland and is secreted in the milk.
(*d*) Recombinant factor VIII appears to be identical to the native human protein.

8.2. FILL IN THE BLANKS

1. In 1907, ... cultured frog tadpole spinal chord in a lymph drop hanging from a cover slip into the cavity of a microscopic slide.
2. The ultimate objective of tissue engineering is to reconstitute .... *in vitro.*
3. Grid method of organ culture was initially devised by ....
4. The explant for preparing artificial skin for the graft must come from the .... to avoid rejection.
5. Glass and metal surfaces are ....charged.
6. Chromosome mapping through somatic cell hybridization is essentially based on fusion of human and .... somatic cells.
7. Abbreviation HGPRT stands for ....
8. Spontaneous cell fusion occurs at a frequency of ....
9. Most commonly used clots, as natural, medium, are............
10. Natural biological fluids have been used for animal .... culture.
11. Tissue extracts can often be substituted by a mixture of .... and certain other organic compounds.
12. .... inhibitors present in the serum protect cells (specially trypsinised cells) from proteolysis.
13. Abbreviation PDGF stands for ....
14. Transferrin usually carries .... in a non basic form.
15. In case of explant isolation from animals, the site of opening is sterilized with .... % alcohol.
16. Usually most of the cell lines will grow for........... subcultures.
17. Abbreviation ATCC stands for ....
18. Subculture of monolayers may be done every .... days.
19. Oxygen transfer rate (OTR) from gas phase into medium is about .... $\mu g/cm^2/hr$.
20. Cloning is generally applied to .... cell lines.
21. The outermost layer of skin consists of dead cells filled with a waterproofing protein called ....
22. Bone marrow and thymus provide the sites for lymphocyte ....
23. A mitogen stimulates a cell to undergo ....
24. Lymphoid stem cells originate from multipotent .... present in the bone marrow.
25. Lymphatic system consists of ...., lymph vessels and lymph nodes.
26. Multiponent stem cells give rise .... and .... stem cells.
27. Those lymphoid stem cells that remain in the bone marrow, develop into ....
28. Tonsils and adenopids are masses of .... tissues.
29. An antibody is a molecule that specifically inactivates an ....
30. The lymph differs from the blood in having .... RBC, and .... WBC.
31. Y-chromosome-bearing sperms are .... than those bearing X-chromosome.
32. Light chain of antibody is of two types, *i.e.,* .... and .... chains.
33. Unlike antibodies, TCR can recognise only those antigens that are displayed on .... molecules.
34. The first test tube baby was born and named as ....
35. Dolly sheep was developed at .... UK.
36. Mammalian immune system is estimated to be able to generate more than .... different antibody specificities.
37. Isozymes are variant forms of an enzyme usually detectable through ....
38. Activation of B cells occurs in .... organs and requires an interacton with the concerned antigens.
39. Cells marked by negative selection usually die by ....

40. The positive and negative selections of lymphocytes are best explained gets by .... model.

41. B1 cells develop from progenitor cells produced in ....

42. When sIg of a B cell specifically binds to the antigen, the B cell is ultimately gets activated and it undergoes repeated cell division to produce a .... of cells.

43. The chief objective of superovulation is to greatly increase the number of .... recovered per female in a single cycle.

44. The heavy chain of antibodies consists of about .... amino acids.

45. A prolonged administration of clomiphene for stimulation of ovulation increases the chances of .... in the treated females.

46. In case of humans, the first division in zygote occurs about .... hours after insemination.

47. Radioimmune assays can detect tumours as small as .... cm, which are otherwise not detectable.

48. Ricin is a natural toxin found in the endosperm of ....

49. B-lymphocyte proliferation, maturation and antibody secretion are dependent on .... produced by activated T-lymphocytes.

50. Monoclonal antibody OKT3 is the most widely used for treatment of acute cases of rejection of .... transplants.

51. Polio vaccine is produced from *in vitro* cultured cells of ....

52. Human lymphocytes are usually collected from .... of volunteers who have been immunized with some antigen, *e.g.*, tetanus toxoid.

53. Production of antibodies by an animal in response to an antigen constitutes a major aspect of ....

54. BCG stands for ....

55. Rabies vaccines are produced in cell lines from .... and ....

56. The leuocyte surface antigens are now given a .... designation in which each individual protein is given a distinct number.

57. The endogenous proteins produced within infected cells are processed by the .... pathway, and the peptides so generated are displayed on .... molecules.

58. Extracellular antigens are eliminated by .... antibodies.

59. When a hapten is linked to a large molecule called ...., it elicits immunogenic response as well, *i.e.*, is able to induce antibody production against itself.

60. A single antigen may induce more than one distinct clone of .... cells, which will produce antibodies of different specificities.

61. When an individual is vaccinated, the antigens of pathogen origin stimulate .... production against themselves.

62. A single plasma cell can secrete more than .... antibody molecules/second.

63. In cell-mediated response, ... are needed to activate B and T_C cells.

64. The components of complement system are synthesized mainly by ....

65. Human factor VIII plays a central role in ....

66. Recombinant factor VIII is now produced in ....

67. Gene encoding factor VIII is over .... kb long having 26 exons.

9.3. MARK TRUE OR FALSE

1. In 1903, Jolly studied the behaviour of animal tissue explants immersed in serum, lymph or ascites fluid.

2. One of the chief disadvantage of all plasma clot methods is that the clot liquefies in the vicinity of explants so that they become partially or fully immersed in the medium.

3. Production of artificial skin is essentially organ culture not cell culture.

4. Animal cell surface has a net negative charge; cross-linking with glycoproteins and/or divalent cations is required for cell adhesion.

5. Glassware can be washed with any detergent.

6. Generally, various growth factors/hormones are added to the basal medium for good cell growth.

7. Animal cell cultures require a gas phase of which O_2 and CO_2 are the critical gases.

8. For animal cell culture, artificial media with or without serum are used.

9. Serum acts as a buffer.

10. Lymph nodes are abundant in neck, armpits and groin.

11. Most of the media available commercially are usually not presterilized.

12. Addition of 5-20% of serum in serum-free media is essential for optimum growth.

13. Monolayer cultures are essential for enchorage dependent cells.

14. Plating efficiency of cell lines can be enhanced by the use of serum, especially foetal calf serum, in the medium and addition of insulin and dexamethasone.

15. Phagocytic cells are crucial to innate immunity; they are ultimately involved in the activation of the acquired immune response.

16. T helper cells and cytotoxic T lymphocytes are effectors of the cell-mediated immune response.

17. Spleen is the smallest lymphatic organ in human body.

18. Thymus and spleen are important lymphatic organs of human body.

19. Antibodies defend the body from invading antigens by combining with them to abolish their free mobility and preventing them from acting in a damaging manner.

20. Anti-Ig and anti-CD3 are the most clear-cut and commonly used means to distinguish between B and T cells.

21. Monoclonal antibodies are produced by genetic engineering.

22. The chief objective of embryo transfter is to obtain several progeny per year from a single female of superior genotype.

23. In general, an antigen molecule has antigenic determinants of one specificity.

24. In 1987, Tonegawa was awarded Nobel Prize for giving the first direct evidence for Dryer and Bennett Model, that is, genetic mechanism that generates antibody diversity.

25. According to avidity model, a high avidity interaction between TCR of double positive (CD_4^+ CD_8^+) T-cells and antigen peptide—MHC complex/MHC molecules leads to positive selection.

26. T cells mature in thymus.

27. The number of B/T cells specific to an antigen increases drastically, when the animal is exposed to that particular antigen, by a process called clonal selection.

28. Each antibody molecule has two antigen binding sites or domains.

29. Immunological assays enable a very early and accurate detection of cancer.

30. Tissue and bone marrow explant rejections are mediated by B lymphocytes.

31. Monoclonal antibodies have been used to isolated mRNAs encoding the proteins to which the monoclonal antibodies are specific.

32. β- and γ-interferons are produced from Chinese hamster ovary cell lines.

33. Class switching affects the specificity of antibodies produced by B lymphocytes.

34. Ability of antigens to interact with specific antibodies is called antibody-antigen interaction.

35. All the molecules of a monoclonal antibody will have the same specificity.

36. In general, inactivation of viruses is always coupled with attenuation to minimise the accidental presence in vaccines of active virulent particles.

37. The endogeneous proteins targetted for proteolysis are often linked to a small protein called ubiquitin.

38. Humoral immune response is based on T cells.

39. A mature B cell that has not yet interacted with the antigen specific to its cell surface antibody (sIg) is called naive B cell.

40. Both B and T cells exhibit clonal selection in response to the specific antigen.

41. T_H cells generally exhibit CD_4 antigen while T_C cells have on their surface CD_8 antigen.

42. Complement system is important in both innate and acquired immunities.

43. The most common form of haemophilia results from an inability to synthesize factor VIII.

44. In case of human blood clotting factor VIII, the functional protein is a tetramer.

45. *Ag* promoter is a hybrid between chicken β-*actin* and rabbit β *globin* promoter sequences.

10

TRANSGENIC ANIMALS

10.1. MULTIPLE CHOICE QUESTIONS

1. Column A lists some events, while column B lists their consequences. Match the two columns carefully and select the correct option from those listed below them.

Column A	Column B
A. Gene disruption	I. Transgenic animal
B. Transfection	II. Nondestructive assay of transgenics
C. XGPRT expression	III. Knockout mice
D. GFP expression	IV. Mycophenolic acid resistance

Options :

(*a*) AIII, BI, CII, DIV
(*b*) AIII, BIV, CII, DI
(*c*) AIII, BI, CIV, DII
(*d*) AIII, BIV, CI, DII

2. The objective of gene transfers in animals is the study of which of the following ?

I. Promoter function
II. Function of transferred gene
III. Regulation of gene expression
IV. Reporter gene expression

Options :

(*a*) I, II, III, IV (*b*) II, III, IV
(*c*) I, III, IV (*d*) I, II, IV

3. Which of the following sequences is required for transgene expression ?

I. The chain termination codon(s)
II. The translation initiation codon
III. Transcription termination sequence including polyadenylation cleavage/addition site.
IV. An efficient promoter/enhancer

Options :

(*a*) I, II, III (*b*) I, II, III, IV
(*c*) II, III, IV (*d*) I, III, IV

4. Which of the following ***is not correct*** about fish vectors ?

(*a*) A typical fish vector is a plasmid.
(*b*) These vectors usually contain a selectable marker.
(*c*) The origin of replication (*ori*) from *E. coli* plasmid *p*BR322.
(*d*) An enhancer/promoter sequence from CaMV.

5. The term transfection is used to denote which of the following ?

(*a*) Genetic transformation of bacteria via virus infection.
(*b*) Genetic transformation of animal cells.
(*c*) Delivery of recombinent DNA into animal cell via a virus.
(*d*) All of the above

6. Early region replacement and late region replacement vectors of SV40 have which of following features ?

(*a*) Transient expression.
(*b*) Produce virions, which infect host cells.
(*c*) Mammalian cells are hosts of SV40-derived vectors.
(*d*) All of the above.

7. Which of the following is correct about a retrovirus vector ?

I. It is a shuttle vector.
II. It produces virions.

III. It integrates as provirus into mammalian genome.
IV. It is used in gene therapy.

Options :
(*a*) I, II, III, IV (*b*) II, III, IV
(*c*) I, III, IV (*d*) III, IV

8. Anti-freeze protein promoter was isolated from which of the following ?
(*a*) Frog (*b*) Fish
(*c*) Snake (*d*) *Drosophila*

9. Transgenics have been produced in which of the following animals ?
(*a*) Cow and goat
(*b*) Sheep and rabbits
(*c*) Mice, fish and pigs
(*d*) All of the above.

10. Which of the following is correct about transgenic fish ?
I. Transgenics have been produced in common carp, Atlantic salmon, etc.
II. Transfection is achieved either by microinjection or by electroporation.
III. Transfected ova are cultured in nutrient medium.
IV. The rate of survival of microinjected embryos varies from 35 to 80% of which 10 -70% may be transgenic.

Options :
(*a*) I, II, III (*b*) I, II, III, IV
(*c*) I, II, IV (*d*) II, III, IV

11. Which of the following is correct ?
I. Scorable markers are used for studying promoter/enhancer activity while selectable markers are utilized to select for transfected cells.
II. The delivery of DNA into cells using liposomes is called lipofection.
III. Homologous recombination refers to exchange of identical segments between two DNA molecules that have identical or almost identical sequences.
IV. When integration of a transgene leads to the loss of function of a host gene, it is called insertional mutagenesis.

Options :
(*a*) I, II, III, IV (*b*) I, II, III
(*c*) I, III, IV (*d*) II, III, IV

12. Mammalian artifical chromosomes and human artificial chromosomes are linear vectors that contain which of the following ?
(*a*) Centromeres and telomeres
(*b*) Origin of replication recognition sequences.
(*c*) Transcriptionally active chromosomal domains.
(*d*) All of the above.

13. Which of the following is correct about *P* elements ?
I. These elements are transposons of 2.9 kb.
II. They contain 3 genes and are flanked by short (31 bp) inverted repeat sequences at their ends.
III. Helper *P* elements are needed to enable recombinant P vector integration into the host genome.
IV. *P* element vectors are derived from flour moth.

Options :
(*a*) I, II, III, IV (*b*) I, II, III
(*c*) I, III, IV (*d*) II, III, IV

14. Which of the following is correct ?
I. Homologous recombination has been exploited to produce 'knockout' mice.
II. In general, transgenes integrate at random sites in any of the chromosomes of the genome of host animals cells.
III. Transgenes are expected to show typical Mendelian inheritance.
IV. Transgenes are always present in homozygous condition.

Options :
(*a*) I, II, III, IV (*b*) I, III, IV
(*c*) I, II, IV (*d*) I, II, III

15. A suitable expression vector ordinarily contains which of the following ?
(*a*) Promoter
(*b*) Transcription termination sequence
(*c*) Usually, a polyadenylation site
(*d*) All of the above.

16. Which of the following ***is not correct*** about promoter/enhancer ?
(*a*) A promoter sequence is the site to which RNA polymerase first binds during the initiation of transcription.

(*b*) Promoter must be located at the 5′-end of the antisense strand of the gene.
(*c*) The promoter sequence determines the level of transcription of the gene and tissue or cell type where the gene will be expressed.
(*d*) A suitable enhancer sequence may be used alongwith the promoter to enhance the promoter activity.

17. Which of the following is correct about Reporter/marker genes ?

I. A reporter gene produces a phenotype, which is either easily and specifically detected or that allows a differential multiplication of the cells.
II. A gene, which permits easy and rapid identification of the organism/cell in which it is present and expressed is called selectable marker.
III. Gene encoding GFP is an excellent scorable marker.
IV. Xanthine-guanine phosphorylaseribosyl transferase (XGPRT) is an example of a selectable marker (reporter) gene.

Options :
(*a*) I, II (*b*) I, III
(*c*) II, IV (*d*) I, III, IV

18. Cells take in calcium phosphate-DNA precipitate particles by which of the following ?
(*a*) Pincocytosis
(*b*) Phagocytosis
(*c*) Both (*a*) and (*b*).
(*d*) Lipofection

19. All the transfection techniques are applicable to cultured animal cells, but microinjection is ordinarily not used due to which of the following ?
(*a*) Limited number of cells can be handled.
(*b*) Tediousness of the technique.
(*c*) Availability of less demanding alternative techniques.
(*d*) All of the above.

20. Mouse is the most preferred mammal for studies on gene transfer due to which of the following ?

I. Production and maintenance of ES cell lines.
II. Short oestrous cycle and gestation period.
III. Convenient *in vitro* fertilization and production of several offspring per pregnancy (*i.e.,* litter)
IV. Short generation time and successful culture of embryos *in vitro* at least for a period of time.

Options :
(*a*) I, II, III (*b*) II, III, IV
(*c*) I, II, III, IV (*d*) I, III, IV

21. Which of the following features are correct about *P* element vectors ?

I. *P* element vectors are shuttle vectors.
II. They are propagated in *E. coli* and are used for gene transfer in *Drosophila.*
III. DNA inserts of upto 40 kb have been cloned using some *P* element vectors.
IV. Their use has made several important contributions to *Drosophila* genetics.

Options :
(*a*) I, II, III, IV (*b*) I, III, IV
(*c*) III, IV (*d*) II, III, IV

22. DEAE-dextran brings about DNA uptake by which of the following mechanisms ?
(*a*) Pincocytosis
(*b*) Endocytosis
(*c*) Active transport
(*d*) Osmosis.

23. The techniques for gene transfer and transgenic animal production were developed using which of the following animals as models ?
(*a*) Sheep (*b*) Rabbits
(*c*) Mice (*d*) Pigs

24. Which of the following factors contribute to high-level transgene expression ?

I. Use of a strong enhancer/promoter
II. Presence of AU rich sequences in the coding region of the gene.
III. Lack of an initiation codon in the 5′-untranslated region.
IV. Lack of secondary structure within the 5′-untranslated region of the mRNA.

Options :
(*a*) I, III, IV (*b*) II, III, IV
(*c*) I, II, IV (*d*) I, II, III, IV

25. Which of the following is correct ?

I. Rabbits are quite promosing for molecular farming.
II. Transgenic sheep have been produced to achieve better growth and meat production.
III. Increased wool production and improved wool quality are important objectives of transgenic sheep research.
IV. More recently, rats and rabbits are being increasingly used for gene transfer research.

Options :

(*a*) I, II, III, IV (*b*) II, III, IV
(*c*) I, III, IV (*d*) I, II, III

26. Which of the following are correct ?

I. DEAE-dextran is water soluble and polycationic.
II. F-virosomes deliver the DNA directly into the cytoplasm via fusion with cell plasma membrane.
III. Many cell lines do not like the calcium-phosphate precipitate adhering to their substrate.
IV. In case of fish embryos, microinjection and electroporation are routinely employed.

Options :

(*a*) I, II, III (*b*) II, III, IV
(*c*) I, II, III, IV (*d*) I, III, IV

27. Which of the following are correct ?

I. Thymidine kinase gene can be used as a selectable marker only when TK^- host cells are used for transfection.
II. Dominant selectable markers are ordinarily used for the selection of transfected/transgenic embryos of mammals.
III. Selectable reporter genes are frequently used for the selection of transgenic fish.
IV. Reporter gene neomycin phosphotransferase (*neo*), specifies resistance to hygromycin-B.

Options :

(*a*) I, II (*b*) I, III
(*c*) I, IV (*d*) II, IV

28. Which of the following is an example of a dominant selectable marker ?

(*a*) CAD protein
(*b*) DHFR and XGPRT
(*c*) Neomycin phosphotransferase
(*d*) All of the above.

29. Which of the following ***is not correct*** ?

(*a*) The enzyme thymidine kinase belongs to the salvage pathway.
(*b*) The F-protein of Sendai Virus envelope mediates the fusion of viral envelope with cell plasma membrane.
(*c*) Lipofection is the method of choice for transfection of mammalian cells *in vitro.*
(*d*) Virosomes contain viral genome.

30. The bacterial XGPRT gene serves as dominant selectable marker on a culture medium containing which of the following ?

(*a*) Xanthine and adenine
(*b*) Mycophenolic acid
(*c*) Aminopterin
(*d*) All of the above.

31. Column A contains a list of promoters, while column B lists tissues in which they specify expression. Match the two columns carefully and select the correct option from those given below them.

Column A	**Column B**
A. Prolactin promoter	I. Stimulus-specific
B. Thymidine kinase promoter	II. Mammary tissue
C. Metallothionein promoter	III. All tissues

Options :

(*a*) AII, BIII, CI (*b*) AI, BII, CIII
(*c*) AIII, BI, CII (*d*) AIII, BII, CI

32. Column A lists some selectable reporter genes, while column B lists their features. Match the two columns carefully and select the correct option from those given below them.

Column A	**Column B**
A. Adenosine deaminase (*Ada*)	I. Resistance to hygromycin-B
B. Hygromycin phosphotrans-ferase (*hpt*)	II. Resistance to indole
C. Tryptophan synthase (*trp*B)	III. Albizzin
D. Asparagine synthase (*as*)	IV. Resistance to Xyl-A and 2′-deoxycoformycin

Options :
(*a*) AI, BII, CIII, DIV
(*b*) AII, BIII, CIV, DI
(*c*) AIV, BI, CII, DIII
(*d*) AIII, BIV, CI, DII

33. Column A lists some transgenes, while column B lists the objective of transgene transfer. Match the two columns carefully and select the correct option from those given below them.

Column A	Column B
A. Blood clotting factor VIII	I. Haemophilia
B. Human growth hormone	II. Improved wool production/quality
C. Bacterial genes *cysE* and *cys M*	III. Proteins for blood transfusion
D. Human haemo-globin	IV. Increased body growth

Options :
(*a*) AII, BIII, CIV, DI
(*b*) AI, BIV. CII, DIII
(*c*) AIII, BII, CI, DIV
(*d*) AIV, BI, CIII, DII

34. Which of the following may serve as edible vaccine for humans ?
(*a*) Honey (*b*) Banana
(*c*) Apple (*d*) All of the above

35. Which of the following ***is not correct*** ?
(*a*) In case of electroporation, circular super-coiled DNA is far more efficient in transfection than linearized DNA
(*b*) The male pronucleus is chosen for microinjection because it is much larger than the female pronucleus.
(*c*) The use of cationic lipids for construction of liposomes offers a distinct advantage.
(*d*) Recombinant retroviruses produce virions.

36. ***Assertion (A)***: Treatment of cells with colcemid before they are electroporated increases the frequency of transfection.

Mechanism (M): Cells at metaphase do not have nuclear envelope, and there may be an unusual permeability of the plasma membranes.

Options :
(*a*) Only A is correct
(*b*) Only M is correct
(*c*) Both A and M are correct, but M does not explain A.
(*d*) Both A and M are correct and M roughly explains A.

37. Which of the following are limitations of retroviral infection ?
I. Limit on the size of DNA insert.
II. Mosaicism of the recovered animals.
III. Possible interference of the proviral LTR sequences with the expression of foreign genes.
IV. Additional steps needed for construction of recombinant retroviruses.

Options :
(*a*) I, II, III, IV (*b*) I, III, IV
(*c*) I, II, III (*d*) II, III, IV

38. Which of the following properties of retro-viruses are useful in their use as vectors ?
I. They have a wide host range, *viz.,* birds, mammals and other animals.
II. Infected cells are not killed and they continue to produce virus particles over an indefinite period.
III. Presence of weak promoters.
IV. Regulation of promoter action in case of some viruses, *viz.,* Murine Mammary Tumour Virus.

Options :
(*a*) I, II, III (*b*) I, II, III, IV
(*c*) I, II, IV (*d*) I, III, IV

39. Retroviral vectors have which of the following features ?
I. Vectors have viral sequences for replication, gene expression and packaging (ψ sequences).
II. DNA inserts may either replace or be located in the non-essential coding region of the viral genome.
III. The vectors and the recombinant DNAs are packaged into virions and used as transducing viruses.
IV. DNA copies of the retroviral genomes are, generally used as shuttle vectors.

Options :
(*a*) I, II, III (*b*) I, III, IV
(*c*) I, II, III, IV (*d*) II, III, IV

40. Which of the following statements are correct about adenovirus vectors ?

I. Adenoviruses are RNA (double-stranded) viruses.

II. The maximum insert size for such vectors is ~6-8 kb.

III. In recombinant DNA, DNA insert replaces genes *E1A/E1B*.

IV. Recombinant adenoviruses have been used to transfect respiratory tract cells for somatic gene therapy of cystic fibrosis, and for gene transfer into skelton muscle.

Options :

(*a*) I, II, III, IV (*b*) II, III, IV
(*c*) I, III, IV (*d*) I, II, III

41. The first animal vector was devised from which of the following ?

(*a*) Simian Virus 40 (SV40)
(*b*) Primate Papova Virus
(*c*) Papilloma Virus
(*d*) Both (*a*) and (*b*)

42. Which of the following is correct about SV40 vectors ?

(*a*) It is a spherical virus with circular, double-stranded 5,243 bp chromosome, which encodes 5 proteins.
(*b*) Large-T is essential for viral replication.
(*c*) VP1 (virion protein 1), VP2 and VP3 form viral capsid.
(*d*) All of the above.

43. SV40 transducing vectors must have which of the following features ?

(*a*) SV40 origin including the surrounding region containing the transcriptional regulatory signals.
(*b*) Genes encoding large-T, VP1, VP2, and VP3.
(*c*) Total size (including, that of the DNA insert) between 3,900 bp and 5,300 bp for packaging into virions.
(*d*) All of the above.

44. SV40 genome has been used to develop which of the following vectors.

I. Plasmid vectors
II. Transforming vectors
III. Transducing vectors
IV. Early replacement vectors

Options :

(*a*) I, II, III, IV (*b*) I, II, III
(*c*) I, III, IV (*d*) I, III

45. Which of the following statements are correct ?

I. The transgene construct is prepared in a buffer solution and is injected into the male pronuclei of fertilized eggs using a microinjection assembly.

II. In mice, the microinjected embryos are cultured *in vitro* upto the morula or blastocyst stage.

III. The surviving embryos are then transferred into the uterus of surrogate mothers.

IV. Embryos in surrogate mothers develop to full term and give rise to normal mice.

Options :

(*a*) I, II, III, IV (*b*) II, III, IV
(*c*) I, II, III (*d*) I, III, IV

46. Which of the following is correct ?

(*a*) The sequences flanking the intein are exeins.
(*b*) Intein sequence is derived from the *VAM1* gene of *Saccharomyces cerevisiae*.
(*c*) The chitin-binding domain (CBD) from *Bacillus circulans* has a high affinity for chitin column.
(*d*) All of the above.

47. Among the given gene transfer techniques, which of the following is the most commonly used in case of mice embryos ?

(*a*) Retroviral infection
(*b*) Microinjection
(*c*) Embryonic stem cell technology
(*d*) Electroporation

48. Late-region replacement vectors contain which of the following features ?

I. Region at which splicing and polyadenylation occur.
II. Origin of replication.
III. Entire early region of SV40.
IV. This vector is used for infection of host cells without a helper virus.

Options :

(*a*) I, II, III (*b*) I, III, IV
(*c*) I, II, III, IV (*d*) II, III, IV

49. Which of the following statements are correct ?

I. Most animal vectors are designed to replicate and express in animal cells.

II. Retrovirus and transposon vectors integrate into the genomes of host cells in a manner similar to the natural retroviruses and transposons, respectively.

III. Circular vectors can integrate into the host genome more frequently than linearized vectors.

IV. Presence of additional vector DNA along with the integrated gene construct interferes with the expression of transgene.

Options :

(*a*) I, II, III, IV (*b*) I, II, IV
(*c*) I, III, IV (*d*) II, III, IV

50. If inducible gene expression is driven by metallothionein promoter, transcription is induced by which of the following metal ions ?

(*a*) Cadmium (*b*) Zinc
(*c*) Iron (*d*) Both (*a*) and (*b*)

51. Which of the following is the chief advantages of both late- and early-region replacement SV40 vectors ?

(*a*) The recombinant DNA replicates to a high copy number.
(*b*) The recombinant DNA is packaged into virions.
(*c*) Both (*a*) and (*b*)
(*d*) The maximum size of DNA insert is ~2.5 kb.

52. Which of the following ***is not correct*** about SV40 plasmid vectors ?

(*a*) Plasmid vectors are generally used for stable transfection.
(*b*) They integrate into the host genome with a frequency of 10^{-5} to 10^{-3}.
(*c*) Plasmid vectors have been mainly used to investigate sequences involved in transcriptional and post-transcriptional regulation.
(*d*) *p*RSV series of vectors are derivatives of *p*SV vectors.

53. Which of the following information ***is not obtained*** by Southern hybridization ?

(*a*) Number of sites of transgene integration per genome.
(*b*) Presence of mRNA/protein produced by transgene.
(*c*) Both (*a*) and (*b*)
(*d*) Confirmation of integration of transgene.

54. Which of the following techniques is used to obtain information on the relative levels of mRNA present in the tissues of different transgenic individuals.

(*a*) Reverse transcription PCR
(*b*) Nuclease protection assay
(*c*) *In situ* hybridization
(*d*) All of the above

55. Which of the following is a more general approach for identification of transgenic animals ?

(*a*) Dot blot techniques
(*b*) PCR amplification
(*c*) Both (*a*) and (*b*)
(*d*) Southern hybridization.

56. Which of the following ***is not correct*** about *Xenopus* oocytes ?

(*a*) Each mature oocyte has a large nucleus called germinal vesicle.
(*b*) Nucleus is located in the darkly pigmented hemisphere of the oocytes.
(*c*) Oocyte nucleus is arrested at first meiotic metaphase.
(*d*) Oocytes serve as a valuable expression system for a wide variety of genes from both animals and plants.

57. Which of following tests can be conducted for detection of the proteins produced by transgenes in transgenic animals ?

I. ELISA

II. Immunohistochemical staining of tissue sections

III. Immunoblotting

IV. Radioimmunoprecipitation

Options :

(*a*) I, II, III, IV (*b*) II, III, IV
(*c*) I, III, IV (*d*) I, II, III

58. Among the given tests which one is the most rapid and convenient ?

(*a*) Immunoblotting
(*b*) ELISA
(*c*) Radioimmunoprecipitation

(*d*) Immunohistochemical staining of tissue sections

59. *Xenopus* oocytes can be used for expression of which of the following ?
(*a*) mRNAs obtained by *in vitro* transcription of eukaryotic genes using T7 RNA polymerase.
(*b*) Eukaryotic mRNAs isolated from various tissues.
(*c*) Genomic eukaryotic DNA micro-injected into the nucleus.
(*d*) All of the above.

60. *Xenopus* oocyte expression system can be used to achieve which of the following objectives ?
I. To study developmental effects of overexpressing normal gene products or of altered gene products.
II. To study functions of various DNA sequences like promoters, enhancers.
III. To investigate the protein product of a gene and the function of this product.
IV. Production of transgenic *Xenopus.*
Options :
(*a*) I, II, III (*b*) II, III, IV
(*c*) I, II, III, IV (*d*) I, III, IV

61. ***Assertion (A)***: Transgene constructs become linked to each other in a head-to-tail manner forming a concatemer.
Reason (R): Linkage of transgene constructs to each other in a head-to-tail manner is possible due to DNA double-strand break repair system.
Options :
(*a*) Both A and R correct, but R does not explain A.
(*b*) Both A and R are correct and R roughly explains A.
(*c*) Only A is correct.
(*d*) Only R is correct.

62. Which of the following is correct about insertional mutagenesis ?
(*a*) It often produces aberrant phenotypes.
(*b*) It occurs by chance and can not be controlled.
(*c*) Occurrence of insertional mutagenesis leads to accidental discovery of unsuspected genes and gene functions.
(*d*) All of the above.

63. Which of the following ***is not correct*** about transgene integration in animal genomes ?
(*a*) Usually, in a given cell, integration occurs at a single location.
(*b*) In general, multiple copies are integrated when small amounts of DNA are used for transfection.
(*c*) When multiple copies are integrated, they are mostly integrated at one site joined to each other head-to-tail.
(*d*) Transgene integration frequently leads to various forms of rearrangements.

64. ***Assertion (A)***: Sequences flanking a gene on either side influence the expression of this gene.
Reason (R): The regulatory elements present in the regions flanking the transgene and the general availability of the region for transcription are responsible for this effect.
Options :
(*a*) Both A and R correct, but R does not explain A.
(*b*) Both A and R are correct and R sufficiently explains A.
(*c*) Only A is correct.
(*d*) Only R is correct.

65. The methotrexate (Mtx) resistant cell lines developed through cell selection show which of the following features ?
(*a*) Reduced Mtx uptake
(*b*) Overproduction of DHFR
(*c*) Reduced affinity of DHFR for Mtx
(*d*) All of the above.

66. Which of the following ***is not correct*** about methotrexate (Mtx) ?
(*a*) Normal nonmutant cultured cells are very sensitive to Mtx.
(*b*) It is a weak inhibitor of dihydrofolate reductase (DHFR).
(*c*) Enzyme DHFR is involved in endogenous synthesis of nucleotides.
(*d*) The Chinese hamster ovary cell line 'A29' overproduces an altered DHFR so that it is extremely resistant to Mtx.

67. Which of the following is based on homologous recombination ?
(*a*) Targetted gene transfer
(*b*) Gene disruption

(*c*) Gene replacement
(*d*) All of the above

68. Which of the following ***is not correct*** about 'Knockout' mice ?
(*a*) In a Knockout mouse, one gene is disrupted by the technique of site directed mutagenesis.
(*b*) The name Knockout signifies the fact that a specific gene in the genomes of these animals has been made non-functional.
(*c*) Production of Knockout mice employs the embryonic stem cell technology.
(*d*) Knockout mice are invaluable for various kinds of basic and applied research.

69. Which of the following features are correct about *cre / lox* system ?
I. The most commonly used recombinase is Cre, isolated from *E. coli* bacteriophage P1.
II. Cre recognizes a specific 34-bp site in DNA known as *loxP* and, upon recognition, catalyzes a site-specific recombination between two *loxP* sites.
III. Expression of the *Cre* recombinase gene can be controlled by the use of a tissue-specific promoter.
IV. Tissue-specific expression (of *Cre* recombinase) allows tissue-specific deletion of the DNA sequence flanked by *loxP*.

Options :
(*a*) I, III, IV (*b*) II, III, IV
(*c*) I, II, III, IV (*d*) I, II

70. Which of the following is correct about CAD (bacterial origin) protein.
(*a*) It is encoded by *Cad* gene.
(*b*) It is a multifunctional enzyme and catalyzes the first three reactions of endogenous pyrimidine synthesis.
(*c*) PALA-resistant cell lines developed through selection overproduce CAD protein due to a high amplification of the *Cad* gene.
(*d*) All of the above

71. F-virosomes are prepared from Sendai Virus; they contain which of the following ?
(*a*) Viral envelope
(*b*) Viral F-protein
(*c*) Recombinant DNA
(*d*) All of the above

72. Which of the following transfection techiques are routinely used for producing transgenic fish ?
I. Lipofection
II. Microinjection
III. Electroporation
IV. Retroviral infection

Options :
(*a*) I, II (*b*) II, IV
(*c*) I, III, (*d*) II, III

73. Which of the options listed in Q. 72 is the preferred transfection method for mice embryos ?

74. Which of the transfection techniques listed in Q. 72 can possibly be used for targetted drug delivery ?
(*a*) I (*b*) II
(*c*) III (*d*) IV

75. Which of the options given in Q. 74 can be used for gene therapy ?

76. Homologous recombination is exploited in which of the following ?
(*a*) Specific gene function 'Knockout' mice
(*b*) Transgenic mice
(*c*) Gene replacement (in gene therapy)
(*d*) Both (*a*) and (*c*)

77. In mouse cell lines, plasmid vectors having which of the following replicons yield stable episomal transformation ?
(*a*) SV40 replicons
(*b*) BPV replicons
(*c*) Murine-polyomavirus
(*d*) EBV replicons

78. Which of options given in Q. 77 produces high level transient expression in COS cell lines ?

79. Which of the options given in Q. 77 generates high level transient expression in some specific mouse cell lines ?

80. Which of the options given in Q. 77 leads to stable episomal transformation in various human cell lines ?

81. Column A lists some animal expression viral transduction vectors, and column B lists their applications. Match the two columns carefully and pick the correct option from those given below them.

Column A	Column B
A. Adeno-associated Virus	I. High level expression in insect larvae
B. Baculovirus vectors	II. High level transient expression
C. Oncoretrovirus vectors	III. Gene therapy
D. Vaccinia Virus	IV. Transgenic mice

Options :

(*a*) AIII, BIV, CI, DII
(*b*) AIII, BII, CIV, DI
(*c*) AIII, BI, CIV, DII
(*d*) AIII, BI, CII, DIV

82. Which of the following viral transduction expression vectors are used for high level transient expression ?

I. Lentivirus
II. Sindbis Virus
III. Semliki Forest Virus
IV. Vaccinia Virus

Options :

(*a*) I, II, III (*b*) II, III, IV
(*c*) I, III, IV (*d*) I, II, III, IV

83. Which of the expression vector systems listed in Q. 82 is designed for *in vivo* gene transfer ?

(*a*) I (*b*) II
(*c*) III (*d*) IV

84. Which of the options listed in Q. 83 is used for expression in nondividing mammalian cell lines ?

85. Which of the options listed in Q. 82 is applicable to mammalian cells ?

86. Which of the following viral transduction expression vectors is used for *in vivo* gene transfer in mammalian hosts ?

(*a*) Adeno-associated virus
(*b*) Baculovirus
(*c*) Both (*a*) and (*b*)
(*d*) Vaccinia Virus

87. Which of the vectors listed in Q. 86 can be used for high level transient expression in insect larvae ?

88. Production of recombinant human protein in insect larvae poses which of the following problems ?

(*a*) Protein folding
(*b*) Downstream processing
(*c*) Both (*a*) and (*b*)
(*d*) Glycosylation

89. Which of the following contributes to high level transgene expression ?

(*a*) Inclusion of an intron in the expression cassette.
(*b*) Codon optimization.
(*c*) Removal of unnecessary untranslated sequences.
(*d*) All of the above.

90. Which of the following polypeptide sequences are used as tags to facilitate recombinant protein purification ?

(*a*) Glutathione-S-transferase
(*b*) Maltose-binding protein
(*c*) *myc* epitope
(*d*) All of the above

91. The chromatography column used to separate recombinant protein having polyhistidine tags has which of the following ?

(*a*) Divalent nickel (*b*) Ca^{2+}
(*c*) K^{+} (*d*) Both (*a*) and (*b*)

92. The 'intein' sequence functions in which of the following ?

(*a*) RNA splicing (*b*) Protein splicing
(*c*) Both (*a*) and (*b*) (*d*) Recombination

93. Intein sequence facilitates which of the following steps in recombinant protein production ?

(*a*) Separation from other proteins
(*b*) Removal of tag
(*c*) Overexpression of the proteins
(*d*) Both (*a*) and (*b*).

94. Which of the following is required for the function of modified intein used in recombinant protein production ?

(*a*) Low (4°C) temperature
(*b*) β-mercaptoethanol
(*c*) High (40°C) temperature
(*d*) Both (*a*) and (*b*)

10.2. FILL IN THE BLANKS

1. A *P* element cloning vector is essentially a .... vector that contains two *P* elements.
2. Retrovirus vectors are usually derived from .... and .... sequences.
3. Baculovirus vectors have been developed for transfection of ....
4. In case of calcium phosphate precipitation, in a small proportion of the transfected cells, the DNA becomes integrated into the cell genome producing .... transfection.
5. Liposomes are small vesicles prepared from a suitable ....
6. ....proteins are found in wool.
7. Abbreviation MMTV stands for ....
8. The bacterial enzyme XGPRT is analogous to the enzyme ....
9. Retroviruses have single-stranded........... genomes.
10. The genome size of Adenovirus is about .... kb.
11. The Bovine Papilloma Virus genome is generally used to produce shuttle vectors by using the .... region of the genome.
12. In laboratory, SV40 vectors are multiplied in cultured kidney cells of ....
13. SV40 transducing vectors produce viral particles after infecting .... cells.
14. In fish ova, the DNA is injected into the ....
15. In mice, the microinjected embryos are cultured *in vitro* upto the ....or ....
16. In case of fish, the microinjected ova are incubated in .... until hatching.
17. The transgene integration occurs at an early stage of embryo development following microinjection, and ordinarily all the cells of an .... are involved.
18. Late-region replacement vectors have been used to study ....
19. In many laboratories .... is routinely used as a first screen for transgenics from thousands of presumptive transgenic individuals.
20. SV40 plasmid vectors replicate in monkey cells but do not get .... into virions.
21. The abbreviation *p*SV stands for ....
22. Integration of transgene into the genome is confirmed by ....
23. *Xenopus* oocytes can be obtained in large numbers by removal of the .... of adult females.
24. In case of animals, the frequency of homologous recombination based transgene integration is only less than .... % that of random integrations.
25. Oncomouse is a special type of .... mouse, that is predisposed to develop cancer.

10.3. MARK TRUE OR FALSE

1. Bovine Papilloma Virus vectors are generally derived from Bovine Papilloma Virus transforming region and *p*BR322 sequences.
2. About 20% or more of the embryos surviving electroporation give rise to transgenic fish.
3. DEAE-dextran-mediated transfection is highly suited for stable transfection.
4. F-virosomes have potential in targetted drug delivery to the liver cells.
5. The chief objective of producing transgenic cattle is increased milk or meat production and molecular farming.
6. Inducible gene expression can be achieved by using metallothionein promoter.
7. Adenoviruses infect respiratory tract.
8. Nonreplicating vectors are generally shuttle vectors.
9. Microinjection of bacterial plasmids or linear copies of genes into the nuclei of mammalian cells is less effective in transferring new genes.

10. Typically, 20 pl (picolitre) of the DNA solution is injected into a pronucleus.
11. Transgenic animals contain the transgene in their germcells and, as a consequence, pass it onto their progeny.
12. Plasmid vectors can be constructed by using the origin of replication and the early region of SV40.
13. *Xenopus* oocyte expression system can be used to isolate a specific gene from a cDNA library.
14. The mechanism of random integration of transgene in genome is well understood.
15. Homologous recombination is the basis of targetted gene transfer.
16. In cell lines overproducing DHFR, the concerned gene is highly amplified, *i.e.*, present in several copies per genome as against the normal one copy.
17. In gene therapy, homologous recombination can be used to replace the normal endogenous gene with a specific mutant from of the same gene.
18. The Cre/*lox* system can be used to turn on gene expression in a particular tissue.
19. Pure transgenic mice can be recovered from the chimaeric mice using a suitable breeding scheme.
20. In general, transgenes integrate at random sites in any of chromosomes of the host cells.

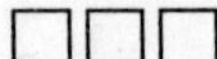

11

MEDICAL BIOTECHNOLOGY

11.1. MULTIPLE CHOICE QUESTIONS

1. Which of the following statements are correct about cancer ?

I. It refers specifically to malignant tumours.

II. Cancers invade healthy tissues by a process called metastasis.

III. They are classified as carcinomas, leukaemias/lymphomas and sarcomas according to the embryonic origin of the tissue from which the tumour is derived.

IV. It is induced by a variety of agents, such as, chemical carcinogens, irradiation and cetain viruses.

Options :

(*a*) I, II, III, IV (*b*) II, III, IV

(*c*) I, III, IV (*d*) I, II, III

2. Which of the following feature ***is not correct*** about ideal vaccine ?

(*a*) It should not contaminate the environment.

(*b*) It should not be tumorigenic or toxic or pathogenic.

(*c*) It should have very low levels of side-effects in normal individuals.

(*d*) The technique of vaccination should be complex.

3. Interferons can be used for the treatment of which of the following ?

(*a*) AIDS (*b*) Cancer

(*c*) Viral diseases (*d*) All of the above

4. The term vaccine is derived from which of the following ?

(*a*) Vascular (*b*) *Vaccinia virus*

(*c*) Vacca (*d*) Vaccination

5. Which of the following techniques are used to study of foetal cells for detection of genetic disorders ?

I. Hybridization with oligonucleotide probes.

II. RFLP analysis.

III. Enzyme assay.

IV. Karyotype analysis.

Options :

(*a*) I, II, III (*b*) II, III, IV

(*c*) I, II, III, IV (*d*) II, IV

6. Conventional vaccines suffer from which of the following limitations ?

I. In many cases, live vaccines have to be used since killed pathogen vaccines are ineffective.

II. Live vaccines are heat labile due to the pathogen inactivation by heat.

III. Conventional vaccines rarely pose a risk of disease development.

IV. Live vaccines are generally produced from cultured animal cells, hence expensive tissue culture set up is essential.

Options :

(*a*) I, II, III, IV (*b*) I, II, IV

(*c*) I, III, IV (*d*) I, II, III

7. Ideal vaccine should have which of the following features ?

I. It should not spread either within the vaccinated individual or to other individuals (live vaccines).

II. It should not cause problems in individuals with an impaired immune system.

III. It should be effective in producing long lasting humoral and cellular immunities.
IV. The vaccine should be cheap.

Options :
(*a*) I, II, III, IV (*b*) II, III, IV
(*c*) I, III, IV (*d*) I, II, IV

8. Recombinant vaccines include which of the following ?
(*a*) DNA vaccines
(*b*) Recombinant polypeptide vaccines
(*c*) Purified antigen vaccines
(*d*) Both (*a*) and (*b*)

9. Tumour necrosis factor can be used for the treatment of which of the following ?
I. Thrombolysis II. Sepsis
III. Tumours IV. Viral diseases

Options :
(*a*) I, II (*b*) II, III
(*c*) I, IV (*d*) III, IV

10. Which of the following is regarded as the third revolution in vaccines ?
(*a*) Recombinant protein vaccines
(*b*) Recombinant polypeptide vaccines
(*c*) DNA vaccines
(*d*) All of the above

11. Which of the following virus vectors can be used for the delivery of immunogen encoding genes into humans ?
I. Vaccinia virus II. Herpes viruses
III. Adenoviruses IV. Retroviruses

Options :
(*a*) I, II, IV (*b*) II, III, IV
(*c*) I, III, IV (*d*) I, II, III, IV

12. DNA vaccines offer which of the following advantages ?
I. Purification and preparation of DNA is easier, cheaper and more rapid.
II. They are safer and more specific.
III. They elicit a more potent immune response than purified protein vaccines.
IV. Their delivery causes no pain.

Options :
(*a*) I, II, IV (*b*) I, II, III, IV
(*c*) I, II, III (*d*) II, III, IV

13. Which of the following statements are correct about purified antigen vaccines ?
I. These vaccines are based on purified antigens of the concerned pathogens isolated from GMOs.
II. They do not contain the organism so that the risk of pathogenicity is avoided.
III. Successful examples of such vaccines are mostly from bacteria.
IV. Cost of purified antigen vaccines is higher than that of conventional vaccines.

Options :
(*a*) I, II, III, IV (*b*) II, III, IV
(*c*) I, III, IV (*d*) II, IV

14. Use of probes for disease diagnosis offers which of the following advantages ?
I. Probes detect even latent viral infections.
II. They are highly specific, relatively rapid and much simpler.
III. They are applicable to non-culturable organisms as well.
IV. They are extremely powerful specially when combined with PCR.

Options :
(*a*) I, II, IV (*b*) I, II, III, IV
(*c*) I, III, IV (*d*) II, III, IV

15. Monoclonal antibodies (Mabs) have which of the following therapeutic applications ?
I. Delivery of radioactivity to cancer cells.
II. Providing passive immunity against diseases.
III. Treatment of diseases like leprosy.
IV. Delivery of toxin molecules (as immunotoxins).

Options :
(*a*) I, II, III, IV (*b*) I, III, IV
(*c*) II, III, IV (*d*) I, II, IV

16. Which of the following diseases occurs due to a single gene mutation ?
(*a*) Tay Sach's disease and sickle cell anaemia.
(*b*) Cystic fibrosis and Huntington's chorea.
(*c*) Haemophilia and Lesch-Nyhan syndrome.
(*d*) All of the above

17. Candidate disorders for gene therapy are selected on the basis of which of the following criteria ?

I. Disease should be life-threatening.
II. Gene responsible for disease should have been cloned.
III. A precise regulation of the gene should be required.
IV. A suitable delivery system should be available.

Options :
(*a*) I, III, IV (*b*) II, III, IV
(*c*) I, II, III, IV (*d*) I, II, IV

18. Application of gene therapy involves which of the following basic developments in genetics, molecular biology and bio-technology ?
I. Identification of the genes that play the key role in the development of gentic disorder.
II. Determination of the role of its product in health and disease.
III. Isolation and cloning of the gene.
IV. Development of an approach for gene therapy.

Options :
(*a*) I, II, III, IV (*b*) II, III, IV
(*c*) I, III, IV (*d*) I, II, IV

19. Granulocyte colony stimulating factor can be used for the treatment of which of the following diseases ?
(*a*) AIDS
(*b*) Cancer
(*c*) Bone marrow transplantation
(*d*) All of the above

20. Recombinant insulin is produced in which of the following ?
(*a*) *E. coli*
(*b*) Continuous cell lines
(*c*) Yeast
(*d*) Both (*a*) and (*c*)

21. Recombinant protein vaccines suffer from which of the following limitations ?
(*a*) Their cost is very high and often prohibitive.
(*b*) They have to be stored at low temperatures.
(*c*) Storage and transportation, especially in developing countries are problematic.
(*d*) All of the above.

22. Which of the following steps is involved in the development of a recombinant protein-based vaccines ?
I. Identification of a protein that is immunogenic and critical for the pathogen.
II. The gene encoding this protein is identified and cloned.
III. The gene is integrated into a suitable cloning vector and introduced into a suitable host.
IV. The recombinant protein is isolated and purified.

Options :
(*a*) I, II, III (*b*) I, II, III, IV
(*c*) II, III, IV (*d*) I, II, IV

23. Ovulation may be stimulated by the administration of which of the following ?
(*a*) Clomiphene
(*b*) Human chorionic gonadotrophin (hCG)
(*c*) Human menopausal gonadotrophin (hMG)
(*d*) Any one of the above

24. Which of the following statements ***is not correct*** about AIDS ?
(*a*) In 1981, it was first reported in India.
(*b*) About 30% of infants from women having AIDS get infected unless the mothers are treated with antiviral agents before delivery.
(*c*) In general, antibodies against HIV proteins appear in the patients 3 months after infection.
(*d*) The decrease in $CD4^+$ T cells is the hallmark of AIDS.

25. Which of the following products generated by genetically engineered microbes is approved for marketing in India ?
(*a*) Granulocyte macrophage colony stimulating factor and interferons.
(*b*) Insulin and hepatitis-B surface antigen.
(*c*) Granulocyte colony stimulating factor and insulin.
(*d*) All of the above.

26. ***Assertion (A)***: Injection of pure DNA into the skeletal muscle leads to the uptake and expression of the DNA in the muscle cells.
Mechanism (M): The DNA most likely enters the skeletal muscle cells through

transient discontinuities in their plasma lemma produced by stretching of the muscle cells during exercise.

Options :

(*a*) Both A and M are correct and M is the correct explanation of A.

(*b*) Both A and M are correct, but M does not explain A.

(*c*) Only A is correct.

(*d*) Only M is correct.

27. Which of the following effects are induced by interferons ?

I. Activation of natural killer (NK) cells.

II. Inhibition of cell division in normal and transformed cells.

III. Inhibition of viral replication.

IV. Inactivaton of macrophage.

Options :

(*a*) I, III, IV (*b*) I, II, III, IV

(*c*) I, II, III (*d*) II, III, IV

28. Which of the following statements are correct about AIDS ?

I. HIV infection produces acquired immuno-deficiency syndrome.

II. HIV-1 has single-stranded DNA genome.

III. In many cases, clinical symptoms indicative of AIDS do not appear for at least 8 years after HIV infection.

IV. Death may occur, on an average, 9-12 years after infection.

Options :

(*a*) I, II, III, IV (*b*) I, III, IV

(*c*) II, III, IV (*d*) I, II, IV

29. Drugs for AIDS are generally designed to block which of the following ?

(*a*) Integrase

(*b*) Reverse transcriptase

(*c*) Viral protease

(*d*) All of the above

30. Probes are being used for the detection of micro-organisms in which of the following samples ?

I. Body fluids II. Tissues

III. Excreta

Options :

(*a*) I, II, III (*b*) II, III

(*c*) I, III (*d*) I, II

31. Which of the following effects are induced by interferon ?

I. Protection of cells against other intracellular parasites.

II. Induction of cytokines.

III. Regulation of cell differentiation.

IV. Enhanced viral replication.

Options :

(*a*) I, II, III, IV (*b*) I, II, III

(*c*) II, III, IV (*d*) I, III, IV

32. Protooncogenes (and their oncogenic counterparts) encode proteins that are involved in which of the following ?

(*a*) Induction of cellular proliferation

(*b*) Regulation of programmed cell death

(*c*) Inhibition of cellular proliferation

(*d*) All of the above

33. Which of the following approaches can be used for the delivery of DNA vaccines.

I. Particle gun.

II. Injection of pure DNA (or RNA) preparation into muscle.

III. Use of expression vectors.

IV. Re-implantation of autologous cells into which the gene has been transferred.

Options :

(*a*) I, II, III, IV (*b*) II, III, IV

(*c*) I, II, III (*d*) I, III, IV

34. Which of the following ***is not correct*** about the drug zidovudin (AZT) ?

(*a*) The first successful drug used for the treatment of AIDS.

(*b*) It is a nucleoside analogue and targetted at reverse transcriptase.

(*c*) Incorporation of this base analogue into a cDNA chain enhances its extension.

(*d*) Long term use produces several side effects and mutant viruses develop in treated patients.

35. ***Assertion (A)***: Long-term use of AZT produces several side effects.

Reason (R): The AZT becomes incorporated into human DNA and, as a result, produces abnormalties.

(*a*) Both A and R are correct and R correctly explains A.
(*b*) Both A and R are correct, but R does not explain A.
(*c*) Only A is correct.
(*d*) Only R is correct.

36. Conventionally disease diagnosis is based on which of the following procedures ?
I. Immunological assays for specific antigens present on the surface of pathogens.
II. Detection and measurement of the pathogen-specific antibodies produced by the patient.
III. Microscopic examination of specimens for the detection of the causal organisms.
IV. Culture of specimens on specific and selective media to allow specific pathogens to grow.

Options :
(*a*) I, II, III (*b*) I, II, III, IV
(*c*) II, III, IV (*d*) I, III, IV

37. Which of the following statements are correct about HIV-1 ?
I. HIV-1 infects T cells that are $CD4^+$.
II. An envelope protein of HIV-1 binds to CD4 antigen, and the infection is assisted by T cell coreceptor CXCR4.
III. HIV-1 can infect monocytes and other cells that have CD4 on their surface.
IV. Virus particles are released from the infected cells, and they infect new $CD4^+$ cells.

Options :
(*a*) I, II, III, IV (*b*) II, III, IV
(*c*) I, III, IV (*d*) I, II, IV

38. Which of the following is correct about conventional vaccines ?
(*a*) Conventional vaccines consist of whole pathogenic organisms.
(*b*) Pathogens may either be killed or live, but attenuated.
(*c*) Conventional vaccines are produced in whole animals or cultured cells.
(*d*) All of the above.

39. ***Assertion (A)***: Antisense oligonucleotides of about 25-30 base length can be used to prevent the expression of genes in a highly specific manner.

Mechanism (M): They prevent gene expression by blocking splicing.

Options :
(*a*) Both A and M are correct and M correctly explains A.
(*b*) Both A and M are correct, but M does not explain A.
(*c*) Only A is correct.
(*d*) Only M is correct.

40. Which of the following statements are correct about recombinant vaccines ?
I. A recombinant vaccine contains either a protein or a gene encoding a protein of pathogen origin.
II. The recombinant protein is immunogenic and critical to the pathogen function.
III. This vaccine is necessarily based on fermentation technology.
IV. Hepatitis-B vaccine is a good example of a recombinant protein vaccine.

Options :
(*a*) I, II, III (*b*) I, II, III, IV
(*c*) I, III, IV (*d*) I, II, IV

41. Which of the following features are correct about recombinant polypeptide/protein vaccines ?
I. The whole immunogen molecule is not necessary for immunogenicity.
II. These vaccines have to be produced from genetically engineered microbes.
III. Recombinant protein/polypeptide vaccines are very safe since whole organisms are not involved.
IV. They are of high efficacy.

Options :
(*a*) I, II, III, IV (*b*) II, III, IV
(*c*) I, III, IV (*d*) I, II, IV

42. Monoclonal antibodies can be used for which of the following ?
(*a*) Disease diagnosis
(*b*) Disease treatment
(*c*) Immunopurification
(*d*) All of the above

43. ***Problem (P)***: Oligonucleotides are rather unstable in serum because of endonuclease action.

Solution (S): Above problem may be resolved by using chemically modified backbone derivatives in the place of normal sugar-phosphate backbone.

Options :
(*a*) Only P is correct.
(*b*) Only S is correct.
(*c*) Both P and S are correct, but S is not likely to solve P.
(*d*) Both P and S are correct and S is likely to solve P.

44. Which of the following statements are correct about Vaccinia Virus ?

I. Vaccinia Virus (VV) is a close relative of the Variola Virus causing small pox.
II. VV was used as the vaccine to generate protection against small pox.
III. VV offers 19 possible sites for integration and expression of foreign genes.
IV. Generally, antigen encoding genes are inserted within its thymidine kinase (*tk*) locus, which makes the virus TK^- and attenuates its pathogenicity.

Options :
(*a*) I, II, III, IV (*b*) II, III, IV
(*c*) I, III, IV (*d*) I, II, IV

45. Which of the following techniques uses probes ?

I. Dot blot assay
II. *In situ* hybridization
III. Ligase chain reaction
IV. Western blotting

Options :
(*a*) I, II, III, IV (*b*) II, III, IV
(*c*) I, II, III (*d*) I, III, IV

46. Which of the following steps are involved in ligase chain reaction (LCR) ?

I. Clinical sample is prepared according to a protocol, which liberates the DNA present in sample.
II. The DNA from the sample is added to a reaction mixture containing a thermostable DNA ligase, a vast excess of two double-stranded oligonucleotide probes specific to the pathogen to be detected, and NAD (nicotinamide adenine dinucleotide).
III. The reaction mixture is heated in a thermocycler to 94°C to ensure strand separation of both the target DNA and the probes.
IV. Temperature is then lowered to 55°C to allow the probes to pair with the target DNA. Now the ligase joins the adjacent 3′-OH of one strand of probe 1 to the 5′-phosphate of probe 2 strand.

Options :
(*a*) I, II, III (*b*) II, III, IV
(*c*) I, II, III, IV (*d*) I, II, IV

47. Therapeutic agents from nonrecombinant organisms may originate from which of the following systems ?
(*a*) Plant cell cultures
(*b*) Animal cell cultures
(*c*) Microorganisms
(*d*) All of the above

48. Which of the following diseases is diagnosed on the basis of probes ?
(*a*) Kala-azar and filaria
(*b*) Malaria and sleeping sickness
(*c*) Herpex Virus type 1, type 2
(*d*) All of the above.

49. Which of the following statements are correct about ligase chain reaction ?

I. It is moderately efficient.
II. It is highly specific and rarely produces false positive signals.
III. It allows automated detection by employing fluorescence.
IV. LCR has been used to detect a wide variety of infectious agents.

Options :
(*a*) I, II, III, IV (*b*) I, II, III
(*c*) II, III, IV (*d*) I, II, IV

50. ***Limitation (L)***: The sensitivity of LCR is limited to between 200-300 target molecules per sample.

Solution (S): Gap-ligase chain reaction (G-LCR) reduces target-independent ligation.

Options :
(*a*) Only L is correct.
(*b*) Only S is correct.
(*c*) Both L and S are correct, but S does not solve L.
(*d*) Both L and S are correct and S adequately solves L.

51. Which of the following features is correct about assymetric gap ligase chain reaction (AG-LCR) ?

(*a*) It utilize reverse transcriptase.
(*b*) It is used for detection of RNA.
(*c*) It is used for detection of antibodies.
(*d*) Both (*a*) and (*b*)

52. In case of AIDS, highly active antiretroviral therapy (HAART) has which of the following features ?

(*a*) It reduces viral load in blood below detection limits.
(*b*) It lowers death rates due to AIDS.
(*c*) This therapy is very expensive (upto US $ 15,000 per day).
(*d*) All of the above.

53. Which of following statements are correct about immuno-PCR ?

I. It is highly precise and more sensitive than ELISA.
II. It can dectect rare antigens.
III. It can be used to diagnose pathological conditions much earlier.
IV. It is extremely versatile.

Options :
(*a*) I, II, III, IV (*b*) I, II, III
(*c*) II, III, IV (*d*) I, III, IV

54. In case of human beings, DNA finger-printing/DNA profiling can be used to solve which of the following problems ?

I. Identification of criminals.
II. Clear-cut identification of victims of crimes/accidents.
III. Identification of sex of an individual, whether dead or alive.
IV. To infer if two or more individuals are members of the same family.

Options :
(*a*) I, II, III (*b*) I, II, III, IV
(*c*) I, III, IV (*d*) II, III, IV

55. Which of following statements are correct about tissue grafts ?

I. Healthy organ, tissue or cells used for implantation in the patient is called graft.
II. Phenomenon of graft acceptance is called graft compatibility.
III. Graft rejection occurs mainly due to cell-mediated immune response.
IV. The process of graft rejection can be divided into sensitization and effector phases.

Options :
(*a*) I, II, III, IV (*b*) II, III, IV
(*c*) I, III, IV (*d*) I, II, IV

56. Column A lists some tumour-associated antigens, while column B lists different types of cancers in which antigen are found. Match both the columns carefully and select the correct option from those given below them.

Column A	Column B
A. CEA	1. Some head, lung, etc. tumours
B. MUC1	2. Breast and ovarian tumours
C. HER 2	3. Breast cancer
D. EGFR	4. Colon cancer

Options :
(*a*) A3, B4, C1, D2 (*b*) A4, B3, C2, D1
(*c*) A2, B1, C3, D4 (*d*) A1, B2, C4, D3

57. Genetic disorders/diseases can be detected through which of the following procedures ?

I. Determination of karyotype of cells.
II. Assay of the concerned enzyme activities.
III. RFLP analysis (applicable to only those disorders in which the gene mutation changes the restriction pattern).
IV. Use of oligonucelotide probes representing the sequence altered by the gene mutation causing genetic disease.

Options :
(*a*) I, II, III, IV (*b*) II, III, IV
(*c*) I, II, IV (*d*) I, III, IV

58. Which of the following is correct about *BRCA1* gene ?

(*a*) It causes human breast cancer.
(*b*) It is ~100 kb long
(*c*) It encodes a protein having over 1800 amino acids.
(*d*) All of the above

59. Which of the following drugs for AIDS ***is not*** a protease inhibitor ?

(*a*) Nelfinavir (*b*) Indinavir
(*c*) Delavirdine (*d*) Saquinavir

60. Which of the following statements are correct about growth factors of humans ?

I. Growth factors belong to the group of proteins called cytokines.
II. They can alter cell proliferation, organogenesis and disease susceptibility in animals.
III. The nomenclature of cytokines is confusing and terms like interleukins, growth factors, colony stimulating factors are used often for a single protein.
III. The various growth factors can be grouped into insulin-like growth factor, nerve growth factor, etc.

Options :
(*a*) I, II, III (*b*) I, III, IV
(*c*) I, II, III, IV (*d*) I, II, IV

61. ***Problem (P)***: The major problem in the use of therapeutic oligonucleotides concerns their delivery to the target tissue as their uptake by cells is rather poor.
Solution (S): Efforts are being made to use liposomes for efficient tissue-specific delivery.
Options :
(*a*) Both P and S are correct, and S seems to be the correct solution of P.
(*b*) Both P and S are correct, but S is not the correct solution of P.
(*c*) Only P is correct.
(*d*) Only S is correct.

62. ***Assertion (A)***: Decrease in the number of $CD4^+$ T cells is hallmark of AIDS.
Reason (R): Most likely infection by HIV leads to death of T cells.
Options :
(*a*) Only A is correct.
(*b*) Only R is correct.
(*c*) Both A and R are correct, but R does not explain A.
(*d*) Both A and R are correct and R adequately explains A.

63. Homologues of *BRCA1* gene ***were not found*** in which of the following ?
(*a*) Mice (*b*) Pig
(*c*) Sheep (*d*) Chickens

64. Which of the following ***can not be used*** for treatment of AIDS ?
(*a*) Interferon
(*b*) Granulocyte macrophage colony stimulating factor.
(*c*) Streptokinase
(*d*) Didanosine

65. Which of the options given in Q. 64 is used for treatment of thrombosis ?

66. Production of recombinant proteins of pharmaceutical value in microorganisms, cultured animal cells or plants offers which of the following advantages over their conventional route of production ?
I. There is no risk of contamination by AIDS.
II. They can be produced in far greater quantities.
III. Production costs are reduced.
IV. Proteins of human origin have become available.

Options :
(*a*) I, II, III, IV (*b*) II, III, IV
(*c*) I, III, IV (*d*) I, II, IV

67. Erythropoietin (EPO) is used to stimulate red blood production in which of the following ?
(*a*) Kidney dialysis (*b*) AIDS patients
(*c*) Cancer patients (*d*) Both (*a*) and (*c*)

68. Which of the following features are correct about interferons ?
I. Interferons are members of a large group of proteins called cytokines.
II. Interferons were originally identified due to their antibacterial activity.
III. Protection from viral infections by interferons is independent of immune system.
IV. They are of three major types: IFN-α, IFN-β and IFN-γ.

Options :
(*a*) I, II, III (*b*) I, II, III, IV
(*c*) I, III, IV (*d*) I, II, IV

69. In general, polymorphism of which of the following is analysed for DNA fingerprinting?
(*a*) Minivariant repeats (MVR)
(*b*) Microsatellites
(*c*) Minisatellites.
(*d*) All of the above.

70. Which of the following features are correct about the drug Saheli (Centchroman) ?

I. It is a contraceptive tablet.
II. It is taken once a week.
III. It produces no side effects.
IV. It was developed by CIMAP, Lucknow.

Options :

(*a*) I, II, III, IV (*b*) I, II, III
(*c*) I, II, IV (*d*) I, III, IV

71. Which of the following approaches have been tried to develop vaccines for fertility control ?

I. Vaccines against human chorionic gonadotrophin (hCG).
II. Antibodies against follicle stimulating hormone (FSH).
III. Antibodies against vitamin carrier proteins.

Options :

(*a*) I, II, III (*b*) II, III
(*c*) I, III (*d*) I, II

72. Which of the following statements are correct ?

I. Heart ailments are mainly due to an excess of the hormones norepinephrine and epinephrine.
II. Propranolol blocks the β-receptor, thereby interfering with the action of the hormones given above.
III. J. Black was awarded Nobel Prize for Physiolology and Medicine for the development of propranolol.
IV. Propranolol is a successful example of drug designing.

Options :

(*a*) I, II, III (*b*) II, III, IV
(*c*) I, II, III, IV (*d*) I, III, IV

73. HIV is transmitted through which of the following routes ?

(*a*) Homosexual and heterosexual intercourse.
(*b*) From infected mothers to their infants (during birth).
(*c*) Transfusion of HIV-infected blood or blood products.
(*d*) All of the above.

74. Which of the following is the most likely first event in colon cancer development ?

(*a*) Loss of APC function.
(*b*) Loss of DCC function.
(*c*) Activation of *k-ras*.
(*d*) Loss of *p53* function.

75. Which of the following chemicals is used to enhance permeability of peptide/protein drugs ?

(*a*) Sodium deoxycholate
(*b*) Dimethyl-β-cyclodextrin
(*c*) Sodium glycocholate
(*d*) All of the above

76. ***Assertion (A)***: Oral route of drug administration is unsuitable for the new class of protein/peptide drugs.

Reason (R): Proteolytic degradation in the gastrointestinal tract and poor permeability of the intestinal mucosa to peptide /protein therapeutic agents.

Options :

(*a*) Only A is correct.
(*b*) Only R is correct.
(*c*) Both A and R is correct, but R does not adequately explain A.
(*d*) Both A and R is correct and R correctly explains A.

77. Among the given various routes for peptide/protein drug delivery, which one is the most promising ?

(*a*) Pulmonary and rectal
(*b*) Buccal and ocular
(*c*) Nasal
(*d*) Vaginal

78. Which of the following approaches are being tried to combat cancer ?

I. Introduction of the antisense construct of the concerned oncogene.
II. The correct functional version of the inactivated tumour suppressor gene.
III. A gene encoding a toxic protein may be introduced into the tumour cells.
IV Gene therapy may be directed at boosting the patient's immune system.

Options :

(*a*) I, II, III, IV (*b*) II, III, IV
(*c*) I, III, IV (*d*) I, II, III

79. Which of the following vectors has been designed for targetted gene transfer in humans ?

(*a*) Insertion vectors
(*b*) Suicide vectors

(c) Replacement vectors
(d) Both (a) and (c)

80. Targetted gene transfer is based on which of the following techniques ?
(a) Heterologous recombination
(b) Homologous recombination
(c) Site-specific recombination
(d) Both (b) and (c)

81. Due to which of the the following, gene targetting is the strategy of choice for gene therapy ?
(a) Target gene is changed in a precise and specific manner.
(b) Introduced functional gene is placed in the same context in the genome.
(c) No other gene of the genome is affected.
(d) All of the above

82. Which of the following ***is not an example*** of systemic autoimmune disease ?
(a) Scleroderma
(b) Multiple sclerosis
(c) Leukaemia
(d) Rheumatoid arthritis

83. Which of the following ***is not an example*** of organ-specific autoimmune disease ?
(a) Grave's disease
(b) Systemic lupus erythematus
(c) Insulin-dependent diabetes mellitus
(d) Myasthenia gravis

84. Autoimmune diseases could arise in which of the following possible ways ?
I. Release into the circulation of a tissue antigen that is normally sequestered from circulation.
II. Infection by a bacterium or virus that has antigenic determinants that are identical or similar to those of normal host cell components.
III. Induction of non-specific polyclonal B cells by a virus or bacterium to produce IgM in the absence of T_H cells.
IV. Expression of MHC II in cells that normally do not express them.

Options :
(a) I, II, III, IV (b) II, III, IV
(c) I, II, III (d) I, II, IV

85. Long-term immunosuppressive therapy increases the risk of which of the following ?
(a) Hypertension
(b) Cancer
(c) Metabolic bone disease
(d) All of the above

86. Which of following ***is not an example*** of immunosuppressive drugs ?
(a) Methotrexate (b) Corticosteroids
(c) Zidovudine (d) Azathioprine

87. Which of the following is correct about Azathioprine ?
(a) A mitotic inhibitor
(b) Acts on S phase cells
(c) Blocks synthesis of inosinic acid
(d) All of the above

88. Which of the following features are correct about variable number of tandem repeats (VNTRs) ?
I. Minisatellite, microsatellite and mini-variant repeat sequences together constitute VNTRs.
II. VNTR sequences are made up of a variable number of end to end duplications of identical or almost identical sequences.
III. These sequences are dispersed throughout the genome.
IV. The repeat units are of 1-13 bp.

Options :
(a) I, II, IV (b) I, II, III
(c) I, II, III, IV (d) II, III, IV

89. Microsatellites are also called which of the following ?
(a) Simple sequence repeats (SSRs)
(b) Short tandem repeats (STRs)
(c) Simple sequence length polymorphism (SSLP)
(d) All of the above

90. Which of the following statements are correct about VNTRs ?
I. The specific site at which a VNTR sequence is present constitutes a VNTR locus.
II. Different alleles of a VNTR locus consist of different numbers of the repeating unit of this VNTR sequence.
III. In humans, the most polymorphic VNTR locus is *MS1* locus (*D1S7*).

IV. The different alleles of a VNTR locus are detected either as RFLP or through PCR.

Options

(*a*) I, II, III, IV (*b*) II, III, IV
(*c*) I, II, III (*d*) I, III, IV

91. Due to which of the following reasons single locus probe (SLP) method is preferred over mutlilocus probe (MLP) method in almost all crime cases ?

I. SLP analysis is more sensitive.
II. Interpretation of SLP data is simpler and more clear cut.
III. It is possible to analyze mixed DNA samples using SLP data, which is not possible with the MLP methods.
IV. When DNA is too degraded, it may often be possible to generate SLP data, while MLP method is not likely to succeed.

Options :

(*a*) I, II, IV (*b*) II, III, IV
(*c*) I, II, III, IV (*d*) I, II, III

92. Which of the following differentiate mutli-locus probe analysis from single locus probe analysis ?

I. In MLP analysis, hybridization is carried out under conditions of low stringency, while in SLP, it is done under the conditions of high stringency.
II. In MLP, hybridization allows the probe to hybridize with those DNA fragments that have similar related sequences, while in SLP, the probe hybrize with only such fragments that are strictly complementary.
III. Many different bands are detected in MLP analyses, while in case of SLP, ordinarily a maximum of two bands develop in each lane of the gel.

Options :

(*a*) I, II, III (*b*) II, III
(*c*) I, III (*d*) III

93. DNA fingerprinting based on probe hybridization analysis of polymorphism for VNTR sequences suffers from which of the following limitations ?

I. Relatively large amounts of DNA are needed.
II. Variations in the intensities of bands may create difficulties in interpretation of the results.
III. There is a small chance that two unrelated individuals could have the same, or atleast very similar, finger-prints.
IV. Their analyses are very slow.

Options :

(*a*) I, II, IV (*b*) I, II, III, IV
(*c*) I, III, IV (*d*) II, III, IV

94. The PCR-based fingerprinting offers which of the following advantages over probe-based DNA fingerprinting ?

I. It is very sensitive.
II. Results are obtained rather quickely.
III. PCR analysis could be done even when DNA is fragmented into short lengths.
IV. A single multiplex PCR reaction enables simultaneous analysis of several loci.

Options :

(*a*) I, II, III (*b*) II, III, IV
(*c*) I, II, III, IV (*d*) I, III, IV

95. Which of the following ***is not used*** in asymmetric gap-LCR ?

(*a*) NAD
(*b*) DNA ligase
(*c*) DNA polymerase
(*d*) Reverse transcriptase

96. Which of the options given in Q. 95 ***is not used*** in gap-LCR ?

97. LCR can detect which of the following molecules.

(*a*) DNA (*b*) Protein
(*c*) RNA (*d*) Both (*a*) and (*c*)

98. Which of the following play the major role in histocompatibility ?

(*a*) MHC loci
(*b*) ABO blood group
(*c*) Rh blood group
(*d*) MN blood group

99. In case of histocompatibility, which of the following is recognized directly (without processing) by T_H cells ?

(*a*) Major histocompatibility complex antigens
(*b*) Minor histocompatibility antigens
(*c*) A and B antigens (ABO blood group)
(*d*) Both (*a*) and (*b*)

100. Column A has some cytokines involved in graft rejection, while their roles are given in column B. Match the two columns carefully, and pick the correct option from those given below them.

Column A	Column B
A. IL-2	1. DTH response
B. IFN-γ	2. Direct cytotoxic effect
C. TNF-β	3. Increased expression of MHC I
D. TNF-α	4. T cell proliferation
	5. Increased avidity

Options :
(*a*) A4, B2, C1, D3 (*b*) A3, B1, C2, D5
(*c*) A4, B3, C5, D1 (*d*) A4, B1, C2, D3

101. At a VNTR locus, which of the following is the basis for different alleles ?
(*a*) Sequence of repeating units
(*b*) Number of repeating units
(*c*) Length of repeating units
(*d*) Both (*a*) and (*c*)

102. Which of the options given in Q. 101 is the basis of different VNTR loci ?

103. A thermostable DNA polymerase is used in which of the following ?
I. Gap-LCR
II. Asymmetric gap-LCR
III. Asymmetric PCR
IV. RT-PCR

Options :
(*a*) I, II (*b*) II, III
(*c*) II, IV (*d*) I, II, III, IV

104. In which of the options given in Q. 103, reverse transcriptase is used ?

105. In which of the options given in Q. 103, DNA ligase is used ?

106. An 'indel' defines a site in the genome that has which of the following ?
(*a*) Insertion of a sequence
(*b*) Deletion of a sequence
(*c*) Either (*a*) or (*b*)
(*d*) Inversion of a sequence

107. Immuno-PCR detects the presence of which of the following ?
(*a*) DNA (*b*) RNA
(*c*) Antigen (*d*) Immunogen

108. Column A lists some growth factors, while column B gives their applications. Match the two columns carefully and pick the correct option from those listed below them.

Column A	Column B
A. Bovine growth hormone	1. Viral infection
B. Streptokinase	2. Thrombolysis
C. Leucocyte protease inhibitor	3. Increased milk yield
	4. Osteoporosis
D. Thymosin α1	5. Cystic fibrosis

Options :
(*a*) A3, B2, C5, D1 (*b*) A3, B4, C5, D1
(*c*) A3, B5, C4, D1 (*d*) A3, B2, C4, D1

109. Which of the following growth factors is used for the treatment of osteoporosis ?
(*a*) Fibroblast growth factor
(*b*) Thymosin α
(*c*) Insulin like growth factor
(*d*) Human growth hormone

110. Anti-RNA polymerase I is used to diagnose which of the following autoimmune diseases ?
(*a*) Polymyositis
(*b*) Scleroderma
(*c*) Systemic lupus erythematus
(*d*) Myasthenia gravis

111. Which of the options given in Q. 110 is diagnosed with anti-dsDNA ?

112. Which of the options given in Q. 110 is diagnosed by anti-acetylcholine receptor ?

113. The lead for development of the antihypertensive drug Captopril came from which of the following ?
(*a*) South American pit viper
(*b*) Banded Krait
(*c*) King cobra
(*d*) Rattle snake

114. Polyesters of lactic acid and glycolic acid are used for achieving slow release of which of the following ?
(*a*) Proteins
(*b*) Oligonucleotides
(*c*) Polysaccharides
(*d*) All of the above

115. Stealth liposomes are made up of which of the following ?

(*a*) Lipid
(*b*) Monoclonal antibodies
(*c*) PEG
(*d*) All of the above

116. SCID may result from a deficiency of which of the following ?
(*a*) RAG-1/RAG-2 (*b*) ADA
(*c*) JAK-3 (*d*) All of the above

117. Which of the following is most likely the last to occur in colon cancer development ?
(*a*) Loss of APC function.
(*b*) Loss of DCC function.
(*c*) Loss of *p*53 function.
(*d*) Activation of κ-ras.

118. Which of the events listed in Q. 117 represents a gain of function ?

11.2. FILL IN THE BLANKS

1. SV40 and Polyoma Viruses have .... genomes.

2. Many bacteria produce exotoxins, which are highly ....

3. Bovine growth hormone is used to increase .... yield.

4. Recombinant protein or polypeptide vaccines are .... safe.

5. Probes are .... bases long nucleotide sequences used to detect the presence of complementary sequences in nucleic acid (DNA/RNA) samples.

6. Abbreviation SCID stands for ....

7. In 1981, AIDS was first reported in ....

8. An immunodeficiency that arises from a genetic or developmental defect in the immune system is called ....

9. Inhibition of viral replication is achieved by ...., ... and .... interferons.

10. Non-nucleoside analogues like nevirapine inhibit the action of ....

11. Abbreviation HAART stands for ....

12. In general, ... grafts are rejected faster than those of other tissues.

13. The second cycle of LCR is initiated by heating the reaction mixture to ....°C.

14. In case of ligase chain reaction, target sequence is .... bases long.

15. Gene *BRCA1* has .... exons.

16. Taxol is used for treatment of .... and .... cancers.

17. Interleukin-2, in conjunction with .... cells, is being used for cancer therapy.

18. In 1986, the technique of DNA finger-printing was developed by ....

19. Saheli tablet was developed by ....

20. DNA fingerprinting is also called ....

21. In human genome, the most common short tandem repeat (STR) has the repeating unit..........., which is usually repeated 5-20 times.

22. Inhibition of HIV protease results in the production of immature and .... viral particles.

23. AZT selectively inhibits the .... of HIV.

24. Loss of immune function as a result of exposure to various agents, such as, human immunodeficiency virus-1 is called ....

25. Cimetidine specially cures .... by blocking the H_2 receptor of histamine.

26. Malignant cells may arise due to .... in oncogenes and tumour suppressor genes.

27. In case of augmentation gene therapy, modified cells contain both the .... and .... copies of the gene.

28. The most effective system for site-directed delivery of drugs and other moieties is based on ....

29. .... syndrome is produced by adenosine deaminase (ADA) deficiency.

30. Target gene transfer uses .... to replace the defective endogenous gene with the functional introduced gene.

31. In minisatellite DNA the repeated units are of .... bp.

32. In case of microsatellite, the repeat units are of .... bp.
33. In case of single probe locus analysis, 3-4 or even more loci can be analyse by using .... for the probes sepecific for individual loci.
34. Chemiluminescent probes have .... attached to them by a linker arm.
35. The duration of exposure in case of radioactive probe is around .... days, while in case of chemiluminescence it is only .... days.

11.3. MARK TRUE OR FALSE

1. The coding sequences of *v-onc* and the homologous *c-onc* genes exhibit a high degree of homology.
2. Most of the purified antigens from pathogens are poorly immunogenic.
3. Some toxoids are very good adjuvants.
4. HIV genome consists of double-stranded RNA.
5. In case of immuno-PCR, all test samples, which yield PCR product, will contain the target DNA sequence.
6. Isografts and autografts are generally accepted, while allografts and xenografts are rejected.
7. TNF-α and TNF-β exhibit direct anti-tumour activities.
8. In case of autoimmune haemolytic anaemias, anti-IgG causes agglutination of RBCs from positive cases since IgG auto-antibodies are present on these cells.
9. Ligase chain reaction can detect as few as 10-20 target molecules in a sample.
10. Erythropoietin is used on a considerable scale for the treatment of anaemia.
11. Aim of drug designing is to develop highly efficient drugs, which have little or no side effects.
12. Histamine induces the release of HCl in stomach leading to the development of stomach ulcer.
13. Oncogenes and tumour suppressor genes are involved in metastasis.
14. Gene therapy can be classified into germ line gene therapy and somatic cell gene therapy.
15. Clinical trials of somatic cell gene therapy have already started mostly for the treatment of AIDS.
16. Tumour cells express tumour-specific transplantation antigens and tumour-associated transplantation antigens.
17. Translation is blocked by pairing of sense oligonucleotide with the selected region of target mRNA.
18. In case of sickle cell anaemia, the mutation from GAG to GTG eliminates a recognition site for the restriction enzyme *Mst*II in the α-globin gene.
19. Amniocentesis is applicable to only 18 week old or older cases of pregnancy.
20. Inhibition of transcription occurs due to the binding of oligonucleotide in the minor groove of double-stranded target DNA resulting in the formation of triplex structure in the selected region.
21. Differences in blood group and major histocompatibility antigens are responsible for most intense graft rejections.
22. A prolonged use of permeability enhancer chemicals causes changes in the mucosal surface.
23. Liposomes hold great promise as DNA delivery system in gene therapy, but they have to be injected into the subjects.
24. Polyesters of lactic acid and glycolic acid are most widely used polyesters for slow release of drugs having small to large molecules.
25. The major limitation of targetted gene transfer is the low frequency of homologous recombination in humans.

26. Systemic lupus erythematus is an example of organ-specific autoimmune diseases.

27. Prevention of rejection of allografts requires administration of drugs that suppress the immune response.

28. Term DNA fingerprinting was used by Alec Jeffreys for multilocus probe analysis.

29. TNF-α (tumour necrosis factor α) and TNF-β exhibit direct antitumour activities.

30. A monoclonal antibody (Mab) against CD4 antigen induces the $CD4^+$ cell to enter an immunosuppressed state.

31. Microsatellite sequences are now used PCR-based STMS markers.

32. In case of single locus probe analysis, only one band develops in each lane of the gel.

33. The multilocus probe and single locus probe analyses differ for the conditions used for hybridization of tandem repeat sequence of interest used as probes.

34. The objective of transplantation is to cure certain diseases by implanting a healthy organ, tissue or cells in the patient.

35. VNTR sequences are made up of a variable number of end-to-end duplications of identical or almost identical sequences of 2-80 bases, 5-50 bases being common in mammals.

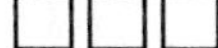

12
ENZYME ENGINEERING

12.1. MULTIPLE CHOICE QUESTIONS

1. Which of the following statements are correct about enzymes ?

I. The term enzyme was introduced by Kühne in 1878.

II. They are proteins that catalyze or speed up a specific chemical reaction.

III. Coenzymes are organic groups, which are readily separated from the apoenzyme.

IV. None-protein groups (both organic and inorganic) attached to an apoenzyme are called cofactors.

Options :

(*a*) I, II, III (*b*) I, II, III, IV
(*c*) I, III, IV (*d*) I, II, IV

2. Which of the following are examples of hydrophobic amino acids ?

(*a*) Leucine and isoleucine
(*b*) Methionine and valine
(*c*) Phenylalanine and often tyrosine
(*d*) All of the above.

3. During 'invert syrup' production, small amounts of xylene are added to achieve which of the following ?

(*a*) To prevent microbial contamination
(*b*) To facilitate product recovery
(*c*) Substrate activation
(*d*) To prevent product inhibition

4. Which of the following are example of hydrophilic amino acid ?

I. Glutamine and glutamic acid

II. Histidine and arginine

III. Aspartic acid and lysine

IV. Asparagine and serine

Options :

(*a*) I, II, III, IV (*b*) I, II, III
(*c*) II, III, IV (*d*) I, III, IV

5. In which of the following, enzymes are used in the largest quantity ?

(*a*) Textile industry
(*b*) Alcohol production
(*c*) Detergents
(*d*) Leather industry

6. Column A lists the names of scientists, while column B lists their contributions. Match both the columns carefully and select the correct option from those listed below them.

Column A	Column B
A. Fisher	1. Mathematical model of enzyme action
B. Michaelis and Menten	2. Crystalization of enzyme (urease)
C. Sumner	3. Lock and key model of enzyme action
D. Pauling	4. Transition state theory of enzyme action

Options :

(*a*) A3, B4, C1, D2 (*b*) A3, B1, C2, D4
(*c*) A3, B4, C3, D1 (*d*) A3, B2, C4, D1

7. In 1953, Sanger determined the amino acid sequence of which of the following proteins ?

(*a*) Casein
(*b*) Insulin
(*c*) Haemoglobin
(*d*) Heat shock protein

8. Penicillin acylases use which of the following substrates ?
(a) Penicillin G (b) Penicillin V
(c) Penicillins (d) Both (a) and (b)

9. In enzymology, abbreviation EC stands for which of the following ?
(a) Exotic collection
(b) Enzyme commission
(c) Enzyme collection
(d) Enzyme cofactor

10. Purified enzymes offer which of the following advantages over whole cells ?
I. There is no risk of by-product formation or product breakdown.
II. The substrate is not converted into biomass.
III. The optimum conditions for an enzyme may be different from those for the organism producing it.
IV. Often purification of the product is simpler.
Options :
(a) I, II, III (b) II, III, IV
(c) I, II, III, IV (d) I, III, IV

11. In 1986, which of the following scientists discovered the catalytic action of some RNA molecules ?
(a) Baltimore (b) Smith
(c) Cech (d) Berg

12. Enzymes are similar to catalysts in respects to which of the following ?
(a) They lower the activation energy of reaction.
(b) They do not participate in the reaction.
(c) They only increase the reaction rate.
(d) All of the above.

13. Purified enzymes have which of the following limitations ?
I. Instability
II. High cost
III. Catalysis of only a single reaction
Options :
(a) I, II (b) I, II, III
(c) II, III (d) I, III

14. Which of the following enzymes catalyses an irreversible reaction of glycolysis ?
(a) Phosphofructokinase
(b) Glucose-6-isomerase
(c) Aldolase
(d) Phosphoglycerate mutase

15. Unit of K_m is which of the following ?
(a) cm (b) moles/litre
(c) s^{-1} (d) It has no unit

16. Which of the following is a multienzyme complex ?
(a) Urease
(b) Tryptophan synthase from *E. coli*
(c) Aldolase
(d) Both (b) and (c)

17. In case of glucose isomerase used for production of high fructose syrup, which of the following is used as cofactor ?
(a) Ca^{2+} (b) Co^{2+}
(c) Mg^{2+} (d) Both (b) and (c)

18. Which of the following statements is the most correct about enzymes ?
(a) They are always proteins
(b) They are heat stable
(c) All the enzymes are highly specific for their substrates
(d) They can be inhibited by substrate analogues.

19. K_m is the substrate concentration at which reaction rate is equal to which of the following ?
(a) V_{max} (b) 1/2 V_{max}
(c) $2V_{max}$ (d) 1/4 V_{max}

20. β-oxidation of palmitic acid produces how many net ATPs ?
(a) 96 (b) 146
(c) 130 (d) 123

21. Which of the following statements is the most correct about ribozymes ?
(a) Enzyme activity associated with ribosomes.
(b) Enzymes which catalyse both synthesis and degradation of small oligonucleotides.
(c) Enzymes that use RNA as substrate.
(d) RNA molecules having enzymatic properties.

22. Which of the following methods is being used in automated amino acid sequencing ?
(a) Sanger's method
(b) Gel filteration
(c) Edman's degradation
(d) Ninhydrin method

23. Helical content of proteins is determined by which of the following techniques ?
(*a*) Circular dichroism
(*b*) Ion-exchange chromatography
(*c*) Polyacrylamide gel electrophoresis
(*d*) Spectrophotometry

24. Which of the following yields highly purified enzymes in a single step ?
(*a*) Gel filteration
(*b*) Affinity chromatography
(*c*) Ion exchange chromatography
(*d*) Both (*b*) and (*c*)

25. As a general rule of thumb, hydrophobic residues in a protein tend to be situated at which of the following positions ?
(*a*) Extending out of the molecule
(*b*) Half exposed on the surface
(*c*) Interior of the molecule
(*d*) Exposed on the surface

26. Na^+–K^+ ATPase is related to which of the following ?
(*a*) Active transport
(*b*) Passive transport
(*c*) Group translocation
(*d*) Both (*a*) and (*c*)

27. Thiamine pyrophosphate (TPP) coenzyme is found in which of the following ?
(*a*) Glutamine synthase
(*b*) Glyceraldehyde 3-phosphate dehydrogenase
(*c*) Pyruvate dehydrogenase complex
(*d*) DNA ligase.

28. Column A lists the type of biosensors and column B lists their applications. Match the two columns carefully and pick the correct option from those listed below them.

Column A	Column B
A. Potentiometric (ion-selective electrode)	1. Nicotinic acid detection
B. Amperometric	2. Bacteria detection
C. Acoustic wave	3. Urea detection
D. Optical	4. Cocaine detection
	5. Glucose biosensor

Options :
(*a*) A3, B4, C5, D2 (*b*) A3, B5, C4, D2
(*c*) A3, B5, C1, D2 (*d*) A3, B1, C4, D2

29. Which of the following hydrolytic enzymes are used for synthetic reactions ?
I. Proteases like thermolysin.
II. Lipase
III. Glycosidases like dextranosucrase

Options :
(*a*) I, II, III (*b*) I, II
(*c*) I, III (*d*) II, III

30. Aspartame is an artificial sweetner. It is chemically which of the following ?
(*a*) Fatty acid (*b*) Carbohydrate
(*c*) Dipeptide (*d*) Oligopeptide

31. Which of the following metal ions is associated with urease enzyme ?
(*a*) Fe (*b*) Ni
(*c*) Mg (*d*) Cu

32. Which of the following are the features of enzymes ?
I. Enzymes increase the rate of reaction at a phenomenal scale.
II. They are highly specific.
III. Their reaction rates show substrate saturation
IV. They are subjected to a variety of regulations.

Options :
(*a*) I, II, III, IV (*b*) II, III, IV
(*c*) I, III, IV (*d*) I, II, IV

33. Due to which of the following features, enzymes are attractive for commerical applications ?
(*a*) They operate under mild conditions of temperature, pressure and pH, which saves energy.
(*b*) Undesirable by-products are not produced.
(*c*) Certain stereochemical reactions are impractical with chemical methods.
(*d*) All of the above.

34. Rennet enzyme is produced by which of the following ?
(*a*) *Mucor miehei* (*b*) Calf stomach
(*c*) Calf liver (*d*) Both (*a*) and (*b*).

35. The bulk of enzymes, both in terms of quantity and variety, are produced from which of the following sources ? The correct option lists these sources in descending order.

(*a*) Animals → plants → microorganisms
(*b*) Microorganisms → animals → plants
(*c*) Microorganisms → plants → animals
(*d*) Plants → microorganisms → animals

36. Which of the following hydrolytic enzymes is produced in bulk quantity from plants ?
(*a*) α- and β-amylase
(*b*) Papain
(*c*) β-Glucanase
(*d*) All of the above.

37. ***Assertion (A)***: Initially, plant and animal enzymes were preferred over microbial enzymes.
Reason (R): Considerations of safety and the fear of contamination by micro-organisms or toxins limited the use of microbial sources.
Options :
(*a*) Both A and R are correct and R roughly explains A.
(*b*) Both A and R correct, but R does not explain A.
(*c*) Only A is correct.
(*d*) Only R is correct.

38. Which of the following advantages are associated with microbes when used as a source of enzyme production ?
I. Large-scale production by fermentation.
II. Easy isolation of those enzymes, which are secreted into the medium.
III. Easy genetic manipulation to enhance enzyme yields.
IV. Opportunities for enzyme engineering.
Options :
(*a*) I, II, III, IV (*b*) I, II, IV
(*c*) I, III, IV (*d*) II, III, IV

39. Isomerases include which of the following ?
(*a*) Intramolecular transferases
(*b*) Epimerases
(*c*) Racemases
(*d*) All of the above

40. The rates of forward and reverse reactions depend on which of the following ?
(*a*) Rate constants for the forward and backward reactions.
(*b*) Concentrations of the products.
(*c*) Concentrations of the reactants.
(*d*) All of the above

41. All chemical reactions possess which of the following major properties ?
(*a*) Kinetic (*b*) Thermodynamic
(*c*) Both (*a*) and (*b*) (*d*) Dynamic

42. Which of the following options lists the correct order of the mechanism of enzyme reaction ?
(*a*) $E + S \rightleftharpoons EP \rightleftharpoons ES \rightleftharpoons E + P$
(*b*) $E + S \rightleftharpoons ES \rightleftharpoons EP \rightleftharpoons E + P$
(*c*) $E + S \rightarrow EP \rightarrow ES \rightarrow E + P$
(*d*) $E + P \rightarrow ES \rightarrow EP \rightarrow E + P$

43. Which of the following enzymes is regarded as catalytically perfect enzyme ?
(*a*) Catalase
(*b*) Triphosphate isomerase
(*c*) Carbonic anhydrase
(*d*) All of the above

44. Oxidoreductase class of enzymes ***does not include*** which of the following ?
(*a*) Aldolases (*b*) Dehydrogenases
(*c*) Oxidases (*d*) Peroxidases

45. Hydrolase class of enzymes ***does not include*** which of the following ?
(*a*) Lipases (*b*) Esterases
(*c*) Oxygenases (*d*) Glycosidases

46. Lyase class of enzymes ***does not contain*** which of following ?
(*a*) Decarboxylases (*b*) Dehydratases
(*c*) Aldolases (*d*) Proteases

47. Column A lists some classes of enzymes, while column B lists the names of some enzymes. Match both the columns carefully and select the correct option from those listed below them.

Column A	Column B
A. Isomerases	1. Aspartate amino-transferase
B. Hydrolases	2. Histidine ammonia lyase
C. Oxidoreductases	3. Chymosin
D. Lyases	4. Xylose isomerase
	5. Glucose oxidase

Options :
(*a*) A4, B5, C2, D1 (*b*) A4, B3, C2, D5
(*c*) A4, B3, C5, D2 (*d*) A4, B5, C3, D1

48. Thermodynamic predictions are based on which of the following ?

(*a*) Stabilities of reactants
(*b*) Stabilities of products
(*c*) Both (*a*) and (*b*)
(*d*) Amounts of enzymes.

49. Column A lists some enzymes, while column B lists the sources from which they are produced. Match both the columns carefully and select the correct option from those given below.

Column A	Column B
A. Catalase	1. *Bacillus*
B. Lipase	2. Liver
C. Protease	3. Pancrease
D. Invertase	4. *Saccharomyces*

Options :
(*a*) A3, B4, C2, D1 (*b*) A2, B3, C1, D4
(*c*) A1, B4, C3, D2 (*d*) A4, B1, C3, D2

50. α-amylase is produced from which of the following ?

(*a*) Malted barley (*b*) *Bacillus*
(*c*) *Aspergillus* (*d*) All of the above

51. Which of the following mechanisms is used by enzymes to lower the activation energy ?

I. Acid-base and redox catalysis.
II. Stabilization of the transition state of substrates.
III. Catalysis by approximation.
IV. Covalent catalysis.

Options :
(*a*) I, II, III, IV (*b*) I, II, IV
(*c*) I, III, IV (*d*) I, II, III

52. Which of the following statements are correct ?

I. The stability of a compound depends on its free energy.
II. A lower free energy is more stable and thermodynamically favoured state.
III. The most useful thermodynamic value in the determination of whether a reaction will occur or not is the change in Gibbs free energy denoted by ΔG.
IV. If the value of ΔG is positive, the reaction will occur, but if it is negative, the reverse reaction will take place.

Options :
(*a*) I, II, III (*b*) II, III, IV
(*c*) II, IV (*d*) I, II, III, IV

53. Column A lists some enzymes, while column B lists the source from which they are commercially produced. Match both the columns carefully and select the correct option from those given below them.

Column A	Column B
A. Lactase (β-galactosidase)	1. Fig latex
B. Raffinase (α-galactosidase)	2. Pancreas
C. Trypsin	3. *Saccharomyces*
D. Ficin	4. *Kluyveromyces*
	5. Liver

Options :
(*a*) A4, B2, C3, D5 (*b*) A4, B1, C3, D5
(*c*) A4, B3, C2, D1 (*d*) A3, B4, C2, D1

54. Which of the following statements are correct ?

I. Thermodynamic predictions about reactions are based on the stabilities of products and reactants.
II. The rate of a chemical reaction depends on the number of reactant molecules that have enough energy to reach the transition state of the slowest step in the reaction.
III. As a rule, very few molecules possess enough energy to reach the transition state.
IV. Higher the value of $G^{\ddagger}$, the higher is the rate of reaction.

Options :
(*a*) I, II, III, IV (*b*) I, II, III
(*c*) II, III, IV (*d*) I, III, IV

55. Column A lists some enzymes, while column B lists their applications. Match both the columns carefully and select the correct option from those given below them.

Column A	Column B
A. Invertase	1. Cheese
B. Lactase	2. Dairy
C. Papain	3. Confectionery
D. Rennet (aspartic proteinase)	4. Detergent
	5. Meat

Options :
(*a*) A1, B4, C2, D3 (*b*) A4, B3, C5, D2
(*c*) A2, B5, C4, D1 (*d*) A3, B2, C5, D1

56. Which of the following enzymes is obtained from bacteria ?
(*a*) α- and β-amylases
(*b*) Glucose isomerase
(*c*) Penicillin amidase
(*d*) All of the above

57. Which of the following enzymes ***is not obtained*** from animals ?
(*a*) Ficin (*b*) Lipase
(*c*) Trypsin (*d*) Catalase

58. Which of the following enzymes ***is not obtained*** from plants ?
(*a*) α-and β-amylase
(*b*) β-glucanase and papain
(*c*) Pectinase
(*d*) Ficin

59. Glucose isomerase enzyme is obtained commercially from which of the following organisms ?
(*a*) *Bacillus* (*b*) *Streptomyces*
(*c*) *Aspergillus* (*d*) Both (*a*) and (*b*).

60. Which of the following enzymes is obtained commercially from *Aspergillus* ?
(*a*) Protease and pectinase
(*b*) α-Amylase and glucoamylase
(*c*) Both (*a*) and (*b*)
(*d*) Papain

61. Which of the following enzymes is obtained commercially from animal pancreas ?
(*a*) Trypsin (*b*) Rennet
(*c*) Lipase (*d*) All of the above

62. Which of the following enzymes ***is not obtained*** commercially from malted barley ?
(*a*) β-Glucanase (*b*) α-Amylase
(*c*) Glucoamylase (*d*) β-Amylase

63. Which of the following enzymes ***is not obtained*** from *Bacillus* ?
(*a*) Protease and glucose isomerase
(*b*) Penicillin amidase
(*c*) α- and β-amylase
(*d*) Pectinase

64. Match the columns A and B and select the correct option from those given below them.

Column A	**Column B**
A. Pectinase	1. Leather
B. Glucose isomerase	2. Food
C. Papain	3. Fructose syrup
D. Catalase	4. Meat
	5. Drinking

Options :
(*a*) A4, B2, C5, D3 (*b*) A5, B3, C4, D2
(*c*) A3, B5, C1, D4 (*d*) A1, B4, C3, D5

65. K_m may be enfluenced by which of the following parameters ?
(*a*) Temperature (*b*) Ionic strength
(*c*) pH (*d*) All of the above.

66. Which of the following enzymes is isolated from hyperthermophiles ?
(*a*) DNA polymerase
(*b*) α-Amylase
(*c*) α-Glucosidase
(*d*) All of the above

67. Which of the following statements are correct about abzymes ?
I. They are antibodies.
II. They catalyse specific chemical reactions.
III. They are not produced naturally.
IV. They are produced in response to molecules that have a structure similar to the proposed/expected transition state of the concerned substrate.

Options :
(*a*) I, II, III, IV (*b*) II, III, IV
(*c*) I, III, IV (*d*) I, II, IV

68. Which of the following features are correct about ribozymes ?
I. They are true catalysts.
II. They are able to cut and splice themselves into a form that is capable of catalysis.
III. Their catalytic ability arises due to their three dimensional structure.
IV. RNA may be the first macromolecule on earth, which catalyzed its own replication.

Options :
(*a*) I, II, III (*b*) I, II, III, IV
(*c*) II, III, IV (*d*) I, III, IV

69. An ideal carrier matrix has which of the following properties ?
I. It is a inert polymer or inorganic material.
II. Its cost is high.
III. It has physical strength.
IV. It has stability.

Options :
(*a*) I, II, III (*b*) I, III, IV
(*c*) I, II, III, IV (*d*) II, III, IV

70. Which of the following methods are used for immobilization of enzymes ?

I. Covalent bonding
II. Adsorption
III. Membrane confinement
IV. Entrapment

Options :

(*a*) I, II, III, IV (*b*) II, III, IV
(*c*) I, III, IV (*d*) I, II, III

71. Carrier matrix has which of the following properties ?

I. It reduces the microbial contamination and non-specific adsorption.
II. It has regenerability after the useful lifetime of the immobilized enzyme.
III. It enhances enzyme specificity.
IV. It reduces product inhibition.

Options :

(*a*) I, II, III (*b*) II, III, IV
(*c*) I, II, III, IV (*d*) I, II, IV

72. Which of the following advantages are associated with immobilization of enzymes ?

I. Enzymes can not be used repeatedly.
II. Recovery of enzyme may reduce effluent handling problems.
III. Thermostability of some enzymes may be increased.
IV. Immobilized enzymes can be used in nonaqueous systems.

Options :

(*a*) I, II, III, IV (*b*) I, III, IV
(*c*) I, II, IV (*d*) II, III, IV

73. Which of the following properties of an enzyme can be modified through enzyme engineering ?

I. Fusion of two or more enzymes.
II. Improved kinetic properties.
III. Elimination of allosteric regulation.
IV. Resistance to proteolytic degradation.

Options :

(*a*) I, II, III, IV (*b*) I, II, III
(*c*) II, III, IV (*d*) I, III, IV

74. Which of the following advantages are associated with immobilization of enzymes.

I. Immobilization permits their repeated use.
II. The product is readily freed from the enzyme.
III. Continuous production systems can be used.
IV. Enzymes can be used at much higher concentrations.

Options :

(*a*) I, II, III (*b*) I, III, IV
(*c*) I, II, III, IV (*d*) II, III, IV

75. Which of the following disadvantages are associated with immobilization of enzymes ?

I. Immobilization of enzyme increases cost.
II. Immobilization often adversely affects the stability.
III. This approach can be used when one of the substrates is insoluble.
IV. Immobilized cells are particularly vulnerable to contamination.

Options :

(*a*) I, II, IV (*b*) II, III, IV
(*c*) I, III, IV (*d*) III, IV

76. ***Problem (P)***: Immobilized cells are particularly vulnerable to contamination.
Solution (S): An antibiotic may have to be used in such cases.

Options :

(*a*) Only P is correct.
(*b*) Only S is correct.
(*c*) Both P and S are correct, but S is not correct remedy of P.
(*d*) Both P and S are correct and S is the correct remedy of P.

77. Proteases are used to digest away proteins present in which of the following ?

(*a*) Blood stains (*b*) Dirt stains
(*c*) Grass stains (*d*) All of the above

78. Which of the following is correct about proteases ?

(*a*) They help in removal of dirt.
(*b*) Serine proteases are produced by *Bacillus licheniformis* and *B. amyloliquefaciens.*
(*c*) They are packed inside dust-free granules for use in detergents.
(*d*) All of the above.

79. Which of the following matrices is commonly used for enzyme adsorption ?

I. Ion-exchange matrices and glasses.
II. Hydrous metal oxides and clays.

III. Porous carbon and polymeric aromatic resins.
IV. Sodium and calcium alginates

Options :
(*a*) I, II, III, IV (*b*) II, III, IV
(*c*) I, II, III (*d*) I, III, IV

80. In case of covalent bonding, the most commonly employed matrix is which of the following ?
(*a*) Celluloses (*b*) Polyacrylamides
(*c*) Agarose (*d*) All of the above

81. Sepharose, an agarose, matrix is activated by treatment with which of the following ?
I. Chloroformates
II. Acrylamide
III. Carbodiimides
IV. Glutaraldehyde

Options :
(*a*) I, II, III, IV (*b*) I, III, IV
(*c*) II, III, IV (*d*) I, IV

82. Which of the following is highly toxic ?
(*a*) Carbodiimides
(*b*) Chloroformates
(*c*) Cyanogen bromide
(*d*) Glutaraldehyde

83. Which of the following is correct about glutaraldehyde ?
I. It is a bifunctional reagent.
II. It can be used to covalently bind the enzyme molecules.
III. It is particularly useful for producing immobilized enzyme membranes for use in biosensors.

Options :
(*a*) I, II (*b*) I, II, III
(*c*) III (*d*) I, III

84. Enzyme kinetics (*i.e.*, activity) may be affected due to which of the following ?
(*a*) Matrix used for immobilization.
(*b*) Conformational changes in the enzyme molecules induced by the procedure of immobilization.
(*c*) Both (*a*) and (*b*)
(*d*) Altered charge of enzyme molecules.

85. An enzyme used in detergents must have which of the following features ?
(*a*) Safe to use
(*b*) Cost-effective
(*c*) Able to function at pH between 8 and 10.5.
(*d*) All of the above.

86. Commercial cellulase obtained from *Trichoderma reesei* is a mixture of which of following synergistic enzymes ?
I. Glucan 1, 4-β-glucosidase
II. Exocellobiohydrolase
III. Cellulose 1, 4-β-cellobiosidase
IV. Cellulase

Options :
(*a*) I, II, III, IV (*b*) III, IV
(*c*) II, III, IV (*d*) II, IV

87. The glucose syrup composition is typcially which of the following ?
(*a*) 90-95% gluclose, 10-15% maltose and 3-5% isomaltose.
(*b*) 95-97% glucose, 1-2% maltose and 0.5-2% isomaltose.
(*c*) 80-90% glucose, 5-10% maltose and 8-10% isomaltose.
(*d*) 85-90% glucose, 5-10% maltose, 5-10% isomaltose.

88. Which of the following ***is not affected*** by enzymes ?
(*a*) Reaction rate (*b*) ΔG
(*c*) $\Delta G^{\ddagger}$ (*d*) Both (*b*) and (*c*)

89. Which of the following ***is not correct*** about aspartame ?
(*a*) It is a dipeptide.
(*b*) It is synthesized from an equal mixture of L-aspartic acid and methyl ester of L-phenylalanine.
(*c*) It is 180 times sweeter than sucrose.
(*d*) It is used as high colorie sweetner.

90. Which of the following is correct about high maltose syrups ?
I. They are produced from liquefied starch.
II. They are produced using fungal α-amylase.
III. Glucoamylase is also used.
IV. They are used to produce hard candy and frozen deserts.

Options :
(*a*) I, II, III (*b*) II, III, IV
(*c*) I, II, IV (*d*) I, III, IV

91. The choice of reactor type depends on which of the following ?
(*a*) Form (free or immobilized) of enzyme to be used.
(*b*) Kinetics of reaction.
(*c*) Scale of operation.
(*d*) All of the above.

92. Which of the following advantages are offered by batch reactors ?
I. They are more useful for large scale productions.
II. They are simple both in use and process development.
III. They provide a close control on the reactor environment.
IV. They can be used where continuous processes can not be used due to viscosity and other problems of the reaction mixture.

Options :
(*a*) I, II, III, IV (*b*) II, III, IV
(*c*) I, III, IV (*d*) I, II, IV

93. Most of the enzymes are used extracellularily for which of the following medical purposes ?
(*a*) Removal of toxic substances.
(*b*) Treatment of disorders within blood circulatory system.
(*c*) Topical applications
(*d*) All of the above.

94. Which of the following statements are correct about medical uses of asparaginase ?
I. Tumour cells are unable to synthesize L-asparagine.
II. When asparaginase is administered, it drastically reduces the levels of free L-asparagine in the blood stream.
III. Asparaginase is injected intravenously.
IV. The enzyme shows half-life of about one day in dogs.

Options :
(*a*) I, II, III, IV (*b*) I, III, IV
(*c*) II, III, IV (*d*) I, II, IV

95. Batch reactors suffer from which of the following limitations ?
I. They are more difficult to scale up.
II. There is batch to batch variation in product quality.
III. Batch mode is costlier than continuous mode.

Options :
(*a*) I, II (*b*) I, II, III
(*c*) I, III (*d*) II, III

96. Enzyme stability in the presence of heavy metals can be improved by which of the following ?
(*a*) Replacing Cys residue
(*b*) Replacing Met residue
(*c*) Removing surface carboxyl groups
(*d*) All of the above.

97. Synzymes must possess which of following functional site(s) ?
(*a*) Substrate binding site.
(*b*) Catalytically effective site.
(*c*) Allosteric site.
(*d*) Both (*a*) and (*b*).

98. Which of the following features are correct about myoglobin ?
I. It functions as oxygen carrier in muscle.
II. When the group $[Ru(NH_3)_5]^{3+}$ is attached to three surface histidine residues of myoglobin, it begins to function like an oxidase.
III. It oxidises ascorbic acid and reduces molecular oxygen.
IV. This derivatised myoglobin is almost as effective as natural ascorbate oxidase.

Options :
(*a*) I, II, III, IV (*b*) I, II, IV
(*c*) II, III, IV (*d*) I, II, III

99. Which of the following statements are correct ?
I. Solvent engineering seeks to usefully modify properties of enzymes simply by using appropriate organic solvents.
II. Suitably alkylated polyethyleneimines behave as synzymes.
III. When pyridoxal coenzyme is attached to a C-6 hydroxyl group of a β-cyclodextrin, it acts as a transaminase specific for L-amino acids.
IV. Aim of enzyme engineering is to modify the properties of an enzyme by making appropriate changes in its amino acid sequence.

Options :
(*a*) I, II, III, IV (*b*) I, III, IV
(*c*) II, III, IV (*d*) I, II, III

100. Enzymes are potential hazards to humans due to which of the following features ?
I. Residual microbiological activity
II. Activity related toxicity
III. Allergenicity

Options :
(*a*) I, II, III (*b*) I, II
(*c*) II, III (*d*) I, III

101. Which of the following statements are concerned with effects of organic solvents on enzyme properties ?
I. Enzymes suspended in organic solvents often show enhanced thermostability.
II. Lyophilized dry enzymes suspended in organic solvents show inhibitor-induced enzyme memory and pH memory.
III. Enzymes may be engineered for a better performance in organic solvents.
IV. In general, stereoselectivity of the enzyme is changed in the organic solvents.

Options :
(*a*) I, III, IV (*b*) II, III, IV
(*c*) I, II, IV (*d*) I, II, III

102. Which of the following techniques is used for obtaining information on three-dimensional structure of enzymes ?
(*a*) SDS-PAGE
(*b*) Nuclear magnetic resonance (NMR)
(*c*) X-ray differaction
(*d*) Both (*b*) and (*c*)

103. Site-directed mutagenesis can be effected by which of the following techniques ?
(*a*) Oligonucleotide-directed mutagenesis
(*b*) Casette mutagenesis
(*c*) Cut-paste mutagenesis
(*d*) Both (*a*) and (*b*)

104. Subtilisin inactivation by oxygen produced by bleaches is due to which of the following ?
(*a*) Oxidation of the methionine residue at position 222.
(*b*) Reduction of the methionine residue at position 222.
(*c*) Oxidation of Ser residue in the active site.
(*d*) All of the above.

105. Which of the following options is an examples of a bi-functional enzyme produced by genetic engineering ?
I. Galactose dehydrogenase-luciferase.
II. β-Galactosidase-galactokinase.
III. β-Galactokinase-galactose dehydrogenase-galactokinase.
IV. β-Galactosidase-galactose dehydrogenase.

Options :
(*a*) I, II, III (*b*) II, III, IV
(*c*) I, II, III, IV (*d*) I, III, IV

106. Which of the following advantages is offered by bi- and multi-functional enzymes ?
I. Two or more enzyme activities required in sequence in a metabolic pathway are located in close proximity.
II. They are useful in preparation of biosensors when two or more enzymes need to be immobilized together.
III. They are easy to separate and purify.

Options :
(*a*) I, II, III (*b*) II, III
(*c*) I, II (*d*) I, III

107. A packed bed reactor can take care of which of the following ?
(*a*) Product inhibition
(*b*) Substrate activation
(*c*) Reaction reversibility
(*d*) All of the above.

108. Which of the following biological materials are used in biosensors ?
I. Enzymes and antibodies
II. Nucleic acids and lectins
III. Whole cells and tissue slices
IV. Entire organs.

Options :
(*a*) I, II, III, IV (*b*) II, III, IV
(*c*) I, III, IV (*d*) I, II, III

109. Which of the following biological materials is most commonly used in biosensors ?
(*a*) Antibodies (*b*) Nucleic acids
(*c*) Enzymes (*d*) Lectins

110. Which of the following statements relates to the effects of organic solvents on enzyme properties ?

I. Organic solvents can modulate enzyme specificity.
II. A hydrophobic solvent changes the three dimensional structure of enzymes.
III. A hydrophilic solvent can extract the water associated with the enzyme molecules, which often leads to their inactivation.
IV. Dry enzyme molecules suspended in a hydrophobic solvent retain their flexibility and, consequently, activity.

Options :
(*a*) I, II, III (*b*) I, III, IV
(*c*) I, II, III, IV (*d*) I, II, IV

111. A biosensor has which of the following types of components ?

I. Chemical II. Biological
III. Physical

Options :
(*a*) I, II (*b*) II, III
(*c*) I, III (*d*) III

112. The nature of interaction between analyte and the biological material used in biosensors may be of which of the following types ?

(*a*) The analyte may be converted into a new chemical molecule by enzymes.
(*b*) The analyte may simply bind to the biological material present on biosensor.
(*c*) The analyte may alter the biological agent used in the biosensor.
(*d*) Both (*a*) and (*b*).

113. A successful biosensor must have which of the following features ?

I. It should be highly specific for the analyte.
II. The reaction used should be ideally independent of factors like stirring, pH, temperature, etc.
III. The response should be linear over a useful range of analyte concentrations.
IV. It should require minimum sample volume.

Options :
(*a*) I, II, III (*b*) I, III, IV
(*c*) II, III, IV (*d*) I, II, III, IV

114. Biosensors convert a chemical information flow into an electrical information flow; this process involves which of the following steps ?

I. The analyte diffuses from the solution to the surface of the biosensor.
II. The analyte reacts specifically and efficiently with the biological component of the biosensor.
III. This reaction changes the physico-chemcial properties of the transducer surface.
IV. This change is measured and converted into electrical signal.

Options :
(*a*) I, II, IV (*b*) I, II, III, IV
(*c*) II, III, IV, (*d*) I, III, IV

115. A successful biosensor must have which of the following features ?

I. The device should be cheap, small and easy to use.
II. Assay should be rapid, accurate and repeatable.
III. It should be robust, stable and sterilizable.
IV. The assay cost should be lower than that of conventional tests.

Options :
(*a*) I, II, III (*b*) I, III, IV
(*c*) I, II, III, IV (*d*) II, III, IV

116. Biological component of biosensors perform which of the following functions ?

(*a*) Recognise the analyte.
(*b*) Interact with the analyte in such a manner, which produces some physical change detectable by the transducer.
(*c*) Both (*a*) and (*b*)
(*d*) Inactivate toxic analytes

117. First generation biosensors suffer from which of the following drawbacks ?

I. They can not be used in oxygen-deprived environments.
II. The electric potential used is sufficient to cause other redox processes which may interfere with the analyses.
III. They use mediators, which reduce the O_2 dissolved in analyte solution.

Options :
(*a*) I, II, III (*b*) II, III
(*c*) I, III (*d*) I, II

118. Whole cells have been used to develop which of the following types of biosensor devices ?
(*a*) Potentiometric
(*b*) Thermometric
(*c*) Amperometric
(*d*) All of the above

119. Colorimetric test strips for glucose contain which of the following ?
(*a*) Horse-radish peroxidase
(*b*) A weakly coloured chromogen
(*c*) Glucose oxidase
(*d*) All of the above

120. Column A contains a list of some enzymes while column B contains their use. Match both the columns carefully and select the correct option from those given below them.

Column A	Column B
A. Lysozyme	1. Gout
B. Uricase	2. Skin ulcer
C. Streptokinase	3. Blood clots
D. Rhodonase	4. Cyanide poisoning
	5. Antibiotic

Options :
(*a*) A1, B3, C2, D4 (*b*) A4, B2, C5, D3
(*c*) A5, B1, C3, D4 (*d*) A2, B5, C4, D3

121. Biosensor for cocaine detection uses which of the following biological agents ?
(*a*) Whole cell (*b*) Antibody
(*c*) Enzyme (*d*) Either (*a*) or (*c*)

122. Enzymatic reactions in biphasic liquid systems have which of the following features ?
I. Ease in separation and recovery of products.
II. Lower yields due to product and enzyme lying in separate phases.
III. Greater solubility of the substrate in the second phase.
IV. Instability of the product in the aqueous phase, but not in the organic phase.

Options :
(*a*) I, II, III, IV (*b*) I, III, IV
(*c*) II, III, IV (*d*) I, II, III

123. Glucose isomerase is obtained from which of the following ?
(*a*) *Streptomyces* sp.
(*b*) *Actinoplanes missouriensis*
(*c*) *Bacillus coagulans*
(*d*) All of the above

124. Which of the following is correct about invertase ?
I. It was perhaps the first enzyme used during 1940s in an immobilized state.
II. This enzyme, obtained by autolysis of yeast cell, was immobilized by adsorption onto bone char.
III. This enzyme has a half life of 90 days at 50°C, pH 5.5.
IV. One kg of granular enzyme produces 16 tons of invert sugar.

Options :
(*a*) I, II, III, IV (*b*) II, III, IV
(*c*) I, II, III (*d*) I, II, III

125. Which of the following features are correct about membrane reactors ?
I. These are useful in producing small scale (g to kg) quantities of the product.
II. They allow easy replacement of enzymes.
III. They permit the use of more than one enzyme to catalyse a chain of reactions.
IV. These reactors are easy to establish.

Options :
(*a*) I, II, III (*b*) II, III, IV
(*c*) I, III, IV (*d*) I, II, III, IV

126. Continuous-flow reactors offer which of the following advantages ?
(*a*) Greater productivity per unit amount of enzyme.
(*b*) Uniform product quality.
(*c*) They can be used for substrates having low solubility.
(*d*) All of the above.

127. Which of the following is the main feature of continuous-flow stirred tank reactors ?
I. Continuous removal of the product (without enzyme).
II. Continuous pumping in of the substrate.
III. Efficient stirring of the tank.
IV. Use of immobilized enzymes.

Options :
(*a*) I, II, III (*b*) II, III, IV
(*c*) I, II, III, IV (*d*) I, III, IV

128. The chief limitations of membrane reactors are which of the following ?
(*a*) Regular replacement of membrane adds to cost.

(*b*) Need for substrate diffusion through the membrane.
(*c*) Useful for production of small quantities of products.
(*d*) All of the above.

129. Continuous-flow reactors may be of which of the following types ?
I. Continuous-flow stirred tank reactors
II. Packed bed reactors
III. Fluidized bed reactors
Options :
(*a*) I, II, III (*b*) II, III
(*c*) I, III (*d*) I, II

130. Packed bed enzyme reactors suffer from which of the following limitations ?
(*a*) Difficulty in temperature control
(*b*) Clogging by colloids
(*c*) Channel formation
(*d*) All of the above

131. Antibodies can be used as biological agent in which of the following types of biosensors ?
(*a*) Optical
(*b*) Acoustic wave
(*c*) Potentiometric
(*d*) Both (*a*) and (*b*)

132. Which of the following biosensor types has the lowest cost ?
(*a*) Potentiometric (*b*) Conductimetric
(*c*) Piezoelectric (*d*) Thermometric

133. Which of the options listed in Q. 132 has the highest cost ?

134. Which of the options given in Q. 132 has the fastest response ?

135. Which of the options given in Q. 132 is the most sensitive ?

12.2. FILL IN THE BLANKS

1. Many enzymes have metal ions, while some others possess low weight organic molecules, which are called .... and are essential for enzyme activity.

2. Catalytic antibodies are called ....

3. Cofactors and coenzymes may be covalently or noncovalently attached to the protein molecule called ....

4. Coenzymes and cofactors generally contribute to enzyme activity and...........

5. Glutathione is made up of .... amino acid residues.

6. Galactose is an .... of glucose.

7. Usually, membrane reactors are used in the case of .... enzymes.

8. Gel filtration separates macromolecules on the basis of their ....

9. The only animal enzyme to be produced in quantities greater than 2 tons/year is .... or .... obtained from calf stomach.

10. Enzymes are classified and named by the commission on ....

11. An enzyme molecule has a highly specific .... or .... to which its substrate binds to produce enzyme subtrate complex.

12. .... is the class of enzymes that contains some pectinases.

13. Dehydrogenases are involved in transfer of ....

14. .... are involved in the transfer of electron to O_2.

15. The value of $\Delta G^{\ddagger}$ (activation energy) for a noncatalyzed breakdown of hydrogen peroxide to water and oxygen is 76 kJ mol^{-1}. This value is lowered to 30 kJ mol^{-1} when the reaction is catalyzed by the enzyme ....

16. Thermodynamic predictions indicate the extent to which the .... will be converted into products.

17. Higher the value of $G^{\ddagger}$, ... the rate of reaction.

18. Proteases are mostly used in .... industry.

19. The phenomenon of substrate saturation is described by the .... equation.

20. DNA polymerase obtained from .... takes 20 hr at 95°C to lose 50% of its catalytic activity while that from........... takes 7 hr.
21. The first DNA molecules are thought to have originated by .... of RNA molecules.
22. The chief objective of enzyme engineering is to produce an enzyme that is more useful for .... and/or other applications.
23. Enzymes ...., at 0.1 –1% w/w are used to remove hair from hides.
24. The commercial callulase is obtained from ....
25. Only .... proteases are suitable for use in detergents.
26. Enzyme loading in the entrapment procedure is usually .... g/g gel or fibre.
27. α-Amylase produced from .... is used in-detergent to digest away starch present in association with dirt and stain.
28. .... are used for digestion of lipids present in stains/dirt.
29. DE (dextrose equivalent) value is obtained from the formula ....
30. Lipases are ordinarily used in .... biphasic systems.
31. High maltose syrup contains .... dextrose equivalent (DE), ... % maltose and 2-7% glucose.
32. Raffinose may be hydrolysed into .... and sucrose by a fungal raffinase.
33. An example of .... synzyme is provided by cyclodextrins.
34. All enzymes are potential allergens due to their proteinaceous nature, especially when .... as dust.
35. Introduction of predetermined changes at a specific site of a DNA molecules is known as ....
36. β-Galactokinase-galactose dehydrogenase-galactokinase is an example of .... enzyme.
37. Potentiometric biosensors use .... electrodes to convert the biological reaction into electronic signal.
38. Optical biosensors measure........... and .... reactions.
39. A .... biosensor has been developed for the detection of enterobacteria.
40. A potentiometric biosensor for the detection of nicotonic acid uses whole cells of .... as the biological component.
41. Acoustic wave biosensor is used for detection of cocaine using .... as biological agent.
42. Lysozyme catalyzes hydrolysis of bacterial ....
43. Rhodonase catalyzes formation of ....
44. β-Lactamase enzyme is used for treatment of .... allergy.
45. The dextran-PEG biphasic system is used to produce .... from starch using α-amylase and glucoamylase.
46. D-glucose is only .... % as sweet as sucrose and is comparatively less soluble in water.
47. For production of soft drinks, a .... % fructose syrup is used.
48. Raffinose present in .... juice is digested with raffinase activity; this leads to a 3% more sugar recovery and reduction in cost of disposal of molasses.
49. Raffinase activity is provided by immobilized cells of the mould ....
50. .... enzyme is used for production of aspartame.
51. Penicillin G amidases may be used to synthesize penicillin and ....

12.3. MARK TRUE OR FALSE

1. In 1951, Pauling and Corey discovered the α-helix and β-sheet structures of enzymes.
2. When a cofactor is so tightly bound to the apoenzyme that it is difficult to remove it without damaging the enzyme, the cofacter is often called prosthetic group.
3. The rate of forward reaction is the highest at the start of a reaction when the concen-

trations of reactants are lower than those of the products.

4. Enzymes increase the overall level of activation energy.

5. Proteases are included in the hydrolases class of enzymes.

6. Oxigenases are responsible for oxygen atom transger from CO_2.

7. In general, the free energy of reactants is higher than that of the products.

8. Only one-half of all the molecules reaching the transition state react to form products, the other half going back to the high energy ground state.

9. Stabilization of the transition state of the substrates reduces the activation energy of the overall reaction; this is the most important feature of enzymatic catalysis.

10. In contrast to substrate saturation, the rate of a non-enzymatically catalyzed reaction increases linearly over the entire range of attainable substrate concentrations.

11. Michaelis-Menten equation is still the most generally applicable equation for describing enzyme-catalyzed reactions.

12. DNA became the primary genetic material in view of its lesser stability than RNA.

13. It may be emphasized that all biological catalysts must possess the ability to bind to their specific substrates.

14. Most of the immobilization strategies present large problems in diffusion of the substrate to reach the enzyme.

15. Bating is necessary for the production of soft leather clothing.

16. Adsorption of enzymes to the matrices is very easy and widely used.

17. Lysine residues, are the most useful in covalent binding of enzymes.

18. Treatment with trialkoxysilanes enables use of glass for covalent binding of enzymes.

19. Enzymes may be entrapped within cellulose acetate fibres.

20. Adsorption method of immobilization usually produces a high loading (about 1 g enzyme/g matrix) of the enzyme.

21. Enzymes can not be enclosed within liposomes.

22. Glucoamylase is generally obtained from *Aspergillus niger*.

23. Fungal α-amylase is used in baking industry to reduce gas production during fermentation.

24. Porcine insulin is converted into human insulin by replacing the C-terminal alanine (B30) residue with a threonine in a single step catalyzed by trypsin.

25. Urokinase is an enzyme that is used for the treatment of disorders within blood circulation system; it is isolated from human urine.

26. Enzyme engineering utilizes recombinant DNA technology to introduce the desired changes in the amino acid sequences of enzymes.

27. Derivatised myoglobin is an example of synzyme.

28. Suitably alkylated polyethyleneimines behave as synzyme

29. Bi- and poly-functional enzymes are produced by genes obtained by fusion of the coding regions of two or more genes encoding different enzymes.

30. Colorimetric biosensor can not be used for turbid and strongly coloured solutions.

31. Conductimetric biosensors detect changes in electrical conductivity produced by changes in concentrations of ionic species.

32. The most promising biosensor involving luminescence uses firefly enzyme luciferase for detection of bacteria in food and clinical samples.

33. One of the major disadvantages of acoustic wave biosensors is the difficulty in using them to determine analytes in solution.

34. Colorimetric test strips are complicated forms of biosensors.

35. Colorimetric test strip is used to detect glucose in blood/urine of diabetes patients.
36. Ribonuclease is used as antiviral agent.
37. The chief limitations of aqueous biphasic systems are related to product separation from the upper phase and loss of enzymes, which enter the upper phase.
38. In general, solvents of lower polarity, *i.e.*, greater hydrophobicity, are less desirable for maintaining enzyme stability.
39. Lipases are used in biphasic systems for the production of isoamyl acetate, a natural aroma.
40. Lactase is used to remove lactose from milk and whey since many people do not relish lactose.
41. A membrane reactor uses a dialysis membrane.
42. Continuous-flow reactors, as a rule, are based on immobilized enzymes.
43. Fluidized bed reactors have kinetic properties between continuous flow stirred tank reactors and packed bed reactors.
44. The complex of an apoenzyme and the cofactor is known as holoenzyme.
45. The rennet (aspartic proteinase) produced by *Mucor miehei* is now widely used for cheese production.

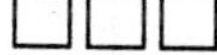

13
INDUSTRIAL BIOTECHNOLOGY

13.1. MULTIPLE CHOICE QUESTIONS

1. Which of the following scientists is recognised as father of microbiology ?
(*a*) Robert Koch (*b*) Edward Jenner
(*c*) Louis Pasteur (*d*) Aristotle

2. Microbiology is widely considered to have begun in 1857 when Pasteur reported his studies on which of the following ?
(*a*) Lactic acid fermentation.
(*b*) Microscopic features of the micro-organisms.
(*c*) A suitable medium for lactic acid fermentation.
(*d*) All of the above

3. Industrial microbiology involve which of the following activities ?
I. Isolation of microorganisms from nature and their screening for product formation.
II. Improvement of product yields.
III. Maintenance of stock cultures.
IV. Mass culture using bioreactors and recovery and purification of products.

Options :
(*a*) I, II, III, IV (*b*) I, II, IV
(*c*) II, III, IV (*d*) I, III, IV

4. An ideal producer strain or economically important strain should have which of the following characteristics ?
I. It should be pure and free from phage.
II. It should be genetically stable, but amenable to genetic modification.
III. It should produce both vegetative cells and spores.
IV. It should grow moderately after inoculation in seed stage vessels.

Options :
(*a*) I, II, III, IV (*b*) II, III, IV
(*c*) I, III, IV (*d*) I, II, III

5. Pure cultures of microorganisms can be obtained from which of following organisations ?
I. Research Institute for Antibiotics, Moscow, Russia.
II. American Type Culture Collection, Rockville, Maryland, USA.
III. Fermentation Research Institute, Tokyo, Japan.
IV. Commonwealth Mycological Institute, Kew, Surrey, England.

Options :
(*a*) I, II, III (*b*) I, II, III, IV
(*c*) II, III, IV (*d*) I, II, IV

6. Among the given sources of industrial micro-organisms, which one is commonly used ?
(*a*) River mud (*b*) Soil
(*c*) Lake (*d*) All of the above

7. Aabomycin A shows which of the following activities ?
(*a*) Antifungal (*b*) Antibacterial
(*c*) Antiviral (*d*) Antiprotozoal

8. Bestatin shows which of the following activities ?
(*a*) Antitumour (*b*) Insecticidal
(*c*) Herbicide (*d*) Antifungal

9. Bestatin is produced by which of the following organisms ?

(a) *Trichoderma polysporum*
(b) *Rhizoctonia leguminicola*
(c) *Streptomyces olivoreticuli*
(d) *Streptomyces avermitilis*

10. Which of the following microbial cultures is used for studies on product isolation, identification and strain improvement ?
(a) Assay culture
(b) Development culture
(c) Research culture
(d) Both (b) and (c)

11. Various cultures can be maintained for long periods using which of the following approaches ?
I. Storage as frozen cultures
II. Storage as lyophilized cells
III. Low temperature storage
IV. Storage in glycerine stabs

Options :
(a) I, II, III (b) I, II, III, IV
(c) II, III, IV (d) I, III, IV

12. Which of the following protective agents reduces the detrimental effects of lyophilization ?
(a) Skimmed milk (b) Salt
(c) Sucrose (d) Both (a) and (c)

13. The objectives of inoculum development methods are which of the following ?
I. To recover the largest possible proportion of cells from dormancy.
II. To obtain a population of cells genetically identical to the preserved strain.
III. To increase microbial cell biomass.
IV. To make the cultures suitable, in physiological terms, for optimum performance in the production stage.

Options :
(a) I, II, III, IV (b) II, III, IV
(c) I, III, IV (d) I, II, IV

14. Piercidin has insecticidal activity; it is isolated from which of following microorganisms ?
(a) *Streptomyces hygrosopicus*
(b) *Streptomyces sagamonensis*
(c) *Streptomyces mobaraensis*
(d) *Streptomyces avermitilis*

15. Which of the following objectives concern sterilization ?
I. To avoid contamination of the environment.
II. To permit only the desired strain to be present in the fermenter vessels.
III. To ensure safety of the products.
IV. To prevent deterioration of the products.

Options :
(a) I, II, III (b) I, II, III, IV
(c) II, III, IV (d) I, II, IV

16. Which of the following is an example of cyanobacteria ?
I. *Nostoc*
II. *Anabaena*
III. *Cylindrospermum*
IV. *Azolla*

Options :
(a) I, II, IV (b) I, III, IV
(c) I, II, III, IV (d) I, II, III

17. Which of the following bacteria increases the solubility/availability of phosphate ?
(a) *Glomus* (b) *Thiobacillus*
(c) *Bacillus* (d) Both (b) and (c)

18. Which of the following is correct about cyanobacteria/blue-green algae (BGA) ?
I. These are prokaryotic photosynthetic organisms.
II. They fix N_2 asymbiotically.
III. Some BGA are known to form symbiotic associations with *Azolla.*
IV. *Azolla* is widely used in Vietnam as biofertilizer for rice.

Options :
(a) I, II, III, IV (b) II, III, IV
(c) I, III, IV (d) I, II, III

19. Column A lists some biocontrol agents while column B lists some target organisms. Match both columns carefully and select the correct option from those given below them.

Column A	Column B
A. NPV (Nucleopolyhedrosis Virus)	1. *Culex larvae*
B. *Bacillus sphaericus*	2. Grasshoppers
C. *Malameba locustae*	3. Bollworm larvae
D. *Agrobacterium radiobacter*	4. *Agrobacterium tumefaciens*

Options :
(*a*) A1, B2, C3, D4 (*b*) A2, B3, C4, D1
(*c*) A3, B1, C2, D4 (*d*) A4, B2, C1, D3

20. Sterilization can be achieved by which of the following ?
(*a*) Heating (*b*) Filtration
(*c*) Radiation (*d*) All of the above

21. Which of the following ***is not correct*** about *Rhizobium* ?
(*a*) These are Gram-positive soil bacteria capable of forming root nodules in most leguminous plants.
(*b*) *Azorhizobium caulinodans* nodulates the stems of *Sesbania rostrata.*
(*c*) Root nodulating rhizobia are of common occurrence.
(*d*) *Rhizobium* cells contain genes for nitrogen fixation (*nif* genes).

22. Biocontrol agents have which of the following features ?
(*a*) They should be specific to the target organism.
(*b*) They should have a high multiplication rate.
(*c*) They should not damage the environment (including human-beings).
(*d*) All of the above.

23. Which of the following is correct about *Bacillus thuringiensis*-based insecticides ?
I. *B. thuringiensis* produces crystal proteins as parasporal inclusions in the vegetative cells containing the spore.
II. Crystal protein is a protoxin, which is processed into a toxin by the proteases present in the insect midgut.
III. Toxin fragment binds to highly specific receptors present in the brush border microvilli membranes of midgut epithelial cells; this binding ultimately causes insect death.
IV. *B. thuringiensis*-based insecticides have been in commercial use.

Options :
(*a*) I, II, III, IV (*b*) I, II, III
(*c*) II, III, IV (*d*) I, III, IV

24. Commercial preparations of *B. thuringiensis* usually contain which of the following ?
(*a*) Crystal proteins (*b*) Spores
(*c*) Inert carriers (*d*) All of the above

25. In 1929, Fleming discovered which of the following antibiotics ?
(*a*) Streptomycin (*b*) Tetracyclin
(*c*) Penicillin (*d*) Gentamycin

26. ***Assertion (A)*** : The crystal protein (produced by *B. thuringiensis*) activity disappears usually within 24-40 hours after application, but the spores may persist for long periods and cause harm to non-target useful insect, *e.g.*, silkworm.

Solution (S) : Above problem is sought to be overcome by developing mutants, which produce the crystal protein, but do not form spores.

Options :
(*a*) Only A is correct.
(*b*) Only S is correct.
(*c*) Both A and S are correct, but S would not solve A.
(*d*) Both A and S are correct and S would adequately solve A.

27. Which of the following viruses is likely to be commercialized in India for control of *Helicoverpa* (*Heliothis*) *armigera* ?
(*a*) Nucleopolyhedrosis viruses (NPV)
(*b*) Granulosis viruses (GV)
(*c*) Advenoviruses
(*d*) All of the above

28. Which of the following is correct about heat sterilization ?
I. It is the most commonly used and the least expensive sterilization method.
II. Heat causes breaks in DNA.
III. Dry heat is suitable for sterilization of solids, while wet heat is used for sterilization of media and fermenter vessels.
IV. In general, dry heat is superior to moist heat.

Options :
(*a*) I, II, IV (*b*) I, II, III, IV
(*c*) I, II, III (*d*) II, III, IV

29. Which of the following disadvantages is associated with chemical pesticides ?
I. Increasing cases of insects developing resistance.
II. Serious health hazards due to the presence of their residues in food, fibre and fodder.

III. Extensive pollution of the environment.

Options :

(*a*) I, II, III (*b*) II, III
(*c*) I, III (*d*) I, II

30. The main criterion for selecting an efficient N_2 fixer is which of the following features ?

I. Fixes nitrogen over a range of environmental conditions.
II. Continues to fix N_2 in the presence of soil nitrogen.
III. Multiplies in broth and survives in the carrier.
IV. Compete with other strains.

Options :

(*a*) I, II, III (*b*) I, II, IV
(*c*) II, III, IV (*d*) I, II, III, IV

31. A germplasm bank of AMF (arbuscular mycorrhizal fungi) cultures was established at which of the following ?

(*a*) National Bureau of Plant Genetic Resources.
(*b*) The Energy and Resources Institute, New Delhi.
(*c*) Indian Institute Pulses Research, Kanpur.
(*d*) Indian Agricultural Research Institute, New Delhi.

32. Chemical fertilizers suffer from which of the following limitations ?

(*a*) They damage the environment
(*b*) They are costly
(*c*) They utilize petroleum (specially nitrogenous fertilizers)
(*d*) All of the above

33. Which of the following advantages are associated with biopesticides ?

I. They do not destroy nontarget species.
II. They do not leave harmful residues.
III. They have very high specificity.
IV. They are often cheaper than chemical pesticides.

Options :

(*a*) I, II, III, IV (*b*) I, II, IV
(*c*) II, III, IV (*d*) I, II, III

34. Biofertilizers have which of the following advantages over inorganic fertilizers ?

I. Biofertilizers require high-cost inputs.
II. They lead to soil enrichment.
III. They are compatible with long-term sustainability.
IV. They are eco-friendly.

Options :

(*a*) I, II, III (*b*) I, II, III, IV
(*c*) II, III, IV (*d*) I, III, IV

35. Genetically modified microbes serve which of the following needs/functions as compared to their natural counterparts ?

I. Produce pharmaceutically useful proteins, and modified or new metabolites.
II. Degrade non-biological wastes and detoxify toxic wastes.
III. Crop protection by control of insects, fungal diseases and frost damage.
IV. Enhanced N_2 fixation.

Options :

(*a*) I, II, III, IV (*b*) I, II, III
(*c*) II, III, IV (*d*) I, III, IV

36. Fungus *Verticillium lecanii* can be used for the control of which of the following insects ?

(*a*) Aphids (*b*) Leaf hopper
(*c*) White flies (*d*) Both (*a*) and (*c*)

37. Fungus *Ampelomyces quisqualis* is used for the control of which of the following powdery mildews ?

(*a*) Grapes (*b*) Tomato
(*c*) Strawberries (*d*) All of the above

38. X-rays cause inactivation of contaminants by which of the following mechanisms ?

I. By inducing single and double-strand DNA breaks.
II. By producing free radicals and peroxidase.
III. By alkylation of DNA.

Options :

(*a*) I, II, III (*b*) I, III
(*c*) I, II (*d*) II, III

39. Column A contains a list of some objectives achieved by genetic engineering and column B contains their respective examples. Match both the column carefully and select the correct option from those given below them.

Column A	Column B
A. Enhanced growth	I. Increased dosage of gene *cefEF of C. acremonium*
B. New substrate utilization	II. Gene encoding D-amino acid oxidase from *Fusarium*
C. Product modification	III. Transgenic yeast capable of using cyclodextrins
D. Enhanced metabolite production	IV. Transfer of *E. coli* glutamate dehydrogenase into *Methalophilus methalotrophus*

Options :
(*a*) AIV, BII, CIII, DI
(*b*) AIV, BIII, CI, DII
(*c*) AIV, BIII, CII, DI
(*d*) AIV, BI, CII, DIII

40. Bioreactors are extensively used for which of the following ?
(*a*) Fermentation
(*b*) Food processing
(*c*) Waste management
(*d*) All of the above

41. In terms of process requirements, bioreactors are of which of the following types ?
I. Solid state bioreactors
II. Immobilized cell bioreactors
III. Aerobic bioreactors
IV. Anaerobic bioreactors

Options :
(*a*) I, II, III, IV (*b*) II, III, IV
(*c*) I, III, IV (*d*) I, II, IV

42. Solid state fermentation is used for the production of which of the following ?
I. Certain valuable biochemicals
II. Fungal toxins
III. Extracellular enzymes
IV. Ascorbic acid

Options :
(*a*) I, II, III, IV (*b*) I, II, III
(*c*) II, III, IV (*d*) I, II, IV

43. Among the given polymer matrices, which one is the most commonly used for cell immobilization ?
(*a*) Polyglycol oligomers
(*b*) Polyacrylamide gel
(*c*) Calcium alginate
(*d*) κ-Carageenan

44. Cell immobilization is advantageous under which of the following situations ?
I. Extracted enzymes are unstable.
II. Enzymes of interest are intracellular.
III. Cells do not have interfering enzymes.
IV. Products are low molecular weight compounds released into the medium.

Options :
(*a*) I, II, III (*b*) I, II, III, IV
(*c*) I, III, IV (*d*) II, III, IV

45. Immobilized cells offer which of the following advantages over enzyme immobilization ?
I. Enzyme purification is not needed.
II. High activity of even unstable enzymes.
III. High operational stability.
IV. Possibility of application in multistep enzyme reactions.

Options :
(*a*) I, II, IV (*b*) I, III, IV
(*c*) I, II, III, IV (*d*) II, III, IV

46. Cell immobilization may be achieved in which of the following ways ?
(*a*) Cells directly bound to water insoluble carriers.
(*b*) They can be cross-linked to bi- or multi-functional reagents.
(*c*) Polymer matrices may be used for entrapping.
(*d*) All of the above.

47. Among the given techniques of filtration, which one is the most commonly used ?
(*a*) Depth filtration
(*b*) Cross-flow filtration
(*c*) Rotary drum vacuum filtration
(*d*) Surface filtration

48. Disruption of microbial cells is usually difficult due to which of the following ?
(*a*) Small cell size
(*b*) Strong cell wall
(*c*) High osmotic pressure inside cells
(*d*) All of the above.

49. Which of the following is the most commonly used to achieve cell disruption ?
(*a*) Drying
(*b*) Lysis
(*c*) Mechanical cell disruption
(*d*) All of the above.

50. Which of the following steps are involved in downstream processing ?
(*a*) Separation of particles and disintegration of cells
(*b*) Extraction and concentration
(*c*) Purification and drying
(*d*) All of the above

51. In case of downstream processing, purification is achieved through which of the following ?
(*a*) Crystallization
(*b*) Chromatographic methods
(*c*) Evaporation
(*d*) Both (*a*) and (*b*)

52. In case of downstream processing, commonly used approach of drying is which of the following ?
(*a*) Spray drying (*b*) Freeze drying
(*c*) Vacuum drying (*d*) All of the above.

53. Typically, fermentation of 100 g glucose by selected strains of *Saccharomyces cerevisiae* and *Saccharomyces carlsbergensis* yields how many grams of ethanol ?
(*a*) 25-29 (*b*) 45-49
(*c*) 60-70 (*d*) 70-89

54. In a batch fermenter, which of the following successive stages occur ?
I. Rapid growth of yeast and parallel increase in ethanol production.
II. Decline in yeast growth coupled with a slower increase in ethanol production.
III. No yeast growth, but low levels of ethanol production, yeast cells begin to die.
IV Finally, ethanol production stops.
Options :
(*a*) I, II, IV (*b*) II, III, IV
(*c*) I, II, III, IV (*d*) I, III, IV

55. *Rhizobium leguminosarum* ***does not nodulate*** which of the following crops ?
(*a*) Clover (*Trifolium species*)
(*b*) Pea (*Pisum sativum*)
(*c*) Khesari (*Lathyrus sativus*)
(*d*) Lentil (*Lens culinaris*)

56. *Bacillus thuringiensis* is used for control of which of the organisms in India ?
(*a*) *Heliothis* and other lepidoptera
(*b*) Coleopteran pests
(*c*) *Spodoptera litura*
(*d*) Both (*a*) and (*b*)

57. *Trichoderma parasitoid* can be used for the control of which of the following ?
(*a*) Bollworms of cotton
(*b*) Stem borer (Sorghum)
(*c*) Sugarcane internode borer
(*d*) All of the above

58. Gluconic acid is produced from which of the following ?
(*a*) *Aspergillus niger*
(*b*) *Penicillium purpurogenous*
(*c*) *Rhizopus stolonifer*
(*d*) *Staphylococcus aureus*

59. Single cell protein (SCP) can be produced from which of the following ?
I. Fungi II. Yeast
III. Bacteria IV. Algae
Options :
(*a*) I, II, III (*b*) II, III, IV
(*c*) I, III, IV (*d*) I, II, III, IV

60. Which of the following yields antibiotic ?
(*a*) *Cladonia* (Lichens)
(*b*) *Streptomyces*
(*c*) *Usnea*
(*d*) All of the above

61. Lactic acid is produced by activity of which of the following microorganisms using molasses/starch as substrate ?
(*a*) *Rhizopus*
(*b*) *Lactobacillus bulgaricus*
(*c*) *Streptococcus lactis*
(*d*) All of the above

62. Which of the following is correct about steroids ?
I. These are complex crystallizable lipids.
II. These are essential components of cell membrane in animals.
III. They are used in treatment of hormonal imbalance.
IV. They are immuno-suppressents.

Options :
(*a*) I, II, III, IV (*b*) I, II, IV
(*c*) I, III, IV (*d*) II, III, IV

63. Which of the following products are obtained from yeast fermentation ?
(*a*) Acetic acid, caproic acid and lactic acid.
(*b*) Glycerol, ethanol, butanol and *n*-propanol
(*c*) Amyl alcohol and ethyl acetate
(*d*) All of the above

64. Which of the following statements are correct about antibiotics ?
I. Broad spectrum anitbiotics are active against common Gram positive and Gram negative pathogens.
II. Narrow spectrum antibiotics are effective against most Gram negative bacteria.
III. Penicillin resistant Gram negative bacteria have a complex cell wall structure that excludes penicillin.
IV. Tetracyclin resistant bacteria develop a protein in the cell surface and cell membrane that prevents the entry of antibiotics.

Options :
(*a*) I, III, IV (*b*) I, II, III
(*c*) I, II, III, IV (*d*) II, III, IV

65. N-butanol is used for making which of the following ?
(*a*) Formaldehyde and urea
(*b*) Petrol
(*c*) Resin
(*d*) All of the above

66. Which of the following is an example of broad spectrum antibiotics ?
(*a*) Chloramphenicol (*b*) Tetracyclin
(*c*) Penicillin (*d*) Both (*a*) and (*b*)

67. Which of the following is based on chemical interaction between the carrier and the product molecules ?
(*a*) Covalent chromatography
(*b*) Gel filtration
(*c*) Group specific affinity chromatography
(*d*) Both (*a*) and (*c*)

68. Complex media contain which of the following ?
(*a*) Molasses (*b*) Cornsteep liquor
(*c*) Soybean meal (*d*) Any of the above

69. In case of downstream processing separation of cells from liquid medium is achieved by which of the following ?
(*a*) Centrifugation
(*b*) Filtration
(*c*) Flocculation and floating
(*d*) All of the above

70. Strain improvement is based on which of the following approaches ?
I. Mutant selection
II. Recombination
III. Recombinant DNA technology

Options :
(*a*) I, II (*b*) II, III
(*c*) I, II, III (*d*) III

71. Acetone-butanol fermentation passes through which of the following phases ?
I. Rapid bacterial growth, production of acetic and butyric acids and evolution of CO_2 and H_2.
II. Rapid conversion of the acids into acetone and butanol leading to a fast decline in the acidity of the broth.
III. Marked decrease in gas evolution, and acetone and butanol production.

Options :
(*a*) I, II, III (*b*) I, II
(*c*) I, III (*d*) II, III

72. Typically, corn medium yields butanol, acetone and ethanol in which of the following ratios ?
(*a*) 3 : 3 : 1 (*b*) 6 : 3 : 1
(*c*) 3 : 6 : 3 (*d*) 1 : 3 : 6

73. During penicillin G production which of the following precursors is used ?
(*a*) Phenylacetic acid
(*b*) Acetaldehyde
(*c*) Phenoxyacetic acid
(*d*) Both (*a*) and (*c*)

74. Which of the following is used as anti-foaming agent during antibiotic production ?
(*a*) Mineral oil (*b*) Vegetable oil
(*c*) Silicones (*d*) Both (*b*) and (*c*)

75. Match the columns A and B carefully and select the correct option from those given below them.

Column A	Column B
A. α-Amylase	1. *Aspergillus niger*
B. Glucoamylase	2. *Bacillus subtilis*
C. Xylose isomerase	3. *Bacillus licheniformis*
D. Alkaline protease	4. *Bacillus coagulans*
	5. *Trichoderma viridae*

Options :
(*a*) A3, B4, C5, D2 (*b*) A3, B2, C5, D1
(*c*) A3, B1, C4, D2 (*d*) A3, B1, C2, D4

76. Which of the following options indicates the correct order of steps involved in production of ethanol from starch substrate ?
(*a*) Starch → pyruvate → glucose → acetaldehyde → ethanol.
(*b*) Starch → glucose → pyruvate → acetaldehyde → ethanol.
(*c*) Starch → acetaldehyde → glucose → pyruvate → ethanol.
(*d*) Starch → pyruvate → acetaldehyde → glucose → ethanol.

77. Column A lists some enzymes, while column B lists their applications. Match both the columns carefully and select the correct option from those given below them.

Column A	Column B
A. α-Amylase	1. Protein digestion in brewing substances
B. Glucoamylase	2. Dextran hydrolysis to glucose
C. Xylose (glucose) isomerase	3. Pure glucose to equilibrium mixture of glucose plus fructose.
D. Neutral proteases	4. Hydrolysis of starch to dextrans

Options :
(*a*) A4, B3, C2, D1 (*b*) A4, B2, C3, D1
(*c*) A3, B1, C4, D2 (*d*) A3, B1, C2, D4

78. Which of the following microorganisms is used for production of xylose (glucose) isomerase ?
I. *Streptomyces olivaceus*
II. *Actinoplanes missouriensis*
III. *Microbacterium arborescens*
IV. *Bacillus coagulans*

Options :
(*a*) I, II (*b*) II, III, IV
(*c*) I, II, III (*d*) I, II, III, IV

79. Column A lists some enzymes, while column B lists their applications. Match both the columns carefully and select the correct option from those given below them.

Column A	Column B
A. Lactase	1. Leather industry
B. β-Glucanase	2. Fruit juice production
C. Pectinase	3. Brewing
D. Acid protease	4. Cheese production
	5. Milk processing

Options :
(*a*) A5, B3, C2, D4 (*b*) A5, B3, C4, D2
(*c*) A5, B1, C3, D4 (*d*) A5, B1, C2, D3

80. Acid protease is produced by which of the following microorganisms ?
(*a*) *Mucor pusillus*
(*b*) *Endothica parasitica*
(*c*) *Mucor miehei*
(*d*) All of the above

81. Biotransformations are performed by which of the following ?
(*a*) Plant cells (*b*) Animal cells
(*c*) Microbes (*d*) All of the above

82. Biotransformation performed by microbes is far more efficient and economical due to which of the following features ?
(*a*) High metabolic rates of microorganisms
(*b*) Rapid microbial growth
(*c*) Both (*a*) and (*b*)
(*d*) More efficient enzymes

83. Which of the following features are correct about amyloglucosidase ?
I. This enzyme is produced by *Aspergillus* or *Rhizopus*.
II. This is an endohydrolase.
III. It removes terminal glucose residues, one by one from dextrins.
IV. It is an extracellular enzyme.

Options :
(*a*) I, II, III, IV (*b*) I, III, IV
(*c*) I, II, III (*d*) II, III, IV

84. The first biotransformation to be commercialized was which of the following ?
(*a*) Deoxycorticosterone to corticosterone.
(*b*) Ethanol to acetic acid

(*c*) Glucose to gluconic acid
(*d*) Fructose to mannitol

85. Which of the following options indicates the correct order of ascorbic acid production ?
(*a*) Glucose → ascorbic acid → D-sorbitol → L-sorbose.
(*b*) Glucose → L-sorbose → D-sorbitol → ascorbic acid
(*c*) Glucose → D-sorbitol → L-sorbose → ascorbic acid.
(*d*) D-sorbitol → L-sorbose → glucose → ascorbic acid.

86. Which of the following ***is not correct*** about α-amylase ?
(*a*) This enzyme is produced by *Bacillus amyloliquefaciens.*
(*b*) This is an exohydrolase.
(*c*) It hydrolyses starch into components, which have 3 or more linear α-1, 4 glucan units.
(*d*) The end products of starch hydrolysis are dextrins.

87. Which of the following acts as an agent of biotransformation ?
(*a*) Resting and dried microbial cells
(*b*) Vegetative cells and spores of microbes
(*c*) Immobilized cells
(*d*) All of the above

88. Which of the following microbes is used for biotransformation ?
(*a*) Fungi (*b*) Eubacteria
(*c*) Streptomyces (*d*) All of the above

89. Which of the following options indicates the correct order for biotransformation of penicillin G and penicillin V ?
(*a*) Penicillin G/penicillin V → 6-aminopenicillanic acid → semisynthetic penicillins and cephalosporins.
(*b*) Penicillin G/penicillin V → semisynthetic penicillins and cephalosporins → 6-aminopenicillanic acid.
(*c*) Penicillin G/penicillin V → natural penicillins → semisynthetic penicillins.
(*d*) Penicillin G/penicillin V → semi-synthetic penicillins and cephalosporins → synthetic antibiotics.

90. Which of the following bacteria induces leaching of copper as copper sulphate from ores ?
(*a*) *Arthrobacter simplex*
(*b*) *Thiobacillus ferrooxidans*
(*c*) *Bacillus subtilis*
(*d*) All of the above

91. The proccess involving *Thiobacillus ferrooxidans* is used to recovers which of the following ?
(*a*) Uranium (*b*) Gold
(*c*) Copper (*d*) All of the above

92. Which of the following advantages is associated with microbial-based ore leaching ?
I. It can be applied both on small and large scales.
II. It does not requires high energy inputs.
III. It is self-regenerating if soluble iron is present.
IV. The process can be used to extract a variety of metals.

Options :
(*a*) I, II, III, IV (*b*) II, III, IV
(*c*) I, II, IV (*d*) I, II, IV

93. Microbial ore leaching is used for which of the following purposes ?
I. To generate ferric sulphate for leaching of other metals.
II. Extraction of metals from ores as their sulphates.
III. Partial leaching of mineral concentrates to remove impurities.
IV. Conversion of a mineral into a form suitable for processing by other means.

Options :
(*a*) I, II, III (*b*) II, III, IV
(*c*) I, II, III, IV (*d*) I, II, IV

94. Which of the following features are associated with microbial ore leaching ?
I. Microorganisms must be kept viable by providing appropriate conditions.
II. Microbial ore leaching is relatively fast process.
III. The desired metal is recovered as a dilute solution of its salts.
IV. Metal recovery requires additional processing.

Options :
(*a*) I, II, III (*b*) I, III, IV
(*c*) II, III, IV (*d*) I, II, IV

95. Which of the following bacteria induces leaching of copper as copper sulphate from ores ?
(*a*) *Thiobacillus organoparus*
(*b*) *T. thiooxidans*
(*c*) *T. acidophilus*
(*d*) All of the above.

96. Column A lists some steroids and column B lists the substrates from which they are produced. Match the two columns carefully and select the correct option from those given below them.

Column A	Column B
A. Campesterol	1. Wool grease
B. Diosgenin	2. *Dioscorea*
C. Hecogenin	3. Soybean
D. Cholesterol	4. African sisal

Options :
(*a*) A3, B2, C4, D1 (*b*) A2, B3, C1, D4
(*c*) A4, B1, C2, D3 (*d*) A1, B4, C3, D2

97. Steroid biotransformation yields which of the following adrenocortical hormones ?
(*a*) Cortisone (*b*) Corticosterone
(*c*) Hydrocortisone (*d*) All of the above

98. Which of the following options indicates the correct order of 11α-Hydroxyprogesterone production ?
(*a*) Diosgenin/stigmasterol → progesterone → 11α-Hydroxyprogesterone.
(*b*) Diosgenin → stigmasterol → 11α-Hydroxyprogesterone
(*c*) Progesterone → diosgenin → 11α-Hydroxyprogesterone.
(*d*) Stigmasterol → 11α-Hydroxyprogesterone → diosgenin.

99. Biotransformation of progesterone to 11α–hydroxyprogesterone is achieved by which of the following microorganisms ?
(*a*) *Rhizopus arrhizus*
(*b*) *Thiobacillus thiooxidans*
(*c*) *Rhizopus nigricans*
(*d*) Both (*a*) and (*c*)

100. Application of the process based on *Thiobacillus* for copper recovery has resulted in which of the following ?
(*a*) Reduction in price of copper by about 2-3 fold.
(*b*) Elimination of the release of SO_2 into the atmosphere.
(*c*) Both (*a*) and (*b*)
(*d*) Increased purity of the product.

101. Which of the following bacteria can adsorb metals on their cell surfaces ?
(*a*) *Proteus* (*b*) *Bacillus*
(*c*) *Streptococcus* (*d*) All of the above

102. *Rhizobium* can be used in which of the following ?
(*a*) Pulses (*b*) Forage crops
(*c*) Cereals (*d*) Both (*a*) and (*b*)

103. *Azotobacter* can be used in which of the following ?
(*a*) Wheat (*b*) Vegetables
(*c*) Rice (*d*) All of the above

104. Column A lists some biocontrol agents, while column B lists their target organisms. Match both the columns carefully and select the correct option from those given below them.

Column A	Column B
A. *Beauveria* sp.	1. Aphids, white flies
B. *Metarrhizium anisopliae*	2. Leaf hoppers, beetles, mosquitoes
C. *Verticillium lecanii*	3. Citrus mites
D. *Hirsutella thompsonii*	4. Many insects, *e.g.*, beetles, caterpillars

Options :
(*a*) A4, B2, C1, D3 (*b*) A3, B4, C2, D1
(*c*) A2, B1, C4, D3 (*d*) A1, B2, C3, D4

13.2. FILL IN THE BLANKS

1. Mycophenolic acid is an .... agent.

2. Bioactivity of a metabolite is commonly identified using ....

3. Low temperature (2-6°C) is useful for periods of .... for the storage of working stock cultures.

4. Lyophilization is easily done by using .... machines in which the cells are first frozen and then their free water is withdrawn under ....

5. *Clostridium* spores require .... for germination.

6. .... help in increasing the solubility/availability of phosphate, which is already present in the soil in sparingly soluble forms.

7. .... is a fern containing symbiotic N_2 fixing BGA, *Anabaena azollae*.

8. In cyanobacteria, N_2 fixation occurs in specialized structures called ....

9. *Rhizobium* cells contain genes for nitrogen fixation on a ....

10. Stigmasterol and β-sitosterol are obtained from ....

11. About .... % of the world copper supply is derived by the process involving *Thiobacillus ferrooxidans.*

12. Crystal protein activity disappears usually within .... hour after application, but the spores may persist for long periods and cause harm to nontarget useful insects, *e.g.*, silkworm.

13. *Rhizobium* species are attacked by viruses, called ....

14. *Azolla* is widely used in .... as biofertilizer for rice.

15. In practice, ... M rad is used for sterilization of pharmaceutical and medical products.

16. Commercial production of nucleopolyhedrosis Viruses and Granulosis Viruses is done in the .... of target insects.

17. Recombination is used to bring the desirable genes present in two or more strains into a single strain to increase product yields or generate new ....

18. *Rhizobium* enters the roots through ....

19. Nitrogenase reduces atmospheric nitrogen into ....

20. Leghaemoglobin is produced by .... and is present in their ....

21. For storage of *Rhizobium* culture packets, a temperature of .... °C is considered satisfactory.

22. National Biofertilizer Development centre is located at ....

23. Fungus .... is used for the control of soil-borne fungal pathogen, *Macrophomina phaseolona.*

24. *Agrobacterium radiobacter* strain K 1026 is used for the control of ....

25. Chemicals used for sterilization cause inactivation by .... or ....

26. In general, filamentous microorganisms are grown for the production of .... metabolites, which begins 1-3 days after inoculation and continues upto 3-4 days thereafter.

27. Generally, ... of fermenter volume is left unfilled with medium as "head space" to allow for splashing, foaming and aeration.

28. The fungi used for solid state fermentations are usually .... aerobes.

29. Recovery of products from .... fermenters does not require anaerobic conditions.

30. Cell immobilization has been used for commercial production of ....

31. Reverse osmosis can separate molecules of the .... size.

32. .... methods are used for the purification of low molecular weight compounds from a mixture of similar molecules.

33. Sugarcane juice has about .... % fermentable sugars.

34. .... culture method is used for the production of large amounts of citric acid.

35. Neomycin and streptomycin inhibit the function of .... of ribosomes.

36. Bacitracin inhibits the synthesis of bacterial ....

37. Penicillinase hydrolyses destroy penicillin and ....

38. One ton molasses produces .... litres of alcohol.

39. Glutamic acid and lysine are produced at .... and .... tons/year, respectively.

40. C-1 dehydrogenation by *Arthrobacter simplex* or *Septomyxa affinis* yields........... from progesterone.

41. During fermentation, starch is digested to yield ...., which is then metabolized to yield acetone and butanol.
42. Typically, molasses medium yields butanol, acetone and ethanol in the ratio of ....
43. Generally, antibiotic yields are much .... on complex media.
44. When immobilized cells are to be used, cell lysis must be ....
45. Extracellular enzymes are recovered directly from ...., while enzymes localized within the cells are isolated by .... the cells.
46. Typically, fermentation of 100 g glucose by selected strains of *Saccharomyces cerevisiae* and *Saccharomyces carlsbergensis* yields .... g ethanol.
47. In general, yeast growth stops at .... % w/v ethanol production.
48. Amyloglucosidase is also called ....
49. The end product of glucose isomerase action is a nearly ....mixture of glucose and fructose.
50. The first biotransformation to be commercialized was the conversion of deoxycorticosterone to corticosterone by ....
51. D-sorbitol is biotransformed to L-sorbose by ....
52. Glycerol is biotransformed by .... to dihydroxyacetone.
53. The longevity of glucose isomerase under practical conditions is about .... hr.
54. The annual production of L-sorbose is about .... tons.
55. Microbial cultures used for biotransformation are usually maintained in frozen state at .... °C.
56. For L-sorbose production, the medium is supplemented with .... % D-sorbitol.
57. Penicillin G and Penicillin V are biotransformed to 6-aminopenicillanic acid by .... reaction.
58. The indirect metal solublizing action of bacteria is based on the reduction of ferric sulphate ($Fe_2(SO_4)_3$) to ....
59. *Thiobacillus ferrooxidans* oxidises .... to H_2SO_4 and converts $FeSO_4$ to $Fe_2(SO_4)_3$.
60. Cassava, potato and yams have Ca. ....% starch on fresh weight basis.

13.3. MARK TRUE OR FALSE

1. In 1860, Pasteur reported the first synthetic medium for microorganisms, and used it to study butanol fermentation.
2. Cyclosporin has antiprotozoal activity.
3. Inoculum development is generally done using flask cultures.
4. Quality and reproducibility of the inoculum are critical factors in determining production levels.
5. *Azolla* multiplies mainly through vegetative reproduction.
6. *Anabaena azollae* is the only species known to be asymbiotically associated with *Azolla* species.
7. Antibiotic cycloheximide is produced from *Streptomyces nodosus*.
8. In canning industry, *Clostridium botulinum* is the chief contaminant.
9. Sterilization involves either inactivation or removal of living organisms.
10. Spores of thermophillic bacteria can survive steam at 30 p.s.i. and 134°C for 1-10 min and dry heat at 180°C for upto 15 min.
11. The energy and carbon requirements of *Rhizobium* sp. are provided by the host and, in return, the ammonium produced by the bacterial cells is made available to the host.
12. Enzyme D-amino acid oxidase converts cephalosporin C into 7-aminocephalosporanic acid, a precursor of several natural antibiotics.
13. Anaerobic fermentation usually liberates CO_2 and H_2, which are collected and used.
14. *E. coli* cells are entrapped in polyacrylamide gel for the production of L-aspartic acid.

15. Foaming is a major problem in synthetic media.
16. Complex media for bioreactors give much higher yields of metabolites.
17. The final step in the recovery of a product is purification.
18. Crystallization is the final stage in purification of products like citric acid, sodium glutamate, etc.
19. Vacuum has been used to remove volatile products like ethanol.
20. At present, both acetone and butanol are obtained by chemical synthesis and their fermentation process is rarely used.
21. Antibiotics are metabolites having preferential antimicrobial activity.
22. Calcium lactate is formed by bacterial fermentation.
23. There is little product loss during downstream processing.
24. Ampicillin is a synthetic antibiotic
25. Fumaric acid is used in resin formation.
26. Citric acid is marketed in the form of white anhydrous crystalline powder.
27. Lactic acid is extracted from whey.
28. Dextran is used in blood transfusion.
29. At lower concentrations biocidal agents become biostatic.
30. *Clostridium acetobutylicum* is a spore forming bacterium.
31. Yeast is an aerobe but fermentation of glucose takes place under anaerobic conditions.
32. India is the third country after America and Brazil where alcohol is produced on large scale.
33. Molasses ('C' grade) obtained after sugar recovery contains total fermentable sugars at nearly 50-55%.
34. A high yielding microbial strain is a prerequisite for antibiotic production.
35. Antibiotics are primary metabolites.
36. Most industrially important enzymes are extracellular.
37. Glucose isomerase is intracellular and best used in the form of immobilized cells.
38. Ascorbic acid is commercially produced from glucose.
39. Dextrins obtained by α-amylase digestion of starch are further digested to glucose by glucoamylase.
40. In the case of direct metal solubilizing action of the bacteria, the metal sulphide is itself converted to metal sulphate.
41. Use of microbes for ore leaching produces toxic or noxious gases as by-products.
42. *Sulfolobus acidocaldarius* can oxidise both iron pyrite as well as organic sulpher compounds.
43. Coal contains usually 0.2-8% sulpher.
44. Some bacteria accumulate metals within their cells.
45. Most of the pesticides are used on cotton (45%), rice (30%) and vegetables (5%).
46. *Azolla-Anabaena* has asymbiotic association with rice.
47. Mycorrhiza (*Glomus*) has associative relation with many crops including pulses.
48. Phosphate solublizing bacteria can be used in many crops.
49. *Arthrobotrys dactyloides* can be used for control of root knot of tomato and brinjal.
50. *Agrobacterium radiobacter* strain K 84 has a plasmid that is responsible for bacteriocin agrocin 84 production.
51. The cost of downstream processing is often more than 50% of the manufacturing cost.
52. Antibiotics are produced by both fungi and bacteria but over 50% of them are obtained from *Streptomyces* alone.

□□□

14

FOOD AND BEVERAGE BIOTECHNOLOGY

14.1. MULTIPLE CHOICE QUESTIONS

1. Kaffir beer is produced from which of the following substrates ?
   (*a*) *Eleusine coracana*
   (*b*) Cassava
   (*c*) *Sorghum caffrorum*
   (*d*) Both (*a*) and (*c*)

2. Which of the following fermented foods is produced from milk ?
   (*a*) Cheese (*b*) Yoghurt
   (*c*) Kefir (*d*) All of the above

3. Koji or solid substrate fermentation presents which of the following problems ?
   I. They are difficult to scale up.
   II. Heat transfer and removal are not as easy and efficient as with liquid fermentation.
   III. It is difficult to monitor and control the various factors during the process.
   IV. Gas exchange, *i.e.,* supply of O_2 and removal of CO_2, presents problems.

   Options :
   (*a*) I, II, III, IV (*b*) II, III, IV
   (*c*) I, II, III (*d*) I, III, IV

4. Which of the following advantages is offered by fermented foods ?
   I. Enhanced nutritional value
   II. Elimination of undesirable flavour
   III. Improved texture
   IV. Increased cooking time

   Options :
   (*a*) I, II, IV (*b*) I, II, III, IV
   (*c*) I, II, III (*d*) II, III, IV

5. Which of the following statements are correct about tempeh ?
   I. It is a fermented food.
   II. It is protein-rich.
   III. It provides good flavoured food.
   IV. It is used as a meat supplement.

   Options :
   (*a*) I, II, III (*b*) I, II, III, IV
   (*c*) II, III, IV (*d*) I, III, IV

6. Yoghurt is produced by which of the following microorganisms ?
   (*a*) *Streptococcus thermophilus*
   (*b*) *Lactobacillus bulgaricus*
   (*c*) *Lactobacillus delbrueckii*
   (*d*) Both (*a*) and (*b*)

7. Fermented food *Gari* is prodcued from which of the following substrates ?
   (*a*) Cassava (*b*) Rice
   (*c*) Milk (*d*) Urad

8. Select the correct order of general procedure for the production of fermented foods ?
   1. Seeds are soaked in water.
   2. The substrate is then inoculated with the appropriate microbial strain.
   3. The seeds are either cooked by boiling or ground into a paste.
   4. The fermented food is either prepared and used, stored or processed further.

   Options :
   (*a*) 1, 2, 3, 4 (*b*) 1, 2, 4, 3
   (*c*) 1, 2, 4, 3 (*d*) 1, 3, 2, 4

9. Which of the following statements are correct about tempeh ?
   I. Soybean seeds are soaked in water for 12-18 hours.

II. Dehulled seeds are boiled in water for 30-60 min, cooled and dried to the desired moisture level.
III. Seeds are inoculated with spore suspension of *Rhizopus oligosporus* and incubated at 30°C for 2-3 days.
IV. The fermented seeds are now pressed into cakes called tempeh cakes, which may be stored or used.

Options :
(*a*) I, II, III, IV (*b*) II, III, IV
(*c*) I, III, IV (*d*) I, II, IV

10. For the production of Ang-Kak (red rice), rice is inoculated with which of the following microorganisms ?
(*a*) *Leuconostoc mesenteroides*
(*b*) *Monascus purpureus*
(*c*) *Endomycopsis burtonii*
(*d*) *Geotrichum candidum*

11. Cheese production involves which of the following steps ?
I. Coagulum formation
II. Separation of curd from whey
III. Ripening of cheese.

Options :
(*a*) I, II (*b*) II, III
(*c*) I, II, III (*d*) I, III

12. For the fermentation of brew, which of the following species of yeast is used ?
(*a*) *Saccharomyces carisbergensis*
(*b*) *Kluyveromyces fragilis*
(*c*) *Saccharomyces cerevisiae*
(*d*) Either (*a*) or (*c*)

13. Pectins are digested by pecteolytic enzymes that are mixtures of which of the following enzyme activities ?
I. Polygalacturonase (random digestion of pectin).
II. Pectin lyase (cleaves pectins into oligosaccharides even without pectin esterase action).
III. Pectin esterase (removal of methyl esters; pectin becomes degradable by polygalacturonase).
IV. Hemicellulase (a mixture of enzymes degrading hemicellulose).

Options :
(*a*) I, II, III, IV (*b*) I, II, III
(*c*) II, III, IV (*d*) I, III, IV

14. Lactose intolerant individuals may suffer from which of following problems when they consume normal milk ?
I. Diarrhoea and flatulence
II. Abdominal cramps
III. Dehydration
IV. Death

Options :
(*a*) I, II, III (*b*) I, II, III, IV
(*c*) II, III, IV (*d*) I, II, IV

15. When lactose is hydrolysed by lactase, which of the following monosaccharides is produced ?
(*a*) D-glucose + D-glucose
(*b*) D-glucose + β-D-galactose
(*c*) β-D-galactose + β-D-galactose
(*d*) D-glucose + D-fructose

16. Which of the following is correct about glucose oxidase ?
I. It is obtained from *Aspergillus oryzae.*
II. It catalyzes the formation of gluconic acid from β-D-glucose.
III. It is used for the removal of glucose or oxygen from foods in order to enhance their storability.
IV. Generally, glucose oxidase and catalase are used in combination.

Options :
(*a*) I, II, III (*b*) II, III, IV
(*c*) I, II, III, IV (*d*) I, III, IV

17. Treatment of fruit pulp with pecteotylic enzyme mixture gives which of the following benefits ?
I. Elimination of cloudiness.
II. Increased juice yields.
III. Enhanced solution viscosity.
IV. Shorter fermentation period in case of wine making.

Options :
(*a*) I, II, III, IV (*b*) II, III, IV
(*c*) I, II, IV (*d*) I, III, IV

18. Mushrooms offer which of the following advantages ?
I. They utilize substrates of poor value.
II. They are delicious to eat.
III. They are rich in protein (about 51% on dry weight basis) and devoid of starch.
IV. They are rich in vitamins particularly nicotinic acid and riboflavin.

Options :
(*a*) I, II, III, IV (*b*) I, II, IV
(*c*) I, III, IV (*d*) II, III, IV

19. Which of the following advantages are offered by single cell protein (SCP) products ?
I. SCP is rich in high quality protein and is rather poor in fats.
II. Some SCPs are good sources of vitamins.
III. At present, SCP appears to be the only feasible approach to bridge the gap between requirement and supply of proteins.
IV. Mushrooms are considered as delicacy in human diet.

Options :
(*a*) I, II, III (*b*) II, III, IV
(*c*) I, III, IV (*d*) I, II, III, IV

20. Cheese production presents example of which of the following ?
I. Use of microorganisms for processing of food to enhance flavour, texture, etc.
II. Use of enzymes in food processing.
III. Rennet modification to suit specific needs.
IV. Use of recombinant DNA technology to produce enzymes for food processing.

Options :
(*a*) I, II, III, IV (*b*) I, II, III
(*c*) I, III, IV (*d*) I, II

21. Which of the following statements are correct about glucose oxidase and catalase ?
I. Generally, glucose oxidase and catalase are used sequentially.
II. An important application of these enzymes is in the processing of egg-white for use in baking industry.
III. They are used for removal of O_2 from the air present in the head-space of bottled and canned drinks.
IV. Reduction of enzymatic browning in wines and mayonnaises.

Options :
(*a*) I, II, III (*b*) I, II, III, IV
(*c*) II, III, IV (*d*) I, III, IV

22. Beer production from fermentation of barley malt uses which of the following species of yeast ?
(*a*) *Kluyveromyces fragils*
(*b*) *Saccharomyces cerevisiae*
(*c*) *Saccharomyces carisbergensis*
(*d*) Both (*b*) and (*c*)

23. Ordinarily, saccharification during beer production is stopped by boiling the wort when about how much of the starch has been converted into fermentable sugars ?
(*a*) 25% (*b*) 50%
(*c*) 75% (*d*) 90%

24. Which of the following statements are correct ?
I. Cellulases are used to digest barley glucans, particularly, when wheat is used as an adjunct.
II. Neutral proteases are added to the wort to hydrolyse proteins and to increase the fermentation rate in the later stages of beer fermentation.
III. For the production of high-gravity beer, extra proteins are added to the wort; neutral proteases are used in such cases to digest the proteins.
IV. Bacterial and fungal α-amylases and β-glucanase are used for increased and rapid saccharification, especially when adjuncts are not added to the malt.

Options :
(*a*) I, II, III, IV (*b*) II, III
(*c*) I, II, III (*d*) I, III

25. Which of the following distilled alcoholic drinks is produced by fermentation of a large number of substrates rich in carbohydrates ?
(*a*) Rum (*b*) Whisky
(*c*) Vodka (*d*) All of the above.

26. Single cell proteins offer which of the following advantages ?
I. They can be produced all round the year.
II. The microbes are very fast growing and produce large quantities of SCP from relatively very small area of land.
III. They use low-cost substrates.
IV. When the substrate used for SCP process is a source of pollution, SCP production helps in reducing pollution.

Options :
(*a*) I, II, III, IV (*b*) I, III, IV
(*c*) I, II, III (*d*) I, II, IV

27. Which of the following statements are correct ?
I. Casing is essential for fruiting bodies of button mushrooms to be produced.
II. Mushroom fruiting bodies appear after about two months of casing.
III. *Agaricus* mushrooms are harvested in the button stage.
IV. Button mushrooms are the most liked and prized of them all.

Options :
(*a*) I, II, III (*b*) II, III, IV
(*c*) I, III, IV (*d*) II, IV

28. The microorganisms used for SCP production must be which of the following ?
I. Fast growing and of good nutritional value.
II. Easy to separate from medium.
III. Nonpathogenic to plants, animals and humans.
IV. Easily and cheaply produced on large scale and free from toxins.

Options :
(*a*) I, II, III, IV (*b*) II, III
(*c*) I, III, IV (*d*) II, IV

29. Fossil carbon sources (non-renewable) of energy include which of the following ?
I. Liquid hydrocarbons
II. Methanol
III. Gaseous hydrocarbons
IV. Ethanol

Options :
(*a*) I, II, IV (*b*) II, III, IV
(*c*) I, III, IV (*d*) I, II, III, IV

30. Which of the following disadvantages are associated with SCP production using bacteria ?
I. Careful evaluation for endotoxin production is essential.
II. Recovery of cells is problematic.
III. High nucleic acid (especially DNA) content.
IV. Risk of contamination by pathogenic bacteria is considerable.

Options :
(*a*) I, II, III, IV (*b*) I, II, III
(*c*) I, II, IV (*d*) I, III, IV

31. Which of the following statements are correct about algae ?
I. The members of genera *Spirulina*, *Chlorella* and *Scendesmus* are generally grown in ponds/tanks.
II. Algal SCP has about 60% crude protein, which is generally good in amino acid composition.
III. They are suitable for animal feed as protein-rich supplements.

Options :
(*a*) I, II (*b*) I, II, III
(*c*) I, III (*d*) II, III

32. ***Assertion (A)***: Algal SCP has about 60% crude protein, but it is not preferred for human consumption.

Reason (R): Algae are rich in chlorophyll content, and serious problems may occur when *Chlorella* and *Scenedesmus* are used in human diet.

Options :
(*a*) Both A and R are correct and R roughly explains A.
(*b*) Both A and R are correct, but R does not explain A.
(*c*) Only A is correct.
(*d*) Only R is correct.

33. The level of RNA in SCP is reduced by which of the following methods ?
I. Activation of endogenous RNases by, usually, a brief heat treatment.
II. Chemical extraction.
III. Suitable manipulation of growth and physiology of microbial cells.
IV. Alkaline hydrolysis.

Options :
(*a*) I, II, III, IV (*b*) I, II, IV
(*c*) II, III, IV (*d*) II, III

34. Which of the following disadvantages are associated with algal SCP ?
I. They are rich in chlorophyll, which is not suitable for human use.
II. They produce only low cell density.
III. There is a serious risk of contamination.
IV. Costly recovery methods have to be used for unicellular algal.

Options :
(*a*) I, II, III (*b*) I, II, III, IV
(*c*) I, III, IV (*d*) II, III, IV

35. Among the given bacteria, which one utilizes methane as well as fixes atmospheric nitrogen ?
(*a*) *Methanomonas methanica*
(*b*) *Methylococcus capsulatus*
(*c*) *Pseudomanas methanitrificans*
(*d*) *Pseudomonas methanica*

36. The renewable carbon sources include which of the following ?
I. Cellulose hydrolysates and cellulosic wastes
II. Starch hydrolysatés and molasses
III. CO_2 and whey
IV. Industrial effluents and cellulosic wastes

Options :
(*a*) I, II, III (*b*) II, III, IV
(*c*) I, II, III, IV (*d*) I, III, IV

37. Which of the following features are associated with filamentous fungi used to produce SCP ?
I. They have high nucleic acid content (upto 15% RNA)
II. They have faster growth rates than bacteria and yeast.
III. Contamination by yeast may be frequent if sterility is not maintained.
IV. Contamination by bacteria can be minimised by keeping the pH of broth below 5.0.

Options :
(*a*) I, II, III, IV (*b*) I, III, IV
(*c*) I, II, III (*d*) II, III, IV

38. Which of the following statements are correct about SCP ?
I. The SCP chemical composition must be characterized in terms of protein, amino acid, lipid, vitamin, nucleic acid contents.
II. Microbiological description should be provided and information on contamination can also be given.
III. The nutritional value should be evaluated on the target species and other species should also be included.
IV. Possible toxic or carcinogenic compounds must be assayed for.

Options :
(*a*) I, II, III, IV (*b*) I, III, IV
(*c*) I, II, III (*d*) II, III, IV

39. Methane is utilized by which of the following bacterium ?
(*a*) *Methanomonas methanica*
(*b*) *Pseudomonas methanica*
(*c*) *Methylococcus capsulatus*
(*d*) All of the above

40. Which of the following statements are correct about yeast-based SCP ?
I. Both *Saccharomyces* and *Candida* are used.
II. The SCP has 55-60% crude protein, which has almost good amino acid balance.
III. The SCP is used as human food and animal feed supplement.
IV. The risk of bacterial contamination is high.

Options :
(*a*) I, II, III, IV (*b*) I, II
(*c*) I, II, III (*d*) I, II, IV

41. Use of methane for SCP production presents which of following problems ?
I. Substrate limitation either due to methane or oxygen.
II. Heat generation necessitating efficient cooling.
III. Hazards of explosion when over 12% O_2 (v/v) is used.

Options :
(*a*) I, II (*b*) II, III,
(*c*) I, III (*d*) I, II, III

42. Algal cultivation offers which of the following advantages ?
I. Year-round cultivation
II. Efficient harvesting of sunlight.
III. Optimal utlilization of mineral nutrients
IV. Cultivation in seawater and alkline lakes

Options :
(*a*) I, II, III, IV (*b*) I, II, III
(*c*) II, III, IV (*d*) I, III, IV

43. Which of the following statements are correct ?
I. Methanol can be produced from coal, gas oil, wood and naphtha.
II. Methanol is fully water soluable.
III. The SCP can be produced from methanol using *Methylophilus methylotrophus* bacterium.

IV. The SCP contains 71% protein, and is marketed as 'Pruteen' in U.K. and used as a milk substitute in calf feeding.

Options :

(*a*) I, II, III (*b*) II, III, IV
(*c*) I, II, III, IV (*d*) I, III, IV

44. In U.S.A., Torula yeast (*Candida utilis*) has been used for commercial SCP production using which of the following as a substrate ?
(*a*) Methanol
(*b*) Ethanol (from fermentation)
(*c*) Ethanol (from ethylene)
(*d*) Dairy effluent

45. In France, SCP production using *Kluyveromyces fragilis* uses which of the following as a substrate ?
(*a*) Whey
(*b*) Molasses
(*c*) Starch hydrolysate
(*d*) Confectionery effluent

46. Which of the following organisms has been used for commercial SCP production from starch hydrolysates ?
(*a*) *Candida utilis*
(*b*) *Saccharomyces cerevisiae*
(*c*) *Fusarium gaminearum*
(*d*) *Kluyveromyces fragilis*

47. Cells of which of the organisms listed in Q. 46 are used for dough fermentation ?

48. Which of the following organisms used for SCP production shows the highest growth rate ?
(*a*) Bacteria
(*b*) Algae
(*c*) Yeast
(*d*) Filamentous fungi

49. Which of the organisms given in Q. 48 shows the lowest growth rate ?

50. SCP from which of the organisms listed in Q. 48 has the highest protein content ?

51. SCP from which of the organisms given in Q. 48 may contain significant amounts of nitrogen in an unavailable form ?

52. Which of the following mushrooms can be grown on straw ?
(*a*) *Coprinus* sp.
(*b*) *Pleurotus ostreatus*
(*c*) *Volvariella volvaceae*
(*d*) All of the above.

53. Which of the mushrooms given Q. 52 is commonly known as Chinese or straw mushrooms ?

54. Which of the mushrooms given in Q. 52 can be cultivated during summer and rainy seasons ?

55. Which of the following proteases is used for meat tenderisation ?
(*a*) Papain
(*b*) Heat labile fungal protease
(*c*) Subtilisin
(*d*) Neutral or alkaline proteases

56. Which of the proteases given in Q. 55 is used to recover meat (in form of slurry) adhering to bones ?

57. Which of the proteases listed in Q. 55 is used for partial hydrolysis of soy protein ?

58. Which of the proteases listed in Q. 55 is used for gluten hydrolysis in dough from high gluten wheat varieties.

59. In cheese production, which of the following agents contributes to the development of flavour ?

I. Lipase
II. Proteases
III. Rennet
IV. *Penicillium roquefortii*

Options :

(*a*) I, II, III, IV (*b*) I, II, III
(*c*) I, III, IV (*d*) I, II, IV

60. Which of the agents listed in Q. 59 are used during curd formation (in cheese production) ?

Options :

(*a*) I, II (*b*) I, III
(*c*) I, IV (*d*) II, III

61. Which of the following leads to curd formation during cheese production ?
(*a*) Cleavage of κ-casein
(*b*) Cleavage of α-casein
(*c*) Lactic acid production
(*d*) Both (*a*) and (*b*)

62. Which of the following are common contaminants of milk ?
(*a*) *Streptococci* (*b*) *Lactobacilli*
(*c*) *Micrococci* (*d*) All of the above

63. Which of the following statements are correct about single cell oil (SCO) ?

I. It refers to the edible oil (triacylglycerol) produced by and extracted from microbial cells.

II. The current interest in SCO began in mid-1970s.

III. Most of the patents have been obtained, in Japan for SCO production using bacteria and fungi.

IV. The cost and year-round availability of the substrate are the greatest limiting factors in SCO production.

Options :

(*a*) I, II, III, IV (*b*) I, II, III

(*c*) II, III, IV (*d*) I, III, IV

64. Which of the following bacteria have been used for production of SCO in Japan ?

(*a*) *Chromobacterium viscosum*

(*b*) *Mycobacterium* sp.

(*c*) *Agrobacterium* sp.

(*d*) All of the above.

65. Which of the following substrates is good and cleanest for SCO production ?

I. Ethanol II. Whey

III. Molasses IV. Starch

Options :

(*a*) I, III, IV (*b*) I

(*c*) IV (*d*) II

66. Which of the options given in Q. 65 serves as good substrate for oil producing microoragnisms ?

67. Which of the options given in Q. 65 is directly utilized by a strain of *Aspergillus oryzae* to achieve good coversion to lipids ?

68. Which of the options given in Q. 65, is too expensive substrate for SCO production ?

69. Which of the following statements are correct ?

I. *Rhizobium* sp. and *Rhizopus delemar* are used for SCO production in Japan.

II. Selected strains of *A. oryzea* could be grown on potato starch, and they accumulated lipids upto 25% of their biomass.

III. *Criptococcus abidus* grown on ethanol could yield 31% lipid.

IV. The substrate used for SCO production must be cheap and available round the year.

Options :

(*a*) I, II, III (*b*) I, II, III, IV

(*c*) II, III, IV (*d*) I, III, IV

70. Due to which of the following features, microorganisms are generally considered promising source of lipids ?

(*a*) They show high growth rate in simple media.

(*b*) They are amenable to numerous bio-transformation reactions.

(*c*) They produce value-added types of fats or oils.

(*d*) All of the above.

71. Among the given microorganisms, which one is the potential producer of oils and fats ?

I. Algae II. Bacteria

III. Fungi IV. Yeast

Options :

(*a*) I, II (*b*) II

(*c*) III, IV (*d*) I

72. Which of the microorganisms given in Q. 71, ***generally does not accumulate*** large amount of lipids and when it does so, it generally produces non-acylglycerol lipids, which are suitable for commercial purposes ?

73. Which of the microorganisms given in Q. 71, produces oils and fats which are rich in polyunsaturated fatty acids (PUFAs) ?

74. High-value (having high nutritive value) microbial lipids that are under current consideration are those used for production of a food product similar to which of the following ?

(*a*) Cocoa butter.

(*b*) Cocoa polyunsaturated fatty acids.

(*c*) Cocoa fat.

(*d*) All of the above.

75. Which of the following is correct ?

I. Oil from *Candida curvata* was used for production of Cocoa butter-like substance.

II. PUFAs are long-chain fatty acids with two or more double bonds in their carbon chain.
III. Docosahexaenoic acid (DHA)-rich oils are used in food products (infant formula and nutrition bars).
IV. Gamma linolenic acid (GLA) contains PUFA.

Options :

(*a*) I, II, III, IV (*b*) II, III, IV
(*c*) I, III, IV (*d*) I, II, III

76. Which of the following are example of PUFAs ?

I. Dihomogammalinolenic (DGLA)
II. Eicosapentaenoic acid (EPA)
III. Arachidonic acid (ARA).
IV. Decosahexaenoic acid (DHA)

Options :

(*a*) I, II, III (*b*) II, III, IV
(*c*) II, IV (*d*) I, II, III, IV

77. Which of the following enzymes is used to prevent 'chill-haze' of beer ?

(*a*) Papain (*b*) Neutral proteases
(*c*) Cellulases (*d*) All of the above

78. Which of the enzymes listed in Q. 77 is used during post-fermentation stages ?

79. Which of the enzymes listed in Q. 77 is used particularly when wheat is added as an adjunct ?

80. Which of the enzymes listed in Q. 77 enhances fermentation rates ?

81. Production of low calorie light bears specifically uses which of the following enzymes ?

(*a*) Glucoamylase
(*b*) Fungal α-amylase
(*c*) Either or both (*a*) and (*b*)
(*d*) Neutral proteases

82. Which of the enzymes listed in Q. 81 is used for production of high gravity beer ?

83. When substrate is rich in fermentable sugars, which of the following enzymes is used for saccharification ?

(*a*) Fungal α-amylase.
(*b*) Heat stable bacterial α-amylase
(*c*) α-Amylase and glucanase
(*d*) Glucanase.

84. In cheese ripening, which of the following generates the strongest bitter flavour ?

(*a*) Medium-sized peptides
(*b*) Small peptides.
(*c*) Large peptides.
(*d*) Both (*b*) and (*c*)

14.2. FILL IN THE BLANKS

1. Idli is produced from .... and ....

2. During cheese production, bricks of cheese may be inoculated with ....

3. κ-Casein .... the colloidal nature of milk.

4. Digestion of κ-casein by .... yields para-κ-casein and ....

5. The cloudiness of fruit juices and wines is mainly due to ....

6. Some individuals are intolerant to lactose due to........... deficiency.

7. Scientific name of button mushrooms is ....

8. Proteins and tannins make the beer hazy when the beer is ....

9. .... is added to the beer during the later post-fermentation stages to hydrolyse the proteins and thereby, prevent the occurrence of ....

10. Brandy and rum are produced from .... and ...., respectively.

11. In button mushrooms, fruiting bodies appear about .... month after casing.

12. Dhingri mushrooms are harvested when the caps become about .... in size.

13. The paddy mushrooms are suited for cultivation during .... and .... seasons.

14. In the rapidly proliferating microbial cells used for SCP, the bulk of nucleic acids is ....

15. Proteases from........... are used to enhance flavour in cheddar cheese.

16. In cheese productions lipolysis is brought about by lipase obtained from ....
17. .... gaseous hydrocarbons have been used for SCP production.
18. The cellulosic material is pretreated thermally and chemically, and is then fermented with the help of the fungus ....
19. Yeast SCP is usually very .... in B-group of vitamin.
20. Generally, *n*-alkanes having .... carbons are used as SCP substrates.
21. Starch hydrolysate is used for SCP production using ....
22. On dry weight basis whey contains .... % lactose, 9-14% protein and 9% ash.
23. .... is the liquid portion of milk remaining after the curd is separated during cheese production.
24. Yeasts (*Kluyveromyces fragilis*, *Candida krusei*) in combination with *Lactobacillus bulgaricus* and *Candida intermedia* are the most widely used for commercial scale production of SCP from ....
25. SCP produced from sulphite liquor using fungus *Paecilomyces varioti* has ....% crude protein and is used as animal feed.

14.3. MARK TRUE OR FALSE

1. Fermented foods offer the advantage of increased digestibility.
2. Tempeh is produced from soybean seeds.
3. During production of *Sake*, rice is inoculated with *A. oryzae.*
4. Rennent cleaves the peptide bond between Phe^{105} and Met^{106} of α-casein.
5. About 70% of Chinese adults can use normal levels of lactose in milk.
6. Mushrooms contain approximately 51% protein on dry weight basis.
7. When normal lactose level milk/whey is condensed or frozen, lactose remains dispersed homogeneously.
8. Beer is an undistilled alcoholic beverage produced from fermentation of barley malt by yeast.
9. Mashing results in partial hydrolysis of starch and proteins.
10. In case of distilled drinks, saccharification is limited to initial stage of fermentation.
11. When substrates are rich in fermentable sugars, saccharification is not required.
12. Recombinant DNA technology has been used to produce dextrin utilizing brewing yeast (*S. cerevisiae*) that hydrolyze the dextrins into glucose.
13. More recently, the demand for low calorie or light beers has grown rapidly.
14. SCP processes are highly aerobic (except those using algae).
15. Dhingri (*Pleurotus*) and button mushrooms are good for winter unless heating/cooling arrangements are available.
16. Substrates like methanol and ethanol can be produced from both renewable and non-renewable carbon sources.
17. Filamentous fungi have been used to produce SCP from polysaccharide hydrolysates and sulphite liquor wood pulp industries.
18. The kind and the degree of flavour in cheese can be controlled by regulating protein hydrolysis.
19. The stronger flavours of Italian cheese are produced by modest protein hydrolysis.
20. Ethanol offers advantages similar to methanol and is even more acceptable as a substrate for SCP production for human use.
21. C_5–C_8 *n*-alkanes are liquid at room temperature, but generally toxic to cells due to their solvent action.
22. SCP produced from bacteria using starch hydrolysate substrate has a meat-like texture, and is approved for human use.
23. The best utilization of cellulosic substrates appears to be mushroom production and for semi-solid fermentation system.
24. SCP produced from pure *n*-alkanes (> 97.5%) having about 60% crude protein was marketed as '*Toprina*'.
25. A very efficient chemical conversion of methane yields methanol.

□□□

15
FUEL BIOTECHNOLOGY

15.1. MULTIPLE CHOICE QUESTIONS

1. The recombinant *E. coli* used for pentose fermentation has transgenes encoding which of the following enzymes ?
(*a*) Pyruvate decarboxylase
(*b*) Alcohol dehydrogenase
(*c*) Acetaldehyde dehydrogenase
(*d*) Both (*a*) and (*c*)

2. Which of the following are the features of biodiesel ?
I. Derived from biomass, which is renewable.
II. Relatively lower CO_2 emission than fossil fuels.
III. They do not emit gases like SO_2, etc.
IV. The substrate for biofuel production is often a waste.

Options :
(*a*) I, II, III (*b*) I, II, III, IV
(*c*) II, III, IV (*d*) I, III, IV

3. The nature of biomass obtained from energy crops is of which of the following type ?
(*a*) Wood (*b*) Sugar and starch
(*c*) Hydrocarbon (*d*) All of the above

4. H_2 is produced by which of the following ?
I. Gasification of biomass
II. Electrolysis of water
III. By biological agents, *e.g.*, bacteria and algae
IV. From oil wells

Options :
(*a*) I, II, III (*b*) II, III, IV
(*c*) I, II, III, IV (*d*) I, III, IV

5. Biogas may be used in which of the following ways ?
I. Direct combustion
II. Generation of electricity
III. For production of petrol

Options :
(*a*) I, III (*b*) II, III
(*c*) I, II, III (*d*) I, II

6. Which of the following undesirable features are associated with biofuels ?
I. Very large volumes are required.
II. Substrate is required in very large volumes.
III. Generally low value.
IV. Rather low profit margin.

Options :
(*a*) I, II, III, IV (*b*) I, II, III
(*c*) II, III, IV (*d*) I, III, IV

7. ***Assertion (A)***: Biofuels are not very attractive commercially.
Reason (R): Their cost of production is over 75% of the sale price.

Options :
(*a*) Both A and R are correct and R sufficiently explains A.
(*b*) Both A and R are correct, but R does not explain A.
(*c*) Only A is correct.
(*d*) Only R is correct.

8. Which of the following ***is not an example*** of an energy crop that yields hydrocarbons ?
(*a*) *Asclepia speciosa*
(*b*) *Copaifera multijuga*
(*c*) *Euphorbia lathyris*
(*d*) *Eucalyptus globulus*

9. Bioethanol can be produced from which of the following crops ?

(*a*) Cereals (*b*) Tuber crops
(*c*) Root crops (*d*) All of the above

10. Biogas is produced by bacterial digestion of organic matter through which of the following processes ?
(*a*) Aerobic digestion
(*b*) Anaerobic digestion
(*c*) Both (*a*) and (*b*)
(*d*) Partially aerobic digestion

11. Which of the following substrates is usually employed for generation of biogas ?
I. Waste products of agricultural origin.
II. Waste products of food processing origin.
III. Waste products of animal husbandary (excreta).
IV. Waste products of domestic and municipal origin.
Options :
(*a*) II, III, IV (*b*) I, III, IV
(*c*) I, II, III, IV (*d*) I, II, III

12. Generally, the wastes are of which of the following types ?
(*a*) Biological (*b*) Physical
(*c*) Chemical (*d*) All of the above

13. Biohydrogen is produced by which of the following routes?
(*a*) By photolysis of water.
(*b*) During anaerobic fermentation.
(*c*) An *in vitro* system created by coupling together the photosynthetic unit and hydrogenase.
(*d*) All of the above.

14. Which of the following statements are correct ?
I. Excreta from ruminant animals are richer in lignocellulose and less favourable for anaerobic digestion than those of nonruminents.
II. Agriculutral biomass like bagasse, straw, stower, etc. show poor digestibility.
III. Domestic and municipal wastes are in the form of solid wastes and sewage, respectively.
IV. The digester design will mainly depend on the type of waste to be handled and level of operation.
Options :
(*a*) I, II, III, IV (*b*) II, III, IV
(*c*) I, III, IV (*d*) I, II, III

15. Which of the following produces hydrogen gas which can be used as a pollution-free fuel ?
(*a*) *Chlamydomonas* (*b*) *Clostridium*
(*c*) Both (*a*) and (*b*) (*d*) Green plants

16. Microorganisms involved in anaerobic digestion and biogas production can be divided into which of the following groups ?
I. Syntrophic H_2 producing bacteria
II. Acetogenic bacteria
III. Methanogenic bacteria
IV. Hydrolytic and fermentative bacteria
Options :
(*a*) I, II, III (*b*) I, II, III, IV
(*c*) II, III, IV (*d*) I, III, IV

17. Hydrolytic and fermentative bacteria hydrolyse and ferment the organic materials and produce which of the following ?
(*a*) Organic acids (*b*) CO_2
(*c*) H_2 (*d*) All of the above.

18. Which of the following is an example of methanogenic bacteria ?
(*a*) *Methanobacterium omelianskii*
(*b*) *Methanosarcina barkeri*
(*c*) Both (*a*) and (*b*)
(*d*) *Methylococcus capsulatus*

19. Which of the following is an example of organic acid ?
(*a*) Long chain fatty acids
(*b*) Formate and butyrate
(*c*) Acetate and propionate
(*d*) All of the above.

20. Direct use of biomass suffers from which of the following disadvantages ?
I. Low efficiency due to a large energy loss on burning.
II. Low bulk density of biomass makes it necessary to use huge equipments.
III. Biomass is biodegradable and difficult to store which necessitates its dyring.
IV. Regulated feeding of combustion plants is practically impossible.
Options :
(*a*) I, II, III, IV (*b*) II, III, IV
(*c*) I, III, IV (*d*) III, IV

21. Biomass may be used in which of the following ways ?
(*a*) Direct burning to generate heat.
(*b*) Thermochemical conversion by pyrolysis/gasification.

(*c*) Biological conversion.
(*d*) All of the above.

22. Which of the following statements are correct about hydrolytic and fermentative bacteria ?

I. They include both obligate and facultative anaerobes.
II. They may occur upto 10^8–10^9 cells/ml of sewage sludge digesters.
III. They remove O_2 and create anaerobic conditions.
IV. Usually, only 50% of the polysaccharides present in the waste may be digested.

Options :
(*a*) I, III, IV (*b*) I, II, III, IV
(*c*) I, II, IV (*d*) I, II, III

23. Syntrophic H_2 producing bacteria are also called which of the following ?
(*a*) Obligate H_2 producing bacteria
(*b*) Obligate proton reducing bacteria
(*c*) Facultative O_2 reducing bacteria
(*d*) Both (*a*) and (*b*)

24. Which of the following statements are correct about methanogenic bacteria ?

I. They belong to the new kingdom *Archaebacteria.*
II. They may occur upto 10^6–10^8 cells/ml of the slurry in digesters.
III. This group of bacteria converts acetate, and $CO_2 + H_2$ into methane.
IV. Methanogenic bacteria are the strictest possible anaerobes known.

Options :
(*a*) I, II, III (*b*) I, II, III, IV
(*c*) I, III, IV (*d*) II, III, IV

25. Which of the following statments are correct about syntrophic H_2 producing bacteria ?

I. They are also called obligate proton reducing bacteria.
II. They breakdown organic acids having greater than 2 carbon atoms in their chain and produce acetate, CO_2 and H_2.
III. Sewage sludge digesters have about $4{\times}10^6$ cells/ml of this group.
IV. *Syntrophomonas wolfei* and *S. wolinii* are examples of syntrophic bacteria.

Options :
(*a*) I, II, III, IV (*b*) II, III, IV
(*c*) I, III, IV (*d*) I, IV

26. Biodiesel can be obtained from which of the following ?
(*a*) Lipids accumulated in plants and algae
(*b*) Hydrocarbons produced by some plants and algae
(*c*) Both (*a*) and (*b*)
(*d*) Anaerobic digestion of domestic waste

27. Which of the following statements are correct about biogas production ?

I. The process of biogas production can explained using 'goḅar gas' as an example.
II. Gobar gas plants are based on excreta of cattle and other farm animals.
III. Generally, spent slurry at about 20% (v/v) of the fresh dung slurry is added back to maintain the microbial population.
IV. The optimal temperature for biogas production are between 35-38°C.

Options :
(*a*) I, III, IV (*b*) II, III, IV
(*c*) I, II, III, IV (*d*) I, II, IV

28. ***Assertion (A)***: Addition of human excreta (upto 3% of slurry) markedly increases the biogas output.
Reason (R): Human excreta has higher nitrogen content, which supports microbial growth.

Options :
(*a*) Both A and R are correct and R roughly explains A.
(*b*) Both A and R are correct, but R does not explain A.
(*c*) Only A is correct.
(*d*) Only R is correct.

29. Which of the following factors affects biogas yields ?

I. Type of waste
II. Temperature during digester operation
III. Retention time
IV. Presence of inhibitors

Options :
(*a*) I, II, IV (*b*) II, III, IV
(*c*) I, II, III, IV (*d*) III, IV

30. Which of the following precautions must be taken during biogas production ?

I. Organic overloading of the digester should be avoided.
II. Adequate provision for moisture should

be made, especially in case of landfil sites.

III. Adequate nutrients should be present in the waste to support good bacterial growth.

IV. The conditions necessary for the formation of anaerobic films should be provided.

Options :

(*a*) I, II, III (*b*) I, II, III, IV
(*c*) II, III (*d*) I, III, IV

31. Any biofuel proposed to be used for transport purposes should have which of the following features ?

I. It should be roughly equivalent to petrol in energy content.

II. It should burn in the internal combustion engines.

III. It should be portable in sufficient quantities in the vehicle.

Options :

(*a*) I, II (*b*) I, II, III
(*c*) I, III (*d*) II, III

32. At present, which of the following routes can be used for producing bioethanol ?

I. From starch or sugar.

II. From cellulose following enzymatic hydrolysis.

III. From cellulose following chemical hydrolysis.

IV. From lipids following enzymatic and chemical hydrolysis.

Options :

(*a*) I, II, III, IV (*b*) I, II, III
(*c*) II, III, IV (*d*) III, IV

33. Among the given options, bioethanol production on commercial scale is based on which of the following crops ?

(*a*) Oil crops (*b*) Starch crops
(*c*) Sugar crops (*d*) Both (*b*) and (*c*)

34. Column A lists various substrates, while column B lists the maximum possible yield of biogas on complete digestion of the substrates. Match both the columns carefully and select the correct option from those listed below them.

Column A	Column B
A. Carbohydrates	1. 0.9 m^3/kg
B. Fatty acids	2. 0.8 m^3/kg
C. Proteins	3. 1.5 m^3/kg

Options :

(*a*) A2, B3, C1 (*b*) A3, B2, C1
(*c*) A1, B3, C2 (*d*) A2, B1, C3

35. Which of the following is correct about biogas ?

I. Generally, mesophilic fermentation at about 35°C gives the maximum gas yields.

II. Gas yield increases with retention time.

III. Toxic components like ammonia, SO_4^{2-}, etc. present in wastes may inhibit biogas production.

IV. Anaerobic digestion is mainly used for pollution control.

Options :

(*a*) I, II, III, IV (*b*) II, III, IV
(*c*) I, III, IV (*d*) I, II, III

36. Which of the following features are correct about *Euphorbia lathyris* ?

I. Its latex has reduced terpenoids (5% of plant dry weight) and hexoses (20% of plant dry weight).

II. The terpenoids can be converted into a gasoline like product.

III. *E. lathyris* can yield about 25 tons biomass/ha/yr.

IV. Certain species of *Euphorbia* produce latex which has about 30% hydrocarbons emulsified in water.

Options :

(*a*) I, II, III (*b*) I, II, III, IV
(*c*) II, III, IV (*d*) I, III, IV

37. Which of the following advantages are offered by biogas ?

I. The technology is cheaper and much simpler than those for other biofuels.

II. Dilute waste materials (2–10% solids) can be used as substrate.

III. Organic pollutants are used to generate biogas.

IV. There is much reduced risk of explosion as compared to pure methane.

Options :

(*a*) I, II, III, IV (*b*) II, III, IV
(*c*) I, II, III (*d*) I, III, IV

38. Lipids are accumulated in seeds of which of the following plant species ?

I. Sunflower and safflower
II. Rapseed and linseed
III. Soybean and peanut
IV. Oil palm

Options :

(*a*) I, II, III, IV (*b*) I, III, IV
(*c*) II, III, IV (*d*) III, IV

39. Fruits of which of the plants listed in Q. 38 accumulate lipids ?

(*a*) I (*b*) II
(*c*) IV (*d*) III

40. ***Problem (P)***: Lipids from many plant species can be used as diesel engine fuel, but the oils are not easily injectable into the engine combustion chamber due to their high viscosity.

Solution (S): Esters of the lipid fatty acids may be produced and used as biodiesel with little or no modification in the engine.

Options :

(*a*) Only P is correct.
(*b*) Only S is correct.
(*c*) Both P and S are correct.
(*d*) Both P and S are correct and S sufficiently overcomes P.

41. Which of the following advantages are offered by biogas ?

I. Any biodegradable matter can be used as substrate.
II. Recovery of the product (methane) is spontaneous.
III. Biogas is suitable for running modified internal combustion engines to generate electricity.
IV. Anaerobic digestion inactivates pathogens.

Options :

(*a*) I, II, III (*b*) II, III, IV
(*c*) I, III, IV (*d*) I, II, III, IV

42. Biogas suffers from which of the following disadvantages ?

I. The product (biogas) value is rather low.
II. The biogas yields are lower due to the dilute nature of substrates used.
III. Biogas contains some gases as impurities, which are corrosive to internal combustion engines.
IV. The process is not very attractive economically.

Options :

(*a*) II, III (*b*) I, II, III, IV
(*c*) I, IV (*d*) I, III, IV

43. The current processes of production of ethanol from cellulose are based on which of the following microorgansims ?

(*a*) *Trichoderma reesei*
(*b*) *Saccharomyces cerevisiae*
(*c*) Recombinant *E. coli*
(*d*) All of the above

44. Conversion of cellulose to ethanol involves which of the following steps ?

I. Production of cellulase
II. Hydrolysis of cellulose
III. Hexose fermentation
IV. Pentose fermentation.

Options :

(*a*) I, II, III, IV (*b*) II, III, IV
(*c*) I, III, IV (*d*) II, IV

45. The cellulase enzyme systems (produced by both bacteria and fungi) carry which of the following function(s) ?

(*a*) Binding to cellulose.
(*b*) Hydrolysis at the end of a cellulose chain.
(*c*) Cleavage of cellulose chain at an internal site.
(*d*) All of the above.

46. In which of the following areas of bio-ethanol production, biotechnology can make a notable contribution ?

I. Development of more efficient organisms for alcoholic fermentation.
II. Devising a more efficient strategy for use of these microorganisms.
III. To develop organisms capable of utilizing cellulose and hemicellulose.
IV. Practical exploitation of the advantageous features of *Zymomonas mobilis.*

Options :

(*a*) I, II, III, IV (*b*) I, III, IV
(*c*) I, II, III (*d*) II, IV

47. Biological conversion can be improved by which of the following approaches ?

I. By making efficient ethanol producers like *Zymomonas mobilis* cabable of increased substrate utilization.

II. By increasing the ethanol producing ability of such organisms, which have the ability to utilize cellulose and hemicellulose, etc.

III. By more efficient and cheaper methods of ethanol recovery.

IV. Enhancing alcohol tolerance of yeast.

Options :

(*a*) I, III, IV (*b*) II, III, IV
(*c*) I, II, IV (*d*) I, II, III, IV

48. Which of the following is correct about *Copaifera multijuga* ?

I. This leguminous tree is native of Brazil.

II. It grows upto 30 m in height.

III. It can be tapped twice a year.

IV. Tapping yields large volumes of liquid quite similar to diesel oil.

Options :

(*a*) I, II, III, IV (*b*) II, III, IV
(*c*) I, II, III (*d*) I, III, IV

49. Which of the following statements is concerned with future directions for research and development for ethanol production ?

I. Increasing the substrate utilizing ability of yeast and *Z. mobilis.*

II. Reducing alcohol tolerance of yeast.

III. Increasing the ethanol production ability of bacteria capable of utilizing cellulose, hemicellulose, pentoses, etc.

IV. Efficient and cost effective process of continuous recovery of ethanol.

Options :

(*a*) I, II, III, IV (*b*) I, II, III
(*c*) I, III, IV (*d*) II, III, IV

50. Ethanol has which of the following advantages over petrol ?

I. Ethanol has a lower latent heat of vaporization than petrol.

II. Ethanol has a higher octane number (99) than petrol (80-100), as a result; preignition does not occur when ethanol is used in engines set for petrol.

III. Higher octane rating of ethanol allows the compression ratio of the engines to be increased; this results in increased production of power.

IV. Ethanol is burnt more completely so that hydrocarbon emission is drastically lower as compared to that in case of petrol.

Options :

(*a*) I, II, III, IV (*b*) I, II, IV
(*c*) I, III, IV (*d*) II, III, IV

51. Ethanol suffers from which of the following disadvantages ?

I. Ethanol-run engines use about 10% more fuel than petrol.

II. Engines run on ethanol may give starting problems when air is cool.

III. The downstream processing for ethanol recovery is costly as it requires lots of energy.

IV. It reacts with metals used in the alloys of carburators, etc.

Options :

(*a*) I, II, III (*b*) I, II, III, IV
(*c*) II, III, IV (*d*) I, III, IV

52. Which of the following is perhaps the chief reason for limiting the use of bioethanol as fuel ?

(*a*) Ethanol run engines use about 10% more fuel than petrol.

(*b*) Due to highly hydrophilic nature, ethanol can absorb moisture from atmosphere, which interferes with combution and also casues corrosion.

(*c*) The downstream processing for ethanol recovery is costly.

(*d*) Ethanol produces engine starting problems when air is cool.

53. Column A lists microorganisms used for conversion of cellulose to ethanol and column B lists the functions they perform. Match the two columns carefully, and select the correct option from those listed below them.

Column A	Column B
A. *Trichoderma reesei*	1. Pentose removal
B. *S. cerevisiae*	2. Hexose fermentation
C. Recombinant-*E. coli*	3. Cellulose hydrolysis
	4. Pentose fermentation

Options :

(*a*) A3, B2, C1 (*b*) A3, B2, C4

(*c*) A1, B2, C4 (*d*) A3, B4, C2

54. Which of the following features are correct about biodiesel ?

I. It is methyl or ethyl ester of fatty acids.

II. Low-level blends (20% and less) generally do not require any engine modification.

III. It can provide the same pay load capacity as diesel.

IV. It is environmentally clean fuel.

Options :

(*a*) I, II, III, IV (*b*) I, II, IV

(*c*) II, III, IV (*d*) I, III, IV

15.2. FILL IN THE BLANKS

1. The ultimate source of energy for both petroleum-derived fuels and biodiesel is .... and both of them are derived from ....

2. Biogas consists mainly of .... and ....

3. In Brazil, bioethanol is produced from .... and ....

4. The decision of digester design will depend mainly on whether the waste is completely .... or it has .... as well.

5. In India, ... is widely used to produce biogass, locally called ....

6. Animal excreta and agricultural wastes are rich in .... and ....

7. Land fill sites are a type of low-cost ....

8. Land fill sites are being used for biogas recovery on commercial scale in .... and ....

9. Plug-flow type of digesters suffer from .... formation, especially in digesters having large diameters.

10. Film reactors have the problem of .... and .... in the filter.

11. Upflow anaerobic sludge blanket digesters are not suited to treat waste water having .... materials.

12. Acetogenic bacteria oxidise .... by reducing CO_2 to acetic acid, which is then used up by methanogens to generate methane, CO_2 and H_2.

13. Diesel-like liquid obtained from materials of biological origin is called ....

14. The feeding rate of a typical dung-based biogas plant is at the rate of .... kg dung/day.

15. The digesters in various biogas production schemes may be operated under ....or ....conditions.

16. Amount of volatile solids are estimated at .... °C.

17. Biogas yield is measured as .... gas/ kg volatile solids.

18. Plant species producing hydrocarbons usually accumulate them in the form of ....

19. Typical gas yields would be .... m^3/kg volatile solids (VS) for sewage sludge, ... m^3/kg VS for pig excreta and .... m^3/kg VS of cowdung.

20. Some microscopic algae produce H_2 when exposed to low levels of ....

21. Hexoses are obtained from hydrolysis of cellulose in the form of glucose and ....

22. Hemicellulose digestion gives rise to ....

23. Milk weeds, *e.g.*, *Asclepias speciosa*, produce a latex having about .... % hydrocarbon.

24. *Botryococcus braunii* accumulates as much as .... % of its biomass in form of hydrocarbons.

25. In USA, a 20% ethanol: 80% petrol mixture is being marketed as ....

15.3. MARK TRUE OR FALSE

1. In general, biofuels are aimed for use in transport as a substitute for nonrenewable and rapidly declining fossil fuels derived from petroleum.
2. Development of fossil fuels caused a rapid reduction in the use of biomass as energy source, especially in developed countries.
3. Biogas consists mainly of methane (60%) and CO_2 (40%) plus traces of hydrogen (H_2) and several other gases.
4. Lignin is degradable under anaerobic conditions.
5. In general, the biomass is much less energy-dense and, very bulky as compared to fossil fuels.
6. Gobar gas plant is an example of low technology aerobic digester.
7. Acetogenic bacteria remove H_2 and enable the obligate H_2-producing bacteria to continue their function.
8. The pH of slurry in gobar gas plants should of around 10.
9. Under both mesophilic and theromophilic conditions, digestion involves the same bacterial species.
10. It is thought that the biogas technology will develop rapidly as a greater emphasis is placed on organic pollution control.
11. Some algae may accumulate upto 60% of their biomass as lipids, especially when they are grown under conditions of mineral nutrient limitation.
12. Yeasts can utilize pentose sugar to produce ethanol.
13. The commercially produced cellulases are very costly and can not be used for fuel production.
14. Billions of litres of ethanol is produced annually mostly in USA (from maize) and Brazil (from sugarcane).
15. *Botryococcus braunii* is a unicellular alga that accumulates as much as 75% of its biomass in thc form of hydrocarbons.
16. Recovery of ethanol from the fermentation broth is by distillation, which exploits the difference in boiling points of ethanol (87°C) and water (100°C).
17. *Zymomonas mobilis is* an aerobic bacterium.
18. *Z. mobilis* is a better producer of ethanol than yeast as it has a relatively slower growth rate coupled with higher sugar conversion rate.
19. Preignition in internal combustion engines leads to power loss and damage to valves and piston.
20. Ethanol is much less likely to catch fire and explode in cases of fuel leakage, say, due to accidents.

16

ENVIRONMENTAL BIOTECHNOLOGY

16.1. MULTIPLE CHOICE QUESTIONS

1. Which of the following abiotic components of environment contributes in various ways to fulfilment of human needs ?

(*a*) Air (*b*) Water
(*c*) Soil (*d*) All of the above

2. Environment consists of which of the following ?

(*a*) Sum total of biotic factors
(*b*) Sum total of abiotic factors
(*c*) Both (*a*) and (*b*)
(*d*) Both (*a*) and (*b*) minus humans

3. Which of the following constitutes environmental biotechnology ?

(*a*) Waste treatment
(*b*) Waste disposal
(*c*) Technologies generating less waste
(*d*) Both (*a*) and (*b*)

4. Which of the options given in Q. 3 constitutes 'end of pipe' technology ?

5. Which of the options given in Q. 3 consitutes 'front of pipe' technology ?

6. Water analysis is done to achieve which of the following objectives ?

I. To safeguard human health.
II. To maintain and improve the quality of water for various uses like recreation, irrigation, etc.
III. To control the pollution level of water bodies.
IV. To protect and conserve aquatic flora and fauna.

Options :

(*a*) I, II, IV (*b*) I, II, III, IV
(*c*) II, III, IV (*d*) I, III, IV

7. Which of the following properties are studied to determine water quality ?

I. Physical properties
II. Biological properties
III. Chemical properities

Options :

(*a*) I, II (*b*) II, III
(*c*) I, II, III (*d*) I, III

8. Which of the following is the contribution of biotechnology to waste treatment and environmental management ?

I. Development of more sensitive and rapid detection techniques for a variety of pollutants.
II. Technologies for degradation and conversion of readily biodegradable wastes.
III. 'Cleaner' technologies of production, which generate less waste and pollutants.
IV. Safer products, which are far less polluting than their conventional alternatives.

Options :

(*a*) I, II, III, IV (*b*) II, III
(*c*) I, II, III (*d*) II, IV

9. Wastes and pollutants may originate from which of the following human activities ?

I. Agriculture and dairy.
II. Manufacturing and transport.
III. Energy production.
IV. House building and house keeping.

Options :

(*a*) I, II, III (*b*) II, III, IV
(*c*) I, II, III, IV (*d*) I, III, IV

10. Which of the following statements are correct about wastes and pollutants ?

I. Transport is a major contributor to atmospheric pollution.

II. Manufacturing industries using biological materials generate wastes of biological substances, which are biodegradable.

III. House-building and domestic activities generate only non-biodegradable wastes.

IV. Manufacturing industries using biological materials generate wastes that can be recycled by microorganisms.

Options :

(*a*) I, II, III (*b*) I, II, IV
(*c*) I, III, IV (*d*) II, III, IV

11. Xenobiotic compounds may be recalcitrant due to which of the following reasons ?

I. They are not recongnised as substrate by the existing degradative enzymes.

II. Their large molecular size prevents their entry into microbial cells.

III. Inability of the compounds to induce the synthesis of degrading enzymes.

IV. Lack of permeases needed for their transport into microbial cells.

Options :

(*a*) I, II, III, IV (*b*) II, III, IV
(*c*) I, III, IV (*d*) I, II, IV

12. Recalcitrant xenobiotic compounds are highly stable due to the presence of which of the following substitution groups ?

(*a*) Halogens and carbamyl groups
(*b*) Nitro- and sulphonate groups
(*c*) Amino- and methoxy groups
(*d*) All of the above.

13. Which of the following hazards is associated with xenobiotics?

I. At low concentrations, they may cause various skin problems and reduce reproductive potential.

II. Many xenobiotics are recalcitrant and persist in the environment.

III. Certain halogenated hydrocarbons have been shown to be carcinogenic.

IV. Many xenobiotics are recalcitrant and lipophilic; as a consequence, they show bioaccumulation.

Options :

(*a*) I, III, IV (*b*) II, III, IV
(*c*) I, II, IV (*d*) I, II, III, IV

14. Bioaccumulation/biomagnification may occurs due to which of the following reasons ?

(*a*) Xenobiotic compounds are continuously taken up from the environment and accumulated in the lipid deposits of the body.
(*b*) Consumption of these organisms by other organisms leads to further accumulation of xenobiotic compounds in the bodies of latter.
(*c*) The xenobiotic compounds are recalcitrant and lipid soluble.
(*d*) All of the above.

15. ***Assertion (A)***: The chief hazard from biological entities present in wastes is disease spread.

Reason (R): The waste may directly contaminate food or water, or it may facilitate pathogen transmission mediated by vectors.

Options :

(*a*) Both A and R are correct and R sufficiently explains A.
(*b*) Both A and R are correct, but R does not explain A.
(*c*) Only A is correct.
(*d*) Only R is correct.

16. Chemical wastes may be classified into which of the following ?

I. Biodegradable

II. Recalcitrant

III. Nonbiodegradable

Options :

(*a*) I, II (*b*) II, III
(*c*) I, II, III (*d*) I, III

17. Which of the following diseases spread through contaminated water/food ?

(*a*) Amoebiosis and typhoid
(*b*) Cholera and diarrhoea
(*c*) Hepatitis (except B)
(*d*) All of the above

18. Which of the following ***is not an example*** of physical pollutants ?

(*a*) Dust and mechanical stress.
(*b*) Sound pollution and electrical storms.

(*c*) Heavy metals.
(*d*) Radiation and fires.

19. ***Assertion (A)***: The enzyme acetylcholinesterase is used to detect organophosphate insecticides/nerve poisons present in water.

Reason (R): Organophosphate insecticides/nerve poisons inhibit the activity of acetylcholinesterase.

Options :
(*a*) Only A is correct.
(*b*) Only R is correct.
(*c*) Both A and R are correct, but R does not explain A.
(*d*) Both A and R are correct and R correctly explains A.

20. Presence of coliform bacteria in water is indicative of contamination by mammalian excreta and suggestive of the presence of which of the following phathogenic bacteria ?
(*a*) *Vibrio cholerae* (*b*) *Salmonella*
(*c*) *Shigella* (*d*) All of the above

21. Water analysis permits which of the following ?
I. Determination of its suitability for various uses.
II. Development of water quality objectives and standards.
III. Determination of polluting effects of various effluents and wastes discharged in water course.
IV. Setting up of safe standards for discharge of effluents in water bodies.

Options :
(*a*) II, III, IV (*b*) I, II, III, IV
(*c*) I, III, IV (*d*) I, II, III

22. Which of the following pollutants pose immediate threat to humans and is included in the black list ?
(*a*) Oils and hydrocarbons from crude oils.
(*b*) Heavy metals, metalloides and compounds containing them.
(*c*) Organophosphates, cyanides and asbestos.
(*d*) All of the above.

23. Various approaches to waste treatment may be grouped into which of the following categories ?
(*a*) Anaerobic digestion.
(*b*) Biofilters and aerobic digestion.
(*c*) Landfill and burning.
(*d*) All of the above.

24. Which of the following is correct about biofilters ?
I. These devices consist of either a solid support or a two-phase (gas/liquid) system.
II. In the solids-support system, gases to be treated are passed through the solid support layer which has the biological agents.
III. In the two-phase biofilters, the biological agents are immobilized on the membrane on the side of liquid phase.
IV. Due to lack of control on the biomass unpredictable results of bioconversion of gases is obtained in the solid support system.

Options :
(*a*) I, II, III, IV (*b*) II, III, IV
(*c*) I, II, IV (*d*) I, III, IV

25. Which of the following statements are correct about liquid wastes ?
I. They are treated by either aerobic or anaerobic digestion.
II. The main objectives of treatment are to reduce the amount of organic material and to inactivate pathogenic organisms.
III. The solids/sludge recovered from liquid waste may be used as fertilizer in agricultural fields.
IV. Agricultural use of sludge is limited by the presence of heavy metals, exotic xenobiotics, and pathogenic micro-organisms.

Options :
(*a*) I, III, IV (*b*) I, II, III
(*c*) I, II, III, IV (*d*) I, II, IV

26. Landfil sites can be useful in which of following ways ?
(*a*) Reclamation of derelict sites to develop landscaped gardens, etc.
(*b*) As a source of biogass.

(c) As a source of organic fertilizers.
(d) Both (a) and (b).

27. In case of water quality, the quality parameter of biological properties includes which of the following ?
I. Total coliform bacteria.
II. *Salmonella* counts.
III. Faecal coliform counts.
IV. Faecal streptococci counts.
Options :
(a) I, II, III, IV (b) II, III, IV
(c) I, III, IV (d) I, II, IV

28. Solid waste is collected and may be pretreated in some way before being placed in the pit. The pre-treatment may be which of the following ?
I. Sorting of the wastes
II. Mechanical pulverization
III. Incineration
Options :
(a) I, II, III (b) II, III
(c) I, III (d) I, II

29. Among the given microorganisms, which one is the most commonly found in aerobic digestion systems ?
(a) Fungi (b) Bacteria
(c) Protozoa (d) Algae

30. Bioremediation of inorganic contaminants is primarily based on which of the following ?
(a) Animal species (b) Microorganisms
(c) Plant species (d) All of the above

31. The disposal of wastes in landfills presents which of the following hazards ?
I. Leaching of toxic and corrosive materials into surface and underground waters.
II. Offensive odours and methane leakage.
III. Increase in the population of disease vectors like flies.
IV. Fire in the waste materials.
Options :
(a) I, II, III, IV (b) II, III, IV
(c) I, III, IV (d) I, II, IV

32. The water (leachate) from landfills may contain which of the following ?
(a) COD value of 1,000–2,000.
(b) Total solids content upto 6,000–7,000 mg/l.
(c) Sodium upto 800 mg/l.
(d) All of the above.

33. Which of the following statements is correct about landfill management ?
(a) The risk due to methane can be removed by burning or tapping.
(b) The risks of fires, offensive odours and increased vector populations may be circumvented by covering the waste with soil on daily basis.
(c) The risk of damage from landfill leachate may be avoided by lining the pit with an immpermeable material.
(d) All of the above.

34. ***Assertion (A)***: The possibilities of creating a 'Super bug' capable of degrading a wide variety of xenobiotic compounds under a number of conditions in stable association with native microorganisms seems unrealistic.
Reason (R): Microorganisms carrying additional recombinant DNA are poor competitors against native microorganisms.
Options :
(a) Both A and R are correct and R adequately explains A.
(b) Both A and R are correct, but R does not explain A.
(c) Only A is correct.
(d) Only R is correct.

35. Which of the following parameters is used to determine the level of pollution in water bodies like rivers ?
I. Ammonical nitrogen and phosphate content.
II. Biochemical and chemical oxygen demands.
III. Presence of biological indicators.
IV. Suspended solids.
Options :
(a) I, III, IV (b) I, II, III, IV
(c) II, III, IV (d) I, II, III

36. The various parameters used to determine the level of pollution in water bodies, usually, determine which of the following ?
(a) Amounts of organic matter present in the water.
(b) Amounts of important inorganic nutrients.

(*c*) Numbers of bacteria per mililitre of waste water.

(*d*) Both (*a*) and (*b*).

37. Which of the following statements are correct ?

I. BOD estimates the amount of biologically oxidisable organic matter present in water.

II. COD is an estimate of the chemically oxidisable inorganic matter present in water.

III. The relative abundance/absence of certain organisms in the river water serves as a good indicator of the level of pollution.

IV. Measurements of phosphates in water are based on colorimetric assay.

Options :

(*a*) I, III, IV (*b*) II, III, IV
(*c*) I, II, III (*d*) I, II, III, IV

38. Recalcitrant xenobiotic compounds can be grouped into which of the following types ?

1. Halocarbons
2. Synthetic polymers
3. Alkylbenzyl sulphonates
4. Polychlorinated biphenyls
5. Polysaccharides.

Options :

(*a*) 1, 3, 4, 5 (*b*) 1, 2, 3, 4
(*c*) 2, 4, 5 (*d*) 2, 3, 4

39. Which of the following structural features makes recalcitrant xenobiotic compounds resistant to microbial degradation ?

I. Branched linear chains.

II. Presence of hydrogen in the place of halogens in the molecule.

III. Cyclic structures.

IV. Substitution of hydrogen by groups like nitro-, sulphonate, etc.

Options :

(*a*) I, II, III (*b*) II, III, IV
(*c*) I, III, IV (*d*) I, II, III, IV

40. Treatment of the water proceeds through five stages; select the correct order of different stages of water treatment

(*a*) Sludge treatment → preliminary treatment → primary treatment → secondary treatment → tertiary treatment.

(*b*) Preliminary treatment → primary treatment → secondary treatment → tertiary treatment → sludge treatment.

(*c*) Preliminary treatment → sludge treatment → primary treatment → secondary treatment → tertiary treatment.

(*d*) Primary treatment → secondary treatment → tertiary treatment → preliminary treatment → sludge treatment.

41. Which of the following waste water treatments is an anaerobic process ?

(*a*) Primary treatment
(*b*) Secondary treatment
(*c*) Tertiary treatment
(*d*) Sludge treatment

42. Preliminary treatment for waste water is necessary to prevent which of the following ?

(*a*) Clogging of pipelines
(*b*) Damage to pump
(*c*) Interference with subsequent process
(*d*) All of the above.

43. Which of the following is correct about aerobic digestion of waste water ?

(*a*) Bacteria are the most common organisms.

(*b*) Bacterial population may be more than 10^9 cells/ml.

(*c*) Bacteria are responsbile for the removal of about 80–90% of the BOD.

(*d*) All of the above

44. Practical application of microbes for xenobiotic degradation is facilitated by which of the following ?

(*a*) Supply of sufficient nutrients or cometabolites.

(*b*) Maintenance of the xenobiotic compounds at nontoxic levels.

(*c*) Provision of microbial population or inoculum.

(*d*) All of the above.

45. Rotating biological contactors offer which of the following advantages ?

I. Low land requirement

II. Very low maintenance

III. Large-scale application

Options :
(*a*) I, II (*b*) I, II, III
(*c*) II, III (*d*) I, III

46. During determination of water quality, which of the following chemical properties are measured ?
I. BOD and COD
II. Total nitrogen and phosphate
III. Total pesticides
IV. pH

Options :
(*a*) I, II, IV (*b*) I, II, III
(*c*) I, II, III, IV (*d*) II, III, IV

47. Aeration in the digester vessel is achieved by which of the following ?
I. Mechanical stirring
II. Generating coarse air bubble stream from a system of pipes.
III. Injecting a fine stream of air bubbles through porous ceramic rocks.
IV. Introducing pure O_2 as a fine stream of bubbles.

Options :
(*a*) I, II, III, IV (*b*) II, III, IV
(*c*) I, III, IV (*d*) II, III

48. The quality of treated effluent from the digester depends mainly on which of the following ?
(*a*) Sludge loading rate
(*b*) Organic loading rate
(*c*) Residence time
(*d*) All of the above

49. NO_3^- is removed from water by the action of which of the following bacteria ?
(*a*) *Pseudomonas* (*b*) *Micrococcus*
(*c*) *Alcaligenes* (*d*) All of the above

50. Which of the following statements are correct about denitrification ?
I. Denitrification bacteria convert NO^{-3} into N_2.
II. Denitrification may also produce various oxides of nitrogen in addition to N_2.
III. Denitrifying bacteria are aerobic.
IV. Denitrification is often achieved by alternating aerobic and anaerobic conditions.

Options :
(*a*) I, II, IV (*b*) I, II, III, IV
(*c*) II, III, IV (*d*) I, III, IV

51. Sewage contains which of the following pathogenic organisms ?
(*a*) Bacteria causing typhoid, cholera, diarrhoea
(*b*) Protozoa causing amoebic dysentry, giardiasis
(*c*) Viruses causing poliomyletis, hepatitis, gastroenteritis
(*d*) All of the above

52. Protozoa are represented in waste waters by which of the following ?
(*a*) Amoebal forms (*b*) Ciliates
(*c*) Flagellates (*d*) All of the above

53. Consider the options given in Q. 52 and select the one that is the most common type of protozoa found in waste waters ?

54. Consider the options given in Q. 52 and select the one which forms the most diverse group ?

55. Efficiency of anaerobic digestion can be enhanced by which of the following ?
(*a*) By using solid support to retain biomass.
(*b*) By recycling the active biomass.
(*c*) By limiting the biomass loss to a rate compatible with high population density in the digester.
(*d*) Any of the above.

56. Bioremediation of organic contaminants is primarily based on which of the following ?
(*a*) Microorganisms naturally present at the site.
(*b*) Microbial inoculants developed in the laboratory and introduced at the site.
(*c*) Suitable plants planted at the site.
(*d*) All of the above.

57. Oil spills cause severe damage to the ecosystems and pose which of the following threats ?
(*a*) Ground water pollution due to percolation
(*b*) Air pollution due to evoporation
(*c*) Fire
(*d*) All of the above

58. Which of the following statements ***is not correct*** ?
(*a*) The U.S. Environment Protection Agency and the Exxon company used microorganisms to clean up Alaskan beaches contaminated by the Valdez oil spill.

(*b*) In India, a consortium of bacterial species has been developed to combat oilspills and oily sludge; the inoculant is aptly called 'Oilzapper'.
(*c*) Inoculation with Oilzapper reduced oil sludge contamination in soil to merely 0.5% in 360 days from the initial 13.41%.
(*d*) Oilzapper has not been effective in field trials.

59. Biofilms contain a complex community of organisms, which degrade carbohydrates, proteins, lipids, etc. into which of the following ?

I. CO_2 II. PO_4^{3-}
III. NO_3^- IV. SO_4^{2-}

Options :
(*a*) I, II, III, IV (*b*) I, II, IV
(*c*) II, III, IV (*d*) I, II, III

60. The anaerobic digestion process involves a wide variety of organisms which digest the organic molecules, such as lipids, proteins, carbohydrates etc., into mainly which of the following ?
(*a*) NO_3^- and PO_4^{3-}
(*b*) CH_4 and CO_2
(*c*) SO_4^{2-} and CO
(*d*) All of the above

61. Which of the following heterotrophic bacteria are responsible for oxidation of organic molecules ?
(*a*) *Pseudomonas* and *Escherichia*
(*b*) *Streptococcus* and *Salmonella*
(*c*) *Shigella* and *Aerobacter*
(*d*) All of the above

62. Which of the following ***is not correct*** about halocarbons ?
(*a*) They contain different numbers of halogen atoms in the place of He atoms.
(*b*) They are used as solvents, in condensor units of cooling systems, etc.
(*c*) The C_1–C_2 haloalkanes escape into the atmosphere where they destroys the protective ozone layer.
(*d*) Pesticides leach into water bodies, where many of them are subjected to biomagnification.

63. Which of the following is correct about alkylbenzyl sulphonates ?
(*a*) These are surface-active detergents.
(*b*) Sulphonate group present at one end resists microbial degradation.
(*c*) At present, alkylbenzyl sulphonates are biodegraded by β-oxidation from their alkyl ends.
(*d*) All of the above.

64. Phytoremediation may occur due to which of the following ?
(*a*) Accumulation of the organic waste in plant tissues.
(*b*) Translocation of the organic waste to leaf and volatilization from there.
(*c*) The organic waste may be metabolized in plant tissues or in the rhizosphere itself.
(*d*) Any of the above.

65. Phytoremediation has which of the following inherent technical limitations ?
I. The contaminant must be present within the root zones of actively growing plants.
II. The site must be sufficiently large for easy plant cultivation.
III. It takes much longer than do 'dig and dump' techniques.

Options :
(*a*) I, II, III (*b*) II, III
(*c*) I, III (*d*) I, II

66. For phytoremediation of flyash, seedlings of which of the following trees are established at abandoned flyash ponds/dams ?
(*a*) *Eucalyptus* (*b*) *Melia*
(*c*) Poplar (*d*) All of the above

67. Continued exposure of microorganisms to xenobiotic compounds can often lead to the evolution of metabolic processes needed to wholly or partly degrade the xenobiotic. These capabilities may arise due to which of the following ?
(*a*) Mutation
(*b*) Transfer of plasmid-borne genes
(*c*) Transformation
(*d*) Both (*a*) and (*b*).

68. Which of the options given in Q. 67 can be expected to modify the active site of an enzyme so that it has an increased affinity for the xenobiotic compounds ?

69. Which of the following is correct about oxidation of aromatic hydrocarbons ?

I. These are oxidized by oxidoreductase to catechol.
II. Catechol is further metabolised by meta-ring cleavage pathway to yield 2-hydroxymyconic semialdehyde.
III. 2-Hydroxymyconic semialdehyde finally yields acetaldehyde and pyruvate.

Options :
(*a*) I, II (*b*) II, III
(*c*) I, II, III (*d*) I, III

70. Which of the following statements are correct about aliphatic hydrocarbons ?

I. They may be saturated or unsaturated
II. Biodegradation of *n*-alkanes is catalyzed by oxygenase to produce carboxylic acid, which is then degraded by β-oxidation.
III. *n*-Alkanes of 10-24 carbons are the most slowly biodegraded.
IV. Saturated aliphatics are easier to degrade than unsaturated ones.

Options :
(*a*) I, II, III, IV (*b*) I, II, IV
(*c*) I, III, IV (*d*) II, III, IV

71. Alicyclic hydrocarbons are present naturally in which of the following?
(*a*) Wax from plants
(*b*) Microbial lipids
(*c*) Crude oils
(*d*) All of the above

72. Which of the following statements are correct about aromatic hydrocarbons ?

I. They are rather stable.
II They are oxidised by di-oxygenases to catechol.
III. Catechol is further metabolised by two separate pathways, called ortho-cleavage pathway and meta-cleavage pathway.
IV. Benzene is degraded by the ortho-cleavage pathway.

Options :
(*a*) I, II, III (*b*) II, III, IV
(*c*) I, II, III, IV (*d*) I, III, IV

73. The aerobic degradation of halogenated aromatic compounds usually involves which of the following ?

I. Addition of –OH group by a di-oxygenase to yeild chlorinated catechols.
II. Cleavage of the ring by ortho- or meta-cleavage.
III. Elimination of the halogen from the straight chain (aliphatic) product.
IV. Degradation.

Options :
(*a*) I, II, III (*b*) I, II, III, IV
(*c*) I, II, IV (*d*) I, III, IV

74. Which of the following is correct about oxidation of aromatic hydrocarbons.

I. These are oxidised by di-oxygenase to catechol.
II. Catechol is further metabolized by ortho-ring cleavage pathway to yield cis, cis-muconate.
III. Subsequent catabolism of cis, cis-muconate yields acetyl-CoA and succinate.

Options :
(*a*) I, II, III (*b*) I, III
(*c*) II, III (*d*) I, II

75. Which of the following ***is not related*** to green-house gas ?
(*a*) CH_2 (*b*) CO_2
(*c*) O_2 (*d*) CFC

76. Fluoride pollution mainly affects which of the following ?
(*a*) Heart (*b*) Kidney
(*c*) Brain (*d*) Teeth

77. Biochemical oxygen demand measures which of the following ?
(*a*) Industrial pollution
(*b*) Air pollution
(*c*) Dissolved O_2 needed by microbes to decompose organic waste.
(*d*) Oxygen need to support microorganism growth.

78. Smog is the product of which of the following ?
(*a*) Smoke (*b*) Fog
(*c*) Soot (*d*) Both (*a*) and (*b*)

79. 'Green-house effect' is related to which of the following ?

(*a*) Global warming
(*b*) Global afforestation
(*c*) Deforestation
(*d*) Both (*a*) and (*c*)

80. Increasing skin cancer and rate of mutation are the result of which of the following ?
(*a*) Acid rain (*b*) Ozone depletion
(*c*) SO_2 pollution (*d*) CO_2 pollution

81. Which of the following diseases is caused by eating fish inhabiting mercury contaminated water ?
(*a*) Minamata disease
(*b*) Osteosclerosis
(*c*) Hashimoto disease
(*d*) Brain fever

82. Depletion of ozone layer is caused by which of the following ?
(*a*) CO_2 (*b*) SO_2^-
(*c*) CFC (*d*) Both (*b*) and (*c*)

83. The atmosphere of metro cities is polluted by which of the following ?
(*a*) Pesticides
(*b*) Automobile exhausts
(*c*) House-hold wastes
(*d*) Radioactive fallout

84. Which of the following associates with the blood haemoglobin more rapidly than oxygen ?
(*a*) CO (*b*) CO_2
(*c*) SO_4 (*d*) NO

85. Which of the following decibles of sound becomes hazardous noise pollution ?
(*a*) > 20 (*b*) > 80
(*c*) > 120 (*d*) > 140

86. Which of the following plants can be used as indicators of SO_2 pollution of air ?
(*a*) Liverworts
(*b*) Hornworts
(*c*) Epiphytic lichens
(*d*) Fern

87. Attack of asthama in certain persons may be due to which of the following ?
(*a*) Inhalation of some airborne pollution.
(*b*) Exposure to cold temperature.
(*c*) Exposure to certain pollen grains.
(*d*) All of the above

88. Which of the following gases contributes the maximum to the 'green-house effect' ?
(*a*) CO_2 (*b*) CFC
(*c*) CH_4 (*d*) N_2O

89. Which of the following poses the greatest risk ?
(*a*) Nuclear plants
(*b*) Thermal power plants
(*c*) Biogas plants
(*d*) Hydroelectric plants

90. Which of the following is an example of non-renewable resources ?
(*a*) Petroleum (*b*) Biological agents
(*c*) Natural gas (*d*) Both (*a*) and (*c*)

91. Maximum deposition of DDT will occur in which of the following ?
(*a*) Phytoplankton (*b*) Fish
(*c*) Crab (*d*) Sea gull

92. Which of the following green-house gases is being generated by agricultural fields ?
(*a*) Sulphur dioxide (*b*) SO_3
(*c*) Nitrous oxide (*d*) Ammonia

93. 'Ozone day' is observed on which of the following ?
(*a*) September 16 (*b*) June 5
(*c*) May 1 (*d*) December 25

94. Which of the following is an example of a renewable resource ?
(*a*) Plants (*b*) Animals
(*c*) Microorganisms (*d*) All of the above

95. Ozone depletion in the stratosphere will cause which of the following ?
(*a*) Global warming
(*b*) Increased sea level
(*c*) Increased incidence of skin cancer
(*d*) All of the above

96. Ozone layer of upper atmosphere is being destroyed by which of the following ?
(*a*) Smog
(*b*) Photochemical oxidants
(*c*) CFC
(*d*) Soot

97. Bioremediation of organic wastes is generally based on which of the following ?
(*a*) Bacteria (*b*) Animal species
(*c*) Plant species (*d*) Both (*b*) and (*c*)

98. Which of the options given in Q. 89 is the most ecofriendly ?

16.2. FILL IN THE BLANKS

1. The term environmental biotechnology is applied only to the end of the pipe technologies using ....
2. Presence of coliform bacteria in water is indicative of contamination by ....
3. Abbreviation HPLC stands for ....
4. Principle of microbial infallibility was proposed by .... in 1965.
5. A .... species strain produces biotin but it can not degrade cyclohexane.
6. Diarrhoea, amoebiosis, hepatitis (except B) diseases spread through contamination of food/water by ....
7. Xenobiotic compounds may be recalcitrant due to a lack of the enzyme .... needed for their transport into the microbial cells.
8. Cleaner technologies are applicable to .... pollutants.
9. When the entire solid waste is dumped into pits, the process is called ....
10. In cell emplacement and trench methods, the soil for covering the waste is dug from the site of the ....
11. Chemical oxygen demand (COD) is always .... than biological oxygen demand (BOD).
12. Primary treatment of waste water reduces BOD by about ....
13. Presence of phosphate in waste water is usually removed by precipation using .... or ....
14. Fungi usually occur as an external biofilm; they help in the removal of ...., ... and ....
15. Most of the pathogens present in sewage are contributed by ....
16. Most of the pathogenic viruses present in sewage are inactivated during ....
17. The protozoa feed on nutrients and ...., and thereby convert smaller particles into larger ones, which may help in the removal by ....
18. In case of aerobic waste water treatment, *Zoogloea ramigera* secretion leads to .... formation, which is recycled in the activated sludge process.
19. The aerobic digestion process involves a wide variety of organisms of which .... are the most predominant.
20. The sewage or municipal sludge is treated to reduce .... and........... and to stabilise the solids before final disposal.
21. The recalcitrant nature of halocarbons is due to their ....
22. Many xenobiotics, including DDT and PCB's are both recalcitrant and lipophilic, as a consequence they show .... often by a factor of 10^4–10^6.
23. The recalcitrant nature of polychlorinated biphenyls is mainly due to their halogenation and .... structure.
24. In case of bioremediation, degradation is the mode of elimination mostly in case of .... compounds, while .... are assimilated.
25. The first plant-based remediation system was installed over 300 year ago in .... for the treatment of municipal sewage.
26. Frequently, oxidation of xenobiotics involves .... or ....
27. Benzene is degraded by the .... cleavage pathway.
28. Usually, the removal of halogens from halogenated aromatic compounds occurs by its subsitution with an .... or ....
29. TOL plasmids encode the enzymes for .... degradation.
30. .... species has plasmid-borne genes for dihydroxylation of one of the ring of 4-chlorobiphenyl, its *meta* ring cleavage and subsequent degradation to produce ....
31. A *Pseudomonas putida* strain cleaves the ring of 4-chlorobenzoate by *ortho* pathway to ultimately generate .... and succinate
32. A mixture of *Nocardia* species degrades cyclohexane but is unable to produce ....

16.3. MARK TRUE OR FALSE

1. Environment consists of all the factors outside an organism.
2. Presence of coliform bacteria in water is suggestive of the presence of pathogenic bacteria like *Vibrio cholerae*, *Salmonella*, *Shigella*, etc.
3. Presence of organic compounds is determined by HPLC.
4. Biotechnological approaches are applied to the management of environmental problems.
5. Xenobiotic compounds, which are recalcitrant in nature are soluble in water.
6. In general, the more complex is the structure of a xenobiotic compound, the more resistant it is to biodegradation.
7. In general, the disease vector population increases with an increase in the accumulation of organic wastes, and it declines with sanitation and hygiene.
8. Cleaning technologies are only feasible option for recalcitrant and non-biodegradable pollutants.
9. Typhoid disease is spread through contamination of water/food with human, poultry, pests and rat excreta.
10. It is highly desirable that landfills are located in an unused area or a derelict land.
11. Waste water promotes microbial and plant growth, which depletes oxygen from the water resulting in the death of fish and other fauna.
12. Rotating biological contractors are suited for large-scale application.
13. The activated sludge process is a typical example of dispersed growth digesters.
14. The sludge loading rate, *i.e.*, the quantity of activated sludge returned to the dispersed growth digesters, is easy to control and can be varied to achieve the maximum possible reduction in BOD.
15. In waste water, the organic materials, are present in lower concentratiȯns than in nature.
16. Synthetic polymers are recalcitrant mainly due to their insolubility in water and molecular size.
17. Carrots are used to absorb DDT, and harvested, air-dired and incinerated to destroy the DDT.
18. Active microbial communities associated with plants may degrade the organic contaminants.
19. Volatalization is useful for the removal of mercury.
20. Xenobiotics degraded by both gratuitous and co-metabolisms need not be similar to the natural substrates of the enzymes involved in their degradation.
21. Release of genetically engineered microbes (GEMs) in the environment is illegal in many countries.
22. *Acinetobactor* and *P. putida* act in tandem to degrade completely the xenobiotic 4-chlorobiphenyl, which neither of them can accomplish on its own.
23. A mixture of *Nocardia* species and *Pseudomonas* species strains would breakdown cyclohexane, but neither of them can do it alone.

17

BIOSAFETY

17.1. MULTIPLE CHOICE QUESTIONS

1. Physical containment relates to which of the following ?

(*a*) Containment equipment
(*b*) Laboratory design
(*c*) Special procedures
(*d*) All of the above.

2. Which of the following is considered as primary physical containment ?

(*a*) Laboratory design
(*b*) Containment equipment
(*c*) Special procedures
(*d*) Both (*a*) and (*b*)

3. Consider the options given in Q. 2 and pick the correct option that lists the secondary physical containment ?

4. It is feared that transgenic plants, may lead to which of the following ?

(*a*) Transfer of their transgenic feature to weeds.
(*b*) May themseleves become weeds.
(*c*) Degrade the environment.
(*d*) All of the above.

5. In the early 1970s which of the following were considered as the possible potential health hazards of cloning recombinant DNA molecules ?

(*a*) Molecular biologists may not be well-versed with the laboratory practices needed to handle serious human and animal pathogens.
(*b*) 'Hybrid organisms' could be created with biological activities of an unpredictable nature.
(*c*) 'Hybrid organisms' may escape from the laboratory with unpredictable consequences.
(*d*) All of the above.

6. Consider the following activities :

1. Risk evaluation
2. Hazard identification
3. Hazard analysis
4. Consequence analysis
5. Risk determination

Select their correct order as involved in the process of risk assessment.

Options :

(*a*) 2, 3, 4, 5, 1 (*b*) 4, 5, 2, 1, 3
(*c*) 1, 2, 3, 5, 4 (*d*) 1, 3, 4, 2, 5

7. The concerns given as the options of Q. 5 were examined by a committee of National Academy of Sciences (USA) in 1974; it made which of the following recommendations.

I. Certain types of experiments, *e.g.*, cloning of genes for bacterial toxins, etc., be deferred.
II. Use of caution in experiments linking animal DNAs to bacterial, phage or plasmid DNAs.
III. NIH, USA be requested to set up an advisory committee on recombinant DNA to oversee experimental programmes to develop procedures to minimize hazards and devise guidelines.
IV. Human cloning experiments can be exempted from scrutiny.

Options :
(*a*) I, II, III, IV (*b*) I, II, III
(*c*) I, III, IV (*d*) II, III, IV

8. A transgenic variety of which of the following crops had to be withdrawn from cultivation following deaths due to allergy ?
(*a*) Maize (*b*) Soybean
(*c*) Tomato (*d*) *Brassica napus*

9. In February 1975, a historic international meeting was convened about cloning of recombinant DNA molecule at Asilomar California; it reached which of the following conclusions ?
I. Certain experiments should be deferred.
II. Most of the work on recombinant DNA could proceed with appropriate safety measures.
III. Potential risks were assigned to different types of experiments.
IV. Such bacteria and plasmids that could not survive in the environment, if they escaped from the laboratory should be developed.

Options :
(*a*) I, II, III, IV (*b*) II, III
(*c*) I, II, IV (*d*) I, III

10. Which of the following ***is not correct*** about NIH guidelines ?
(*a*) The first NIH guidelines were prepared in 1975.
(*b*) NIH guidelines were more liberal than the recommendations of the Asilomar Conference.
(*c*) The guidelines were revised after two years.
(*d*) In 1977, NIH prepared an Environmental Impact Statement.

11. By 1981, most cloning experiments in which of the following microorganisms were considered exempt from other requirements of NIH guidelines ?
I. Certain strains of *Bacillus subtilis*
II. *E. coli* K12
III. *Saccharomyces cerevisiae*
IV. *Xanthomonas oryzae*

Options :
(*a*) II, III, IV (*b*) I, II, III, IV
(*c*) I, II, III (*d*) I, III, IV

12. Which of the following ***is not correct*** about NIH guidelines ?
(*a*) A major revision of the guidelines was effected in 1982.
(*b*) In the revision, the containment levels were made more stringent
(*c*) Experiments that were previously prohibited, were changed to category requiring review and approval by NIH.
(*d*) In USA, the NIH guidelines are followed by all federal agencies that fund research on recombinant DNA.

13. For biosafety considerations, modern biotechnology includes which of the following ?
I. Recombinant DNA techniques.
II. Direct injection of nucleic acids into cells or organelles.
III. Fusion of cells beyond the taxonomic family that overcomes natural physiological, reproductive or recom-bination barriers.

Options :
(*a*) I, II, III (*b*) I, III
(*c*) I, II (*d*) II, III

14. Which of the following terms ***is not used*** as synonym of planned introduction ?
(*a*) Field testing
(*b*) Deliberate release
(*c*) Contained use
(*d*) Deliberate introduction

15. The biosafety guidelines are developed to ensure an adequate level of protection during which of the following activities of modern biotechnology ?
(*a*) Safe transfer (*b*) Handling
(*c*) Use of GMOs (*d*) All of the above

16. The NIH, USA guidelines specify the practices for constructing and handling which of the following ?
(*a*) Recombinant DNA molecules.
(*b*) Organisms and viruses containing recombinant DNA molecules.
(*c*) Products obtained from (*b*).
(*d*) Both (*a*) and (*b*).

17. Risk assessment involves determination of the potential and anticipated adverse effects of which of the following ?

I. Recombinant DNA research to the concerned workers.
II. Product of recombinant DNA research on human health.
III. Environment consequent to accidental or deliberate release of genetically modified organisms or as a result of their consumption.

Options :

(*a*) I, II (*b*) I, II, III
(*c*) I, III (*d*) II, III

18. In case of which of the following products, an empirical approach based on data obtained through experimentation about the source of potential hazards has proved satisfactory ?

(*a*) Pesticides (*b*) Drugs
(*c*) Vaccines (*d*) All of the above

19. In risk assessment, a lack of scientific knowledge or scientific consensus should not necessarily be interpreted as indicating which of the following ?

(*a*) A particular level of risk
(*b*) Absence of risk
(*c*) Acceptable risk
(*d*) Any of the above.

20. The assessment of risk during laboratory research is usually done in which of the following steps ?

(*a*) Initial risk assessment
(*b*) Comprehensive risk assessment
(*c*) Advanced risk assessment
(*d*) Both (*a*) and (*b*)

21. The chief objectives of risk assessment during laboratory research are to decide about which of the following of the proposed research ?

(*a*) Laboratory procedures
(*b*) Biological containment
(*c*) Physical containment
(*d*) All of the above

22. On the basis of their potential effects on a healthy adult human, organisms can be classified into which of the following ?

I. Risk group 1 II. Risk group 2
III. Risk group 3 IV. Risk group 4

Options :

(*a*) I, II, III, IV (*b*) II, III, IV
(*c*) I, III, IV (*d*) I, II, IV

23. In which of the following risk groups, ***agents are not associated*** with disease in healthy humans ?

(*a*) Risk group 3 (*b*) Risk group 1
(*c*) Risk group 2 (*d*) Risk group 4

24. Which of options given in Q. 23 is concerned with agents which are associated with such serious or lethal human diseases for which preventive or therapeutic interventions may be available ?

25. In Q. 23, which of the options is concerned with organisms which are associated with such human diseases, which are rarely serious and for which preventive or therapeutic interventions are often available ?

26. In Q. 23, which of the options is concerned with organisms, which cause serious or lethal disease for which preventive or therapeutic invention are not usually available ?

27. ***Statement (S)***: In India, the Ministry of Environment and Forests (MOEF) promulgated in Dec. 1989 the rules and procedures for the manufacture, import, use, research and relase of GMOs as well as products made from such organisms; these were done under the provisions of Environment Protection Act (EPA), 1986.

Misuse (M): Any violation and noncompliance, would attract the punitive actions provided under the EPA.

Options :

(*a*) Both S and M are correct and M applies to S.
(*b*) Both S and M are correct, but M does not apply to S.
(*c*) Only S is correct.
(*d*) Only M is correct.

28. Which of the following ***is not correct*** about Biosafety Guidelines in India ?

(*a*) Initially, the Indian Recombinant DNA Safety Guidelines and Regulations were prepared in 1990 by Recombinant DNA Advisory Committee, Deptt. of Biotechnology, New Delhi.
(*b*) The Indian Recombinant DNA Safety Guidelines and Regulations were revised in 1994.
(*c*) Field trials, in India, using transgenic plants began in 1995.

(*d*) Cananda become the first country to begin commercial use of virus resistant transgenic tobacco and tomato in the early 1990.

29. Which of the following statements is correct about comprehensive risk assessment ?

(*a*) It is done after the initial risk assessment.

(*b*) The level of containment appropriate for an experiment is decided on the basis of comprehensive risk assessment.

(*c*) The containment level for the experiment may, in the end, be comparable to that of the risk group (RG) of the agent or it may be raised or lowered as a result of the comprehensive risk assessement.

(*d*) All of the above.

30. It is feared that genetically engineered microorganisms may disturb the ecosystem and its processes, in which of the following ways ?

(*a*) They may rapidly multiply and out-complete the native microbes.

(*b*) They may transfer genes related to virulence or pathogenesis into the native bacterial populations.

(*c*) Both (*a*) and (*b*)

(*d*) They may cause unexpected health hazards.

31. Genetically modified plants could pose biological and ecological risks that may be summed up as which of the following ?

I. Production of toxic or allergenic metabolites.

II. Unexpected new susceptabilities to pathogens.

III. Transmission of new traits to related sexually compatible weed species.

IV. The ecosystems may be disturbed by their dispersal, persistence or altered reaction to parasites, symbionts or competitors.

Options :

(*a*) I, II, III (*b*) I, II, III, IV
(*c*) I, II, IV (*d*) II, III, IV

32. During assessment of risk on a case-by-case basis, which of the following factors should be considered ?

I. The biological characteristics of the recipient organisms.

II. Taxonomic status and the relevant biological characteristics of the donor organisms.

III. Characteristics of the vector, including its origin, source and host range.

IV. Genetic characteristics of the DNA insert, the function it specifies and/or characteristics of the modification introduced.

Options :

(*a*) I, II, III, IV (*b*) I, III, IV
(*c*) I, II, III (*d*) II, III, IV

33. Risk assessment in case of planned release of transgenic crops may take into account which of the following ?

I. Nature of marker genes.

II. The characteristics of promoters in terms of whether they are organ-specific or consitutive.

III. Location and proximity of related crops in relation to isolation distance needed for prevention for pollination.

IV. Proximity of wild relatives and the distance of interpollination with such relatives.

Options :

(*a*) I, II, IV (*b*) II, III, IV
(*c*) I, III, IV (*d*) I, II, III, IV

34. In case of transgenic plants, which of the following are the main concerns related to their planned introduction ?

I. Virus resistance genes may provide opportunities for evolution of newer virulent strains by recombination.

II. Insect resistant plants, would be cultivated on a large scale; this may lead to evolution of resistant insect biotypes.

III. Transgenic plants may affect the flora and fauna of their phyllosphere and rhizosphere.

IV. The products of transgenes may pose health hazards.

Options :

(*a*) I, III, IV (*b*) II, III, IV
(*c*) I, II, III, IV (*d*) I, II, III

35. During assessment of risk from food obtained from transgenic varieties of crops, which of the following is evaluated ?

I. The food crop that has been modified.

II. The potential for introduced DNA to encode harmful substances.

III. The safety of proteins encoded by transgenes.

IV. Proof that known plant toxicants and important nutrients are within acceptable levels in the new variety.

Options :

(*a*) I, II, III, IV (*b*) II, III
(*c*) I, II, III (*d*) I, III

36. ***Assertion (A)*** : Cry proteins, in general, have no adverse effect on higher animals, including mammals.

Reason (R) : The specific receptors [at least for CryIA(b)] are absent from the gastrointestinal tracts of mammals, including humans.

Options :

(*a*) Only A is correct.
(*b*) Only R is correct.
(*c*) Both A and R are correct, but R does not explain A.
(*d*) Both A and R are correct, and R sufficiently explains A.

37. Which of the following is correct about GM foods ?

I. GM foods include foods and additives obtained from genetically modified organisms.

II. Japan has announced mandatory evaluation of GM food for potential health risk.

III. European Union has adopted legislation requiring mandatory labelling of all GM food.

IV. US Food and Drug Administration (FDA) requires the food to be labelled as genetically modified only if the changes introduced through genetic engineering have an impact on the safety or nutrition of the food itself.

Options :

(*a*) I, II, III, IV (*b*) II, II, IV
(*c*) I, III, IV (*d*) I, II, III

38. ***Assertion (A)***: Labelling of GM food is considered desirable.

Reason (R): It gives the consumer the choice of decision to have GM food.

Options :

(*a*) Only A is correct.
(*b*) Only R is correct.
(*c*) Both A and R are correct but R does not explain A.
(*d*) Both A and R are correct and R roughly explains A.

39. Which of the following ***is not correct*** ?

(*a*) Oral exposure to transgenic tomoto containing Cry protein poses no additional risk to human and animal health.
(*b*) In general, the quality of produce from *cry* gene carrying transgenic crops is regarded different from that from the nontransgenic plants of the same variety.
(*c*) Cowpea trypsin inhibitors do show some adverse effects on rats in nutritional studies.
(*d*) Significant hypertrophy of small intestine and altered enzyme activities in brush border cells occur due to wheat germ agglutinin.

40. The α-amylase inhibitor from *Phaseolus vulgaris* (rajma) caused allergy when expressed in which of the following by Australian Scientists ?

(*a*) Soybean (*b*) Tomato
(*c*) Peas (*d*) Maize

41. The α-amylase inhibitor gene described in Q. 40 was transferred to modify which of the following traits ?

(*a*) Insect resistance
(*b*) Amino acid balance
(*c*) Food digestibility
(*d*) Both (*a*) and (*c*)

42. In case of biological containment, initially, NIH guidelines required the use of *E. coli* strains and vectors that were severely debilitated, so that they could not infect humans, survive and spread outside the laboratory, and transfer the introduced foreign genes readily into other organisms.

These objectives can be achieved using which of the following ?

I. Autotrophic mutants of *E. coli.*
II. *rec*A$^-$ strains
III. Plasmid vectors that are non-self transmissible and non-mobilizable
IV. *E. coli* strains not carrying a transposon or antibiotic resistance gene.

Options :
(*a*) II, III, IV (*b*) I, II, III, IV
(*c*) I, II, III (*d*) I, III, IV

43. The host-vector (HV) systems for prokaryotes are grouped into which of the following ?

I. Host vector 1 systems
II. Host vector 2 systems
III. Host vector 3 systems
IV. Host vector 4 systems

Options :
(*a*) I, II, IV (*b*) I, II, III
(*c*) I, II (*d*) I, II, III, IV

44. In case of *E. coli,* the host for any HV1 system is which of the following ?
(*a*) Strain K-12
(*b*) A derivative of strain K-12
(*c*) Either (*a*) or (*b*)
(*d*) Strain chi 1776

45. The vector under host-vector 1 system includes which of the following ?
(*a*) Nonconjugative plasmids
(*b*) Derivative of nonconjugative plasmids
(*c*) Variants of bacteriophages
(*d*) All of the above

46. ***Risk (R)***: Dispersal of pollen and/or seeds produced by transgenic plants may cause damage to the environment.

Solution (S): Use of male sterile lines has been advocated.

Options :
(*a*) Both R and S are correct and S provides real solution for R.
(*b*) Both R and S are correct, but S does not provide adequate solution for R.
(*c*) Only R is correct.
(*d*) Only S is correct.

47. Effective dissemination of plant-associated microorganisms beyond the green house can be prevented by using which of the following ?
(*a*) Organisms that have been genetically disabled to survive in nature.
(*b*) Organisms whose natural mode of transmission requires injury to the host.
(*c*) Organisms which require another organisms for their survival.
(*d*) Both (*a*) and (*b*).

48. The type of regulation necessary during field trials should depend on which of the following ?
(*a*) Ability of the modified plants to survive in nature.
(*b*) Their ability for dispersal and reproduction.
(*c*) Their ability to hybridize with crop and weed plants.
(*d*) All of the above.

49. Which of the following is correct about transmission of transgenes from one crop species to another ?
(*a*) In case of cross-pollinated species, isolation by distance is rarely sufficient to prevent inter-population mating.
(*b*) If male sterility is introduced into transgenic cross-pollinated crops, it can check the movement of transgenes through pollen.
(*c*) If transgenes are integrated in the chloroplast genome, it would almost eliminate the transmission of transgene through pollen grains.
(*d*) All of the above.

50. Which of the following ***is not correct*** about Cry proteins.
(*a*) Cry proteins are rapidly degraded by the stomach juices of vertebrates.
(*b*) They could have harmful effects on non-target insect species.
(*c*) It has been reported that Cry proteins leak into soil from transgenic maize roots, where they persist for over 3 weeks.
(*d*) The Cry proteins present in the soil become associated with soil clay/humus, and become prone to microbial degradation.

51. *Assertion (A)*: Use of biological containment for genetically engineered microbes (GEMs) is strongly advocated.
Reason (R): A higher survival of genetically modified microbes will enhance the risk.
Options :
(*a*) Both A and R are correct and R advocates A.
(*b*) Both A and R are correct, but R does not advocate R.
(*c*) Only A is correct.
(*d*) Only R is correct.

52. The survival of GEMs in nature, and gene transfer from them to native bacterial population can be minimized by which of the following strategies ?
1. Use of *RecA*$^-$ strains.
2. Use of auxotrophic mutants.
3. Integration of the transgene into the bacterial chromosome.
4. Use of appropriate lethal genes to limit the survival of GEMs to the specified niches.
Options :
(*a*) 1, 2, 3 (*b*) 1, 2, 3, 4
(*c*) 2, 3 (*d*) 1, 2, 4

53. Which of the following ***is not correct*** ?
(*a*) *RecA*$^-$ strains lack recombination.
(*b*) Transposon vectors lacking transposase gene are not able to transpose to other bacteria.
(*c*) Auxotrophic mutants can survive in nature.
(*d*) Transgenes integrated into plasmids may be transferred to other bacteria.

54. The *gef* containment system is based on which of the following elements ?
I. The *xylS* regulator gene, which is expressed constitutively
II. The regulator gene *lacI* linked to the promoter *Pm*.
III. The structural gene *gef* driven by *E. coli* promoter *Plac.*
Options :
(*a*) I, II, III (*b*) II, III
(*c*) I, III (*d*) I, II

55. The first recombinant microorganism (Tn5-containing strain of *Pseudomonas fluorescens*) was released in which of the following countries ?
(*a*) USA (*b*) Canada
(*c*) Netherlands (*d*) Germany

56. Most of the recombinant microorganism released in the environment consisted of only a simple inactivation of genes by which of the following ?
(*a*) Transposon insertion.
(*b*) Deletion of genes by molecular genetic procedure *in vitro.*
(*c*) Genetic tagging of bacteria with specific markers.
(*d*) Any of the above.

57. Which of the following non-infectious illnesses is associated with production of steroids ?
(*a*) Increased body weight
(*b*) Feminization of males
(*c*) Hypertension
(*d*) All of the above

58. Which of the following non-infectious illnesses is associated with endotoxin production ?
(*a*) Flu symptoms (*b*) Dermatitis
(*c*) Asthama (*d*) All of the above

59. Which of the following hazards is associated with operation of bioreactor fermentation ?
(*a*) Spillage
(*b*) Effluent contamination of gases
(*c*) Aerosols from reactor
(*d*) All of the above

60. Non-infectious illnesses like allergic asthama and dermatitis are associated with which of the following production processes ?
(*a*) Brewing (*b*) Single cell protein
(*c*) Antibiotic (*d*) All of the above.

61. Which of the following is correct about guidelines and regulations of biosafety ?
I. Appropriate legislation should be promoted in those countries that lack them.
II. Public consciousness of biosafety issues should be increased.
III. A licensing may be imposed on the export of genetically manipulated organisms.
IV. A voluntary code of conduct, *i.e.*, an international agreement between industry and governments on various

biotechnological products and processes, may be promoted.

Options :

(*a*) I, II, III, IV (*b*) II, III, IV
(*c*) I, III, IV (*d*) I, II, IV

62. Which of the following standard microbiological practices are concerned with biosafety level 1 (BL1) experiments with microorganisms ?

1. Access to the laboratory is restricted at the discretion of principal investigaror, when the experiments are in progress.
2. Work surfaces are decontaminated once a day and after any spill of viable material.
3. All contaminated liquid or solid wastes are decontaminated before disposal.
4. Mouth pipetting is prohibited

Options :

(*a*) 1, 2, 3 (*b*) 2, 3, 4
(*c*) 1, 2, 3, 4 (*d*) 3, 4

63. Which of the following laboratory facilities are concerned with BL1 experiments with microorganisms ?

1. Laboratory design must facilitate easy cleaning.
2. Bench tops must be impervious to water, and resistant to acids, alkalies, organic solvents and moderate heat.
3. Laboratory furniture must be sturdy and spaces between benches, cabinets and equipments must be accessible for cleaning.
4. Each laboratory must have a sink for hand washing.

Options :

(*a*) 1, 2, 3 (*b*) 1, 2, 3, 4
(*c*) 2, 3, 4 (*d*) 1, 3, 4

64. Which of the following standard microbiological practices are concerned with BL1 experiments with micro-organism ?

1. Persons wash their hands every times after they handle materials and animals involving organisms containing recombinant DNA molecules, and before leaving the laboratory.
2. Eating, drinking, smoking and applying cosmetics are not permitted in the laboratory premises.
3. All procedures must be performed carefully so that a minimum of aerosols are created.
4. Facilities for good personal hygiene and protective clothing, *e.g.*, uniforms and laboratory coats, must be provided.

Options :

(*a*) 1, 2, 3, 4 (*b*) 1, 3, 4
(*c*) 2, 3, 4 (*d*) 1, 2, 3

65. In case of experiments with microorganisms, BL2 differs from BL1 with respect to which of the following ?

1. Laboratory personnel must be specifically trained in handling pathogenic agents and are directed by competent scientists
2. Access to the laboratory is limited when the experiments are in progress.
3. Certain procedures in which infectious aerosols are created are done in biological safety cabinets
4. Spills and accidents involving organisms containing recombinant DNA molecules are immediately reported to the Institutional Biosafety Committee (IBC) and higher bodies concerned with biosafety.

Options :

(*a*) 1, 2, 4 (*b*) 1, 2, 3, 4
(*c*) 2, 3, 4 (*d*) 1, 3, 4

66. In case of experiments with microorganisms, BL3 has which of the following additional chief safety measures over BL2 ?

1. Laboratory personnel have specific training in handling pathogenic and potentially lethal agents.
2. All procedures involving the manipulation of infectious material are conducted with biological safety cabinets.
3. Laboratory has special engineering and design features.
4. Laboratory clothing may be worn outside the laboratory.

Options :
(*a*) 1, 2, 3, 4 (*b*) 2, 3, 4
(*c*) 1, 2, 3 (*d*) 1, 3, 4

67. In case of experiments with microorganisms, which of the following is related to BL 4 ?
1. Entry in the laboratory is limited to only those who work in the area.
2. Personnel enter and exit the facility only through the clothing change and shower rooms.
3. All procedures with microorganisms are done in class III safety cabinets.
4. Biological materials to be removed from Class III cabinets in a viable state are transferred into a non-breakable sealed primary and secondary containers.

Options :
(*a*) 1, 2, 3, 4 (*b*) 2, 3, 4
(*c*) 1, 2, 4 (*d*) 1, 3, 4

68. In case of experiments with animals, which of the following procedures is followed at all biosafety levels ?
(*a*) Animal carcass is disposed off to avoid its use as food.
(*b*) A permanent record is maintained of the experimental use and disposal of each animal.
(*c*) The animals are confined to security-fenced areas.
(*d*) All of the above.

69. Which of the following is correct about biosafety level 1 for animals (BL1-N) ?
1. Access to the containment area shall be limited or restricted when experimental animals are being held.
2. The containment area shall be monitored at frequent intervals
3. All transgenic new borns should be permanently marked within 72 hours of their birth.
4. The animals shall be confined to security fenced areas.

Options :
(*a*) 1, 3, 4 (*b*) 1, 2, 3, 4
(*c*) 2, 3, 4 (*d*) 1, 2, 3

70. Biosafety level 3 for animals differs from BL-2-N in which of the following respects ?
1. Animal room doors shall be kept closed when experiments are in progress.
2. The work surfaces of containment equipment shall be decontaminated when work with organsisms containing recombinant DNA is finished.
3. All animals shall be euthanized at the end of their experimental usefulness.
4. Special procedures and IBC approval shall be required to transfer specimens to a low biosafety level area.

Options :
(*a*) 1, 3, 4 (*b*) 1, 2, 3, 4
(*c*) 2, 3, 4 (*d*) 1, 2, 3

71. In which of the following respects, BL4 for animals represents greater stringency than BL-3-N ?
1. Individuals under 16 years of age shall not be allowed entry.
2. Individuals shall enter and exit the animal facility only through the clothing change and shower room.
3. All waste from the animal rooms and laboratories shall be decontaminated before disposal.
4. The animal/personnel shower entrance/exit area shall be equipped with a chemical disinfectant shower.

Options :
(*a*) 1, 2, 3, 4 (*b*) 2, 3, 4
(*c*) 1, 2, 3 (*d*) 1, 3, 4

72. Which of the following are related to biosafety level 2 for animals ?
1. Viable biological materials are removed from the containment as in the case of BL4-plants.
2. Appropriate steps should be taken to prevent exposure of laboratory personnel.
3. Eating, drinking, smoking and applying cosmetics shall be prohibited.
4. Animals shall be contained in animal rooms with provision to avoid entry or escape of anthropods.

Options :
(*a*) 1, 2, 3, 4 (*b*) 2, 3, 4
(*c*) 1, 3, 4 (*d*) 1, 2, 3

73. Which of the following is correct about biosafety guidelines in India ?
1. Every organization involved in research and development using recombinant

DNA is required to set up an Institutional Biosafety Committee (IBC).
2. The DBT has a Review Committee for Genetic Manipulation (RCGM) which reviews all the approvals of ongoing projects on GMOs.
3. Each state has, in addition, a State Biotechnology Coordination Committee, and a District Level Commitee.
4. The Ministry of Environment and Forestry (MOEF) has an interministrial committee, called The Genetic Engineering Approval Committee (GEAC).

Options :
(*a*) 1, 2, 3, 4 (*b*) 1, 3, 4
(*c*) 1, 2, 3 (*d*) 3, 4

74. Which of the following is related to biosafety guidelines in India ?
1. The guidelines recognise three levels of risk in the case of experiments with microorgaisms.
2. Four different *biosafety levels* are recognised and containment facilities for each level are recommended for necessary safegaurd.
3. Biological containment consists of the use of vectors and hosts in such way so that it limits the host-vector survival in the environment.
4. Experiments with plants are to be done under two types of speical environments that may be achieved by using galss-house containment .

Options :
(*a*) 1, 2, 3 (*b*) 2, 3, 4
(*c*) 1, 2, 3, 4 (*d*) 1, 3, 4

75. According to biosafety guidelines of India, physical containment envisages to limit the spread of dangerous microorganisms by which of the following ?
(*a*) Laboratory design and facilities
(*b*) Laboratory practices
(*c*) Safety equipment
(*d*) All of the above.

76. According to biosafety guidelines of India, experiments with microorganisms, plants and animals are grouped into which of following categories ?
I. Exempt category for self-cloning experiments.
II. Category requiring intimation of initiation to competent authority.
III. Category requiring review and approval by the competent authority.

Options :
(*a*) I, II (*b*) II, III
(*c*) I, II, III (*d*) I, III

77. Which of the following is related to biosafety guidelines of India ?
I. Application for recognition of research facility to carry out genetic manipulation should be made to the Department of Environment before the commencement of work.
II. All products obtained using recombinant DNA technology shall be subject to the general regulations normally applicable for such products.
III. The controlled release of GMOs should be done under appropriate containment facilities.
IV. Pre-release tests of GMOs in agriculture should include elucidation of requirements for vegetative growth and persistence and stability in small plots and experimental fields.

Options :
(*a*) I, II, III, IV (*b*) II, III, IV
(*c*) I, II, III (*d*) I, II

78. Risk assessment for transgenic plants takes into account which of the following ?
I. Promoter sequence and target gene sequence.
II. Regulatory mechanism utilized in the expression cassette.
III. Diagram of the expression cassette to describe fully the marker genes used.
IV. Cell lines used for shuttling and amplification of the cassette.

Options :
(*a*) I, III, IV (*b*) I, II, III, IV
(*c*) II, IV (*d*) I, II, III

79. ***Feature (F)*** : Transgenic varieties will help in reduction of pollution by permitting the use of biodegradable agrochemicals ?

Benefit (B): The above feature will help to reduce detrimental effects of agrochemicals on the ecosystem like non-target species, water-bodies, etc.

Options :

(*a*) Both F and B are correct.
(*b*) Only F is correct.
(*c*) Only B is correct.
(*d*) Both F and B are incorrect.

80. Crop yields can be stabilized by introducing which of following genes in transgenic varieties ?

(*a*) Genes for improved nutritional quality.
(*b*) Genes for better tolerance/resistance to biotic and/or abiotic stresses.
(*c*) Genes for herbicide resistance.
(*d*) All of the above.

81. GM food may differ from those prepared from the conventionally developed varieties with respect to which of the following ?

I. Protein(s) encoded by the transgene(s) in question.
II. A metabolic product generated by the transgene products.
III. Altered levels of natural toxins and important nutrients.
IV. The enzyme encoded by the selectable marker gene.

Options :

(*a*) I, II, III (*b*) I, III, IV
(*c*) I, II, III, IV (*d*) II, III, IV

82. The potential risks from novel DNA sequences used during transgenic development may be summed up as which of the following ?

(*a*) Protein products of transgenes or products generated by them may be toxic.
(*b*) The transgene product may be allergenic.
(*c*) Antibiotic resistance genes may be taken up by human intestinal microflora, which, as a consequence, become resistant to these antibiotics.
(*d*) All of the above.

83. Transgenic plants could serve as vectors for transgene dissemination through which of the following ?

(*a*) Seed
(*b*) DNA released from debris of transgenic plants
(*c*) Pollen
(*d*) All of the above

84. Which of the following ***is not correct*** ?

(*a*) In European Union, the maximum permissible limit for GMO content in conventional food products and food ingredients is 1% at the marketing stage.
(*b*) All foods that contain more than 1% GMOs related to the different ingredients have to be labelled.
(*c*) In case of organic farming, utilization and presence of GMOs is excluded.
(*d*) Volunteers are not likely to pose problems in crops like rapeseed and mustard.

85. The rate of gene-flow is affected by which of the following factors ?

(*a*) Mode of seed dispersal
(*b*) Mating system
(*c*) Mode of pollination
(*d*) All of the above

86. Which of the following ***is not correct*** about lectins ?

(*a*) They are polysaccharides.
(*b*) They are involved in defence mechanism of plants.
(*c*) Several lectins have been identified as food allergens.
(*d*) α-Amylase/tripsin inhibitor family proteins are potential allergens.

87. The International Life Science Institute advocates which of the following criteria tfor assessing whether a protein poses no risk of allergy ?

I. Not known to cause allergies.
II. Lacks amino acid sequences similar to that of known allergens.
III. Is digested rapidly.
IV. Is expressed at low levels.

Options :

(*a*) I, II, III (*b*) I, II, III, IV
(*c*) I, III, IV (*d*) II, III, IV

88. In the assessment of allergenicity, the source of transgene is the first consideration; the trangene may be obtained from which of the following ?

(*a*) Commonly allergenic food
(*b*) Less commonly allergenic food
(*c*) No documented history of food allergenicity.
(*d*) Any one of the above.

89. Which of the following toxic effects is associated with proteinase inhibitors ?

I. Pancrease enlargement
II. Adenoma
III. Hyperplasia
IV. Weight loss

Options :

(*a*) I, II, III, IV (*b*) II, III, IV
(*c*) I, II, III (*d*) I, IV

90. Which of the following compounds is associated with toxic effects and is also involved in plant defence reaction/ mechanism ?

I. Phytoalexins II. β-1-3 Glucanases
III. Thionin IV. Alkaloids

Options :

(*a*) I, II, III (*b*) I, III, IV
(*c*) I, IV (*d*) I, II, III, IV

91. Which of the following is known to be a food allergen ?

I. Wheat germ agglutinin (WGA)
II. Soybean Kunitz trypsin inhibitor
III. Trypsin inhibitor
IV. Peanut lectins

Options

(*a*) I, II, III, IV (*b*) II, III
(*c*) I, III, IV (*d*) I, IV

92. Which of the following is correct about wheat germ agglutinin ?

(*a*) It is effective against insects at concentration of 10 mg/kg body weight.
(*b*) It produces cytotoxic effects in rats at a lower concentration (7 mg/kg)
(*c*) Safe food has it only at 0.3 mg/kg.
(*d*) All of the above.

93. Which of the following ***is not correct*** ?

(*a*) Transgene isolation from a food crop guarantees the food safety of the transgene product.
(*b*) Acute toxic effect depends on the concentration of the compound in question.
(*c*) Psoralen is known to be toxic, carcinogenic and mutagenic.
(*d*) Any outstanding insect resistance whose biochemical basis is not known should be considered as the prime candidate for toxicological evaluations.

94. Which of the following ***is not correct*** about bromoxynil ?

(*a*) It is a non-biodegradable herbicide.
(*b*) It causes birth defects in laboratory animals.
(*c*) It is toxic to fish and may cause cancer in humans.
(*d*) Bromoxynil is absorbed through the skin.

95. Transgenic crops are perceived by many to pose which of the following threats to the environment ?

I. They may have adverse impact on biodiversity.
II. Insect resistant transgenic crops may affect non-target species.
III. They may encourage use of agrochemicals.
IV. They may alter the composition of rhizosphere and phyllosphere microflora.

Options :

(*a*) I, II, IV (*b*) I, II, III
(*c*) I, II, III, IV (*d*) II, III, IV

96. A careful evaluation of toxin encoding genes for toxic action on non-target insects is warranted since it seems to be a function of which of the following ?

I. The toxin encoding gene
II. Crop species
III. Target insect pest
IV. Non-target insect species

Options :

(*a*) I, II, IV (*b*) I, IV
(*c*) II, III, IV (*d*) III, IV

97. ***Assertion (A)***: Transgenic plants may accelerate genetic erosion and consequent loss of biodiversity.

Reason (R): A large-scale adoption of transgenic varieties would replace traditional varieties.

Options :

(*a*) Both A and R are correct and R adequately explains A.

(*b*) Both A and R are correct, but R does not explain A.
(*c*) Only A is correct.
(*d*) Only R is correct.

98. Which of the following techniques can be used for minimising pollen-mediated gene flow from transgenic varieties of crops ?
I. Integration of transgene into the chloroplast genome.
II. Male sterility.
III. Terminator technology.
IV. Gene silencing.

Options :
(*a*) I, II, III (*b*) II, III
(*c*) I, II, IV (*d*) I, IV

99. For minimising pollen-mediated gene-flow from transgenic varieties of *Solanum tuberosum*, how many meters of isolation distance is recommended ?
(*a*) 10 (*b*) 20
(*c*) 30 (*d*) 40

100. Which of the following can be used to minimise transgene transfer from transgenic varieties of crops ?
I. Transgenic mitigation
II. Cleistogamy
III. Temporal transgene expression
IV. Apomixis

Options :
(*a*) I, II, III (*b*) II, III, IV
(*c*) I, II, IV (*d*) I, II, III, IV

101. Seed sterility can be reduced by using which of the following techniques ?
I. Terminator technology
II. Transgenic mitigation
III. Recoverable block of function (RBF)
IV. Apomixis

Options :
(*a*) I, III (*b*) I, II, III, IV
(*c*) I, II, III (*d*) I, II, IV

102. Strategy of temporal and tissue-specific expression for preventing transgene transfer from transgenic varieties of crops is based on which of the following techniques ?
(*a*) Tapetum-specific promoters allow expression only when the suppressor is present.
(*b*) Terminator technology
(*c*) Recoverable block of function
(*d*) Inducible promoters allow expression only when the inducer is present.

103. ***Statement (S)***: Strategy of transgenic mitigation can be used to prevent transgene transfer from transgenic varieties of crops.
Consequence (C): Transgenics may accelerate or even cause extinction of wild relatives of crops.

Options :
(*a*) Both S and C are correct.
(*b*) Both S and C are incorrect.
(*c*) Only S is correct.
(*d*) Only C is correct.

104. ***Assertion (A) :*** Strategy of temporal and tissue specific expression may prevent transgene transfer from transgenic varieties of crops.
Mechanism (M) : The transgene is either activated only when the product is required or it is excised before flowering.

Options :
(*a*) Only A is correct.
(*b*) Only M is correct.
(*c*) Both A and M are corect and M adequately explains A.
(*d*) Both A and M are correct, but M does not explain A

105. Which of the following concerns has been expressed about the agricultural performance of transgenic varieties ?
I. Yield drag.
II. Unstable transgene expression over environments.
III. Resistance of target pests to the transgene product.
IV. Genetic vulnerability due to large-scale cultivation of single varieties.

Options :
(*a*) I, II, III (*b*) II, III, IV
(*c*) I, II, III, IV (*d*) I, III, IV

106. Roundup Ready transgenic variety of soybean showed, on an average, how much yield decrease as compared to the non-transgenic parent varieties in USA, in a comparison based on field trials at 8,200 different locations ?
(*a*) 15% (*b*) 10%
(*c*) 5% (*d*) –5%

107. The risk assessment in relation to transgenic crop varieties should include which of following considerations ?

I. Occurrence of wild relatives of the concerned crop in the area where transgenic varieties are to be cultivated.
II. The extent of domestication of the crop whose transgenic varieties are to be produced.
III. The degree of pollinator insect activity.
IV. The pest diversity of the given crop and their relative economic importance.

Options :

(*a*) II, III, IV (*b*) I, II, III, IV
(*c*) I, III, IV (*d*) I, II, III

108. In India, it is insisted upon that field trials with transgenic plants observe which of the following ?

I. The isolation distance recommended for the foundation seed crop of the concerned crop be maintained.
II. Beyond the isolation distance, a few rows of a non-transgenic variety of the same crop may be planted to serve as a pollen trap.
III. Within the isolation distance, nontransgenic varieties of the crop should be planted to assess the extent and distance of pollen transfer from the transgenic plants.
IV. Data on genetic marker persistence and stability in small plots, etc. should be collected at least for two years.

Options :

(*a*) I, II, III, IV (*b*) I, II
(*c*) I, II, III (*d*) II, IV

109. In India, it is insisted upon that field trials with trangenic plants observe which of the following ?

I. All the vegetative plants and leftover seeds be destroyed by burning after the experiment.
II. The land may be left fallow next year, and any volunteer plants that emerge be destroyed.
III. The experimental field be visited by the company authorised personnel only.
IV. Full account of transgenic seeds produced be maintained and no transgenic seeds be transacted or further propagated without authorization.

Options :

(*a*) I, III, IV (*b*) II, III, IV
(*c*) I, II, III, IV (*d*) I, II, III

110. The principal purpose of transgenic plant containment is to avoid the unitentional transmission of a recombinant DNA containing plant genome including which of the following ?

(*a*) Organellar hereditary material.
(*b*) Nuclear hereditary material.
(*c*) Release of recombinant DNA-derived organisms associated with plants.
(*d*) Any of the above.

111. Which of the following points is considered during research involving biosafety level-1 plants (BL-1P) ?

I. Greenhouse access is limited when experiments are in progress.
II. A programme to control undesired species shall be in effect.
III. Experimental and other motile micro-organisms shall be housed in appropriate places under containment.
IV. Experimental organisms shall be rendered biologically inactive before their disposal outside the green house.

Options :

(*a*) I, II, IV (*b*) I, II, III, IV
(*c*) II, III, IV (*d*) I, II, III

112. Biosafety level 2 for plants (BL-2P) differs from BL-1P in respect to which of the following ?

I. When work is in progress, access is limited to personnel directly involved with the experiment.
II. A record of experimental plants, micro-organisms or small animals that are brought into or removed from the green-house facility may be kept, if desired.
III. The principal investigaror (PI) shall report any inadvertent release or spill of organisms to green house incharge, bodies concerned with biosafety.
IV. Periodical treatment should be done to inactivate organisms present in the gravel present in the green house.

Options :
(*a*) I, II, III, IV (*b*) I, III, IV
(*c*) I, II, III (*d*) I, III

113. Biosafety level 3 for plants (BL-3P) has the features of BL-2P plus which of the following additional ones ?

I. The entry into greenhouse shall be restricted to those who are needed for the programme or support purposes.
II. All experimental materials shall be sterilized before disposal.
III. Experimental materials that are brought into the greenhouse facility in a viable or intact state, shall be kept into a non-breakable sealed secondary container as well.
IV. Disposable clothing shall be worn in the greenhouse whereever considcred necessary.

Options :
(*a*) I, II, III, IV (*b*) II, III, IV
(*c*) I, III, IV (*d*) I, II, III

114. Biosafety level 4 for plants (BL-4P represents a greater stringency in containment over BL-3P in which of the following respects ?

I. Access to the greenhouse shall be limited by means of secure, locked doors.
II. Individuals shall be advised about the potential hazards and of appropriate safeguards to be followed, which they shall comply with.
III. Personnel shall enter and exit the greenhouse facility only through the clothing change and shower rooms.
IV. Standard microbiological procedures shall bc followed for decontamination of equipment and materials.

Options :
(*a*) I, II, III (*b*) I, II, III, IV
(*c*) II, III, IV (*d*) I, III, IV

17.2. FILL IN THE BLANKS

1. Abbreviation NIH stands for ....

2. The hazards due to GMOs are far more difficult to identify than those, for instance, associated with .... pesticides.

3. The initial risk assessment is made by the .... on the basis of the risk group to which the organism, on which he proposes to conduct experiments, belongs

4. Environment in which planned introduction is proposed is known as the ....

5. The food and additives obtained from genetically modified organisms are called ....

6. As the biosafety level ...., the laboratory design and facilities, and the operational procedures become more and more rigid and stringent.

7. .... physical containment is used where experiments of moderate to high potential hazard are performed.

8. Biological containment is based on the .... used for the construction of .... and the host (bacterial, plant, or animal cells) in which the recobinant DNA is propagated in the laboratory.

9. In case of *E. coli,* the host for any HV1 system is strain K 12, and this system is generally called ....

10. In case of .... systems, escape of the recombinant DNA either via survival of the organisms or via transmission of the recombinant DNA to other organisms should be less than 10^{-8} under specific conditions designed to represent the natural environment.

11. A biologically contained GEM has been developed by engineering strain EEZ 30 of *Pseudomonas putida* to degrade ....

12. The first release of recombinant microorganism, was done in...........

13. Allergenic dusts are associated with material .... during production.

14. Non-infectious illnesses like cardiovascular disorders, candidiasis are associated with production process of ....

15. Bronchitis is associated with production process of .... and ....

16. Abbreviation IWGB stands for ....

17. In 1991, IWGB, the main body of UN on .... issued the draft voluntry code of conduct for .... into the environment.

18. In case of biosafety level 2 (involving experiments with microorganism) an autoclave for decontaminating .... must be available.

19. Abbreviation RDAC stands for ....

20. The recommended safety assessment strategies for GM foods are, generally, based on the concept of ....

21. In case of *Gossypium hirsutum*, the extent of pollen dissemination from transgenic varieties containing transgene *tfdA* (for 2,4-D resistance) and *Bt* gene to other varieties of the same crops is about .... % and ....% at 1 m and 50 m, respectively.

22. All known allergens causing type 1 allergies are ....

23. The risk of food allergy .... with the increased duration of consumption of the concerned food.

24. Abbreviation ILSI stands for ....

25. Increased seed production in wild sunflower as a result of the transfer of .... gene has been reported.

26. Lectins caused loss of .... and hypergrowth of the .... in rats.

27. Psoralen is a ....

28. Glyphosate accumulates in .... and .... since plants cannot degrade it.

29. Transgenic varieties may pose a greater risk only if they spread to such areas where the .... developed varieties did not/could not reach.

30. The exent of pollen dissemination from *Brassica napus* transgenic variety containing *bar* transgene to other varieties of the same crops was 1.5% at .... m and 0.00033 % at .... m respectively.

31. The transgene may be integrated into the chloroplast genome to ensure its ...., although species like tobacco may show upto ....% pollen transfer of chloroplast traits.

32. Herbicide resistance gene transfer from transgenic *Oryza sativa* to .... has been reported.

33. In case of transgenic *Brassica napus*, planting of .... m wide continuous borders of a nontransgenic variety of the same crop is recommended for minimising pollen-mediated ....

34. In India, for all transgenic crops, isolation distance as recommended for the .... crop of the same crop species is recommended.

35. Transfer of the transgene conferring hygromycin resistance from transgenic plants of *Datura innoxia* via soil to .... has been reported.

36. Preventing transgene transfer through male sterility has been commericalized in glufosinate tolerant ....

37. Preventing transgene transfer through seed sterility (using RBF system) has been demonstrated in ....

38. If apomixis is used to prevent transgene transfer from transgenic varieties of crops, transgenics have to be .... to prevent outcrossing.

39. Concerns have been voiced about the risk of evolution of new virus strains due to .... and .... that may occur in transgenic varieties created by employing viral DNA sequences.

40. Transgenes may become deleted or modified by recombination, following their integration into the plant genome; this phenomenon is called ....

41. The consequences of transgene instability and transgene .... are the same.

42. It was found that one male out of .... gypsy moth males had a recessive gene conferring resistance to the insecticidal protein CryIA(c).

43. Farmers are expected to plant .... per cent refugea in case of cotton and ....per cent or even 30-40 per cent in case of maize.

44. In case of plants, the containment principles are based on the recognition that the organisms that are used present .... to humans or higher animals.

17.3. MARK TRUE OR FALSE

1. The term GMO applies to all organisms, including microorganisms.
2. The ultimate objective of guidelines that regulate research and development activities using recombinant DNA technology should be to minimise risk from such activities and, at the same time, encourage these activities.
3. Risk is a function of the level of hazard and the probability of occurrence of the hazard.
4. Synthetic DNA sequences that are not expressed *in vivo* as biologically active polynucleotides or polypeptides are not exempt from NIH guidelines.
5. Consumption of a certain transgenic variety of soybean caused servere allergic reactions is some people in Mexico.
6. Opportunities for transfer of transgene would be greater in the centres of origin where crop-weed complexes occur.
7. A strict adherence to a set of standard laboratory practices that are generally used in microbial laboratories is the basic principle of containment.
8. In case of biological containment for prokaryotes, certification of a host-vector system covers the modifications of either the host or the vector component of that system.
9. HV2 systems provide a low level of biological containment as demonstrated by data from suitable tests performed in the laboratory.
10. In case of plants, biological containment procedures aim at minimising the risk of dispersal of pollen and seeds of plants, and dissemination and establishment of plant associated microorganisms and insects.
11. Use of lethal genes, *e.g.*, *gef*, to limit the survival of GEMs to the specified niches is an example of biological containment.
12. GEMs may be constructed so that they contain an active biological containment system that minimizes the survival and dissemination of recombinant DNA outside the target area.
13. Gef protein causes a collapse of the membrane potential which leads to cell death.
14. Many of the biotechnological processes of manufacture have the potential to generate biohazards.
15. Malt fever is associated with sugar industry.
16. Aerosol and spillage hazards are associated with process of product purification.
17. Biosafety level 3 is applicable to clinical diagnostic, teaching, research or production facilities in which work is done on microorganisms, which may cause serious or potentially lethal disease as a result of exposure by the inhalation route.
18. In case of experiments with microorganisms, BL 4 is appropriate for organisms that are likely to cause serious or lethal human disease for which preventive or therapeutic interventions are usually available.
19. In case of biosafety level 3, research involving animals, creation of aerosols must be minimized.
20. In case of biosafety level 3 experiments with microorganism, persons under 16 years of age shall not enter the laboratory.
21. In case of BL3 for animals, the animal rooms are as in the case of BL1 animals, but their windows are closed, sealed and breakage-resistant.
22. The DBT implements the research and development experiments utilizing GMOs and recombinant DNA products, while MOEF implements the large-scale commercial use of these.

23. The presence of transgenic volunteers in a conventional crop would contaminate the conventional harvest with transgenic seed and prevent the farmer from obtaining a non-trangenic crop label for the product.
24. The consequence of allergic reactions does not depend on the quantity of allergen ingested.
25. A safe general policy would be not to grow transgenic crops in such areas where their wild relatives occur in proximity of cultivated fields.
26. Experimental findings indicate that a non-immunogenic protein does not become immunogenic when it is expressed in another species.
27. The toxic effects of wheat germ agglutinin (WGA) were found to be more severe than those due to other lectins.
28. Glyphosate is reported to be toxic to target soil organisms.
29. Transfer of oil quality modification gene from *Brassica napus* to *B. campestris* has been reported.
30. Transgene instability and gene silencing can influence the agricultural performance of transgenic varieties.
31. Transgene expression does not vary with the environment.
32. A higher frequency of Bt resistance allele in the Bt-cotton fields than in non-Bt-cotton fields has already been reported.
33. Genetic vulnerability is the unwanted gift from modern agriculture.
34. In India, large-scale use of GMOs is approved by the Genetic Engineering Approval Committee (GEAC) of the Ministry of Environment and Forest.

□□□

18

INTELLECTUAL PROPERTY RIGHTS

18.1. MULTIPLE CHOICE QUESTIONS

1. Which of following statements are correct ?

I. Intellectual property is an idea, a design, an invention, a manuscript, etc. which can ultimately give rise to a useful product/application.

II. The earliest record of rewarding the inventors for their inventions by societies and governments relates to food recipes.

III. The first law on patent was passed in Venice in 1474.

IV. In 1623, the House of Commons of U.K. passed the act of properietarship.

Options :

(*a*) I, II, III (*b*) I, II, III, IV

(*c*) I, III, IV (*d*) II, III, IV

2. Which of the following statements are correct about intellectual property rights (IPR) ?

I. It is the right of an inventor to derive economic benefits from an invention to the exclusion of others.

II. The protection of IPR may take several forms depending mainly on the type of intellectual property and the type of protection sought.

III. Intellectual property may be a design, an idea, an invention, a manuscript, etc.

IV. The main forms of IPR protection are trade secret, patent, copyright, plant breeder's right, trade mark and geographical indications.

Options :

(*a*) II, III, IV (*b*) I, II, III

(*c*) I, II, III, IV (*d*) I, III, IV

3. Trade secret relates to which of the following ?

(*a*) Certain materials, *e.g.*, bacterial strains

(*b*) Processes

(*c*) Formulae

(*d*) Any one of the above

4. Which of the following ***is not correct*** about patent ?

(*a*) It is the right of an individual or a group of individuals to gain profit from a particular invention or unique manufacturing process.

(*b*) It is granted by the Government of a country to the applicant for an unlimited period of time.

(*c*) When a patent is granted, the inventor becomes the owner of the patent like any other form of property.

(*d*) Patents are granted for an invention (including a product), innovation/ improvement in an invention, process/ product of an invention and a concept.

5. In the area of biotechnology, which of the following materials can be kept as trade secret ?

(*a*) Cell lines

(*b*) Strains of microorganism

(*c*) Production processes

(*d*) All of the above

6. Which of the following is the chief requirements for the grant of a patent ?

1. Novelty
2. Inventiveness
3. Industrial application and usefulness
4. Disclosure

Options :
(*a*) 1, 3 (*b*) 2, 3, 4
(*c*) 1, 2, 3, 4 (*d*) 1, 2, 3

7. Trade secret offers which of the following advantages ?
I. Effective for unlimited duration.
II. No need to satisfy the requirements for protection under, say, patent.
III. The risk of innovation by someone else is minimized.
IV. Low cost of maintaining the secret.

Options :
(*a*) I, II, III (*b*) II, III, IV
(*c*) I, III, IV (*d*) I, II, III, IV

8. Trade secrets suffer from which of the following disadvantages ?
I. Maintaining a trade secret itself is costly.
II. It offers protection from independent innovation/invention.
III. Nondisclosure hampers progress.
IV. It can not be applied to many inventions.

Options :
(*a*) I, II, III, IV (*b*) II, III, IV
(*c*) I, III, IV (*d*) I, II, III

9. Which of the following statements are correct about patents ?
I. The subject matter must be patentable.
II. Organisms and natural products as such are not patentable in U.S.A.
III. In U.S.A., a patent could be claimed for any 'new form or composition'.
IV. In 1980, the American Supreme Court ruled that a live, human-made (genetically engineered) microorganism can be patented under the American patent law as a "manufacture" or "composition of matter"

Options :
(*a*) I, II, III, IV (*b*) I, II, III
(*c*) I, III, IV (*d*) II, III, IV

10. Trade secret ***can not be applied*** for which of the following inventions ?
(*a*) Plant varieties
(*b*) Equipment designs
(*c*) Books
(*d*) All of the above.

11. ***Drawback (D)***: In case of trade secret, non-disclosure of the invention/innovation is ensured.

Loss (L): Nondisclosure prevents or at least delays, progress in the area of a trade secret, and society/nation/humanity is the loser in such cases.

Options :
(*a*) Both D and L are correct and L is the result of D.
(*b*) Both D and L are correct, but L does not result from D.
(*c*) Only D is correct.
(*d*) Only L is correct.

12. Which of the following statements are correct about plant breeder's rights (PBRs) ?
I. These are the rights granted by the government to a plant breeder, or owner of a variety to exclude others from producing or commercializing the propagating material of that variety.
II. A person holding PBR title to a variety can not authorize other interested persons/organizations to produce and sell the propagating material of that variety.
III. The object of protection in PBR is the variety and the genetic components and the breeding procedures are not protected.
IV. PBR systems contains some form of 'breeder's exemption' and 'farmer's privilege'.

Options :
(*a*) I, II, III (*b*) I, II, III, IV
(*c*) I, III, IV (*d*) II, III, IV

13. Which of the following ***is not correct*** about breeder's exemption ?
(*a*) The use of a protected variety for the development of new varieties is exempted from protection.
(*b*) The PBR for a new variety evolved from the initial variety will be of the breeder who developed the new variety and of the holder of PBR title of the initial variety as well.
(*c*) Under the UPOV 1978 Act, all new varieties evolved using a protected variety were exempted from protection under this provision.

(*d*) The UPOV 1991 Act has limited breeders exemption in that 'essentially-derived varieties' are covered by the PBR granted to the initially variety.

14. Which of the following is correct about an essentially-derived variety ?

I. It is a variety produced by mutation or transfer of (a single) gene through backcross method into another variety.

II. It may be obtained by genetic transformation of a single gene into another variety.

III. It will be covered under the PBR title granted to the initial variety.

IV. The breeder of such a variety will be required to obtain permission from PBR title holder of the intial variety.

Options :

(*a*) I, II, III (*b*) II, III, IV
(*c*) I, III, IV (*d*) I, II, III, IV

15. Which of the following is correct about farmer's rights ?

I. The farmers should be allowed a share in the profit earned from the sale of modern high yielding varieties in recognition of their contribution to the development of germplasms of various crops.

II. It should be obligatory and should not be relegated as privilege.

III. The key questions relating to farmer's rights remain as to whom to reward, to what extent and in what manner.

Options :

(*a*) I, II, III (*b*) II, III
(*c*) I, II (*d*) I, III

16. Which of the following people are considered under farmer's rights for sharing the profit earned from the development of high yielding varieties evolved from the use of raw materials/plant genetic resources ?

(*a*) Tribal people
(*b*) Rural communities
(*c*) Traditional farming families
(*d*) All of the above

17. An otherwise excellent transgenic variety of which of the following crops developed during 1990s ***could not be released*** due to IPR problems ?

(*a*) Potato (*b*) Tomato
(*c*) Tobacco (*d*) *Brassica napus*

18. India has created a National Biodiversity Authority with headquarters at which of the following ?

(*a*) New Delhi (*b*) Kolkata
(*c*) Chennai (*d*) Hyderabad

19. Which of the following intellectual properties can be protected by copyright ?

I. Authored and edited books
II. Audio and video cassettes
III. Computer software
IV. DNA sequences

Options :

(*a*) I, II, III (*b*) I, II, III, IV
(*c*) II, III, IV (*d*) I, III, IV

20. The copyright of a book may be held by which of the following ?

(*a*) Author(s) (*b*) Editor(s)
(*c*) Publisher (*d*) Any of the above

21. Which of the following steps are involved in the procedure of patenting ?

I. An inventor files a properly prepared application with the patent office of the concerned country.

II. If it is found suitable for patenting the invention alongwith adequate details of the desired patent is published for the information of all concerned.

III. Anyone can challenge the award of patent within a specified period of time.

IV. In case a patent is not challenged, the patent is awarded immediately after the expiry of the specified period.

Options :

(*a*) I, II, III, IV (*b*) II, III, IV
(*c*) I, II, III (*d*) I, III, IV

22. In USA, which of the following systems are available for protection of IPRs related to plants ?

(*a*) The Plant Patents Act (1930)
(*b*) The Plant Variety Protection Act of 1970.
(*c*) The Utility Patents Act (1985)
(*d*) All of the above

23. Which of the options given in Q. 22 is considered to be the most powerful and the most expansive in scope of coverage ?

24. Which of the following is correct ?

I. A patent act to provide patents on plants was first introduced in Germany in 1866.

II. The International Organisation for Plant Variety Protection (ASSINSEL) was established in 1938 with the objective of persuading governments of different countries for introducing laws to protect plant varieties.

III. The first International Union for Protection of New Plant Varieties (UPOV) convention was signed in 1961 in Paris.

IV. In 1993, UPOV had 24 member states.

Options :

(*a*) I, III, IV (*b*) I, II, III, IV
(*c*) I, II, IV (*d*) I, II, III

25. Which of the following is correct about farmer's privilege ?

I. Under UPOV 1978 Act, there was explict provision for farmer's privilege.

II. In the UPOV 1991 Act, farmer's privilege was made 'optional'.

III. PBR systems generally allow the farmers to use the seeds of protected varieties produced by themselves.

IV. It is a very important provision for countries like India, where over 90% of the total cropped area is sown by seeds produced by the farmers themselves.

Options :

(*a*) I, II, III, IV (*b*) II, III, IV
(*c*) I, III, IV (*d*) I, III

26. The copyright suffers from which of the following limitations ?

(*a*) It provides protection for a specific period and only from reproduction as such of the copyright material.

(*b*) It does not prevent another person from using either the idea or the information contained in a copyright material.

(*c*) In case of DNA sequences, one may get around this protection by designing an alternative sequence to encode the same protein.

(*d*) All of the above.

27. Which of the following is correct ?

I. The UPOV 1978 Act is now revised as UPOV 1991 Act.

II. The UPOV 1991 Act has strengthened the PBR in comparison to the UPOV 1978 Act.

III. India has enacted the Protection of Plant Varieties and Farmer's Rights (PPVFR) Act (2001).

IV. The PPVFR Act (2001) is similar to UPOV Act (1978) in some respects, has same features of UPOV Act (1991) and is unique in respect to some of its other features.

Options :

(*a*) I, II, III (*b*) I, II, III, IV
(*c*) I, III, IV (*d*) II, III, IV

28. PPVFR Act 2001 is similar to UPOV Act (1978) with respect to which of the following ?

I. Protection of varieties of nationally recognized plant species.

II. The duration of protection is 15 years or more.

III. Provision for farmer's privilege.

Options :

(*a*) I, II (*b*) I, II, III
(*c*) II, III (*d*) I, III

29. PPVFR Act (2001) is comparable to UPOV Act (1991) with respect to which of the following ?

(*a*) Requirement of novelty, distinctiveness, uniformity and stability for registration of a variety.

(*b*) Protection extended to commercial use of all the material of the protected variety.

(*c*) Essentially-derived varieties being subjected to PBR protection granted to the concerned initial varieties.

(*d*) Both (*a*) and (*c*).

30. PPVFR Act (2001) has which of the following unique features which ***are not provided*** for the UPOV Acts (1978, 1991) ?

I. Registration of extant varieties

II. Registration of farmer's varieties

III. It permits farmers to 'exchange, share or sell' their farm produce, including seed, except as branded seed.

IV. It provides protection to farmer's from innocent infringement of PBR.

Options :

(*a*) I, II, III, IV (*b*) I, II, IV
(*c*) I, II, III (*d*) II, III, IV

31. Under the provisions of UPOV Act 1991, a plant variety must satisfy which of the following criteria for protection ?

I. Novelty II. Stability
III. Distinctiveness IV. Uniformity

Options :

(*a*) I, II, III, IV (*b*) I, II, III
(*c*) II, III, IV (*d*) I, III, IV

32. The provisions of UPOV 1991 Act offer which of the following protections to the concerned variety ?

I. Sale of materials becomes the exclusive right of the holder of the PBR title.
II. A grower may be allowed to reserve a portion of his harvest for use as seed for his own next crop.
III. Farmers can exchage small amounts of seeds/propagating materials.
IV. The use for scientific purpose is not subject to PBR title.

Options :

(*a*) I, II, III (*b*) II, III, IV
(*c*) I, II, IV (*d*) I, II, III, IV

33. Which of the following countries has 30 years protection for inbred lines of maize and for clovers and a few grasses ?

(*a*) France (*b*) Germany
(*c*) U.S.A. (*d*) U.K

34. The PPVFR Act (2001) aims to provide for the establishment of suitable systems for which of the following ?

I. Protection of plant varieties
II. Providing for rights of the farmers
III. Implementing plant breeder's rights
IV. Development of new breeds of animals

Options :

(*a*) I, II, III, IV (*b*) I, II, III
(*c*) II, III, IV (*d*) I, II, IV

35. Which of the following is the main considerations for the development of PBR systems ?

(*a*) It allows breeders to benefit from the varieties developed by them.
(*b*) It encourages plant breeding activities.
(*c*) Private sector is encouraged to invest in plant breeding and seed industry.
(*d*) All of the above.

36. Which of the following statements are correct about historical development of intellectual property rights in India ?

I. In 1856, the Act of Protection of Inventions was introduced.
II. In 1872, Patents and Designs Protection Act was passed.
III. In 1883, the Protection of Inventions Act was introduced; it was consolidated as Inventions and Designs Act in 1888.
IV. On August 15, 1947, the Indian patents and designs came under the management of Controller of Patents and Designs.

Options :

(*a*) I, II, III (*b*) II, III, IV
(*c*) I, II, III, IV (*d*) I, II, IV

37. Which of the following is correct about historical development of Intellectual Property Rights in India ?

I. The Indian Patents Act (1970) was introduced in the Parliament in 1965.
II. Protection of designs is covered by the Indian Patent and Design Act (1911) with subsequent amendments.
III. Trademark protection is in force since June 1, 1946 under the 1940 Act.
IV. The Indian copyright Act 1957, ammended in 1999, is comparable to international standards.

Options :

(*a*) I, II, III, IV (*b*) II, III
(*c*) I, III, IV (*d*) I, IV

38. Which of the following is correct about international harmonization of patent laws ?

I. The first concrete efforts were made by the Paris Convention for the Protection of Industrial Property signed in 1983
II. The Paris Convention established equal protection of industrial IPR under the laws of member countries for both nationals and residents of other member countries of the convention.
III. The Paris Convention also allows inventors to claim in all the member

countries by filing a patent application initially in one of the member states.

IV. The Paris Convention has 100 member states; India joined the convention on December 7, 1998.

Options :
(*a*) I, III, IV (*b*) I, II, III
(*c*) I, II, III, IV (*d*) I, II, IV

39. Government of India has now established the PPVFR Authority (PPVFRA) with head-quarters at which of the following place ?
(*a*) Chennai (*b*) Kolkata
(*c*) New Delhi (*d*) Hyderabad

40. Which of the following is correct about international harmonization of patent laws ?

I. IPRs are administered but not enforced, by the World Intellectual Property Organization (WIPO), Geneva.

II. WIPO operates by asking member states to ratify a convention and to introduce the agreed basic principles into their national laws.

III. The Trade Related Intellecutal Property Rights (TRIPs) agreement is the most comprehensive multilateral agreement on IPR.

IV. TRIPs became effective on January 1, 1998.

Options :
(*a*) I, II, IV (*b*) I, II, III
(*c*) II, III, IV (*d*) I, II, III, IV

41. Which of the following is correct ?

I. Member countries of WTO are obliged to meet all the articles of TRIPs.

II. The provisions of GATT are administered and enforced by WTO, Geneva.

III. The member countries of WTO have been given a period of 5 years to suitably ammend their IPR laws according to TRIPs.

IV. Each member country has the option to frame its own patent laws within the broad framework defined in the GATT agreement.

Options :
(*a*) I, II, III, IV (*b*) I, II, IV
(*c*) I, II, III (*d*) I, III, IV

42. Which of the following is correct ?

I. Pending modification of patent laws as per TRIPs provision, the developing countries are expected to provide for a 'mailbox protection'.

II. Under 'mail box provision', a country will accept patent applications for products related to pharmaceuticals and agricultural chemicals from January 1, 1995 and keep them for consideration after the patent laws are suitably ammended.

III. The member countries are required to guarantee exclusive marketing rights for 5 years to each invention.

Options :
(*a*) I, II, III (*b*) II, III
(*c*) I, III (*d*) I, II

43. Which of the following is correct about TRIPs in relation to India ?

I. In 1997, USA complained to WTO that India has failed to meet the basic commitments to TRIPs.

II. The Dispute Settlement Body of WTO, observed that India has failed to provide 'mailbox' system of protection.

III. India was given time till April 1999 to meet the basic commitment to TRIPs, failing which USA could call for appropriate sanctions.

IV. India is required to change its patent laws as per the broad framework of TRIPs latest by 2008.

Options :
(*a*) I, III, IV (*b*) I, II, III, IV
(*c*) I, II, III (*d*) II, III, IV

44. In India, which of the following is correct ?

I. A provision for grant of exclusive marketing rights has been made upto December 31, 2004.

II. Product patents are not allowed.

III. The provision in relation to compulsory license shall, apply to 'exclusive marketing rights' all well.

IV. In the interest of security of India, the government of India may not disclose any information relating to any patentable invention.

Options :

(*a*) I, III, IV (*b*) II, III, IV
(*c*) I, II, III, IV (*d*) I, II, IV

45. Which of the following features are concerned with Protection of Plant Varieties and Farmers Rights (PPVFR) Act, 2001 ?

I. Registration of farmer's varieties.

II. A new variety must meet criteria of novelty, distinctiveness, uniformity and stability.

III. Any variety involving any technology, which is injurious to life or health of human beings, animals or plants may be registered.

IV. A variety that has been 'essentially-derived' from an initial variety can be registered as a new variety.

Options :

(*a*) I, II, III, IV (*b*) I, II, IV
(*c*) I, II, III (*d*) II, III, IV

46. The PPVFR Act (2001) recognizes the farmer's rights in which of the following respects ?

I. Registration of farmer's varieties.

II. Reward for the farmers engaged in the conservation of genetic resources provided that the materials have been used as donors of genes in varieties registered under PPVFR Act.

III. Freedom of farmers to save, use, sow, resow, exchange, share or sell their own farm produce, including seed.

IV. Requirement for the breeder to disclose to the farmers the expected performance of the variety under given conditions; the farmers can claim compensation if this expectation is not fulfilled.

Options :

(*a*) I, II, III, IV (*b*) II, III, IV
(*c*) I, III, IV (*d*) I, II, IV

47. Which of the following features are concerned with the PPVFR Act (2001) ?

I. The duration of protection of the varieties will be 15 years for the extant varieties and for varieties of most food crops.

II. Registration of a variety confers an exclusive right 'to produce, sell, market, distribute, import or export the variety'.

III. Freedom to use any registered variety for research and for creation of new varieties, except essentially derived varieties.

IV. Compulsory license may be granted after 3 years of registration of a variety if seed of the variety is not available to the public.

Options :

(*a*) I, II, III (*b*) II, III, IV
(*c*) I, III, IV (*d*) I, II, III, IV

48. Which of the following biotechnological inventions can be patented ?

(*a*) Microorganisms, cell lines, plant/animal lines obtained through biotechnolgical approaches.

(*b*) DNA sequences/genes and the proteins encoded, if any, by them.

(*c*) Biotechnological process/technologies for modification of the properties of various organisms.

(*d*) All of the above.

49. Which of the following features are concerned with PPVFR Act (2001) ?

I. The procedure for making a 'claim attributable to the contribution to the evolution of any variety' and seeking award from the 'gene fund' has been specified.

II. The Central Government shall establish the Protection of Plant Varieties and Farmer's Rights Authority.

III. The Central Govt. shall establish a Plant Varieties Registry for the registration of plant varieties.

IV. The breeder shall be required to deposit specified quantities of seeds/propagules of the registered variety as well as it parental lines in the National Gene Bank.

Options :

(*a*) I, II, III, IV (*b*) I, III, IV
(*c*) I, II, III (*d*) II, III, IV

50. Which of the following features ***is not concerned*** with the PPVFR Act (2001) ?

(*a*) The Central Govt. is to constitute a National Gene Fund.
(*b*) Citizens of convention countries will have the same rights as citizens of India under the Act.
(*c*) Application for registration of a variety may be made in India within 2 years from the date of application for registration of the same plant variety made in the covention country.
(*d*) The rights of PBR holder 'shall not be deemed infringed by a farmer who was not aware of the existence of such right'.

51. Which of the following biotechnology-related matters can be patented ?
(*a*) Method/process of production.
(*b*) Products, etc.
(*c*) Applications of the various processes/ products.
(*d*) Any of the above.

52. In case of PPVFR Act (2001), the gene fund shall be used for which of the following ?
(*a*) Paying compensation to communities for their contributions to the development of a variety.
(*b*) Conservation of genetic resources.
(*c*) Sustainable use of genetic resources.
(*d*) All of the above.

53. Methods for which of the following ***can not be patented*** ?
(*a*) Treatment of disease
(*b*) Diagnosis of disease
(*c*) Prevention of disease
(*d*) All of the above

54. Which of the following is correct about patenting of genes and DNA sequences isolated from naturally occuring organisms ?
I. Patents are allowed in U.S.A.
II. The first patent was for the gene *aroA*.
III. The patent for *aroA* is held in terms of a DNA sequence containing this gene.
IV. The US patent statute (35 USC 101) requires an invention to be 'useful' for being patented.

Options :
(*a*) I, II, III (*b*) II, III, IV
(*c*) I, II, III, IV (*d*) I, III, IV

55. Which of the following is correct about gene *Xa21* ?
I. The gene was originally discovered by Dr. R.C. Chaudhary in the wild species *Oryza longistaminata.*
II. Dr. G.S. Khush transferred it into *Oryza sativa*, named it as *Xa21* and located it on chromosome 11.
III. Dr. Tanksley (USA) identified the molecular markers flanking *Xa21*.
IV. This gene was isolated and patented.

Options :
(*a*) I, II, III, IV (*b*) I, II, III
(*c*) I, III, IV (*d*) I, II, IV

56. Which of the following life forms ***can not be patented*** in India under the provisions of Indian Patents Act (1970) ?
(*a*) Microorganisms (*b*) Animals
(*c*) Plants (*d*) All of the above

57. ***Statement (S)***: In 1992, European Patent Office (EPO) awarded a patent for onco-mouse.
Reason (R): The European Patent Office did not consider oncomouse as an animal variety.

Options :
(*a*) Both S and R are correct and R adequately explains S.
(*b*) Both S and R are correct, but R does not explain S.
(*c*) Only S is correct.
(*d*) Only R is correct.

58. Patent activity is the lowest in which of the following ?
(*a*) USA (*b*) Japan
(*c*) Europe (*d*) India

59. Which of the following is concerned with broad patents in biotechnology ?
I. Protection of all kinds of transgenic cotton granted to Agracetus (Middleton, USA).
II. Patent listed in item I was challenged and the US PTO revoked it in December 1994 as a consequence of its reexamination.
III. The final position of this revocation will be clear only after Agracetus (U.S.A.) has exhausted all the opportunities of appeal.

IV. A similar patent to Agracetus was granted in India in 1991, but it was revoked in 1994.

Options :

(*a*) I, II, IV (*b*) I, II, IV
(*c*) I, II, III, IV (*d*) I, III, IV

60. Column A lists the names of companies and column B lists names of the transgenic plants for which broad patents were granted. Match both the columns carefully and select the correct option from those listed below them.

Column A	Column B
A. W.R. Grace & Co.	1. *Brassica* family
B. DNA Plant Technology	2. Pepper
C. Calgene, Inc.	3. Cotton, soybean

Options :

(*a*) AIII, BII, CI (*b*) AII, BI, CIII
(*c*) AI, BIII, CII (*d*) AI, BII, CIII

61. Column A lists the names of the companies and column B lists the traits for which broad patents were granted. Match both the columns carefully and select the correct option from those given below them.

Column A	Column B
A. Pioneer Hi-Bred	I. Insect resistance- (*cry* gene)
B. Dekalb Genetic Corp	II. Low level of saturated fatty acids
C. Plant Genetic Systems	III. Increased lysine content.

Options :

(*a*) AI, BII, CIII (*b*) AII, BIII, CI
(*c*) AIII, BI, CII (*d*) AII, BI, CIII

62. Column A lists the names of companies and column B lists names of technologies/processes for which broad patents were granted. Match both the columns carefully and select the correct option from those listed below them.

Column A	Column B
A. Mycogen Corp	I. Gene gun method of genetic engineering of soybean
B. Enzo Biochem, Inc.	II. Any method of modifying the *cry gene* of *B. thuringiensis*
C. W.R. Grace & Co.	III. 'Antisense' RNA technology

Options :

(*a*) AIII, BI, CII (*b*) AI, BIII, CII
(*c*) AII, BI, CIII (*d*) AII, BIII, CI

63. Which of the following is correct about the Convention on Biological Diversity (CBD) ?

I. On December 29, 1993, India and 172 other nations singed this.

II. CBD recognizes the sovereign rights of nations over their genetic resources.

III. India was a signatory to the International Undertaking on Plant Genetic Resources developed by the FAO in 1983.

IV. The CBD has recognized two outstanding issues: the mechanism for implementing farmer's rights and the status of *ex situ* germplasm collected prior to December, 1993.

Options :

(*a*) I, II, III (*b*) II, III, IV
(*c*) I, II, III, IV (*d*) I, III, IV

64. Which of the following technologies and/or raw materials were used to develop Endless Summer tomato by DNA Plant Technology ?

(*a*) Selectable marker *npt*II.

(*b*) CaMV 35S promoter and the ACC synthase gene.

(*c*) Antisense RNA technology and *Agrobacterium tumefaciens* mediated genetic transformation.

(*d*) All of the above.

65. DNA Plant Technology faced difficulties during release of Endless Summer due to the use of which the options listed in Q. 64 ?

66. The PPVFR Authority (PPVFRA) began registration of plant varieties in which of the following years ?

(*a*) 2005 (*b*) 2006
(*c*) 2007 (*d*) 2008

67. In order to survive in an IPR hungry world, systematic, effective and continued effort must be made to train Indian scientists and technologists to enable to provide technical support for which of the following ?

I. Writing 'world-class' patents based on their innovations.

II. Defending patents.
III. Formulating opposition/revocation cases.
IV. Identifying infringements.

Options :
(*a*) I, II, III (*b*) I, II, III, IV
(*c*) I, III, IV (*d*) II, III, IV

68. Which of the following is offered by PBR ?
I. Opportunity for breeders to benefit from varieties developed by them.
II. Increased competition among various organizations engaged in plant breeding.
III. Disincentive to private companies to invest in plant breeding activities.
IV. Access to varieties developed in other countries and protected by IPR laws.

Options :
(*a*) I, II, III, IV (*b*) II, III, IV
(*c*) I, II, IV (*d*) I, III, IV

69. In order to survive in an IPR hungry world, efforts must be made to bring about which of the following in India ?
I. Introduction of IPR into curriculum.
II. Modernisation of Indian Patent Office (IPO).
III. Drastic reform of educational system to produce vibrant, innovative, committed and motivated individuals.
IV. Creation of databases of our national resources.

Options :
(*a*) I, II, III, IV (*b*) I, III, IV
(*c*) I, II, III (*d*) II, III, IV

70. IPR management involves which of the following ?
I. Transfer of the IPR appropriately and at optimum value.
II. Establishment of collaborative linkages to facilitate exploitation of the IPR.
III. Monitoring infrigements and enforcing IPRs.
IV. Renewal of patents and designs periodically.

Options :
(*a*) I, III, IV (*b*) II, III, IV
(*c*) I, II, III, IV (*d*) I, II, III

71. Which of the following benefits is offered by IPR ?
I. It encourages and safeguards intellectual and artistic creations.
II. It enables the dissemination of new ideas and technologies quickly and widely.
III. Discourage investments in R&D efforts.
IV. Provides consumers with the results of creations and inventions.

Options :
(*a*) I, II, IV (*b*) I, II, III, IV
(*c*) I, II, III (*d*) II, III, IV

72. Which of the following may be associated with PBR ?
I. Increased cost of seed.
II. Lower than the demand of seed production in order to achieve more profits.
III. Monopolies in genetic materials for specific traits.
IV. Dilution/elimination of farmer's privilege.

Options :
(*a*) I, II, III (*b*) I, II, IV
(*c*) I, III, IV (*d*) I, II, III, IV

73. Which of the following may be the consequence of IPR regime ?
I. Threat to food security.
II. Adverse effects on biological diversity and ecological balance.
III. Detrimental to the livelihood of poor in developing countries.
IV. IPR may discourage monopolies.

Options :
(*a*) I, II, III (*b*) I, II, IV
(*c*) I, II (*d*) II, III, IV

74. Which of the following is an example of geographical indications ?
(*a*) Champagne wine
(*b*) Scotch whiskey
(*c*) California wine
(*d*) All of the above.

75. Geographical indications includes which of the following ?
(*a*) Natural products
(*b*) Agricultural goods
(*c*) Goods of handicraft
(*d*) All of the above

76. Which of the following ***is not correct*** about geographical indications (GIs) ?
   (*a*) Once enforced by legislation, GIs exclude others from using a GI as trademark.
   (*b*) The chief requirements for GI protection is that a given quality, reputation or some other characteristics of the product be essentially attributable to the locality of its origin.
   (*c*) The GIs do not cover manufactured products and even food products.
   (*d*) India has enacted the Geographical Indication Act (1999) to claim GI for a variety of goods, including 'Basmati' rice.

77. Monitoring and tackling the IPR aspects of inventions has which of the following features ?
   (*a*) Demands time.
   (*b*) Enhances cost.
   (*c*) May act as a disincentive for R&D efforts.
   (*d*) All of the above

78. PPVFR Act (2001) allows registration of which of the following ?
   (*a*) Farmer's varieties
   (*b*) Extant varieties
   (*c*) New varieties
   (*d*) All of the above.

79. In the first instance, PPVFR began registration of varieties in how many of the crops ?
   (*a*) 6 (*b*) 12
   (*c*) 2 (*d*) 20

18.2. FILL IN THE BLANKS

1. The IPR is recognized by governments only so long as it is not .... to the society.
2. The best guarded secret of the modern times concerns the .... of Coca Cola.
3. In India, computer software are now protected under the ....
4. A patent entitled 'Basmati Rice Line and Grain' for a novel, high yielding, medium dwarf, photoinsensitive rice having all the desirable features of basmati rice, was awarded to ...., Texas (U.S.A.) on Sept. 2, 1997.
5. A purified natural compound like azadirachtin isolated from .... has been patented.
6. A patent was granted to A.M. Chakraborty for a .... developed from a natural isolate through genetic manipulation.
7. In most of the countries, patent is awarded for a period of .... years.
8. The Indian Patent Act (1970) granted protection for .... or .... years.
9. The PPVFR Act (2001) recognises farmer's right and provides for monetary compensation for these rights from ....
10. The UPOV 1991 Act has strengthned the PBR in comparison to UPOV 1978 Act and has made PBR more comparable to a .... protection.
11. The use of protected cultivar for the creation of .... for plant breeding purposes is not dependent on permission of the holder of PBR title.
12. The Protection of Plant Varieties and Farmer's Rights Act (2001) was passed in .... by the Lok Sabha.
13. The European Patent Convention (EPC) began to operate in .... and has 17 member states.
14. Abbreviation WIPO stands for ....
15. TRIPs became effective on January 1, ...
16. Abbreviation GATT stands for ....
17. The office of World Trade Organization (WTO) is located at ....
18. India is required to change its patent laws as per the broad framework of TRIPs latest by ....
19. In case of PPVFR Act (2001), definition of an essentially derived variety is comparable to that given in UPOV Act (.............) with an additional clarification that such a variety must be distinguishable from the 'initial variety' and otherwise confirm to the latter

in the expression of heritable essential characteristics.

20. In case of PPVFR Act (2001), the criterion of novelty requires a food crop variety to be in commercial use for .... year in India, or less than .... years outside India.
21. In case of PPVFR Act (2001), application for registration of a variety may be made in India within .... from the date of application for registration of the same plant variety made in a convention country.
22. In 1998, the .... approved provisions for patenting of DNA sequences where the use of the technological process is specified.
23. In U.S.A., European Union and other developed countries, microorganisms isolated from nature or obtained by simple mutagenesis and/or selection from natural isolates are .... patentable.
24. Among the higher organisms modified by biotechnology, ... were the first to be patented in U.S.A., in 1985, when a .... overproducing tryptophan was allowed a patent.
25. Geographical indication (GI) protection is recognized under the provisions of .... of GATT (1994).
26. The first animal patent in the world was awarded in U.S.A. in 1988 to ....
27. In Europe, U.S.A. and Japan, over .... of the patent applications are filed both of total applications and of applications in high technology areas, including biotechnology.
28. The rice gene *Xa21*, specifies resistance to ....
29. Abbreviation ICBD stands for ....
30. National Biodiversity Act has a mandate to control .... and prevent unauthorized transfer of information about biological resources of the country to a person who is not a citizen of India or a corporate body that is not registered in the country.

18.3. MARK TRUE OR FALSE

1. The development of an intellectual property, as a rule, requires intellectual inputs, ingenuity and innovativeness.
2. The Indian Patent Act of 1970 allows product patents in pharmaceuticals, foods and agrochemicals.
3. The concept of patentable subject matter is bound to change with time.
4. The Indian Patent Act (1970) has now been amended as Indian Patents (Amendment) Act 1999; it allows product patents, except for some specified medicines/drugs.
5. The disclosure of an invention gives an opportunity to other inventors to improve upon the various features of the invention so that it becomes more efficient and/or useful.
6. PBR protection covers breeding methods.
7. PBR protection covers the new variety, but does not protect the parents of the variety, except in the case of hybrid varieties.
8. The concept of PBR originated in the developed countries, where private companies have been important/major players in plant breeding and seed production/marketing.
9. A plant variety should be regarded as an intellectual property, the rights to benefit from which needs legal protection.
10. India has now enacted its own PBR law called Protection of Plant Varieties and Farmer's Rights, Act, 2004.
11. The provision of TRIPs covers a variety of intellectual properties, including patents and protection of new varieties of plants.
12. The techniques of surgery are patentable.
13. The European Patent Office (EPO) has suggested that isolation of a substance from nature is merely a 'discovery' and, therefore, should not be patentable. However, the process developed for the isolation of this product is patentable.
14. According to the EPO, if natural substance is characterized and is found to be 'new' having 'no previously recognized' existence, the substance *per se* should be patentable.

15. In U.S.A., the U.S. Patent and Trademark Office (USPTO) held that natural products were not patentable. But in 1977, the U.S. Court of Customs and Appeals clarified that, although a natural product *per se* is not patentable a *new* 'form' or 'composition' of the product can be patented.
16. The processes used for genetic modification of various organisms are not patentable virtually in all countries, including India.
17. An artificially synthesized gene is considered patentable in almost all developed countries, but patenting of genes isolated from naturally occurring organisms is controversial.
18. Microorganisms modified by genetic engineering are patentable.
19. In U.S.A., non-naturally occurring, non-human mutlicellular organisms are considered patentable by the U.S. Patent and Trademark Office.
20. The varius objections raised against patenting of life forms are largely ethical and political in nature.
21. Most patents in biotechnology, especially agricultural biotechnology, are rather broad in nature.
22. India has enacted the Biological Diveristy Act (2002), and created a National Biodiveristy Authority (NBA), Chennai.
23. IPR management involves qualitative evaluation of factors such as ratio of the R&D investments to the royalty.
24. IPR may be detrimental to the livelihood of poor in developing countries.

SECTION III

MODEL QUESTION PAPERS (I–VII)

MODEL QUESTION PAPER – I

MULTIPLE CHOICE QUESTIONS

1. Which of the following is often called molecular glue ?
(*a*) DNA ligase (*b*) Synthetase
(*c*) DNA polymerase I (*d*) RNA polymerase

2. Which of the following assays involves antigen-antibody interaction ?
(*a*) Southern hybridization
(*b*) Dot-blot assay
(*c*) ELISA
(*d*) Colony hydridization

3. Ordinarily, the recognition sites of restriction enzymes are, which of the following ?
(*a*) Palindromes
(*b*) Nonpalindromic
(*c*) Asymmetrical
(*d*) Palindromes with rotational symmetry

4. A RAPD fragment is generated when sequences complementary to the single arbitrary primer used in the PCR reaction are located at two sites in the target DNA, having which of the following features ?
(*a*) In the same direction
(*b*) In the opposite directions
(*c*) Within 5 Kb distance
(*d*) Both (*b*) and (*c*) together

5. Totipotency is reflected by which of the following ?
(*a*) Somatic embryogenesis
(*b*) Shoot regeneration
(*c*) Pollen embryogenesis
(*d*) All of the above

6. Plant tissue culture is regarded to have began when Haberlandt attempted to culture *in vitro*, which of the following ?
(*a*) Leaf discs (*b*) Isolated leaf cells
(*c*) Cambium tissue (*d*) Zygotic embryos

7. In which of the following, somatic embryos are used for micropropagation ?
(*a*) Coconut (*b*) Oil palm
(*c*) Orchids (*d*) Date palm

8. Eukaryotic DNA segments are usually cloned initially in which of the following ?
(*a*) *Bacillus* (*b*) Yeast
(*c*) *E. coli* (*d*) Both (*a*) and (*b*)

9. Guide RNA is involved in which of the following ?
(*a*) RNA processing
(*b*) *Trans*-splicing
(*c*) RNA editing
(*d*) Alternative splicing

10. Production of which of the following ***does not constitute*** biotechnology ?
(*a*) Plastic (*b*) Antibiotic
(*c*) Idli (*d*) α-Amylase

11. Air-lift fermenters ***do not have provision*** for which of the following ?
(*a*) Aeration
(*b*) Stirring
(*c*) Temperature control
(*d*) Sterilization

12. A vaccine contains which of the following ?
(*a*) Inactivated pathogen
(*b*) Attenuated pathogen
(*c*) Purified antigen from pathogen
(*d*) Any of the above

13. Viruses from plants can be eliminated by which of the following ?
(*a*) Thermotherapy (*b*) Cryotherapy
(*c*) Chemotheraphy (*d*) Any of the above

14. In case of single cell proteins, high content of which of the following is problematic ?
(*a*) Nucleic acids (*b*) Lipids
(*c*) Carbohydrates (*d*) Proteins

15. 'Edible vaccines' belong to which of the following category ?
(*a*) Conventional vaccines
(*b*) Purified antigen vaccines
(*c*) Recombinant vaccines
(*d*) Both (*a*) and (*b*)

16. The term 'clonal selection' signifies which of the following in response to an antigen ?
(*a*) B cell proliferation
(*b*) T cell proliferation
(*c*) B/T cell maturation
(*d*) Both (*a*) and (*b*)

17. Which of the following mapping populations is immortal ?
(*a*) Recombinant inbred lines
(*b*) Near-isogenic lines
(*c*) Both (*a*) and (*b*)
(*d*) F_2 population

18. Which of the following molecular markers is expected to produce a single band ?
(*a*) Sequence-tagged microsatellite marker
(*b*) RAPD
(*c*) Amplified fragment length polymorphism
(*d*) ISSR (inter-simple sequence repeats)

19. Single cell proteins are obtained from which of the following ?
(*a*) Bacteria (*b*) Fungi
(*c*) Algae (*d*) All of the above

20. Which of the following generates more number of different proteins from the same number of genes ?
(*a*) Autosplicing
(*b*) *Trans*-splicing
(*c*) Alternative splicing
(*d*) RNA editing

21. 'Single cell protein' is represented by which of the following ?
(*a*) Protein from microbes
(*b*) Protein from cell cultures
(*c*) Microbial biomass
(*d*) Both (*a*) and (*b*)

22. Which of the following markers behaves as dominant marker ?
(*a*) RFLP (*b*) RAPD
(*c*) AFLP (*d*) Both (*b*) and (*c*)

23. In India, a transgenic variety can be protected by which of the following ?
(*a*) Patent
(*b*) Plant Breeder's Rights
(*c*) Both (*a*) and (*b*)
(*d*) Trade Secret

24. Trade secret can be used to protect which of the following ?
(*a*) A formula (*b*) A design
(*c*) A manuscript (*d*) A transgene

25. In immune response, antibodies are produced by which of the following ?
(*a*) T cells (*b*) Memory B cells
(*c*) Plasma cells (*d*) Naive B cells

26. MHC molecules are present on the surface of which of the following ?
(*a*) Helper T cells
(*b*) T_C cells
(*c*) Antigen presenting cells
(*d*) Pathogens

27. A monoclonal antibody is specific to a single epitope because of which of the following ?
(*a*) It is produced by a single B cell
(*b*) It is produced by a single hybrid cell clone obtained by fusing a single B cell with a fusion partner.
(*c*) A single antigen is used for immunization of the animal from which the B cell is obtained.
(*d*) A single antigen epitope is used for the immunization of the animal from which the B cell is obtained.

28. PEG promotes which of the following ?
(*a*) Protoplast fusion
(*b*) Animal cell fusion
(*c*) DNA uptake by protoplasts
(*d*) All of the above.

29. Monoclonal antibodies are used for which of the following ?
(*a*) Disease diagnosis
(*b*) ELISA
(*c*) Immunopurification
(*d*) All of the above

30. The melting temperature for a DNA sequence having 6 G : C and 4 A : T base pairs will be which of the following ?

(*a*) 32°C (*b*) 28°C
(*c*) 36°C (*d*) 30°C

31. In PCR, primer length affects the temperature used for which of the following ?
(*a*) Denaturation
(*b*) Annealing
(*c*) Primer extension
(*d*) Storage of PCR product

32. Which of the following markers uses restriction enzymes ?
(*a*) RFLP
(*b*) Microsatellite markers
(*c*) AFLP
(*d*) Both (*a*) and (*c*)

33. In which of the following PCR procedures, target DNA is cut and circularised, then cut open to produce linear molecules ?
(*a*) Anchored PCR (*b*) Asymmetric PCR
(*c*) Inverse PCR (*d*) Nested PCR

34. Which of the following uses two pairs of PCR primers ?
(*a*) Nested PCR (*b*) Asymmetric PCR
(*c*) Inverse PCR (*d*) Anchored PCR

35. In case of a plasmid, which form will move the fastest in gel ?
(*a*) Linear form
(*b*) Supercoiled circular
(*c*) Both (*a*) and (*b*)
(*d*) Relaxed circular

36. The site where a protein binds a DNA molecule is determined by which of the following techniques ?
(*a*) DNA footprinting
(*b*) DNA fingerprinting
(*c*) Gel retardation assay
(*d*) FISH

37. Nick translation uses which of the following enzymes ?
(*a*) *E. coli* DNA polymerase III
(*b*) *E. coli* Klenow fragment
(*c*) *E. coli* DNA polymerase II
(*d*) DNA polymerase I of *E. coli*

38. Which of the following involves restriction mapping of DNA fragments ?
(*a*) Chromosome jumping
(*b*) Primer walking
(*c*) Chromosome walking
(*d*) Both (*b*) and (*c*)

39. The whole genome of which of the following was the first to be sequenced ?
(*a*) Baker's yeast
(*b*) *E. coli*
(*c*) *Bacillus subtilis*
(*d*) *Haemophilus influenzae*

40. The Human Genome Project was officially completed in which of the following years ?
(*a*) 2001 (*b*) 2003
(*c*) 2005 (*d*) 2007

41. The human genome is estimated to contain how many genes ?
(*a*) 35,000 (*b*) 25,000
(*c*) 45,000 (*d*) 55,000

42. Which of the following growth regulators suppresses callus formation ?
(*a*) GA_3 (*b*) Auxin
(*c*) Cytokinin (*d*) Both (*a*) and (*b*)

43. Which of the following human chromosomes has the highest extent of segmental duplications ?
(*a*) Autosome 1 (*b*) X chromosome
(*c*) Y chromosome (*d*) Autosome 13

44. A single-nucleotide polymorphic site has how many alleles ?
(*a*) 1 (*b*) 4
(*c*) 2 (*d*) 3

45. In which of the following, gene integration occurs generally by homologous recombination ?
(*a*) Yeast (*b*) Mammals
(*c*) Tobacco (*d*) Tomato

46. Which of the following vectors can be used to clone DNA inserts of about 40 kb ?
(*a*) Plasmid (*b*) Cosmid
(*c*) Phagemid (*d*) M13

47. Which of the following vectors ***can not be used*** to efficiently clone DNA inserts longer than 5 kb ?
(*a*) Cosmid (*b*) Plasmid
(*c*) Lambda phage (*d*) M13

48. A BAC vector can be used to efficiently clone DNA inserts of upto which of the following ?

(*a*) 1 Mb (*b*) 100 Kb
(*c*) 300 Kb (*d*) 500 Kb

49. A helper Ti of binary vector system ***does have*** which of the following ?
(*a*) *vir* region
(*b*) DNA insert
(*c*) Origin of replication for *E. coli*
(*d*) T-DNA

50. Which of the following molecules functions as a protein kinase ?
(*a*) VirA (*b*) VirB
(*c*) VirD (*d*) VirG

51. Which of the following Vir proteins functions as activator of *vir* operons ?
(*a*) VirE (*b*) VirG
(*c*) VirH (*d*) VirD

52. The intermediate vector of Ti plasmid cointegrate vector system ***does not have*** which of the following ?
(*a*) T-DNA borders
(*b*) T DNA sequence
(*c*) *E. coli* plasmid sequence
(*d*) Origin of replication for *E. coli*

53. Which of the following proteins is active against Diptera ?
(*a*) CryI (*b*) CryIII
(*c*) CryIV (*d*) CryVI

54. Which of the following proteins is active against nematodes ?
(*a*) CryII (*b*) CryIA
(*c*) CryIII (*d*) CryVI

55. Which of the following approaches for virus resistance has been the most successful ?
(*a*) Coat protein gene
(*b*) cDNA of satellite RNA
(*c*) Antisense RNA approach
(*d*) Ribozyme approach

56. Which of the following can be used to suppress the expression of endogenous genes ?
(*a*) Cosuppression (*b*) Antisense RNA
(*c*) RNAi (*d*) All of the above

57. 'Laurical' variety of *B. napus* has, which of the following transgenes ?
(*a*) Lauroyl-ACP desaturase
(*b*) Lauroyl-ACP thioesterase
(*c*) Lauroyl-ACP saturase
(*d*) Stearoyl-ACP desaturase

58. 'Golden Rice' grains mainly accumulate, which of the following ?
(*a*) β-carotene (*b*) Lycopene
(*c*) Zeta-carotene (*d*) Phytoene

59. Phytate is used for phosphate storage in seeds, and it interferes with absorption of which of the following in human intestine ?
(*a*) β-Carotene (*b*) Zinc
(*c*) Iron (*d*) Phosphate

60. In case of 'Flavr Savr' tomato, the expression of which of the following has been suppressed ?
(*a*) ACC synthase
(*b*) Polygalacturonase
(*c*) β-galacturonidase
(*d*) β-glucuronidase

61. In the case of *barnase-barstar* male sterility system, phosphinothricin resistance gene *bar* is used to achieve, which of the following ?
(*a*) Restoration of male fertility.
(*b*) Reinforcing male sterility.
(*c*) Enhancing Barstar action.
(*d*) Eliminating male fertile plants.

62. Which of the following research reagents is being produced from transgenic plants on a commercial scale ?
(*a*) Avidin
(*b*) β-glucuronidase
(*c*) Both (*a*) and (*b*)
(*d*) Polygalacturonidase

63. Which of the following would reduce transgene silencing ?
(*a*) Single copy integration in genome.
(*b*) Transgene AT composition similar to host genome.
(*c*) Each transgene having a different promoter and polyadenylation signal.
(*d*) All of the above.

64. The 'slow-growth' cultures of tropical plants would suffer cold damage at which temperatures ?
(*a*) 4°C (*b*) 8°C
(*c*) Both (*a*) and (*b*) (*d*) 15°C

65. A somatic hybrid plant may have chloroplasts from which of the following ?

(*a*) Both the parents
(*b*) First fusion parent
(*c*) Second fusion parent
(*d*) Any of the above

66. Somatic hydridization has been the most successful in which of the following ?
(*a*) Solanaceae (*b*) Papilionaceae
(*c*) Graminae (*d*) Malvaceae

67. 'Pusa Jai Kisan' variety of *B. juncea* is which of the following ?
(*a*) Transgenic
(*b*) Somaclonal variant
(*c*) Somatic hybrid
(*d*) Doubled haploid

68. Haploid plants can be obtained by which of the following ?
(*a*) Anther culture
(*b*) Ovary culture
(*c*) Interspecific hybridization
(*d*) All of the above

69. Haploid plants through anther culture were first produced in which of the following ?
(*a*) Potato (*b*) Tobacco
(*c*) Datura (*d*) *Brassica*

70. In which of the following, heat shock induces androgenesis ?
(*a*) Rice (*b*) *Brassica* sp.
(*c*) Barley (*d*) Datura

71. Androgenesis in which of the following would yield a dihaploid ?
(*a*) Barley (*b*) Potato
(*c*) Tobacco (*d*) Both (*b*) and (*c*)

72. In which of the following crops, somatic hybridization has yielded a commercial variety ?
(*a*) Tobacco (*b*) Tomato
(*c*) *Brassica juncea* (*d*) Rice

73. Which of the following contains nuclear genome from a single fusion parent ?
(*a*) Asymmetric hybrids
(*b*) Cybrids
(*c*) Symmetric hybrids
(*d*) Both (*a*) and (*b*)

74. 'Hybrid sorting' has relevance to which of the following ?
(*a*) Somatic hybridization
(*b*) Molecular markers
(*c*) Haploid production
(*d*) Marker-assisted selection

75. Somatic embryo maturation is promoted by which of the following ?
(*a*) Auxin (*b*) ABA
(*c*) Cytokinin (*d*) GA_3

76. Which of the following promotes somatic embryo conversion ?
(*a*) BAP (*b*) Auxin
(*c*) 2,4-D (*d*) GA_3

77. Which of the following is the least reliable strategy for virus indexing ?
(*a*) Indicator plants
(*b*) Serological tests
(*c*) Visible disease symptoms
(*d*) Both (*b*) and (*c*)

78. Negative cell selection allows which type of cells to divide ?
(*a*) Wild type cells (*b*) Variant cells
(*c*) Both (*a*) and (*b*) (*d*) Neither (*a*) nor (*b*)

79. Somaclonal variations due to epigenetic changes ***are generally not transmitted*** through which of the following ?
(*a*) Mitotic cell division
(*b*) Meiotic cell division
(*c*) Plantlet regeneration
(*d*) Both (*b*) and (*c*)

80. Disease resistant plants can be developed by cell selection using which of the following as selection agents ?
(*a*) Specific toxins
(*b*) Nonspecific toxins
(*c*) Both (*a*) and (*b*)
(*d*) Neither (*a*) nor (*b*)

81. Embryo culture is routinely used for propagation of which of the following ?
(*a*) Lily (*b*) Orchids
(*c*) Rose (*d*) Apple

82. Tissue culture raised plantlets require hardening due to which of the following ?
(*a*) Poor cuticle development
(*b*) Poor vascular bundle development
(*c*) Improper stomatal function
(*d*) All of the above

83. Hardening of tissue culture raised plantlets can be achieved by which of the following ?

(*a*) Modified culture conditions
(*b*) Chemical additives in medium
(*c*) Bacterization
(*d*) All of the above

84. Selection for hybrid cells based on which of the following is the most widely applicable ?
(*a*) Visual markers
(*b*) Complementation
(*c*) Transgenic selectable markers
(*d*) Both (*a*) and (*b*)

85. Which of the following serves as cryoprotectant ?
(*a*) DMSO (*b*) Proline
(*c*) Glycerol (*d*) All of the above.

86. Plant vitrification solutions are used for which of the following ?
(*a*) Slow-growth cultures
(*b*) Cryopreservation
(*c*) Micropropagation
(*d*) Prevention of hyperhydration

87. In case of pollen culture, which of the following is the most responsive stage of pollen development ?
(*a*) Around first mitosis
(*b*) Early uninucleate
(*c*) Late binucleate
(*d*) Trinucleate

88. Unfertilized ovaries/ovules are cultured for which of the following ?
(*a*) Gynogenesis (*b*) *In vitro* pollination
(*c*) Both (*a*) and (*b*) (*d*) Embryo rescue

89. In which of the following, GA_3 promotes shoot regeneration ?
(*a*) Tobacco (*b*) *Arabidopsis*
(*c*) Carrot (*d*) *Citrus*

90. *In vitro* regeneration potential is affected by which of the following ?
(*a*) Oligogenes (*b*) Polygenes
(*c*) Plasmagenes (*d*) All of the above

91. Which of the following is the most commonly used for root regeneration ?
(*a*) IBA (*b*) IAA
(*c*) 2,4-D (*d*) ABA

92. Which of the following is the strongest auxin?
(*a*) IAA (*b*) 2,4-D
(*c*) NAA (*d*) 2,4,5-T

93. Which of the following cytokinins is the most commonly used in micropropagation ?
(*a*) BA (*b*) Zeatin
(*c*) 2-ip (*d*) TDZ

94. Which of the following solubilizes phosphate ?
(*a*) *Thiobacillus* sp.
(*b*) *Glomus* sp.
(*c*) Both (*a*) and (*b*)
(*d*) *Azospirillum*

95. *Bacillus papillae* is used for biocontrol of which of the following ?
(*a*) *Heliothis* (*b*) Mosquitoes
(*c*) Leaf hoppers (*d*) Aphids

96. *Trichoderma viridae* is used for the control of which of the following ?
(*a*) Fungal pathogens
(*b*) Bacterial pathogens
(*c*) Weeds
(*d*) Nematodes

97. Which of the following enzymes is produced in the largest quantity ?
(*a*) β-Amylase (*b*) Lipase
(*c*) Lactase (*d*) α-Amylase

98. In production of glucose syrup, α-amylase brings about which of following ?
(*a*) Gelatinization
(*b*) Liquefaction
(*c*) Saccharification
(*d*) All of the above

99. Affinity biosensors are based on which of the following ?
(*a*) Enzyme (*b*) Antibody
(*c*) Nucleic acid (*d*) Either (*b*) or (*c*)

100. In cheese production, Rennet leads to curd formation by digesting, which of the following ?
(*a*) α-casein
(*b*) β-casein
(*c*) κ-casein
(*d*) All of the above

□□□

MODEL QUESTION PAPER – II

MULTIPLE CHOICE QUESTIONS

1. The two strands of a DNA double helix are held together due to which of the following ?
   (*a*) Hydrogen bonds
   (*b*) Hydrophobic interactions
   (*c*) Covalent bonds
   (*d*) Ionic interactions
2. Frame-shift mutations may result from which of the following ?
   (*a*) Base substitution
   (*b*) Trinucleotide expansion
   (*c*) Tautomeric shift
   (*d*) Transposition
3. A test-cross is made mainly to demonstrate which of the following ?
   (*a*) 1 : 1 ratio of gametes in monohybrids.
   (*b*) Random union of gametes.
   (*c*) Equal survival of zygotes.
   (*d*) Both (*a*) and (*b*).
4. Somatic hybridization has been the most successful in which of the following families ?
   (*a*) Cruciferae (*b*) Solanaceae
   (*c*) Graminae (*d*) Both (*a*) and (*b*)
5. The term 'wound reponse' refers to the production of which of the following by the plant cells at wound sites ?
   (*a*) Protein VirA (*b*) Acetosyringone
   (*c*) Protein VirG (*d*) Lectins
6. In hypersensitive response, the *avr* gene of pathogen is responsible for generating, which of the following ?
   (*a*) Toxin (*b*) Receptor
   (*c*) Elicitor (*d*) Repressor
7. In case of species propagated by asexual reproduction, germplasm is represented by which of the following ?
   (*a*) Pollen grains
   (*b*) Seed
   (*c*) Vegetative propagules
   (*d*) Zygotic embryos
8. Which of the following eukaryotic enzymes essentially functions as reverse transcriptase ?
   (*a*) DNA polymerase (*b*) Primase
   (*c*) RNA polymerase (*d*) Telomerase
9. Golgi bodies function in which of the following ?
   (*a*) Protein synthesis
   (*b*) Protein modification
   (*c*) Protein packaging
   (*d*) Both (*b*) and (*c*)
10. Which of the following is the most correct ?
    (*a*) Each normal chromosome has, as a rule, a single centromere.
    (*b*) The centromeric activity is always confined to a single locus in the chromosomes.
    (*c*) In most species, the centromeric activity is confined to a single locus in the chromosomes.
    (*d*) Polycentric chromosomes represent structural aberrations.
11. Which of the following is the chief reason for the reduction in chormosome number from $2n$ to n as a result of meiosis ?
    (*a*) Chromosome pairing during MI.
    (*b*) Separation of chromosomes during AI.
    (*c*) The (*a*) above, followed by (*b*).
    (*d*) Two nuclear divisions without an intervening S phase.
12. Which of the following is a transgene ?
    (*a*) A human gene transferred into *E. coli*

(*b*) A human gene used for gene therapy
(*c*) Both (*a*) and (*b*)
(*d*) An *Aegilops* sp. gene transferred into *Triticum* sp. by backcrossing

13. 'Hirudin' protein produced in *Brassica napus* is which of the following ?
(*a*) An antigen (*b*) An antithrombin
(*c*) An enzyme (*d*) A hormone

14. Beer production is estimated to have began about how many years ago ?
(*a*) 4000 (*b*) 6000
(*c*) 400 (*d*) 600

15. Which of the following is the first recombinant protein to be approved for use in humans ?
(*a*) Insulin (*b*) Interferon
(*c*) Hirudin (*d*) Erythropoietin

16. Department of Biotechnology, New Delhi supports, which of the following programmes in biotechnology ?
(*a*) M.Sc./M.Tech. (*b*) Post-doctoral
(*c*) Diploma (*d*) All of the above

17. A biotechnological production process may use which of the following ?
(*a*) A microbe
(*b*) An animal/a plant cell
(*c*) An enzyme
(*d*) Any of the above

18. A restriction enzyme has six-base recognition sequence. This sequence may be expected to occur at which of the following intervals ?
(*a*) 4^6 bp (*b*) 6^4 bp
(*c*) 4×6 bp (*d*) $4^6/6$ bp

19. Which of the following enzymes is used to prevent circularization of opened vectors during recombinant DNA production ?
(*a*) Acid phosphatase
(*b*) Polynucleotide kinase
(*c*) Alkaline phosphatase
(*d*) Klenow fragment

20. S1 nuclease is used for, which of the following ?
(*a*) DNA footprinting
(*b*) Production of blunt ends from protruding ends
(*c*) DNA fingerprinting
(*d*) DNA sequencing

21. Klenow fragment is used for which of the following ?
(*a*) Filling up of protruding ends
(*b*) Nick translation
(*c*) DNA sequencing
(*d*) Both (*a*) and (*c*)

22. 'Nick translation' is used for which of the following ?
(*a*) DNA labelling
(*b*) Recombinant protein production
(*c*) DNA replication
(*d*) Expression-based screening

23. Production of which of the following involves recombinant DNA technology ?
(*a*) Polyclonal antibodies
(*b*) Monoclonal antibodies
(*c*) Hybrid antibodies
(*d*) Both (*b*) and (*c*)

24. Which of the following uses insertional mutagenesis ?
(*a*) Gene tagging
(*b*) Exon trapping
(*c*) Differential screening
(*d*) Chromosome jumping

25. Which of the following is used for positional cloning of genes ?
(*a*) Chromosome walking
(*b*) Chromosome jumping
(*c*) Chromosome sorting
(*d*) Both (*a*) and (*b*)

26. Colony hydridization ***is not based*** on which of the following ?
(*a*) DNA : DNA hybridization
(*b*) Nucleic acid hybridization
(*c*) Antigen-antibody interaction
(*d*) RNA : DNA hybridization

27. Which of the following techniques ***does not*** use antigen-antibody interaction for screening of expression libraries ?
(*a*) Complementation
(*b*) ELISA
(*c*) FACS
(*d*) Both (*a*) and (*c*)

28. Genes encoding which of the following proteins are identified by South-western screening ?

(*a*) Binding to an RNA segment
(*b*) Binding to a protein
(*c*) Binding to a DNA segment
(*d*) Binding to an antibody

29. North-western screening is based on which of the following ?
(*a*) Antigen-antibody interaction
(*b*) RNA-protein interaction
(*c*) DNA : protein interaction
(*d*) RNA : DNA interaction

30. In case of retrovirus vectors, ψ sequence is required for which of the following ?
(*a*) Transcription
(*b*) Replication
(*c*) Reverse transcription
(*d*) Packaging into virions

31. Which of the following is indispensable for PCR ?
I. Target DNA
II. dNTPs
III. Primers
IV. Thermal cycler/PCR machine
V. Thermostable DNA polymerase

Options :
(*a*) I, II, III, IV (*b*) I, II, III, V
(*c*) I, II, III, IV, V (*d*) I, II, III

32. Thymine is found in which of the following ?
I. Unique DNA II. Satellite DNA
III. tRNA IV. mRNA

Options :
(*a*) I, II, III, IV (*b*) I, II, III
(*c*) I, II (*d*) I, II, IV

33. Which of the following has more than one chromosome in its genome ?
(*a*) *E. coli* (*b*) *B. subtilis*
(*c*) *Agrobacterium* (*d*) *Vibrio cholerae*

34. Genome means which of the following ?
I. Haploid set of chromosomes
II. Complete genetic information present in a cell
III. Proteins expressed in a cell/tissue at a given time.
IV. Proteins expressed in a cell during its entire life time

Options :
(*a*) I, II (*b*) I, II, III
(*c*) I, II, III, IV (*d*) I, II, IV

35. Which of the options given in Q. 34 describes transcriptome ?
(*a*) III, IV (*b*) IV
(*c*) III (*d*) II

36. Which of the options given in Q. 34 describes proteome ?
(*a*) II (*b*) III
(*c*) III, IV (*d*) IV

37. Paralogues means 'homologous' genes within which of the following ?
(*a*) Same cell (*b*) Same organism
(*c*) Same genus (*d*) Both (*a*) and (*b*)

38. Orthologue means 'homologous' genes in which of the following ?
(*a*) Different tissues of an organism
(*b*) Same tissue of an organism
(*c*) Individuals of different species
(*d*) Different individuals of the same species

39. Which of the following can perform genetic functions ?
I. DNA II. RNA
III. Proteins

Options :
(*a*) I (*b*) I, II
(*c*) II (*d*) III

40. Which of the options given in Q. 39 performs only nongenetic functions ?
(*a*) III (*b*) II
(*c*) II, III (*d*) I, II

41. Which of the options given in Q. 39 performs both genetic and nongenetic functions ?
(*a*) I (*b*) I, II
(*c*) II (*d*) II, III

42. Which of the options given in Q. 39 performs nongenetic functions ?
(*a*) III (*b*) I, III
(*c*) II (*d*) II, III

43. Which of the options given in Q. 39 is involved in gene regulation ?
(*a*) II (*b*) II, III
(*c*) III (*d*) I, III

44. Which of the following processes involves DNA-protein interaction ?
I. Replication initiation
II. Transcription activation

III. Transcription repression
IV. Transcription initiation

Options :

(*a*) I, II, III (*b*) I, II, III, IV
(*c*) II, III, IV (*d*) I, III, IV

45. Among the processes listed in Q. 44, which one also involves protein-protein interaction ?

(*a*) IV (*b*) III
(*c*) II (*d*) I

46. Which of the processes listed in Q. 44 involves separation of the two strands of DNA duplex ?

(*a*) I, II (*b*) I, IV
(*c*) II, III (*d*) I, III

47. Translation involves which of the following interactions ?

I. RNA-protein II. Protein-protein
III. RNA-RNA IV. RNA-DNA

Options :

(*a*) I, III, IV (*b*) II, III, IV
(*c*) I, II, III (*d*) I, II, III, IV

48. Restriction site recognition is affected by which of the following ?

(*a*) Base substitution
(*b*) Base deletion/addition
(*c*) Base methylation
(*d*) All of the above

49. Which of the following techniques identifies the DNA fragment to which a given protein binds ?

(*a*) DNA footprinting
(*b*) DNA fingerprinting
(*c*) Gel retardation assay
(*d*) Restriction mapping

50. Which of the options given in Q. 49, identifies the region of the given DNA fragment to which the concerned protein binds ?

51. Which of the options given in Q. 49 is used for physical mapping ?

52. Which of the techhiques given in Q. 49 may use PCR ?

53. In which of the options given in Q. 49, DNase I digestion of DNA is involved ?

54. In which of the following, unique sequence-specific primers are used ?

I. SCAR II. STMS
III. ISSR IV. RAPD

Options :

(*a*) I, II (*b*) II, III
(*c*) I, II, III (*d*) I, II, III, IV

55. In which of the options given in Q. 54, random or arbitrary sequence primers are used ?

(*a*) IV (*b*) III, IV
(*c*) II, III (*d*) I, II, IV

56. In which of the options given in Q. 54, short tandem repeats are used as primers ?

(*a*) II (*b*) III
(*c*) III, IV (*d*) I, II

57. Which of the following genetic transformation techniques can be used in monocots ?

(*a*) Particle gun
(*b*) *Agrobacterium*-mediated
(*c*) Electroporation
(*d*) All of the above

58. Acetosyringone triggers which of the following events ?

I. T-DNA transfer
II. VirA phosphorylation
III. VirG dimerization
IV. *vir* regulon activation
V. Low level transcription of *virA* operon

Options :

(*a*) I, II, III, IV (*b*) II, III, IV, V
(*c*) I, II, III, IV, V (*d*) I, III, IV, V

59. During *Agrobacterium*-mediated gene transfer, which of the following depicts the correct order of events listed in Q. 58 ?

(*a*) I, II, III, IV, V (*b*) V, III, II, I, IV
(*c*) V, III, II, IV, I (*d*) V, II, III, IV, I

60. Which of the following has enabled successful transformation of monocots using *Agrobacterium* ?

(*a*) Exogenous acetosyringone
(*b*) *Agrobacterium* strain
(*c*) Explant tissue
(*d*) Plant variety

61. Which of the following techniques of genetic transformation ***does not depend*** on plantlet regeneration protocol ?

(*a*) *Agrobacterium*-mediated
(*b*) Particle gun
(*c*) Electroporation
(*d*) Both (*a*) and (*b*)

62. Which of the following *Agrobacterium* proteins has helicase activity ?
(*a*) VirC (*b*) VirG
(*c*) $VirD_2$ (*d*) VirE

63. Which of the proteins listed in Q. 62 is single-strand binding protein ?

64. The satellite RNA present in some RNA viruses may produce which of the following effects on disease severity ?
(*a*) Enhance disease severity
(*b*) Decrease disease severity
(*c*) No effect on disease severity
(d) All of the above

65. Column A lists the class of Cry proteins and column B gives the class of target insects. Match the two columns carefully, and pick the correct option from those listed below.

Column A	Column B
A. CryI	1. Lepidoptera and Diptera
B. CryII	2. Coleoptera
C. CryIII	3. Nematodes
D. CryV	4. Lepidoptera

Options :
(*a*) A4, B2, C1, D3 (*b*) A4, B1, C2, D3
(*c*) A4, B3, C2, D1 (*d*) A4, B1, C3, D2

66. Which of the following proteins is specific to Diptera ?
(*a*) CryI (*b*) CryII
(*c*) CryIV (*d*) CryIII

67. Improved Pusa Basmati 1 (Pusa 1460), the first variety developed in India through MAS, has been improved for which of the following traits ?
(*a*) VitA content
(*b*) Cooking quality
(*c*) Bacterial leaf blight resistance
(*d*) Blast resistance

68. Which of the following marker systems would be preferred for testing the purity of hybrid seeds ?
(*a*) RAPD (*b*) RFLP
(*c*) STMS (*d*) AFLP

69. Column A contains substratum/cell type used for animal tissue culture, while column B lists the treatment required for them. Compare the two columns carefully and pick the correct option from those listed below ?

Column A	Column B
A. Plasticware	I. Polylysine
B. Soda-lime glass	II. Magnesium acetate
C. Muscle cells	III. Strong acids
D. Repeatedly washed glassware	IV. Boiling in weak acid

Options :
(*a*) AIII, BI, CIV, DII
(*b*) AIII, BIV, CII, DI
(*c*) AIII, BIV, CI, DII
(*d*) AIII, BI, CII, DIV

70. In which of the following types of cultures, a constant volume of spent medium is regularly replaced by equal volume of fresh medium ?
(*a*) Perfusion cultures
(*b*) Fed-batch cultures
(*c*) Agar cultures
(*d*) Batch cultures

71. In which of the options given in Q. 70 fresh medium is added gradually ?

72. In which of the options given in Q. 70, there is an increase in culture volume during the culture period ?

73. F-virosomes derived from Sendai virus ***do not contain*** which of the following ?
(*a*) Viral envelope
(*b*) Viral HN protein
(*c*) Recombinant DNA
(*d*) Viral F protein

74. Which of the following generally produces transient transfection ?
(*a*) DEAE-Dextran-mediated transfection
(*b*) Calcium-phosphate precipitation
(*c*) Microinjection
(*d*) Retroviral infection

75. In case of mice, DNA is microinjected into which of the following ?
(*a*) Male pronucleus
(*b*) Female pronucleus
(*c*) Ovum cytoplasm
(*d*) Both (*a*) and (*c*)

76. In which of the options given in Q. 75, DNA is microinjected in the case of fish ?

77. An intein sequence functions in which of the following ?
(*a*) DNA (*b*) RNA
(*c*) Protein (*d*) Both (*a*) and (*b*)

78. Which of the following vectors is the most promosing for development of DNA vaccines ?
(*a*) Vaccinia virus (*b*) Retrovirus
(*c*) Herpes virus (*d*) Adenovirus

79. Which of the following is used in gap-ligase chain reaction ?
(*a*) Thermostable DNA ligase
(*b*) Thermostable DNA polymerase
(*c*) NAD
(*d*) All of the above

80. The biological component of biosensors is responsible for which of their following features ?
(*a*) Detection of analyte
(*b*) Specificity of biosensor
(*c*) Sensitivity of biosensor
(*d*) All of the above

81. Column A lists the physical change generated by the analyte, while column B lists the type of biosensor. Match the two columns carefully and pick the correct option from those listed below ?

Column A	**Column B**
A. Change in mass	1. Amperometric
B. Redox reaction	2. Optical
C. Heat released or absorbed	3. Potentiometric
D. Light produced or absorbed	4. Calorimetric
	5. Acoustic wave

Options :
(*a*) A5, B1, C4, D2 (*b*) A5, B4, C1, D2
(*c*) A5, B4, C1, D2 (*d*) A5, B3, C4, D2

82. Glucose biosensor based on glucose oxidase detects which of the following changes ?
(*a*) Evolution of a gas
(*b*) Change in temperature
(*c*) Redox reaction
(*d*) Fluorescence

83. Lipases are used in biphasic systems during the production of which of the following ?
(*a*) Wax
(*b*) Isoamyl acetate
(*c*) Fatty acids (from lipid)
(*d*) Both (*a*) and (*c*)

84. Conversion of palm oil to cocoa butter is based on which of the following enzymes ?
(*a*) Lipase
(*b*) Fatty acid synthase I
(*c*) Fatty acid desaturase
(*d*) Fatty acid thioesterase

85. In 1860 the first synthetic medium for microorganisms was used to study which of the following fermentations ?
(*a*) Lactic acid (*b*) Alcohol
(*c*) Acetic acid (*d*) Citric acid

86. The phenomenon of Pasteur effect was demonstrated with which of the fermentation processes listed in Q. 85

87. Lectins are used as ligands in affinity chromatography for the separation of which of the following ?
(*a*) Antigens (*b*) Glycoproteins
(*c*) Polysaccharides (*d*) Both (*b*) and (*c*)

88. Which of the following is the most gentle method of drying ?
(*a*) Spray drying (*b*) Vacuum drying
(*c*) Freeze drying (*d*) Both (*b*) and (*c*)

89. Which of the following can be used for *in situ* recovery of products ?
(*a*) Vacuum
(*b*) Two-phase systems
(*c*) Dialysis
(*d*) All of the above

90. The first industrial production of enzymes by fermentation was for which of the following applications ?
(*a*) Food (*b*) Pharmaceutical
(*c*) Detergent (*d*) Textile

91. Solid state fermentation is used for which of the following ?
(*a*) Food processing
(*b*) Enzyme production
(*c*) Organic acid production
(*d*) All of the above

92. Which of the following serves as inducer of pullulanase production ?

(*a*) Maltose (*b*) Sucrose
(*c*) Dextrin (*d*) Starch

93. Column A lists some precursors and column B lists the production process. Match the two columns carefully and select the correct option from those listed below them ?

Column A	Column B
A. Phenoxy acetic acid	1. Penicillin G
B. Chloride	2. Chlortetracycline
C. D-Threonine	3. Vitamin B_{12}
D. Phenylacetic acid	4. Penicillin V
	5. Isoleucine

Options :
(*a*) A3, B2, C5, D1 (*b*) A4, B2, C5, D1
(*c*) A4, D2, C3, D1 (*d*) A4, B3, C5, D1

94. Which of the following is used as the main nitrogen source for riboflavin production ?
(*a*) Pancreatic digest of gelatin
(*b*) Peanut granules
(*c*) Corn-steep liquor
(*d*) Soybean meal

95. Which of the options given in Q. 94 is used as the nitrogen source for pencillin production ?

96. Which of the following constitutes 'process development' ?
(*a*) Laboratory scale experiments
(*b*) Scaling-up using small to medium fermenters
(*c*) Production scale experiments
(*d*) All of the above

97. Enhanced metabolite production may be achieved by selection for which of the following ?
(*a*) Auxotrophic mutants
(*b*) Analogue resistant mutants
(*c*) Revertant of a nonproducing mutant
(*d*) All of the above

98. Change in medium pH is used as screen for detection of microbial strains producing which of the following ?
(*a*) Protease (*b*) Urease
(*c*) Lipase (*d*) Amylase

99. Chitin synthase inhibition is used as screen for detection of microorganisms producing which of the following ?
(*a*) Antibiotics (*b*) Antivirals
(*c*) Antifungals (*d*) Antitumour agents

100. Which of the following programmes converts the submitted nucleotide sequence into amino acid sequence then campares it with a protein database ?
(*a*) $BLAST_x$ (*b*) $BLAST_n$
(*c*) $tBLAST_n$ (*d*) $tBLAST_x$

□□□

MODEL QUESTION PAPER – III

MULTIPLE CHOICE QUESTIONS

1. Chromosome walking is used in case of eukaryotes to generate which of the following ?
   (*a*) Linkage map (*b*) Restriction map
   (*c*) Physical map (*d*) Both (*b*) and (*c*)
2. In plants, mitosis occurs during which of the following ?
   (*a*) Embryogenesis (*b*) Parthenogenesis
   (*c*) Gametogenesis (*d*) All of the above
3. The term vitrification is related to which of the following ?
   I. Cryopreservation
   II. Abnormal morphology of shoots *in vitro*
   III. Somatic hybridization
   Options :
   (*a*) I (*b*) II
   (*c*) I, III (*d*) I, II
4. Which of the following supports somatic embryo maturation ?
   I. High sugar concentration
   II. ABA
   III. Partial desiccation
   IV. BAP
   Options :
   (*a*) I, II, III (*b*) II, III, IV
   (*c*) I, III, IV (*d*) I, II, IV
5. The K_m of the substrate for any enzyme is increased by which of the following ?
   (*a*) Competitive inhibitor
   (*b*) Noncompetitive inhibitor
   (*c*) Substrate concentration
   (*d*) Both (*a*) and (*c*)
6. Anther culture is related to which of the following ?
   (*a*) Gynogenesis (*b*) Androgenesis
   (*c*) Parthenogenesis (*d*) Embryogenesis
7. Nucleic acids are transferred from a gel onto a membrane filter in which of the following techniques ?
   (*a*) Northern hybridization
   (*b*) Dot blot hybridization
   (*c*) Calony hybridization
   (*d*) Zoo blot hybridization.
8. Which of the following elements ***is not essential*** for plant cells ?
   (*a*) Ni (*b*) Na
   (*c*) K (*d*) P
9. Choose the name of enzyme used for ligation of blunt ends of DNA ?
   (*a*) DNA polymerase (*b*) T_4 ligase
   (*c*) DNA gyrase (*d*) Topoisomerase
10. Which of the following ***is not an operation*** in a biotechnological process ?
    (*a*) Strain development
    (*b*) Downstream processing
    (*c*) Process engineering
    (*d*) Safety evaluation
11. Conditioned medium is the nutrient medium that has been optimised by which of the following ?
    (*a*) Nutrient enrichment
    (*b*) By adding tissue extract
    (*c*) By growing plant cells
    (*d*) By adding amino acid mixture
12. Which of the following is a Zn containing enzyme ?
    (*a*) Urease
    (*b*) Alkaline phosphatase
    (*c*) Hexokinase
    (*d*) Phosphoglycerate kinase
13. Haploid plants can be obtained by which of the following ?

I. Anther culture
II. Unfertilized ovule culture
III. Interspecific hybridization
IV. Colchicine treatment

Options :

(*a*) I, II, IV (*b*) II, IV
(*c*) I, III (*d*) I, II, III, IV

14. Which of the options given in Q. 13 has been used to develop commerical varieties ?

15. Abzymes are which of the following ?
(*a*) Antigen-antibody complexes
(*b*) Antigens with enzyme activity
(*c*) Antibodies with enzyme activity
(*d*) RNA molecules with enzyme activity

16. Which of the following techniques yields high purification of molecules in a single step ?
(*a*) Affinity chromatography
(*b*) Gel filtration
(*c*) SDS-PAGE
(*d*) Column chromatography

17. Inactive precursors of enzymes are called which of the following ?
(*a*) Isozymes
(*b*) Zymogenes
(*c*) Allozymes
(*d*) Pre-enzymes

18. Somaclonal variation is the least likely to occur in which of the following ?
(*a*) Protoplast culture
(*b*) Suspension culture
(*c*) Meristem culture
(*d*) Callus culture

19. The least used growth regulator in plant tissue cultures is which of the following ?
(*a*) Kinetin (*b*) GA_3
(*c*) BAP (*d*) 2,4-D

20. Antisense RNA technology may be used to achieve which of the following ?
(*a*) Minimise the expression of a gene.
(*b*) Enhance the expression of a gene.
(*c*) Stablize the expression of a gene.
(*d*) Change the expression pattern of a gene.

21. The chief problem in the commercial exploitation of pharmaceutically valuable recombinant protein production in plants is which of the following ?
(*a*) Purification of the proteins
(*b*) Folding of the proteins
(*c*) Glycosylation of the proteins
(*d*) Stability of the proteins

22. Enzyme technology concerns with which of the following ?
(*a*) Modification of the amino acid sequence of the enzymes.
(*b*) Enzyme immobilization
(*c*) Both (*a*) and (*b*)
(*d*) Modification of glycosylation pattern of enzymes.

23. The term 'single cell protein' refers to which of the following ?
(*a*) Protein recovered from microbes
(*b*) Protein recovered from single cells
(*c*) Protein recovered from cultured plant and animal cells.
(*d*) Microbial biomass used as food/feed supplement.

24. The rate of filtration in downstream processing is a function of which of the following ?
(*a*) Viscosity of the fluid and filter area.
(*b*) Filter area and pressure.
(*c*) Pressure and compressibility of filter cake.
(*d*) Filter area, pressure, fluid viscosity and compressibility of the filter cake.

25. Gel filtration separates macromolecules on the basis of the which of the following ?
(*a*) Colour (*b*) Mass
(*c*) Charge (*d*) Specific binding

26. Aspartame is an artificial sweetner, it is chemically which of the following ?
(*a*) Dipeptide (*b*) Disaccharide
(*c*) Oligopeptide (*d*) Both (*a*) and (*b*)

27. Which of the following statements is correct ?
(*a*) All enzymes are heat stable.
(*b*) Enzymes are always proteins.
(*c*) Enzymes are always specific for a single substrate.
(*d*) Enzymes can be inhibited by substrate analogues.

28. Penicillin acylase (amidase) is being used industrially for production of which of the following ?
(*a*) Detergents
(*b*) Semisynthetic penicillins

(*c*) Secondary metabolites
(*d*) Mitigation of penicillin allergy

29. Phenotypic variability having nongenetic basis is called which of the following ?
(*a*) Epigenetic variation
(*b*) Somaclonal variation
(*c*) Gametoclonal variation
(*d*) Protoclonal variation

30. Which of the following enzymes breaks phosphodiester bonds located inside a nucleic acid molecule ?
(*a*) Epimerase (*b*) Exonuclease
(*c*) Endonuclease (*d*) Isomerase

31. Introduction of purified phage DNA molecules into bacterial cells is called which of the following ?
(*a*) Conjugation (*b*) Transfection
(*c*) Transduction (*d*) Transformation

32. Which of the options given in Q. 31 shall be used when naked recombinant DNA is introduced into a bacterial cell ?

33. Which of the following ***is not a feature*** of an enzyme ?
(*a*) Affects the rate of reaction
(*b*) Has a pH optima
(*c*) It is always a protein
(*d*) It is specific for a chemcial reaction

34. In which of the following, RNA acts as the genetic material ?
(*a*) Tobacco mosaic virus
(*b*) *Rhizobium*
(*c*) Fungi
(*d*) Archaebacterium

35. Which of the following agents is used for virus elimination ?
(*a*) Ribavirin (*b*) Actinomycin D
(*c*) 2-Thiouracil (*d*) All of the above

36. A protein has isoelectric pH of 5.7. What will be the net charge of this protein at pH 7.0 ?
(*a*) Negative (*b*) Positive
(*c*) Neutral (*d*) Either (*a*) or (*b*)

37. The virus titre in shoot-tip meristem cells is much lower than that in the differentiated cells; this may be due to which of the following ?
(*a*) Absence of plasmodesmata
(*b*) Rapid cell division
(*c*) Inhibitory action of growth regulators
(*d*) All of the above

38. The *nic-bom* region of *p*BR322 does which of the following ?
(*a*) Interferes with extrachromosomal replication in monkey cells.
(*b*) Reduces replication of *p*BR322 in *E. coli.*
(*c*) Governs mobilization of *p*BR322
(*d*) All of the above

39. Plant cell suspension cultures are continuously agitated to achieve which of the following ?
(*a*) Break cell clumps
(*b*) Facilitate aeration
(*c*) Improve nutrient availability
(*d*) All of the above

40. Plants obtained by chromosome doubling of haploids are known as which of the following ?
(*a*) Amphidiploids (*b*) Dihaploids
(*c*) Doubled haploids (*d*) Diploids

41. Virus resistant transgenic plants can be produced by transferring into them which of the following ?
(*a*) cDNA of the satellite RNA of the RNA virus
(*b*) Coat protein gene of the virus
(*c*) Defective genome of the virus
(*d*) Any of the above

42. Which of the options given in Q. 41 has been exploited commerically ?

43. Production of biochemicals by cultured plant cells is markedly improved by which of the following ?
(*a*) Treatment with elicitors
(*b*) Selection of high producing clones
(*c*) Optimisation of culture conditions
(*d*) All of the above

44. It is feared that transgenic plants may cause which of the following ?
(*a*) Degrade the environment
(*b*) Themselves become weeds
(*c*) Foster increasingly stringent IPR regimes
(*d*) All of the above

45. Alcohol dehydrogenase gene is induced by which of the following ?
(*a*) Anaerobiosis (*b*) Wound
(*c*) Oxygen (*d*) Pathogen invasion

46. Stable integration of a gene into plant genome can be conclusively shown by which of the following ?
(*a*) PCR
(*b*) Northern hybridization
(*c*) Dot blot assay
(*d*) Southern hybridization

47. Genes whose products are necessary for the maintenance of all types of cells of a species are called which of the following ?
(*a*) Smart genes
(*b*) House-keeping genes
(*c*) Luxury genes
(*d*) Both (*a*) and (*b*)

48. *Azolla* contains an endosymbiont, which fixes nitrogen; this organism belongs to which of the following genera ?
(*a*) *Nostoc* (*b*) *Plectonema*
(*c*) *Anabaena* (*d*) *Aulosira*

49. Immobilization of enzymes may involve which of the following ?
(*a*) Covalent bonds (*b*) Cross-linking
(*c*) Ionic bonds (*d*) Any of the above

50. Biological extraction of copper and uranium utilizes which of the following ?
(*a*) *Thiobacillus thiooxidans*
(*b*) *T. ferroxidans*
(*c*) Both (*a*) and (*b*)
(*d*) *T. organoparus*

51. *Bacillus thuringiensis* strains are active against which of the following groups of insects ?
(*a*) *Diptera* (*b*) Nematodes
(*c*) *Coleoptera* (*d*) All of the above

52. Cross-flow membrane filtration in downstream processing is suitable for application in the case of which of the following ?
(*a*) Small scale, high value product
(*b*) Small scale, low value product
(*c*) Large scale, high value product
(*d*) Large scale, low value product

53. Nick-translation utilizes which of the following enzymes ?
(*a*) DNase I
(*b*) DNA polymerase I
(*c*) Klenow fragment
(*d*) Both (*a*) and (*b*)

54. Denaturation is essential part of which of the following ?
(*a*) Southern hybridization
(*b*) PCR
(*c*) Nick-translation
(*d*) Both (*a*) and (*b*)

55. Which of the following techniques ***does not use*** radioactivity ?
(*a*) RFLP
(*b*) Western hybridization
(*c*) RAPD
(*d*) Southern blotting

56. Dot blot assay detects the presence of which of the following ?
(*a*) Polypeptide (*b*) DNA sequence
(*c*) mRNA (*d*) Both (*b*) and (*c*)

57. PCR can be used for obtaining which of the following ?
(*a*) Amplification of a specific cDNA from a mixture of cDNAs
(*b*) Site-directed mutagenesis
(*c*) RAPD maps
(*d*) All of the above

58. RFLP patterns depend on which of the following ?
I. The restriction enzyme used
II. The probe employed
III. The strains used for DNA isolations
IV. The stringency of hybridization
Options :
(*a*) I, II (*b*) I, II, III, IV
(*c*) I, III (*d*) II, III

59. An endonuclease like DNase I is used in which of the following techniques ?
(*a*) Nick translation
(*b*) DNA foot printing
(*c*) Both (*a*) and (*b*)
(*d*) Chromosome walking

60. Which of the options given in Q. 59 employs Type II endonucleases ?

61. In thermotherapy for virus elimination, the best results are obtained when high temperature treatment is applied to which of the following ?
(*a*) Shoot-tip cultures
(*b*) Seeds
(*c*) Whole plants, followed by culture of their shoot-tips
(*d*) Whole plants

62. A polyprotein is a protein that has which of the following features ?
(*a*) Several functions
(*b*) Homopolymer
(*c*) Heteropolymer
(*d*) Cleaved into two or more functional proteins

63. Some introns perform which of the following functions ?
(*a*) Enhance promoter action in expression vectors.
(*b*) Encode enzymes
(*c*) Perform self-splicing
(*d*) Any of the above

64. The first functional gene was chemically synthesized by which of the following approaches ?
(*a*) Phosphate diester
(*b*) Phosphate triester
(*c*) Phosphite triester
(d) Phosphoramidite

65. Lectins are proteins that have which of the following features ?
(*a*) DNA binding proteins
(*b*) Bind to glycoproteins
(*c*) Bind to lipoproteins
(*d*) Hormone binding proteins

66. Which of the following uses restriction enzymes ?
(*a*) Chromosome jumping
(*b*) Restriction mapping
(*c*) AFLP
(*d*) All of the above

67. Fibroin is found in which of the following ?
(*a*) Silk
(*b*) Insect wing hinges
(*c*) Hair
(*d*) Blood vessels and ligaments.

68. The recognition sites for restriction enzymes used in gene cloning are which of the following ?
(*a*) Random sequences
(*b*) Palindromes with rotational symmetry
(*c*) Simple palindromes
(*d*) Nonpalindromic sequences

69. Ti binary vectors have which of the following ?
(*a*) Two copies of the *vir* region
(*b*) T-DNA and the *vir* region in the same plasmid
(*c*) *vir* region within the T-DNA
(*d*) *vir* region and the T-DNA in separate plasmids.

70. T-DNA is transferred into the plant cells most likely as which of the following ?
(*a*) Single-stranded circular molecule
(*b*) Doble-stranded circular molecule
(*c*) Single-stranded linear molecule
(*d*) Doble-stranded linear molecule

71. Which of the *Agrobacterium tumefaciens* proteins is activated by acetosyringone ?
(*a*) VirA (*b*) VirC
(*c*) VirG (d) $VirD_2$

72. The *A. tumefaciens vir* region is positively regulated by which of the following proteins ?
(*a*) VirA protein (*b*) VirC protein
(*c*) VirG protein (d) VirD protein

73. The polysaccharides necessary for attachment of *A. tumefaciens* cells to plant cells is encoded by genes present in which of the following ?
(*a*) *vir* region
(*b*) Bacterial chromosome
(*c*) T-DNA
(*d*) Both (*b*) and (*c*)

74. The most effective fusion treatment for plant protoplasts is which of the following ?
(*a*) High pH and high Ca^{2+}
(*b*) PEG
(*c*) PEG combined with high pH and high Ca^{2+}
(*d*) $NaNO_3$

75. ***Assertion (A)*** : Vaccines based on recombinant proteins are very safe.
Reason (R) : This is because whole organism is involved.

Options :
(*a*) Both A and R are correct and R sufficiently explains A
(*b*) Both A and R are correct, but R does not explain A.
(*c*) Only A is correct.
(*d*) Only R is correct.

76. Which of the following is correct about vaccines ?
I. First generation vaccines are obtained by killing or attenuation of the pathogens.

II. Second generation vaccines are made up of pure surface antigens of the pathogens.
III. Third generation vaccines are made up of DNA molecules.
IV. Recombinant protein vaccines are second generation vaccines.

Options :
(*a*) I, II, III (*b*) I, III, IV
(*c*) I, II, III, IV (*d*) II, III, IV

77. *Bacillus thuringiensis* Cry protein is inactivated by which of the following ?
(*a*) UV light (*b*) Humidity
(*c*) Red light (*d*) Both (*a*) and (*b*)

78. When very young embryos are cultured, it is critical to isolate them with intact suspensor since it provides which of the following to the developing embroys ?
(*a*) ABA (*b*) GA_3
(*c*) Auxin (*d*) Cytokinin

79. In a disarmed Ti plasmid, which of the following genes are deleted ?
(*a*) *iaaM* and *iaaH* (*b*) *ipt*
(*c*) *nos* (*d*) Both (*a*) and (*b*)

80. Which of the following is correct about vaccines ?
I. Conventional vaccines consist of pathogenic organism either killed or live.
II. Recombinant vaccines are based on recombinant proteins.
III. DNA vaccines are the latest.
IV. DNA vaccines are inferior to conventional vaccines.

Options :
(*a*) I, III, IV (*b*) I, II, III
(*c*) I, II, IV (*d*) I, II, III, IV

81. ABA is related to which of the following ?
(*a*) Flowering in plants
(*b*) Dormancy
(*c*) Abscission of leaves
(*d*) Both (*b*) and (*c*)

82. RuBISCO functions in which of the following ?
(*a*) Photorespiration in C_3 plants
(*b*) Fixation of CO_2 in C_3 plants
(*c*) Respiration
(*d*) Both (*a*) and (*b*)

83. Selection of toxin resistant cells for the development of disease resistant plant is the most successful in the case of pathogens producing which of the following ?
(*a*) Toxin (*b*) Specific toxin
(*c*) Nonspecific toxin (*d*) No toxin

84. Which of the following is an approach of germplasm`conservation ?
(*a*) Slow-growth shoot cultures
(*b*) DNA banks
(*c*) Cryopreservation
(*d*) All of the above

85. Which of the following pre-determined antibody is present in saliva ?
(*a*) IgA (*b*) IgD
(*c*) IgM (*d*) IgG

86. Which of the following ***is not optically active*** ?
(*a*) Glycine (*b*) Serine
(*c*) Leucine (*d*) Alanine

87. Isozymes are variants of a single enzyme differing in which of the following ?
(*a*) Catalysis function
(*b*) Mobility during electrophoresis
(*c*) Substrate preference
(*d*) All of the above

88. Match the columns A and B carefully and select the correct option from those given below them.

Column A	Column B
A. α-Amylase	I. Protein
B. Cellulase	II. Fats
C. Protease	III. Cellulose
D. Lipase	IV. Starch

Options :
(*a*) AI, BII, CIII, DIV
(*b*) AIV, BIII, CI, DII
(*c*) AII, BIII, CIV, DI
(*d*) AIII, BI, CII, DIV

89. In response to stress, which of the following amino acids accumulates ?
(*a*) Phenylalanine (*b*) Lysine
(*c*) Proline (*d*) Histidine

90. Which of the following advantages is associated with immobilization of enzymes ?
I. Higher concentrations of enzymes can be used.
II. Product is readily freed from enzyme.
III. Repeated use of the enzyme.
IV. Enzyme thermostability may be increased.

Options

(*a*) I, II, IV (*b*) II, III, IV
(*c*) I, II, III, IV (*d*) I, III, IV

91. Monoclonal antibodies are being used for diagnosis of which of the following diseases ?
(*a*) Hepatitis B
(*b*) Cancer
(*c*) Venereal diseases
(*d*) All of the above

92. Nitrate reductase consists of which of the following ?
(*a*) Mo cofacter and one polypeptide
(*b*) One polypeptide
(*c*) Two polypeptides
(*d*) Three polypeptides

93. WHO has launched Global Immunization Programme for which of the following diesases ?
(*a*) Pertusis and Tetanus
(*b*) Diphtheria and Measles
(*c*) Polio and T.B.
(*d*) All of the above

94. Which of the following is correct about ribozyme ?
I. These RNA molecules have catalytic action.
II. Catalytic action was discovered by Cech in 1986.
III. Ribozymes catalyze cleavage of DNA and RNA.
IV. Ribozymes are used for treatment of cancer.

Options :

(*a*) I, II, III, IV (*b*) I, II, III
(*c*) I, III, IV (*d*) I, II, IV

95. Southern hybridization differs from northern hybridization in respect to which of the following ?
(*a*) Membrane filter
(*b*) Need for denaturation
(*c*) Type of nucleic acid involved
(*d*) All of the above

96. In case of some plant genes, light is known to affect which of the following ?
(*a*) mRNA degradation rates
(*b*) Induction of transcription
(*c*) Enhanced transcription rates
(*d*) All of the above

97. The main features of light induced promoters of dicots relates to which of the following ?
(*a*) An upstream AG or AGGA box
(*b*) TATA box
(*c*) Both TATA and AG/AGGA boxes
(*d*) CAAT box

98. A yeast minichromosome vector ***does not contain*** which of the following molecules ?
(*a*) ARS sequence
(*b*) Telomere sequence
(*c*) CEN sequence
(*d*) A functional yeast gene

99. Plant cell cultures are being used for the production of which of the following ?
(*a*) Berberine
(*b*) Shikonin
(*c*) Ginseng (as biomass)
(*d*) All of the above

100. Crystal formation in plant cells preserved in liquid nitrogen would take place if their temperature rises above which of the following ?
(*a*) –130°C (*b*) –5°C
(*c*) –190°C (*d*) –160°C

□□□

MODEL QUESTION PAPER – IV

MULTIPLE CHOICE QUESTIONS

1. Cosmids contain which of the following sequences from the λ phage genome ?
   (*a*) Terminase binding site
   (*b*) *cos* site
   (*c*) *cos* and terminase binding sites
   (*d*) *cos*, terminase binding and cleavage sites.
2. Chloramphenicol acetyltransferase gene has been used in gene transfer experiments as which of the following ?
   (*a*) Bacterial resistance gene
   (*b*) Selectable marker
   (*c*) Scorbale marker
   (*d*) Both (*b*) and (*c*)
3. A phagemid vector has which of the following functional modules ?
   (*a*) Plasmid origin of replication
   (*b*) λ phage lytic genes
   (*c*) *cos* and terminase binding sites
   (*d*) All of the above
4. The action of chloramphenicol involves which of the following ?
   (*a*) Inhibition of DNA replication
   (*b*) Inhibition of transcription
   (*c*) Inhibition of peptidyl transferase
   (*d*) Prevention of initiator tRNA from entering the P site
5. The number of copies per bacterial cell of plasmids having stringent replication control is which of the following ?
   (*a*) 5–10 (*b*) 1–2
   (*c*) <10 (*d*) 10
6. Hydrogen peroxide is degraded by the enzyme catalase in which of the following organelles ?
   (*a*) Peroxisomes (*b*) Lysosomes
   (*c*) Mitochondria (*d*) Glyoxysomes
7. An extremozyme is an enzyme that has which of the following features ?
   (*a*) Extremely active
   (*b*) Extremely long-lived
   (*c*) Extremely mobile during electrophoresis
   (*d*) Stable and active under extreme environments
8. The two complementary strands of a DNA molecule are held together cheifly by which of the following ?
   (*a*) Salt bridges
   (*b*) Ionic interactions
   (*c*) Hydrogen bonds
   (*d*) Hydrophobic interactions.
9. Which of the following amino acids disturbs the α-helical configuration of proteins ?
   (*a*) Alanine (*b*) Proline
   (*c*) Serine (*d*) Glutamine
10. A conditioned medium permits, which of the following ?
    (*a*) Subculture at low cell density
    (*b*) Elimination of lag phase
    (*c*) Production of greater biomass
    (*d*) Both (*a*) and (*b*)
11. In India, molecular markers ***can not be used*** to resolve issues related to which of the following ?
    (*a*) Biodiversity
    (*b*) Plant breeding rights
    (*c*) Plant breeder's rights
    (*d*) Farmer's rights

12. N-linked oligosaccharide biosynthesis occurring in the endoplasmic reticulum membrane is blocked by which of the following ?
(*a*) Tunicamycin
(*b*) Chloramphenicol
(*c*) Puromycin
(*d*) Actinomycin D

13. The marker enzyme for mitochondria is which of the following ?
(*a*) Cytochrome C
(*b*) Catalase
(*c*) Amino acid permease
(*d*) 5′-Nucleotidase

14. Acid phosphatase acts as a marker for which of the following ?
(*a*) Mitochondria
(*b*) Lysosome
(*c*) Golgi complex
(*d*) Endoplasmid reticulum.

15. A transgene stably integrated into the plant genome shows which of the following ?
(*a*) Cytoplasmic inheritance
(*b*) Segregation distortion
(*c*) Mendelian inheritance
(*d*) All of the above

16. Molecular markers can be used for which of the following ?
I. Assessment of genetic variability
II. Creation of genetic variability
III. Selection of desriable genotype
IV. Selection of desirable phenotype
Options :
(*a*) I, II, III, IV (*b*) I, III
(*c*) II, III, IV (*d*) I, II, IV

17. A double-stranded DNA molecule of 100,000 bp length has about how many complete turns ?
(*a*) 8,000 (*b*) 10,000
(*c*) 20,000 (*d*) 12,000

18. For double-stranded DNA, which of the following base ratios always equals one ?
(*a*) (A + T)/(G + C) (*b*) (A + G)/(C + T)
(*c*) C/T (*d*) A/G

19. Which of the following is naturally occurring auxin ?
(*a*) IAA (*b*) IBA
(*c*) NAA (*d*) 2,4-D

20. Affinity chromatography techniques can be best used for which of the following ?
(*a*) Enzyme identification
(*b*) Enzyme classification
(*c*) Enzyme purification
(*d*) Quantitative assays of enzyme activity

21. AFLPs utilize which of the following ?
(*a*) Chromosome walking
(*b*) Southern hybridization
(*c*) PCR
(*d*) *In situ* hybridization

22. Restriction endonucleases are sometimes unable to digest the DNA even in the presence of the correct recognition sequence; this may be due to which of the following ?
(*a*) Acetylation of DNA
(*b*) Methylation of DNA
(*c*) Phosphorylation of DNA
(*d*) All of the above

23. Map-based cloning requires which of the following ?
(*a*) Saturated RFLP map
(*b*) Genetic map
(*c*) Karyotype
(*d*) Integrated (*a*) and (*b*)

24. Many of the *Bacillus* species are pathogenic to Lepidopteran pests due to which of the following ?
(*a*) Endotoxin production
(*b*) Exotoxin production
(*c*) Antibiotic production
(*d*) Chitinase production

25. Match the columns A and B carefully and select the correct option from those listed below them ?

Column A	Column B
A. ARS	I. Gene transfer
B. Pulsed-field gel electrophoresis	II. DNA finger-printing
C. Electroporation	III. YAC
D. Microsatellite DNA	IV. Separation of whole chromosome
	V. Transcription

Options :

(*a*) AI, BII, CIII, DV
(*b*) AIII, BII, CIV, DI
(*c*) AIII, BIV, CI, DII
(*d*) AV, BI, CIII, DII

26. Match the columns A and B and select the correct option from those listed below them.

Column A	Column B
A. Multiple origin of replication	I. Geomic Library
B. Shot-gun cloning	II. PEG
C. Somatic hybridization	III. Vacuole
D. Maintenance of turgor	IV. Shuttle vector

Options :

(*a*) AI, BIV, CIII, DII
(*b*) AIV, BI, CII, DIII
(*c*) AII, BIII, CIV, DI
(*d*) AIII, BII, CI, DII

27. Match the columns A and B and select the correct option from those given below them.

Column A	Column B
A. Restriction enzymes	I. Chromosome walking
B. CaMV	II. Palindromes with rotational symmetry
C. Amplicon	III. PCR
D. Map-based cloning	IV. 35*S* promoter
	V. STMS

Options :

(*a*) AII, BIV, CIII, DI
(*b*) AV, BIII, CII, DI
(*c*) AIII, BI, CII, DV
(*d*) AI, BII, CIV, DIII

28. Match the columns A and B carefully and select the correct option from those given below them.

Column A	Column B
A. Maxam and Gilbert	I. Protoplast isolation
B. E.C. Cocking	II. PCR
C. Kary Mullis	III. DNA sequencing
D. Temin and Baltimore	IV. Reverse transcriptase
	V. Inverse PCR

Options :

(*a*) AII, BIV, CV, DI
(*b*) AIV, BI, CIII, DII
(*c*) AIII, BI, CII, DIV
(*d*) AI, BIII, CV, DII

29. A eukaryotic nuclear gene with a bacterial promoter can not be expressed in bacteria because of which of the following differences between prokaryotes and eukaryotes ?

(*a*) Translation
(*b*) RNA processing
(*c*) DNA replication
(*d*) Genetic code

30. A circular plasmid DNA gives two bands of 6.5 kb and 5.5 kb with EcoRI and only one band of 12 kb with BamHI. How many bands will be expected when it is digested with both the enzymes ?

(*a*) 2 (*b*) 4
(*c*) 3 (*d*) 5

31. A mutant of *Agrobacterium tumefaciens* defective in VirG shows which of the following features ?

(*a*) Can be used to transform dicots
(*b*) Can be used to transform monocots
(*c*) Can not be used for plant transformation
(*d*) Both (*a*) and (*b*)

32. The base composition of genome of a virus is as follows:

A, 26%; U, 26.2%; G, 24.1%; C, 23.7%

The genome of this virus is which of the following ?

(*a*) Single-stranded DNA
(*b*) Single stranded RNA
(*c*) Double-stranded RNA
(*d*) Double-stranded DNA

33. Match the columns A and B and select the correct option from those given below them ?

Column A	Column B
A. Site directed mutagenesis	I. Camphor degradation
B. *Streptomyces antibioticus*	II. Protein engineering
C. *Pseudomonas putida*	III. Removal of S from coal
D. *Thiobacillus ferroxidans*	IV. Mitomycin

Options :
(*a*) AII, BIII, CIV, DI
(*b*) AII, BIV, CI, DIII
(*c*) AIII, BI, CII, DIV
(*d*) AIV, BII, CIII, DI

34. Match the columns A and B and select the correct option from those given below them.

Column A	**Column B**
A. Ricin	I. H_2 receptor
B. Cimetidin	II. Biotransformation
C. Feedback inhibition	III. Toxin polypeptide
D. L-sorbose	IV. Regulatory enzyme

Options :
(*a*) AII, BIII, CIV, DI
(*b*) AIV, BII, CI, DIII
(*c*) AIII, BI, CIV, DII
(*d*) AI, BIV, CII, DIII

35. Match the columns A and B and select the correct option from those given below them.

Column A	**Column B**
A. *Spirulina*	I. Competence for transformation
B. Monoclonal antibody	II. SCP
C. Alternative vaccine	III. Hybridoma techn-ology
D. $CaCl_2$	IV. DNA molecules

Options :
(*a*) AIII, BIV, CII, DI
(*b*) AI, BII, CIV, DIII
(*c*) AIV, BI, CIII, DII
(*d*) AII, BIII, CIV, DI

36. Match the columns A and B and select the correct option from those given below them.

Column A	**Column B**
A. Shuttle vector	I. *E. coli* and yeast
B. *E. coli lac* promoter	II. Cyclic AMP
C. CEN sequence	III. Minichromosome vector
	IV. Terminase binding site
D. Cosmid	V. *p*UC18

Options :
(*a*) AI, BII, CIII, DIV
(*b*) AII, BIII, CI, DIV
(*c*) AIII, BI, CV, DII
(*d*) AIV, BI, CII, DIII

37. Which of the following is correct about monoclonal antibodies ?

I. For producing monoclonal antibodies, Milstein and Kohler were awarded Nobel Prize in 1984.
II. B-cells are fused with cancer cells to produce hybrid cells which are immortal.
III. Large quantities of antibodies are produced by hybridoma cells.
IV. Monoclonal anitbodies are also called magic bodies.

Options :
(*a*) I, II, III, IV (*b*) II, III
(*c*) I, III, IV (*d*) I, II, III

38. Which plant is used as a model system for transgenic plant production ?
(*a*) Potato (*b*) *Arabidopsis*
(*c*) Tobacco (*d*) Datura

39. Somatic embryogenesis was first demonstrated in which of the following ?
(*a*) Carrot (*b*) Tobacco
(*c*) *Arabidopsis* (*d*) Datura

40. Which of the following is a prokaryote ?
(*a*) Yeast (*b*) Green algae
(*c*) Blue-green algae (*d*) Mushroom

41. Which of the following generates lymphocytes ?
(*a*) Lymph nodes (*b*) Thymus
(*c*) Liver (*d*) Bone marrow

42. Which of the following is known as *Drosophila* of plant kingdom ?
(*a*) *Nicotiana tobaccum*
(*b*) *Arabidopsis thaliana*
(*c*) *Daucus carota*
(*d*) *Capsicum annuum*

43. Which of the following organs is involved in diabetes ?
(*a*) Kidney (*b*) Spleen
(*c*) Pancreas (*d*) Liver

44. Which of the following is a Gram-positive bacterium ?

(*a*) *Bacillus subtilis*
(*b*) *Agrobacterium* species
(*c*) *Rhizobium* species
(*d*) *E. coli*

45. Rabies virus affects which of the following organs ?
(*a*) Thymus (*b*) Liver
(*c*) Kidney (*d*) Spinal cord

46. Ribose and deoxyribose differ at which position of ribose ?
(*a*) 3′ (*b*) 2′
(*c*) 5′ (*d*) 1′

47. Which of the following causes oncogenesis ?
(*a*) DNA viruses (*b*) Retroviruses
(*c*) Mutation (*d*) All of the above

48. The genetic material of an organism shows the following relationship: $A \neq U$ and $G \neq C$; this genetic material will be which of the following ?
(*a*) Double-stranded DNA
(*b*) Single-stranded DNA
(*c*) Double-stranded RNA
(*d*) Single-stranded RNA

49. Genetic material of tobacco mosaic virus will show which of the following ?
(*a*) $A \neq T$ (*b*) $G = C$
(*c*) $A = U$ (*d*) $A \neq U$

50. Who published the first observations on microorganisms ?
(*a*) Pasteur (*b*) Schwann
(*c*) Leeuwenhoek (*d*) Spallanzani

51. In which of the following organelles, phosphorylation is a common reaction ?
(*a*) Chloroplast (*b*) Mitochondria
(*c*) Golgi bodies (*d*) Both (*a*) and (*b*)

52. The first ever vaccination was against which of the following diseases ?
(*a*) Polio (*b*) Rabies
(*c*) Cholera (*d*) Small pox

53. RNA ***is not involved*** in which of the following ?
(*a*) Enzymatic activity
(*b*) Protein synthesis
(*c*) Chromosome structure (eukaryotes)
(*d*) Heredity

54. Which of the following has eukaryotic regulatory sequences ?
(*a*) T-DNA (*b*) vir regulon
(*c*) ϕX174 (*d*) λ phage

55. Which of the following ***is not correct*** about immortalized vertebrate cells cultured *in vitro* ?
(*a*) Flat and extended shape
(*b*) Serum-independence
(*c*) Anchorage dependence
(*d*) Contact inhibition

56. Units of K_m is which of the following ?
(*a*) Moles/litre
(*b*) cm
(*c*) s^{-1}
(*d*) It does not have a unit

57. Na^+— K^+ ATPase is related to which of the following ?
(*a*) Group translation
(*b*) Active transport
(*c*) Passive transport
(*d*) All of the above

58. Which of following has a higher iodine number (g) ?
(*a*) Lard (*b*) Coconut oil
(*c*) Beef fat (*d*) Sunflower oil

59. As a general rule of thumb, hydrophobic residues in a protein tend to be situated at which of the following ?
(*a*) C-terminal
(*b*) N-terminal
(*c*) Interior of the molecule
(*d*) Surface of the molecule

60. Column A contains a list of some enzymes, while column B contains their use in diagnosis of various disorders/diseases. Match both the columns carefully and select the correct option from those given below them.

Column A	Column B
A. Ficin	I. Skin ulcers
B. Collagenase	II. Leukaemia
C. Lysozyme	III. Deworming
D. Glutaminase	IV. Antibiotic

Options :
(*a*) AIII, BI, CIV, DII
(*b*) AII, BIII, CI, DIV
(*c*) AIV, BII, CIII, DI
(*d*) AI, BII, CIII, DIV

61. Which of the following statements are correct about terminator technology ?

I. Patented by Delta and Pineland Company in over 52 countries.

II. Plants containing terminator technology produce normal looking seeds that can not germinate.

III. This technology forces farmers to purchase seeds every year.

IV. Indian Government has allowed the import of seed bearing terminator technology.

Options :

(*a*) I, II, III, IV (*b*) I, II, III
(*c*) I, III, IV (*d*) II, III, IV

62. Which of the following statements are correct ?

I. Tissue plasminogen activator is used to disolve blood clots in heart attack victims.

II. Superbug was developed by Dr. Anand Mohan Chakraborty.

III. DNA chips of healthy BRCA-I and BRCA-II genes have been prepared to study breast cancers.

IV. The first commercial example of enzymatic modification of a protein for human use is the conversion of pig insulin to human insulin.

Options :

(*a*) I, II, III (*b*) I, II, III, IV
(*c*) II, III, IV (*d*) I, III, IV

63. Which of the following statements are correct ?

I. A reporter gene produces an enzyme that allows an easy identification or selection of the cells in which it is expressed.

II. A vector which is used for propagation of DNA insert in a suitable host is known as expression vector.

III. Process of producing clones is called cloning

IV. A circular DNA molecule, which has autonomous replicating property in host cell it is called plasmid.

Options :

(*a*) I, II, III, IV (*b*) I, II, IV
(*c*) I, III, IV (*d*) II, III, IV

64. Technology of haploid production leads to which of the following ?

(*a*) Genetic variation
(*b*) Hybrid sorting
(*c*) Homozygous lines
(d) All of the above

65. Which of the following hydrocarbons present in oil is borken down by genetically engineered strain of *Pseudomonas putida* ?

I. Naphthalenes II. Camphors
III. Octanes IV. Xylenes

Options :

(*a*) I, II, III, IV (*b*) II, III, IV
(*c*) I, III, IV (*d*) I, II, IV

66. Which of the following is correct about vinegar ?

(*a*) Acetic acid is commonly called vinegar.
(*b*) Used as souring agent, preservative and condiment.
(*c*) It is 10–13% ripened acetic acid.
(*d*) All of the above.

67. Which of the following vitamins is commercially produced by microbes ?

(*a*) Riboflavin (*b*) B_{12}
(*c*) Carotene (*d*) All of the above

68. Which of the following is correct about insulin ?

1. It is a protein hormone secreted by pancreas.
2. Banting and Best showed the role of dog's pancreas on diabetes in 1921.
3. It regulates the sugar (glucose) concentration in blood.
4. Humulin is the first genetically engineered product.

Options :

(*a*) 1, 2, 3, 4 (*b*) 2, 3, 4
(*c*) 1, 3, 4 (*d*) 1, 2, 4

69. Which of the following features are correct about DNA chips ?

I. Single-stranded DNA or genes are fixed on silica.

II. DNA chips for single nucleotide polymorphism (SNP) are available.

III. It can be used to detect hereditary defects.

Options :
(*a*) I, II, III (*b*) II, III
(*c*) I, III (*d*) I, II

70. Synthetic vaccines have been developed for which of the following ?
(*a*) Typhoid and rabies
(*b*) Cancer (Feline leukaemia virus)
(*c*) Cholrea and foot and mouth diesase of cattle
(*d*) All of the above

71. Which of the following strains of bacteria is used for the degradation of petroleum and management of oil spills ?
(*a*) *Clostridium acetobutylicum*
(*b*) *Methylophilus methylotrophus*
(*c*) *Pseudomonas putida*
(*d*) *Pseudomonas fluorescens*

72. During gynogenesis, haploid plants generally originate from which of the following ?
(*a*) Polar nuclei (*b*) Egg cell
(*c*) Antipodals (*d*) Synergids

73. In case of which of the following vectors, selection for recombinant clones is based on replica plating technique ?
(*a*) *p*BR322 (*b*) *p*UC18
(*c*) *p*UC8 (*d*) Both (*b*) and (*c*)

74. In case of which of the options given in Q. 73, selection for recombinant clones is based on blue/white colonies ?

75. Which of the following can be used for DNA delivery into *E. coli* cells ?
(*a*) $CaCl_2$ treatment (*b*) Microinjection
(*c*) Electroporation (*d*) Both (*a*) and (*c*)

76. Which of the following is the most suitable transfection technique for animal ova ?
(*a*) Lipofection
(*b*) Calcium phosphate precipitation
(*c*) Microinjection
(*d*) Particle gun

77. In which of the following, transgene integation by homologous recombination is almost the rule ?
(*a*) Yeast (*b*) *Drosophila*
(*c*) Mice (*d*) Humans

78. In which of the following, random transgene integration is far more frequent than that by homologous recombination ?
(*a*) Animals (*b*) Plants
(*c*) Yeast (*d*) Both (*a*) and (*b*)

79. The gene encoding which of the following proteins serves as a selectable marker for animal cells ?
(*a*) Neomycin phosphotransferase
(*b*) Dihydrofolate reductase
(*c*) Thymidine kinase
(*d*) All of the above

80. Consider the options given in Q. 79. Which of the marker genes leads to an amplification of the DNA insert linked to it ?

81. In which of the following animals, electroporation is the preferred method for ova transfection ?
(*a*) Fish (*b*) Cattle
(*c*) Mice (*d*) Both (*b*) and (*c*)

82. Physical containment relates to which of the following ?
(*a*) Laboratory design
(*b*) Special procedures
(*c*) Containment equipments
(*d*) All of the above

83. Which of the following is considered as primary physical containment ?
(*a*) Containment equipment
(*b*) Laboratory practices
(*c*) Both (*a*) and (*b*)
(*d*) Special laboratory design

84. Consider the options given in Q. 83 and pick the option that lists secondary physical containment.

85. It is feared that transgenic plants may pose which of the following risks ?
(*a*) Transfer their transgenic features to weeds.
(*b*) Degrade the environment.
(*c*) Themselves become weeds.
(*d*) All of the above.

86. Match the columns A and B and pick the correct option from those listed below.

Column A	Column B
A. Sexual hybridization	I. Transgenic organisms
B. Cell fusion	II. Limited to closely related species
C. Recombinant DNA technology	III. Difficult to predict outcome
D. *Barnase*	IV. *Bacillus amyloliquefaciens*

Options :
(*a*) AIII, BI, CII, DIV
(*b*) AI, BII, CIII, DIV
(*c*) AII, BIII, CI, DIV
(*d*) AII, BI, CIII, DIV

87. Which of the following viruses has acquired a gene from its host genome ?
(*a*) Adenoviruses
(*b*) Acute transforming retroviruses
(*c*) Epstein-Barr Virus
(*d*) Replication competent tumour retroviruses.

88. Which of the following is correct about patents ?
I. It is the right of an individual to gain profit from a particular invention or unique manufacturing process.
II. The inventor is the owner of the patent.
III. It is granted by the government of a country to an applicant for a limited period of time.
IV. Like any other form of property, a patent can be transacted, purchased, sold or even mortgaged.

Options :
(*a*) I, II, III, IV (*b*) I, II, III
(*c*) II, III, IV (*d*) I, III, IV

89. Which of the following statements are correct about biodiversity ?
I. It is the total variability within all living organisms and the ecological complexes in which they exist.
II. It is a product of hundreds of millions of years of evolutionary processes.
III. The direct benefits of biological diversity to humanity are virtually innumerable.
IV. Once it is lost, this heritage can not be recovered or restored.

Options :
(*a*) I, II, IV (*b*) I, II, III
(*c*) I, II, III, IV (*d*) II, III, IV

90. Which of the following is correct ?
I. Trade mark can be a logo, a symbol, word, phrase, etc., which is used to distinguish one work/service from another.
II. Trade mark provides a distinct identity to a particular goods/service.
III. Copyright is a tool for protecting original literary works.
IV. Trade secret is a safeguard to protect the secrets of a production process/ formulation

Options :
(*a*) I, II, IV (*b*) I, II, III, IV
(*c*) II, III, IV (*d*) I, III, IV

91. Who said, "the cost of conserving biodiversity is far less than the penalty for allowing its degradation".
(*a*) M.S. Swaminathan
(*b*) Edouard Sauma
(*c*) Suman Sahai
(*d*) S.J. Britto

92. The term 'biological diversity' was for the first time introduced by Norse and McManus in 1980. This term was shortened as 'biodiversity' in 1985 by which of the following scientists ?
(*a*) W.G. Rosen
(*b*) M.S. Swaminathan
(*c*) N.I. Vavilov
(*d*) J.R. Harlan

93. Which of the following is responsible for the loss of biodiversity ?
(*a*) Deforestation and overgrazing
(*b*) Biological invasion and hunting
(*c*) Destruction of habitats and overexploitation.
(*d*) All of the above.

94. Biological diversity, called biodiversity in short, refers to which of the following ?
(*a*) Diversity among species
(*b*) Diversity among ecosystems
(*c*) Genetic diversity within a given species
(*d*) All of the above

95. Which of the following ***is not correct*** about biodiversity ?
(*a*) It is a product of hundreds of millions of years of evolution
(*b*) It represents all the mutations that have occured and survived since the life originated on earth.
(*c*) Chances of biodiversity loss are not linked to developmental activities.
(*d*) Biodiversity can be conserved *in situ* as well as *ex situ*.

96. Which of the following is correct about *ex situ* conservation of biodiversity ?
I. *Ex situ* biodiversity convervation is in common use.
II. *Ex situ* conservation of plant biodiversity can be done in the form of seed gene banks, field gene banks, etc.
III. Seed gene banks are vulnerable to technical problems, earth quakes, etc.
IV. *Ex situ* conservation disrupts the processes of evolution.

Options :
(*a*) I, II, III (*b*) I, II, III, IV
(*c*) II, III, IV (*d*) I, II, IV

97. Which of the following ***is not correct*** about *in situ* conservation of biodiversity ?
(*a*) Plants are conserved in their natural habitats.
(*b*) Only the wild relatives are condidates for *in situ* conservation.
(*c*) Plants can continue to evolve.
(*d*) *In situ* conservation is rather simple.

98. Which of the following reasons has already been responsible for extinction of biodiversity ?
(*a*) Introduction of foreign species
(*b*) Habitat destruction
(*c*) Infrastructure development
(*d*) All of the above

99. Among the given countries, which one became the first country to begin commerical use of virus resistant transgenic tobacco and tomato in early 1990s ?
(*a*) India (*b*) USA
(*c*) China (*d*) Canada

100. Risk assessment consists of which of the following ?
(*a*) Hazard indentification and hazard analysis.
(*b*) Consequence analysis and determination
(*c*) Risk evaluation
(*d*) All of the above

□□□

MODEL QUESTION PAPER – V

MULTIPLE CHOICE QUESTIONS

1. Which of following ***is not correct*** about BIBAC2 and TAC plant vectors ?

(*a*) Both have ampicillin resistance marker for selection in bacteria.

(*b*) Both contain hygromycin resistance marker for selection of transformed plant cells.

(*c*) Both have the *sacB* marker (containing a polylinker for DNA insert integration) for negative selection in bacteria.

(*d*) Both have the Ri origin of maintenance in *Rhizobium.*

2. ***Problem (P)***: Standard vectors for plants generally do not afford transfer of larger than 30 kb inserts due to instability in the bacterial host.

Solution (S): High capacity binary vector constructed on the pattern of aritificial chromosome vectors, like BAC (*e.g.* BIBAC2) and PAC (*e.g.* TAC)

Options :

(*a*) Only P is correct.

(*b*) Only S is correct.

(*c*) Both P and S are correct, but S does not solve P.

(*d*) Both P and S are correct, and S adequately solves P.

3. Consider the following statements.

1. Binary vector *p*GV3850 is nonconjugative.
2. Mobilization of recombinant intermediate vector from *E. coli* to *Agrobacterium* is induced by a helper plasmid, *e.g.*, *p*RK2013
3. The maximum size of DNA insert acceptable by T-DNA appears to be greater than 50 kb.
4. The intermediate vector (IV) must contain origin of replication in *Agrobacterium.*

Which of the above statements is correct.

(*a*) 1, 2, 3, 4 (*b*) 1, 2, 3

(*c*) 2, 3, 4 (*d*) 2, 3

4. Which of the following features is correct about BIBAC2 and TAC plant vectors ?

(*a*) They can transfer multiple genes.

(*b*) They can be used for positional cloning of genes identified by mutation.

(*c*) Genomic libraries have been constructed using these vectors.

(*d*) All of the above

5. *In vitro* pollination can be used to produce which of the following ?

I. Inbred progeny of self-incompatible species.

II. Hybrids that are not obtainable sexually.

III. Doubled haploid plants.

IV. Stress tolerant plants.

Options :

(*a*) I, II, III, IV (*b*) I, II

(*c*) I, II, III (*d*) I, III, IV

6. Consider the following statements.

1. The *35S* promoter is the most commonly used constitutive promoter in dicots.
2. The *35S* promoter is 10-40-fold more efficient than the *nos* promoter
3. The *35S* promoter is isolated from CaMV 35*S* RNA gene.
4. Promoter is located at the 3′-end of the sense strand.

Which of these statements is correct.

(*a*) 1, 2, 4 (*b*) 1, 3, 4
(*c*) 1, 2, 3, 4 (*d*) 1, 2, 3

7. Which of the following can be used for induction of mutations in plants and also to serve as molecular tags for the genes so mutated ?

(*a*) T-DNA
(*b*) Transposable elements
(*c*) EMS
(*d*) Both (*a*) and (*b*)

8. Transgenic plants have proved to be extremely valuable tools in studies of which of the following ?

I. Identification of regulatory sequences
II. Identification of promoters
III. Plant molecular biology
IV. Regulation of gene action

Options :

(*a*) I, II, III, IV (*b*) II, III
(*c*) I, II, IV (*d*) I, IV

9. Consider the following statements.

1. Biosource technology permits a rapid and effective elucidation of function of unknown genes/DNA sequences.
2. Transgenic plants permit the analysis of metabolic pathways.
3. Development of transgenic plants resistant to certain biodegradable herbicides was the first major achievement from genetic engineering.
4. Flavr Savr tomato was the second transgenic variety to reach the market.

Which of these statements is correct.

(*a*) 1, 2, 3 (*b*) 1, 2, 4
(*c*) 2, 3, 4 (*d*) 2, 3

10. Which of the following is correct about nutraceuticals ?

I. In 1989, Stephen Dfelice coined the term nutraceuticals derived from nutrition and pharmaceutical.
II. A nutraceutical is a product isolated or purified from foods that is generally sold in medicinal forms not usually associated with foods.
III. The food substances used as nutraceuticals contain antioxidants, probiotics and omega-3 fatty acids.
IV. It is demonstrated to have a physiological benefit or provide protection against chronic diseases.

Options :

(*a*) I, III, IV (*b*) I, II, III
(*c*) I, II, III, IV (*d*) II, III, IV

11. Nutraceuticals differ from dietary supplements in respect to which of the following ?

(*a*) They must not only supplement the diet, but should also aid in prevention or treatment of diseases or disorders.
(*b*) They are represented for use as the conventional food or as the sole item of meal or diet.
(*c*) They include some products from nonfood sources.
(*d*) Both (*a*) and (*b*)

12. Functional food provides the body with the required amount of which of the following needed for healthy survival ?

(*a*) Carbohydrates (*b*) Proteins and fats
(*c*) Vitamins (*d*) All of the above

13. Which of the following ***is not correct*** ?

(*a*) In 1960, Cocking produced large quantities of protoplasts by using cell wall degrading enzymes.
(*b*) In 1970, Powers and coworkers achieved protoplast fusion.
(*c*) In 1971, Takebe and coworkers reported plant regeneration from protoplasts.
(*d*) In 1972, Melchers regenerated somatic hybrids through fusion of protoplasts of two species of *Nicotiana*.

14. ***Constraint (C)***: A wide spread use of antibiotic resistance genes as selectable markers in transgenic plants could increase the incidence of antibiotic resistance in human pathogens ?

Remedy (R): Removal of antibiotic resistance genes from GM plants and utilization of alternative markers for the development of transgenic varieties could be the answer to this problem.

Options :

(*a*) Both C and R are correct and R would remedy C.

(*b*) Both C and R are correct, but R does not remedy C.

(*c*) Only C is correct

(*d*) Only R is correct

15. Today hotly debated issue regarding use of GM crops relates to which of the following ?

(*a*) Biodiversity, ecology and biosafety

(*b*) Environmental and social concerns

(*c*) Ethical concerns

(*d*) All of the above

16. Consider the following statements.

1. Quantitative trait loci control the expression of most of the economically relevant traits.
2. In plant breeding, gene tagging is commonly used to denote a close linkage of a molecular marker with an economic trait.
3. Map based gene cloning and transposon tagging techniques provide opportunities to isolate genes governing particular phenotypes.
4. Molecular markers can not be used for identification of somatic hybrids.

Which of these statements is correct ?

(*a*) 1, 2, 3, 4 (*b*) 1, 2, 4

(*c*) 1, 2, 3 (*d*) 2, 3, 4

17. Which of the following is correct about transgenic crop varieties ?

I. Cultivation of transgenic varieties will help in stablizing yield.

II. They would reduce the use of agrochemicals.

III. Transgenic varieties like Golden Rice will help in improvement of human health.

IV. Transgenic varieties will increase pollution by permitting the use of biodegradable agrochemicals.

Options :

(*a*) I, II, III (*b*) I, II, III, IV

(*c*) II, III, IV (*d*) I, III, IV

18. Transgenic varieties are being designed to produce which of the following ?

(*a*) Research reagents (*b*) Edible vaccines

(*c*) Pharmaceuticals (*d*) All of the above

19. Molecular markers offer which of the following advantages over morphological/ other conventional markers ?

(*a*) They show high degree of polymorphism.

(*b*) They can be established at cellular and tissue levels.

(*c*) They are not influenced by the environmental fluctuation.

(*d*) All of the above.

20. In vegetable crops, molecular markers are now increasingly being used for which of the following purposes ?

I. Comparative mapping

II. Hybrid purity testing

III. Indentification of heterotic parents

IV. Characterization of germplasm

Options :

(*a*) I, II, III (*b*) I, II, III, IV

(*c*) I, III, IV (*d*) I, II, IV

21. Construction of saturated molecular maps and ability to map any gene of economic importance to a defined chromosomal site opens the possibility of isolating genes via chromosome walking. This method is sometimes referred to as which of the following ?

I. Reverse genetics

II. Top-down approach

III. Forward genetics

IV. Map-based cloning

Options :

(*a*) I, II, III, IV (*b*) II, III, IV

(*c*) I, II, IV (*d*) I, III, IV

22. Which of the following methods can be applied to plant genome analysis ?

(*a*) Minisatellites can be hybridized to restricted and electrophoretically separated DNA blotted onto nylon membranes.

(*b*) Microsatellites can be hybridized to DNA in dried gels.

(*c*) Microsatellites can be cloned, sequenced and amplification fragment length

polymorphisms detected by PCR, using oligonucleotides from surrounding monomorphic DNA as primers.
(*d*) All of the above

23. Which of the following features is relavant to an ideal herbicide ?
(*a*) No toxicity towards humans, animals or soil organisms.
(*b*) Kills selectively weeds.
(*c*) Biodegradability.
(*d*) All of the above.

24. Which of the following appraches are used for development of fungal disease resistant transgenic crops ?
(*a*) Transgene encoding antifungal compounds.
(*b*) Transgenes which encodes a product that leads to cell death upon pathogen infection.
(*c*) The R gene may be transferred to initiate resistance response.
(*d*) All of the above.

25. ***Assertion (A)***: Chitinase genes of plant and/or bacterial origin are used for engineering plants resistant to fungal diseases.

Reason (R): Chitinase enzyme degrades chitin rich cell walls of fungi.

Options :
(*a*) Both A and R are correct and R sufficiently explains A.
(*b*) Both A and R are correct, but R does not explain A.
(*c*) Only A is correct.
(*d*) Only R is correct.

26. Which of the following strategies can be used for selection of hybrid cells ?
I. Visual marker
II. Complementation
III. Staining with fluorescent dyes
IV. Trangenic selectable markers

Options :
(*a*) I, II, III (*b*) II, III, IV
(*c*) I, III, IV (*d*) I, II, III, IV

27. The ability to design and execute molecular strategies for generating male sterility has been possible due to which of the following ?
(*a*) Isolation, cloning and characterization of anther/pollen specific genes.
(*b*) Anther/pollen specific promoters
(*c*) Chemically inducible promoters.
(*d*) All of the above.

28. The genes given in the options of Q. 27 are expressed either in the pollen grains themselves (gametophytic expression) or in cells and tissues that directly or indirectly support pollen development (sporophytic expression); such tissues are which of the following ?
(*a*) Tapetum (*b*) Anther wall
(*c*) Connective tissue (*d*) All of the above.

29. Which of the following features is correct about ribosome-inactivating proteins (RIPs) ?
(*a*) An effective antifungal protein from barley seeds called RIP has been isolated.
(*b*) It acts by inhibiting protein synthesis via N-glycosidase modification of fungal 28S rDNA.
(*c*) Transgenic crop plants expressing RIP proteins are now being tested against many fungi.
(*d*) All of the above.

30. ***Technology (T)***: Transgenic plants expressing the coding region of the *iaaH* gene under the control of ovule-specific *DefH9* promoter showed parthenocarpic fruit development.

Utility (U): Parthenocarpy transgenics of fruit vegetables have tremendous potential under adverse climatic conditions which adeversely affect pollen survival/function.

Options :
(*a*) Both T and U are correct and U adequately supports the use of T.
(*b*) Both T and U are correct, but U does not support the use of T.
(*c*) Only T is correct.
(*d*) Only U is correct.

31. ***Statement (S)***: Development of less seeded fruit vegetables like eggplant, tomato, sweet pepper, etc. increases their consumer acceptance.

Mechanism (M): Gene consturcts derived from *Pseudomonas syringae* code for an enzyme involved in IAA biosynthesis. Expression of this gene construct under ovule-specific promoter enhances the level of IAA in ovules and stimulates growth and development of unfertilized ovules, which promotes fruit set.

Options :

(*a*) Only S is correct.

(*b*) Only M is correct.

(*c*) Both S and M are correct and M adequately supports S.

(*d*) Both S and M are correct, but M does not support S.

32. Which of the following is correct about transgenic development ?

I. In 1983, the first transgenic plant was produced in a tobacco line expressing kanamycin resistance gene.

II. The development of virus resistant transgenic plants using coat protein gene was the first useful transgenic trait.

III. First report of transgenic insect resistant plants was published in 1987.

IV. In 1994, Flavr Savr tomato became the first transgenic variety to be commercially cultivated in USA.

Options :

(*a*) I, II, III (*b*) I, II, III, IV

(*c*) II, III, IV (*d*) I, III, IV

33. Selection of an appropriate molecular markers system for applied plant breeding would depend on which of the following ?

(*a*) Breeding objective(s)

(*b*) Breeding material

(*c*) Cost effectiveness

(*d*) All of the above

34. In the coming years, which of the following research areas have been predicted to be very important in the improvement of plant species ?

(*a*) Apomixis to fix and exploit heterosis in hybrids.

(*b*) Transgenic male sterility for hybrid seed production.

(*c*) Parthenocarpy for seedless vegetables and fruits.

(*d*) All of the above.

35. In Q. 34 which of the given areas is applicable to most of the vegetable crops ?

36. Selection of appropriate molecular marker for applied plant breeding would depend on which of the following ?

(*a*) Trait(s) under consideration

(*b*) Crop in question

(*c*) Reproducibility of molecular marker

(*d*) All of the above

37. Which of the following proteins involved in plant defence is known to be an allergen ?

I. Soybean Kunitz trypsin inhibitor

II. Pea lectin

III. Wheat germ agglutinin (WGA)

IV. 15 kDa α-amylase

Options :

(*a*) II, III, IV (*b*) I, II, III, IV

(*c*) I, III, IV (*d*) I, II, III

38. ***Bottleneck (B)***: Besides high cost, reproducible molecular markers like RFLP or AFLP may also have other drawbacks like general applicability.

Decesion (D): Before incorporating above markers in breeding programme, their validity either in the same cross or other crosses should be tested.

Options :

(*a*) Both B and D are correct and D accounts for B.

(*b*) Both B and D are correct, but D does not account for B.

(*c*) Only B is correct.

(*d*) Only D is correct.

39. Which of the following statements is correct about molecular markers ?

(*a*) The utlimate goal of molecular marker research is to develop plant varieties more efficiently and effectively.

(*b*) Molecular markers tightly linked to male sterility gene can be used to identify male fertile sister plants at very early stage.

(*c*) RAPD is cost effective and simple, but its reproducibility is not high.
(*d*) All of the above.

40. Transgenic plants suffer from which of the following problems ?

I. Position effect II. Co-suppression
III. Adverse pleiotropy IV. Gene silencing

Options :

(*a*) I, II (*b*) I, II, III, IV
(*c*) II, III, IV (*d*) I, II, III

41. Which of the following is correct ?

I. Seven transgenes were incorporated in the rice genome to enable synthesis of beta-carotene and iron in the body of the grain.
II. Just 300 grams of golden rice can provide a full daily complement of vitamin A and iron.
III. A gene, *ama1*, isolated in India from *Amaranthus* encodes a protein that has well balanced amino acid content
IV. Transgenic potatoes expressing *ama1* are undergoing field trials.

Options :

(*a*) I, II, III (*b*) I, II, III, IV
(*c*) II, III, IV (*d*) I, III, IV

42. Somatic hybridization yields which of the following ?

I. Symmetric hybrids
II. Homozygous lines
III. Cybrids
IV. Asymmetric hybrids

Options :

(*a*) I, II, IV (*b*) I, III, IV
(*c*) I, II, III, IV (*d*) I, II, III

43. For which of the following, toxicity or allergenicity ***is not reported*** ?

(*a*) Cry protein
(*b*) Trypsin inhibitor
(*c*) Virus coat protein
(*d*) Both (*a*) and (*c*)

44. Which of the following ***is not correct*** about *Bacillus thuringiensis* ?

(*a*) Ishiwata discovered this bacterium in 1902 from diseased silkworm (*Bombyx mori*) larvae.
(*b*) In 1911, Berliner isolated it from larvae of Mediterranean flour moth, *Anagastra* (*Ephestia*) *kuehniella* and designated it as *Bacillus thuringiensis*.
(*c*) It is a Gram-negative bacterium.
(*d*) This bacterium produces parasporal proteinaceous crystalline inclusion (bodies) during sporulation.

45. Glass bead sterilizers are being employed for the sterilization of forceps, scalpels, etc. These devices use which of the following ?

(*a*) Moist heat (*b*) Dry heat
(*c*) X-rays (*d*) All of the above

46. Which of the following is an example of heat labile compound ?

(*a*) Urea
(*b*) Zeatin
(*c*) Enzymes
(*d*) All of the above

47. Which of the following ***is not correct*** about electrofusion ?

(*a*) It utilizes high voltage nonuniform alternating electric current pulses to bring the protoplast in close contact.
(*b*) Fusion of protoplasts is brought about by a short pulse (few microseconds) of high voltage (500-1,000 V/cm).
(*c*) The entire operation is carried out manually in a specially designed equipment, called electroporator.
(*d*) Electrofusion has been mostly used with the members of solanaceae often with very high rate (over 50%) of fusion.

48. Terminator seed technology is seen to result in which of the following ?

(*a*) Encourage monopoly of multinational seed companies.
(*b*) Force the farmers to purchase seeds of even self-pollinated crops every year.
(*c*) Jeoparadise food security.
(*d*) All of the above.

49. For optimum callus growth, which of the following vitamins is required ?

(*a*) Pyridoxin (*b*) Inositol
(*c*) Thiamine (*d*) All of the above

50. Among the given options in Q. 49 which one is essential for optimum callus growth ?

51. Which of the following statements ***is not correct*** ?

(*a*) Autoclave maintains temperature of 121°C at 15 p.s.i. (1.06 kg/cm^2)

(*b*) A few drops of a surfactant may be added to the sterilant solution.

(*c*) In case of tissue culture, 6 macro-nutrients are needed in concentrations of >0.5 m mol l^{-1}.

(*d*) Maltose is the most commonly used carbon source for cultured plant materials.

52. Which of the following features ***is not correct*** about micropropagation ?

(*a*) Mass clonal propagation of desired genotypes.

(*b*) Plantlets are usually pathogen free.

(*c*) Shoot cultures of some species are maintained as 'slow-growth cultures' for germplasm conservation.

(*d*) There is no chance of somaclonal variation.

53. The technique of micropropagation suffers from which of the following limitations ?

I. High cost of propagules
II. Bacterial contamination
III. Browing of the media/explants
IV. Hyperhydration

Options :

(*a*) I, II, IV (*b*) I, II, III, IV
(*c*) II, III, IV (*d*) I, II, III

54. In 1974, Murashige proposed which of the following groups of activities involved in micropropagation ?

I. Selection and preparation of mother plants.
II. Selection of suitable explants and establishment of axenic cultures.
III. Proliferation and multiplication of shoots from the cultured explants.
IV. Rooting of shoots and transfer of the plantlets into soil.

Options :

(*a*) II, III, IV (*b*) I, III, IV
(*c*) I, III, IV (*d*) I, II, III

55. At present, micropropagation is considered to consist of which of the following stages ?

I. Selection and preparation of mother explants.
II. Culture initiation
III. Multiplication
IV. Rooting of shoots
V. Transfer of plantlets to soil

Options :

(*a*) I, II, III, IV (*b*) II, III, IV, V
(*c*) I, II, III, IV, V (*d*) I, II, IV, V

56. Electrofusion possesses which of the following features ?

(*a*) Fusion conditions can be easily controlled.

(*b*) Even a single pair of protoplasts can be fused.

(*c*) Even very fragile protoplasts may survive electrofusion.

(*d*) All of the above

57. Expressed sequence tags (ESTs) have been used for which of the following ?

(*a*) Identification of genes in genomic clones.

(*b*) Designing of PCR primers to generate large numbers of target sequences for cDNA microarrays.

(*c*) Gene expression analyses.

(*d*) All of the above.

58. Expressed sequence tags have been used for which of the following ?

(*a*) As physical markers for genome maps.

(*b*) Discovery of genes.

(*c*) Differential-display PCR.

(*d*) All of the above

59. Which of the following ***is not correct*** ?

(*a*) Culture initiation consists of surface sterilization of explants and establishing them *in vitro*.

(*b*) Micropropagation can not be carried out throughout the year.

(*c*) IAA is a natural auxin.

(*d*) In carrot, NH_4^+ has a promotive effect on somatic embryo regeneration.

60. Which of the following treatments are commonly used for rejuvenation ?

I. Repeated subculture of shoot-apices in a cytokinin containing medium.
II. Etiolation of shoots/branches before the excision of shoot-tip.
III. Repeated grafting of scion from mature trees onto seedling rootstocks.
IV. Selection of current year's basal spouts/ twigs from adult trees for culture.

Options :

(*a*) II, III, IV (*b*) I, III, IV
(*c*) I, II, III, IV (*d*) I, II, III

61. Cell viability can be determined by staining with which of the following ?

(*a*) Evan's blue
(*b*) 2, 3, 5-triphenyltetrazolium chloride
(*c*) Fluorescein diacetate
(*d*) All of the above

62. The protoplast fusion products recovered after a treatment with a fusion inducing agent consist of which of the following ?

(*a*) Homokaryons
(*b*) Heterokaryons
(*c*) Unfused protoplasts of the two species/ strains
(*d*) All of the above

63. For the recovery of virus-free stocks of clonal crops, meristem culture is combined with which of the following ?

(*a*) Thermotherapy (*b*) Chemotherapy
(*c*) Cryotherapy (*d*) Any of the above

64. Evan's blue is usually used in conjunction with which of the following ?

(*a*) Fluorescein diacetate (FDA)
(*b*) TTC
(*c*) Hematoxylin
(d) All of the above

65. Which of the following ***is not correct*** about TTC ?

(*a*) It stands for 2, 3, 5-triphenyltetrazolium chloride.
(*b*) Cell masses can be stained with 1-2% solution of TTC.
(*c*) TTC is reduced by living cells to formazon that yields red colour
(*d*) TTC is suitable for study of single cells.

66. Which of the following is correct about fluorescein diacetate (FDA) ?

(*a*) During testing of viability, cells are treated with 0.01% solution of FDA.
(*b*) Live cells cleave FDA by esterase activity and produce fluorescein.
(*c*) When stained cells are exposed to UV rays, living cells appear green.
(*d*) All of the above.

67. Consider the following statements about ontogeny of shoot bud development.

1. Clusters of meristematic cells, called meristemoids, appear in the explant/ callus.
2. Meristemoids are considered to arise in areas that accumulate starch.
3. Meristemoids may develop vascular elements inside them, while their outside may be made of cambium like cells.
4. Initially, the meristemoids may either produce a root or shoot.
5. In general, roots originate from inside the meristemoids while shoots develop from the outside.

Which of the above statements is correct ?

(*a*) 1, 2, 3, 4, 5 (*b*) 1, 2, 3, 4
(*c*) 2, 3, 4 (*d*) 3, 4, 5

68. Shoot regeneration is affected by which of the following factors ?

I. Electrical stimulation
II. Growth regulator regime
III. Explant genotype
IV. Physical factors of the culture system

Options :

(*a*) I, II, III (*b*) I, II, III, IV
(*c*) I, III, IV (*d*) II, III, IV

69. Which of the following ***is not correct*** about somatic embryo ?

(*a*) It is an embryo derived from a non-zygotic/somatic cell.
(*b*) Somatic embryo has vascular connection with the tissue from which it develops.
(*c*) It generally originates from a single cell.

(*d*) In 1978, somatic embryogenesis was independently reported by Steward and coworkers, and Reinert in cell suspension of carrot.

70. Centre for the Application of Molecular Biology to International Agriculture (CAMBIA) is located at which of the following palces ?

(*a*) Stockholm (Sweden)
(*b*) Vienna (Austria)
(*c*) Canberra (Australia)
(*d*) Trieste (Italy)

71. ***Problem (P)***: Somatic embryos (SEs) often show abnormal developmental features, *e.g.*, three or more cotyledons, bell-shaped cotyledon, larger size, etc.

Solution (S): Addition of ABA or a suitable concentration of manitol in the medium leads to more normal development of SEs.

Options :

(*a*) Both P and S are correct, and S adequately overcomes P.
(*b*) Both P and S are correct, but S does not overcome P.
(*c*) Only P is correct
(*d*) Only S is correct.

72. In which of the following situations, micropropagation can be used ?

I. Seeds show long dormancy period.
II. Seeds are nongerminable/poorly germinable/short-lived.
III. Plants do not produce seeds.
IV. Species/variety is highly heterozygous.

Options :

(*a*) I, II, III, IV (*b*) II, III, IV
(*c*) I, III, IV (*d*) I, II, III

73. The chief objective of clonal/vegetative propagation is to produce progeny plants, which are identical in genotype to their parent plants. This is achieved by which of the following processes ?

(*a*) Somatic embryogenesis.
(*b*) Proliferation of axillary buds.
(*c*) Induction of adventitious buds, bulbs, protocorms.
(*d*) All of the above

74. Which of the following ***is not correct*** about meristem culture ?

(*a*) Cultivation of axillary or apical shoot meristems.
(*b*) The shoot apical meristem is the portion lying distal to the youngest leaf primordium and is 250 μm in length.
(*c*) The shoot apex/shoot-tip consists of the apical meristem plus 1-3 young leaf primordia.
(*d*) Meristem culture usually involves the regeneration of a new shoot meristem.

75. Consider the following statements.

1. In practice, shoot-tips of upto 1 mm are used when the objective is virus elimination.
2. Shoot-tip culture is widely used for rapid clonal propagation for which much larger, *e.g.*, 5-10 mm, explants are used.
3. Most cases of meristem culture are essentially shoot-tip cultures.
4. Nodal explants of various sizes are also commonly employed for rapid clonal propagation.

Which of the above statements is correct ?

(*a*) 2, 3, 4 (*b*) 1, 2, 3
(*c*) 1, 3, 4 (*d*) 1, 2, 3, 4

76. Which of the following ***is not correct*** about somatic embryogenesis ?

(*a*) It is amenable to scaling up.
(*b*) It gives a moderate multiplication rate.
(*c*) Embryogenic cultures can be maintained for long periods of time.
(*d*) There is no need for a rooting stage.

77. Somatic embryos can be stored for prolonged periods through which of the following ?

(*a*) Cryopreservation (*b*) Desiccation
(*c*) Cold storage (*d*) All of the above

78. Which of the following restricts the use of somatic embryo route of micropropagation ?

I. There is risk of somaclonal variation.
II. Somatic embryo quality is often poor.
III. Field conversion frequencies of somatic embryos and artificial seeds are low (15–20%)

IV. Large scale (>1 million somatic embryos) production is difficult.

Options :

(*a*) I, II, III (*b*) II, III, IV
(*c*) I, II, III, IV (*d*) I, III, IV

79. Artificial seed is a bead of gel that contains which of the following ?

(*a*) Pesticides and antibiotics
(*b*) Nutrients and growth regulators
(*c*) Shoot bud/somatic embryo
(*d*) All of the above

80. *Ex vitro* rooting offers which of the following advantages over *in vitro* rooting ?

I. Structurally and functionally better roots.
II. Better rooting of difficult to root species.
III. No risk of root damage during transfer to soil.
IV. Saving of labour and media reagents required for *in vitro* rooting and hardening steps.

Options :

(*a*) I, II, III, IV (*b*) II, III, IV
(*c*) I, III, IV (*d*) I, II, III

81. Which of the following steps is necessary for the production of artificial seeds by desiccated system ?

(*a*) Somatic embryos (SEs) are first hardened to withstand desiccation.
(*b*) Hardened SEs are encapsulated in a suitable coating material.
(*c*) SEs may be hardened either by coating/treating mature SEs with a suitable polymer followed by drying during their maturation phase.
(*d*) All of the above.

82. Which of the following ***is not correct*** about production of hydrated artificial seed ?

(*a*) Somatic embryos are enclosed in gels, which are then desiccated.
(*b*) Calcium alginate is the most suitable gel.
(*c*) The artificial seeds are sticky and difficult to handle.
(*d*) The seeds are difficult to store for long periods.

83. ***Problem (P)***: Hydrated artifical seeds are sticky and difficult to handle on a large scale, and dry rapidly in the open air.
Solution (S): A waxy coating over the beads can be provided.

Options :

(*a*) Both P and S are correct and S sufficiently resolves P.
(*b*) Both P and S are correct, but S does not solve P.
(*c*) Only P is correct.
(*d*) Only S is correct.

84. Consider the following statements.

1. A gradual reduction in sucrose content of the medium is reported to favour photoautotrophy.
2. Paclobutrazol and polyethylene glycol 8,000 are reported to promote cuticular biosynthesis and the development of normal anatomical features in plantlets raised *in vitro*.
3. Bacterization of potato plantlets with *Pseudomonas* significantly decreased their root number, root dry weight, stem length and leaf area.
4. Improved survival of microbe-treated plantlets is thought to be the result of expression of defence-related proteins in these plants.

Which of the above statements is correct ?

(*a*) 1, 2, 3 (*b*) 1, 2, 4
(*c*) 2, 3, 4 (*d*) 1, 3, 4

85. The problem of phenolics leaching in the medium from cut surfaces of explants can be overcome by which of the following ?

I. The cut ends of the explants may be inserted into the agar medium or they may be sealed with paraffin wax.
II. Adsorbants like activated charcoal or PVP added into the medium.
III. A brief period of culture in the liquid medium.
IV. Frequent subculture of explants on agar-medium.

Options :

(*a*) I, III, IV (*b*) II, III, IV
(c) I, II, III, IV (*d*) I, II, III

86. Problems of hyperhydration can be over-come by which of the following ?

I. Reducing relative humidity in the culture vessels.
II. Decreased agar concentration of the medium.
III. Adddition of agar hydrolysate to the medium.
IV. Using a desiccant like $CaSO_4$ or silica gel.

Options :

(*a*) I, II, III (*b*) I, III, IV
(*c*) I, II, IV (*d*) II, III, IV

87. In case a plant variety is a chimera, which of the following route of micropropagation can be used to conserve the chimaeric state ?

(*a*) Somatic embryogenesis
(*b*) Adventitious shoot buds
(*c*) Shoot-tip culture
(*d*) Both (*a*) and (*b*)

88. In Q. 87, which of the options disrupts chimaeras and produces nonchimeric progeny plants ?

89. In Q. 87, which of the options shows the lowest frequency of genetic variation and chromosomal aberrations ?

90. Those cases where the desirable feature of a variety is due to the presence of a virus, *e.g.*, the clear vein character of geranium variety 'Crocodile', which of the options given in Q. 87 will be used to retain the viral infection in the progeny plants ?

91. Which of the following options given in Q. 87 is the mostly likely to eliminate the virus and consequently, the desirable feature of the variety say, Crocodile ?

92. In difficult cases, where browning persists at each subculture, which of the following antioxidants may be used to check the oxidation of polyphenols ?

(*a*) Cysteine-HCl (*b*) Citric acid
(*c*) Ascorbic acid (*d*) All of the above

93. Which of the following treatments can reduce the problem of hyperhydration ?

(*a*) Lowered NH_4^+ level.
(*b*) Lowered level of cytokinin.
(*c*) Lower salt concentration in the medium.
(*d*) All of the above.

94. Addition of which of the following chemicals in the medium can reduce the problem of hyperhydration ?

(*a*) $CoCl_2$ (*b*) Phloroglucinol
(*c*) Phlorizin (*d*) Any of the above

95. ***Assertion (A)***: The ELISA test can not be used for those diseases, which involve several related luteoviruses *e.g.*, Potato Leaf Roll Virus.

Reason (R): All the viruses may not react with the antiserum prepared against the main virus.

Options :

(*a*) Both A and R are correct and R sufficiently explains A.
(*b*) Both A and R are correct, but R does not explain A.
(*c*) Only A is correct.
(*d*) Only R is correct.

96. In cryopreservation, which of the following favours storage of plant cells, tissues or organs in liquid nitrogen at –196°C ?

(*a*) All metabolic processes and growth are suppressed.
(*b*) Occurrance of genetic, karyotypic morphological and biochemical changes are prevented.
(*c*) It is the most reliable method for long-term prevention of cell cultures.
(*d*) All of the above.

97. Which of the following difficulties are encountered in distant hybridization ?

(*a*) Failure of zygote formation.
(*b*) Zygotes fail to develop into a mature embryos.
(*c*) Hybrid seedlings may fail to survive.
(*d*) All of the above.

98. ***Assertion (A)***: In distant crosses, the zygote produced by fertilization may fail to develop into a mature embryo and give rise to hybrid seedlings.

Reason (R): Often the young endosperm fails to continue development and provide nutrition to the developing young embryo.

Options :

(*a*) Only A is correct.
(*b*) Only R is correct.
(*c*) Both A and R are correct, but R does not explain A.
(*d*) Both A and R are correct and R sufficiently explains A.

99. The problem of endosperm abortion can be overcome by excising and culturing which of the following ?

(*a*) Hybrid endosperms
(*b*) Hybrid fruits
(*c*) Hybrid embryos
(*d*) Hybrid zygotes

100. Which of the following is correct about omega 3 fatty acids ?

I. They are found in flax seeds, walnut and soybean.

II. They are long chain polyunsaturated fatty acids like eicosapentaenoic acid (EPA) which increase the fluidity of membranes.

III. They protect against prostate and breast cancer by stimulating the death of tumour cells.

IV. They increase HDL chloesterol and reduce triglycerides, a condition that is favourable for the heart.

Options :

(*a*) I, II, III
(*b*) I, II, III, IV
(*c*) II, III, IV
(*d*) I, III, IV

□□□

MODEL QUESTION PAPER – VI

FILL IN THE BLANKS

1. India permitted cultivation of insect resistant transgenic cotton varieties in the year ....

2. Introduction of DNA into cells with the help of electricity is called ....

3. A somatic cell that performs all the functions of a zygote is known as .... cell.

4. Cereals can be transformed by *A. tumefaciens* provided exogenous .... is supplied during the bacterial coculture.

5. Nonconjugative plasmids can also be transmitted from one cell to another provided a .... plasmid is present in the same cell; this phenomenon is called ....

6. Hairy root cultures used for isolation of biochemicals are produced following transformation by ....

7. .... somatic hybrids contain the complete somatic complement of one species and some chromosomes of the other species involved in fusion.

8. A vector that can replicate in the cells of more than one organism is called ....

9. Detection of DNA or RNA molecules in cytological preparations is based on .... hybridization.

10. .... PCR is the geometric amplification of unknown DNA sequences that flank the region of known sequence.

11. To be useful in crop improvement, somatic hybrid cells must regenerate .... plants.

12. During protoplast isolation, generally, a mixture of pectinase or macerozyme (0.1–1.0%) and .... is appropriate for most plant materials.

13. *nptII* gene confers resistance to .... and is used as a .... in gene transfer experiments.

14. When a prokaryotic gene is transferred into an eukaryote often its activity declines with time, this phenomenon is known as ....

15. A synthetic oligonucleotide having the recognition site for a restriction enzyme is known as ....

16. Many bacteria accumulate ...., which is used to make biodegradable plastic.

17. Butanol production is based on the bacterium ....

18. Biogas consists mainly of .... and ....

19. The recognition site for *Eco*RI is .... and its cleavage site is between the bases .... and ....

20. The identification of antibiotic sensitive cells present in a culture having antibiotic resistant ones as well is achieved by ....

21. The Klenow fragment lacks .... activity.

22. According to the .... model, biological membranes are composed of a lipid bilayer within which protein molecules are embedded.

23. Teichoic acid is present in the cell wall of .... bacteria.

24. The toxin function of the *B. thuringiensis* crystal proteins is located in its .... region.

25. For easy selection of the recombinant clones, a plasmid vector should have atleast ....

selectable markers containing unique target sites for ....

26. Cosmids are essentially plasmid vectors containing .... for their easy packaging in .... λ phage head.

27. Typically, vector molecules produce several copies per bacterial cell; this feature is due to their .... of DNA replication which is subject to a .... control.

28. Vectors designed to be propagated in two distinct hosts are called ....; they have atleast one .... functional in the cells of each host.

29. During anther culture pollen embryos, in general, originate from .... cell.

30. Two plant species are valued as ornamentals due to their variegation patterns. Variegation in species A is due to chimaera, while in species B it is due to a virus. Shoot-tip culture is the method of choice for propagation of .... but not of ....

31. In 1972, the hybrid *Nicotiana glauca* + *N. langsdorfii* was produced by the .... method.

32. The osmoticum used in the medium for plant protoplasts generally has .... m mol/l mannitol, sorbitol or sucrose; often 50–100 m mol/l ...... is also added to this solution.

33. When a viral genome is placed within T-DNA of .... plasmid and this construct is introduced into plant host of the virus, it is called ....

34. Encapsulated somatic embryos that behave like true seed are called ....

35. The phenomenon where the terminal bud of a shoot suppresses the growth of axillary buds is called ....

36. The ability of different states of DNA and proteins, which may have different phenotypic effects, to be inherited is called .... inheritance.

37. A Ti plasmid that has some or all of the T-DNA genes removed so it is no longer able to promote cancerous growth of plant cells is said to be a .... Ti plasmid.

38. Carbon fixation is catalysed by the enzyme ...., which is widely claimed to be most abundant protein on the earth.

39. .... is the total amount of DNA in a haploid genome.

40. Doubling of the number of chromosomes without division of nucleus, resulting in polyploid cells is called ....

41. Right-handed DNA helix is known as .... and the most stable left-handed DNA helix called ....

42. The development of a haploid individual from a pollen grain is called ....

43. An usually circular piece of DNA, existing primarily independent of host chromosome and found in bacteria is called ....

44. Production of an embryo from a female gamete without its fusion with a male gamete is called ....

45. CryIA protein is an endotoxin; it is potentially insecticidal to Lepidopteran insects and is derived from ....

46. .... cells are obtained by fusion of B lymphocytes with myeloma cells and used for monoclonal antibody production.

47. .... is the red pigment containing protein present in nodules of legumes.

48. The .... cycle accounts for about two-thirds of the total oxidation of carbon compounds in most cells and its major end products are CO_2 and NADH.

49. Electrofusion technique utilizes .... voltage nonuniform alternating electric current pulses to bring the protoplasts in close contact.

50. The enzyme ...., transcribes RNA chains into complementary DNA molecules.

51. .... is a technique used to identify a series of overlapping restriction fragments to determine their relative positions in the large DNA segment from which they were derived.

52. .... is a protein that is 10,000 times sweeter than sucrose and is flavour enhancer.

53. A cloning vector comprising the chromosomal components of *Saccharomyces* and

able to clone very large pieces of DNA is called ....

54. A plasmid capable of integration into the host cell chromosome is called ....

55. A cell/an individual having less than the gametic chromosome complement of the species is known as ....

56. .... is common if the shoot has too much water available, usually, in medium with low agar concentration.

57. Detection of unfractioned DNA or RNA molecules immobilized on a membrane is called ....

58. In B-DNA, the number of base pairs per turn of the helix is roughly ....

59. Abbreviation MAC stands for .... vector.

60. A plant cell can have .... types of functional ribsomes.

61. Electron microscope was invented by ....

62. The storage of plant material unders ultra-low temperatures is called ....

63. The enzyme used for joining of two DNA fragments is known as ....

64. Prefertilization barriers can be overcome by .... and ....

65. Urease was the first enzyme discovered by .... in 1926.

66. Two major sources of cryoinjury are mechanical damage due to .... and toxic solution effects due to the excessive concentration of intracellular solution resulting from .... formation.

67. In general, about .... % (v/v) DMSO is used in medium for cryopreservation.

68. Selection of somatic hybrid cells from protoplast fusion products is the .... step in somatic hybridization.

69. Pore size in the membrane filter for sterilization of culture medium should be ....

70. In 2002, herbicide resistant soybean varieties occupied .... % of global area under transgenic crops, and insect resistant maize was grown on .... % of the area.

71. .... cells do not stain with Evan's blue.

72. ELISA test can not be used for viroids and viruses that have lost their ....

73. In case of distant hybridization, hybrid seedlings may fail to survive due to .... or fail to reproduce due to ....

74. Maximum level of monoclonal antibodies production can be acheived by growing hybridoma cells in ....

75. Beads of microcarrier culture system for .... cells are usually made of dextrans, polysaccharide, etc.

76. During young embryo culture, ... to .... % sucrose is generally used.

77. Most of the tetraploid and hexaploid wheats carry two dominant genes, namely *Kr1* and *Kr2*, which prevent seed development in crosses with ....

78. In India the importance of biotechnology was highlighted by the 69th session of the Indian Science Congress held at .... in 1982.

79. International Laboratory for Tropical Agricultural Biotechnology (ILTAB) is located at ....

80. When embryo fails to develop due to endosperm degeneration, embryo culture is used to recover hybrid plants; this is called ....

81. In case a plant variety is a chimaera, it should be propagated through ....

82. Cocking obtained large number of protoplasts through .... of cell walls.

83. .... were the first to report fusion of protoplast.

84. .... were the first to regenerate plants from protoplasts.

85. In 1972, Calson *et al.* reported for the first time interspecific hybridization through protoplast fusion in two speceis of ....

86. Marton *et al.* developed cocultivation prodcedure for transformation of plant protoplasts with ....

87. .... introduced the term somaclonal variation in 1981.

88. India ranked .... worldwide in the cultivation of transgenic varieties of crops during 2006.

89. In 1986, Powel-Abel *et al.* developed virus resistant .... transgenic plants using cDNA of coat protein gene of TMV.

90. In 1988, Okamura developed pomato by fusion of protoplasts of ....with those of tomato (*Lycopersicon pimpinellifolium*).

91. In 1953, ... determined the amino acid sequence of insulin.

92. Glucose syrup is produced from liquefied starch of .... dextrose equivalent (DE).

93. .... is used to breakdown lactose present in milk and butter milk.

94. Rabies vaccine is obtained from cultures of .... cell lines.

95. Cell viability can be determined by .... microscopy.

96. Enzyme .... is used in cheese making to produce curd.

97. The first DNA molecules are thought to have originated by .... molecules.

98. Gallic acid is obtained from *Aspergillus niger* and is used in manufacture of ....

99. L-sorbose is precursor of .... acid.

100. .... are dominant markers, and are obtained due to differential amplification of DNA fragments produced by restriction digestion.

□□□

MODEL QUESTION PAPER – VII

MARK TRUE OR FALSE

1. The aim of genetic engineeers is to usually maintain all the desirable properties of target plant and include an additional phenotype predicted from the insertion of a foregin gene.
2. Transfection of bacteria is the same as transformation, except for the introduction of phage DNA in place of plasmid/other DNA.
3. Gynogenesis is related to *in vitro* pollination.
4. An epigenetic change is an alternation in gene expression associated with alternative chromatin or methylation states (or both) of DNA with or without a change in its sequence.
5. Most antigens induce a polyclonal response.
6. A large protein antigen can, generally, interact with many different antibody moelcules.
7. A hapten can induce antibody formation against itself and interact with these antibody moelcules.
8. *Agrobacterium tumefaciens* is called natural genentic engineer.
9. Guha and Maheshwary were the first to report haploid production through pollen culture of *Datura.*
10. Biotechnology can be used as an alternative of plant breeding.
11. *Bacillus thuringiensis* is a gram-positive bacterium.
12. B-cell epitopes of antigens are often nonsequential amino acids brought together by the tertiary conformation of a protein antigen.
13. Abbreviation IIB stands for International Institute of Biotechnology.
14. AFLP is expanded as amplified fragment length polymorphism.
15. Professor Haberlandt is regarded as father of plant tissue culture.
16. LD medium is used for culture of plant protoplasts.
17. Germplasm is also called genetic resource.
18. Genetic engineering provides an opportunity to transfer genes from tertiary gene pool.
19. StarLink is a transgenic variety of tobacco.
20. *Azosprillium* fixes nitrogen symbiotically.
21. The term photophosphorylation is related to photosynthesis.
22. The technique of micropropagation is used for true-to-type multiplication of self-pollinated species.
23. Cybrids can also be produced by fusion of protoplasts.
24. Both T_H and T_C cells recognize antigens that have been processed and presented with a MHC molecule.
25. Many of somaclonal variations occur due to methylation in the promoter regions of genes.
26. Ligase is regarded as molecular glue.
27. A.C. Chang is a somaclonal variety of tobacco.
28. Parasexual hybrids are also called somatic hybrids.
29. AIDS is transmitted through mosquito bite.

30. MHC genes play a major role in determining the degree of immune responsiveness to an antigen.

31. Hyperhydration occurs only during shoot multiplication.

32. Orthodox seeds are conserved in seed banks, while short-lived seeds are difficult to store.

33. The term cryobiology is concerned with cryopreservation of germplasm.

34. Haploid breeding helps in reducing the duration of breeding cycle in comparison to conventional breeding.

35. During cryopreservation, step by step reducing temperature of stored plant materials is called freezing.

36. Rapeseed/canola transgenic Laurical has reduced level of lauric acid.

37. Cell lines resistant to herbicide glyphosate have been isolated in tobacco using technique of *in vitro* cell selection.

38. Alloplasmic lines can be produced by somatic hybridization.

39. Molecular markers can not be used for identification of somatic hybrids.

40. Antigen tolerance can be induced more easily in neonatal animals than in adult animals.

41. VNTR stands for variable number of tandem repeats.

42. The term amplicon is related to PCR.

43. Fermentation Research Institute (FERM) is located at Tokyo, Japan.

44. An autoclave uses steam for sterilization at 121°C and 15 pounds per square inch.

45. IFN-γ and IL-4 act antagonistically

46. New Leaf is transgenic variety of maize.

47. Polymerase chain reaction is also called people's choice reaction.

48. Antihistamines are effective for the treatment of type III hypersensitivity.

49. Ratan is a somaclonal variety of khesari.

50. Most of the modern plant tissue culture media have been derived from the work of Skoog and coworkers during 1950's and 1960s.

51. Kinetin and benzyl aminopurine are occasionally used cytokinins in plant tissue culture.

52. Virus elimination generally improves the yield by 20-90% over the infected control.

53. Heat labile compounds are filter sterilized.

54. Laminar air flow cabinets are used to create aspectic working space.

55. In 1970, Kasha and Kao reported chromosome elimination technique for production of haploids in barley using embryo culture.

56. Viruses are ultra-microscopic, obligate parasitic pathogens, and are highly infectious nucleoproteins, which behave as living *in vivo* and nonliving *in vitro*.

57. Antigens are usually proteins or glycoproteins.

58. Lactase is used in cheese making.

59. Shikonin is used for cosmetics.

60. In general, rooting medium has full salt strength of MS medium.

61. RNA is proposed to be the first macromolecule on earth that catalyzed its own replication.

62. Presence of human chorionic gonadotrophin (hCG) in urine is detected by using monoclonal antibodies.

63. In general, the essential features of SE development, especially after the globular stage, are comparable to those of zygotic embryos.

64. Xenobiotic compounds, which are recalcitrant in nature, are highly toxic or give rise to toxic products due to microbial activity.

65. AFLP uses restriction enzyme-digested genomic DNA as template for PCR amplicfication.

66. In general, GA_3 inhibits shoot-bud regeneration, most likely by inhibiting meristemoid formation.

67. Ribavirin is a nucleotide analogue.

68. The first commercial production of shikonin through cultured plant cells was achieved in Japan using a two-stage process.

69. In general, individual shoots of ~ 2 cm are transferred to the rooting medium.

70. Herbicide resistance deployed in soybean, maize and cotton, remains the predominant trait in GM crops, followed by insect resistance due to *cry* genes.

71. Lysozyme is a hydrolytic enzyme present in mucous secretions.

72. Lymphocytes are specialized cells responsible for immune response in animals.

73. Ag promoter is a hybrid between chicken β-actin and rabbit β-globulin promoter sequence.

74. Lysozyme cleaves peptidoglycan layer of the bacterial cell wall.

75. When functional food aids in the prevention or treatment of diseases or disorders other than anaemia, it is called a nutraceutical.

76. Examples of nutraceuticals include fortified dairy products, *e.g.,* milk, and citrus fruit products, *e.g.,* orange juice.

77. Decision regarding safety of GM crops should be based on the nature of the product rather than the method by which it has been modified.

78. Co-suppression can result in high gene expression.

79. Many companies in France are producing cabbage and cauliflower hybrids utilizing cytoplasmic male sterile cybrids.

80. MS and B_5 nutrient media are mostly used for plant tissue culture.

81. Nitrate is superior to ammonium as the sole N source, and use of NH_4^+ increases the drift of pH towards, alkalinity.

82. Virus elimination through meristem culture is of direct commercial significance in clonal crops.

83. Amelioration of polluted soil cannot be achieved by growing appropriate transgenic plants.

84. Marker-assissted selection (MAS) can not be used to improve complex traits like yield.

85. *In vitro* germplasm conservation is particularly useful in clonal crops, especially in those producing tubers, storage roots, etc.

86. Commercial utilization of many transgenic lines is plagued by transgene silencing.

87. Triton-X and Tween 80 are examples of surfactants.

88. Thidiazuron (TDZ) having cytokinin activity is employed to promote cell division particularly in monocots.

89. Evan's blue (0.025%) is taken up by live cells.

90. The various events occuring during shoot regeneration may be divided into shoot induction, and shoot differentiation and development.

91. A shoot-tip of upto 500 μm would contain 1-3 leaf primorida in addition to the apical meristem.

92. When the objective is vegetative propagation, the size of shoot-tip used for culture is important.

93. In case of artificial seeds, gels contain inorganic nutrients, a carbon source, a fungicide, a bactericide and growth promoting substances necessary for SE germination and seedling establishment in the field.

94. Transfer of plantlets to soil is the most critical step in micropropagation.

95. In general, the older an embryo, the more complicated are its nutritional needs.

96. Suspensor begins to degenerate after the formation of cotyledons and the GA_3 is now mainly synthesized by the cotyledons.

97. Generally, growth regulators are used during embryo culture, since embryo is usually heterotrophic in this respect.

98. Generally, MS and B5 media and their modifications are used for protoplast culture.

99. In majority of freeze preservation protocols, a mixture of DMSO, glycerol and sucrose is used as cryoprotectant.

100. The *in vitro* strategies of germplasm storage are useful when many improved cell clones may need to be preserved for future use.

□□□

SECTION IV

ANSWERS

CHAPTER 1

INTRODUCTION

1.1. MULTIPLE CHOICE QUESTIONS

1. (*d*) Bioinformatics
2. (*b*) Genetically ...... microbes
3. (*b*) B cells ...... cells
4. (*c*) I, II, III
5. (*d*) Both (*b*) and (*c*)
6. (*a*) I, II, III, IV
7. (*d*) All of the above
8. (*a*) I, II, III, IV
9. (*b*) Sodium alginate
10. (*a*) *Agrobacterium tumefaciens*
11. (*d*) All of the above
12. (*c*) AIII, BI, CIV, DII
13. (*b*) G. Haberlandt
14. (*d*) Both (*b*) and (*c*)
15. (*d*) All of the above
16. (*a*) AII, BI, CIV, DIII
17. (*b*) *Penicillium notatum*
18. (*c*) I, II, III, IV
19. (*b*) Precursor ...... maleic acid.
20. (*a*) Both A ...... explains A.
21. (*b*) I, II, III, IV
22. (*d*) All of the above
23. (*a*) Plant cells
24. (*b*) Genetic ...... animal cells.
25. (*c*) ABA
26. (*c*) Ministry of ...... Technology
27. (*d*) Both (*a*) and (*c*)
28. (*b*) Special laboratory design
29. (*a*) I, II, III, IV
30. (*c*) I, II, III, IV
31. (*d*) All of the above
32. (*c*) Neomycin phosphotransferase II
33. (*b*) Chimpanzee
34. (*d*) Both (*a*) and (*b*)
35. (*d*) Both (*a*) and (*b*)
36. (*d*) All of the above
37. (*c*) I, II, III
38. (*a*) *Pseudomonas putida*
39. (*d*) All of the above
40. (*c*) I, II, III, IV
41. (*d*) I, IV
42. (*c*) II, III
43. (*b*) I, II, III, IV
44. (*a*) *Aspergillus niger*
45. (*d*) All of the above
46. (*c*) Ministry of ...... Forests
47. (*d*) Department of Biotechnology
48. (*b*) I, II, III, IV
49. (*c*) I, II, III, IV
50. (*b*) Food crops
51. (*a*) I, II, III, IV
52. (*c*) I, IV
53. (*a*) Bt-cotton
54. (*d*) All of the above
55. (*c*) Lipids
56. (*a*) Carbohydrates
57. (*d*) All of the above
58. (*b*) I, II, III, IV
59. (*d*) I, II, III, IV
60. (*b*) AIII, BIV, CII, DI
61. (*b*) In case of ...... peroxysomes.
62. (*a*) Both A ...... explanation of A
63. (*d*) All of the above
64. (*a*) It is a non-essential fatty acid.
65. (*a*) To accumulate ...... soil.

66. (*d*) All of the above
67. (*d*) I, II, III, IV
68. (*c*) *Spirulina*
69. (*d*) All of the above
70. (*b*) *Pseudomonas*
71. (*d*) All of the above
72. (*a*) I, II, III, IV
73. (*a*) They would ...... pollution
74. (*b*) I, II, III, IV
75. (*c*) I, II, III
76. (*c*) A somaclonal ...... Lucknow
77. (*b*) I, II, III, IV
78. (*d*) All of the above
79. (*d*) AII, BIV, CI, DIII
80. (*a*) I, II, III, IV
81. (*b*) I, II, III, IV
82. (*c*) I, II, III
83. (*b*) I, II, III, IV
84. (*d*) I, II, III, IV
85. (*a*) I, II, III, IV
86. (*d*) I, II, III, IV
87. (*a*) It is ...... potato.
88. (*d*) Selection of ...... easy.
89. (*a*) Both P ...... takes care of P.
90. (*b*) I, II, III
91. (*c*) I, II, III
92. (*a*) I, II, III, IV
93. (*c*) $tBLAST_n$
94. (*a*) Both A and ...... explains A.
95. (*d*) Both (*a*) and (*b*)
96. (*b*) I, II, III, IV
97. (*d*) All of the above
98. (*c*) DMSO ...... used
99. (*d*) All of the above
100. (*a*) Both P and ...... explains P.
101. (*d*) Protoplasts ...... light.
102. (*d*) All of the above
103. (*c*) This technology ...... growth.
104. (*b*) I, II, III, IV
105. (*a*) Both A and ...... explains A.
106. (*b*) M.C. Mehta
107. (*d*) All of the above
108. (*b*) Rabies
109. (*a*) Severe protein deficiency
110. (*c*) Systemic expression.
111. (*b*) I, II, III, IV
112. (*d*) All of the above.
113. (*a*) Blue-green algae
114. (*b*) Sieve cell of phloem
115. (*c*) Fungi
116. (*d*) All of the above
117. (*b*) I, II, III, IV
118. (*a*) I, II, III
119. (*b*) mRNA
120. (*d*) All of the above
121. (*a*) 10^7–10^9
122. (*a*) Chromosome jumping
123. (*b*) I, II, III, IV
124. (*c*) GM food
125. (*a*) Both P and ...... result of P.
126. (*d*) All of the above
127. (*b*) I, II, III, IV
128. (*d*) All of the above
129. (*c*) I, II, III, IV
130. (*a*) Both P and ...... the P.
131. (*d*) All of the above
132. (*d*) All of the above
133. (*b*) Broccoli (Sulforaphane)
134. (*c*) Soy or clover products
135. (*a*) *Psyllium* seed husk
136. (*d*) Resveratrol
137. (*a*) I, II, III, IV
138. (*d*) All of the above
139. (*d*) All of the above
140. (*d*) All of the above
141. (*d*) All of the above
142. (*d*) All of the above
143. (*c*) I, II, III
144. (*d*) All of the above
145. (*a*) I, II, III
146. (*d*) All of the above
147. (*d*) All of the above

1.2. FILL IN THE BLANKS

1. April, 2003
2. information technology
3. International Rice Genome Sequencing Project
4. ABA
5. dominant
6. endosperm
7. Delta and Pineland Company
8. Issacs and Lindemann
9. antigen-antibody
10. Humulin
11. L-ascorbic acid
12. mouse fibroblasts
13. Sanger
14. Miller and coworkers
15. Knockout
16. blood
17. RNA
18. *Nicotiana*
19. protoplast fusion
20. double
21. petroleum diesel
22. Morton
23. Southern blotting
24. does not
25. plastids (chloroplasts)
26. 500 to 600
27. cauliflower mosaic virus (CaMV)
28. transgene silencing
29. Evening primerose (*Oenothera* sp.), borage (*Borage officinalis*)
30. iron
31. additive effects (partial dominance)
32. Whitehead Institute of Biomedical Research, USA
33. Lalji Singh
34. Monsanto, USA
35. *tissue culture response* (TCR) genes.
36. spinal cord
37. deficient
38. Pancreas
39. Gram positive
40. 3.2
41. helper plasmid
42. spheroplast
43. phosphorylation
44. transfection
45. biofortification

1.3. MARK TRUE OR FALSE

1. True	**2.** False	**3.** True	**4.** True
5. True	**6.** False	**7.** False	**8.** False
9. False	**10.** True	**11.** True	**12.** True
13. False	**14.** True	**15.** True	**16.** False
17. True	**18.** True	**19.** False	**20.** True
21. True	**22.** False	**23.** True	**24.** True
25. True	**26.** True	**27.** True	**28.** True
29. False	**30.** True	**31.** False	

CHAPTER 2

RECOMBINANT DNA TECHNOLOGY

2.1. MULTIPLE CHOICE QUESTIONS

1. (*a*) Griffith
2. (*b*) Tobacco mosaic virus
3. (*a*) T_2 phage ...... *E. coli*
4. (*c*) AIV, BI, CIII, DII
5. (*d*) Nucleoproteins
6. (*b*) 5′C and 3′C
7. (*c*) DNA molecule ...... bonds.
8. (*b*) RNA molecules ...... cytosine.
9. (*a*) *E. coli* ...... cloning.
10. (*d*) Hydrophobic ...... transcription.
11. (*b*) The smallest ...... tRNA.
12. (*d*) Both (*a*) and (*b*).
13. (*d*) Semiconservative ...... *E. coli.*
14. (*c*) Both strands ...... continuously.
15. (*b*) Length of ...... 34Å.
16. (*a*) Crick
17. (*c*) AIII, BII, CI
18. (*a*) Joining ...... of DNA.
19. (*b*) Repetition of ...... same order.

20. (*b*) DNA replication
21. (*d*) I, II, III
22. (*b*) Both A and R ...... explanation of A.
23. (*c*) It has ...... property.
24. (*d*) All of the above
25. (*c*) I, II, III
26. (*b*) DNA ligase
27. (*a*) I, II, IV
28. (*a*) Capillary action
29. (*b*) I, II, III
30. (*d*) F. Griffith
31. (*c*) Restriction enzyme
32. (*d*) P. Berg
33. (*a*) Boliver Rodriguez
34. (*c*) Type II endonuclease
35. (*b*) AII, BIII, CI, DIV
36. (*b*) Nick translation
37. (*d*) I, II, III, IV
38. (*b*) I, III, IV
39. (*a*) *Aspergillus oryzae*
40. (*d*) All of the above
41. (*a*) Shuttle vectors
42. (*c*) I, II, III, IV
43. (*b*) 49 kb
44. (*b*) II, III, IV
45. (*d*) Both (*a*) and (*c*)
46. (*d*) *Pst*I
47. (*a*) I, II, III, IV
48. (*b*) Genomic ...... organism.
49. (*d*) I, II, III, IV, V
50. (*c*) I, II, III
51. (*a*) G/AATT C
C TTAA/G
52. (*c*) I, II, III
53. (*c*) 4096 bp
54. (*d*) 4–6 bp
55. (*a*) I, II, III
56. (*c*) I, II, III
57. (*b*) I, II, III, IV
58. (*b*) *Alu*I
59. (*d*) All of the above
60. (*b*) Luria-Bertani (LB) medium
61. (*a*) *Eco*K
62. (*c*) *p*BAC108L
63. (*d*) All of the above
64. (*b*) I, III, IV
65. (*a*) AII, BIII, CI, DIV
66. (*b*) 300 kb
67. (*c*) II, I, III
68. (*b*) Two
69. (*b*) Phosphite triester
70. (*a*) I, II, III, IV
71. (*d*) All of the above
72. (*c*) AII, BI, CIII
73. (*a*) I, II, III, IV
74. (*d*) All of the above.
75. (*a*) I, II, III
76. (*b*) λEMBL4
77. (*d*) All of the above
78. (*b*) Wallace and Birnstiel
79. (*a*) I, II, IV
80. (*a*) I, II, III, IV
81. (*c*) I, II, III
82. (*c*) I, II, III, IV
83. (*d*) All of the above
84. (*c*) I, III
85. (*a*) I, II, III
86. (*d*) All of the above
87. (*b*) 20 kb
88. (*a*) I, II, III, IV
89. (*b*) 2^n
90. (*c*) I, II, III
91. (*b*) 4^8 bp
92. (*a*) I, II, III, IV
93. (*c*) IV, I, II, III
94. (*d*) I, II, III, IV
95. (*a*) I, III
96. (*b*) RFLP
97. (*d*) All of the above
98. (*a*) I, II, III, IV
99. (*b*) I, II, III
100. (*c*) I, II, III, IV
101. (*a*) I, II, III, IV
102. (*d*) I, II, III, IV

103. (*c*) Sanger and coworkers
104. (*b*) [4(G + C)] + [2(A + T)]
105. (*a*) Only intact ...... PCR
106. (*d*) All of the above
107. (*c*) I, II, III
108. (*d*) All of the above
109. (*d*) All of the above
110. (*a*) I, II, III
111. (*c*) I, II, III, IV
112. (*b*) I, II, III, IV
113. (*c*) Khorana and coworkers
114. (*b*) I, III, IV
115. (*d*) Both (*a*) and (*c*)
116. (*a*) I, II, III, IV
117. (*d*) All of the above
118. (*c*) I, II, III, IV
119. (*d*) I, II, III
120. (*b*) I, II, III, IV
121. (*a*) I, II, III, IV
122. (*a*) Asymmetric
123. (*b*) Nested
124. (*d*) Inverse
125. (*d*) Inverse
126. (*d*) Inverse
127. (*d*) Inverse
128. (*c*) I, II, III
129. (*a*) Protein function
130. (*b*) DNA sequence homology
131. (*c*) Protein-protein interaction
132. (*d*) DNA-protein interaction
133. (*b*) I, IV
134. (*a*) I, II
135. (*c*) Probe
136. (*c*) *E. coli*
137. (*d*) Both (*a*) and (*b*)
138. (*c*) *E. coli*
139. (*d*) All of the above
140. (*a*) Yeast
141. (*d*) Both (*b*) and (*c*)
142. (*b*) A vector ...... integrated.
143. (*d*) Both (*b*) and (*c*)
144. (*a*) In one ...... markers.
145. (*b*) Selection of ...... single step.
146. (*d*) Packaging ...... particles.
147. (*d*) All of the above.
148. (*d*) All of the above.
149. (*d*) Both (*a*) and (*c*)
150. (*b*) S1 nuclease
151. (*a*) DNase I
152. (*c*) *Eco*RI
153. (*c*) GAATTC
154. (*a*) GAAAAG
155. (*b*) GAAGAA
156. (*a*) GAAAAG
157. (*c*) Alkaline phosphatase
158. (*c*) *E. coli* exonuclease III
159. (*d*) λ exonuclease
160. (*a*) S1 nuclease
161. (*a*) S1 nuclease
162. (*b*) Exonuclease *Bal*31
163. (*d*) Both (*b*) and (*c*)
164. (*c*) Klenow ...... polymerase I
165. (*c*) Terminal ...... transferase
166. (*c*) I, II, III, IV
167. (*a*) I
168. (*b*) II, III, IV
169. (*a*) I
170. (*d*) II, IV
171. (*c*) I, III
172. (*b*) II, III, IV
173. (*a*) I, II, III
174. (*d*) Specified ...... amplified.
175. (*c*) I, II, III, IV
176. (*c*) Phage M13 vectors
177. (*c*) Both (*a*) and (*b*)
178. (*d*) Both (*a*) and (*c*)
179. (*d*) All of the above
180. (*b*) Differential screening
181. (*d*) All of the above.
182. (*a*) Overlap extension PCR
183. (*c*) Touchdown PCR
184. (*d*) Anchored PCR
185. (*b*) Hotstart PCR

186. (*c*) Differential amplification of alleles
187. (*a*) Primer sequence
188. (*d*) ARMS PCR
189. (*a*) Single nucleoticle overhang
190. (*a*) A at the 3′-end
191. (*b*) 5′-end having P residue
192. (*d*) It always …… primers

2.2. FILL IN THE BLANKS

1. Arthur Korenberg
2. Meischer
3. DNA
4. 3
5. RNA primers
6. antibody, antigen
7. pulsed-field gel electrophoresis
8. RNA
9. genotype
10. plasmids, bacteriophage genomes
11. T_4
12. adenine, cytosine
13. genus
14. poison
15. agarose
16. double
17. conjugation
18. genomic
19. marker/reporter
20. 1 kb
21. alkali
22. phosphodiester bond
23. W. Arber
24. pancrease
25. replication control system
26. University of California
27. 30–40
28. selectable marker
29. *p*BR322
30. proof-reading
31. protein
32. low
33. phosphate
34. 24
35. scorable
36. One
37. probe
38. 5′
39. polyacrylamide gel electrophoresis
40. 3′
41. negatively
42. 1000-2000 kb
43. RNA
44. cut ends
45. cDNA

2.4. MARK TRUE OR FALSE

1. True	**2.** False	**3.** True	**4.** True
5. False	**6.** True	**7.** True	**8.** True
9. False	**10.** True	**11.** True	**12.** True
13. True	**14.** True	**15.** False	**16.** True
17. True	**18.** False	**19.** True	**20.** True
21. True	**22.** True	**23.** False	**24.** True
25. True	**26.** False	**27.** True	**28.** False
29. True	**30.** True	**31.** True	**32.** True
33. False	**34.** True	**35.** True	**36.** False
37. True	**38.** True	**39.** True	**40.** True

CHAPTER 3

GENOME MAPS

3.1. MULTIPLE CHOICE QUESTIONS

1. (*d*) All of the above
2. (*a*) International Rice …… Project.
3. (*c*) AIV, BI, CII, DIII
4. (*b*) I, II, IV
5. (*d*) All of the above
6. (*c*) I, II, III
7. (*b*) II, III

8. (*a*) Recombination frequency
9. (*c*) Codominant
10. (*c*) A3, B4, C1, D2
11. (*a*) I, II, III, IV
12. (*d*) J.D. Watson
13. (*a*) I, II, III, IV
14. (*b*) I, II, III, IV
15. (*d*) All of the above
16. (*c*) I, II, III
17. (*b*) I, II, III
18. (*b*) I, II, III, IV
19. (*a*) A single arbitrary primer
20. (*d*) All of the above
21. (*b*) Morton
22. (*d*) All of the above
23. (*c*) Backcross method
24. (*d*) All of the above
25. (*d*) All of the above
26. (*a*) They are ...... DNA fragments.
27. (*d*) They are ...... human genome.
28. (*a*) *Mycoplasma genitalium*
29. (*d*) *Haemophilus influenzae*
30. (*c*) 4
31. (*b*) I, II, III, IV
32. (*c*) I, II
33. (*a*) II, IV
34. (*b*) I
35. (*d*) III, V
36. (*c*) II
37. (*a*) I, II, III
38. (*b*) III, V
39. (*a*) I, III, IV, V
40. (*d*) More than ...... by (*b*).
41. (*b*) 25000
42. (*c*) Protein-protein interaction
43. (*a*) I, II
44. (*b*) I, III, IV
45. (*b*) RFLP
46. (*d*) STMS (STR loci)
47. (*c*) AFLP
48. (*c*) AFLP
49. (*d*) Both (*a*) and (*b*)
50. (*b*) III, IV
51. (*a*) I, II
52. (*a*) I
53. (*d*) *Arabidopsis thaliana*
54. (*d*) *Arabidopsis thaliana*
55. (*c*) *Hordeum vulgare*
56. (*b*) Yeast
57. (*b*) Yeast
58. (*d*) *Drosophila*
59. (*a*) *Arabidopsis*
60. (*b*) Yeast
61. (*c*) *Vibrio cholerae*
62. (*b*) Sequence interpretation

3.2. FILL IN THE BLANKS

1. DNA amplification fingerprint
2. polytene
3. 1000
4. large, smaller
5. International Human Genome Sequencing Consortium.
6. dominant
7. linked
8. chromosome sorting
9. fluorescence activated cell sorting
10. contig
11. H. Winkler
12. October 1, 1990

3.3. MARK TRUE OR FALSE

1. True	**2.** True	**3.** False	**4.** False
5. True	**6.** True	**7.** False	**8.** True
9. True	**10.** True	**11.** False	**12.** True

CHAPTER 4
GENOMICS AND BIOINFORMATICS

4.1. MULTIPLE CHOICE QUESTIONS

1. (*c*) Bioinformatics
2. (*b*) A4, B1, C2, D3
3. (*a*) Thomas H. Roderick
4. (*c*) *Haemophilus influenzae*
5. (*b*) June 26, 2001
6. (*a*) Craig Venter
7. (*c*) 3.2×10^9
8. (*d*) Both (*a*) and (*c*)
9. (*a*) *E. coli*
10. (*b*) I, II, III, IV
11. (*a*) Horizontal
12. (*c*) 1986
13. (*a*) I, II, III, IV
14. (*b*) 10^6 bp
15. (*a*) I, II, III, IV
16. (*a*) Single letter
17. (*c*) I, II, III
18. (*a*) I, II, III, IV
19. (*d*) All of the above
20. (*d*) All of the above
21. (*b*) Pseudogenes ...... genomes.
22. (*d*) Introns ...... sequences.
23. (*d*) All of the above
24. (*c*) I, II, III, IV
25. (*b*) I, II, IV
26. (*d*) All of the above
27. (*a*) I, II, III
28. (*c*) Functional genomics
29. (*a*) Zuckerkandl and Pauling
30. (*b*) National ...... Foundation
31. (*d*) All of the above
32. (*c*) A2, B3, C1, D4
33. (*a*) A1, B2, C4, D3
34. (*b*) I, II, III, IV
35. (*d*) All of the above
36. (*b*) These chips ...... 20-25 bases.
37. (*a*) I, II, III, IV
38. (*a*) Exchange of ...... chromosomes.
39. (*d*) All of the above
40. (*c*) RNA Data ...... Japan.
41. (*d*) This vector ...... *thuringiensis*
42. (*c*) I, II, III
43. (*b*) Base sequence ...... 5′-direction.
44. (*d*) All of the above
45. (*a*) I, II, III, IV
46. (*c*) A2, B3, C4, D1
47. (*d*) All of the above
48. (*a*) I, II, III, IV
49. (*b*) PubMed
50. (*c*) A3, B4, C2, D1
51. (*b*) I, II, III, IV
52. (*a*) I, II, III
53. (*c*) I, II, III, IV
54. (*d*) Both (*a*) and (*b*)
55. (*c*) I, III, IV
56. (*b*) I, II, III
57. (*d*) All of the above
58. (*d*) All of the above
59. (*c*) I, II, III, IV
60. (*a*) BLAST*n*
61. (*c*) tBLAST*x*
62. (*d*) tBLAST*n*
63. (*b*) BLAST*x*
64. (*b*) I, II
65. (*c*) Pigeonpea
66. (*d*) Humans
67. (*c*) 2006
68. (*d*) 2008
69. (*b*) 600
70. (*c*) 25%
71. (*a*) *C. elegans*
72. (*d*) Humans
73. (*b*) *Drosophila*

74. (*b*) I, II, III, IV
75. (*c*) I
76. (*c*) Real-time PCR
77. (*d*) The fluorescence ...... amplification.
78. (*d*) All of the above
79. (*d*) All of the above
80. (*a*) Real time ...... amplicon
81. (*c*) Multiplexing does ...... sequences
82. (*d*) The sequencing ...... approach.
83. (*a*) Sequencing ...... genomics.
84. (*d*) Assigning ...... genomics.
85. (*b*) I, II, III, IV

4.2. FILL IN THE BLANKS

1. bioinformatics
2. RNA
3. Biotechnology Information System.
4. shot-gun procedure
5. October 1, 1990
6. 26,000
7. Dystrophin
8. Hinxton (U.K.)
9. 2(1–3)
10. nucleotides
11. 250, 350
12. 2.9×10^6
13. Japanese puffer fish
14. smaller
15. 2,000
16. fruit fly (*D. melanogaster*)
17. alpha proteobacteria
18. proteome
19. 105,000
20. gene expression
21. gene expression
22. 100, 300
23. cDNA
24. 1,000,000
25. mutational genomics
26. insertional mutagenesis
27. Virus-induced Gene Silencing
28. European Bioinformatics Institute, Hinxton, U.K.
29. complete
30. Mnase (Mungbean nuclease)
31. database
32. genetic map
33. http ://www.ncbi.nlm.nih.gov
34. gene
35. reading frame
36. April, 2003
37. India

4.3. MARK TRUE OR FALSE

1. True	2. False	3. True	4. False
5. True	6. True	7. True	8. False
9. True	10. True	11. False	12. True
13. True	14. True	15. False	16. True
17. True	18. False	19. False	20. True
21. False	22. False	23. True	24. True
25. True			

CHAPTER 5

PLANT PHYSIOLOGY AND MOLECULAR BIOLOGY

5.1. MULTIPLE CHOICE QUESTIONS

1. (*b*) I, II, III, IV
2. (*c*) I, II, IV
3. (*d*) All of the above
4. (*a*) I, II, III, IV
5. (*d*) All of the above
6. (*b*) *Moricandia arvensis*
7. (*d*) Both (*a*) and (*c*)
8. (*c*) CAM plants
9. (*d*) All of the above
10. (*a*) Blackman reaction
11. (*b*) Hill reaction
12. (*a*) I, II, III, IV
13. (*c*) Sucrose
14. (*c*) O_2
15. (*d*) All of the above

16. (*b*) Thylakoids
17. (*a*) Stroma
18. (*d*) Both (*a*) and (*b*)
19. (*c*) 1, 2, 3, 4
20. (*d*) Wheat
21. (*b*) H_2O
22. (*b*) Bundle sheath
23. (*d*) Both (*b*) and (*c*)
24. (*b*) Heterocyst formation
25. (*d*) Both (*a*) and (*b*)
26. (*a*) Homomeric dimer
27. (*c*) Fatty acids
28. (*b*) Mitochondria
29. (*c*) Fe
30. (*a*) N_2-fixation
31. (*c*) Cytoplasm
32. (*b*) 8
33. (*a*) Chloroplast
34. (*d*) I, II, III, IV
35. (*d*) Both (*a*) and (*c*)
36. (*b*) O_2 supply
37. (*c*) Glutamine synthetase
38. (*d*) Nitrogenase
39. (*c*) Tetraploid
40. (*b*) PSII
41. (*a*) Cold treatment
42. (*b*) Mitochondria
43. (*d*) All of the above
44. (*b*) Transpiration
45. (*d*) Glycolysis
46. (*a*) 2
47. (*c*) Both (*a*) and (*b*)
48. (*a*) Glyoxysomes
49. (*b*) Chloroplasts
50. (*a*) Mitochondria
51. (*a*) Mitochondria
52. (*c*) Leucoplasts
53. (*d*) Both (*a*) and (*c*)
54. (*a*) Chlorophyll
55. (*a*) Glucose
56. (*d*) Mitochondrial matrix
57. (*d*) All of the above
58. (*b*) 1, 2, 3, 4
59. (*c*) Both TATA and AG/AGGA boxes.
60. (*b*) Anaerobiosis
61. (*d*) I, II, III, IV
62. (*b*) Flowering
63. (*a*) Proline
64. (*d*) Both (*a*) and (*c*)
65. (*c*) ABA and ethylene
66. (*a*) Siroheme ...... cluster
67. (*b*) *D* and *K* ...... DNA
68. (*d*) *Anabaena*
69. (*b*) F_0 factor
70. (*d*) Some ...... and (*b*)
71. (*b*) *Clostridium*
72. (*b*) Enzymes for DNA replication
73. (*c*) Homodimer
74. (*c*) 4
75. (*a*) I, II, III, IV
76. (*b*) Water
77. (*a*) Mammals
78. (*d*) All of the above
79. (*d*) All of the above
80. (*a*) Auxin
81. (*c*) 24
82. (*a*) Cytoplasm
83. (*a*) Oxysome
84. (*a*) Mesophyll cells ...... plants.
85. (*c*) Night
86. (*d*) All of the above
87. (*d*) All of the above
88. (*b*) 38
89. (*a*) 36
90. (*a*) Acetyl-CoA
91. (*d*) AII, BI, CIV, DIII
92. (*b*) C_4 plants
93. (*a*) Both A and ...... explains A.
94. (*b*) I, II, III, IV
95. (*c*) *Gleotrichia*

96. (*a*) I, II, III, IV
97. (*d*) Both P and S ...... solves P.
98. (*b*) 38
99. (*c*) 2
100. (*d*) I, II, III, IV
101. (*a*) I, II, III
102. (*d*) All of the above
103. (*b*) 1, 2, 3, 4
104. (*d*) Both (*a*) and (*c*)
105. (*d*) All of the above
106. (*a*) I, II, III, IV
107. (*d*) All of the above
108. (*c*) I, II, III
109. (*a*) Both A and ...... explains A.
110. (*d*) Starch molecule ...... grains.
111. (*d*) All of the above.
112. (*a*) All of the above.
113. (*a*) I, II, III, IV
114. (*b*) I, II, III, IV
115. (*b*) I, II, III, IV
116. (*a*) I, II, III, IV
117. (*b*) 1, 2, 3, 4
118. (*c*) Transcription ...... polymerases.
119. (*a*) I, II, III, IV
120. (*d*) Enhancer sequence ...... promoter.
121. (*d*) All of the above
122. (*b*) Pribnow box
123. (*c*) GC box
124. (*a*) TATA box
125. (*a*) TATA box
126. (*c*) Octamber sequence
127. (*d*) Both (*b*) and (*c*)
128. (*b*) I, III
129. (*d*) All of the above
130. (*a*) I, II, III
131. (*d*) All of the above
132. (*d*) All of the above
133. (*a*) Both A and R ...... explains A.
134. (*c*) Nucleus
135. (*d*) All of the above
136. (*b*) I, II, III, IV
137. (*a*) I, II, III, IV
138. (*c*) IV
139. (*b*) I, II, III, IV
140. (*a*) Both A and R ...... explains A.
141. (*c*) 3
142. (*d*) 7
143. (*a*) 14
144. (*b*) RNA editing
145. (*a*) Histone mRNA
146. (*c*) mRNA
147. (*d*) Replication ...... genome.
148. (*b*) Pol α
149. (*a*) Methylation ...... origin.
150. (*c*) Licensing factor
151. (*c*) Pol γ
152. (*b*) I, II, III, IV
153. (*a*) Plastids
154. (*c*) Endoplasmic reticulum
155. (*d*) Both (*a*) and (*c*)

5.2. FILL IN THE BLANKS

1. large subunit
2. 7
3. Mo-Fe factor
4. ammonia
5. glyoxylate
6. RuBISCO
7. Kreb's cycle
8. Starch
9. apical dominance
10. PS I
11. nuclear
12. PS I, PS II
13. 30
14. stomatal
15. 18
16. β-D glucose
17. two
18. ATP
19. EMP pathway
20. 686 Kcal (2870 KJ)

21. light
22. aerobic
23. non-heterocystous
24. 6 molecules
25. C_4, C_3
26. heat shock
27. leaves
28. fructans
29. eight
30. nine
31. mitochondria, *E. coli*
32. Photosynthetic bacteria
33. large
34. light
35. C_4 plants

5.3. MARK TRUE OR FALSE

1. True	**2.** True	**3.** False	**4.** False
5. True	**6.** False	**7.** True	**8.** True
9. False	**10.** True	**11.** True	**12.** True
13. True	**14.** True	**15.** False	**16.** True
17. False	**18.** True	**19.** True	**20.** True
21. True	**22.** False	**23.** True	**24.** True
25. True	**26.** False	**27.** True	**28.** True
29. True	**30.** True	**31.** True	**32.** True
33. Flase	**34.** True	**35.** True	

CHAPTER 6

PLANT TISSUE CULTURE

6.1. MULTIPLE CHOICE QUESTIONS

1. (*d*) All of the above
2. (*c*) AIV, BIII, CI, DII
3. (*d*) All of the above
4. (*a*) I, II, III, IV
5. (*b*) AIII, BIV, CII, DI
6. (*a*) A3, B1, C4, D2
7. (*c*) Parthenogenesis
8. (*b*) I, II, IV
9. (*d*) All of the above
10. (*a*) I, III, IV
11. (*d*) Both (*a*) and (*b*)
12. (*c*) Haploid
13. (*d*) All of the above
14. (*a*) I, II, III, IV
15. (*b*) II, III, IV
16. (*a*) A2, B1, C3
17. (*b*) A4, B3, C1, D2
18. (*d*) All of the above
19. (*d*) All of the above
20. (*a*) I, II, III, IV
21. (*d*) All of the above
22. (*a*) I, II, III
23. (*b*) Sodium alginate
24. (*a*) I, II, III, IV
25. (*d*) All of the above
26. (*a*) Poor respiration ...... capsule.
27. (*d*) All of the above
28. (*b*) *Datura*
29. (*b*) Mutation breeding
30. (*a*) A3, B1, C4, D2
31. (*b*) A3, B4, C2, D1
32. (*d*) A4, B2, C3, D1
33. (*d*) Precursor ...... malic acid.
34. (*b*) Carlson and coworkers
35. (*a*) A2, B4, C3, D1
36. (*d*) Both A and M ...... of A.
37. (*a*) I, II, III, IV
38. (*d*) Both (*a*) and (*b*)
39. (*c*) I, II, III, IV
40. (*a*) Both A and C ...... explains A.
41. (*d*) All of the above.
42. (*b*) Indian mustard
43. (*d*) All of the above
44. (*d*) Both (*a*) and (*c*)
45. (*b*) Sigma
46. (*b*) I, II

47. (*a*) I, II, III, IV
48. (*d*) All of the above
49. (*a*) New Delhi
50. (*c*) Liquid nitrogen
51. (*d*) All of the above
52. (*b*) Gottlieb Haberlandt
53. (*a*) I, II, III
54. (*d*) All of the above
55. (*c*) Liquid nitrogen
56. (*d*) All of the above
57. (*b*) 4-6 weeks
58. (*a*) Cytokinin
59. (*d*) Both (*a*) and (*b*)
60. (*b*) Larkin and Scowcroft
61. (*d*) All of the above
62. (*c*) 3-10 days
63. (*a*) 2, 4-D
64. (*c*) Varuna
65. (*a*) I, II, III
66. (*b*) *Nicotiana tabacum*
67. (*c*) DMSO
68. (*d*) All of the above
69. (*a*) F211
70. (*b*) Virus
71. (*c*) Sweet potato
72. (*b*) DMSO ...... proline
73. (*b*) Flue-cured tobacco
74. (*a*) Braun
75. (*c*) Egg cell
76. (*d*) I, II, III, IV
77. (*c*) III
78. (*d*) IV
79. (*d*) Solanaceae and Cruciferae
80. (*d*) All of the above
81. (*b*) Black rot
82. (*a*) Blackberry
83. (*c*) Calcium ...... hypochlorite
84. (*d*) Both (*b*) and (*c*)
85. (*a*) Skin colour
86. (*d*) Gibberellic acid
87. (*c*) Canada
88. (*b*) Shin Shu
89. (*a*) Flax
90. (*a*) Salt tolerance
91. (*d*) It inhibits ...... regeneration
92. (*d*) Both (*a*) and (*c*)
93. (*b*) High pH ...... medium
94. (*d*) All of the above
95. (*a*) Jinghua 1
96. (*a*) Rust immunity
97. (*d*) *Citronella java*
98. (*d*) All of the above
99. (*b*) I, IV, II, III
100. (*a*) I, II, III, IV
101. (*c*) I, II, III, IV
102. (*a*) Haploid plants
103. (*d*) All of the above
104. (*b*) Pindar
105. (*b*) I, II, IV
106. (*b*) Somaclonal variation
107. (*c*) AIV, BII, CI, DIII
108. (*a*) AIII, BI, CII, DIV
109. (*c*) AIII, BIV, CII, DI
110. (*b*) I, II, III, IV
111. (*b*) Suitable ...... species.
112. (*d*) It is ...... *Trichosanthes* sp.
113. (*d*) All of the above
114. (*d*) Both (*a*) and (*b*)
115. (*a*) I, II, III, IV
116. (*c*) Camphor
117. (*d*) All of the above
118. (*a*) Parasexual hybrid
119. (*c*) Asymmetric hybrid ...... other species.
120. (*d*) Arbutin ...... biotransformation.
121. (*d*) All of the above
122. (*b*) Continuous-flow bioreactor
123. (*d*) All of the above
124. (*b*) II, III, IV
125. (*a*) I, II, III, IV
126. (*c*) I, II, III, IV
127. (*d*) All of the above
128. (*a*) I, II, III, IV
129. (*c*) I, II, IV
130. (*b*) I, II, III

131. (*d*) I, II, III, IV
132. (*d*) I, II, III, IV
133. (*d*) All of the above
134. (*c*) Somaclonal ...... low frequency.
135. (*a*) I, II, III, IV
136. (*d*) II, III, IV
137. (*c*) I, II, III, IV
138. (*d*) Either (*a*) or (*b*)
139. (*c*) II, III, IV
140. (*b*) I, III, IV
141. (*d*) All of the above
142. (*a*) Ni
143. (*a*) I, II, III, IV
144. (*a*) Both A and ...... explains A
145. (*b*) I, II, IV
146. (*d*) All of the above
147. (*d*) All of the above
148. (*d*) All of the above
149. (*b*) Both A and ...... explains A
150. (*a*) I, II, III, IV
151. (*d*) All of the above
152. (*d*) All of the above
153. (*b*) II, III
154. (*c*) I, IV
155. (*a*) 0°C
156. (*a*) Controlled freezing
157. (*d*) Both (*a*) and (*c*)
158. (*d*) Glycerol ...... permeable.
159. (*b*) Dividing...... cells.
160. (*b*) A2, B4, C1, D3
161. (*a*) Thiamine
162. (*a*) Embryo culture
163. (*a*) Embryo culture
164. (*c*) Somatic hybridization
165. (*d*) All of the above
166. (*c*) Microdrop method
167. (*c*) II, III
168. (*a*) SE induction
169. (*d*) SE conversion
170. (*c*) SE maturation
171. (*d*) All of the above
172. (*b*) Culture establishment
173. (*d*) Rooting
174. (*a*) I, II, III
175. (*d*) All of the above
176. (*d*) All of the above
177. (*d*) Both (*a*) and (*b*)
178. (*d*) All of the above
179. (*a*) Thaumatin
180. (*c*) Diosgenin
181. (*d*) Pyrethrin
182. (*b*) I, III
183. (*d*) II, IV
184. (*d*) All of the above
185. (*d*) All of the above
186. (*b*) Organ cultures
187. (*d*) I, II, III, IV
188. (*a*) Chemical reactions
189. (*b*) Potato
190. (*c*) *Asparagus*
191. (*b*) Analytical breeding
192. (*d*) Both (*a*) and (*b*)
193. (*c*) Binucleate pollen
194. (*d*) I, II, III, IV
195. (*d*) All of the above
196. (*d*) All of the above
197. (*a*) I, II, III, IV
198. (*d*) Both (a) and (b)
199. (*b*) I, II, III, IV
200. (*c*) I, II, III, IV, V

6.2. FILL IN THE BLANKS

1. endosperm
2. stimulates
3. *Trichoderma viride*
4. protoplast
5. somatic hybridization/protoplast fusion
6. pectin
7. carrot
8. 160, 180
9. meristem
10. somaclonal variation
11. E.C. Cocking

12. *Agrobacterium rhizogenes*
13. antileukaemic
14. artificial seed
15. *Secale*
16. cytoplasmic
17. secondary metabolite
18. selfed progeny
19. plantlet
20. NBPGR
21. dimethylsulphoxide
22. ice crystal
23. diploid
24. –196
25. *Brassica napus*
26. thermotherapy
27. Skoog
28. clonal
29. 35, 40
30. haploid
31. 5–10
32. oil
33. organogenesis, somatic embryogenesis
34. R_0
35. regeneration
36. pectinase/macerozyme, cellulase
37. 5, 8
38. + (plus) sign
39. cybrids
40. meiotic
41. Central Institue for Medicinal and Aromatic Plants (CIMAP).
42. Polyethylene glycol (PEG)
43. barley
44. 500, 800, bursting
45. totipotency
46. freezing
47. endopolyploidy
48. diplochromosome
49. somatic embryo
50. plant tissue culture, genetic engineering
51. R.J. Gautheret, P.R. White
52. Sucrose
53. ABA
54. regeneration
55. Rescue
56. induction
57. leaf mesophyll
58. increase
59. androgenic
60. endoreduplication
61. mixoploid
62. 2, 4-D
63. aseptic
64. 0.5, 2.0
65. antiviral
66. Letham
67. 100, 1000
68. Meristem
69. cell wall
70. X- or γ-irradiated
71. Florin
72. LN refrigerator
73. –130°C, ice crystals
74. 15-45, washing
75. secondary metabolites
76. cytokinins
77. homozygous
78. high Ca^{2+}
79. polycross/hybridization
80. aeration
81. regeneration
82. Cybridization
83. somaclone
84. instability
85. doubling, colchicine
86. Direct selection
87. 25
88. embryo culture
89. androgenesis
90. embryo culture
91. cytoplast
92. somatic back hybridization
93. symmetric hybrid
94. dihaploid
95. field bank

96. embryo culture
97. uninucleate
98. gene amplification
99. callus, pollen embryos
100. variant
101. interspecific/distant
102. regeneration
103. viruses
104. micropropagation
105. viruses
106. enhances
107. DMSO, zero
108. dominance
109. Fiji disease
109. *H. vulgare*, *H. bulbosum*
111. binucleate
112. first pollen
113. *Helminthosporium maydis*, mitochondrial
114. tryptophan
115. incompatible
116. banana
117. –196°C, liquid nitrogen
118. interspecific hybrids
119. *Hordeum bulbosum*
120. Shikonin, *Lithospermum erythrorhizon*
121. kheshari (*Lathyrus sativus*)
122. another
123. ABA
124. 2.5, 5.0

6.3. MARK TRUE OR FALSE

1. True	**2.** False	**3.** True	**4.** True
5. False	**6.** True	**7.** True	**8.** False
9. True	**10.** True	**11.** False	**12.** True
13. True	**14.** True	**15.** False	**16.** True
17. False	**18.** False	**19.** False	**20.** True
21. True	**22.** False	**23.** True	**24.** False
25. False	**26.** True	**27.** False	**28.** False
29. False	**30.** True	**31.** True	**32.** True
33. True	**34.** True	**35.** True	**36.** False
37. False	**38.** True	**39.** False	**40.** True
41. True	**42.** False	**43.** False	**44.** False
45. False	**46.** True	**47.** False	**48.** True
49. True	**50.** True	**51.** False	**52.** False
53. True	**54.** True	**55.** False	**56.** False
57. True	**58.** True	**59.** True	**60.** True
61. False	**62.** True	**63.** True	**64.** False
65. True	**66.** False	**67.** False	**68.** True
69. False	**70.** False	**71.** True	**72.** True
73. True	**74.** True	**75.** True	**76.** True
77. False	**78.** False	**79.** True	**80.** True
81. False	**82.** True	**83.** True	**84.** True
85. False	**86.** True	**87.** True	**88.** False
89. True	**90.** False		

CHAPTER 7
TRANSGENIC PLANTS

7.1. MULTIPLE CHOICE QUESTIONS

1. (*c*) A gene ...... technology.
2. (*d*) Both A and M ...... explanation of A.
3. (*a*) I, II, III, IV
4. (*b*) Avery, MacLeod and McCarty
5. (*a*) Both A and R ...... explains A
6. (*d*) All of the above
7. (*c*) Papaya Ring Spot Virus
8. (*d*) Corn
9. (*b*) Novartis
10. (*c*) It is a ...... bacterium.
11. (*a*) DNA → RNA → ...... Trait
12. (*d*) Both (*a*) and (*b*)
13. (*c*) I, II, III, IV
14. (*a*) Both A and R ...... explains A.
15. (*d*) Both A and M ...... explains A
16. (*b*) Neomycin phosphotransferase II
17. (*a*) I, II, III
18. (*d*) All of the above
19. (*d*) All of the above

20. (*c*) I, II, III, IV
21. (*d*) All of the above
22. (*a*) Both A and M ...... correctly explains A.
23. (*b*) They are not useful ...... transformants.
24. (*a*) Tobacco
25. (*c*) Flavr Savr
26. (*b*) Kanamycin resistance
27. (*c*) Only A is correct
28. (*a*) 24 bp.
29. (*b*) 60 kDa
30. (*a*) Squash
31. (*d*) Virus coat ...... gene
32. (*c*) Tobacco
33. (*d*) All of the above
34. (*b*) Lepidoptera
35. (*d*) All of the above
36. (*a*) U.S.A
37. (*c*) Opine
38. (*b*) Diptera
39. (*d*) Both (*b*) and (*c*)
40. (*d*) *Bacillus amyloliquefaciens*
41. (*c*) Rural ...... International, Canada
42. (*b*) Colorado potato beetle
43. (*c*) Tissue specificity
44. (*a*) M.S. Swaminathan
45. (*d*) All of the above
46. (*a*) *Streptomyces* sp.
47. (*d*) All of the above
48. (*d*) All of the above
49. (*b*) β-glucuronidase (*gus*)
50. (*d*) All of the above
51. (*c*) Mariani and coworkers
52. (*d*) Glyphosate
53. (*a*) Tapetum
54. (*b*) Antisense RNA technology
55. (*c*) Tapetum
56. (*a*) I
57. (*a*) Delayed ripening
58. (*d*) All of the above
59. (*b*) Maize
60. (*c*) Reverse transcription
61. (*a*) Macroinjection
62. (*c*) 35*S* promoter
63. (*b*) Ti plasmid vectors
64. (*d*) *Agrobacterium* ...... transformation
65. (*a*) Inability to ...... meristem cells.
66. (*c*) I
67. (*a*) Release of a signal ...... wounds.
68. (*d*) All of the above
69. (*c*) II, III, IV
70. (*d*) Both (*b*) and (*c*).
71. (*a*) I, II, III, IV
72. (*d*) All of the above
73. (*c*) I, II, III, IV
74. (*a*) II, III
75. (*c*) IV
76. (*c*) III
77. (*a*) I, II
78. (*d*) IV
79. (*a*) VirA
80. (*b*) VirG
81. (*d*) VirD2
82. (*c*) VirD1
83. (*b*) VirG
84. (*d*) VirD2
85. (*d*) Both (*a*) and (*c*)
86. (*b*) VirB11
87. (*d*) Both (*a*) and (*b*)
88. (*d*) All of the above
89. (*d*) All of the above
90. (*d*) All of the above
91. (*a*) β-glucuronidase
92. (*d*) Both (*b*) and (*c*)
93. (*a*) *Vicilin*
94. (*c*) *35S*
95. (*d*) *Adh1*
96. (*a*) I, II, IV
97. (*b*) I, III
98. (*d*) Both (*a*) and (*b*)
99. (*b*) I, II, IV
100. (*b*) Origin ...... *Agrobacterium*
101. (*b*) II, III, IV
102. (*c*) V

103. (*d*) I, II, III, IV
104. (*b*) II, III, IV
105. (*a*) I, II, III
106. (*d*) IV, V
107. (*b*) Introduction …… cells
108. (*d*) All of the above
109. (*b*) Pressurised helium
110. (*d*) A3, B1, C4, D2
111. (*d*) I, II, III, IV
112. (*c*) III
113. (*d*) IV
114. (*a*) I
115. (*b*) Acyl-ACP thioesterase
116. (*c*) Fused with …… orientation.
117. (*a*) Acetyl-CoA
118. (*c*) Malonyl-CoA
119. (*c*) They are …… quantities.
120. (*b*) Honey …… vaccine
121. (*d*) All of the above
122. (*c*) High level …… generations.
123. (*d*) All of the above
124. (*d*) Both (*a*) and (*b*)
125. (*a*) Endless Summer Tomato
126. (*d*) 1, 2, 3, 4
127. (*b*) 1, 2, 3, 4
128. (*d*) Conusmption …… iron.
129. (*c*) 1, 2, 3, 4
130. (*b*) 1, 2, 3, 4
131. (*c*) I, II, III
132. (*d*) 1, 2, 3, 4
133. (*d*) 1, 2, 3, 4
134. (*d*) Both A and …… explains A.
135. (*b*) I, II, III, IV
136. (*a*) I, II, III, IV
137. (*d*) I, II, III, IV
138. (*c*) I, II, III, IV
139. (*d*) All of the above
140. (*b*) I, II, III, IV
141. (*a*) I, II, III, IV
142. (*d*) I, II, III, IV
143. (*a*) 1, 2, 3, 4
144. (*d*) Any of the above
145. (*a*) I, II, III, IV
146. (*d*) Transgenes …… of expression.
147. (*b*) The uptake …… transfection.
148. (*d*) The siRNA …… respect.
149. (*c*) I, II, III
150. (*b*) I, II, III, IV
151. (*c*) I, II, III, IV
152. (*d*) All of the above
153. (*c*) 1, 2
154. (*b*) 3, 4, 5
155. (*c*) Both A and …… result of A.
156. (*a*) MAHYCO …… in India.
157. (*d*) In 2004 …… countries.
158. (*c*) USA
159. (*b*) Brazil
160. (*b*) Ideal for …… expression.
161. (*a*) Cry I
162. (*b*) Cry III
163. (*c*) Cry IV
164. (*d*) Both (*b*) and (*c*)
165. (*a*) Cry II
166. (*d*) All of the above
167. (*a*) 3′ ⌉GAGGAA …… GGTGTA⌈ 5′
P—
5′ ⌋CTCCTT …… CCACAT⌊ 3′
168. (*c*) I, II, III, IV
169. (*d*) Both (*b*) and (*c*)
170. (*d*) All of the above
171. (*b*) I, II, III, IV
172. (*c*) *Plodia interpunctella*
173. (*b*) *Cadra cautella*
174. (*d*) *Plutella xylostella*
175. (*d*) All of the above
176. (*a*) 1, 2, 3
177. (*a*) Suppression of endogenous genes
178. (*b*) Alteration of …… transgenes.
179. (*c*) Over expression …… phytochrome A.
180. (*d*) Any of the above
181. (*c*) I, II, III, IV
182. (*b*) I, II, III, IV
183. (*a*) I, II, III, IV
184. (*c*) I, II, III, IV

185. (*d*) I, II, III, IV
186. (*d*) As a result ...... usefulness.
187. (*d*) All of the above
188. (*a*) *sacB*
189. (*c*) *betB*
190. (*d*) *ala3*
191. (*b*) *hsf*
192. (*b*) I, II, III, IV
193. (*c*) I, II, III, IV
194. (*a*) AII, BI, CIV, DIII
195. (*b*) Lauric acid ...... species.
196. (*d*) All of the above
197. (*d*) All of the above
198. (*c*) I, II, IV
199. (*d*) All of the above
200. (*a*) I, II, IV
201. (*d*) All of the above
202. (*b*) I, II, III, IV
203. (*b*) Maharashtra
204. (*c*) Madhya Pradesh

7.2. FILL IN THE BLANKS

1. reduces
2. transformed
3. *iaaM, iaaH*
4. gold, tungston
5. acetosyringone
6. *Agrobacterium tumefaciens*, crown gall
7. *Agrobacterium rhizogenes*
8. *nptII* (resistance to kanamycin)
9. serological test
10. pectin
11. Diptera
12. phosphinothricin or bialophos
13. Avian Myeloblastosis Virus
14. viral genomes
15. antisense RNA
16. terminator technology
17. plant growth, verminator technology
18. boll worm, bud worm
19. transferred DNA
20. RNase
21. *ipt*
22. *virD2*
23. isopentenyl adenine
24. transient, plasma lemma
25. *Bacillus thuringiensis*
26. T-DNA
27. pea, sulpher containing
28. male sterility
29. Delta and Pineland Company, United States Department of Agriculture (USDA)
30. Rural Advancement Foundation International
31. hairy root, dicot
32. Canada
33. bromoxynil
34. eight, T-DNA
35. ~ 70 kDa
36. midgut
37. blank cartridges
38. transposon
39. *barstar*
40. Chalcone synthase (CHS)
41. Cruciferae
42. Brush border, midgut
43. random
44. papaya
45. Lepidoptera, Diptera
46. tobacco
47. membranes, nonspecific
48. influx, lysis
49. Graminae
50. methionine
51. tobacco
52. Cry
53. *gt*1
54. Tobacco Mosaic Virus (TMV)
55. virus coat protein
56. uncoating, replication
57. transformation
58. acetosyringone
59. eukaryotic
60. Taipei 309

7.3. MARK TRUE OR FALSE

1. True 2. False 3. True 4. False
5. False 6. False 7. True 8. True
9. True 10. False 11. True 12. False
13. True 14. False 15. True 16. True
17. True 18. False 19. False 20. True
21. True 22. True 23. False 24. False
25. True 26. False 27. True 28. False
29. True 30. True 31. False 32. True
33. True 34. Flase 35. False 36. True
37. True 38. True 39. True 40. True
41. True 42. True 43. True 44. False

CHAPTER 8

MOLECULAR MARKERS AND MARKER–ASSISTED SELECTION

8.1. MULTIPLE CHOICE QUESTIONS

1. (*d*) Both P and ...... explains P.
2. (*c*) The indirect ...... case of latter.
3. (*b*) 2, 3, 4
4. (*a*) 1, 2, 3
5. (*d*) 1, 2, 3 4
6. (*a*) I, II, III
7. (*d*) All of the above
8. (*b*) 2, 3, 4
9. (*d*) Both (*a*) and (*b*)
10. (*a*) 1, 2, 3, 4
11. (*a*) I, II, IV
12. (*a*) 1, 2, 3, 4
13. (*d*) All of the above
14. (*a*) I, II, III, IV
15. (*b*) 2, 3, 4
16. (*a*) 1, 2, 3, 4
17. (*a*) 1, 2, 3, 4
18. (*c*) >70
19. (*d*) All of the above
20. (*b*) I, II, III
21. (*a*) STMS ...... dominant.
22. (*c*) CAPS was ...... pea.
23. (*d*) 1, 2, 3, 4
24. (*d*) All of the above
25. (*b*) 1, 3, 4
26. (*c*) I, II, III, IV
27. (*a*) I, II, III
28. (*b*) 2, 3, 4
29. (*d*) All of the above
30. (*d*) All of the above
31. (*c*) I, II, III, IV
32. (*b*) II, III, IV
33. (*b*) Molecular ...... populations.
34. (*d*) All of the above
35. (*d*) Any of the above
36. (*d*) All of the above
37. (*c*) Linkage ...... traits.
38. (*c*) I, II, III
39. (*a*) Molecular ...... disease test.
40. (*d*) All of the above
41. (*a*) RILs are ...... lines.
42. (*b*) RFLP
43. (*b*) MAS ...... yield.
44. (*c*) I, II, III, IV
45. (*d*) RIL ...... mortal.
46. (*d*) All of the above
47. (*a*) 1, 2, 3, 4
48. (*a*) I, II, III
49. (*c*) Near-isogenic lines
50. (*d*) All of the above
51. (*b*) Sax
52. (*c*) I, II, III
53. (*d*) I, II, III, IV, V
54. (*d*) Improved Pusa Basmati 1
55. (*c*) Disease resistance
56. (*a*) Bacterial leaf blight
57. (*c*) Both (*a*) and (*b*)

58. (*b*) STMS
59. (*a*) I
60. (*d*) II, III, IV
61. (*c*) I, II, III, IV
62. (*b*) III, IV
63. (*a*) I, II, III, IV
64. (*b*) I, II, IV
65. (*a*) I
66. (*b*) II
67. (*d*) I, II
68. (*c*) III, IV
69. (*c*) I, IV
70. (*d*) IV
71. (*b*) II, III
72. (*c*) III
73. (*d*) NILs
74. (*a*) F_2
75. (*a*) F_2
76. (*c*) NILs
77. (*a*) Seed size ...... seed colour.
78. (*b*) RFLP ...... in 1980s.
79. (*d*) All of the above

8.2. FILL IN THE BLANKS

1. morphological, environment
2. unlimited
3. single copy sequences
4. less
5. RAPD, RFLP
6. sequence tagged sites (STS)
7. dominant
8. single-strand conformation polymorphism
9. AFLP
10. presence/absence
11. gel electrophoresis
12. codominant
13. random amplified hybridization microsatellites
14. *Arabidopsis*
15. retrotransposon-microsatellite amplified polymorphism
16. tight linkage
17. linkage
18. disease test
19. five
20. F_2
21. marker-assisted selection
22. near isogenic lines
23. backcrosses
24. recurrent, donor
25. 'Rapids'
26. environment, genetic background
27. Vivek QPM9
28. Marker assisted selection
29. pearlmillet
30. phenotype

8.3. MARK TRUE OR FALSE

1. True	**2.** True	**3.** False	**4.** True
5. True	**6.** False	**7.** True	**8.** True
9. True	**10.** True	**11.** True	**12.** False
13. True	**14.** True	**15.** True	**16.** True
17. True	**18.** False	**19.** False	**20.** True
21. True	**22.** True	**23.** True	**24.** True

CHAPTER 9

ANIMAL TISSUE CULTURE AND HYBRIDOMA TECHNOLOGY

9.1. MULTIPLE CHOICE QUESTIONS

1. (*c*) Arnold
2. (*d*) All of the above
3. (*c*) Loeb noted ...... 13 days.
4. (*a*) I, II, III, IV
5. (*d*) All of the above
6. (*b*) I, III, IV
7. (*d*) All of the above
8. (*c*) Substrate

9. (*b*) Skin cells ...... adult skin.
10. (*a*) I, II, III
11. (*c*) I, II, III, IV
12. (*d*) All of the above
13. (*d*) All of the above
14. (*a*) I, II, III, IV
15. (*c*) I, III, IV
16. (*c*) All the ...... positively charged.
17. (*b*) Cells harvested ...... at 20°C.
18. (*a*) I, II, III, IV
19. (*c*) I, II, III, IV
20. (*d*) All of the above
21. (*d*) Both (*a*) and (*b*)
22. (*a*) Serum
23. (*b*) Chick embryo extract
24. (*d*) All of the above
25. (*c*) Foetal calf serum
26. (*d*) All of the above
27. (*c*) Alkaloids
28. (*c*) Peptone and salts
29. (*a*) I, II, III, IV
30. (*b*) I, II, III, IV
31. (*d*) All of the above
32. (*a*) I, II, III
33. (*b*) AII, BIII, CIV, DI
34. (*d*) All of the above
35. (*a*) I, II, III, IV
36. (*d*) All of the above
37. (*c*) Trypsin and collagenase
38. (*d*) All of the above
39. (*a*) I, II, III, IV
40. (*d*) All of the above
41. (*b*) 12
42. (*d*) All of the above
43. (*d*) All of the above
44. (*c*) I, II, III
45. (*d*) All of the above
46. (*b*) I, II, IV
47. (*d*) All of the above
48. (*a*) I, II, III
49. (*c*) II, III, IV
50. (*a*) I, II, III, IV
51. (*d*) All of the above
52. (*c*) I, II, IV
53. (*a*) Cells derived ...... clone.
54. (*c*) Results from ...... animals.
55. (*a*) Intact skin explant ...... medium.
56. (*c*) Differentiated cells
57. (*b*) Stem cells
58. (*d*) All of the above
59. (*c*) I, III, IV
60. (*a*) I
61. (*d*) I, IV
62. (*a*) I
63. (*b*) Trypsin
64. (*d*) All of the above
65. (*b*) Epithelium
66. (*d*) All of the above
67. (*b*) I, II, III, IV
68. (*a*) I
69. (*a*) I
70. (*d*) IV
71. (*a*) I, II
72. (*a*) I
73. (*b*) II
74. (*d*) All of the above
75. (*d*) Both (*b*) and (*c*)
76. (*d*) All of the above
77. (*d*) All of the above
78. (*b*) I, III, IV
79. (*a*) I, II, III, IV
80. (*c*) I, II, III, IV
81. (*d*) All of the above
82. (*b*) I, II, III, IV
83. (*c*) I, II, IV
84. (*c*) I, III, IV
85. (*a*) T lymphocytes ...... stem cells.
86. (*d*) All of the above
87. (*c*) Infection
88. (*c*) Destruction of bacteria
89. (*d*) All of the above
90. (*d*) All of the above
91. (*b*) Sephadex gel column

92. (*a*) I, II, III, IV
93. (*d*) TCR-gene ...... genes.
94. (*c*) I, II, III
95. (*b*) II, III, IV
96. (*a*) I, II, III, IV
97. (*d*) All of the above
98. (*d*) Monoclonal ...... myeloma cell
99. (*d*) I, II, III
100. (*b*) I, II, III
101. (*a*) IgD
102. (*b*) I, II, III, IV
103. (*c*) I, II, III, IV
104. (*b*) I, III, IV
105. (*d*) Both (*a*) and (*b*)
106. (*b*) 220
107. (*c*) Laproscopy ...... ovulation.
108. (*a*) 1, 2, 3, 4
109. (*a*) I, II, III, IV
110. (*d*) All of the above
111. (*a*) I, II, III, IV
112. (*b*) 1, 2, 3, 4, 5
113. (*b*) II, III, IV
114. (*a*) I, II, III, IV
115. (*c*) I, II, IV
116. (*b*) A3, B1, C2
117. (*d*) All of the above.
118. (*c*) 1, 2, 3, 4
119. (*c*) Interferons are ...... tumours.
120. (*a*) Polio
121. (*b*) A2, B3, C4, D1
122. (*c*) Both (*a*) and (*b*)
123. (*d*) All of the above
124. (*a*) Both A and R ...... explains A.
125. (*c*) I, II, III, IV
126. (*b*) I, II, III, IV
127. (*a*) Both A and R ...... explanation of A.
128. (*a*) I, II, III, IV
129. (*a*) I, II, III
130. (*d*) All of the above
131. (*a*) I, II, III, IV
132. (*c*) I, II, IV
133. (*d*) All of the above
134. (*d*) All of the above
135. (*b*) A3, B1, C4, D2
136. (*a*) I, II, III, IV
137. (*a*) Recombinant ...... factor VIII.

9.2. FILL IN THE BLANKS

1. Harrison
2. body parts
3. Trowell
4. patient
5. negatively
6. mouse
7. hypoxanthine-guanine phosphoribosyl transferase (HGPRT)
8. 10^{-6}
9. plasma clots
10. organ
11. amino acids
12. Protease
13. platelet-derived growth factor
14. Fe (iron)
15. 70
16. 8–10
17. American Type Culture Collection (ATCC)
18. 7
19. 17
20. continuous
21. keratin
22. maturation
23. mitosis
24. stem cells
25. lymph
26. lymphoid, myeloid
27. B cells
28. lymphatic
29. antigen
30. no, many
31. lighter
32. kappa, lambda
33. MHC
34. Loise Joy Brown
35. Roslin Institute
36. 10^8

37. electrophoresis
38. peripheral lymphoid
39. apoptosis
40. avidity
41. foetal liver
42. clone
43. embryos
44. 440–450
45. abortion
46. 24–30
47. 0.5
48. castor
49. interleukin-4
50. kidney
51. primate kidney
52. blood
53. acquired immunity
54. *Bacillus* Calmette Guerien
55. chick embryo, human diploid cells
56. CD (cluster of differentiation)
57. cytosolic, MHC I
58. secreted
59. carrier
60. plasma
61. antibody
62. 2000
63. cytokines
64. liver hepatocytes
65. blood clotting
66. pig
67. 186

9.3. MARK TRUE OR FALSE

1. True	**2.** True	**3.** False	**4.** True
5. False	**6.** True	**7.** True	**8.** True
9. True	**10.** True	**11.** False	**12.** True
13. True	**14.** True	**15.** True	**16.** True
17. False	**18.** True	**19.** True	**20.** True
21. False	**22.** True	**23.** False	**24.** True
25. False	**26.** True	**27.** True	**28.** True
29. True	**30.** False	**31.** True	**32.** True
33. False	**34.** False	**35.** True	**36.** True
37. True	**38.** False	**39.** True	**40.** True
41. True	**42.** True	**43.** True	**44.** False
45. True			

CHAPTER 10
TRANSGENIC ANIMALS

10.1. MULTIPLE CHOICE QUESTIONS

1. (*c*) AIII, BI, CIV, DII
2. (*a*) I, II, III, IV
3. (*b*) I, II, III, IV
4. (*d*) An enhancer …… CaMV.
5. (*d*) All of the above
6. (*d*) All of the above
7. (*a*) I, II, III, IV
8. (*b*) Fish
9. (*d*) All of the above
10. (*c*) I, II, IV
11. (*a*) I, II, III, IV
12. (*d*) All of the above
13. (*b*) I, II, III
14. (*d*) I, II, III
15. (*d*) All of the above
16. (*b*) Promoter must …… gene.
17. (*d*) I, III, IV
18. (*b*) Phagocytosis
19. (*d*) All of the above
20. (*c*) I, II, III, IV
21. (*a*) I, II, III, IV
22. (*b*) Endocytosis
23. (*c*) Mice
24. (*a*) I, III, IV
25. (*a*) I, II, III, IV
26. (*c*) I, II, III, IV
27. (*b*) I, III
28. (*d*) All of the above
29. (*d*) Virosomes …… genome.

30. (*d*) All of the above
31. (*a*) AII, BIII, CI
32. (*c*) AIV, BI, CII, DIII
33. (*b*) AI, BIV, CII, DIII
34. (*d*) All of the above
35. (*a*) In case ...... DNA.
36. (*d*) Both A and M ...... explains A.
37. (*a*) I, II, III, IV
38. (*c*) I, II, IV
39. (*c*) I, II, III, IV
40. (*b*) II, III, IV
41. (*d*) Both (*a*) and (*b*)
42. (*d*) All of the above
43. (*d*) All of the above
44. (*c*) I, III, IV
45. (*a*) I, II, III, IV
46. (*d*) All of the above
47. (*b*) Microinjection
48. (*a*) I, II, III
49. (*b*) I, II, IV
50. (*d*) Both (*a*) and (*b*)
51. (*c*) Both (*a*) and (*b*)
52. (*a*) Plasmid ...... transfection.
53. (*b*) Presence ...... by transgene.
54. (*d*) All of the above
55. (*c*) Both (*a*) and (*b*)
56. (*c*) Oocytes nucleus ...... metaphase
57. (*a*) I, II, III, IV
58. (*b*) ELISA
59. (*d*) All of the above
60. (*c*) I, II, III, IV
61. (*b*) Both A and R ...... explains A.
62. (*d*) All of the above
63. (*b*) In general ...... transfection.
64. (*b*) Both A and R ...... explains A.
65. (*d*) All of the above
66. (*b*) It is ...... (DHFR)
67. (*d*) All of the above
68. (*a*) In a Knockout ...... mutagenesis.
69. (*c*) I, II, III, IV
70. (*d*) All of the above
71. (*d*) All of the above
72. (*d*) II, III
73. (*b*) II, IV
74. (*a*) I
75. (*d*) IV
76. (*d*) Both (*a*) and (*c*)
77. (*b*) BPV replicons
78. (*a*) SV40 replicons
79. (*c*) Murine-polymavirus
80. (*d*) EBV replicons
81. (*c*) AIII, BI, CIV, DII
82. (*b*) II, III, IV
83. (*a*) I
84. (*a*) I
85. (*d*) I, II, III, IV
86. (*c*) Both (*a*) and (*b*)
87. (*b*) Baculovirus
88. (*d*) Glycosylation
89. (*d*) All of the above
90. (*d*) All of the above
91. (*a*) Divalent nickel
92. (*b*) Protein splicing
93. (*b*) Removal of tag
94. (*d*) Both (*a*) and (*b*)

10.2. FILL IN THE BLANKS

1. bacterial plasmid
2. *p*BR322, retrovirus.
3. insects
4. stable/permanent
5. lipid
6. Keratin
7. Mouse Mammary Tumour Virus
8. HGPRT
9. RNA
10. 36
11. transforming
12. African green monkey
13. monkey
14. egg cytoplasm

15. morula, blastocyst
16. water
17. embryo
18. post-transcriptional processing
19. PCR
20. packaged
21. Plasmid Simian Virus
22. Southern hybridization
23. ovary
24. 0.1, 1
25. Knockout

10.3. MARK TRUE OR FALSE

1. True	**2.** True	**3.** False	**4.** True
5. True	**6.** True	**7.** True	**8.** True
9. False	**10.** False	**11.** True	**12.** False
13. True	**14.** False	**15.** True	**16.** True
17. False	**18.** True	**19.** True	**20.** True

CHAPTER 11

MEDICAL BIOTECHNOLOGY

11.1. MULTIPLE CHOICE QUESTIONS

1. (*a*) I, II, III, IV
2. (*d*) The technique …… complex.
3. (*d*) All of the above
4. (*c*) Vacca
5. (*c*) I, II, III, IV
6. (*b*) I, II, IV
7. (*a*) I, II, III, IV
8. (*d*) Both (*a*) and (*b*)
9. (*d*) III, IV
10. (*c*) DNA vaccines
11. (*d*) I, II, III, IV
12. (*c*) I, II, III
13. (*b*) II, III, IV
14. (*b*) I, II, III, IV
15. (*a*) I, II, III, IV
16. (*d*) All of the above
17. (*d*) I, II, IV
18. (*a*) I, II, III, IV
19. (*d*) All of the above
20. (*d*) Both (*a*) and (*c*)
21. (*d*) All of the above
22. (*a*) I, II, IV
23. (*d*) Any one of the above
24. (*a*) In 1981 …… in India.
25. (*d*) All of the above
26. (*a*) Both A and M …… explanation of A.
27. (*c*) I, II, III
28. (*b*) I, III, IV
29. (*d*) All of the above
30. (*a*) I, II, III
31. (*b*) I, II, III
32. (*d*) All of the above
33. (*a*) I, II, III, IV
34. (*c*) Incorporation of …… its extension
35. (*a*) Both A and R …… explains A.
36. (*b*) I, II, III, IV
37. (*a*) I, II, III, IV
38. (*d*) All of the above
39. (*c*) Only A is correct.
40. (*d*) I, II, IV
41. (*c*) I, III, IV
42. (*d*) All of the above
43. (*d*) Both P and S …… solve P.
44. (*a*) I, II, III, IV
45. (*c*) I, II, III
46. (*c*) I, II, III, IV
47. (*d*) All of the above
48. (*d*) All of the above
49. (*c*) II, III, IV
50. (*d*) Both L and S …… solves L.
51. (*d*) Both (*a*) and (*b*)
52. (*d*) All of the above
53. (*a*) I, II, III, IV
54. (*b*) I, II, III, IV
55. (*c*) I, III, IV
56. (*b*) A4, B3, C2, D1

57. (*a*) I, II, III, IV
58. (*d*) All of the above
59. (*c*) Delavirdine
60. (*c*) I, II, III, IV
61. (*a*) Both P and ...... solution of P.
62. (*d*) Both A and R ...... explains A.
63. (*d*) Chickens
64. (*c*) Streptokinase
65. (*c*) Streptokinase
66. (*a*) I, II, III, IV
67. (*d*) Both (*a*) and (*c*)
68. (*c*) I, III, IV
69. (*d*) All of the above
70. (*a*) I, II, III, IV
71. (*a*) I, II, III
72. (*c*) I, II, III, IV
73. (*d*) All of the above
74. (*b*) Loss of APC function.
75. (*d*) All of the above
76. (*d*) Both A and R ...... explains A.
77. (*c*) Nasal
78. (*a*) I, II, III, IV
79. (*d*) Both (*a*) and (*c*)
80. (*b*) Homologous recombination
81. (*d*) All of the above
82. (*c*) Leukaemia
83. (*b*) Systemic ...... erythematus
84. (*a*) I, II, III, IV
85. (*d*) All of the above
86. (*c*) Zidovudine
87. (*d*) All of the above
88. (*b*) I, II, III
89. (*d*) All of the above
90. (*a*) I, II, III, IV
91. (*c*) I, II, III, IV
92. (*a*) I, II, III
93. (*b*) I, II, III, IV
94. (*c*) I, II, III, IV
95. (*c*) DNA polymerase
96. (*d*) Reverse transcriptase
97. (*d*) Both (*a*) and (*c*)
98. (*a*) MHC loci
99. (*a*) Major ...... antigens
100. (*d*) A4, B1, C2, D3
101. (*b*) Number ...... units
102. (*d*) Both (*a*) and (*c*)
103. (*d*) I, II, III, IV
104. (*c*) II, IV
105. (*a*) I, II
106. (*c*) Either (*a*) or (*b*)
107. (*c*) Antigen
108. (*a*) A3, B2, C5, D1
109. (*c*) Insulin ...... factor
110. (*b*) Scleroderma
111. (*c*) Systemic ...... erythematus
112. (*d*) *Myasthenia gravis*
113. (*a*) South ...... viper
114. (*d*) All of the above
115. (*d*) All of the above
116. (*d*) All of the above
117. (*c*) Loss of p^{53} function.
118. (*d*) Activation of κ-ras.

11.2. FILL IN THE BLANKS

1. DNA
2. immunogenic
3. milk
4. very
5. 15-30
6. severe combined immuno deficiency (SCID)
7. USA
8. primary immunodeficiency
9. IFN-α, IFN-β, IFN-γ
10. reverse transcriptase
11. highly active antiretroviral therapy
12. skin
13. 94
14. 35-60
15. 22
16. breast, ovarian
17. LAK
18. Alec Jeffreys
19. Central Drug Research Institute, Lukcnow
20. DNA profiling

21. CA
22. noninfectious
23. reverse transcriptase
24. secondary/acquired immunodeficieny
25. peptic ulcers
26. mutations
27. defective (endogenous), normal (introduced)
28. monoclonal antibodies
29. SCID
30. homologous recombination
31. 15–60
32. 1–13
33. different labels
34. alkaline phosphatase
35. 10, 1–2

11.3. MARK TRUE OR FALSE

1. True	**2.** True	**3.** True	**4.** False
5. False	**6.** True	**7.** True	**8.** True
9. False	**10.** True	**11.** True	**12.** True
13. False	**14.** True	**15.** False	**16.** True
17. False	**18.** False	**19.** True	**20.** False
21. True	**22.** True	**23.** True	**24.** False
25. True	**26.** False	**27.** True	**28.** True
29. True	**30.** True	**31.** True	**32.** False
33. True	**34.** True	**35.** True	

CHAPTER 12

ENZYME ENGINEERING

12.1. MULTIPLE CHOICE QUESTIONS

1. (*b*) I, II, III, IV
2. (*d*) All of the above
3. (*a*) To prevent ...... contamination.
4. (*a*) I, II, III, IV
5. (*c*) Detergents
6. (*b*) A3, B1, C2, D4
7. (*b*) Insulin
8. (*d*) Both (*a*) and (*b*)
9. (*b*) Enzyme commission
10. (*a*) I, II, III
11. (*c*) Cech
12. (*d*) All of the above
13. (*b*) I, II, III
14. (*a*) Phosphofructokinase
15. (*b*) Moles/litre
16. (*b*) Tryptophan ...... *E. coli*
17. (*d*) Both (*b*) and (*c*)
18. (*d*) They can ...... analogues.
19. (*b*) 1/2 V_{max}
20. (*c*) 130
21. (*d*) RNA molecules ...... properties
22. (*c*) Edman's degradation
23. (*a*) Circular dichroism
24. (*b*) Affinity chromatography
25. (*c*) Interior of the molecule
26. (*a*) Active transport
27. (*c*) Pyruvate ...... complex
28. (*b*) A3, B5, C4, D2
29. (*a*) I, II, III
30. (*c*) Dipeptide
31. (*b*) Ni
32. (*a*) I, II, III, IV
33. (*d*) All of the above
34. (*d*) Both (*a*) and (*b*)
35. (*c*) Microorganisms → plants → animals
36. (*d*) All of the above
37. (*a*) Both A ...... explains A.
38. (*a*) I, II, III, IV
39. (*d*) All of the above
40. (*d*) All of the above
41. (*c*) Both (*a*) and (*b*)
42. (*b*) $E + S \rightleftharpoons ES \rightleftharpoons EP \rightleftharpoons E + P$
43. (*d*) All of the above
44. (*a*) Aldolases
45. (*c*) Oxygenases
46. (*d*) Proteases
47. (*c*) A4, B3, C5, D2
48. (*c*) Both (*a*) and (*b*)
49. (*b*) A2, B3, C1, D4

50. (*d*) All of the above
51. (*a*) I, II, III, IV
52. (*a*) I, II, III
53. (*c*) A4, B3, C2, D1
54. (*b*) I, II, III
55. (*d*) A3, B2, C5, D1
56. (*d*) All of the above
57. (*a*) Ficin
58. (*c*) Pectinase
59. (*d*) Both (*a*) and (*b*)
60. (*c*) Both (*a*) and (*b*)
61. (*d*) All of the above
62. (*c*) Glucoamylase
63. (*d*) Pectinase
64. (*b*) A5, B3, C4, D2
65. (*d*) All of the above
66. (*d*) All of the above
67. (*a*) I, II, III, IV
68. (*b*) I, II, III, IV
69. (*b*) I, III, IV
70. (*a*) I, II, III, IV
71. (*c*) I, II, III, IV
72. (*d*) II, III, IV
73. (*a*) I, II, III, IV
74. (*c*) I, II, III, IV
75. (*a*) I, II, IV
76. (*d*) Both P …… remedy of P
77. (*d*) All of the above
78. (*d*) All of the above.
79. (*c*) I, II, III
80. (*d*) All of the above
81. (*b*) I, III, IV
82. (*c*) Cyanogen bromide
83. (*b*) I, II, III
84. (*c*) Both (*a*) and (*b*)
85. (*d*) All of the above
86. (*a*) I, II, III, IV
87. (*b*) 95–97% glucose …… isomaltose.
88. (*b*) ΔG
89. (*d*) It is …… sweetner.
90. (*c*) I, II, IV
91. (*d*) All of the above
92. (*b*) II, III, IV
93. (*d*) All of the above
94. (*a*) I, II, III, IV
95. (*b*) I, II, III
96. (*d*) All of the above
97. (*d*) Both (*a*) and (*b*)
98. (*a*) I, II, III, IV
99. (*a*) I, II, III, IV
100. (*a*) I, II, III
101. (*d*) I, II, III
102. (*d*) Both (*b*) and (*c*)
103. (*d*) Both (*a*) and (*b*)
104. (*a*) Oxidation …… position 222.
105. (*c*) I, II, IV
106. (*a*) I, II, III
107. (*d*) All of the above
108. (*a*) I, II, III, IV
109. (*c*) Enzymes
110. (*b*) I, III, IV
111. (*b*) II, III
112. (*d*) Both (*a*) and (*b*)
113. (*a*) I, II, III
114. (*b*) I, II, III, IV
115. (*c*) I, II, III. IV
116. (*c*) Both (*a*) and (*b*)
117. (*d*) I, II
118. (*d*) All of the above
119. (*d*) All of the above
120. (*c*) A5, B1, C3, D4
121. (*d*) Either (*a*) and (*c*)
122. (*b*) I, III, IV
123. (*d*) All of the above
124. (*a*) I, II, III, IV
125. (*d*) I, II, III, IV
126. (*d*) All of the above
127. (*c*) I, II, III, IV
128. (*d*) All of the above
129. (*a*) I, II, III
130. (*d*) All of the above
131. (*d*) Both (*a*) and (*b*)
132. (*b*) Conductimetric
133. (*d*) Thermometric
134. (*c*) Piezoelectric
135. (*d*) Thermometric

12.2. FILL IN THE BLANKS

1. cofactors
2. abzymes
3. apoenzyme
4. stability
5. three
6. epimer
7. soluble
8. mass
9. rennet, chymosin
10. Biochemical Nomenclature of the International Union of Biochemistry
11. active site, binding site
12. Lyases
13. hydrides
14. Oxidases
15. catalase
16. reactants/substrate
17. lower
18. detergent
19. Michaelis-Menten
20. *Pyrococcus furiosus*, *Thermococcus litoralis*
21. reverse transcription
22. industrial
23. alkaline proteases
24. *Trichoderma reesei*
25. serine
26. 1 (one)
27. *Bacillus licheniformis*
28. Lipases
29. $\dfrac{\text{Amount of reducing sugar expressed as glucose}}{\text{Total amount of carbohydrates}} \times 100$
30. aqueous-organic
31. 40-50, 45-60
32. galactose
33. nonprotein (nontraditional)
34. inhaled
35. site directed mutagenesis
36. multifunctional
37. ionselective
38. catalytic, affinity
39. Piezoelectric (Acoustic wave)
40. *Lactobacillus arabinosus*
41. antibodies
42. cell wall
43. cyanide sulphide
44. penicillin
45. glucose
46. 70
47. 55
48. sugarbeet
49. *Mortierella vinacea* var. *raffinoseutilizer*
50. Thermolysin
51. cephalosporins

12.3. MARK TRUE OR FALSE

1. True	**2.** True	**3.** False	**4.** False
5. True	**6.** False	**7.** True	**8.** False
9. True	**10.** True	**11.** True	**12.** False
13. True	**14.** False	**15.** True	**16.** True
17. True	**18.** True	**19.** True	**20.** True
21. False	**22.** True	**23.** True	**24.** True
25. True	**26.** True	**27.** True	**28.** True
29. True	**30.** False	**31.** True	**32.** True
33. True	**34.** False	**35.** True	**36.** True
37. True	**38.** False	**39.** True	**40.** True
41. True	**42.** True	**43.** True	**44.** True
45. True			

CHAPTER 13

INDUSTRIAL BIOTECHNOLOGY

13.1. MULTIPLE CHOICE QUESTIONS

1. (*c*) Louis Pasteur
2. (*d*) All of the above
3. (*a*) I, II, III, IV
4. (*d*) I, II, III
5. (*b*) I, II, III, IV
6. (*d*) All of the above
7. (*c*) Antiviral

8. (*a*) Antitumour
9. (*c*) *Streptomyces olivoreticuli*
10. (*c*) Research culture
11. (*b*) I, II, III, IV
12. (*d*) Both (*a*) and (*c*)
13. (*a*) I, II, III, IV
14. (*c*) *Streptomyces mobaraensis*
15. (*b*) I, II, III, IV
16. (*d*) I, II, III
17. (*d*) Both (*b*) and (*c*)
18. (*a*) I, II, III, IV
19. (*c*) A3, B1, C2, D4
20. (*d*) All of the above
21. (*a*) These are ...... leguminous plants.
22. (*d*) All of the above.
23. (*a*) I, II, III, IV
24. (*d*) All of the above
25. (*c*) Penicillin
26. (*d*) Both A and ...... solve A.
27. (*a*) Nucleopolyhedrosis viruses
28. (*c*) I, II, III
29. (*a*) I, II, III
30. (*d*) I, II, III, IV
31. (*b*) The Energy ......, New Delhi.
32. (*d*) All of the above
33. (*b*) I, II, IV
34. (*c*) II, III, IV
35. (*a*) I, II, III, IV
36. (*d*) Both (*a*) and (*c*)
37. (*d*) All of the above
38. (*c*) I, II
39. (*c*) AIV, BIII, CII, DI
40. (*d*) All of the above
41. (*a*) I, II, III, IV
42. (*b*) I, II, III
43. (*c*) Calcium alginate
44. (*b*) I, II, III, IV
45. (*c*) I, II, III, IV
46. (*d*) All of the above
47. (*c*) Rotary ...... filtration
48. (*d*) All of the above
49. (*a*) Drying
50. (*d*) All of the above
51. (*d*) Both (*a*) and (*b*)
52. (*d*) All of the above
53. (*b*) 45–49
54. (*c*) I, II, III, IV
55. (*a*) Clover (*Trifolium* species)
56. (*d*) Both (*a*) and (*b*)
57. (*d*) All of the above
58. (*b*) *Penicillium purpurogenous*
59. (*d*) I, II, III, IV
60. (*d*) All of the above
61. (*d*) All of the above
62. (*a*) I, II, III, IV
63. (*d*) All of the above
64. (*c*) I, II, III, IV
65. (*d*) All of the above
66. (*d*) Both (*a*) and (*b*)
67. (*d*) Both (*a*) and (*c*)
68. (*d*) Any of the above
69. (*d*) All of the above
70. (*c*) I, II, III
71. (*a*) I, II, III
72. (*b*) 6 : 3 : 1
73. (*d*) Both (*a*) and *c*)
74. (*d*) Both (*b*) and (*c*)
75. (*c*) A3, B1, C4, D2
76. (*b*) Starch → ...... ethanol
77. (*b*) A4, B2, C3, D1
78. (*d*) I, II, III, IV
79. (*a*) A5, B3, C2, D4
80. (*d*) All of the above
81. (*d*) All of the above
82. (*c*) Both (*a*) and (*b*)
83. (*b*) I, III, IV
84. (*a*) Deoxycorticosterone ...... corticosterone
85. (*c*) Glucose → ...... ascorbic acid
86. (*b*) This ...... exohydrolase.
87. (*d*) All of the above
88. (*d*) All of the above
89. (*a*) Penicillin G ...... cephalosporins
90. (*b*) *Thiobacillus ferrooxidans*

91. (*d*) All of the above
92. (*a*) I, II, III, IV
93. (*c*) I, II, III, IV
94. (*b*) I, III, IV
95. (*d*) All of the above
96. (*a*) A3, B2, C4, D1
97. (*d*) All of the above
98. (*a*) Diosgenin → …… 11 α-Hydroxy-progesterone.
99. (*d*) Both (*a*) and (*c*)
100. (*c*) Both (*a*) and (*b*)
101. (*d*) All of the above
102. (*d*) Both (*a*) and (*b*)
103. (*d*) All of the above
104. (*a*) A4, B2, C1, D3

13.2. FILL IN THE BLANKS

1. antiviral
2. high performance liquid chromatography (HPLC)
3. 2-6 months
4. automated freeze-drying, high vacuum
5. heat shock
6. Mycorrhizal fungi
7. *Azolla*
8. heterocysts
9. megaplasmid
10. soybean
11. 10–20
12. 24–40
13. rhizobiophage
14. Vietnam
15. 2.5
16. larvae
17. products
18. root hairs
19. ammonia
20. legumes, root nodules
21. 20–25
22. Ghaziabad (U.P.)
23. *Trichoderma viridae*
24. *Agrobacterium tumefaciens*
25. oxidation, alkylation
26. secondary
27. 20–25%
28. obligate
29. anaerobic
30. amino acids
31. same
32. Chromatographic
33. 12
34. Continuous
35. 30*S* subunit
36. cell wall
37. cephalosporin
38. 225
39. 3,00,000; 40,000
40. 1-dehydroprogesterone
41. glucose
42. 6.5 : 3 : 1
43. higher
44. absent
45. broth, rupturing
46. 45–49
47. 6–9
48. glucoamylase
49. 1 : 1
50. ox adrenals
51. *Acetobacter suboxydans*
52. *Gluconobacter melanogenus*/*A. suboxydans*
53. 2000-4000
54. 35,000
55. –20 to –170
56. 15–30
57. deacylation
58. ferrous sulphate
59. sulpher
60. 30

13.3. MARK TRUE OR FALSE

1. False	**2.** False	**3.** True	**4.** True
5. True	**6.** False	**7.** False	**8.** True
9. True	**10.** True	**11.** True	**12.** False
13. True	**14.** True	**15.** False	**16.** True
17. True	**18.** True	**19.** True	**20.** True

21. True 22. True 23. False 24. False
25. True 26. True 27. True 28. True
29. True 30. True 31. True 32. True
33. True 34. True 35. False 36. True
37. True 38. True 39. True 40. True
41. False 42. True 43. True 44. True
45. True 46. False 47. True 48. True
49. True 50. True 51. True 52. True

CHAPTER 14
FOOD AND BEVERAGE BIOTECHNOLOGY

14.1. MULTIPLE CHOICE QUESTIONS

1. (*d*) Both (*a*) and (*c*)
2. (*d*) All of the above
3. (*a*) I, II, III, IV
4. (*c*) I, II, III
5. (*b*) I, II, III, IV
6. (*d*) Both (*a*) and (*b*)
7. (*a*) Cassava
8. (*d*) 1, 3, 2, 4
9. (*a*) I, II, III, IV
10. (*b*) *Monascus purpureus*
11. (*c*) I, II, III
12. (*d*) Either (*a*) or (*c*)
13. (*a*) I, II, III, IV
14. (*b*) I, II, III, IV
15. (*b*) D-glucose + β-D-galactose
16. (*b*) II, III, IV
17. (*c*) I, II, IV
18. (*a*) I, II, III, IV
19. (*d*) I, II, III, IV
20. (*a*) I, II, III, IV
21. (*c*) II, III, IV
22. (*d*) Both (*b*) and (*c*)
23. (*c*) 75%
24. (*c*) I, II, III
25. (*d*) All of the above
26. (*a*) I, II, III, IV
27. (*c*) I, III, IV
28. (*a*) I, II, III, IV
29. (*d*) I, II, III, IV
30. (*c*) I, II, IV
31. (*b*) I, II, III
32. (*a*) Both A ...... explains A.
33. (*a*) I, II, III, IV
34. (*b*) I, II, III, IV
35. (*c*) *Pseudomonas methanitrificans*
36. (*c*) I, II, III, IV
37. (*b*) I, III, IV
38. (*a*) I, II, III, IV
39. (*d*) All of the above
40. (*c*) I, II, III
41. (*d*) I, II, III
42. (*a*) I, II, III, IV
43. (*c*) I, II, III, IV
44. (*c*) Ethanol (from ethylene)
45. (*a*) Whey
46. (*c*) *Fusarium gaminearum*
47. (*b*) *Saccharomyces cerevisiae*
48. (*a*) Bacteria
49. (*b*) Algae
50. (*a*) Bacteria
51. (*d*) Filamentous fungi
52. (*d*) All of the above
53. (*c*) *Volvariella volvaceae*
54. (*c*) *Volvariella volvaceae*
55. (*a*) Papain
56. (*d*) Neutral ...... proteases
57. (*c*) Substilisin
58. (*b*) Heat ...... proteases
59. (*d*) I, II, IV
60. (*b*) I, III
61. (*d*) Both (*a*) and (*b*)
62. (*d*) All of the above
63. (*a*) I, II, III, IV
64. (*d*) All of the above
65. (*b*) I
66. (*d*) II
67. (*c*) IV

68. (*a*) I, III, IV
69. (*b*) I, II, III, IV
70. (*d*) All of the above
71. (*c*) III, IV
72. (*b*) II
73. (*d*) I
74. (*d*) All of the above
75. (*a*) I, II, III, IV
76. (*d*) I, II, III, IV
77. (*a*) Papain
78. (*a*) Papain
79. (*c*) Cellulases
80. (*b*) Neutral proteases
81. (*c*) Either or both (*a*) and (*b*)
82. (*d*) Neutral proteases
83. (*b*) Heat ...... α-amylase.
84. (*a*) Medium-sized peptides.

14.2. FILL IN THE BLANKS

1. rice, urd
2. *Penicillium camembertii* or *P. roquefortii*
3. stabilizes
4. rennet, casein macropeptide
5. pectins
6. lactase
7. *Agaricus bisporus*
8. chilled
9. Papain, chill-haze
10. grapes, molasses
11. one
12. 8–10 cm
13. summer, rainy
14. RNA
15. *Bacillus amyloliquefaciens*
16. *Mucor miehei/Aspergillus niger*
17. C_1–C_4
18. *Chaetomium cellulolyticum*
19. rich
20. 9–18
21. *Fusarium graminearum*
22. 70
23. Whey
24. whey
25. 52–57

14.3. MARK TRUE OR FALSE

1. True	2. True	3. True	4. False
5. False	6. True	7. False	8. True
9. True	10. False	11. True	12. True
13. True	14. True	15. True	16. True
17. True	18. True	19. False	20. True
21. True	22. False	23. True	24. True
25. True			

CHAPTER 15
FUEL BIOTECHNOLOGY

15.1. MULTIPLE CHOICE QUESTIONS

1. (*d*) Both (*a*) and (*c*)
2. (*b*) I, II, III, IV
3. (*d*) All of the above
4. (*a*) I, II, III
5. (*d*) I, II
6. (*a*) I, II, III, IV
7. (*a*) Both A ...... explains A.
8. (*d*) *Eucalyptus globulus*
9. (*d*) All of the above
10. (*b*) Anaerobic digestion
11. (*c*) I, II, III, IV
12. (*d*) All of the above
13. (*d*) All of the above
14. (*a*) I, II, III, IV
15. (*c*) Both (*a*) and (*b*)
16. (*b*) I, II, III, IV
17. (*d*) All of the above
18. (*c*) Both (*a*) and (*b*)
19. (*d*) All of the above
20. (*a*) I, II, III, IV
21. (*d*) All of the above
22. (*c*) I, II, IV
23. (*d*) Both (*a*) and (*b*)

24. (*b*) I, II, III, IV
25. (*a*) I, II, III, IV
26. (*c*) Both (*a*) and (*b*)
27. (*d*) I, II, IV
28. (*a*) Both A ...... explans A.
29. (*c*) I, II, III, IV
30. (*b*) I, II, III, IV
31. (*b*) I, II, III
32. (*b*) I, II, III
33. (*d*) Both (*b*) and (*c*)
34. (*a*) A2, B3, C1
35. (*a*) I, II, III, IV
36. (*b*) I, II, III, IV
37. (*a*) I, II, III, IV
38. (*a*) I, II, III, IV
39. (*c*) IV
40. (*d*) Both P ...... overcomes P.
41. (*d*) I, II, III, IV
42. (*b*) I, II, III, IV
43. (*d*) All of the above
44. (*a*) I, II, III, IV
45. (*d*) All of the above
46. (*a*) I, II, III, IV
47. (*c*) I, II, IV
48. (*a*) I, II, III, IV
49. (*c*) I, III, IV
50. (*d*) II, III, IV
51. (*b*) I, II, III, IV
52. (*c*) The downstream ...... energy.
53. (*b*) A3, B2, C4
54. (*a*) I, II, III, IV

15.2. FILL IN THE BLANKS

1. sun, biomass
2. methane, CO_2
3. sugarcane, sugarbeet
4. soluble, particulate matter
5. cowdung, gobar gas
6. cellulose, lignocellulose
7. batch digester
8. USA, U.K.
9. scum
10. clogging, channelling
11. particulate
12. H_2
13. biodiesel
14. 3,500
15. mesophilic, thermophilic
16. 500
17. m^3
18. latex
19. 0.6, 0.4, 0.2
20. sunlight
21. cellobiose
22. pentoses
23. 30
24. 75
25. gasohol

15.3. MARK TRUE OR FALSE

1. True	2. True	3. True	4. False
5. True	6. False	7. True	8. False
9. False	10. True	11. True	12. False
13. True	14. True	15. True	16. True
17. False	18. True	19. True	20. True

CHAPTER 16
ENVIRONMENTAL BIOTECHNOLOGY

16.1. MULTIPLE CHOICE QUESTIONS

1. (*d*) All of the above
2. (*d*) Both (*a*) and (*b*) minus humans
3. (*d*) Both (*a*) and (*b*)
4. (*d*) Both (*a*) and (*b*)
5. (*c*) Technologies ...... waste
6. (*b*) I, II, III, IV
7. (*c*) I, II, III
8. (*a*) I, II, III, IV
9. (*c*) I, II, III, IV
10. (*b*) I, II, IV
11. (*a*) I, II, III, IV

12. (*d*) All of the above
13. (*d*) I, II, III, IV
14. (*d*) All of the above
15. (*a*) Both A ...... explains A.
16. (*c*) I, II, III
17. (*d*) All of the above
18. (*c*) Heavy metals
19. (*d*) Both A and ...... explains A.
20. (*d*) All of the above
21. (*b*) I, II, III, IV
22. (*d*) All of the above
23. (*d*) All of the above
24. (*a*) I, II, III, IV
25. (*c*) I, II, III, IV
26. (*d*) Both (*a*) and (*b*).
27. (*a*) I, II, III, IV
28. (*a*) I, II, III
29. (*b*) Bacteria
30. (*c*) Plant species
31. (*a*) I, II, III, IV
32. (*d*) All of the above
33. (*d*) All of the above
34. (*a*) Both A and R ...... explains A.
35. (*b*) I, II, III, IV
36. (*d*) Both (*a*) and (*b*).
37. (*a*) I, III, IV
38. (*b*) 1, 2, 3, 4
39. (*c*) I, III, IV
40. (*b*) Preliminary ...... sludge treatment.
41. (*d*) Sludge treatment
42. (*d*) All of the above
43. (*d*) All of the above
44. (*d*) All of the above
45. (*a*) I, II
46. (*b*) I, II, III
47. (*a*) I, II, III, IV
48. (*d*) All of the above
49. (*d*) All of the above
50. (*a*) I, II, IV
51. (*d*) All of the above
52. (*d*) All of the above
53. (*c*) Flagellates
54. (*b*) Ciliates
55. (*d*) Any of the above
56. (*d*) All of the above
57. (*d*) All of the above
58. (*d*) Oilzapper ...... trials.
59. (*a*) I, II, III, IV
60. (*b*) CH_4 and CO_2
61. (*d*) All of the above.
62. (*a*) These compound ...... He atoms.
63. (*d*) All of the above
64. (*d*) Any of the above
65. (*a*) I, II, III
66. (*d*) All of the above
67. (*d*) Both (*a*) and (*b*)
68. (*a*) Mutation
69. (*b*) II, III
70. (*b*) I, II, IV
71. (*d*) All of the above
72. (*a*) I, II, III
73. (*b*) I, II, III, IV
74. (*a*) I, II, III
75. (*c*) O_2
76. (*d*) Teeth
77. (*c*) Dissolved ...... waste.
78. (*d*) Both (*a*) and (*b*)
79. (*d*) Both (*a*) and (*c*)
80. (*b*) Ozone deplition
81. (*a*) Minamata disease
82. (*c*) CFC
83. (*b*) Automobile exhausts
84. (*a*) CO
85. (*b*) > 80
86. (*c*) Epiphytic lichens
87. (*d*) All of the above
88. (*a*) CO_2
89. (*a*) Nuclear plants
90. (*d*) Both (*a*) and (*c*)
91. (*d*) Sea gull
92. (*c*) Nitrous oxide
93. (*a*) September 16
94. (*d*) All of the above

95. (*c*) Increased ...... cancer
96. (*c*) CFC
97. (*a*) Bacteria
98. (*c*) Biogas plant

16.2. FILL IN THE BLANKS

1. biological agents
2. mammalian excreta
3. high performance liquid chromatography (HPLC)
4. Alexander
5. *Pseudomonas*
6. human excreta
7. permease
8. biodegradable
9. landfill
10. next trench/cell
11. higher
12. 40%
13. lime, alum
14. nintrogen, phosphorus, other nutrients
15. faeces
16. water treatment
17. bacteria, sedimentation
18. floc
19. bacteria
20. odours, pathogens
21. halogenation
22. bioaccumulation
23. cyclic
24. organic compounds, heavy metals
25. Germany
26. cytochrome P_{450}, ruberdoxin
27. meta
28. –H, –OH
29. toluene
30. *Acinetobacter*, 4-chlorobenzoate
31. acetyl-CoA
32. biotin

16.3. MARK TRUE OR FALSE

1. True	**2.** True	**3.** True	**4.** True
5. False	**6.** True	**7.** True	**8.** False
9. True	**10.** True	**11.** True	**12.** False
13. True	**14.** True	**15.** False	**16.** True
17. True	**18.** True	**19.** True	**20.** False
21. True	**22.** True	**23.** True	

CHAPTER 17
BIOSAFETY

17.1. MULTIPLE CHOICE QUESTIONS

1. (*d*) All of the above
2. (*d*) Both (*a*) and (*b*)
3. (*c*) Special procedures
4. (*d*) All of the above
5. (*d*) All of the above
6. (*a*) 2, 3, 4, 5, 1
7. (*b*) I, II, III
8. (*b*) Soybean
9. (*a*) I, II, III, IV
10. (*b*) NIH guidelines ...... conference.
11. (*c*) I, II, III
12. (*b*) In the revision ...... stringent.
13. (*a*) I, II, III
14. (*c*) Contained use
15. (*d*) All of the above
16. (*d*) Both (*a*) and (*b*).
17. (*b*) I, II, III
18. (*d*) All of the above
19. (*d*) Any of the above
20. (*d*) Both (*a*) and (*b*)
21. (*d*) All of the above
22. (*a*) I, II, III, IV
23. (*b*) Risk group 1
24. (*a*) Risk group 3
25. (*c*) Risk group 2
26. (*d*) Risk group 4
27. (*a*) Both S and M ...... applies to S.

28. (*d*) Canada become ...... early 1990.
29. (*d*) All of the above
30. (*c*) Both (*a*) and (*b*)
31. (*b*) I, II, III, IV
32. (*a*) I, II, III, IV
33. (*d*) I, II, III, IV
34. (*c*) I, II, III, IV
35. (*a*) I, II, III, IV
36. (*d*) Both A and ...... explains A.
37. (*a*) I, II, III, IV
38. (*d*) Both A and ...... explains A.
39. (*b*) In general ...... variety
40. (*c*) Peas.
41. (*a*) Insect resistance
42. (*a*) II, III, IV
43. (*c*) I, II
44. (*c*) Either (*a*) or (*b*)
45. (*d*) All of the above
46. (*b*) Both R and ...... solution for R.
47. (*d*) Both (*a*) and (*b*)
48. (*d*) All of the above
49. (*d*) All of the above
50. (*d*) The Cry ...... degradation.
51. (*a*) Both A and ...... advocates A.
52. (*b*) 1, 2, 3, 4
53. (*c*) Auxotropic ...... nature.
54. (*a*) I, II, III
55. (*c*) Netherlands
56. (*d*) Any of the above
57. (*d*) All of the above
58. (*a*) Flu symptoms
59. (*d*) All of the above
60. (*b*) Single cell protein
61. (*a*) I, II, III, IV
62. (*c*) 1, 2, 3, 4
63. (*b*) 1, 2, 3, 4
64. (*a*) 1, 2, 3, 4
65. (*b*) 1, 2, 3, 4
66. (*c*) 1, 2, 3
67. (*a*) 1, 2, 3, 4
68. (*d*) All of the above
69. (*b*) 1, 2, 3, 4
70. (*b*) 1, 2, 3, 4
71. (*a*) 1, 2, 3, 4
72. (*a*) 1, 2, 3, 4
73. (*a*) 1, 2, 3, 4
74. (*b*) 2, 3, 4
75. (*d*) All of the above
76. (*c*) I, II, III
77. (*a*) I, II, III, IV
78. (*d*) I, II, III
79. (*a*) Both F ...... are correct.
80. (*b*) Genes ...... abiotic stresses.
81. (*c*) I, II, III, IV
82. (*d*) All of the above
83. (*d*) All of the above
84. (*d*) Volunteers ...... mustard.
85. (*d*) All of the above
86. (*a*) They are polysaccharides.
87. (*b*) I, II, III, IV
88. (*d*) Any one of the above
89. (*c*) I, II, III
90. (*b*) I, III, IV
91. (*a*) I, II, III, IV
92. (*d*) All of the above
93. (*a*) Transgene ...... product.
94. (*a*) It is ...... herbicide.
95. (*c*) I, II, III, IV
96. (*b*) I, IV
97. (*a*) Both A and ...... explains A.
98. (*a*) I, II, III
99. (*b*) 20
100. (*a*) I, II, III
101. (*a*) I, III
102. (*d*) Inducible ...... inducer is present.
103. (*a*) Both S ...... correct.
104. (*c*) Both A ...... explains A.
105. (*c*) I, II, III, IV
106. (*c*) 5%
107. (*b*) I, II, III, IV
108. (*a*) I, II, III, IV
109. (*c*) I, II, III, IV
110. (*d*) All of the above
111. (*b*) I, II, III, IV
112. (*a*) I, II, III, IV

113. (*a*) I, II, III, IV
114. (*b*) I, II, III, IV

17.2. FILL IN THE BLANKS

1. National Institute of Health, USA
2. chemical
3. investigator
4. receiving environment
5. GM food.
6. increases
7. Secondary
8. vector, recombinant DNA
9. *E. coli* K-12 host-vector 1 (Ek1) system.
10. HV2
11. alkylbenzoates
12. Netherlands
13. weighing/mixing
14. antibiotics
15. fungal fermentation, citric acid
16. Informal Working Group on Biosafety
17. biosafety, release GMOs
18. laboratory waste
19. Recombinant DNA Advisory Committee
20. substantial equivalence
21. 11, less than 0.1
22. proteins
23. increases
24. International Life Science Institute
25. Bt toxin
26. weight gain, small intestine
27. phytoalexin
28. fruits, tubers
29. conventionally
30. 1, 47
31. maternal transmission, 0.5
32. red rice (weed form)
33. 10, gene-flow/transmission
34. foundation seed
35. *Aspergillus niger*
36. rapeseed/*B. napus*
37. tobacco
38. male sterile
39. recombination, heteroencapsidation
40. transgene instability
41. silencing
42. 350
43. 4, 5–15
44. no health hazard

17.3. MARK TRUE OR FALSE

1. True	**2.** True	**3.** True	**4.** False
5. True	**6.** True	**7.** True	**8.** False
9. False	**10.** True	**11.** True	**12.** True
13. True	**14.** True	**15.** False	**16.** True
17. True	**18.** False	**19.** True	**20.** True
21. False	**22.** True	**23.** True	**24.** False
25. True	**26.** False	**27.** True	**28.** False
29. True	**30.** True	**31.** False	**32.** True
33. True	**34.** True		

CHAPTER 18
INTELLECTUAL PROPERTY RIGHTS

18.1. MULTIPLE CHOICE QUESTIONS

1. (*b*) I, II, III, IV
2. (*c*) I, II, III, IV
3. (*d*) Any one of the above
4. (*b*) It is granted ...... time.
5. (*d*) All of the above
6. (*c*) 1, 2, 3, 4
7. (*a*) I, II, III
8. (*c*) I, III, IV
9. (*a*) I, II, III, IV
10. (*d*) All of the above
11. (*a*) Both D ...... result of D.
12. (*c*) I, III, IV
13. (*b*) The PBR ...... as well.
14. (*d*) I, II, III, IV

15. (*a*) I, II, III
16. (*d*) All of the above
17. (*b*) Tomato
18. (*c*) Chennai
19. (*b*) I, II, III, IV
20. (*d*) Any of the above
21. (*a*) I, II, III, IV
22. (*d*) All of the above
23. (*c*) The utility ...... (1985)
24. (*b*) I, II, III, IV
25. (*a*) I, II, III, IV
26. (*d*) All of the above.
27. (*b*) I, II, III, IV
28. (*b*) I, II, III
29. (*d*) Both (*a*) and (*c*)
30. (*a*) I, II, III, IV
31. (*a*) I, II, III, IV
32. (*c*) I, II, IV
33. (*a*) France
34. (*b*) I, II, III
35. (*d*) All of the above
36. (*c*) I, II, III, IV
37. (*a*) I, II, III, IV
38. (*c*) I, II, III, IV
39. (*c*) New Delhi
40. (*b*) I, II, III
41. (*a*) I, II, III, IV
42. (*a*) I, II, III
43. (*c*) I, II, III
44. (*a*) I, III, IV
45. (*b*) I, II, IV
46. (*a*) I, II, III, IV
47. (*d*) I, II, III, IV
48. (*d*) All of the above.
49. (*a*) I, II, III, IV
50. (*c*) Application ...... convention country.
51. (*d*) Any of the above
52. (*d*) All of the above
53. (*d*) All of the above
54. (*c*) I, II, III, IV
55. (*a*) I, II, III, IV
56. (*d*) All of the above
57. (*a*) Both S ...... explains S.
58. (*d*) India
59. (*c*) I, II, III, IV
60. (*a*) AIII, BII, CI
61. (*b*) AII, BIII, CI
62. (*d*) AII, BIII, CI
63. (*c*) I, II, III, IV
64. (*d*) All of the above.
65. (*d*) All of the above.
66. (*c*) 2007
67. (*b*) I, II, III, IV
68. (*c*) I, II, IV
69. (*a*) I, II, III, IV
70. (*c*) I, II, III, IV
71. (*a*) I, II, IV
72. (*d*) I, II, III, IV
73. (*a*) I, II, III
74. (*d*) All of the above
75. (*d*) All of the above
76. (*c*) The GIs ...... products.
77. (*d*) All of the above
78. (*d*) All of the above
79. (*b*) 12

18.2. FILL IN THE BLANKS

1. detrimental
2. formulation
3. Information Technology Act (2000)
4. Rice Tech
5. *Azadirachta Indica* (neem)
6. *Pseudomonas* strain
7. 15–20
8. 7, 14
9. National Gene Fund
10. patent
11. genetic variability
12. 2001
13. 1978
14. World Intellectual Property Organization (WIPO)
15. 1995
16. General Agreement on Tariffs and Trade (GATT)

17. Geneva
18. 2004
19. 1991
20. less than one, four
21. 12 months (one year)
22. European Parliament
23. not considered
24. plants, maize line
25. TRIPs
26. oncomouse
27. 90%
28. bacterial leaf blight
29. International Convention on Biological Diversity
30. biodiversity use

18.3. MARK TRUE OR FALSE

1. True	**2.** False	**3.** True	**4.** True
5. True	**6.** False	**7.** True	**8.** True
9. True	**10.** False	**11.** True	**12.** False
13. True	**14.** True	**15.** True	**16.** False
17. True	**18.** True	**19.** True	**20.** True
21. True	**22.** True	**23.** False	**24.** True

MODEL QUESTION PAPER – I

(MULTIPLE CHOICE QUESTION)

1. (*a*) DNA ligase
2. (*c*) ELISA
3. (*d*) Palindromes .... symmetry
4. (*d*) Both (*b*) and (*c*) together
5. (*d*) All of the above
6. (*b*) Isolated leaf cells
7. (*b*) Oil palm
8. (*c*) *E. coli*
9. (*c*) RNA editing
10. (*a*) Plastic
11. (*b*) Stirring
12. (*d*) Any of the above
13. (*d*) Any of the above
14. (*a*) Nucleic acids
15. (*c*) Recombinant vaccines
16. (*d*) Both (*a*) and (*b*)
17. (*c*) Both (*a*) and (*b*)
18. (*a*) Sequence .... marker.
19. (*d*) All of the above
20. (*c*) Alternative splicing
21. (*c*) Microbial biomass
22. (*d*) Both (*b*) and (*c*)
23. (*b*) Plant Breeder's Rights
24. (*a*) A formula
25. (*c*) Plasma cells
26. (*c*) Antigen presenting cells
27. (*b*) It is ...... partner.
28. (*d*) All of the above
29. (*d*) All of the above
30. (*a*) 32°C
31. (*b*) Annealing
32. (*d*) Both (*a*) and (*c*)
33. (*c*) Inverse PCR
34. (*a*) Nested PCR
35. (*b*) Supercoiled circular
36. (*a*) DNA footprinting
37. (*d*) DNA polymerse .... *coli*
38. (*c*) Chromosome walking
39. (*d*) *Haemophilus influenzae*
40. (*b*) 2003
41. (*b*) 25,000
42. (*a*) GA_3
43. (*c*) Y chromosome
44. (*b*) 4
45. (*a*) Yeast
46. (*b*) Cosmid
47. (*d*) M13
48. (*c*) 300 kb
49. (*a*) *vir* region
50. (*a*) VirA
51. (*b*) VirG
52. (*a*) T-DNA borders

53. (*c*) CryIV
54. (*d*) CryVI
55. (*a*) Coat protein gene
56. (*d*) All of the above
57. (*b*) Lauroyl-ACP thioesterase
58. (*a*) β-carotene
59. (*c*) Iron
60. (*b*) Polygalacturonase
61. (*d*) Eliminating .... plants.
62. (*c*) Both (*a*) and (*b*)
63. (*d*) All of the above
64. (*c*) Both (*a*) and (*b*)
65. (*d*) Any of the above
66. (*a*) Solanaceae
67. (*b*) Somaclonal variant
68. (*d*) All of the above
69. (*c*) Datura
70. (*b*) *Brassica* sp.
71. (*d*) Both (*b*) and (*c*)
72. (*a*) Tobacco
73. (*b*) Cybrids
74. (*c*) Haploid production
75. (*b*) ABA
76. (*d*) GA_3
77. (*c*) Visible disease symptoms
78. (*a*) Wild type cells
79. (*d*) Both (*b*) and (*c*)
80. (*a*) Specific toxins
81. (*b*) Orchids
82. (*d*) All of the above
83. (*d*) All of the above
84. (*c*) Transgenic .... markers
85. (*d*) All of the above
86. (*b*) Cryopreservation
87. (*a*) Around first mitosis
88. (*c*) Both (*a*) and (*b*)
89. (*b*) *Arabidopsis*
90. (*d*) All of the above
91. (*a*) IBA
92. (*b*) 2, 4 -D
93. (*a*) BAP
94. (*c*) Both (*a*) and (*b*)
95. (*b*) Mosquitoes
96. (*a*) Fungal pathogens
97. (*d*) α-Amylase
98. (*b*) Liquefaction
99. (*d*) Either (*b*) or (*c*)
100. (*c*) κ-casein

MODEL QUESTION PAPER – II

(MULTIPLE CHOICE QUESTION)

1. (*b*) Hydrophobic interactions
2. (*d*) Transposition
3. (*a*) 1 : 1 ratio .... monohybrids.
4. (*d*) Both (*a*) and (*b*)
5. (*b*) Acetosyringone
6. (*c*) Elicitor
7. (*c*) Vegetative propagules
8. (*d*) Telomerase
9. (*d*) Both (*b*) and (*c*)
10. (*c*) In most .... chromosomes.
11. (*d*) Two nuclear .... S phase
12. (*c*) Both (*a*) and (*b*)
13. (*b*) An antithrombin
14. (*b*) 6000
15. (*a*) Insulin
16. (*d*) All of the above
17. (*d*) Any of the above
18. (*a*) 4^6 bp
19. (*c*) Alkaline phosphatase
20. (*b*) Production .... ends
21. (*d*) Both (*a*) and (*c*)
22. (*a*) DNA labelling
23. (*c*) Hybrid antibody
24. (*a*) Gene tagging
25. (*d*) Both (*a*) and (*b*)
26. (*c*) Antigen .... interaction

27. (*a*) Complementation
28. (*c*) Binding .... segment
29. (*b*) RNA-protein interaction
30. (*d*) Packaging into virions
31. (*d*) I, II, III
32. (*b*) I, II, III
33. (*d*) *Vibro cholerae*
34. (*a*) I, II
35. (*c*) III
36. (*c*) III, IV
37. (*d*) Both (*a*) and (*b*)
38. (*c*) Individuals .... species
39. (*b*) I, II
40. (*a*) III
41. (*c*) II
42. (*d*) II, III
43. (*b*) II, III
44. (*b*) I, II, III, IV
45. (*a*) IV
46. (*b*) I, IV
47. (*c*) I, II, III
48. (*d*) All of the above
49. (*c*) Gel retardation assay
50. (*a*) DNA footprinting
51. (*d*) Restriction mapping
52. (*b*) DNA fingerprinting
53. (*a*) DNA footprinting
54. (*a*) I, II
55. (*a*) IV
56. (*b*) III
57. (*d*) All of the above
58. (*a*) I, II, III, IV
59. (*d*) V, II, III, IV, I
60. (*a*) Exogenous acetosyringone
61. (*b*) Particle gun
62. (*a*) VirC
63. (*d*) VirE
64. (*d*) All of the above
65. (*b*) A4, B1, C2, D3
66. (*c*) CryIV
67. (*c*) Bacterial .... resistance
68. (*c*) STMS
69. (*c*) AIII, BIV, CI, DII
70. (*a*) Perfusion cultures
71. (*b*) Fed-batch cultures
72. (*b*) Fed-batch cultures
73. (*b*) Viral HN protein
74. (*a*) DEAE .... transfection
75. (*a*) Male pronucleus
76. (*c*) Ovum cytoplasm
77. (*c*) Protein
78. (*a*) Vaccinia virus
79. (*d*) All of the above
80. (*d*) All of the above
81. (*a*) A5, B1, C4, D2
82. (*c*) Redox reaction
83. (*d*) Both (*a*) and (*c*)
84. (*a*) Lipase
85. (*b*) Alcohol
86. (*b*) Alcohol
87. (*d*) Both (*b*) and (*c*)
88. (*c*) Freeze drying
89. (*d*) All of the above
90. (*b*) Pharmaceutical
91. (*d*) All of the above
92. (*a*) Maltose
93. (*b*) A4, B2, C5, D1
94. (*a*) Pancreatic digest of gelatin
95. (*c*) Corn-steep liquor
96. (*d*) All of the above
97. (*d*) All of the above
98. (*b*) Urease
99. (*c*) Antifungals
100. (*a*) $BLAST_x$

MODEL QUESTION PAPER – III

(MULTIPLE CHOICE QUESTION)

1. (*d*) Both (*b*) and (*c*)
2. (*d*) All of the above
3. (*d*) I, II
4. (*a*) I, II, III
5. (*a*) Competitive inhibitor
6. (*b*) Androgenesis
7. (*a*) Northern hybridization
8. (*a*) Ni
9. (*b*) T_4 ligase
10. (*d*) Safety evalution
11. (*c*) By growing .... cells
12. (*b*) Alkaline phosphatase
13. (*d*) I, II, III, IV
14. (*c*) I, III
15. (*c*) Antibodies .... activity
16. (*a*) Affinity chromatography
17. (*b*) Zymogenes
18. (*c*) Meristem culture
19. (*b*) GA_3
20. (*a*) Minimise .... a gene.
21. (*a*) Purification .... proteins
22. (*c*) Both (*a*) and (*b*)
23. (*d*) Microbial .... supplement.
24. (*d*) Filter area .... cake
25. (*b*) Mass
26. (*a*) Dipeptide
27. (*d*) Enzymes .... analogues.
28. (*b*) Semisynthetic penicillins
29. (*a*) Epigenetic variation
30. (*c*) Endonuclease
31. (*b*) Transfection
32. (*d*) Transformation
33. (*c*) It is .... protein
34. (*a*) Tobacco mosaic virus
35. (*d*) All of the above
36. (*a*) Negative
37. (*d*) All of the above
38. (*d*) All of the above
39. (*d*) All of the above
40. (*c*) Doubled haploids
41. (*d*) Any of the above
42. (*b*) Coat .... virus
43. (*d*) All of the above
44. (*d*) All of the above
45. (*a*) Anaerobiosis
46. (*d*) Southern hybridization
47. (*b*) House-keeping genes
48. (*c*) *Anabaena*
49. (*d*) Any of the above
50. (*c*) Both (*a*) and (*b*)
51. (*d*) All of the above
52. (*a*) Small .... value product
53. (*d*) Both (*a*) and (*b*)
54. (*d*) Both (*a*) and (*b*)
55. (*c*) RAPD
56. (*b*) Both (*b*) and (*c*)
57. (*d*) All of the above
58. (*b*) I, II, III, IV
59. (*c*) Both (*a*) and (*b*)
60. (*d*) Chromosome walking
61. (*c*) Whole plants .... shoot-tips.
62. (*d*) Cleaved into .... proteins.
63. (*d*) Any of the above
64. (*a*) Phosphate diester
65. (*b*) Bind to glycoproteins
66. (*d*) All of the above
67. (*a*) Silk
68. (*b*) Palindromes .... symmetry
69. (*d*) *vir* region .... plasmids
70. (*c*) Single-stranded linear molecule
71. (*a*) VirA
72. (*c*) VirG protein.
73. (*b*) Bacterial chromosome
74. (*c*) PEG combined .....Ca^{2+}
75. (*c*) Only A is correct.
76. (*c*) I, II, III, IV
77. (*d*) Both (*a*) and (*b*)
78. (*b*) GA_3

79. (*d*) Both (*a*) and (*b*)
80. (*b*) I, II, III
81. (*d*) Both (*b*) and (*c*)
82. (*d*) Both (*a*) and (*b*)
83. (*b*) Specific toxin
84. (*d*) All of the above
85. (*a*) IgA
86. (*a*) Glycine
87. (*b*) Mobility .... electrophoresis
88. (*b*) AIV, BIII, CI, DII
89. (*c*) Proline
90. (*c*) I, II, III, IV
91. (*d*) All of the above
92. (*a*) Mo cofactor .... polypeptide
93. (*d*) All of the above
94. (*b*) I, II, III
95. (*d*) All of the above
96. (*d*) All of the above
97. (*c*) Both TATA .... boxes
98. (*b*) Telomere sequence
99. (*d*) All of the above
100. (*a*) –130°C

MODEL QUESTION PAPER – IV

(MULTIPLE CHOICE QUESTION)

1. (*d*) *cos* .... cleavage sites
2. (*c*) Scorable marker
3. (*d*) All of the above
4. (*b*) Inhibition of transcription
5. (*b*) 1–2
6. (*a*) Peroxisomes
7. (*d*) Stable and .... environments
8. (*d*) Hydrophobic interactions
9. (*b*) Proline
10. (*d*) Both (*a*) and (*b*)
11. (*d*) Farmer's rights
12. (*a*) Tunicamycin
13. (*d*) Cytochrome C
14. (*b*) Lysosome
15. (*c*) Mendelian inheritance
16. (*b*) I, III
17. (*b*) 10,000
18. (*b*) (A + G)/(C + T)
19. (*a*) IAA
20. (*c*) Enzyme purification
21. (*c*) PCR
22. (*b*) Methylation of DNA
23. (*d*) Integrated (*a*) and (*b*)
24. (*a*) Endotoxin production
25. (*c*) AIII, BIV, CI, DII
26. (*b*) AIV, BI, CII, DIII
27. (*a*) AII, BIV, CIII, DI
28. (*c*) AIII, BI, CII, DIV
29. (*b*) RNA processing
30. (*c*) 3
31. (*c*) Can not .... transformation.
32. (*c*) Doble-stranded RNA
33. (*b*) AII, BIV, CI, DIII
34. (*c*) AIII, BI, CIV, DII
35. (*d*) AII, BIII, CIV, DI
36. (*a*) AI, BII, CIII, DIV
37. (*a*) I, II, III, IV
38. (*c*) Tobacco
39. (*a*) Carrot
40. (*c*) Blue-green algae
41. (*d*) Bone marrow
42. (*b*) *Arabidopsis thallana*
43. (*c*) Pancreas
44. (*a*) *Bacillus subtilis*
45. (*d*) Spinal cord
46. (*b*) 2′
47. (*d*) All of the above
48. (*d*) Single-stranded RNA
49. (*d*) A ≠ U
50. (*c*) Leeuwenhoek
51. (*d*) Both (*a*) and (*b*)
52. (*b*) Rabies
53. (*c*) Chromosome structure (eukaryotes)
54. (*a*) T-DNA

55. (*b*) Serum independence
56. (*a*) Moles/litre
57. (*b*) Active transport
58. (*d*) Sunflower oil
59. (*c*) Interior of the molecule
60. (*a*) AIII, BI, CIV, DII
61. (*b*) I, II, III
62. (*b*) I, II, III, IV
63. (*c*) I, III, IV
64. (*d*) All of the above
65. (*a*) I, II, III, IV
66. (*d*) All of the above
67. (*d*) All of the above
68. (*a*) 1, 2, 3, 4
69. (*a*) I, II, III
70. (*d*) All of the above
71. (*c*) *Pseudomonas putida*
72. (*b*) Egg cell
73. (*a*) *p*BR322
74. (*d*) Both (*b*) and (*c*)
75. (*d*) Both (*a*) and (*c*)
76. (*c*) Microinjection
77. (*a*) Yeast
78. (*d*) Both (*a*) and (*b*)
79. (*d*) All of the above
80. (*b*) Dihydrofolate reductase
81. (*a*) Fish
82. (*d*) All of the above
83. (*c*) Both (*a*) and (*b*)
84. (*d*) Special laboratory design
85. (*d*) All of the above
86. (*c*) AII, BIII, CI, DIV
87. (*b*) Acute .... retroviruses.
88. (*a*) I, II, III, IV
89. (*c*) I, II, III, IV
90. (*b*) I, II, III, IV
91. (*b*) Edouard Sauma
92. (*a*) W.G. Rosen
93. (*d*) All of the above
94. (*d*) All of the above
95. (*c*) Chances .... activities.
96. (*b*) I, II, III, IV
97. (*d*) *In situ* .... simple.
98. (*d*) All of the above
99. (*c*) China
100. (*d*) All of the above

MODEL QUESTION PAPER – V

(MULTIPLE CHOICE QUESTION)

1. (*a*) Both .... in bacteria.
2. (*d*) Both P and S .... solves P.
3. (*b*) 1, 2, 3
4. (*d*) All of the above
5. (*b*) I, II
6. (*d*) 1, 2, 3
7. (*d*) Both (*a*) and (*b*)
8. (*a*) I, II, III, IV
9. (*a*) 1, 2, 3
10. (*c*) I, II, III, IV
11. (*d*) Both (*a*) and (*b*)
12. (*d*) All of the above
13. (*d*) In 1972 .... *Nicotiana.*
14. (*a*) Both C and R .... remedy C.
15. (*d*) All of the above
16. (*c*) 1, 2, 3
17. (*a*) I, II, III
18. (*d*) All of the above
19. (*d*) All of the above
20. (*b*) I, II, III, IV
21. (*b*) II, III, IV
22. (*d*) All of the above
23. (*d*) All of the above
24. (*d*) All of the above
25. (*a*) Both A and R .... explains A.
26. (*d*) I, II, III, IV
27. (*d*) All of the above
28. (*d*) All of the above
29. (*d*) All of the above
30. (*a*) Both T and U .... use of T.

31. (*c*) Both S and M .... supports S.
32. (*b*) I, II, III, IV
33. (*d*) All of the above
34. (*d*) All of the above
35. (*d*) All of the above
36. (*d*) All of the above
37. (*b*) I, II, III, IV
38. (*a*) Both B and D ...... accounts for B.
39. (*d*) All of the above
40. (*b*) I, II, III, IV
41. (*b*) I, II, III, IV
42. (*b*) I, III, IV
43. (*d*) Both (*a*) and (*c*)
44. (*c*) It is a .... bacterium.
45. (*b*) Dry heat
46. (*d*) All of the above
47. (*a*) It utilizes .... contact.
48. (*d*) All of the above
49. (*d*) All of the above
50. (*c*) Thaimine
51. (*d*) Maltose is .... materials.
52. (*d*) There is .... variations.
53. (*b*) I, II, III, IV
54. (*a*) II, III, IV
55. (*c*) I, II, III, IV, V
56. (*d*) All of the above
57. (*d*) All of the above
58. (*d*) All of the above
59. (*b*) Micropropagation .... year.
60. (*c*) I, II, III, IV
61. (*d*) All of the above
62. (*d*) All of the above
63. (*d*) Any of the above
64. (*a*) Fluorescein diacetate (FDA)
65. (*d*) TTC is .... single cells.
66. (*d*) All of the above
67. (*a*) 1, 2, 3, 4, 5
68. (*b*) I, II, III, IV
69. (*b*) Somatic embryo .... develops.
70. (*c*) Canberra (Australia)
71. (*a*) Both P and S .... overcomes P.
72. (*a*) I, II, III, IV
73. (*d*) All of the above
74. (*d*) Meristem culture .... meristem.
75. (*d*) 1, 2, 3, 4
76. (*b*) It gives .... multiplication rate.
77. (*d*) All of the above
78. (*c*) I, II, III, IV
79. (*d*) All of the above
80. (*a*) I, II, III, IV
81. (*d*) All of the above
82. (*a*) Somatic embryos .... desiccated.
83. (*a*) Both P and S .... resolves S.
84. (*b*) 1, 2, 4
85. (*c*) I, II, III, IV
86. (*b*) I, III, IV
87. (*c*) Shoot-tip culture
88. (*d*) Both (*a*) and (*b*)
89. (*c*) Shoot-tip culture
90. (*b*) Adventitious shoot buds.
91. (*c*) Shoot tip culture.
92. (*a*) All of the above
93. (*d*) All of the above
94. (*d*) Any of the above
95. (*a*) Both A and .... explains A.
96. (*d*) All of the above
97. (*d*) All of the above
98. (*d*) Both A and .... explains A.
99. (*c*) Hybrid embryos
100. (*b*) I, II, III, IV

MODEL QUESTION PAPER – VI

(FILL IN THE BLANKS)

1. 2000
2. electroporation
3. totipotent
4. acetosyringone

5. conjugative, mobilization
6. *Agrobacterium rhizogenes*
7. Asymmetric
8. shuttle vector
9. *in situ*
10. inverse
11. fertile
12. cellulase (1–2%)
13. kanamycin, selectable marker
14. gene silencing
15. linker
16. PHB (polyhydroxy butyrate)
17. *Clostridium*
18. methan, CO_2
19. GAATTC, G, A
20. replica plating
21. 5′ → 3′ exonuclease
22. fluid-mosaic
23. Gram-positive
24. N-terminal
25. two, restriction enzymes
26. *cos* sequence, empty
27. origin, relaxed
28. shuttle vector, origin of DNA replication.
29. vegetative
30. species A, species B
31. somatic hybridization or protoplast fusion
32. 500-800, $CaCl_2$
33. Ti, agroinfection
34. synthetic seeds (artificial seeds)
35. apical dominance
36. epigenetic
37. disarmed
38. RuBISCO
39. Haplome
40. endomitosis (endoreduplication)
41. B-DNA, Z-DNA
42. androgenesis
43. plasmid
44. parthenogenesis
45. *Bacillus thuringiensis*
46. Hybridoma
47. Leghaemoglobin
48. Kreb's
49. low
50. reverse transcriptase
51. Chromosome walking
52. Thaumatin
53. YAC (yeast artificial chromosomes)
54. episome
55. hypohaploid
56. Vitrification/hyperhydracity
57. dot blot
58. 5-10
59. mammalian artificial chromosome
60. two
61. Ernest Ruska
62. cryopreservation
63. DNA ligase
64. *in vitro* pollination, *in vitro* fertilization
65. Sumner
66. ice crystals, ice
67. 10
68. most critical
69. 0.22 μm
70. 62, 13
71. Viable
72. coat proteins
73. hybrid chlorosis, hybrid sterility
74. ascites
75. animal
76. 8, 12
77. *Secale*
78. Mysore
79. La Jolla, Ca, USA
80. hybrid rescue
81. shoot-tip culture
82. emzymatic degradation
83. Powers and coworkers
84. Takebe and coworkers
85. *Nicotiana*
86. *Agrobacterium*
87. Larkin and Scowcroft
88. Fifth

89. tobacco
90. potato (*Solanum tuberosum*)
91. Sanger
92. 8-12
93. Lactase
94. chick embryo
95. phase contrast
96. rennet
97. reverse transcription of RNA
98. ink
99. L-ascorbic
100. AFLPs

MODEL QUESTION PAPER – VII

(MARK TRUE OR FALSE)

1. True	**2.** True	**3.** False	**4.** False
5. True	**6.** True	**7.** False	**8.** True
9. True	**10.** False	**11.** True	**12.** True
13. True	**14.** True	**15.** True	**16.** False
17. True	**18.** True	**19.** False	**20.** False
21. True	**22.** False	**23.** True	**24.** True
25. True	**26.** True	**27.** False	**28.** True
29. False	**30.** True	**31.** True	**32.** True
33. True	**34.** True	**35.** True	**36.** False
37. True	**38.** True	**39.** False	**40.** True
41. True	**42.** True	**43.** True	**44.** True
45. True	**46.** False	**47.** True	**48.** False
49. True	**50.** True	**51.** False	**52.** True
53. True	**54.** True	**55.** True	**56.** True
57. True	**58.** False	**59.** True	**60.** False
61. True	**62.** True	**63.** True	**64.** True
65. True	**66.** True	**67.** True	**68.** True
69. True	**70.** True	**71.** True	**72.** True
73. True	**74.** True	**75.** True	**76.** True
77. True	**78.** False	**79.** True	**80.** True
81. False	**82.** False	**83.** False	**84.** False
85. True	**86.** True	**87.** True	**88.** False
89. False	**90.** True	**91.** True	**92.** False
93. True	**94.** True	**95.** False	**96.** True
97. False	**98.** True	**99.** True	**100.** True

SECTION V

APPENDICES

APPENDIX I

A List of Some Important Abbreviations and Symbols

α, Alpha

Å, Angstrome

Ab, Antibody

ABA, Abscisic acid

AB-QTL, Advanced backcross QTL

Ac, Activator (element)

ACC, 1-Aminocyclopropane-1-carboxylic acid

ACLSV, Apple Chlorotic Leafspot Virus

ACMV, African Cassava Mosaic Virus

ACP, Acyl-carrier protein

ADA, Adenosine deaminase

ADCC, Antibody dependent cell-mediated cytotoxicity

ADP, Adenosine diphosphate

adh-1, *alcohol dehydrogenase 1*

AEV, Avian Erythroblastosis Virus

AFGC, *Arabidopsis* Functional Genomic Consortium

AFLPs, Amplified fragment length polymorphisms

AFP, Antifreeze protein

Ag, Antigen

AGF, Angiogenesis factor

AG-LCR, Asymmetric gap ligase chain reaction

AGP, Arabinogalactan protein

AGPase, Adenosine diphosphate glucose pyrophosphorylase

AIDS, Acquired immunodeficiency syndrome

ALL, Acute lymphoblastic leukaemia

ALS, Acetolactate synthase

AMF, Arbuscular mycorrhizal fungi

AMP, Adenosine monophosphate

AMP-PCR, Anchored microsatellite primed-PCR

AMV, Avian Myeloblastosis Virus; Arabis Mosaic Virus

ANF, Atrial natriuretic factor

APCs, Antigen presenting cells

APHIS, Animal and plant health inspection service

AP-PCR, Arbitrary primer-PCR

ARDRA, Amplified ribosomal DNA restriction analysis

ARMS-PCR, Amplification refractive mutation system-PCR

ARS, Autonomously replicating sequences

ASAPs, Allele specific associated primers

AS-PCR, Allele specific-PCR

asRNA, Antisense RNA

ASSINSEL, International Organization for Plant Variety Protection

ASSR, Anchored simple sequence repeats

ASV, Avian Sarcoma Virus

ATCC, American Type Culture Collection

ATL, Adult T cell leukaemia

ATP, Adenosine triphosphate

AZT, Azidothymidine

β, Beta

B_1, Backcross of an F_1 with its first parent

B_2, Backcross of an F_1 with its second parent

BAC, Bacterial artificial chromosome

BAP, 6-Benzylaminopurine

BC, Before Crist

BC_1, BC_2, etc., Generation from F_1 crossed with its recurrent parent, BC_1 crossed with its recurrent parent, etc., respectively.

BC_1F_2, Generation obtained by selfing of BC_1

BC_2F_2, Generation obtained by selfing of BC_2

BCG, Bacillus of Calmette Guerien

BCIG, 5-Bromo, 4-chloro, 3-indolyl glucuronide

BCIL, Biotech Consortium India Limited

BEM, Biological effect monitoring

BIBCOL, Bharat Immunological and Biological Corporation Limited

BL, Biosafety level

BL-1, Biosafety level-1

BL-1-P, Biosafety level 1-Plant

BL-1-N, Biosafety level 1-Animal

BLAST, Basic Local Alignment Search Tool

BMV, Brome Mosaic Virus
BOD, Biochemical/biological oxygen demand
bp, Base pairs
BPV, Bovine Papilloma Virus
BSA, Bulked segregant analysis
BTH, Benzo (1, 2, 3) thiadiazol-7-carbothionic acid 5-methyl-ester
BTIC, Biotechnology Information Centre
BTIS, Bioinformatics Information Service
5-BUdR, 5-Bromodeoxyuridine

C, Colchicin generation
Ca., Approximately (circa)
cAMP, Cyclic-AMP
CAMIA, Centre for the Application of Molecular Biology to International Agriculture
CAMM, Computer-aided molecular modelling
CaMV, Cauliflower Mosaic Virus
CAPSs, Cleaved amplified polymorphic sequences
Cat, Chloramphenicol acetyl transferase
CbBRSV, Cabbage Black Ringspot Virus
CBD, Convention on Biological Diversity
CCC, 2-Chloroethyltrimethylammonium chloride
CCMB, Centre for Cellular and Molecular Biology
CCMV, Chrysanthemum Chlorotic Mottle Virus
CDC (*cdc*) genes, Cell division cycle genes
CDFD, Centre for DNA Fingerprinting and Diagnostic
CDK, Cyclin dependent kinases
CDR, Complementarity determining region
cDNA, Copy DNA; complementary DNA
CEA, Carcinoembryonic antigen
CEN, Centromere(ic)
CFCs, Chlorofluorocarbons
CFSTR, Continuous-flow stirred tank reactor
CGIAR, Consultative Group on International Agricultural Research
CGMS, Cytoplasmic genetic male sterility
CGT, Cyclodextrin glucosyltransferase
C_H, Constant region of heavy chain (antibodies)
CHEFE, Countour-clamped Homogeneous Electric Field Electrophoresis
CHO, Chinese hamster ovary
CHS, Chalcone synthase
chv, Chromosomal virulence (genes)
CIE, Counter immunoelectrophoresis
CIFOR, Centre for International Forestry Research
CIM, Composite interval mapping
CIMAP, Central Institute of Medicinal and Aromatic Plants
CITES, Convention on Trade in Endangered Species
C_L, Constant region of light chain (antibodies)
CLIP, Class II-associated invariant chain processing
cM, centiMorgan
CMI, Commonwealth Mycological Institute
CMRTD, Consortium on Micropropagation Research and Technology Development
CML, Chronic myelogenous leukaemia
CMS, Cytoplasmic male sterility
CMV, Cucumber Mosaic Virus
CNPs, Copy number polymorphisms
COD, Chemical oxygen demand
cos, cohesive sequence
COS, Cv1 origin of SV40 (Cv1 is a monkey cell line)
CP, Coat protein
cpDNA, Chloroplast DNA
CPG, Cyclopentadienyl guanosine
CpG, Cytidine-phosphate-guanosine
CPMB, Centre for Plant Molecular Biology
CPMV, Cowpea Mosaic Virus
CPTI, Cowpea Trypsin Inhibitor
C-region, Constant region
cry genes, Crystal protein genes
CSF, Cytostatic factor
CSIR, Council for Scientific and Industrial Research
CSL, Corn steep liquor
CSV, Chrysanthemum Stunt Virus
CT, Cholera toxin
CTA, Technical Centre for Agricultural and Rural Development
CTLs, Cytotoxic T lymphocytes
CTP, Chloroplast transit peptide; Cytidine triphosphate

δ, Delta
Da, Dalton
2,4-D, 2,4-Dichlorophenoxy acetic acid
DAF, DNA amplification fingerprinting
dATP, Deoxyadenosine triphosphate
DArT, Diversity array technology
DASH, Dyanamic allele specific hybridization
DBT, Department of Biotechnology
dCTP, Deoxycytidine triphosphate
ddATP, 2′,3′-dideoxyadenosine triphosphate
ddCTP, 2′,3′-dideoxycytidine triphosphate
ddGTP, 2′,3′-dideoxyguanosine triphosphate
ddTTP, 2′,3′-dideoxythymidine triphosphate
DGGE, Denaturing gradient gel electrophoresis
dGTP, Deoxyguanosine triphosphate
DH, Doubled haploid
DHFR, Dihydrofolate reductase
DHPLC, Denaturing high performance liquid chromatography
DHPS, Dihydropteroate synthase
DLCs, District Level Committees
DIMBOA, 2,4-Dihydroxy-7-methoxy-1, 4-benzoxazine-3-one
DMEM, Dulbecco's minimal essential medium
DMGT, DNA-mediated gene transfer
DMSO, Dimethyl sulphoxide
DNA, Deoxyribonucleic acid
DNase, Deoxyribonuclease
DO, Dissolved oxygen
DOPE, Dioleoyl phosphatidylethanolamine
DRE, Dehydration responsive element
DSBR, Double strand break repair
Ds, Dissociator (element)
dsRNA, Double-stranded RNA
DST, Department of Science and Technology
DTA, Diphtheria Toxin A chain

ε, Eata
EBI, European Bioinformatics Institute
EBV, Epstein-Barr Virus
EDTA, Ethylenediaminetetracetic acid
EEC, European Economic Community
ε-ACA, ε-Aminocaproic acid
EGF, Epidermal growth factor
EI, Ethylene imine
EIS, Environment Impact Statement
ELISA, Enzyme-linked immunosorbant assay
EMBL, European Molecular Biology Laboratory
EMCV, Eggplant Mottled Crinkled Virus
EMS, Ethylmethane sulphonate
EMU, Ethylmethylurea
EPA, Environment Protection Act; U.S. Environmental Protection Agency
EPC, European Patent Convention
EPG, Endopolygalacturonase
EPO, Erythropoietin; European Patent Office
EPSP, 5-Enolpyruvylshikimate-3-phosphate
EPSPS, 5-Enolpyruvylshikimate-3-phosphate synthase
ES (cell line), Embryonic stem (cell line)
EST, Expressed sequence tag
ET, Embryo transfer

F, Filial (generation)
F_{AB}, Fragment with antigen binding (of antibodies)
FACS, Fluorescence activated cell sorter
FAD, Ferridoxin adenine dinucleotide
FAP, Fatty acid analysis profiles
FBR, Fluidized bed reactor
F_C, Crystal forming fragment (of antibodies)
FDA, Fluorescein diacetate; Federal Food and Drug Administration
FERM, Fermentation Research Institute
FGF, Fibroblast growth factor
FIGE, Field inversion gel electrophoresis
FISH, Fluorescence *in situ* hybridization
FLV, Feline Leukaemia Virus
FMD, Foot and mouth disease
FQPA, Food Quality Protection Act
FR, Framework region
FSH, Follicle stimulating hormone

γ, Gamma
ΔG, Gibbs free energy denoted by ΔG

GA, Gibberellic acid
GAI, Genetic annotation index
GATT, General Agreement on Tariffs and Trade
GBA, Genetic bit analysis
GBSS-I, Granule-bound starch synthase I
GDP, Guanosine diphosphate
GEAC, Genetic Engineering Approval Committee
GEMs, Genetically engineered microbes/microorganisms
GFLV, Grapevine Fanleaf Virus
GFP, Green fluorescent protein
GIBP, Green Industry Biotechnology Plateform
GISH, Genomic *in situ* hybridization
G-LCR, Gap-ligase chain reaction
GMOs, Genetically modified organisms
GMS, Genetic male sterility
GMV, Garlic Mosaic Virus
GOGAT, Glutamate synthase
GOX, Glyphosate oxidoreductase
GR, Growth regulator
GRAIN, Genetic Resources Action International
GRAS, Generally regarded as safe
GST, Glutathione-S-transferase
GTP, Guanosine triphosphate
GURT, Gene use restriction technology
gus, β-glucuronidase
GV, Granulosis Virus
Gy, Gray
GYSV, Garlic Yellow Streak Virus

HAC, Human artificial chromosome
HaMuSV, Harvey Murine Sarcoma Virus
HAART, Highly active antiretroviral therapy
HART, Hybrid arrested translation
HAT medium, Hypoxanthine aminopterin and thymidine medium
HBsAg, Hepatitis B surface antigen
hCG, Human chorionic gonadotropin
HDACs, Histone deacetylases
HEPA filter, High efficiency particulate air filter
HGF, Hepatocyte growth factor
hGH, Human growth hormone
HGPRT, Hypoxanthine-guanine phosphoribosyl transferase
HIV, Human Immunodeficiency Virus
HLA, Human leucocyte antigen
hMG, Human menopausal gonadotropin
hnRNA, heterogeneous nuclear RNA
HPLC, High performance liquid chromatography
h, Hours
HSA, Human serum albumin
HSP, Heat shock protein
HSV, Herpes Simplex Virus
HSV-tk, Herpes Simplex Virus thymidine kinase
HTLV-1, Human T-cell Leukaemia Lymphoma Virus-1

IAA, Indole-3-acétic acid
IAM, Indole-3-acetamide
IBA, Indole-3-butyric acid
IBC, Institutional Biosafety Committee
IBPGR, International Board for Plant Genetic Resources (now called Bioversity International)
IBS, Intermediary Biotechnology Service
IBSD, Institute of Bioresources and Sustainable Development
ICAR, Indian Council of Agricultural Research
ICBD, International Convention on Biological Diversity
ICGEB, International Centre for Genetic Engineering and Biotechnology
ICRAF, International Centre for Research on Agrofostery.
IEDC, Induced embryogenic determined cells
IFN, Interferon
Ig, Immunoglobulin
IGF, Insulin-like growth factor
IHF, Integration host factor
IIB, International Institute of Biotechnology
IICA, International Institute for Co-operation in Agriculture
IL, Interleukin
IL-2, Interleukin-2
ILSI, International Life Sciences Institute

ILTAB, International Laboratory for Tropical Agricultural Biotechnology
IMDM, Iscoves modified Dulbecco's medium
IMGT Database, International ImmounoGenetics Database
IMP, Inosine monophosphate
IMTECH, Institute of Microbial Technology
INA, 2,6-Dichloroisonicotinic acid
2-ip, Isopentenyl adenine
IPG, Isopropyl-β-D-thiogalactoside
IPP, Intellectual Property Protection
IPR, Intellectual Property Rights
IPTG, Isopropylthiogalactoside
IRGSP, International Rice Genome Sequencing Project
IS, Insertion sequence
ISA, Inter-SSR amplification
ISAAA, International Service for the Acquisition of Agri-biotech Applications
ISGPB, Indian Society of Genetics and Plant Breeding
ISH, *In situ* hybridization
ISSR, Inter-simple sequence repeats
ITMI, International Triticeae Mapping Initiative
IV, Intermediate vector
IVCOL, Indian Vaccines Corporation Limited
IVF, *In vitro* fertilization
IWGB, Informal Working Group on Biosafety

JH, Juvenile hormone

kb, Kilobase pairs (10^3 bp)
KEGG, Kyoto Encyclopedia of Genes and Genomes.
kg, Kilogram
KiMuSV, Kirsten Murine Sarcoma Virus
kR, kiloRoentgen
KTI, Soybean Kunitz trypsin inhibitor

λ, Lambda
l, Litre
LAK cells, Lymphokine activated killer cells
LB, Left border (of T-DNA)
LCR, Ligase chain reaction
LGL, Large granular lymphocytes
LH, Luteinising hormone
LINES, Long interspersed sequences
LMV, Lily Mosaic Virus
LMWHSP, Low molecular weight heat shock protein
LRE, Light responsive element
LT-B, Heat labile enterotoxin B subunit (of *E. coli*)
LTP, Lipid transfer protein
LTR, Long terminal repeats

μ, Micron
M, Molar (=gram molecular weight/l)
Mab, Monoclonal antibody
MAC, Mammalian artificial chromosome
MAAP, Multiple arbitrary amplicon profiling
MAS, Marker-assisted selection
Mb, Megabase pairs (10^6 bp)
McFISH, Multicolour fluorescent *in situ* hybridization
MCB, Master cell banks
MCPA, 4-Chloro-2-methylphenoxyacetic acid
MCT, Metabolic control theory
Met, Methyl transferase
MEM, Eagles' minimum essential medium
MFC, Microbial fuel cell
MGI, Mouse Genome Informatics
MGSC, Mouse Genome Sequencing Consortium
MH, Maleic hydrazide
MHC, Major histocompatibility complex
min, Minutes
MIM, Multiple interval mapping
MLP, Multilocus probe
MLV, Moloney Murine Leukaemia Virus
mM, Millimolar (= mg molecular weight/l)
MMC, Megaspore mother cell
MMDB, Molecular Modelling Database
mmol l^{-1}, Millimole per litre
MMS, Methylmethane sulphonate
MMTV, Mouse Mammary Tumour Virus
MNCs, Multinational Corporations
MNNG, N-methyl-N-nitro-N-nitrosoguanidine

MoMuSV, Moloney Murine Sarcoma Virus
MoEF, Ministry of Environment and Forests
MP-PCR, Microsatellite primed-PCR
mRNA, Messenger RNA
μs, Microsecond
MS, Male sterility
MSV, Maize Streak Virus
mtDNA, Mitochondrial DNA
MTPs, Micropropagation Technology Parks
Mtx, Methotrexate
MVR, Minisatellite variant repeat
MW, Molecular weight
MWCB, Master working cell bank

n, Gametic chromosome number
2*n*, Sporophytic/somatic chromosome number
NAA, Naphthalene acetic acid
NAAP, National *Azola* Action Programme
NAAQS, National Ambient Air Quality Standard
NAAS, National Academy of Agricultural Sciences
NAD, Nicotinamide adenine dinucleotide
NADH, Nicotinamide adenine dinucleotide (reduced)
NBPGR, National Bureau of Plant Genetic Resources
NBRC, National Brain Research Centre
NBRI, National Botanical Research Institute
NBTB, National Biotechnology Board (now DBT)
NCBI, National Centre for Biotechnology Information
NCL, National Chemical Laboratory
NEP, Naked eye polymorphism
NESHAPs, National Emission Standards for Hazardous Air Pollutants.
NFATCC, National Facility for Animal Tissue and Cell Culture
NFPTCR, National Facility on Plant Tissue Culture Repository
NGF, Nerve growth factor
NGO, Non-government organizations
NHGRI, National Human Genome Research Institute
NIH, National Institute of Health, USA
NII, National Institute of Immunology, New Delhi
NILs, Near isogenic lines
NIPGR, National Institute for Plant Genome Research
NK cells, Natural killer cells
NLS, Nuclear localization signal
NoA, Naphthoxy acetic acid
NPDES, National Pollution Discharge Elimination System
*npt*II, Neomycin phosphotransferase II
NPV, Nucleopolyhedrosis Virus
NRC, National Research Centre; U.S. National Research Council
NRCPB, National Research Centre on Plant Biotechnology
NVCP, Norwalk Virus Capsid Protein

OBA, Office of Biotechnology Activities
OD, Optical density
OECD, Organization for Economic Corporation and Development
OLA, Oligonucleotide ligation assay
OMIM, Online Mendelian Inheritance in Man
OMV, Odontoglossum Mosaic Virus
ORF, Open reading frame
ORSV, Ornithogalum Ringspot Virus
OTR, Oxygen transfer rate
OYDMV, Onion Yellow Dwarf Mosaic Virus

φ, Phi
ψ, Psi
PAG, P1-derived artificial chromosome
PAGE, Polyacrylamide gel electrophoresis
PAL, Phenylalanine ammonialyase
PALA, N-phosphonacetyl-L-aspartate
PAMPs, Pathogen-associated molecular patterns
PANs, Peroxyacetylnitrates
PBR, Plant breeder's rights; Packed bed reactor
PC, Phosphatidylcholine
PCBs, Polychlorinated biphenyls
PCPA, Para-chlorophenoxy acetic acid
PCR, Polymerase chain reaction
PDB, Protein Data Bank
PDGF, Platelet-derived growth factor

PEDC, Preembryogenic determined cells
PEG, Polyethylene glycol
5′, 5-Prime
3′, 3-Prime
PFGE, Pulsed-field gel electrophoresis
Pg, picogram
PG, Polygalacturonase
PGR, Plant growth regulator, plant genetic resources
PHAs, Polyhydroxyalkanoates
PHB, Polyhydroxybutyrate
PIR, Protein Information Resource
P-Lec, Pea lectin
PLRV, Potato Leaf Roll Virus
PMCs, Pollen mother cells
PMSG, Pregnant mare serum gonadotropin
POPs, Persistent organic pollutants
ppb, Parts per billion
PPFD, Photosynthetic photon flux density
ppm, Parts per million
PPRs, Pattern recognition receptors
PPT, Phosphinothricin
PPVFR Act, Protection of Plant Varieties and Farmer's Rights Act
PRF, Papilla regulatory factor
PR proteins, Pathogenesis-related proteins
PS, Phosphatidyl serine, Pedigree selection
PSTV, Potato Spindle Tuber Virus
p.s.i., Pounds per square inch
PVA, Potato Virus A
PVC, Polyvinyl carbonate
PVG, Potato Virus G
PVM, Potato Virus M
PVP, Plant variety protection; Polyvinyl pyrrolidon
PVS, Potato Virus S
PVX, Potato Virus X
PVY, Potato Virus Y

QTL, Quantitative trait loci

R, Regenerant generation
R, Resistance gene
RACE, Rapid amplification of cDNA ends
RAFI, Rural Advancement Foundation International
RAHM, Random amplified hybridization microsatellites
RAMs, Random amplified microsatellites
RAMP, Random amplified microsatellite polymorphism
RAPDs, Randomly amplified polymorphic DNAs
RB, Right border (of T-DNA)
RBCs, Red blood cells
RCGM, Review Committee for Genetic Manipulation
RDAC, Recombinant DNA Advisory Committee
REMAP, Retrotransposon microsatellite amplified polymorphism
RFLPs, Restriction fragment length polymorphisms
RG1, Risk Group 1
RHdb, Radiation hybrid database
Ri Plasmid, Root inducing plasmid
RIA, Radio-immuno assay
RILs, Recombinant inbred lines
RIP, Ribosome inactivating protein
RNA, Ribose nucleic acid
RNA_i, RNA interference
RNase, Ribonuclease
r.p.m., Revolutions per minute
rRNA, Ribosomal RNA
RSSs, Recombination signal sequences
RSV, Ring Spot Virus, Rous Sarcoma Virus
RTF, Resistance transfer factor
RuBISCO, Ribulose 1,5-bisphosphate carboxylase/oxygenase

σ, Sigma
s, second
S, Svedberg
SA, Salicylic acid
SAM, S-Adenosyl methionine
SAMPL, Selective amplification of microsatellite polymorphic loci
SAR, Systemic acquired resistance
SBEs, Starch branching enzymes
SCARs, Sequence characterized amplified regions
SCID, Severe combined immunodeficiency

SCO, Single cell oil
SCP, Single cell protein
scRNAs, Small cytoplasmic RNAs
scRNP, Small cytoplasmic ribonucleoprotein
SDBEs, Starch debranching enzymes
SDS, Sodium dodecyl sulphate
SE, Somatic embryo
SERK, Somatic embryogenesis receptor kinase
SGSC, Swine Genome Sequencing Consortium
SIM, Simple interval mapping
SINEs, Short interspersed sequences
SINGER, System-wide Information Network of Genetic Resources
siRNAs, Small interfering RNAs
SLP, Single locus probe
SMV, Soybean Mosaic Virus
SNP, Single nucleotide polymorphism
snRNA, Small nuclear RNA
snRNP, Small nuclear ribonucleoprotein
SPARs, Single primer amplification reactions
SSBP, Single strand binding protein
SSCP, Single-strand conformational polymorphism
SSD, Single seed descent
SSLP, Simple sequence length polymorphism
SSR-A PCR, SSR-anchored PCR
SSRs, Simple sequence repeats
SSS, Soluble starch synthase
STD, Sexually transmitted disease
STMS, Sequence-tagged microsatellite sites
STR, Stirred tank reactor
STRs, Sequence-tagged repeats; Short tandem repeats
STS, Sequence-tagged sites
SV40, Simian Virus 40
2,4,5-T, 2,4,5-Trichlorophenoxyacetic acid
TAFE, Transverse alternating field electrophoresis
TAP, Transporters associated with antigen processing
TAV, Tomato Aspermy Virus
TBGRI, Tropical Botanical Garden and Research Institute
TCD, Tapeto-choroidal dystrophy
TCR, Tissue culture response (gene); T cell receptor
TDC, Tryptophan decarboxylase
TCPPs, Tissue Culture Pilot Plants
TDZ, Thidiazuron
T-DNA, Transferred DNA
TEL, Telomeric sequence
TERI, The Energy and Resources Institute
TF, Transcription factor
TGF-β, Transforming growth factor β
TGGE, Thermal gradient gel electrophoresis
TGMS, Temperature sensitive genetic male sterility
Ti plasmid, Tumour inducing plasmid
TIBA, 2,3,5-Tri-idobenzoic acid
TIGR, The Institute for Genome Research
TILs, Tumour-infiltrating lymphocytes
TILLING, Targetting Induced Local Lesions in Genomes
Tk, Thymidine kinase
TLCV, Tomato Leaf Curl Virus
TMGMV, Tobacco Mild Green Mosaic Virus
TMV, Tobacco Mosaic Virus
Tn, Transposon
TNF, Tumour necrosis factor
TobRV, Tobacco Ringspot Virus
ToMV, Tomato Mosaic Virus
TOSCA, Toxic Substances Control Act
tPA, Tissue plasminogen activator
TP, Transit peptide
TRIPs, Trade Related Intellectual Property Rights
tRNA, Transfer RNA
tSMS, True single molecule sequencing
TSTAs, Tumour specific transplantation antigens
TTC, 2,3,5-Triphenyl tetrazolium chloride; Triple test cross
TuMV, Turnip Mosaic Virus
USPTO, U.S. Patents and Trademark Office
UV, Ultraviolet (light)
V_H, Variable region of heavy chain (antibodies)
VIGS, Virus-induced gene silencing

VIP, Vegetative insecticidal protein
vir region, Virulence region
V_L, Variable region of light chain (antibodies)
VLP, Virus-like particle
VNTRs, Variable number of tandem repeats
VP1, 2, or 3, Virion protein 1, 2 or 3
V region, Variable region (in antibodies)
VS, Volatile solids
V/V, Volume/volume
VV, Vaccinia Virus

WBC, White blood cells
WDV, Wheat Dwarf Virus
WGA, Wheat germ agglutinin
WIPO, World Intellectual Property Organisation
WTO, World Trade Organisation
W/v, Weight/volume
W/w, Weight/weight

x, Basic or genomic chromosome number
2*x*, Diploid chromosome number
XGPRT, Xanthine-guanine phosphoribosyltransferase

YAC, Yeast artificial chromosome
ζ, Zeta

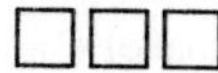

APPENDIX II

A Chronology of Important Developments Related to Biotechnology

Year	Scientist	Contribution/Discovery
Before 6000 BC	—	Man began employing microorganism (yeast) for making wine, vinegar, beer, curd, etc.; conversion of wine into vinegar was practice in Babylon as early as 5000 BC.
About 4,000 BC	—	Man used yeast for making leavened bread.
3000 BC	—	Sumerian people prepared 20 different types of beer.
7 BC	—	In the Greek colony of Saberis, south of Italy, the discoverer of a food recipe was given the exclusive right to use this recipe for one year.
1150 AD	—	Ethanol was first obtained by distillation of alcoholic beverages.
1474 AD	—	The first law on patent was passed in Venice, which gave monopoly rights to artisans for their inventions.
1623	—	The House of Commons of U.K. passed the Act of Proprietorship.
Before 1670	—	Copper mined with the aid of microbes (Rio Tinto, Spain).
1677	A. van Leeuwenhoek	First observation of microorganism; observation published by the Royal Society, London in 1677 and latter in 1684.
1680	A. van Leeuwenhoek	Observed first yeast cell.
1818	Erxleben	Discovered fermentative property of yeast.
1833	Payen and Persoz	First observation of enzyme activity in a test tube much earlier in 1833.
1852	—	British Patent Law
1856	—	Government of India introduced the Act of Protection of Inventions; this Act was based on the British Patent Law of 1852.
1857	Louis Pasteur	Microbiology is widely considered to have began in 1857 when Pasteur reported his studies on lactic acid fermentation, including microscopic features of the microorganisms, and suitable medium for the processes; the scientific basis of industrial microbiology began with 1857 paper of Pasteur.
1860	Louis Pasteur	Reported first synthetic medium for microorganisms and used it to study alcohol fermentation.
1861	Louis Pasteur	Showed that growth and physiology of microorganism differ, depending on the presence or absence of O_2.
1866	G.J. Mendel	Postulated concept of genes (hypothetical unit of inheritance).
1871	F. Meischer	Isolated nucleic acid; called them nuclein.
1872	—	Patents and Designs Protection Act was passed by Government of India.
1876	Cohn	Showed that bacterial spores have a level of heat resistance and developed the technique of intermittant sterilization for their inactivation.
1878	Kühne	Introduced the term enzyme.

	Lister	Describe the dilution technique for obtaining the first pure microbial culture of lactic acid bacterium.
1880	Arnold	Showed that leucocytes can be divide outside the body; this mark the beginning of animal tissue culture.
1881	Robert Koch	Described a simple and more effective technique of obtaining pure culture from isolated separate colonies developed on solidified medium.
1883	—	In India, protection of Inventions Act was introduced; it was consolidated as Inventions and Designs Act in 1888.
1885	Louis Pasteur	Reported first case of vaccination against rabies; used the fluid from the spinal cord of another mad dog for vaccination.
1887	Petri	Devised Petri plate.
1890	Fisher	During 1890s suggested the lock and key model of enzyme action.
1892	Klercker	Plant protoplasts were first isolated by cutting plasmolysed cell with fine knife.
1896	Nobbe and Hilter	Obtained U.S. patent for production of *Rhizobium* inoculant.
1897	Buchner	Demonstrated alcohol fermentation by cell free yeast juice; suggested that a proteinaceous enzyme was responsible for fermentation.
	Loeb	Maintained adult rabbit liver, kidney, thyroid and ovary on small plasma clots in tubes and noted that these organs retained their normal histological features for 3 days; there was first attempt of organ culture.
1901	Wildiers	Demonstrated that yeast required growth factors (vitamins) for growth, especially at low inoculum level.
1902	L. Sutton and T. Bovery	Chromosomal theory of inheritance, *i.e.,* genes are located in chromosomes and chromosomes are unit of inheritance of traits from parents to offspring.
	Haberlandt	First attempt to culture isolated single palisade cells from leaves in Knob's salts solution enriched with sucrose; postulated the concept of cellular totipotency.
	Ishiwata	Discovered *Bacillus thuringiensis* from diseased silk worm (*Bombyx mori*) larvae.
1903	Jolly	Studied the behaviour of animal tissue explants immersed in serum, lymph or ascites fluid.
1904	Hanning	Attempt were made to culture embryo of selected crucifers.
1907	Ross Harrison	Cultured frog tadpol spinal cord in a lymph drop hanging from a coverslip into the cavity of a microscopic slide; this is regarded as turning point in animal tissue culture.
1910	T.H. Morgan	Proposed concept of linkage in *Drosophila melanogaster.*
	—	Sewage treatment using microbes developed/established in about 1910.
1911	—	Protection of design is covered by the Indian Patent and Design Act (1911) with amendments in 1978 and amended rules in 1985.
	Berliner	Isolated *Bacillus thuringiensis* from larvae of Mediterranean flour moth (*Anagastra kuehiella*) and designed it as *Bacillus thuringiensis*.

Year	Scientist	Contribution/Discovery
1912-14	—	Large scale production of acetone, butanol and glycerol using bacteria.
1913	A.H. Sturtevant	First genetic/linkage map of *Drosophila melanogaster.*
	Alexis Carrel	Developed a complicated methodology for maintaining cultures free from contamination, especially by bacteria.
	Michaelis and Menten	Proposed a mathematical model of enzyme action.
1915	Delbenk and Henneberg	Discovered the large scale use of yeast in food and fodder industry.
1917	d'Herelle	Described the biological properties of the parasite of dysentery *Bacillus*, and called it bacteriophage.
1919	Loeb and Fleischer	Reported that the enzyme culture tube must be filled with O_2 to prevent central necrosis of the explants.
1920	Chaim Weismann	Used *Clostridium acetobutylicum* for converting starch into butanol and acetone in 1920s.
	H. Winkler	Introduced the term genome.
1922	Knudson	Reported asymbiotic germination of orchid seed *in vitro.*
	Robbins	Develop a technique for isolated root culture and effect of peptone, yeast on it.
1923	Sax	Theory of QTL mapping was first described.
1925	Laibach	Technique of embryo culture used to recover hybrid progeny from interspecific crosses in *Linum*.
1926	J.B. Sumner	Crystalized enzyme (urease) for the first time.
1928	F. Griffith	Discovered phenomenon of transformation in *Diplococcus pneumoniae.*
1929	Alexander Fleming	Discovered penicillin produced by growing as contaminant in a Petri plate of *Staphylococcus*; developed technique of assay of antibacterial activity of penicillin using bacteria and showed it low toxicity to man and animals.
1930	—	In U.S.A., the Plant Patent Act (1930) cover varieties of asexually propagated crops, *e.g.,* ornamentals and fruit trees.
1934	P.R. White	Grew the excised roots of tomato in a liquide medium contains inorganic salts, yeast extract and sucrose or vitamin B.
	R.J. Gautheret	*In vitro* culture of the cambial tissue of few trees and shrubs, although failed to sustain cell division.
1936	—	*B. thuringiensis* was first used as a commercial insecticide in France.
1938	—	The International Organization for Plant Variety Protection (ASSINSEL) was established with the objective of persuading governments of different countries from introducing law to protect plant varieties.
1939	R.J. Gautheret, P.R. White and Nobecourt (independently)	The first continuous growing callus cultures were established from cambium tissue.
1940	R.J. Gautheret	Cultured *in vitro* cambial tissue of *Ulmus* to study adventitious shoot formation.
	—	Invertase was perhaps the first enzyme used during 1940s in an immobilized state; the enzyme obtained by autolysis of yeast cells was immobilized by adsorption onto bone char.

1942	van Overbeak	Coconut milk containing a cell division factor was for the first used in *Datura*.
	Braun	Cultured crown gall *in vitro*.
1944	O.T. Avery, C.M. MacLeod and McCarty	Demonstrated that DNA is the transforming principle in *Diplococcus pneumoniae*.
	—	Large scale production of penicillin.
	S.A. Wakesman	Discovered streptomycin.
	Duggar	Discovered chlorotetramycin.
	F. Skoog	Reported shoot bud differentiation from tobacco pith tissues cultured *in vitro*.
1946	Ball	Regenerated whole plants of *Lupinus* and *Tropaeolum* from shoot-tip cultures.
1947	—	The Indian Patents and Designs come under the management of Controller of Patents and Designs.
	—	It was discovered that the bacterium *Thiobacillus ferrooxidans* induces leaching of copper sulphate from ores.
1948	Pauling	The transition state theory of enzyme action.
	Holmes	Recovered virus free plants of *Dahlia* from virus infected mother plants through shoot-tip cutting.
	—	Trademark protection is enforce since June 1, 1948 under the 1940 Act; this Act was amended as Indian Trade and Merchandise Marks Act (1958), which came enforce on November 25, 1959.
1950	Morgan and coworkers	Develop medium 119 with serum for animal cell and tissue culture.
	Ball	Reported organ regenerations from callus tissue of *Sequoia sempervirens*.
	—	Discovery of several antibiotics as wonder drugs.
1951	Pauling and Corey	Discovered the α-helix and β-sheet structure of enzymes.
	Ziebur and Brink	Reported beneficial effects of excised barley endosperm tissues placed around cultured young barley embryo.
1952	N.D. Zinder and J. Lederberg	Described transduction in *Salmonella*.
	A.D. Hershey and Chase	DNA is the genetic material in *E. coli* phage T_2.
	Morel and Martin	They excised 100 μm long meristems from virus infected plants of *Dahlia* and cultured them to obtain virus-free shoots.
	—	Birth of a calf by artificial insemination was achieved.
	—	Cloning of frog embryo cells was successfully done.
1953	J.D. Watson and F.H.C. Crick	Propose the double helix model of DNA.
	F. Sanger	Determined amino acid sequence of a protein (insulin).
	Tulecke	Reported occurrence of chromosomal variation in *Ginkgo biloba* cell culture derived from anther; haploid callus of *Ginkgo biloba* produced from pollen.
1954	G. Gammow	Proposes the codon to be a triplet.
	Trowell	Initially devised Grid method for animal organ culture.
	Muir and coworkers	First reported regeneration of plant from a single cell.
1955	Volkin and Astrachan	Existence of mRNA (studies on T_2 infected *E. coli*).
	H. Frankel-Conrate and R.C. Williams	Demonstrated that RNA is genetic material in TMV.

Year	Scientist	Contribution/Discovery
	F. Jacob and E.Z. Wollman	Reported bacterial conjugation involves transfer of a piece of DNA from donor to recipient cells.
	S. Ochoa and coworkers	*In vitro* synthesis of RNA.
	Eagle	Develop minimum essential medium (MEM) with serum for animal cell and tissue culture.
	R.A. Miller and coworkers	Discovered kinetin; enables initiation of callus cultures from differentiated tissue.
1956	A. Korenberg and coworkers	*In vitro* synthesis of DNA.
1957	V.M. Ingram	Presented first evidence that gene control the amino acid sequences of proteins.
	Parker and coworkers	Develop CMRL 1066 medium with serum for animal cell and tissue culture.
	Alick Issacs and Jean Lindemann	Discoverd interferon.
	F. Skoog and R.A. Miller	Reported that root and shoot differentiation in cultured pith tissue of tobacco was regulated by auxin-cytokenin ratio.
	—	The copyright law in India [The Indian Copyright Act (1957), ammended in 1999] are as per international standard.
1958	F.H.C. Crick	Propose the participation of an adopter (= tRNA) in protein synthesis; DNA (albeit via RNA) determines the amino acids; propose concept of central dogma.
	Maheshwary and Rangaswamy	Reported regeneration of somatic embryoes *in vitro* from the nucellus of *Citrus* ovules.
1958-59	Reinert and Steward (independently)	Reported development of somatic embryos from callus clump and cell suspension of carrot.
1959	S.B. Weiss, K. McQuillen, R.B. Robert anbd R.J. Britten	RNA polymerase activity in rats liver. *E. coli* ribosomes are site of protein synthesis.
	Braun	Regenerated first plant from mature plant cell.
	R.J. Gautheret	Published first handbook on Plant Tissue Culture.
	Street	Role of vitamins in root culture.
1960	S.B. Weiss	Discovered RNA polymerase activity.
	G. Morel	The technique of clonal propagation developed; used Knudson C medium for culturing shoot-tips and protocorms.
	E.C. Cocking	Produce large amounts of protoplasts using cell wall degrading enzyme cellulase, isolated from fungus *Myrothecium verrucaria.*
	Bergmann	Filtration of cell suspensions and isolation of single plant cells by plating.
	Jones and coworkers	Used microculture method for growing single plant cells in hanging drops in a conditional medium.
	W. Arber	The existence of restriction enzyme was postulated in 1960s.
1961	S.B. Weiss and T. Nakamoto	Isolated RNA polymerase.
	F. Jacob and J. Monod	Propose the operon concept of gene regulation, and the existence and function of RNA.
	G. von Ehrenstein and F. Lipman	Cell free system for protein synthesis.
	Thoday	Concept of QTL mapping was further eloborated.

	F.H.C. Crick, L. Barnett, S. Brenner and R.J. Watts-Tobin	Genetic code was 3 letter (= three bases together code for one amino acid); genetic code is non-overlapping, commaless and degenerate.
	M.W. Nirenberg and J.H. Mathaei	The meaning of first triplet codon, UUU encodes phenylalanine.
	—	The first international Union for Protection of New Plant Varieties (UPOV) convention was signed in Paris.
	Torrey and Reinert	Develop cell suspension culture procedure in plants.
1962	Kanta and coworkers	The first time reported successful test tube fertilization/*in vitro* pollination in *Papaver rhoeas.*
	Zuckerkandle and Pauling	Proposed that amino acid sequences of protein may be used to study evolutionary relationship among organisms.
	T. Murashige and F. Skoog	Develop MS nutrient medium for culture of plant cell/tissue.
	—	The process involving *Thiobacillus ferrooxidans* is being used for mining of Uranium in Canada.
1963	P.R. White	Develop white Medium for plant tissue culture.
1964	A.S. Sarabhai and coworkers; C. Yanofski and coworkers (independently)	Colinearity of genes and their products.
	Guha and Maheshwary	First time produced haploid plants from anther culture of *Datura.*
1965	R.W. Holley and coworkers	Complete base sequence of alanine transfer RNA of yeast synthesized *in vitro.*
	S. Brenner, A.O.W. Stretton and S. Kaplan	Deduced that UAG and UAA signal polypeptide chain termination.
	H. Harris and J.F. Watkins	Fusion of man and mouse cell using sendai virus.
	Ham	Develop F12 medium with serum for animal cell and tissue culture.
	Dryer and Bannett	First time propose the basic idea that organization of immunoglobulin genes and the mechanism generating the diversity are essentially a combination of both germline and somatic variation theories.
	Hugh Wallac and Max L. Birnstiel	For the first time ribosomal RNA genes were isolated from an amphibian, *Xenopus.*
	Vasil and Hilderbrandt	Cell has totipotency so it can divide and give rise to a whole plant.
	Eriksson	Develop Eriksson nutrient medium for plant tissue culture.
1966	S.B. Weiss and C.C. Richardson	Isolated DNA ligase.
	J. Adams and M. Cappecchi	N-formylmethionyl-tRNA functions as the initiator of polypeptide chain termination.
1967	H.G. Khorana and coworkers	Use synthetic polynucleotides of known repeating di- or tri-nucleotide sequences to resolve the genetic code.
	Moore and coworkers	Developm RPMI 1640 medium with serum for animal cell and tissue culture.
	van Wenzel	Initially dextron beads (Sephadex A-50) were used.
1968	Takebe and coworkers	Use both pectinase and cellulase enzymes to isolated mesophyll protoplasts. Both enzymes use subsequently *i.e.,* pectinase use preceded that of cellulase.
	Power and E.C. Cocking	Use both pectinase and cellulase enzymes simultaneously to isolate protoplasts.
	O.L. Gamborg and coworkers	Develop B_5 nutrient medium for plant tissue culture.
1969	Nitsch	Develop N_6 nutrient medium for plant tissue culture.

Year	Scientist	Contribution/Discovery
1970	H.O. Smith, K.W. Wilcox and T.J. Kelley	Isolated and characterized the first restriction endonuclease enzyme, *Hind*III.
	H.G. Khorana and 12 coworkers	Total synthesis of gene for an alanine tRNA from yeast.
	D. Baltimore and H.M. Temin	Discovered reverse transcriptase in two oncogenic RNA viruses.
	Krishnamurthi and coworkers	In Fiji, isolated sugarcane variants that showed improved resistance to Fiji disease, caused by an aphid-transmitted virus and downy mildew (casual agent *Sclerospora sacchari*).
	—	The Indian Patent Act (1970) was introduced in the Parliament in 1965, was modified in 1967 and was passed in 1970; this Act did not allow patents in pharmaceuticals, foods and agrochemicals; this Act has now been amended as Indian Patents (amended) Act (1999); the new Act allows products patents, except for some specific medicines/drugs.
	—	The Plant Variety Protection Act of 1970 is U.S. version of the plant breeder's rights followed by European Union and several other countries.
	—	Discussion on the possible hazards of cloning recombinant DNA molecules began in early 1970s.
1971	K. Dona and D. Nathans	First time prepared restriction map of SV40 genome.
	Takebe and coworkers	Regeneraed plants from protoplasts.
	Heinz and Mee	The first morphological variation in plants generated from cell cultures concerned those of sugarcane.
1972	R. Silber, V.G. Malathi and J. Hurwitz	Discover RNA ligase.
	D.A. Jackson, R.H. Symons and P. Berg	Produced first recombinant DNA molecule by joining DNA of SV40 and phage λ using restriction enzyme.
	P.S. Carlson, H.H. Smith and R.D. Dearing	The first somatic hybrid plants produced by fusion of the protoplast of *Nicotiana glauca* and *N. longsdorfi*.
	Lobban and Kaiser	Develop a procedure in which appropriate enzyme can be added to fill in any single-stranded gap and use of DNA ligase to join the two fragments which giving rise to recombinant DNA.
1973	Herbert Boyer and Stanley Cohen	Technique of Lobban and Kaiser was used to develop hybrid plasmid-insertion of EcoRI fragment of DNA molecule into circular plasmid DNA of bacteria using DNA ligase. Gene from African clawed toad inserted into plasmid DNA of bacteria.
	W. Fiers, W.M. Jou, G. Haegerman and M.Y. Ysebaert	First to sequence a gene encoding a protein; the coat-protein gene of the male-specific phage MS2.
	P.S. Carlson	The first report of selection for disease resistance (resistance to *Pseudomonas syringae* pv. *tabacci*), using methionine sylfoximine as selection agent by exploiting gametoclonal variation.
	Pierik and coworkers	Found that cytokinin is capable of breaking dormancy in excised capitulum explants of Gerbera.
1974	J. Shine and L. Dalgarno	Discover Shine-Dalgarno sequence at the 3′-end of *E. coli* 16*S* rRNA, which is complementary to the ribosome binding sites of mRNA.
	Zaenen and coworkers	Discovered tumour inducing plasmid *i.e.,* Ti plasmid, of *Agrobacterium tumefaciens.*
	—	First expression of a gene from a different species in a bacterium.

	Reinchard	Reported biotransformation in plant tissue cultures.
	Binding	Produce haploid *Petunia hybrida* plants from protoplast.
	—	National Insitute of Health (NIH), U.S.A. established the Recombinant Advisory Committee (RAC).
1975	G. Köhler and C. Milstein	Develop the hyridoma technology for the production of monoclonal antibody.
	M. Grunstein and D.S. Hogness	Develop technique of colony hybridization.
	D. Pribnow	Develop a model for prokaryotic promoter structure.
	E.M. Southern	Southern blotting and hybridization technique.
	F. Sanger and A.R. Coulson	Enzymatic method of DNA sequencing was developed.
	O' Farrel	Develop high resolution two dimensional gel electrophoresis procedure, which led to the development of proteomics.
	—	In February 1975, an international meeting was convended at Asilomar, California; the conclusions from the conference were as follows : (*i*) Certain experiments should be deferred, (*ii*) most of work on recombinant DNA could proceed with appropriate safety measures, (*iii*) potential risks were assigned to different types of experiments and (*iv*) such safe bacteria and plasmids that could not survive in the environment, if they escaped from the laboratory, should be developed.
	—	The first guidelines about research on recombinant DNA experiments were prepared; they were more strict than the recommendation of the Asilomar Conference; the guidelines were revised after two years; these had major changes and were much less restrictive about conditions for conducting experiments. The guidelines specified types of research, often according to the organisms, and the described the physical and biological principles of containment.
	Gengenbach and Green	Reported positive *in vitro* selection of maize callus cultures, show resistant to T toxin of *Helminthosporium maydis.*
1976	M.F. Gilbert and coworkers	Discover DNA gyrase and its functions.
	B.G. Borrel and coworkers	Overlapping genes in phage ϕX176.
	Tonegawa and Hozumi	Presented first direct evidence for Dryer and Bennette model, *i.e.,* germline and somatic variation theories are responsible for generating antibodies.
	Bomhoff and coworkers	Reported that octopine and nopaline synthesis and breakdown found to be genetically controlled by the Ti plasmid of *Agrobacterium tumefaciens.*
	—	NIH, U.S.A. issues guidelines regulating recombinant DNA research.
	San Noem	First reported gynogenesis in barley.
	Park and coworkers	Develop 100 lines through each of the three procedures, *viz.,* SSD (F_6), pedigree (visual selection; F_6) and DH (haploids obtained through interspecific hybridization with *Hordeum bulbosum* from two barley crosses).
	Seibert	Reported shoot regeneration from cryopreserved shoot apices of carnation.
1977	C. Jacq, J.R. Miller and G.G. Brownlee	Discover pseudogenes within the 5*S* DNA cluster of *Xenopus laevis.*

Year	Scientist	Contribution/Discovery
	J.C. Alwine, D.J. Kemp and G.R. Stark	Develop the technique of northern blotting.
	F. Sanger and coworkers	Base sequence of the complete genome of ϕX174.
	A.M. Maxam and W. Gilbert	Develop chemical method of DNA sequencing based on degradation of DNA chain.
	P.A. Sharp and R.J. Roberts	Discover split genes
	D.S. Hogness and coworkers	Reported introns in some 28*S* rRNA genes of *Drosophila melanogaster.*
	A. Jefferes and R.A. Flawell	Disover introns in rabbit betaglobin gene.
	P. Chambdon	Introns in chicken ovalbumin gene.
	J. Collins and Bolm	Develop cosmid.
	—	The NIH, U.S.A. prepared an Environmental Impact Standard (EIS), which estimated the possible undesirable impacts of experiments and the likelihood of their occurrence based on probabilities of creating and dispersing potentially hazardous agents.
	—	It was clarified by the U.S. Court of Customs and Appeals that a natural product *per se* could not be patented, but a patent could be claimed for any new form or composition, this interpretation permitted the patenting of purified natural compounds like azadirachtin (purified from neem).
1978	W. Gilbert	Coins the term introns and exons.
	T. Maniatis and others	First genomic library for gene isolation.
	Y.W. Kan and A.M. Dozy	Use RFLP for prenatal diagnosis of sickle cell anaemia.
	C.A. Hutchinson and coworkers	Site-directed mutagenesis in isolated DNA.
	—	The genes (DNA sequences for chain A and B) of insulin were synthesized separately as early as 1978.
	—	Bacteria produce human somatostatin from a synthetic gene.
	—	The first baby named Louise Joy was born on July 25, 1978 by *in vitro* fertilization and embryo transfer followed by normal development of fetus.
	—	Under the UPOV 1978 Act, all new varieties evolved using a protected variety where exempted from protection under this provision, there was explicit provision for farmers privilege.
	—	The European Patent Convention (EPC) began to operate in 1978; it has 17 member states (countries).
1979	H.G. Khorana	Reported completion of the total synthesis of a biologically functional tyrosine suppressor t-RNA gene carrying all regulatory sequences.
	D.V. Goeddel and coworkers	Using recombinant DNA technology, prepared a gene construct encoding human growth hormone (hGH) and express it in *E. coli;* a hGH-like polypeptide produced.
	M.R. Lerner and J.A. Steitz	Discover small nuclear RNAs.
	Morton and coworkers	Develop co-cultivation procedure for the transformation of protoplasts with *Agrobacterium.*
	—	The first animal vector was devised from the primate papova virus; simian virus 40 (SV40); it was used for cloning in 1979.

	—	Twin lambs born through artificial embryo splitting.
1980	J.W. Gordon and coworkers	Developed first transgenic mice.
	C. Weismann and coworkers	Published the nucleotide sequence of first interferon-α (IFN-α) gene derived from cloned IFNα cNDA.
	Botstein and coworkers	Developed RFLP technique.
	C. Weismann	Produced human interferon in bacteria.
	—	Eli Lilly International Corporation began commercial production of insulin through genetic engineering in *E. coli.*
	—	Marketing of human food of fungal origin in U.K.
	—	Gene synthesis machine was developed in 1980s.
	—	The European Molecular Biology Laboratory (EMBL) established their data library to collect, organize and distribute nucleotide sequence data and related information. This function is now performed by the European Bioinformatics Institute (EBI), Hinxton, U.K.
	—	During 1980s, the National Centre for Bioinformatics Information (NCBI) was established in USA; NCBI serves primary information databank and provider of information.
	—	The American Supreme Court ruled that a live, human-made (genetically engineered) microorganism can be patented under the American patent law as a manufacture or composition of matter (Diamond *vs.* Chakraborty).
	—	The first patent to a microorganism was allowed by the American Supreme Court.
	Shepard and coworkers	Reported their finding on the variants isolated from the American potato variety Russet Burbank.
	Zambryski and coworkers	Studied the structure of T-DNA by cloning complete EcoRI digest of T37 tobacco crown gall DNA into phage vector, allow the isolation and study of T-DNA border sequences.
	Alferman and coworkers	Use immobilized whole cells for biotransformation of digitoxin into digoxin.
1981	T.R. Cech, A.J. Zaug and P.J. Grabuski	Discover self-splicing rRNA in *Tetrahymena thermophila.*
	S. Anderson and 13 others	Complete base sequence and organization of human mitochondrial genome.
	Larkin and Scowcroft	Introduced the term somaclonal variation; use to describe the variants obtained from cell cultures of geranium and potato protoplasts; it has replaced the earlier term like caliclone, protoclone.
	—	The use of monoclonal antinbodies for dignosis approved in U.S.A.
	—	A patent was allowed in European Union for a microorganism by EPO.
	—	Most cloning experiments in *E. coli* K12, certain strains of *Bacillus subtilis* and *Saccharomyces cerevisiae* was considered exempt from other requirements of NIH guidelines.
1982	Krens and coworkers	Reported that protoplasts are capable of receiving naked DNA; leads to transformation of isolated naked DNA.
	Fujita and coworkers	Shikonin is the first example of biochemical production from cultured plant cells.

Year	Scientist	Contribution/Discovery
	—	First transgenic animal Knockout mice produced.
	—	ELi Lily International Corporation is first to market insulin, produced by genetically engineered bacteria; insulin is marked as Humulin; to be approved for use in Britain and USA.
	—	A major revision of the NIH guidelines was effected 1982; containment level were lowered, and experiments, that were previously prohibited, including deliberate release of recombinant DNA-containing organisms into the environment, were change to category requiring review and approval by NIH. In addition, institutional biosafety committees were delegated the powers to approve all but few experiments, and to instruct investigators in containment conditions recommended and described in the guidelines.
	—	The importance of biotechnology was highlighted by the 69th session of the Indian Science Congress held at Mysore. As a consequence, the Government of India constituted a National Biotechnology Board (NTBT) to encourage and coordinate research activities in biotechnology.
	—	The Government of Philippines implemented the National *Azolla* Action Programme (NAAP) to develop farm-based technology for the use of *Azolla* as an organic fertilizers for irrigated low land rice field.
1983	—	The concrete effort in international hormonization of patent laws was the Paris Convention for the Protection of Industrial Property signed in 1983; it has 100 member states.
	—	India was a signatory to the International Undertaking on Plant Genetic Resources develop by the FAO; it was adopted by 112 countries; this undertaking was based on the concept that plant genetic resources were the common heritage of mankind.
	E.A. Miele, D.R. Mills and F.R. Kramer	Produced first recombinant RNA molecule.
	A. Murray and J. Szostak	Constructed the first working artificial chromosome.
	J. Gusella and coworkers	Developed gene probes to detect Huntington's disease and locate a genetic marker for Huntington's disease on chromosome 4.
	—	Approval for the use of insulin produced by genetically engineered microbes in U.S.A. and U.K.
	E.L. Herrera-Estella, A. Depicker, M. Van Montagu and J. Schel	First transgenic plant containing kanamycin resistance gene was produced by transformation of tobacco with *Agrobacterium*.
1984	—	Animal inferon produced by GEMS approved for the protection of cattle against diseases.
	—	The idea of genome sequencing was discussed in the scientific community in 1984 onwards.
	—	The National Biomedical Research Foundation established the Protein Information Resource (PIR) in 1984; PIR helps researchers in the identification and interpretation of protein sequence information.
	Evans and coworkers	The term gametoclonal variation was introduced for the variability among pollen-derived cells/plants but *this term is only occasionally used.*

1985	C.W. Greider and E.H. Blackburn	Isolated telomerase from *Tetrahymena pyriformis*.
	R.K. Saiki, K.B. Mullis and five others	Discover polymerase chain reaction to amplify β-globin gene fragments *in vitro*.
	Alec Jeffreys	Use term DNA fingerprinting, and develop the technique of DNA fingerprinting to identify individuals by analysing polymorphism at DNA level.
	Oliver Smithies	For the first time technique of targetted gene transfer was successfully used to disrupt the human β-globin gene in cultured cells.
	—	The first plant, a maize line overproducing trytophan was allowed patent in USA.
	—	Herbicide resistance transgenic develop.
	—	Attempt to produce transgenic fish started.
	—	Software LINKAGE was used for the preparation of several linkage maps.
	—	The Utility Patent Act (1985) was originally meant to cover man-made industrial inventions and processes.
	G.P. Smith	He opened a new area of functional genomics by developing a filamentous fusion phage vector to display cloned antigen expression on virion surface.
1986	Cech	Discovered catalytic RNA, *i.e.,* ribozyme.
	Lerner and Schutlz	Developed catalytic antibodies.
	Powell-Abel and coworkers	TMV resistant tobacco transgenic plants were developed using cDNA of coat protein gene of TMV.
	—	First field trial of transgenic plant approved in USA and Europe.
	M.C. Shih, G. Lazar and H.M. Goodman	In higher plants, nuclear genes encoding chloroplast glyceroldehyde-3-phosphate dehydrogenase are derived from the genomes of symboints, which gave rise to chloroplasts.
	—	The transgenic ewes were born in early summer of 1986.
	—	Method of DNA sequencing automated.
	—	A proposal was prepared for sequencing of human genome.
	—	The first release of a recombinant microorganism in environment was done.
	B. Horvitz	Proposed programmed cell death during development of the nematode worm.
	—	In India, a separate Department of Biotechnology (DBT) was created within the Ministry of Science and Techonology.
	Feidt and Foroughi-Wehr	The performance of barley lines developed through pedigree selection and DH (anther culture) technique were compared.
	Snape and coworkers	The relative merit of anther culture and interspecific hybridization with *Hordeum bulbosum* has been examined in some detail.
1987	Thomas H. Roderick	Introduced the term genomics.
	P. Ledev and T. Steward	Developed oncomouse; Harvard University receives the patent for oncomouse; first U.S. patent for a genetically altered animals.
	Sanford and coworkers Klein and coworkers	Both group develop biolistic gene transfer method for transformation of plants.

Year	Scientist	Contribution/Discovery
	Barton and coworkers	Isolated *cry* gene from bacterium, *Bacillus thuringiensis* and transferred it into *N. tobacum* which provided resistance against lepidoptern insects.
	—	Cotton transformation.
	—	USDA/APHIS propose guidelines for field testing of transgenic plants.
	D.C. Wraith and coworkers	Proposed that the nucleoprotein of influenza virus can be used as universal vaccine for influenza.
	—	An International Centre for Genetic Engineering and Biotechnology has been established by the UNO; it has two centres; one centre is located at Trieste, Italy while other is located in New Delhi, India; In India, this centre began operate in 1987.
1988	—	Soybean transformation.
	—	Rice transformation.
	—	Ripening control in tomato.
	—	Antisense RNA technology in plants.
	Paterson and coworkers	One of the first published reports of QTL mapping with DNA marker involved fruit size, fruit pH and soluble solids in tomato.
	Okamura	Produce 'Pomato' by fusion of potato and tomato mesophyll protoplasts.
	J.P. Simons	Published first reports on transgenic sheep.
	A.F. Francoeur	Develop autoantibody fingerprinting.
	—	The National Institute of Health (NIH), Bethesda, Maryland, U.S.A. established an office of Human Genome Project with James Watson as its director.
	—	The European Commission proposed a Council Directive on the Legal Protection of Biotechnology Inventions; this directive seeks patent protection for biological materials, including plants and animals.
	—	The progress of biofertilizers exploitation in Asian countries was survey by FAO.
1989	—	Journal of Science (U.S.A.) recognised that PCR is the major scientific development of the year and chosen *Taq* DNA polymerase used in PCR is the molecule of the year 1989.
	—	The first successful transformation of chloroplast in higher plants.
	—	Despite the provision of *Article 53(b)* of EPC, the first patent on a plant was awarded in 1989 by European Patent Office (EPO).
	—	In India, the Ministry of Environment and Forests promulgated in December 1989, the rules and procedure for the manufacture, import, use, research and release of GMOs as well as product made from such organism.
	—	The Consultative Group on International Agricultural Research (CGIAR) treated a taskforce on biotechnology (BIOTASK).

1990	Williams and coworkers	Develop RAPD marker.
	—	First transgenic in maize is produced.
	Ingo Potrykus	In early 1990s began a research programme that would focus on development of 'golden rice'; over a period of seven years, Potrykus colleague Peter Beyer and other workers incorporated seven transgenes into rice genome that would enable plant to synthesize beta-carotane and iron in the grain.
	R.M. Blaese and coworkers	Allowed somatic cell therapy.
	J.C. Sanford and W. Wolf	Transferred gene through bioslistic method.
	—	European community directive on deliberate release and commercialization of transgenic plants.
	—	The Human Genome Project officially began on October 1, 1990.
	—	Mammalian artificial chromosomes (MACs) and human artificial chromosomes (HACs) have been developed.
	C. Mariani and coworkers	Successfully produce transgenic male sterility in *Brassica napus* using a gene construct having anther specific promoter (*TA29* gene from tobacco) and *barnase* gene from *Bacillus amyloliquefaciens.*
	—	First successful gene therapy for SCID in USA.
	—	The Indian Recombinant DNA Safety Guidelines and Regulations have been prepared initially in 1990.
	—	China become the first country to begin commercial use of virus resistance transgenic tobacco and tomato in the early 1990s.
	Griffith and coworkers	Culture nodal cutting from virus infected potato plants on MS medium containing 0.8 mM virazola; plants recovered from these cultures were free from potato virus X (PVX), PVS, and PVM.
1991	Fodor	Develop DNA microassay system using light directed chemical synthesis.
	Prof. A. Dutta (of JNU)	Dutta's laboratory reported for the first time cloning and characterization of the oxalate decarboxylase gene which degrades and will reduce the content of oxalate or oxalic acid.
	—	In the Netherlands, a technique has been developed for *in vitro* embryo production.
	—	The Informal Working Group on Biosafety, the main body of UN on biosafety, issued the draft voluntary code of conduct for Release of Organisms into the Environment.
	—	In India, patent for all the transgenic cotton granted to Agracetus (Revoked but still effective till all the appeals are exhausted).
	—	UPOV 1991 Act somewhat limited the scope of breeder's exemption by bringing 'essentially-derived' varieties under the cover of PBR protection granted to the initial variety; farmer privilege has been made 'optional' and each UPOV member state (country) can either allow or disallow this privilege.
	J. Craig Ventor	Develop strategy to find expressed genes with ESTs.
1992	C. Mariani and coworkers	Produce transgenic fertility restorer (*Barnase/barstar*) using a gene construct having anther specific promoter (*TA29* gene from tobacco) and *barstar* gene from *Bacillus amyloliquefaciens.*

Year	*Scientist*	*Contribution/Discovery*
	—	First transgenic in wheat is developed.
	—	Transgenic for modified fatty acid composition is produced.
	Prof. A. Dutta (of JUN)	Dutta's laboratory reported for the first time isolation of gene from *Amaranthus* that encodes a seed specific protein rich in all essential amino acids; composition of this protein correspond to that of WHO recommended protein standard for the optimum human nutrition.
	—	Regulations for deliberate release of GMOs established in USA.
	—	First complete base sequence of a chromosome *i.e.,* yeast chromosome III was discovered.
	—	European Patent Office awarded a patent for oncomouse.
	—	The most widely discussed case concerns patent protection of all kinds of transgenic cotton granted in October, 1992 to Agracetus (Middleton, U.S.A.) a subsidiary to W.R. Grace and Co.
	—	Over 400 field tests of transgenic varieties performed worldwide.
	—	USDA/APHIS deregulates controlled ripening tomato.
	—	USDA/APHIS established framework for food safety evalu ation.
	—	FDA established framework for food safety evaluation.
1993	—	First human gene therapy trial in U.K.; gene therapy for SCID and cystic fibrosis began U.K.
	—	During 1993, UPOV had 24 member states.
	—	India and 172 other nations signed the International Convention on Biological Diversity (CBD) on December 29, 1993; this treaty recognizes the sovereign rights of nations over their genetic resources.
	—	US Patent on insect resistant transgenic plants issued.
	—	National Research Centre on Plant Biotechnology came into operation in 1993.
	Kranz and coworkers	Although gametic fusion was achieved in 1990, but complete plant regeneration was achieved in 1993.
1994	—	Flavr Savr become the first transgenic variety (of tomato) to reach market and commercially cultivated in U.S.A.
	—	A germplasm bank of AMF (arbuscular mycorrhizal fungi) cultures was established at Tata Energy Research Institute, New Delhi.
	—	The Indian Recombinant DNA Safety Guidelines and Regulation is revised.
	—	The International Agricultural Research Centre under the CGIAR system have placed their global germplasm collection under the auspices of FAO upon joining the International Network of *ex situ* collection through an agreement signed on October, 1994.
	—	The patent granted for all the transgenic cotton to Agracetus in India was challenged by ICAR and DBT, New Delhi, and the USPTO revoked it in December 1994 as a consequence of its re-examination. However, the final position of this revocation

		will be clear only after Agracetus (USA) has exhausted all the opportunities of appeal against it, and till such time the patent will be effective and operative.
1995	R.D. Fleischmann and coworkers	The first genome to be sequenced was that of *Haemophilus influenzac;* announced by Institute for Genomic Research.
	Vos and coworkers	Develop technique of DNA fingerprinting based on amplified fragment length polymorphism (AFLP).
	—	The field trials of transgenic plants started in India.
	—	The Trade Related Intellectual Property Rights (TRIPs) agreement which forms a part of the Uruguay Round of GAAT (signed by India and other states) is to date the most comprehensive multi-lateral agreement on IPR; it become effective on January 1, 1995.
1996	—	A carnation transgenic variety with longer vase-life developed by cosuppression of its ACC synthase gene. This delayed senescence variety was to be release in 1996.
	—	In Britain, gentically engineered tomato marketed.
	A. Goffeau and coworkers	The first eukaryotic genome to be sequenced was that of yeast (*Saccharomyces cerevisiae*).
1997	Ewan Bilmuit	First cloned mammal, 'Dolly' was produced from a single udder cell.
	Blatter and coworkers	The *E. coli* genome was completely sequenced.
	—	Transgenic carnation was approved for commercial cultivation in Australia; the vase-life of flower by 200%.
	—	A patent entitled 'Basmati Rice Line and Grain' for a novel, high yielding, medium dwarf, photoinsenstive rice having all the desirable features of basmati rice was awarded to Rice Tech, Texas (U.S.A.) in USA on Sept. 2, 1997 (Patent No. 5663484).
1998	—	In USA, a patent entitled Control of Plant Gene Expression was granted jointly to USDA and Delta and Pineland Company on March 3, 1998.
	—	India joined the Paris Convention on Dec. 7, 1998.
	—	The European Parliament has approved provision for patenting of DNA sequences where a use or technological process is specified.
	R. Waterston and J.E. Sulston	Genome of worm, *Caenorhabditis elegans* sequenced.
1999	—	India has enacted the Geographical Indication (GI) Act 1999 to claim GI for a variety of goods including, basmatic rice; GI protection is recognized under the provision of TRIPs of GAAT (1944).
2000	—	Genome of *Arabidopsis thaliana* sequenced by The *Arabidopsis* Initiative (TAI).
	—	Rough draft of human genome sequence prepared and announced on June 26, 2000.
	—	Automated DNA sequencing and more refine technique enabled the preparation of draft sequence of genome in 2000.
	—	In India, permitted cultivation of insect resistant transgenic cotton varieties.

Year	*Scientist*	*Contribution/Discovery*
	—	Computer software has been included in the list of copyright properties [Protected under the Information Technology Act (2000)].
	—	At the end of 2000, there were 281 databases related to bioinformatics.
2001	—	About 93.5% of the human genome had been sequenced, of which only 32.5% is finished, while the remaining 61% is as draft.
	—	Sequencing of human genome successfully completed jointly by Human Genome Project Consortium, and Ventor workers of Celera Genomics.
	—	The complete sequence of human genome was obtained in 2001, much before the project.
	—	In India, the Protection of Plant Varieties and Farmer's Right (PPVFR) Act 2001 was passed. On August 9, 2001 by the Lok Sabha; this Act aims to provide for the establishment of an effective system for protection of plant varieties, the rights of farmers and plant breeders and to encourage the development of new varieties of plants.
2002	—	Four countries, *viz.,* U.S.A., Argentina, Canada and China, grew 99% of total global area under transgenic crops.
	—	India has enacted the Biological Diversity Act (2002) and created a National Biodiversity Authority (NBA), Chennai.
	Shekhawat and coworkers	Develop a regeneration protocol for *Azadirechta indica.*
	—	MAHYCO released three Bt cotton hybrids (MECH12, MECH 162 and MECH 184) for commercial cultivation in India.
	R.H. Waterston and coworkers	Sequenced mouse genome.
	—	Released of world's first cloned cat.
2003	—	The complete sequence of human genome euchromatin became available.
2006	G.A. Tuskan and coworkers	Sequenced popular genome.
2007	R. Velasco and coworkers	Sequenced grape genome.
2008	R. Ming and coworkers	Sequenced papaya genome.
	D.G. Gibson and coworkers	Synthesized genome of *Mycoplasma genitalium.*
	—	The Human Fertilization and Embryo Bill approved in U.K.; will now make it legal to create GM embryos for research but bans implantation of such embryos in the womb.
2009	—	World's first blue rose approved for commercial cultivation in Australia.

APPENDIX III

A Chronological List of the Scientists Awarded Nobel Prize for Discoveries in Biotechnology and Related Areas

Year of award	*Name of scientist(s)*	*Work for which awarded*
1901	E. von Behring	Studies on antiserum therapy.
1930	K. Landsteiner	Studies in immunology.
1933	T.H. Morgan	*Drosophila* genetics, including sex-linkage and linkage, *i.e.*, development of theory of gene.
1935	H. Spemann	Studies on embryonic induction.
1945	A. Fleming, E.B. Chain, and H.W. Florey	Discovery, purification and chemical characterization of penicillin.
1946	H.J. Muller	Discovery of mutagenic action of X-rays in *Drosophila melanogaster.*
	J.B. Sumner	Crystallisation of enzymes.
	W.M. Stanley	Purification and chemical characterization of viruses.
1952	A.J.P. Martin and R.L.M. Synge	In chemistry; for chromatography technique.
	S.A. Waksman	For the discovery of streptomycin, the first antibiotic effective against tuberculosis.
1954	J.F. Enders, T.H. Weller and F.C. Robbins	Ability of poliomyelitis viruses to grow in cultures of various types of tissues.
1957	A. Todd	Studies on the structure of nucleosides and nucleotides.
1958	G.W. Beadle, E.L. Tatum and J. Lederberg	*Neurospora* biochemical genetics (Beadle, Tatum) and bacterial conjugation (Tatum, Lederberg).
	F. Sanger	Studies on protein chemistry.
1959	S. Ochoa and A. Kornberg	*In vitro* synthesis of DNA (Kornberg) and RNA (Ochoa).
1960	P.B. Medawar and F.M. Burnet	Discovery of acquired immunological tolerance.
1962	J.D. Watson, F.H.C. Crick, and M.H.F. Wilkins	The double helix model of DNA (studies on DNA structure).
1962	M.F. Perutz and J.C. Kendrew	Studies on the structures of haemoglobin and myoglobin.
1965	F. Jacob, J. Monod, and A. Lwoff	Operon concept of gene regulation (Jacob and Monod); microbial genetics (Lwoff).
1966	P. Rouse	Studies on oncogenic viruses.
1968	M.W. Nirenberg, Hargovind Khorana and R.W. Holley	Deciphering of genetic code (Nirenberg, Khorana, Holley) and *in vitro* synthesis of DNA/gene (Khorana).
1969	M. Delbrück, S.E. Luria and A.D. Hershey	Contributions to viral genetics.
1970	N.E. Borlaug	Development of semi-dwarf varieties of wheat.
1972	G.M. Edelman and R.R. Porter	Studies on chemical structure of antibodies.
1974	A. Claude, C. de Duve and G. Palade	Contributions to cell biology.
1975	R. Dulbecco, H. Temin and D. Baltimore	Studies on oncogenic viruses (reverse transcription).
1977	R. Yalow	Development of radioimmunoassay procedure.

Year of award	*Name of scientist(s)*	*Work for which awarded*
1978	H.O. Smith, D. Nathans and W. Arber	Development of techniques utilizing restriction endonucleases for the study of genetic organization.
1980	P. Berg, W. Gilbert and F. Sanger	In chemistry : for experimental manipulation of DNA, including production of recombinant DNA.
	G.D. Snell, J. Dausset and B. Benacerraf	In physiology and Medicine; for contributions to immuno-genetics.
1982	A. Klug	Analysis of crystalline structures of biological importance, especially virus particles, tRNA and nucleosomes.
1983	B. McClintock	Discovery of transposable elements (*Ac* and *Ds*) in maize.
1984	N.K. Jerne, G. Köhler and C. Milstein	Contributions to immunology, including hybridoma technology.
	R.B. Merrifield	In chemistry; automated peptide synthesis.
1985	M.S. Brown and J.L. Goldstein	Identification of low density lipoprotein receptor pathway; familial hypercholesterolemia is a genetic defect in this pathway.
1986	E. Ruska	Designing of first electron microscope.
1987	S. Tonegawa	Genetic mechanism that generates antibody diversity.
1988	Sir J.W. Black, G.B. Elion and G.H. Hichings	Development of drug propranolol; used for the treatment of heart attack and hypertension.
1989	J.M. Bishop and H.E. Varmus	In Medicine; studies on oncogenes of retroviruses.
	T.R. Cech and S. Altman	In chemistry; enzymatic RNAs (= ribozymes).
1990	Murray and Thomas	Organ and cell transplantation.
1992	E.H. Fischer and E.G. Krebs	Discoveries concerning reversible protein phosphorylation as a biological regulatory mechanism.
1993	K.B. Mullis	In chemistry; invention of the PCR method.
	M. Smith	In chemistry; fundamental contributions to the establishment of oligonucleotide-based, site-directed mutagenesis and its development for protein studies.
	R.J. Roberts and P.A. Sharp	For the discovery of split genes.
1994	A.G. Gilman and Martin Rodbell	Discovery of G-proteins and the role of these proteins in signal transduction in cells.
1995	E.B. Lewis, C. Nüsslein-Volhard and E.F. Wieschaus	The discoveries concerning the genetic control of early embryonic development.
1996	Doherty and Zinkernagel	Discovery of cell mediated immune defence.
1997	S.B. Prusiner	The discovery of prions; a new biological principle of infection.
1999	G. Blobel	The discovery that proteins have intrinsic signals that govern their transport and localisation in the cell.
2000	Carlsson, Greengard and Kandel	Discovery of signal transduction in the nervous system.
2001	L.H. Hartwell, R.T. Hunt and Sir P.M. Nurse	Discoveries of the key regulators of the cell cycle.
2002	Sidney Brenner, H.R. Horvitz and J.E. Sulston	Discoveries concerning genetic regulation of organ development and programmed cell death.
	J.B. Fenn	In chemistry; development of methods for identification and structure analyses of biological macromolecules.
2004	A. Ciechanover, A. Hershko and I. Rose	In chemistry; for the discovery of ubiquitin mediated protein degradation.
2006	Andrew Z. Fire and Craig C. Mello	In medicine; how RNA interference can switch genes on or off.
	R.D. Kornberg	In chemistry; for the study of molecular basis of eukaryotic transcription.

2007	M.J. Evans and O. Smithies	In medicine; production of Knock-out mice
2008	O. Shimomura, M. Chalfie and R.Y. Tsien	In chemistry; discovery and development of the green fluorescent protein (GFP).
	H. zur Hausen	In medicine; for the finding of human papilloma viruses causing cervical cancer.
	F. Barre-Sinoussi and L. Montagnier	In medicine; for discovery of human immunodeficiency virus.
2009	E.H. Blackburn, C.W. Greider and J.W. Szostak	In medicine; how chromosomes are protected by telomere and telomerase enzyme.
	Venkataraman Ramakrishanan, T.A. Steitz and A.E. Yonath	In chemistry; for studies of the structure and function of ribosomes.

APPENDIX IV

Sobriquets (Nick-names)

Sobriquet	*Entity/Event*
Drosophila of plant kingdom	*Arabidopsis thaliana*
Genetic bit	Nucelotide
Genetic parasite	T-DNA
Jumping genes	Transposons
Molecular glue	DNA ligase
Natural genetic engineer	*Agrobacterium tumefaciens*
People's choice reaction	Polymerase chain reaction
Queen of genetics	*Drosophila melanogastor*
Stress hormone	Abscisic acid
DNA scissor	Restriction enzyme

APPENDIX V

DBT Sponsored Regular Teaching and Training Courses in Biotechnology in Different Universities/Institutions in India (as on 01.01.2001)

University/Institution	*Year of start*	*Annual intake*
M.Sc. General Biotechnology (2 year course)		
1. Jawaharlal Nehru University, New Delhi	1985-86	20
2. Madurai Kamaraj University, Madurai	1985-86	20
3. MS University, Baroda	1985-86	20
4. University of Poona, Pune	1985-86	20
5. Banaras Hindu University, Varanasi	1986-87	12
6. Indian Institute of Technology, Mumbai	1987-88	10
7. Roorkee University, Roorkee	1991-92	10
8. Aligarh Muslim University, Aligarh	1991-92	10
9. Guru Nanak Dev University, Amritsar	1991-92	10
10. Devi Ahilya Viswavidyalaya, Indore	1991-92	10

11. University of Hyderabad, Hyderabad	1991-92	10
12. Himachal Pradesh University, Shimla	1994-95	10
13. University of Calicut, Kerala	1994-95	12
14. Banasthali Vidyapeeth, Banasthali, Rajasthan (for girls only)	1994-95	10
15. Tezpur University, Tezpur	1998-99	12
16. Gulberga University, Gulbarga	1998-99	10
17. Jammu University, Jammu	1999-2000	10
18. Gujarat University, Ahmedabad	1999-2000	10
19. Mysore University, Mysore	1999-2000	10
20. University of Allahabad, Allahabad	1999-2000	12
21. Guru Jambeshwar University, Hisar	2000-2001	10
22. University of Kashmir, Srinagar	2000-2001	10
23. Kumaun University, Nainital	2000-2001	10
M.Sc. Agricultural Biotechnology (2 years)		
1. Assam Agricultural University, Jorhat	1988-89	10
2. Tamil Nadu Agricultural University, Coimbatore	1988-89	10
3. GB Pant University of Agriculture and Technology, Pantnagar	1988-89	10
4. Birsa Agricultural University, Ranchi	1999-2000	12
5. Himachal Pradesh Krishi Vishavavidhalaya, Palampur	1999-2000	05
6. Indira Gandhi Agricultural University, Raipur	2000-2001	10
7. Marathwada Agricultural University, Parbhani	2000-2001	10
Master in Medical Biotechnology (2 years)		
1. All India Institute of Medical Sciences, New Delhi	1986-87	10
M.Sc. Marine Biotechnology (2 years)		
1. Goa University, Goa	1988-89	10
M.Sc. Neurosciences (3 years)		
1. Tata Institute of Fundamental Research, Mumbai	2000-2001	
M.Tech/M.Sc. (Tech.) Biochemical Engineering and Biotechnology *(5 years integrated/3 semesters/1.5 year course)*		
1. Indian Institute of Technology, Kharagpur	1986-87	10
2. Indian Institute of Technology, New Delhi (Now converted into a 5 year integrated course since 1993-94)	1986-87	10
3. Anna University, Chennai	1991-92	15
4. University Institute of Chemical Technology, Mumbai	1993-94	10
Post-Doctoral Research and Training Programme (2 years)		
1. Indian Institute of Science, Bangalore	1986-87	15
2. Centre for Cellular and Molecular Biology, Hyderabad	1988-89	12
3. Bose Institute, Calcutta	1989-90	6
4. Indian Agricultural Research Institute, New Delhi	1994-95	6
Post MD/MS Certificate Course in Medical Biotechnology (1 year)		
1. All India Institute of Medical Sciences, New Delhi		4
2. Post Graduate Institute of Medical Education & Research, Chandigarh		4
3. Sanjay Gandhi Post Graduate Institute of Medical Sciences, Lucknow	2000-2001	(1st yr. 5, then 10)
PG Diploma Course in Clinical Biochemistry & Biotechnology (1 year)		
1. Utkal University, Bhubaneshwar	1999-2000	12

APPENDIX VI

International Organizations that Facilitate the Transfer of Plant Biotechnologies to Developing Countries

International organization	*Description of activities*
Food and Agriculture Organization (FAO) of the United Nations, Rome, Italy	Conducts, research on and facilitates transfer of plant biotechnologies that can benefit developing countries through its Plant Production and Protection Division in Rome, its regional offices and the Joint FAO/IAEA Division of Nuclear Techniques in Food and Agriculture in Vienna.
International Atomic Energy Agency (IAEA), Vienna, Austria	Conducts collaborative research with national agencies and provides training in mutation breeding and other plant biotechnologies through the Joint FAO/IAEA Division of Nuclear Techniques in Food and Agriculture.
International Laboratory for Tropical Agricultural Biotechnology (ILTAB), La Jolla, CA, USA.	An advanced research laboratory developed through a collaboration between the Scripps Research Insitute and the French technical assistance organization ORSTOM; conducts research and offers training on development of disease resistant tropical plants through genetic engineering.
International Centre for Genetic Engineering and Biotechnology (ICGEB), Trieste, Italy and New Delhi, India	Originally established by the United Nations Industrial Development Organization and now an independent reseach and training organization with crop biotechnology programmes in New Delhi and information dissemination provided through Trieste.
Center for the Application of Molecular Biology to International Agriculture (CAMBIA), Canberra, Australia	A research and technology transfer organization specializing in the production and dissemination of inexpensive biotechnology tools that can be employed in developing countries.
International Service for the Acquisition of Agri-biotech Applications (ISAAA), Ithaca, NY, USA	An international organization committed to the acquisition and transfer of proprietary agricultural biotechnologies from the industrial countries for the benefit of the developing world.
Intermediary Biotechnology Service (IBS), The Hague, The Netherlands	A unit of the International Service for National Agricultural Research, which provides national agricultural research agencies with information, advice, and assistance to help strengthen their biotechnology capacities.
Biotechnology Advisory Commission (BAC), Stockholm, Sweden	A unit of the Stockholm Environment Insitute that provides biosafety advice and helps developing countries assess the possible environmental, health, and socio-economic impacts of proposed biotechnology introductions.
Technical Center for Agricultural and Rural Development (CTA), Wageningen, The Netherlands	A unit of the European Union that collects, disseminates and facilitates exchange of information on research innovations including plant biotechnologies for the benefit of Asian, Caribbean and Pacific States.
International institute for Co-operation in Agriculture (IICA), San José, Costa Rica	Assists countries in Latin America and the Caribbean with policy issues related to biotechnology, including the formulation and harmonization of biosafety procedures.

APPENDIX VII

Differences between DNA and RNA

S.No.	*Characteristic*	*DNA*	*RNA*
1.	Pentose sugar	**Deoxyribose***	**Ribose**
2.	Base	Ordinarily **thymine present and uracil absent**	Ordinarily, **uracil present and thymine absent**
3.	Number of strands	Generally, double-stranded	Generally, single-stranded
4.	Native form	Double-stranded DNA usually in B Form	Double-stranded RNA usually in A form
5.	Origin	(*i*) Replication of pre-existing DNA (*ii*) In case of infection by RNA viruses, reverse transcription of genetic RNA	(*i*) **Genetic RNA** either through transcription of DNA or (*ii*) Through replication of RNA by RNA-dependent RNA polymerase. (*iii*) **Nongenetic RNA** from transcription of DNA.
6.	Function	Genetic material only	(*i*) Generally, nongenetic functions, *e.g.*, mRNA, rRNA, tRNA, etc. (*ii*) In some viruses, it serves as genetic material.

*Main differences are depicted in bold letters.

APPENDIX VIII

A List of Some Restriction Endonucleases

Restriction endonuclease	*Source (organism and strain)*	*Recognition sequence*
*Ava*I*	*Anabaena variabilis* (ATCC 27892)	C/PyCGPu G G PuGCPy/C
*Alu*I	*Arthrobacter luteus*	AG/CT TC/GA
*Bam*HI	*Bacillus amyloliquefaciens* H	G/GATC C C CTAG/G
*Bgl*II	*Bacillus globigii*	A/GATC T T CTAG/A
*Eco*RI	*Escherichia coli* Ry 13	G/AATTC C TTAA/G
*Eco*RII**	*E. coli* R 245	/CCA(T)GG GGT(A)CC/
*Hae*III	*Haemophilus aegypius*	GGCC CCGG
*Hind*II	*Haemophilus influenzae* R_d	GTPy/PuAC CAPu/PyTG
*Hind*III	*H. influenzae* R_d	A/AGCTT T TCGA/A
*Hinf*I*	*H. influenzae* Rf	G/ANT C C TNA/G
*Hin*PH	*H. influenzae* P_1	G/GCC CCG/G
*Hpa*I	*H. parainfluenzae*	GTT/AAC CAA/TTG
*Hpa*II	*H. parainfluenzae*	C/CGG GGC/C
*Nla*III	*Neisseria lactamica*	CATG/ /GTAC
*Not*I	*Nocardia otitidis-caviarum*	GCGGCCGC CGCCGGCG
*Pst*I	*Providencia stuartii*	CTGCA/G G/A CGTC
*Pvu*I	*Proteus vulgaris*	CGATCG GCTAGC
*Pvu*II	*Proteus vulgaris*	CAGCTG GTCGAC
*Sau*3A	*Staphylococcus aureus* 3A	/GATC CTAG/
*Sfi*I	*Streptomyces fimbriatus*	GGCCNNNNNGGCC CCGGNNNNNCCGG
*Taq*I	*Thermus aquaticus* YTI	T/CG A A GC/T

*Pu, either of the two purines (adenine or guanine), Py, either of the two pyrimidines (thymine or cytosine); N, any of the four bases (adenine, guanine, thymine or cytosine).

**The base given with parenthesis, *e.g.*, (T) may occur in place of the preceding base, *e.g.*, A.

APPENDIX IX

A Comparison Among the Salient Features of Morphological /Naked Eye Polymorphism (NEP), Protein-based and DNA Markers

Feature	*NEP Markers*	*Isozyme Markers*	*DNA Markers*
Effort required for detection	Simple (visual observation)	Moderate	Moderate to difficult
Easy in use	Easy	Moderately difficult	Moderately difficult to difficult
Number of different markers per cross	< 10	< 30	Unlimited
Plant material required for detection	Intact plant	Little amount of tissue	Little to medium amount of tissue
Reproducibility	High	High	Moderate to high
Dominant/codominant	Generally dominant	Codominant	Dominant (RAPD), codominant
Feature of the organism scored	Phenotype	Protein product	DNA base-sequence
Biological meaning of markers	Consequences of gene action	Genes that are expressed	Arbitary DNA sequences, may or may not represent genes

APPENDIX X

A Comparison Among Commonly Used DNA Markers

(Modified from Gupta, 2000)

Molecular markers	*RFLPs*	*RAPDs*	*DAF*	*STS (CAPSs)*	*SSRs*	*AFLPs*	*SNPs*
Principle	*Endonuclease restriction, Southern blot hybridization*	*DNA amplification with random primers*	*DNA amplification with random-primers*	*May need endonuclease restriction of PCR products*	*Amplification of simple sequence repeats using specific primers*	*Endonuclease restriction, use of adaptors and selective primers*	*Sequence analysis, DNA chips*
Number of loci detected	1-5	1-10	20-30	1-4	1-3	>70	1 (biallelic)
Inheritance	Codominant	Dominant	Dominant	Codominant	Codominant	Generally dominant	Codominant
Type of polymorphism detected	Base changes, deletion, duplications	Base changes	Base changes	Base changes	Variation in length of repeats	Base changes	Single base changes
Reproducibility	High	Low	Low	High	High	High	High
Sequence information needed	No	No	No	Yes	Yes	No	Yes
Automation possible	No	No	No	Yes	Yes	Yes	Yes
Cost	Medium	Low	Medium	Medium-high	High initially	High	High
Technical difficulties	Medium	Low	Medium	Low	Low	Medium/high	Medium/High
Uses							
1. Varietal fingerprinting	Yes	Yes	Yes	Yes	Yes	Yes	Yes
2. QTL mapping	Yes	Yes	Yes	Yes	Yes	Yes	Yes
3. Genetic diversity	Yes	Yes	Yes	Yes	Yes	Yes	Yes
4. Marker assisted selection	Yes	No/Yes	No	Yes	Yes	Yes	Yes
5. Qualitative gene tagging	Yes	Yes	Yes	Yes	Yes	Yes	Yes

APPENDIX XI

The Maximum Size of DNA Inserts that can be Efficiently Cloned in Various *E. coli* Vectors

Vector	*Size (in kb) of DNA insert (Max.)*	*Remarks*
M13 vector	3	1.5 Kb is the most common
Plasmid	8	Most plasmids
Phagmid vectors	10	Provide the facilities of M13 vector as well
λ Vectors		
λgt 10	8	Insertion vector
λ ZAP II	10	Insertion vector
λ EMBL 4	20	Replacement vector
λGEM11, λGEM12	23	Replacement vector
Cosmid vectors	40	Some cosmids
Bacterial artificial chromosomes (BACs)	300	Based on *E. coli* F plasmid
P1 derived artificial chromosomes (PACs)	300	Based on *E. coli* bacteriophage

APPENDIX XII

The Genome Size and the Estimated Number of Genes of Some Selected Organisms

Organism	*Number of chromosomes in the genome (n)*	*Genome size (Mb)**	*Number of genes*
Archaea			
Archaeoglobus fulgidus	1	2.2	2,493
Eubacteria			
Escherichia coli	1	4.64	4,408
Bacillus subtilis	1	4.21	4,212
Haemophilus influenzae	1	1.83	1,791
Mycoplasma genitalium	1	0.58	503
Eucaria			
Yeast (*Saccharomyces cerevisiae*)	16	12.8	6,548
Round worm (*Caenorhabditis elegans*)	6	97	>20,000
Arabidopsis thaliana	5	130	26,000
Drosophila melanogaster	4	180	~16,000
Rice (*Oryza sativa*)	12	415	~20,000
Maize (*Zea mays*)	10	2,500	~20,000
Human (*Homo sapiens sapiens*)	23	3,300	~35,000**
Barley (*Hordeum vulgare*)	7	5,300	~20,000

* Mb, megabase pairs (10^6 bp).

** Estimates range from 28,000–1,50,000.

APPENDIX XIII

A List of Some Diseases/Syndromes that have been Mapped onto Specific Sites on Human Chromosomes

(Information collected from genome database; cancer genome anatomy project website and NCBI's genome resource site)

Chromosome	*Disease/Syndrome*
1	Ductal breast cancer, Charcot-Marie Tooth Neuropathy 2a, Chediak-Higashi syndrome, Gaucher disease, Usher syndrome type 2.
2	Tibial muscular dystrophy, Alstrom syndrome, Autosomal recessive deafness 9, Limb Girdle muscular dystrophy 2b, Holoprosencephaly 2.
3	*Alkaptonuria*, Acute Myeloid leukaemia, von Hippel-Lindau syndrome, Cornelia de Lange syndrome.
4	*Huntington disease*, Wolf Hirschhorn syndrome, Wolfram syndrome, Juvenile Periodontitis.
5	Spinal muscular atrophy, *Cri-du-chat*, Coloractal cancer, Diastrophic dysplasia, Teacher Collins syndrome.
6	Hemochromatosis, Lafora myoclonus epilepsy, Celiac disease, Spinocerebellar atrophy 1.
7	*Cystic fibrosis*, Type 1 Williams-Beuren syndrome, Pendred syndrome, Split hand/foot malformation, Pallister-Hall syndrome.
8	Werner syndrome, Nijmegen-breakage syndrome, Lipoprotein lipase: Human, Cohen syndrome, Langer-Giedion syndrome.
9	Torsion Dystonia 1, Fanconi anemia type C, Dysautonomia, Friedreich ataxia, Nail-Patella syndrome.
10	Wolman disease, Cowden disease, Jackson-Weiss syndrome, Hermansky-Pudlak syndrome.
11	Long QT syndrome 1, Wilms tumour type 1, Ataxia-telangiectasia, Beckwith-Wiedemann syndrome, Bardet-Biedl syndrome 1.
12	*Phenylketonuria,* Darier disease, Familial periodic fever, Dentatorubro-pallidoluysian atrophy, Noonan syndrome.
13	Wilson disease, Stargardt disease-2, Retinoblastoma, Rieger syndrome type 2.
14	Graves disease, Machato-Joseph disease, Alzheimer disease, Spastic paraplegia 3A.
15	*Tay-Sachs disease*, Amytrophic lateral sclerosis-5, Bloom's syndrome, Prader-Willi syndrome,
16	Fanconi anemia type A, Familial Mediterranean fever, Inflammatory bowel disease 1, Polycystic kidney disease adult 1.
17	*Breast cancer 1,* Canavan disease, TP53 tumour suppressor gene, Miller-Dieker, Lissencephaly, Neurofibromatosis type 1.
18	Colorectal cancer, Niemann-pick disease type C, Tourette syndrome, Holoprosencephaly 4.
19	Diamond-Blackfan anemia, *Acute T cell leukaemia,* Myotonic dystrophy.
20	Corneal dystrophy, polymorphous SCID due to ADA deficiency, Alagille syndrome.
21	*Down syndrome*, Usher syndrome type 1E, Holoprosencephaly 1.
22	Cat eye syndrome, Ewing sarcoma, DiGeorge syndrome, Velocardiofacial syndrome, Neurofibromatosis type 2.
X	Duchenne muscular dystrophy, Adrenoleukodystrophy, Lowe syndrome, Norrie disease, Rett syndrome.
Y	Gonadal dysgenesis, *Prostrate cancer*, Mobius syndrome, *Acute myeloid-leukaemia,* Adenocarcinoma.

APPENDIX XIV

A List of Different Types of Arrays and Chips

S.No.	*Type of array*	*Array contains*	*Application*
1.	Spotted DNA array	dsDNA : genomic or cDNA	Gene expression pattern
2.	Printed oligonucleotide chips	ssDNA synthesized on the solid support	Gene expression pattern
3.	Protein arrays	Proteins or molecules that recognize proteins	See, below
	(*i*) Antibody arrays (Microimmunoassay arrays)	Antibodies immobilized on array surface**	Standard immuno-assay or a variation
	(*ii*) Antigen arrays	Protein antigens attached to array surface	Detection of antibodies in solution
	(*iii*) Arrays of specific capture agents	Specific capture agents that interact with proteins	Detection of specific proteins
4.	Protein chips	Artificial recognition sites for proteins, *e.g.*, those imprinted on polymers	Not yet in practical use
5.	Protein chips (Broad capture agent biochips)	Broad specificity capture agents	Bind to specific class of proteins

* Prepared by contact printing, inkjetting and photolithography.

**Prepared by using recombinant antibodies expressed in bacteria.

APPENDIX XV

A List of Some Important Databases

Database	Information available	Source
dbEST	EST sequences (redundant nucleotide sequences)	NCBI, U.S.A.; EBI, U.K.
dbSTS	A nonredundant database of GeneBank, EMBL and DDBJ STS entries.	NCBI, U.S.A.; EBI, U.K.
DDBJ (DNA DataBank of Japan)	Nucleotide sequences.	GenomeNet, Japan
EMBL (European Molecular Biology Laboratory)-Nucleotide Sequence Databank	DNA sequence.	EBI, U.K.
GenBank	Nucleotide sequences (nonredundant or less redundant nucleotide sequences)	NCBI, U.S.A.
HomoloGene	Homologous genes in human, mouse, rat, zebrafish, cow, represented in Unigene.	
IMGT Database	Nucleotide sequences of immunologically important genes.	EBI, U.K.
KEGG (Kyoto Encyclopedia of Genes and Genomes)	Metabolic pathways in many microorganisms, complete genomes.	GenomeNet, Japan
Mito	Mitochondrial DNA sequences.	NCBI, U.S.A.
NR	Nonredundant entries from GeneBank, EBML, DDBJ, and PDB databases.	
PALI database	Phylogenetic analysis and alignment of proteins.	
PDB (Protein DataBank)	Sequences of those proteins whose 3-D structures are known.	NCBI, U.S.A.; EBI, U.K.
PIRs (Protein Identification Resources)	Redundant protein sequences.	NCBI, U.S.A.
RefSeq	Messenger RNAs and proteins of human, mouse and rat	
Ribosomal RNA database	Ribosomal RNA sequences.	
SWISS-PROT	Annotated protein sequences.	NCBI, U.S.A.; EBI, U.K.
TrEMBL	Protein sequence database obtained by translation of cell coding sequences in EMBL.	NCBI, U.S.A.
UniGene	EST sequences; ESTs for separate genes grouped into distinct sets to avoid redundancy.	
Vector	Vector sequences from GeneBank.	NCBI, U.S.A.; EBI, U.K.
Yeast	Yeast genomic sequences.	NCBI, U.S.A.

APPENDIX XVI

A List of Some Important Database Search Tools

Search Tools	*Function provided*
BLAST (Basic Local Alignment Search Tool) (NCBI, U.S.A.)	A group of tools used to analyse sequence information and detect homologous sequences.
ENTREZ (NCBI, U.S.A.)	Used to access literature (abstracts), sequence and structure databases.
DNAPLOT (EBI, U.K.)	Sequence alignment tool.
LOCUS LINK (NCBI, U.S.A.)	Accessing information on homologous genes, *i.e.,* genes of different species that are similar due to common ancestry.
LIGAND (GenomeNet, Japan)	A database that allows search for a combination of enzymes and metabolic enzymes; links to all other publicly accessible databases.
BRITE (GenomeNet, Japan)	Biomolecular relations information transmission and expression database; links to all other publicly accessible databases.
TAXONOMY BROWSER (NCBI, U.S.A.)	Taxonomic classification of various species as well as genetic information.
STRUCTURE	It supports Molecular Modeling Database (MMDB) and software tools for structure analysis.
PROSITE	A collection of functional sites and sequence patterns found in many proteins; has search tools for matching patterns.

APPENDIX XVII

A List of Software Used for Analysis and Interpretation of Genome Sequence Databases

Software	*Used for*
GeneFinder, GENEMARK, GeneScan, GENIE, Glimmer, HMMGene, GRAIL	Detection of genes from genome sequence.
tBLASTx, FASTA, HMMER,	Prediction of the function of a new gene.
PRINTS, PROSITE, SMART, BLOCKS	Identification of functional domains/motifs of proteins.
tRNA ScanSE	Detection of tRNA genes.
FGENEH	Identification of presence of genes
Genquest	Sequence assembly, analysis and comparison
MAPMAKER, LINKAGE, GMendel, Mapmanager, Joinmap	Analysis of genetic data and preparation of molecular map
MUMmer	Whole genome alignment
PSI-Blast and variants	The most commonly used programme for homology search
REPEATMASKER	Screening of a sequence against a library of repetitive sequences and search for complexity regions
	Genome Annotation :
GAME	Description of experimental evidence
DAS	Indexing and visualization
BioJava 2001, BioPerl 2001	Storage, manipulation and visualization
AAT	Analysis and annotation

APPENDIX XVIII

A Summary of the Main Objectives Achieved/Achievable through Plant Biotechnology

Activity	*Objectives*	*Remarks*
Embryo culture	Rescue otherwise inviable hybrids, recovery of haploid plants from interspecific hybrids, micropropagation of orchids, etc.	The first two applications are the most remarkable.
Micropropagation	Rapid clonal multiplication usually through meristem culture, *e.g.*, of many fruit and forest trees.	Very high rates of multiplication; conventional rates are very low.
Virus elimination	Recovery of virus and other pathogen-free stocks of clonal crops; meristem culture is generally combined with thermotherapy/ cryotherapy.	Very useful in clonal crops, particularly for germplasm exchange.
Germplasm conservation	Germplasm conservation through storage in liquid nitrogen (at –196°C, cryopreservation) or through slow growth.	Particularly useful in clonal crops, especially in those producing tubers, storage roots, etc.
Haploid production	Rapid isolation of homozygous lines by chromosome doubling of haploids produced through anther culture/interspecific hybridization/ovary culture.	Very successful in variety development in China, *e.g.*, in rice and wheat.
Somaclonal variants	Isolation of stable somaclonal variants with improved yield/yield traits/disease resistance/ resitance to cold, herbicides, metal toxicity, salt and other abiotic stresses.	Many examples of successful isolation; many variations are stable and heritable; often due to gene mutations, which may, sometimes, be novel.
Genetic engineering	Gene transfers of insect resistance, protection against viruses, herbicide resistance, storage protein improvement, etc.	Mainly using the Ti plasmid of *Agrobacterium;* also through particle gun, free DNA uptake, a ***Revolutionary development*** in crop improvement.
Marker-assisted selection (MAS)	Molecular markers, *e.g.*, RFLPs, RAPDs, SSRs, etc., for linkage mapping and mapping of quantitative trait loci.	A ***powerful tool for indirect selection*** for quantitative traits; several other important applications.
Biochemical production	Production of valuable pharmaceuticals, etc, from cell culture, transgenic plants.	Transgenic plants are emerging as an attractive source of pharmaceuticals and research reagents.
Somatic hybridization	Production of distant hybrids by protoplast fusion to produce symmetric and asymmetric somatic hybrids, and cybrids.	Suitable for gene and cytoplasm transfers; some commercial examples are available.
Phytoremediation	Amelioration of polluted soils by growing appropriate transgenic plants.	In experimental stages; some encouraging results obtained.

APPENDIX XIX

A Comparison Between Shoot Buds and Somatic Embryos

Sl. No.	*Characteristics*	*Shoot bud*	*Somatic embryo*
1.	Origin	Many cells, usually superficial.	Single cell, usually superficial.
2.	Polarity	Unipolar; only the shoot/root pole present.	Bipolar, both shoot and root poles present.
3.	Vascular connection with callus/explant	Present; vascular strands connected with those present in callus/explant.	Absent; there is no vascular connection with callus/explant.
4.	Separation from callus/ explant	Not easily separated unless cut off.	Easily separated since the radicular end is cutinized.
5.	Developmental stage	Organogenesis does not exhibit well defined stages of development.	Somatic embryogenesis progress through well defined developmental stage, *viz.*, globular, heart-shaped, torpedo, and cotyledonary stages.
6.	Induction	It is induced by cytokin.	Induced by auxin (in mature tissues) or cytokinin (in case of embryonic tissues).
7.	Amenable to scale-up	Difficult	Yes
8.	Number	The number of organs regenerated is comparatively much lower than that in case of SEs.	Very high number of SEs can be produced in a relatively small culture volume.
9.	Applicable to	Organogenic calli are relatively less suitable for transformation.	Embryogenic calli are highly suitable for production of transformed cells and transgenic plants.

APPENDIX XX

A Summary of the Various Strategies Used for Virus Elimation

Strategy	*Treatment*	*Remarks*
Thermotherapy	Plants exposed to 35-40°C for few minutes to seven weeks; small shoot-tip cuttings excised and grafted onto healthy root stocks.	Usually, effective against isometric and thread-like viruses.
Meristem culture	Shoot apical meristem of less than 500 μm excised from virus-infected plants and cultured *in vitro*.	Explant size is critical; requires considerable skill and is tedious; many viruses may be present in the apical meristem as well.
Thermotherapy plus meristem culture	Plants subjected to thermotherapy, and shoot-tip excised and cultured; shoot cultures may also be given heat treatment and shoot-tips excised and cultured.	Perhaps the most effective strategy; in case like potato virus S, two cycle of thermotherapy plus meristem culture may be used; mm length shoot-tips may be used.
Cryotherapy plus meristem culture	Plants subjected to low temperature (~5°C) treatment for several months, followed by shoot-tip culture.	Less severe on host plant than thermotherapy.
Chemotherapy	Chemical agents like ribavirin added to the culture medium.	Ribavirin has been the most successful.
Plantlet regeneration from callus cultures	Callus culture initiated from infected plants and plantlets regenerated from them.	Some plantlets may be virus-free.

APPENDIX XXI

Commercial Examples of Biochemical Production from Cultured Plant Cells

Biochemical	*Plant species*	*Produced by*
Berberine	*Coptis japonica*	Mitsui Petrochemical Industries Ltd., Japan.
Ginseng (cell biomass)	*Panax ginseng*	Nitto Denko Corp., Japan.
Ginsenoides	*P. ginseng*	Nitto Denko Crop., Japan.
Purpurin	*Rubia akane*	Mitsui Petrochemical Industries Ltd., Japan.
Rosmarinic acid	*Coleus blumei*	—
Shikonin*	*Lithospermum erythrorhizon*	Mitsui Petrochemical Industries Ltd., Japan.
Taxol	*Taxus species*	Phyton Gesellschaft far Biotechnik mbH (in 75,000 l bioreactors).

*The first example of commercial production achieved by Fujita and coworkers in 1982.

APPENDIX XXII

A Comparison Among Various Approaches of Germplasm Conservation

	Approach		
Activities	*Conventional*	**In vitro** ***technique***	*Molecular*
Collection	Seed, vegetative bud, wood, tubers	Meristems, embryos, vegetative parts *in vitro*	Fixed material, raw DNA
Conservation	Seed, Field and gene banks	*In vitro* cultures, slow-growth, cryopreservation	Raw DNA, gene libraries
Multiplication	Normal sexual cycle, vegetative propagation	Micropropagation, subculturing	Plasmids, bacteria, viral clones
Characterization	Morphology	Isozymes, proteins	RFLPs, gene sequencing
Evaluation	Field trials, tolerance	Range of *in vitro* possibilities	Gene indentification
Distribution/quarantine	Culturing pathogens, indexing by grafting	ELISA	DNA probes
Medium	Seed, plants, plant parts	Plantlets, cultures	Bacterial clones, raw DNA
Utilization-through	Normal sexual hybridization	Wide hybridization (with embryo rescue in cell fusion)	Gene transfer through *Agrobacterium*, micro-injection, etc.
Scope/exploitation	Primary gene pool	Secondary and tertiary gene pool	All sources of DNA
Nature of new variation	Alleles reassortment	Alleles reassortment, gene addition/replacement, somaclonal variation.	Gene addition

Chopra (1993). Biotechnological tools for conserving biodiversity, Indian Farming. 43(7): 13-16.

APPENDIX XXIII

A Comparison of Three Approaches for *In Vitro* Germplasm Conservation

Feature	*Cryopreservation*	*Slow growth*	*DNA clones*
Tissue/organ conserved	Shoot-tips, zygotic or somatic embryos, cells, protoplasts	Slow growing shoot	DNA piece as phage clones
Metabolic activity	Nil	Slow	Nil
Storage temperature	–196°C	4-9 or 15-20°C	4°C; in lyophylised state
Storage in	Liquid nitrogen refrigerators	Ordinary refrigerators	Ordinary refrigerator/deep freezer
Attention needed during storage	Replenishing liquid nitrogen	Subculture every 6-36 months	Virtually nil
Risks	Loss in variability with time	Contamination	Virtually nil
Applicable to	All species amenable to tissue culture	All species amenable to tissue culture	Conservation of valuable genes
Sophistication	Sophisticated	Less sophisticated	Highly sophisticated
Cost involved	Costly equipments required	Standard tissue culture facilities needed	Very costly as it is based on recombinant DNA technology.

APPENDIX XXIV

A List of Some Somaclonal Variants Released as Varieties

Crop	*Parent variety*	*Somaclonal variety*	*Remarks*
Alfalfa	—	Sigma	Improved yield and disease resistance; a synthetic from somaclones of commercial varieties.
Blackberry	—	Evergreen	Thornless
Carrot	—	Vegisnax	Crunchier and more palatable than the parental varieties.
Celery	—	UC-T3 somaclone	Fusarium wilt resistance
Citronella java	—	Bio-13	37% and 39% more oil and citronellol, respectively than the parent variety (developed by CIMAP, Lucknow)
Geranium	Rober's Lemon Rose	Velvet Rose	Polyploid somaclone; sturdiness, vigour and attractiveness.
Indian Mustard	Varuna	BIO-902	17.4% yield advantage (by IARI, New Delhi)
Khesari (*Lathyrus sativus*)	—	Ratan	Low neurotoxin (by IARI, New Delhi)
Linseed (Flax)	McGregor	Andro	Rust immunity, salt tolerance.
Princes Tree (*Paulownia tomentosa*)	—	Somaclone Snowstorm	Irregular variegated foliage.
Sugarcane	Pindar	Ono	Resistant to Fiji disease
Sweet potato	—	Scarlet	Darker and more stable skin colour

APPENDIX XXV

A Comparison Among the Various Approaches for Gene Transfer in Terms of the Problems That can be Resolved/ Objectives That can be Achieved by Them

Problem/Objective	*Method of gene transfer*			
	Conventional	*Somatic hybridization*	*Genetic engineering*	*Others*
Intervarietal crosses :				
Non-flowering or sterile parents	None	Yes	Yes	None
Interspecific crosses :				
Hybrid sterility	Chromosome doubling	Yes	Yes	None
Sexual incompatibility :				
(*i*) Endosperm abortion	None	Yes	Yes	Embryo-rescue
(*ii*) Prefertilization barriers	Stigma/style manipulations, etc.	Yes	Yes	*In vitro* pollination/ fertilization
(*iii*) Very distant crosses	None	Yes	Yes	None
Combining mitochondria of one parent with chloroplasts of the other parent	None	Yes	No	None
Production of recombinant mtDNA/cpDNA	None	Yes	No	None
Entirely unrelated organisms :				
Animals, bacteria, viruses, etc.	None	No	Yes	None
Synthetic genes	None	No	Yes	None

APPENDIX XXVI

A Comparison Among the Techniques Used for Transfer of Gene(s) into Plant Cells

Feature	*Gene transfer technique*			
	Agrobacterium mediated	*Chemical and electrical*	*Microinjection*	*Particle gun*
Size of DNA construct (Max.)	< 50 kb	5-20 kb	16 kb	—
Range of plants	Limited	All plants	All plants	All plants
Efficiency	High	High	—	—
DNA insert integrity	Not affected by rearrangement	High degree of rearrangement	—	High degree of rearrangement
Number of copies integrated	Mostly single or few copies	High frequency of multicopy insertions	1-5	High frequency of multicopy insertions
Need for special equipment	No	No (chemical) Yes (electrical)	Yes	Yes

Regeneration protocol	Needed	Needed	Needed (often)	Not necessary (use of embryos, shoot-tips, etc.)
Protoplast culture	Not needed	Necessary	May be needed	Not needed
Applicable to organised meristems	Generally, No	No	Yes	Yes
Applicability to cereals	Applicable	Frequently used	Possible	High applicability
Chimaeric plants	No	No	Often (when mersitems are used)	Often (when meristem are bombarded)

APPENDIX XXVII

A List of Some of the Promoters Used for Driving the Expression of Transgenes in Different Plant Species

Promoter	*Source*	*Relative activity*
nos	*Agrobacterium* nopaline synthase gene	Moderate activity; constitutive
ocs	*Agrobacterium* octopine synthase gene	Moderate activity; constitutive
mas	*Agrobacterium* mannopine synthase gene	Moderate activity; constitutive
35*S*	CaMV 35*S RNA* gene	Constitutive, high activity; most commonly used in dicots
35*S* + *Adh*1-I 1	35*S* promoter + first intron of maize *Adh* gene	Enhanced promoter activity; constitutive
35*S* + *sh*1-I 1	35S promoter + first intron of maize *shrunken* 1 gene	Better than 35S + *Adh1*-I 1 in monocots; constitutive
19*S*	CaMV 19*S RNA* gene	Constitutive; moderate activity
Gene VI	CaMV *gene VI* encoding the matrix protein	Constitutive expression
*Adh*1	Promoter of alcohol dehydrogenase gene of maize	Moderate activity in cereals; anaerobic expression
Emu	Modified from *Adh*1 promoter and its first intron	Moderate activity in cereals; anaerobic expression
*Act*1 + *Act*1-I 1	Rice *actin* gene + its first intron	Moderate activity; constitutive
*Ubi*1 + *Ubi*1-I 1 (or I6)	Maize *ubiquitin*1 gene promoter + its first (or sixth) intron	High activity in cereals; constitutive
PHA-L	*Phytohaemagglutinin* gene of *P. vulgaris*	Strong, seed-specific activity
Vicilin promoter	Pea vicilin storage protein gene	Seed-specific activity
Extensin promoter	Carrot extensin gene long transcript promoter	—

APPENDIX XXVIII

A List of Some Selected Examples of Regulatory Sequences Determining Tissue-Specific and/or Stimulus-Specific Gene Expression

Regulatory sequence of gene	*Source organism*	*Expressed in tissue*	*Expressed in response to*
Ribulose, 1, 5-bisphosphate-carboxylase/oxygenase-small subunit (*rbcs*)	Pea, soybean, *Nicotiana-plumbaginifolia*	Leaves (high) and stem (low)	Light
Chlorophyll a/b binding protein (*cab*)	Pea, wheat, *N. plumbaginifolia*	Leaves and stem	Light
Chalcone synthase	*Antirrhinum majus*	—	Light
ST-LS 1	Potato	Green tissue	Light
Heat shock protein (Hsp)	Maize, soybean, *Drosophila*	—	Heat shock
Protease inhibitor	Potato	—	Wound
Patatin	Potato	Tuber	—
Leghaemoglobin	Soybean	Nodule	—
Nodulin	Soybean	Nodule	—
β-Phaseolin	French bean (rajma)	Seed	—
Lectin	Soybean	Seed + root	—
Glutenin	Wheat	Seed	—
Hordein	Barley	Seed	—
5-Enolpyruvylshikimate-3-phosphate synthase (EPSPS)	Petunia	Pollen	—
Sucrose synthase-1	Maize	Phloem cells	—

APPENDIX XXIX

A List of Some of Reporter or Marker Genes Used for Gene Transfers into Plants

Gene	*Source*	*Characteristic*
	Scorable Markers	
ocs (Octopine synthase)	*Agrobacterium*	Octopine production
nos (Nopaline synthase)	*Agrobacterium*	Nopaline production
cat (Chloramphenicol acetyltransferase)	*E. coli*	Acetylation of chloramphenicol
lux (Luciferase)	Bacteria, firefly	Phosphorescence
lacZ (β-galactosidase)	*E. coli*	Blue colour
uidA (β-glucuronidase)	*E. coli*	Blue colour (substrate X-gluc)
Green fluorescent protein (GFP)	Jelly fish (*Aequorea victoria*)	Fluoresces bright green under UV light (long wavelength) or blue light due to the presence of a β-hydroxy benzylidine imidazolinone chromophore.

Diverse regulatory factors involved in anthocyanin biosynthesis	Maize	Enhanced anthocyanin pigmentation
	Selectable Markers	
Antibiotic resistance		
dhfr (dihydrofolate reductase)	Tn7, mouse, plasmid R67	Methotrexate resistance
nptII (Neomycin phosphotransferase)	Tn5	Kanamycin, neomycin and G418 resistance
hptIV (Hygromycin phosphotransferase)	*E. coli, Streptomyces-hygroscopicus*	Hygromycin B resistance
Kan^r [Aminoglycoside 3′-phosphotransferase II; APH(3′) II]	Bacteria	Resistance to kanamycin
Streptomycin and spectinomycin phosphotransferase	*E. coli*	Resistance to streptomycin and spectinomycin
Herbicide resistance		
bar (Phosphinothricin acetyltransferase)	*Streptomyces hygroscopicus*	Phosphinothricin or bialaphos resistance
*deh*1 (Dehalogenase)	*Pseudomonas putida*	Dalapon resistance
ALS (Mutant acetolactate synthase)	*Arabidopsis thaliana,* tabocco (*N. tabacum*), *E. coli*, yeast	Resistance to sulfonyl ureas and imidazolinones
bxn (Bromoxynil nitrilase)	*Klebsiella ozaene*	Detoxifies herbicides bromoxynil, which inhibits photosystem II.
aroA [5-Enolpyruvylshikimate phosphate (EPSP) synthase]	*Agrobacterium* sp. CP4	Herbicide glyphosate inhibits EPSP synthase, which is essential for synthesis of Phe, Tyr and Trp (aromatic amino acid) in plants.
GOX (Glyphosate oxido-reductase)	*Achromobacter* sp.	Detoxifies glyphosate by degradation; resistance to glyphosate
	Unusual GR/Substrate Utilization Markers	
β-glucuronidase (*vidA*)	*E. coli*	Releases BAP from benzyladenine N-3-glucuronide, which is used in selection medium.
Mannose-6-phosphate-isomerase	—	Converts mannose-6-phosphate to fructose-6-phosphate; selection medium has mannose as a carbon source.
Xylose isomerase	—	Isomerises xylose to xylulose; xylose used in selection medium.

APPENDIX XXX
A List of Some Chromosomal Genes of *Agrobacterium tumefaciens* Involved in Attachment of Bacterial Cells to Plant Cells

Chromosomal gene	*Function*
chvA	Encodes on inner membrane protein essential for the transport of β-1, 2-glucan from cytoplasm to periplasm.
chvB	Encodes an inner membrane protein most likely involved in the synthesis of β-1, 2-glucan.
chvD and chvE	Needed for an optimal expression of *vir* genes of *p*Ti.
exo locus genes	Biosynthesis of attachment polysaccharides.
*exo*C	Encodes an enzyme directly involved in the biosynthesis of β-1, 2-glucan.
cel genes	Cellulose fibril synthesis especially during the early phases of infection so that bacterial cell become firmly adhered to plant cells.

APPENDIX XXXI
A List of Some of the Important Genes/Sequences of *p*Ti (nopaline type) and Their Functions

Gene/Operon	*Function*
	T-DNA
iaaM (*aux1, tms1*)*	Auxin biosynthesis; encodes the enzyme tryptophan-2-mono-oxygenase, which converts tryptophan into indoel-3-acetamide (IAM)
iaaH (*aux2, tms2*)	Auxin biosynthesis; encodes the enzyme indole-3-acetamide hydrolase, which converts IAM into IAA (indole-3-acetic acid)
ipt (*tmr, Cyt*)	Cytokinin biosynthesis; encodes the enzyme isopentenyl transferase, which catalyzes the formation of isopentenyl adenine.
nos	Nopaline biosynthesis; encodes the enzyme nopaline synthase which produces nopaline from arginine and pyruvic acid.
24 bp left and righ border sequences	*Sites of endonuclease action during T-DNA transfer; the only sequences of T-DNA essential for its transfer.*
	vir* Region (*vir* Regulon)*
virA (1)+	Encodes a sensor protein; receptor for acetosyringone and functions as an autokinase, also phosphorylates VirG protein; *constitutive expression.*
virB (11)	Membrane proteins; possibly form a channel for T-DNA transport (conjugal tube formation); VirB11 has ATPase activity.
virC (2)	Helicase; binds to the overdrive region just outside the right border; involved in unwinding of T-DNA.
virD (4)	VirD1 has topoisomerase activity; it binds to the right border of T-DNA; VirD2 is an endonuclease; it nicks the right border.
virE (2)	Single-strand binding proteins (SSBP); bind to T-DNA during its transfer.

virF (1)	Not well understood.
virG (1)	DNA binding protein; probably forms dimer after phosphorylation by virA, and induces the expression of all *vir* operons (operons A to H); *constitutive expression.*
virH (2)	Not well known.

* The symbols within parentheses are the earlier symbols for the genes.

** virA, virB, etc. are the various operons of the *vir* region (*vir* regulon).

+ Figures within the parentheses are the numbers of genes in the operons.

APPENDIX XXXII

A List of *cry* genes of *Bacillus thuringiensis*, Their Proteins and Target Insects*

Gene	*Protein (Mol. mass in kDa)*	*Bacterial strain*	*Target insect*	*Remarks*
*cry*IA(*a*)	133.2	HD-1	Lepidoptera	Each Cry I protein has a distinct insecticidal spectrum. Most *cry* genes are situated on large conjugative plasmids.
*cry*IA(*b*)	131.0	Berliner 1715	Lepidoptera	
*cry*IA(*c*)	133.3	HD-73	Lepidoptera	
*cry*IB	138.0	HD-2	Lepidoptera	
*cry*IC	134.8	HD-110	Lepidoptera	
*cry*ID	132.5	HD-68	Lepidoptera	
*cry*IE	132.5	HD-146	Lepidoptera	
*cry*IIA	70.9	HD-263	Lepidoptera and Diptera	
*cry*IIB**	70.8	HD-1	Diptera	
*cry*IIIA	73.1	tenebrionis	Coleoptera	
*cry*IIIB	74.2	tolworthi	Coleoptera	
*cry*IIIC	129.4	gallariae	Coleoptera	
*cry*IVA	134.4	israelensis	Diptera	
*cry*IVB	127.8	israelensis	Diptera	
*cry*IVC	77.8	israelensis	Diptera	
*cry*IVD	72.4	israelensis	Diptera	
*cry*V	—	—	Nematodes	
*cry*VI	—	—	Nematodes	
*cyt*A+	27.4	israelensis		

* Several additional subgroups has to be created to accommodate newly discovered *cry* genes. Therefore, the total number of subgroups is much greater than the 18 listed in this table.

** Homology with other *cry* proteins is rather limited.

+ No sequence homology to the *cry* genes; cytolytic for a variety of vertebrate and invertebrate cells; no insecticidal activity.

APPENDIX XXXIII

A List of Some Transgenes for Insect Resistance (other than the *cry* genes from *B. thuringiensis*). None of These Genes has yet Generated a Transgenic of Practical Value)

Transgene	*Source*	*Expressed in crop species*	*Conferred resistance to the insects*
Insecticidal protein gene	Streptomyces	Tobacco	Boll weevil (*Spodoptera litura*)
Trypsin inhibitor gene	Sweet potato	Tobacco	*Spodoptera litura*
α-Amylase inhibitor gene	Adzuki bean, common-bean	Pea	Bruchus beetle and pea weevil
Lectin gene*	Snowdrop-(*Galanthus nivalis*)	Potato	Tomato moth (*Lacanobia oleracea*)
		Sweet potato	Sweet potato weevil
Cholesterol oxidase gene	*Streptomyces* sp.	Tabacco	Boll weevil
Stunt virus genome	*Helicoverpa* stunt virus	Cotton	Cotton bollworm
Chitinase	Bean	Potato	Tomato moth
Vegetative insecticidal protein (VIP)	*Bacillus thuringiensis* (strain AB88, AB424)	Bacterium *E. coli*	Resistance to *A. ipsilon*, *S. frugiperda*, *H. virescens*, *H. zea* etc.

* Lectins are plant glycoproteins, which act against piercing and sucking insects like aphids. But they are effective only when ingested in microgram quantities. As a result, it has poor insecticidal effectiveness in transgenic plants to be of practical usefulness.

APPENDIX XXXIV

A List of Some Strategies for Engineering Resistance to Bacterial and Fungal Pathogens

Transgene description			*Transgene*	*Consequence of transgene*
Transgene	*Source*	*Function*	*expressed in*	*expression*
		Genes from Plants		
Stilbene synthase (*vst*)	*Vitis vinifera*	Synthesis of the phytoalexin resveratrol	Tobacco	Lower susceptibility to *Botrytis cinerea*
Ribosome-inactivating-protein A	Barley	Inhibits protein synthesis by removing a specific A residue from 28*S* rRNA	Tobacco	Increased resistance *Rizoctonia solani*
α-Thionins	Barley	Toxic *in vitro* to several phytopathogenic bacteria	Tobacco	Increased resistance to *P. syringae* pv. *tabaci*; bacterial growth severely inhibited.
PRI	Tobacco	A PR protein, function not known	Tobacco	Consitutive ectopic expression did not produce resistance to TMV and several other pathogens.
Chitinase	Bean (Class I chitinase)	Hydrolysis of chitin, major component of cell walls of most fungi	Tobacco *B. napus*	Significant degree of protein from *R. solani*; no effect on symbiotic association with micorrhizal fungus *Glomus mosseae*.
		Genes from other organism		
argK	*Pseudomonas syringae* pv. *phaseolicola*	Ornithine carbamoyl transferase (arginine synthesis)	Tobacco	No chlorosis on treatment with very high concentration of phaseolotoxin, which causes chlorosis in control plants.
			P. vulgaris	Inoculation with *P. syringae* pv. *phaseolicola* produced HR, no systemic infection.
ttr (tabtoxin resistance)	*P. syringae* pv. tabaci	Tabtoxin acetylase; inactivates tabtoxin	Tobacco	Inoculation with *P. syringae* pv. *tabaci* did not produce chlorotic halos typical of the wildfire disease.
Cecropin B	Silk moth-(*Hyalophora cecropia*)	Lytic peptide; anti-microbial activity	Tobacco	Increased resistance to *P. solanacearum* on stem inoculation.
Lysozyme	T_4 bacteriophage	Hydrolysis of bacterial cell	Potato	Higher level of resistance to *Erwinia carotovora atroseptica* (soft rot and black leg symptoms)
avr9 and *cf9*	*Cladosporium-fulvus* Tomato	Wall Elicitor Resistance gene corresponding to *avr9*	—	Expected to generated resistance; *avr9* driven by an elicitor inducible; promoter; yet to be tested.
barnase	*Bacillus amyloliquefaciens*	Encodes an RNase, which is cytotoxic	Potao	Resistance to *Phytophthora infestans*.

APPENDIX XXXV

A Comparison of the Various Strategies Used for Producing Virus Resistant Transgenic Plants

Feature	*Type of Protection*				
	Coat protein gene	*cDNA of satellite RNA*	*Defective viral genomes*	*Antisense RNA approach*	*Ribozyme/RNase P*
Mode of action	Interferes with capsid uncoating; virus spread; generates recovery*	Interferes with virus assembly	Interferes with replication of virus	Binding to RNA prevents translation	Cleavage of RNA genome/mRNA
General applicability	Yes	No	No	Yes	Yes
Effectiveness against unrelated viruses	Some effect on systematic spread	None	None	Possibly, if conserved sequences in the viral genomes can be identified.	Possibly, if conserved sequences in the viral genomes can be identified.
Required level of expression of host plants	Possibly high	Low	Possibly high	Possibly high	Possibly high
Efficacy	High in many cases	High	Medium	Low	Probably low

*Recovery has been reported to potyviruses; the plants develop disease symptoms, but the symptoms abate as plants grow. There is reduction or elimination of virus accumulation in symptomless parts of these plans.

APPENDIX XXXVI

A List of Some Transgenes that have been Shown to Confer Resistance to One or More Abiotic Stresses

Transgene	*Isolated from*	*Function*	*Transferred into*	*Protection from abiotic stress*
mtlID	*E. coli*	Mannitol-1-phosphate dehydrogenase (mannitol production)	Tobacco	Salt (250 mM NaCl) stress
			Arabidopsis	Seeds germinated in high NaCl medium
P5CS	Mothbean	Pyrroline-5-carboxylate synthetase (overproduction of proline)	Tobacco	Salt stress
hsf	—	Heat shock factor (transcription factor)	Tobacco	Heat stress
sacB	*Bacillus subtilis*	Fructan accumulation	Tobacco	Drought
**ala3*	Chemically synthesized	Antifreeze protein (AFP)	Tobacco	Freeze stress
	Squash	Glycerol-3-phosphate acetyl transferase	Tobacco	Chilling stress
hav1	Barley	**A class 3 Lea protein	Rice	Salt stress
Cor47	—	A low temperature responsive gene product	Rice	Water and salt stress
betA	*E. coli*	+Choline dehydrogenase	Tobacco	Salt stress
betB	*E. coli*	++Betaine aldehyde dehydrogenase	Tobacco	Osmotic stress
codA	*Arthrobacter globiformis*	†Choline oxidase (glycine-betaine production)	*Arabidopsis*, rice	Salt and cold stress
sal1	*Arabidopsis* sp.	Sulphur assimilation	Yeast	High salt stress
—	*E. coli*	TPS1 subunit of trehalose synthase (trehalose production)	Tobacco	Drought

* Found in polar arctic fishes.

** Lea, late embryogenesis abundant proteins.

+ Converts choline into betaine aldehyde.

++ Converts betaine aldehyde into glycine-betaine.

† Converts choline to glycine-betaine.

APPENDIX XXXVII

A List of Transgenes for Herbicide Resistance and the Mechanisms of Their Action

Gene	*Source organism*	*Confers resistance to the herbicide*	*Mechanism of action/ Remarks*
*aroA**	*Agrobacterium* sp. strain CP4	Glyphosate/Roundup	Encodes 5-enolpyruvylshikimate-3-phosphate synthase (EPSPS) enzyme that is insenstive to glyphosate.
*bar***	*Streptomyces hygroscopicus*	Bialaphos/Basta/Glufosinate	Acetylation of phosphinothricin (enzyme phosphinothricin acetyl transferase)
bxn†	*Klebsiella ozaene*	Bromoxynil	Converts the herbicide into 3,5-dibromo-4-hydroxy benzoic acid
gox††	*Achromobacter* sp. strain LBAA	Glyphosate/Roundup	Detoxifies glyphosate by oxidizing it into amino ethylphosphonic acid and glyoxylate.
Hra, csr1-1, C3 and *uhas 3r genes**	*Arabidopsis thaliana, N. tabacum,* yeast *E. coli*	Sulphonylurease and imidazolinones	Encode acetolactate synthase (ALS) enzyme that is insensitive to the herbicides.

* EPSPS and ALS enzymes are involved in amino acid biosynthesis pathways.

** Encodes the enzyme phosphinothricin acetyltransferase.

† Encodes the enzyme bromoxynil nitrilase.

†† Encodes the enzyme glyphosate oxidoreductase.

APPENDIX XXXVIII

A List of Some Enzyme Activities that must be provided by Transgenes to Enable the Production of β-carotene, and the Transgenes Transferred to Generate High Iron Rice

Enzyme activity	*Function*
Golden Rice	
Phytoene synthase (a plant gene)	Produces phytoene by condensation of two molecules of geranyl-geranyl pyrrophosphate, the last precursor of β-carotene biosynthesis found in rice endosperm.
* Phytoene desaturase	Converts phytoene into zeta-carotene.
* ζ-carotene desaturase	Converts zeta-carotene into lycopene.
Lycopene β-cyclase (a plant gene)	Converts lycopene into β-carotene, the cyclic C_{40} carotene, which is commonly known as provitamin A.
High Iron Rice	
Ferritin gene from *Phaseolus*	Endosperm iron content increased by a factor of 2.5.
A metallothionin-like gene from *Oryza.*	Endosperm cystein content increased 7-fold; cystein enhances iron absorption in intestine.
A mutant phytase gene from *Aspergillus fumigatus* encoding a thermostable enzyme.	Hydrolyses phytate to inorganic phosphate and myoinositol. The mutant enzyme refolds to 80% activity after 20 min. at 100°C, but the phytase expressed in rice, for some reason, failed to do so.

*In golden rice, both these activities were provided by *Erwinia* phytoene desaturase encoded by gene *crt1*. The enzymes contained signal sequence for localization in plastids. Conversion of phytoene to lycopene involves a total of four desaturation steps.

APPENDIX XXXIX

A List of Some Transgenes Encoding Valuable Polypeptides/Enzymes Expressed in Plants

Polypeptide/Enzyme	*Source*	*Expressed in*	*Applications*	*Remarks*
Polypeptides				
Enkephalin	Human	*B. napus*	Opiate activity	Expressed in fusion with the storage protein 2*S* albumin.
Antibodies (IgG, IgM, chimaeric, single chain, V_H chains, etc.)	Mouse	—	Various applications	Expressed at levels of 2% of the extractable proteins
Hirudin	Synthetic	*B. napus*	Thrombin inhibitor	Expressed in fusion with olesin; ***first commercial example.***
α-Trichosanthin	Chinese-medicinal plant	—	Inhibition of HIV replication	High level of expression
Epidermal growth factor	Human	—	Proliferation of specific cells	—
Erythropoietin	Human	—	Regulation of erythocyte levels	—
Growth horomone	Trout	—	Growth stimulation	—
Human serum albumin	Human	—	Plasma expander	—
Interferon	Human	—	Antiviral activity	—
Enzymes				
α-Amylase	*Bacillus-licheniformis*	Tobacco	Liquefaction of starch	Industrial applications
(1-3, 1-4)-β-Glucanase	*Trichoderma reesei*; hybrid of two *Bacillus* species	Tobacco, barley	Brewing	Industrial applications
Manganese-dependent lignin peroxidase	*Phanerochaete chrysosporium*	Alfalfa, tobacco	Bleaching and pulping of paper	Industrial applications
Phytase	*Aspergillus niger*	Alfalfa, tobacco	Increased phosphate utilization from feed	Upto 14% of soluble protein in leaves close to senescence
β(1, 4) Xylanase	*Clostridium thermocellum; Cryptococcus albidus*	Tabacco, canola	Animal feed, paper and pulp, baking	Industrial applications
Research Reagents				
*Avidin	Chicken	Maize	Research reagent	2-3% of seed dry mass; ***marketed by Sigma***
β-glucuronidase	Bacteria (*E. coli*)	Maize	Research reagent	0.4-0.7% of seed dry weight; ***marketed by Sigma***

* Cost reduced to 1/50 of that of avidin recovered from chicken egg.

APPENDIX XL

A List of Oraly Active and Other Antigenic Proteins Produced in Transgenic Plants

Antigen encoding gene	*Organism*	*Expressed in*	*Antigenic activity tested*	*Remarks*
Integrated in Plant Genome				
Surface protein gene *spaA*	*Streptococcus mutans*	Tobacco (0.02% of total leaf protein)	Orally; s-IgA production in saliva stimulated	—
Surface antigen (HBsAg)	Hepatitis B-virus	Tobacco (as 22 nm virus-like particles)	Parenterally in mice; similar to that of yeast derived HBsAg	Both B- and T-cell epitopes preserved
Heat-liable enterotoxin B subunit (LT-B)	*E. coli*	Tobacco, potato (low level of expression)*	Orally in mice; comparable to bacteria-derived LT-B	A proportion of LT-B is pentamerised
Viral Vectors				
(*a*) *Foreign gene transcription driven by subgenomic promoter of TMV*				
α-Trichosanthin	Chinese medicinal plant	High level of expression	—	An antiviral protein
(*b*) *Capsid protein fusions*				
Malarial epitope	Malarial sporozoites	Tobacco (TMV capsid protein fusion)	By ELISA, western blot, positive	Both internal and C-terminal fusions
ZP3 protein epitope (13 amino acids)	Mammalian oocyte zona pellucida	Tobacco (TMV capsid protein fusion); high expression	Parenterally in mice; antibodies produced	Ovarian pathology; no effect on fertility
HIV-1 epitope	Human immunodeficiency virus	Fusion with small coat protein of cowpea mosaic virus (CPMV)**	Immunogenic in animals	CPMV-HIV1 antibodies active against 3 strains of HIV 1
Rhinovirus 14 epitope	Human rhinovirus 14			

* Accumulation enhanced when a C-terminal microsomal-retension sequence (Ser-Glu-Lys-Asp-Glu-Leu) was added to LT-B sequence.

** Epitopes of upto 30 amino acids have used in CPMV.

APPENDIX XLI

A List of Transgenic Varieties Released for Commercial Cultivation in U.S.A.

Crop	*Engineered trait(s)*	*Sources from which gene(s) is/are isolated*	*Transgenic variety*	*Year of release*	*Institution/ company*
Canola	Resist glyphosate herbicide to control weeds	Arabidopsis, bacteria, virus	Roundup Ready*	1999	Monsanto
	Altered oil (high lauric acid) use in soap and food products	California bay, turnip rape, bacteria, virus	Laurical*	1995	Monsanto
Chicory (radicchio)	Male sterility to facilitate hybrid seed production	Bacteria	SeedLink*	1997	Bejo Zaden
Corn	*cry* gene to control insect pests (European corn borer)	Bacteria (*B. thuringiensis*)	YieldGard*	1995	Monsanto
	Resistance to glufosinate herbicide to control weeds/ male sterility to facilitate hybrid seed production	Bacteria, virus	SeedLink*	—	Aventis
	cry gene to control insect pests (European corn borer)	Bacteria (*B. thuringiensis*)	NatureGard*	1995	Dow/Mycogen
	cry gene to control insect pests (European corn borer)	Bacteria (*B. thuringiensis*)	Bt-Xtra*	1997	Monsanto/DeKalb
	Resistance to glufosinate herbicide to control weeds/ *cry* gene to control insect pests (European corn borer)	Bacteria, virus	StarLink*	1998	Aventis
	Resistance to glyphosate herbicide to control weeds	Arabidopsis, bacteria, virus	Roundup Ready*	1998	Monsanto
	Resistance to glufosinate herbicide	Bacteria, virus	Liberty Link	—	Aventis
Pop corn	*cry* gene to control insect pests (European corn borer)	Bacteria (*B. thuringiensis*)	Bt II*	1996	Novartis
Sweet corn	*cry* gene to control insect pests (European corn borer)	Bacteria (*B. thuringiensis*)	Knock Out*	1995	Novartis
Cotton	*cry* gene to control insect pests (cotton boll worms)	Bacteria (*B. thuringiensis*)	Knock Out*	1998	Novartis

	cry gene to control insect pests (cotton boll worms)	Bacteria (*B. thuringiensis*)	Bt II*	1998	Novartis
	cry gene to control insect pests (cotton boll worms and tobacco budworm)	Bacteria	Bollgard*	1995	Monsanto
	Resistance to glyphosate herbicide to control weeds	*Arabidopsis*, bacteria, virus	Roundup Ready*	1996	Monsanto
	Resistance to bromoxynil herbicide to control weeds	Bacteria, virus	BXN Cotton*	1995	Monsanto/Rhone-Poulenc
Flax	Resistance sulfonylurea herbicides to grow in soil contaminated with herbicide residues	*Arabidopsis*, bacteria	CDC Triffid*	1999	University of Sasketchewan
Papaya	Resistance to papaya ring spot virus	Bacteria, virus	Sunup, Rainbow*	1997	Cornell Univ./Univ. Hawaii
Potato	*cry* gene to control insect pests (Colorado potato beetle)	Bacteria (*B. thuringiensis*)	New Leaf*	1995	Monsanto
	cry gene to control insect pests (Colorado potato beetle)/resist potato leaf roll virus Y	Bacteria, virus	New Leaf Y*	1999	Monsanto
	cry gene to control insect pests (Colorado potato beetle)/resist potato leaf roll virus	Bacteria, virus	New Leaf Plus *	1998	Monsanto
Soybean	Resistance to glyphosate herbicide to control weeds	Petunia, soybean, bacteria, virus	Roundup Ready	1995	Monsanto
	Resistance to virus	Virus	Freedom	1995	Asgrow
Squash	Resistance to watermelon mosaic 2 and Zucchini yellow mosaic viruses	Bacteria, virus	Freedom II	1995	Seminis seeds
Tomato	Altered ripening to enhance fresh market value	Tomato, bacteria, virus	Endless Summer**	1995	DNA plant technology
	Altered ripening to enhance fresh market value	Tomato, bacteria, virus	Flavr Savr**	1994	Monsanto/Calgene

* Trade name

** Achieved regulatory exemption status in 1996.

APPENDIX XLII

A Comparison of UPOV Act (1978) with UPOV Act (1991), PPVFR Act (2001) and Patents

Feature	*UPOV Act (1978)*	*UPOV Act (1991)*	*PPVFR Act (2001)**	*Patent*
Protection coverage	Plant varieties of nationally defined plant species	Plant varieties of all plant genera and species	Varieties of nationally specified genera and species	Inventions
Requirements for protection	1. Distinctness 2. Uniformity 3. Stability	1. Novelty 2. Distinctiveness 3. Uniformity 4. Stability	1. Novelty** 2. Distinctiveness† 3. Uniformity 4. Stability	1. Novelty 2. Inventiveness 3. Non-obviousness 4. Industrial application and usefulness
Duration of protection	Minimum 15 yr	Minimum 20 yr	Maximum 15 yr for extant varieties and new varieties of crops; 18 yr for varieties of trees and vines	17-20 yr (OECD)††
Scope of protection	Commercial use of the ***reproductive*** material of protected variety	Commercial use of ***all material*** of the protected variety	Commercial use of all material of the protected variety	Commercial use of protected subject matter
Breeders' exemption	Yes	Yes, ***except for essentially-derived varieties***	Yes, except for essentially-derived varieties, and use as parents of hybrid varieties	No
Farmers' privilege	Yes (in practice)	Optional; left to the national laws	Yes, as 'farmers' right'; more extensive than in UPOV Act (1978)	No

* PPVFR Act, 2001, The Protection of Plant Varieties and Farmers' Right Act, 2001.

** A variety not in commercial use for more than one year in India, or 4 years (6 years in case of trees and vines) outside India.

† In case of extant varieties, distinctiveness, uniformity and stability.

†† OECD, Organization for Economic Cooperation and Development.

APPENDIX XLIII

A List of Some Different Types of Vectors Used for Gene Transfers in Animals

Vector	*Derived from*	*Features*
1. SV40 vector		
(*a*) Early region replacement vectors	Replacement of large-T gene of SV40	1. Produce virions, which infect host cells
(*b*) Late region replacement vectors	Replacement of *VP1*, *VP2*, and *VP3* genes of SV40, *e.g.,* SVGT-5	2. Transient gene expression 3. Mammalian cells are hosts of SV40
(*c*) Plasmid vectors	Origin of replication and large-T gene of SV40	—
(*d*) Shuttle plasmid vectors	Plasmid vector [item 1(c)] plus *p*BR322 origin and amp^r gene, *e.g.,* *p*SV2, *p*SV3, etc.	—
	Rous Sarcoma Virus promoter in place of SV40 early promoter, *e.g.,* *p*SRV.	Strong expression of the marker gene
(*e*) Passive transfecting vectors	SV40 transcription regulatory and polyadenylation sequences, plus *p*BR322 origin and amp^r gene	Shuttle vectors; used for gene integration in mammalian cells
2. BPV vectors	Bovine Papilloma Virus "transforming region" + *p*BR322.	Shuttle vector; often *p*BR322 sequence deleted prior to transfection; plasmid-like vector
3. Retrovirus vectors	*p*BR322 + retrovirus sequences	Shuttle vector; integrates as provirus into mammalian genome; produces virions; used in gene therapy
4. Polyoma virus vectors	Polyoma virus origin and early region + *p*BR322 sequences	Similar to SV40 vectors; mouse cells used as host
5. Vaccinia virus vectors	DNA insert placed within the thymidine kinase gene of the virus by a process of recombination.	Promising as live vaccines; DNA insert is a pathogen gene encoding an antigen
6. *P* element vectors	*Drosophila* transposable element *P*; minimum of 31 bp inverted repeat borders and the neighbouring regions, plus an *E. coli* vector, *e.g.,* *p*UC8; DNA insert of upto 40 kb placed within the two borders.	Gene transfer in *Drosophila*; a helper *P* element is needed to provide the transposase necessary for transposition or insertion of the recombinant *P* vector into the *Drosophila* genome
7. Bacculovirus vectors	Nuclear polyhedroma virus (NPV) polyhedrin gene replaced by DNA insert; *e.g.,* AcNPV (*Autographa californica* nuclear polyhedroma virus) and BmNPV (*Bombyx mori* nuclear polyhedroma virus) vectors.	Produce virions; expression vector for production of transgenic proteins in silk worm larvae (BmNPV vectors and in *Spodoptera frugiperda* larvae or cultured cells (AcNPV vectors)

APPENDIX XLIV

A List of Promoter/Enhancer Sequences Used for Driving Transgenes in Different Transgenic Animal Species

*Promoter/enhancer sequence**	*Source*	*Used in animal species*	*Gene expression in the tissue*
Metallathionein promoter	Fish	Fish	Stimulus-specific
	Mouse	Fish, mouse, pig	
	Sheep	Sheep	
	Human	Rabbit, pig	
β-actin	Fish	Fish	
	Chicken	Fish	
cd-crystalline SV	SV40	Pig	All tissues
SV40 early promoter	SV40	Mammalian cells, fish	All tissues
Moloney murine leukaemia virus (MLV)	MLV	Pig	All tissues
RSV promoter	Rous Sarcoma Virus (RSV)	Mammalian cells, fish	All tissues
Thymidine kinase promoter	Herpes Simplex Virus (HSV)	Mammalian cells	All tissues
SV40 enhancer	72 bp sequence having tandem repeats near SV40 origin	Enhances transcription of all genes transcribed by RNA polymerase II	All tissues
Anti-freeze protein promoter	Fish	Fish	
β-Casein promoter	Mouse	Goat	Mammary tissue
β-Lactoglobulin promoter	Sheep	Sheep	Mammary tissue
Prolactin promoter	Cow	Pig	Mammary tissue
Immunoglobulin heavy chain promoter	Rabbit	Rabbit	—

* A promoter/enhancer sequence is usually designated by the gene with which it is naturally associated.

APPENDIX XLV

A List of Reporter/Marker Genes Used in Gene Transfers in Animal Cells

Reporter gene	*Source*	*Remarks*
Scorable reporter genes		
Chloramphenicol acetyltransferase (CAT)	*E. coli* transposon Tn9	Used in fish, mammalian cells
β-Galactosidase	*E. coli*	Used in fish
Luciferase (*lux*)	Bacteria, firefly	Used in fish
Selectable reporter genes		
Thymidine kinase (*Tk*)	Herpes simplex virus (HSV)	Used in TK^- cells; HSV gene promoter is weak in mammalian cells
Dihydrofolate reductase (DHFR)	1. Chinese hamster ovary (CHO) cell line 'A29'	Resistance to methotrexate due to overproduction of DHFR; DHFR gene is amplified during integration
	2. Bacteria	DHFR intrinsically resistant to methotrexate.
CAD protein gene (*Cad*)	Syrian hamster gene cloned in *E. coli*	Overproduction of CAD protein confers resistance to N-phosphon-acetyl-L-aspartate (PALA); *Cad* gene is also amplified during integration.
Adenosine diaminase (*Ada*)	—	Resistance to Xyl-A (9-β-D-xylofuranosyl adenosine) and 2′-deoxycoformycin
Adenine phosphoribosyl transferase (*Aprt*)	—	Selection agent: adenine + azaserine (blocks *de novo*) dATP synthesis)
Asparagine synthase (*as*)	*E. coli*	Albizzin (a toxic analogue of glutamine)
Blasticidin deaminase (*bsd*)	*Aspergillus terrcus*	Resistance to blacticidin S
Hygromycin phosphotransferase (*hpt*)	*E. coli*	Resistance to hygromycin-B
Tryptophan synthase (*trpB*)	*E. coli*	Resistance to indale
Xanthine-guanine phosphoribosyl-transferase (XGPRT)	*E. coli*	Resistance to mycophenolic acid
Neomycin phosphotransferase (*neo*)	Bacterial transposons Tn5 and Tn601	Resistance to antibiotic G-418

APPENDIX XLVI

A List of Some Notable Gene Transfers and Their Consequences in Animals of Economic Importance

Gene transferred	*Objective*	*Achievements*	*Remarks*
Cattle, goat, sheep and swine			
Human genes α_1 anti-trypsin, tissue plasminogen activator, blood clotting factor IX, and protein C.	Gene farming	Genes expressed in mammary tissue; proteins secreted in milk in functional form.	Experimental stages; α-antitrypsin recovered from Tracey's (a sheep) milk at the rate of 1.5 kg per lactation.
Sheep			
Bacterial genes, *cysE* and *cysM* concerned with cysteine biosynthesis)	Improved wool production/ quality	Gene expressed in transgenic animals	—
Mice and Swine			
Human haemoglobin and specific circulating immunoglobulins (antibodies)	Proteins from blood serum for blood transfusion and disease diagnosis	Gene expressed; proteins released in blood serum	Experimental stages
Swine and Sheep			
Human growth hormone	Increased desirable body growth	Improvements in body weight gain, feed efficiency, lean meat/fat ratio, fat composition, etc.	Produces joint pathology, skeletal defects, ulcers, infertility, etc.
Rabbits			
Human genes : Interleukin 2, growth hormone, tissue plasminogen activator, α_1-antitrypsin, etc. *Bovine gene* : α-lactoglobulin	Molecular farming or gene farming	Genes expressed in mammary tissue; proteins harvested from milk	Experimental stage
Fish			
Salmon or rainbow trout growth hormone	Increased body growth	Upto 60% increase in size	Transgene stably inherited; growth improved by selection
Anti-freeze protein gene, α-globin gene, chicken δ-crystalline protein gene, etc.	Variable	Genes expressed in transgenic individuals	Transgenes are stably integrated

APPENDIX XLVII

A List of Products Generated from Genetically Engineered Microbes (GEMs). The Products are Either in Current Therapeutic Use or in Advanced Stages of Development

Product	*GEM*	*Application*
Currently in therapeutic use		
Insulin*	*E. coli* and yeast	Diabetes
Human growth hormome	*E. coli*	Dwarfism
Interferons*	*E. coli*	Viral diseases, cancer, AIDS
Interleukins	*E. coli*	Various cancers
Hepatitis-B surface antigen*	Yeast	Vaccine against hepatitis B
Streptokinase	*E. coli*	Thrombolysis
Epidermal growth factor	*E. coli*	Wound and burn healing
Granulocyte macrophage colony stimulating factor*	Yeast	Cancer, AIDS
Granulocyte colony stimulating factor*	Yeast	Cancer, AIDS, bone marrow transplantation
Bovine growth hormone	*E. coli*	Increase milk yield
Tumour necrosis factor	*E. coli*	Sepsis, cancer
In advanced stages of development		
Atrial natriuretic factor (ANF)	Yeast	Hypertension and kidney diseases
Plasminogen activator (including chimaerics and modifications)	*E. coli*	Thrombolysis
Superoxide dismutase	*E. coli*	Cardiac treatment and organ transplants
Tumour necrosis factor (TNF)	*E. coli*	Antitumour and antiviral therapy
Urokinase	*E. coli*	Thrombolysis
Fibroblast growth factor	*E. coli* and yeast	Neuropathic ulcers
Insulin like growth factor (IGF)	*E. coli* and yeast	Osteoporosis, metabolism
Nerve growth factor	*E. coli* and yeast	Peripheral neuropathies
Platelet-drived growth factor	*E. coli* and yeast	Diabetic ulcers
Haemoglobin (adult)	*E. coli*	Blood substitute
Leucocyte protease inhibitor	Yeast	Cystic fibrosis
Thymosin $\alpha 1$	*E. coli*	Viral infection

* Approved for marketing in India

Source : P.K. Ghosh, 1995. Role of biotechnology in health care in India : Present and future. Biotch. Dev. Rev. June-Dec. 1995, pp. 1-22.

APPENDIX XLVIII

A List of Products (recombinant proteins) Generated Using Recombinant DNA technology. The genes are Expressed in Animal Cell Cultures, and Their Products are Either Already in Therapeutic Use or in Advanced Stages of Development

Product (protein)	*Gene expressed in (host)*	*Application*
Currently in therapeutic use		
Human growth hormone (hGH)	Mouse mammary tumour cell line	Dwarfism
Tissue plasminogen activator (tPA)	Chenese hamster ovary (CHO) cell line	Thrombolysis
Erythropoietin*	Chenese hamster ovary (CHO) cell line	Anaemia
Blood clotting factor VIII*	CHO cell line	Haemophilia
In advance stages of development		
Antithrombin VIII	CHO cell line	Anticoagulant
Blood factor VIII	BHK-21 cell line	Haemophilia
Blood factor IX	CHO cell line	Haemophilia-B
Interleukin-2 (IL-2)	—	Cancer therapy
Human recombinant antibodies	CHO cell line and Mouse myeloma lines	Infections, various cancers
Hepatitis-B surface antigen (HBsAg)	CHO cell line and C-127 cell line	As vaccine against Hepatitis-B
Interferons (IFN)	—	Tumours
Plasminogen activator (including chimaeric and modified)	CHO cell line and *Spodoptera frugiperda*	Thrombolysis
CD4 Protein	Mammalian cell line	AIDS vaccine
gp160 protein	Mammalian cell line	AIDS vaccine
p24 protein	Mammalian cell line	AIDS vaccine
Interleukin-1 receptor antagonist	Mammalian cell line	Severe sepsis
Atrial natriuretic	Mammalian cell line	Kidney failure
Ciliary neurotropic factor	Mammalian cell line	Amyotrophic sclerosis
DNase	Mammalian cell line	Cystic fibrosis

* Approved for marketing in India

Source : P.K Ghosh, 1995. Role of biotechnology in health care in India : Present and future. Biotch. Dev. Rev. June-Dec. 1995, pp. 1-22.

APPENDIX XLIX

A List of Some of the Products Generated/Likely to be Generated from Cultured Animal Cells

Product	*Cell line*	*Remarks*
Virus vaccines		
Canine distemper	Dog kidney	
Foot and mouth disease (FMD)	Cow kidney	
Hepatitis-B	Human plasma-derived	From blood of infected individuals
Influenza	Chick embryo	
Measles	Chick embryo	
Mumps	Chick embryo	
* Polio	Primate kidney	First vaccine from cell culture
* Rabies	1. Chick embryo 2. Human diploid cells	
* Rubella (German measles, MMR)	Human diploid cells	
Cellular biochemicals		
Angiogenic factor	Human tumour	
β-Interferon	Mouse fibroblast	
β- and γ-interferons	Chinese hamster ovary (CHO) cell lines	
α-Interferon	Human leucocytes	
Immunoregulatory biochemicals		
Interleukin-2	Lymphoblastoid T-cell line	Continuous cell line
Lymphokines	—	
Enzymes		
Collagenase, pepsin, renin, trypsin	—	
Urokinase (plasminogen activator)	Human kidney	
Tissue-type plasminogen activator	CHO cell line	
Single chain urokinase type Plasminogen activator	Human kidney transformed cell line TCL598	
Tyrosine hydroxylase	—	
Hormones		
Luteinizing hormone	—	
Follicle stimulating hormone	—	
Chorionic hormone	—	
Erythropoietin	—	
Growth hormone	—	
ACTH (adenocorticotrophic hormone)	—	
Immunobiologicals		
Monoclonal antibodies	Hybridoma clone	Most dominant activity

*Being manufactured in India

APPENDIX L

A Comparison Between Transgenic Mice and Knockout mice

Sl. No.	Feature	Transgenic mice	Knockout mice*
1.	Cells into which DNA is introduced	Zygote	Embryonic stem (ES) cells
2.	The transgene that is introduced	Natural gene or cDNA of the desired gene	A mutated or disrupted gene.
3.	Identity of the transgene	Any gene from any organism that is desired for some specific region	The particular mouse gene that is to be knocked out.
4.	Means of diversity of DNA	Microinjection into the zygote, and implantation into foster mother.	ES cells are transfected and selected for homologous recombination; ES cells introduced into blastocyst, which are implanted into foster mothers.
5.	The outcome	Mouse gains a transgene function	A particular mouse gene is rendered non-functional.

* Knockout mice are a special type of transgenic mice.

APPENDIX LI

White Blood Cells, Types and Their function

Cell type	Function
A. Phagocytes	
1. Neutrophil	It participates in early stage of defence against microorganisms.
2. Monocyte	It arrives at site after neutrophils transfer into macrophages; Engulf's foreign materials, present antigen to lymphocytes, stimulates lymphocyte proliferation.
3. Eosinophil	It responds to allergies and parasitic infections.
B. Lymphocytes	
1. B-cells	When they are activated by foreign molecules, produce plasma and memory cells.
2. Plasma cells	They secrete antibodies.
3. Memory cells	They respond to antigens during secondary response.
4. Natural killer cells	They directly destroy virus infected and cancerous cells.
5. Cytotoxic T-cells	They destroy virus-infected and cancerous cells.
6. Helper T-cells	They stimulate B cell and killer T-cell proliferation.
7. Suppressor T-cells	They slow down immune response.
C. Basophils	They release histamine in inflammatory response.

APPENDIX LII

A Comparison Between Human B and T Cells With Respect to Certain Features

Sl. No	*Feature*	*B cells*	*T cells*
1.	Maturation	Bone marrow	Thymus
2.	Antigen receptors		
	I. Surface Ig	Present	Absent
	II. TCR/CD3	Absent	Present
3.	Other receptors		
	I. EBV receptors (= CR2**)	Present	Absent
	II. Measle receptors	Absent	Present
4.	Other markers	CD*5/19/23/40/45	CD2*4/5/*8/45
	I. MHC class I	Present	Present only in activated cells
	II. MHC class II	Present	Present only in activated cells
5.	Polyclonal activation (by nonspecific mitogens)††	Anti-Ig$^+$	Anti-CD_3^+
		Phytohaemagylutinin (PHA)	*Staphylococcus aureus* strain Cowan I
		Conanavalin A	EBV**

* Present only on a subset (= subpopulation) of cells.

** Complement receptor; EBV, Epstein-Barr virus.

\+ The most clear-cut and commonly used procedure to distinguish between B and T cells.

†† A mitogen stimulates a cell to undergo mitosis.

APPENDIX LIII

A List of Some Autoimmune Diseases of Human beings

Autoimmune disease	*Self-antigen*	*Immune response*
	Organ-specific autoimmune diseases	
Autoinmune haemolytic anaemia	RBC membrane proteins	Autoantibodies
Grave's disease	Thyroid-stimulating receptor	Autoantibody (stimulation of the receptor)
Insulin-dependent diabetes	Pancreatic beta cells	T_{DTH} cells*, autoantibody
Myasthenia gravis	Acetylcholine receptors	Autoantibody (blockage of the receptor)
Spontaneous infertility	Sperm	Autoantibodies
	Systemic autoimmune diseases	
Multiple sclerosis	Brain	T_{DTH} and T_C cells, autoantibodies
Rheumatoid arthritis	Connective tissue, IgG	Autoantibodies, immune complexes
Scleroderma	Nuclei, heart, lungs, kidney, gastrointestinal tract	Antoantibodies
Systemic lupus erythematus	DNA, nuclear protein, RBC and platelet membranes.	Autoantibodies, immune complexes

* T_{DTH} = T cells involved in delayed hypersenstivity.

APPENDIX LIV

A List of Some Immunodeficiency Diseases of Human beings

Disease	Specific defect	Impaired immune function	Genetic basis*
Severe combined immunodeficiency (SCID)	RAG-1/RAG2 deficiency	TCR or Ig gene rearrangement	AR
	ADP deficiency, PNP deficiency	Toxic metabolites accumulate in T and B cells	AR
	JAK-3 deficiency	Defective signals from IL-2, IL-4 IL-7, IL-9, IL-15	AR
	IL-2R γ-deficiency		XL
	ZAP-70 deficiency	Defective signal from TCR	AR
Bare lymphocyte syndrome	Defect in MHC class II gene promoter	Lack of MHC class II molecules	AR
Interferon-gamma receptor	IFN-γ receptor defect	Impaired immunity to mycobacteria	AR
Ataxia telangiectasia	Defective cell cycle kinase	Low IgA, IgE	AD
Di George syndrome	Thymic aplasia	T cell and B cell development	AD
Gammaglobulinemias	X-linked agamma-globulinemia	Burton's tyrosine kinase (Btk; no mature B cells)	XL
	X-linked hyper-IgM syndrome	Defective CD40 ligand	XL
	Common variable immuno-deficiency	Low IgG, IgA; variable IgM	Complex
	Selective IgA deficiency	Low or no IgA	Complex

* AR, autosomal recessive; XL, X-linked; AD, autosomal dominant; complex, precise genetics not known and may be multigenic; TCR, T cell receptor; Ig, immunoglobulin; ADA, adenosine deaminase; IL-2Rγ, gamma chain of interleukin-2 receptor; JAK-3, Janus kinase 3; RAG-1/RAG-2, recombination activating proteins; ZAP-70, a tyrosine kinase involved in T cell signal transduction.

APPENDIX LV

A List of Some Tumour-Associated Antigens being Evaluated as Targets for Cancer Therapy Using Monoclonal Antibodies

Tumour type	*Tumour antigen*	*Target antigen*
	Limphoid cell-surface markers	
T-cell leukaemia/lymphoma	T-cell marker	CD5
B-cell lymphoma	B-cell marker	CD20
B-cell lymphoma	Anti-idiotype	Immunoglobulin
	Nonlymphoid tissue markers	
Colon cancer	Carcinoembryonic antigen (CEA)	Glycoprotein
Neurorectodermal tumours	Gangliosides like GD2 and GD3	Glycolipids associated with neutral tissues
Breast cancer	MUC1	Glycoprotein
Some lung, head, neck and breast-tumour	Epidermal growth factor receptor (EGFR)	EGF-binding cell surface protein
Breast and ovarian tumours	HER2 (an EGF like receptor)	Cell surface EGF binding protein*

*It is homology to EGFR

APPENDIX LVI

The Mode of Action of the Common Immuno-Suppressive Drugs Used to Prevent Graft Rejection

Immunosuppressive drug	*Mode of action*
Azathioprine (Imuran)	Mitotic inhibitor; acts on S phage cells; blocks synthesis of inosinic acid*
Cyclophosphamide	Mitotic inhibitor; an alkylating agent.
Methotrexate	Mitotic inhibitor; blocks purine biosynthesis by acting as a folic acid antagonist.
Corticosteroids	Anti-iflammatory agents; affects immune response at many levels.
Cyclosporin A**, FK506**	Block activation of resting T cells by inhibiting transcription of genes encoding IL-2 and IL-2 receptor; they prevent formation and the translocation of factors needed for transcription.
Rapamycin**	Blocks the proliferation and differentiation of activated T_H cells and in G1 phase.

* Inosinic acid is a precursor of the purines.

** Fungal metabolites.

APPENDIX LVII

A List of Selected Antibiotics Produced Commercially

Antibiotic	*Produced by*	*Activity*	*Chemical nature*
Amphotericin B	*Streptomyces nodosus*	Antifungal	Polyene
Bacitracin	*Bacillus subtilis*	Gram$^+$ bacteria	Peptide
Cephalosporin C	*Cephalosporium acremonium*	Gram$^+$ and $^-$ bacteria	Peptide
Cycloheximide	*S. griseus*	Antifungal	—
Fungimycin	*S. coelicolor*	Antifungal	Polyene
Gentamycin	*Micromonospora purpurea*	Gram$^+$ bacteria	Aminoglycoside
Gramicidin	*Bacillus brevis*	Gram$^+$ bacteria	Peptide
Griseofulvin	*Penicillium griseofulvum*	Gram$^+$ and $^-$ bacteria	Spirolactone
Kanamycin	*S. kanamyceticus*	Gram$^+$ and $^-$ bacteria, and mycobacteria	Aminoglycoside
Neomycin	*S. fradiae*	Gram$^+$ and $^-$ bacteria	Aminoglycoside
Pimaricin	*S. natalensis*	Antitumour	Polyene
Penicillin G	*P. chrysogenum*	Gram$^+$ bacteria	Peptide
Polymixin B	*Bacillus polymyxa*	Antifungal	Peptide
Streptomycin	*S. griseus*	Gram$^+$ and $^-$ bacteria, and mycobacteria	Aminoglycoside
Tetracyclines	*Streptomyces* sp.	Gram$^+$ and $^-$ bacteria	Tetracycline
Trichomycin	*S. hachijoensis*	Antifungal	Polyene

APPENDIX LVIII

A Comparison of the Various Features of Available and Effective Vaccines and Those for the HIV-1 virus

Feature	*In the case of most vaccines*	*In the case of HIV-1*
Mode of function	Mimic natural immunity against reinfection generally seen in those recovered from infection.	HIV-1 is able to infect and cause AIDS even in the presence of circulating antibodies against itself.
Protection from	Disease production, and not from infection.	Remains latent as provirus for long periods before causing AIDS.
Maturation rate in the infection	Very low; viruses are remain stable overtime.	High mutation rate.
Nature	Whole killed or live-attenuated pathogens.	Killed HIV 1 nonantigenic; attenuated virus poses risk.
Frequency of infection	Infrequent contact with the pathogens	Very frequent (even daily) contact in high risk groups.
Infection through	Mucosal surface of the respiratory or gastrointestinal tract.	The genital tract.
Evaluation and test carried out in	Animal models before trials with human volunteers.	A suitable animal model is not available for HIV-1/AIDS.

APPENDIX LIX

A List of Some Selected Microorganisms Against Which Probes are Available for Diagnosis of Diseases

Protozoa	*Helminths*	*Bacteria*	*Viruses*
Leishmania (Kala-azar)	*Schistosomes* (Human blood flukes)	*Legionella*	Herpex virus type 2
Trypanosoma (Sleeping sickness)	*Wuchereria* and *Brugia* (Filaria)	*Mycobacterium tuberculosis* complex *Mycobacterium* species	Herpex virus type 1 and 2
Plasmodium (Malaria)	*Onchocera* (River blindness) *Trichinella* *Taenia solium*	*Mycobacterium avium-sutracellulare* *Mycoplasma pneumoniae* *Chlamydia* *Campylobacter* species	—

APPENDIX LX

A List of Some Antibiotics and the Mode of Their Action

Antibiotic	*Mode of action*
Amino glycoside Manamycin Neomycin Streptomycin	Inhibit protein synthesis by interacting with 30*S* or 50*S* subunit of ribosome.
β-Lactams Ampicillin Carbenicillin Penicillin	Inhibit synthesis of bacterial cell wall.
Trimethoprim and sulphonamides	Inhibit synthesis of tetrahydrofolate.
Chloramphanicol	Inhibits protein synthesis by acting on 50*S* subunit of ribosome.
Tetracyclines	Inhibits protein synthesis by interacting with 30*S* subunit of ribosome.
Glycopeptides Vancomycin	Interfere with synthesis of bacterial cell wall.
Macrolides and lincosamides Erythromycin Lincomycin	Inhibit protein synthesis by interacting with 50*S* subunit of ribosome.
Polymixins Polymixin B Polymixin E	Attach to cell membrane and modify ion flux, resulting in cell lysis.
Quinolones Nalidic acid Norfloxin Ofloxacin	Interfere with replication of DNA by inhibition of DNA gyrase.
Rifampicin	Interferes with formation of mRNA by binding to RNA polymerase.

APPENDIX LXI

A List of Different Types of Interferons and Their Main Features

Interferon (IFN)	*Number of amino acids*	*Produced by*	*Induced by*	*Receptors*
IFN-αI subfamily	166-172	Leucocytes	Viral infection	IFN-α and IFN-β share common receptors
IFN-α-II subfamily (= IFN-ω)	166-172	Leucocytes	Viral infection	
IFN-β	166	Fibroblasts and leucocytes	Viral infection	
IFN-γ	143	T-lymphocytes	Antigenic stimulation of T-lymphocytes	Distinct receptor

APPENDIX LXII

A List of Some Selected Applications of Enzymes Used in Treatment of Diseases

Enzyme	*Reaction catalyzed*	*Used for*
α-Amylase	Starch hydrolysis	Digestive disorders
Asparaginase	Asparagine → aspartate	Leukaemia
Collagenase	Collagen hydrolysis	Skin ulcers
Ficin	Protein hydrolysis	Deworming
Glutaminase	L-Glutamine → L-glutamate	Leukaemia
Lysozyme	Bacterial cell wall hydrolysis	Used as antibiotic
Lipase	Lipid hydrolysis	Digestive disorders
Papain	Protein hydrolysis	Deworming
Proteases	Protein hydrolysis	Digestive disorders
Rhodonase	Formation of cyanide sulphide	Cyanide poisoning
Ribonuclease	RNA digestion	As antiviral agent
β-Lactamase	Penicillin → penicilloate	Penicillin allergy
Streptokinase	Plasminogen → plasmin	Blood clots
Uricase	Urate → allantoin	Gout
Urokinase	Plasminogen → plasmin	Blood clots

APPENDIX LXIII

A List of Some Examples of Solid State Fermentation Used Commercially in Japan

Product	*Substrate*	*Primary genus*	*Product used as*	*Remarks*
Soy sauce (shoyu)	Soybean, wheat	*Aspergillus soyae* or *A. oryzae*	Food	Processed further
Hamanatto	Soybean, wheat	*Aspergillus* sp.	Food	Processed further
Miso	Rice/barley, soybean	*A. oryzae*	Food	Processed further
Sufu	Tofu	*Actinomucor* sp.	Food	Processed further
Tempeh	Soybean	*Rhizopus* sp. (*R. oligosporus*)	Food	No further processing
Cellulase*	Wheat bran	*Trichoderma reesei* (syn. *T. viride*)	Enzyme	
Citric acid	Cooked vegetable residue	*Aspergillus niger*	Organic acid	Occasionally; in Japan
Amylase*	Rice	*A. oryzae*	Enzyme	

*The enzymes are produced commercially, other enzymes pectinase, protease and lipase.

APPENDIX LXIV

A List of Some Selected Fermented Foods Used in the Various Countries

Fermented food	*Substrate*	*Microorganism*	*Country/Region*
Ang-Kak (red rice)	Rice	*Monascus purpureus*	China
Cheese (processing)	Milk	*Penicillium roquefortii* *P. camembertii*	Worldwide
Gari	Cassava	*Corynebacterium manihot* *Geotrichum candidum*	West Africa
Idli	Rice and urad	*Leuconostoc mesenteroides* *Streptococcus faecalis*	India
Kaffir beer	*Sorghum caffrorum* or *Eleusine coracana*	*Lactobacillus delbrueckii* *Saccharomyces cerevisiae*	South Africa
Kefir	Milk	*Lactobacillus* sp. and yeast	USSR
Sake (rice wine)	Rice	*A. oryzae*	Japan
Tape ketan, tape katella	Rice	*Amylomyces rouxii* *Endomycopsis burtonii*	Indonesia
Yoghurt	Milk	*Streptococcus thermophilus* *Lactobacillus bulgaricus*	Worldwide

APPENDIX LXV

A List of Microorganisms/Enzymes Used for Cheese Production and Their Functions

Process	*Organism/Enzyme*	*Function*
Curd formation	1. Bacterial cultures : *Streptococcus lactis, S. cremoris* or *S. thermophilus* plus *Lactobacillus lactis, L. bulgaricus*	Produce lactic acid from lactose, lower pH to 4.6 and lead to coagulation of milk.
	2. Rennet (calf or *Mucor miehei**)	Digests κ-casein, which leads to coagulation of α- and β-caseins; results in curd formation. It cleaves the peptide bond between Phe 105 and Met 106 of κ-casein.
	3. Lipase (before rennet is added; from *Mucor miehei*) or *Aspergillus niger*)	Lipid digestion (modest) and accumulation of butytic acid; produces strong flavours of Italian cheese.
Ripening	1. Proteases (from *Bacillus amyloliquefuciens*), or 2. *Penicillium roquefortii P. camembertii*	Flavour production, *e.g.*, in cheddar cheese by proteolysis. 1. Peptides with terminal acidic amino acid residues—meaty appetising flavours. 2. Nonterminal hydrophobic amino acid residues : (*a*) Medium-sized peptides, bitter flavour (*b*) Intensity of bitter flavour decreases with decrease in peptide size. (*c*) Bitter flavour disappears with larger peptides.

* Rennet from *M. Miehei* is treated with oxidizing agents, *e.g.*, H_2O_2, etc.; this converts methionine residues to their sulphoxides, reduces its thermostability to 10°C, and makes it more comparable to calf rennet.

APPENDIX LXVI

A List of Enzymes Used in Food Processing (other than cheese)

Enzyme	*Substrate*	*Action/Objective*
A. Proteases		
1. Endogenous proteases	Meat ('hanging' of meat)	Tenderisation of meat, flavour development.
2. Subtilisin	Soy protein	Partial hydrolysis; increases whipping expansion, emulsifying capacity; hydrolysate may be added to cured meats
3. Neutral or alkaline proteases	Animal and fish bones (contain about 5% meat)	Mashed bone incubated at 60°C for 4 hours; meat slurry used in canned meats and soups.
4. Subtilisin	Red blood cells (RBCs)	RBC haemolysate subjected to hydrolysis; haeme molecules precipitate and are removed; purified hydrolysate spray-dried and used in cured meats, sausages, luncheon meats, etc.
5. Papain (in active form)	Meat (tenderisation)	Injected into the jugular vein shortly before slaughter; after slaughter, papain is activated and tenderises the meat, only 2-5 ppm (of body weight) enzyme injected.
6. Heat labile fungal protease	Dough from high gluten wheat varieties	Hydrolysis of gluten; makes dough suitable for biscuit, pie-pastry making.
B. Glucose oxidase	D-glucose	D-glucose oxidized to gluconic acid, O_2 utilized, H_2O_2 produced.
C. Catalase	H_2O_2	Degrades H_2O_2 into water and O_2; used in combination with glucose oxidase to *remove glucose and/or O_2 from foods, drinks,* etc.
D. Amylases (α- and β-), glucoamylase, pullulanase, invertase, glucose isomerase (immobilized)	Starch, sucrose, D-glucose	Production of glucose, maltose and high fructose syrups.

APPENDIX LXVII

A List of Enzymes Widely Used in the Production of Fruit Juices, Beer and Distilled Alcoholic Drinks

Product	*Substrate*	*Problem*	*Enzyme(s)*	*Action/purpose*
Fruit juices, wines	Pectins	Cloudiness	A mixture of : (*i*) polygalacturonase (*ii*) pectin esterase, (*iii*) pectin lyase, and (*iv*) hemicellulases	Reduced viscosity, no cloudiness, increased juice yield, enhanced flavour, shorter fermentation time (wines)
Beer	1. Starch	Nonfermentable	Barley malt + bacterial and fungal α-amylases, β-glucanase	Saccharification; stopped by boiling the 'wort' when 75% starch is saccharified
	2. Protein	—	Proteases (neutral)	Hydrolysis of protein and increased fermentation rate (later); especially to obtain high gravity beer
	3. Cellulose and barley β-glucans	—	Cellulases	Used to hydrolyse cellulose and barley β-glucans, especially when wheat is added as adjunct*
	4. Protein (in association with tannin)	Chill-haze on cooling the beer	Papain	Used in post-fermentation stages
	5. Starch	More total solids in beer	Glucoamylase of fungal α-amylase	Higher degree of saccharification, reduced alcohol and total solids; to produce 'light' beers
	6. Dextrins**	Nonfermentable; more total solids in beer	Genetically engineered yeast (*S. cerevisiae*)	Utilizes dextrins to produce alcohols: to produce light beers
Distilled alcoholic drinks	Starch	Nonfermentable	More heat stable bacterial α-amylases	Saccharification of starch present in the substrate

* An adjunct is a starch containing material added to barley malt in order to increase the amount of fermentable sugars.

** Up to 25% of the carbohydrates in original fermentation liquid.

APPENDIX LXVIII

A List of Some Selected Valuable Products (other than antibiotics) From Microorganisms; These Represent Potential Targets for Directed Screening

Product	*Activity*	*Source (producing microorganism)*
Avermectin	Antihelmintic	*Streptomyces avermitilis*
Bestatin	Antitumour	*S. olivoreticuli*
1, 3-Diphenethylurea	Antidepressant	*Streptomyces* sp.
Detoxin	Detoxicant	*S. caespitosus*
Herbicidin	Herbicide	*S. sagamonensis*
Cyclosporin	Immunosuppressor	*Trichoderma polysporum*
Piercidin	Insecticide	*S. mobaraensis*
Tetranactin	Miticide	*S. aureus*
Gibberellic acid	Plant growth regulator	*Gibberella fujikuroi*
Slaframine	Salivation inducer	*Rhizoctonia leguminicola*
Azalomycin	Antiprotozoal	*S. hygroscopicus*
Aabomycin A	Antiviral	*S. hygroscopicus*

APPENDIX LXIX

A List of Some Enzymes Used for Commercial Activlties

Enzyme	*Source*	*Application*	*Use in the form*
α-Amylase	*Bacillus licheniformis, B. amyloliquefaciens*	Hydrolysis of starch to dextrans	Extracellular, soluble
Glucoamylase	*Aspergillus niger*	Dextran hydrolysis to glucose	Extracellular, soluble
Xylose (Glucose)–isomerase	*Bacillus coagulans**	Pure glucose to equilibrium mixture of glucose + fructose	Immobilized whole cells
Alkaline protease	*B. licheniformis, B. subtilis*	Detergents (protein digestion)	Extracellular, soluble
Neutral protease	*B. amyloliquefaciens, B. subtilis*	Protein digestion in brewing substances	Extracellular, soluble
Acid protease, *e.g.*, rennet	*A. niger***	Milk coagulation and cheese flavour enhancement	Extracellular, soluble
Pectinase	*A. niger, B. subtilis*	Pectin hydrolysis in fruit juices	Extracellular, soluble
Glucanase	*A. niger, B. subtilis*	In fruit juices	Extracellular, soluble
Cellulase	*A. niger, Trichoderma reesei Rhizopus* species[+]	Cellulose hydrolysis in fruit juices	Extracellular, soluble
Lipase	*A.. niger*	Detergents, lipid hydrolysis	Extracellular, soluble
Lactase		Milk lactose hydrolysis to glucose + galactose	Immobilized on glass beads

* Other source organisms : *Streptomyces olivaceus, Microbacterium arborescens, Actinoplanes missouriensis.*

** Other source organisms : *Mucor miehei, Mucor pusillus, Endothica parasitica.*

[+] Other source organisms : *Candida lipolytica, Geotrichum candidum.*

APPENDIX LXX

A List of Some Industrially Important Enzymes and Their Applications

Enzyme	*Source*	*Annual production (tons/yr)*	*Application*
Animal enzyme			
Catalase	Liver	<1	Food
Lipase	Pancreas	<1	Food
Rennet (= chymosin)	Pancreas	>1	Cheese
Trypsin	Pancreas	<1	Leather
Plant enzymes			
α-Amylase	Malted barley	>100	Brewing
β-Amylase	Malted barley	>100	Brewing
β-Glucanase	Malted barley	>10	Brewing
Ficin	Fig latex	<1	Food
Papain	Papaya latex	>10	Meat
Bacterial enzymes			
α-Amylase	*Bacillus*	>100	Starch
β-Amylase	*Bacillus*	>1	Starch
Glucose (xylose) isomerase	*Bacillus, Streptomyces*	>10	Fructose syrup
Penicillin amidase	*Bacillus*	<1	Pharmaceutical
Protease	*Bacillus*	>100	Detergent
Fungal enzymes			
α-Amylase	*Aspergillus*	>10	Baking
Glucoamylase	*Aspergillus, Rhizopus*	>100	Starch
Rennet (aspartic proteinase)	*Mucor miehei*	>10	Cheese
Pectinase	*Aspergillus*	>10	Drinks
Protease (aspartic proteinase)	*Aspergillus*	>10	Baking
Yeast enzymes			
Invertase	*Saccharomyces*	<1	Confectionery
Lactase (β-galactosidase)	*Kluyveromyces*	<1	Dairy
Raffinase (α-galactosidase)	*Saccharomyces*	<1	Food

APPENDIX LXXI

A Sample of the Screening Approaches Used for Detection of Microbial Isolates Producing Useful Products. Of Necessity, the Description is Generalized and Highly Simplified

Product	*Screening*
Extracellular enzymes	
Amylase	Starch in agar; detected by clear zones on idoine staining
Proteases	Protein suspended in agar; detected by cleared zones
Lipases	Target lipid emulsified in agar; detected by cleared zones (or precipitation of liberated fatty acid by Ca^{2+} in agar)
Urease	pH indicator in urea agar (indicator, phenol red)
Enzyme inhibitors	Enzyme-containing agar; the procedure for enzyme detection is suitably modified.
Antimicrobials	1. *Primary screening* is based on a broad range of specific resistant or hypersensitive microorganisms, *e.g., Penicillium avellaneum*, and recombination-deficient strains of *Bacillus subtilis* and *E. coli* for antitumour agents; *Acholeplasma laidlawii* for polyether antibiotics, etc. 2. Secondary screening uses more specialized media and conditions.
Antifungals	Chitin synthase inhibition (chitin, *i.e.,* ($1 \rightarrow 4$)-β-homopolymer of N-acetylglucosamine, is a major constituent of fungal cell wall).
Antiviral agents	Agar-diffusion tissue culture method for *in vitro* and *in vivo* screenings using complex fermentation broths; antiviral agents pyrazomycin and mycophenolic acid identified in this manner.
Antitumour agents	1. *Prescreening* uses microorganisms known to be sensitive to antitumour agents, *e.g., P. avellaneum,* mutants of *B. subtilis, E. coli,* etc., mycoplasma *Acholeplasma laidlawii* etc. 2. Initial screenings are based on *in vivo* animal testing, which is complex and time consuming.

APPENDIX LXXII

A Summary of Different Approaches used for Mutation and Genetic Recombination for Strain Improvement

Approach	*Chief feature*	*Example/Remark*
A. Mutant Selection : Types		The main approach to strain improvement; *produces new alleles of existing genes.*
1. Spontaneous mutation	Occurs without any treatment with a mutagen	Used in the initial stages of strain improvement; also for maintenance of improved strians
2. Induced mutation	Induced by chemical (mainly) or physical mutagens	Mutagenesis followed by selection ; several cycles employed
3. Major mutation	Affects the pattern of metabolite production	Production of 6-demethyltetracycline in place of tetracycline by *S. aureofaciens.*
4. Minor mutation	Affects the rate of metabolite production	Small gains in each cycle of selection; substantial improvement after several cycles
B. Mutant Selection : Strategies		
1. Auxotrophic mutant	Defective biosynthesis of a biochemical	Enhanced production of an amino acid, *e.g.*, *phe*$^-$ mutants accumulate tyrosine
2. Analogue-resistant mutant	Feed-back insensitive enzymes	Overproduction of metabolites, *e.g.*, amino acids by *C. glutamicus*
3. Revertant of a nonproducing mutant		Some mutants are high producers, *e.g.*, chlortetracycline by *S. viridifaciens*
4. Revertant of an auxotrophic mutant		Some mutants are high producers, *e.g.*, chlortetracycline by *S. viridifaciens*
5. Resistance to the antibiotic produced by the organism itself.		Increased production, *e.g.*, chlortetracycline by *S. aureofaciens*
C. Recombination		Produces new combinations of existing alleles
1. Sexual reproduction	Conjugation; fusion of gametes	Some bacteria and Actinomycetes; fungi and yeast
2. Heterokaryosis	Nuclear fusion followed by mitotic recombination and mitotic reduction	Fungi
3. Protoplast fusion	Protoplasts produced by lytic enzymes; fusion by PEG, recombinant recovery	Bacteria, Actinomycetes, fungi, quite successful.

APPENDIX LXXIII

A Summary of the Types of Changes in Metabolite Production Induced by Recombinant DNA Technology/Genetic Engineering

Approach	*Features*	*Example/Remark*
Recombinant DNA technology	Genes from other organisms transferred into microorganisms.	New genes transferrred; entirely new products, modified products, enhanced product yield, etc.
1. Recombinant proteins	Protein encoded by the transgenes are the products of interest.	Examples are insulin, interferons, human growth hormone, bovine growth factor, etc.
2. Metabolic engineering	Motabolites generated by the transgene encoded enzymes are the products of interest.	Existing metabolic pathways modified, extended, made more efficient or new pathways introduced.
I. Product modification	The new enzyme modifies the product of existing biosynthetic pathway.	Conversion of cephalosporin C into 7-aminocephalosporanic acid by D amino acid oxidase (in *A. chrysogenum*).
II. New substrate utilization	Inaccessible substrate converted into accessible form.	Beer fermentation by yeast : cyclodextrins coverted into glucose, which is utilized by yeast.
III. Completely new metabolite	All the genes of a new pathway transferred.	*E. coli*, transfer of two genes for poly-hydroxybutyrate synthesis from *Alcaligenes eutrophus.*
IV. Enhanced metabolite production	Amplification of the gene encoding that enzyme whose activity is rate limiting.	Gene *cefEF* of *C. acremonium* catalysing the conversion of penicillin N; increased cyclosporin yield.
V. Enhanced growth	Enhanced substrate utilization.	*E. coli* glutamate dehydrogenase into *M. methylotrophus*; carbon conversion increased from 4% to 7%.

APPENDIX LXXIV

A List of Some Important Microorganisms Used for Single Cell Protein (SCP) Production

Microorganism	*Substrate*	*Used as*	*Used commercially*
Algae			
Chlorella species	CO_2 + sunlight	Feed	Yes (Japan and Taiwan)
Scenedesmus acutus	CO_2 + sunlight	—	—
Spirulina maxima	CO_2 + sunlight	Feed	Yes (Mexico)
Yeasts			
Candida utilis	1. Confectionery effluents	—	Yes (U.K.); Symba process
(Torula yeast)	2. Ethanol	Food	Yes (U.S.A.)
	3. Sulphite liquor	—	Yes (Europe, U.S.A. and Russia)
C. intermedia	Whey	—	Yes; Vienna process
C. krusei (+ *Lactobacillus bulgaricus*)	Whey	—	Yes; Kiel process
C. lipolytica	*n*-alkanes (C_{10}–C_{23}) + ammonia	—	Yes (Russia)
Kluyveromyces fragilis	Whey	Food	Yes (France); Le Bel process
Saccharomyces cerevisae (Baker's yeast)	Molasses	(Food)*	Yes
Fungi			
Chaetomium cellulolyticum	Cellulosic wastes	—	Promising
Fusarium graminearum	Starch hydrolysate	Food	Yes (U.K.)
Paecilomyces varioti	Sulphite liquor	Feed	Yes (Finland); Pekilo process
Bacteria			
Brevibacterium species	C_1–C_4 hydrocarbons	—	Process developed
Methylophilus methylotrophus	Methanol	Feed	Yes (U.K.)

* Mainly used for fermentation of dough in bakeries; thus eaten indirectly as components of food.

APPENDIX LXXV

A List of Some Important Features of Different Microorganisms and the SCP Produced from Them

Feature	*Algae*	*Bacteria*	*Yeasts*	*Filamentous fungi*
Growth Rate	Low	Highest	Quite high	Lower than bacteria and yeast
Substrate	Light, inorganic carbon sources, *e.g.*, CO_2 (preferably)	A wide range of substrates	Most substrates, except hydrocarbons and CO_2	Limited substrates (mostly starchy and cellulosic materials)
pH range	Up to 11	5-7	5-7	3-8
Cultivated in	Open ponds, tanks; in sunlight	Bioreactors	Bioreactors	Bioreactors
Risk of contamination	Serious	High; precautions necessary	Low	Low if grown below pH 5
Biomass recovery	Difficult and costly with unicellular algae	Problematic; improved methods are needed	Easy; by centrifugation	Easy for filamentous or pellet forms
Protein content (crude)	Up to 60%	80% or more	55-60%	50-55%
Amino acid profile	Generally, good; low in S-containing amino acids	Generally, good; a small deficit in S-containing amino acids	Generally, good; deficit in S-containing amino acids	Low in S-containing amino acids
Nucleic acid content	—	Very high (20% RNA)	High (15% RNA)	High (15% RNA)
Removal of nucleic acids	—	Necessary	Necessary	Necessary
Toxins	—	Gram negative bacteria may produce endotoxins	None	Many species produce mycotoxins
Other features	1. Low yield (1-2 g dry wt./l) 2. High chlorophyll content; unsuitable for human	—	High B-vitamin content	Chitin may contain a significant proportion of N-content, which is unavailable.

APPENDIX LXXVI

A List of Various Substrates Used for SCP Production Using Different Microorganisms

Substrate	*Microorganisms*	*Status*
A. Fossil carbon sources		
1. Liquid hydrocarbons (C_{16}–C_{23} *n*-alkanes + ammonia)	*Candida lipolytica*	Product 'Toprina' released and approved; commercial production only in Soviet Union (Ca. 200,000 tons/year)
2. Gaseous hydrocarbons		
(*i*) Methane (CH_4)	*Pseudomonas methanica, Methanomonas methanica, Methylococcus capsulatus, Pseudomonas methanitrificans*	Only upto pilot scale; commercial production presents many technical problems.
(*ii*) C_1 to C_4 hydrocarbons	*Brevibacterium* sp.	Process developed
3. Methanol (produced by chemical conversion of CH_4, etc.)	***Bacteria*** : *Methylophilus methylotrophus* ***Other Bacteria*** : *Methylomonas methanolica, Streptomyces* sp., *P. utilis, P. extroquens* ***Yeast*** : *Torulopsis glabrata, Candida boidinii,* etc.	Grows at 35-40°C; commercial production in U.K.; marketed as 'Pruteen'; 71% protein.
4. Ethanol (by catalytic addition of water to ethylene)	*Candida utilis* (Torula yeast)	Commercial production in U.S.A.; used as human food supplement.
B. Renewable carbon sources		
1. Carbon dioxide (CO_2)	*Spirulina*	Grows in alkaline lakes (up to pH 11); commercial production in Mexico in 1 m deep ponds; yield, 50 tons/ha/yr.
	Chlorella	Commercial production in Japan and Taiwan.
2. Molasses	*Saccharomyces cerevisiae* (baker's yeast)	Over 200,000 tons (dry wt)/yr; produced as by-product of ethanol production; used in dough fermentation.
3. Whey (world production, 74 million tons/yr in 1973)	1. *Kluyveromyces fragilis*	23,000 tons/yr SCP; used as human food in France of over 2 decades.
	2. *Lactobacillus bulgaricus* + *Candida krusei*	—
	3. *Candida intermedia*	—
4. Starch hydrolysates	*Fusarium gramineurum*	Meat like product approved for human use; marketed as 'Mycoprotein' in U.K.
5. Industrial effluents		
(*i*) Confectionery effluents	*Candida utilis*	Commercial production in U.K.
(*ii*) Sulphite-liquor (from wood pulp mills)	1. *Paecilomyces varioti*	Commercial production in Finland; used as animal feed.
	2. *Candida utilis*	Used in USA, Europe and Soviet Union.
6. Cellulosic wastes, *e.g.,* straw, bagasse, sawdust (thermally and chemically pretreated)	1. *Chaetomium cellulolyticum*	Semisolid fermentation; rapid degradation of cellulose (in 4 hr or so).
	2. *Mushrooms*	See Appendix LXXVII

APPENDIX LXXVII

A List of Some of the Mushrooms Cultivated on Commercial Scale

Mushroom	*Substrate*	*Temperature for fruiting body formation*	*Country/Region*
Agaricus bisporus (Button or common edible mushroom)	Compost (horse manure, rice straw)	10–20°C	Europe, U.S.A.
Auricularia species	Saw dust, rice bran	20–30°C	—
Coprinus species	Straw	20–40°C	—
Lentinus edodes (Shii-take)	Logs, saw dust, rice bran	12–20°C	Japan, China
Pleurotus ostreatus	Straw, paper, saw dust	10–20°C	—
Volvariella volvaceae (Chinese or straw mushroom)	Straw, cotton	30–50°C	India, China, South-East Asia

APPENDIX LXXVIII

A Comparison Between Biopesticides and Chemical Pesticides

S.No.	*Biopesticides*	*Chemical pesticides*
1.	Biopesticides do not harm nontarget species.	Nontarget species are also harmed.
2.	They do not pollute the environment.	Cause pollution; sometimes serious.
3.	No harmful residues remain in food, fodder and fibres.	Harmful residues may often remain in food, fodder and fibres.
4.	Relatively cheaper.	Relatively costlier.
5.	Insects are expected not to develop resistance to biopesticides.	Insects may become resistant, *e.g., Heliothis,* has become resistant to most insecticides.
6.	Since they are highly specific, correct identification of the pest is essential.	It is often not critical.
7.	High specificity may often make the use of two or more biopesticides necessary.	Often not required.
8.	Performance may be variable due to the influence of biotic and abiotic factors of the environments.	This is not often the case.

APPENDIX LXXVIX

A List of Some Biocontrol Agents Used Against Insects, Pathogens and Weeds

Microorganism	*Target organism*	*Production process*	*Remarks*
A. Insect control			
(*i*) ***Viruses***			
Nucleopolyhedrosis viruses (NPV)	Asiatic rice borer, bollworm, cotton leafworm, cabbage looper, etc.	In *Heliothis* larvae	Commercially used in U.S.A.
Granulosis viruses (GV)	larvae	—	Not in commercial use
(*ii*) ***Bacteria***			
Bacillus thuringiensis	Lepidopteran and Dipteran larvae, cockroaches, mosquitoes (both *Culex* and *Anopheles*)	Fermentation	Commercially used
Bacillus papillae	—	Fermentation	Commercially used
Bacillus sphaericus	Mosquito larvae (*Culex*)	Fermentation	Used by Government agencies
(*iii*) ***Fungi***			
Beauveria sp.	Many insects, *e.g.*, beetles, caterpillars	Fermentation	Used in USSR
Hirsutella thompsonii	Citrus mites	Fermentation	Commercially used.
Verticillium lecanii	Aphids, white flies	Fermentation	Commercially used in Europe
Metarrhizium anisopliae	Leaf hoppers, beetles, mosquitoes	Fermentation	Commercially used in South Africa
(*iv*) ***Protozoa***			
Malameba locustae	Grasshoppers	—	Promising
Mattesia sp.	Lepidoptera, Coleoptera	—	Promising
(*v*) ***Mites***			
Hypoaspis mites	*Sciarid* larvae and other invertebrates	—	Developmental stages
B. Weed control			
Phytophthora palmivora	—	Fermentation	Commercially used in U.S.A
Colletotrichum gleospirodes		Fermentation	Commercially used in U.S.A.
C. Disease control			
(*i*) ***Fungi***			
Trichoderma viride	Fungal plant pathogens, usually soil-borne	Fermentation	Commercially used in U.K.
Ampelomyces quisqualis	Powdery mildew of grapes, tomatoes, strawberries, etc.	—	Being commercialized in Israel
Arthrobotrys oligospora	Root knot of brinjal, rice	—	Promising in field trials
Arthrobotrys dactyloides	Root knot of tomato, brinjal	—	Promising in field trials
	(In both the above cases, pathogen is *Meloidogyne* sp.)		
(*ii*) ***Bacteria***			
Agrobacterium radiobacter (strain K1026)	*Agrobacterium tumefaciens* (crowngall disease)	Fermentation	Commercially used in U.S.A., Australia.

APPENDIX LXXX

A List of Biological Control Agents Being Developed for Commercial Use in India

Microorganism	*Target organism*	*Crops*	*Remarks*
Bacillus thuringiensis	*Heliothis* and other Lepidopteran and Coleopteran pests	Cotton, chickpea, maize, tomato, groundnut, etc.	Commercially produced by Wockhardt Ltd.
Heliothis NPV*	*Heliothis armigera*	Cotton, chickpea, etc.	To be commercialized.
Spodoptora NPV	*Spodoptera litura*	Cotton, tobacco, pulses, oilseeds, etc.	
Chilo GV**	*Chilo infuscatellus*	Sugarcane	To be commercialized.
Trichograma parasitoid	Sugarcane internode borers, bollworms of cotton, stem borer (sorghum)	Sugarcane, cotton, sorghum	To be commercialized.
Trichoderma	*Macrophomina phaseolona;* seed treatment	Groundnut, chickpea, sunflowers, etc.	To be commercialized.

* NPV, Nucleopolyhedrosis virus.
** GV, Granulosis virus.

APPENDIX LXXXI

A List of Some Important Microorganisms Used as Biofertilizers

Organism	*Activity*	*Association, if any*	*Crops in which used*
Rhizobium (*leguminosarum, japonicum, phaseoli,* etc.)	N_2-fixation	Symbiotic	Legumes (pulses, oilseeds, forage crops)
Azospirillum	N_2-fixation	Associative	Crops like wheat, rice, sugar-cane jowar
Azotobacter	N_2-fixation	Asymbiotic	Wheat, rice, vegetables
Blue-green algae (*Anabaena, Nostoc, Plectonema,* etc.)	N_2-fixation	Asymbiotic	Rice
Azolla-Anabaena complex	N_2-fixation	Symbiotic	Rice
Phosphate solubilzing bacteria (*Thiobacillus, Bacillus,* etc.)	Phosphate solubilization	Asymbiotic	Many crops
Mycorrhiza (*Glomus*)	Phosphate solubilization	Associative	Many crops, including pulses.

APPENDIX LXXXII

A Comparison of Enzyme Engineering and Solvent Engineering

Sl. No.	Feature of enzyme	Enzyme engineering	Solvent engineering
1.	Amino acid sequence	Changed	Unchanged
2.	Recombinant DNA technology	Must be used	Not used
3.	Site-specific mutagenesis	Must be used	Not used
4.	Catalytic activity	Modified	Modified
5.	Enzyme specificity	Modified	Modified
6.	Thermostability	Increased	Increased
7.	pH dependence	Modified	Modified
8.	Allosteric function	Modified	Unchanged
9.	Creation of new enzyme actitivities	Possible	Possible
10.	Stability against denaturants	Acheived	Not achieved
11.	Stereospecificity	Modified	Modified
12.	Use of organic solvent for enzyme action	Not necessary	Essential

APPENDIX LXXXIII

A Comparison Between Enzymes and Non-biological Catalysts

Feature	Enzymes	Non-biological catalysts
Specificity	Highly specific; binding to substrate may be less specific, but the catalyzed reaction is highly specific.	Nonspecific
Rate of reaction	Enhanced by a factor of 10^3–10^6.	Enhancement only a fraction of that by enzymes.
Regulation	Enzymes are subject to a variety of regulations, which increase/decrease reaction rate.	They are not subject to regulation.
Saturation	Enzymes have a maximum reaction rate with respect to substrate concentration.	Most catalysts do not show substrate saturation.
Chemical nature	Enzymes are ordinarily proteins (RNA with enzymatic action is called ribozyme).	Metal and nonmetal inorganic molecules.
Temperature, pressure and pH	Mild biologically compatible.	Often high temperature, and high pressure.
Side reactions (other than the main reaction)	Do not occur	Occur.

APPENDIX LXXXIV

A Comparison of the Various Features of the Different Enzyme Immbolization Systems

Feature	*Immobilization system*			
	Adsorption	*Covalent bonding*	*Entrapment*	*Membrane confinement*
Matrices (example)	Ion-exchange matrices, clays, glasses, etc.	Sepharose, cellulose acrylamide, etc.	Acrylamide, cellulose acetate, etc.	Semipermeable membranes, *e.g.*, hollow-fibres, etc.
Preparation	Simple	Difficult	Difficult	Simple
Immobilization mechanism	Hydrophobic effects, salt links	Covalent bonds	Trapping in gel/ fiber; even covalent bonds	Confinement by a semipermeable membrane.
Binding force	Variable	Strong	Weak	Strong
Enzyme loading	High (Ca 1 g/g matrix)	Small (Ca 0.02 g/g)	High (upto 1 g/g matrix)	—
Enzyme leakage during use	Yes	No	Yes	No
Applicability	Wide	Selective	Wide	Very wide
Problems during operation	High	Low	High	High
Matrix effects on enzyme	Yes	Yes	Yes	No
Diffusional barriers to substrate and product molecules	Absent	Absent	Large	Large
Protection from microbial attack	No	No	Yes	Yes
Cost	Low	High	Moderate	High

APPENDIX LXXXV

A List of Some Important Applications of Immbolized Enzymes

Enzyme	*Substrate*	*Enzyme reactor used**	*Product*
Aminoacylase (immobilized on anion exchange resins)	N-acyl-DL-amino acids	PBR	L-amino acids
Aspartate ammonialyase	Fumaric acid + NH_4^+	PBR	L-aspartic acid
Cyanidase	Cyanide present in industrial waste, food or feed	—	Formic acid
Glucoamylase	Dextrins produced by α-amylase	—	D-glucose
Glucose isomerase- (immobilized with glutar-aldehyde by cross linking)	D-glucose in glucose syrup	PBR	High fructose corn syrup
Invertase	Sucrose	PBR	Invertase sugar
Lactase (immobilized in cellulose triacetate fibres)	Milk and whey	STR	Lactase-free milk and whey
Lipase	Vegetable oils, *e.g.*, palm oil		Cocoa butter substitute
Nitrile hydratase (immobilized cells)	Acrylonitrile		Acrylamide
Penicillin acylases	Penicillin G, penicillin V	STR, PBR	Penicillins
Raffinase (immobilized cells)	Raffinase in beet juice, soybean milk	STR	Raffinose-free solutions
Thermolysin	L-aspartic acid and L-phenylalanine methyl ester	—	Aspartame

* PBR, packed bed reactor; STR, stirred tank reactor.

APPENDIX LXXXVI

A List of the Various Types of Biosensors and the Biological Materials Used in Their Construction

Type of biosensor (detection device or transducer)	*Type of change detected*	*Biological component*	*Example/Remark*
Calorimetric (thermal, thermometric)*	Temperature	Enzyme	Can detect temperature difference of 0.0001°C.
Potentiometric (ion selective electrode)	Evolution/consumption of a gas	Enzyme	Urea detection using urease
Amperometric	Redox reaction (e^- evolution)	Enzyme	Glucose biosensor based on glucose oxidase
Conductimetric	Electrical conductivity (due to ion concentration changes)		Urea detection using urease
Optical	Fluorescence/absorbance/optical properties of biosensor surface	Enzyme, antibody, DNA/RNA	Luciferase for bacteria detection
Acoustic wave (piezoelectric)	Resonant frequency of certain crystals due to changes in mass	Antibodies	Detection of cocaine using antibodies
Whole cell	Based on amperometric, potentio-metric and thermometric devices	Live/dead microbial cells	Nicotinic acid using *Lactobacillus arabinosus*.

* The terms in parenthesis are the other names used for the biosensor.

APPENDIX LXXXVII

A Comparison Among Different Types of Biosensors

	Type of biosensor					
Feature	***Amperometric***	***Conductimetric***	***Potentiometric***	***Piezoelectric***	***Thermometric****	***Optical***
Reliability	High	Medium	Medium	Low	High	Low
Sensitivity	Medium	Medium	Medium	Low	High	Medium
Cost	Low	Very low	Low	Low	High	Low
Complexity	High	Low	Medium	Low	Very high	Medium
Speed of response	Medium	Medium	Medium	Fast	Slow	Medium
General utility	Small	Small	Medium	Narrow	Wide	Small
Current usage	High	Medium	High	Small	Medium	High

* Also called calorimetric biosensor.

APPENDIX LXXXVIII

A List of Some Energy Crops and the Predominant Mode of Their Utilization

Nature of biomass	*Plant species*	*Estimated annual production (tons)*	*Predominant mode of energy use*
Wood (lignocellulose)*	*Beta monosperma, Casurina equisetifolia, Eucalyptus globulus, Leucaena leucocephala, Melia azadirachta, Tamarix dioica*	1.3×10^{10}	Firewood (Ca. 50% of the harvest)
Starch	Cereals, millets, root and tuber crops, *e.g.*, potato	1.9×10^{9}	Bioethanol
Sugar	Sugarcane, sugarbeet	1.2×10^{8}	Bioethanol, *e.g.*, in Barzil
Hydrocarbons	*Euphorbia lathyris, Asclepia speciosa, Copaifera multijuga*, algae		Biodiesel
Wastes**	Crop residues, animal/human refuge, sewage		Biogas
Hydrogen†	Algae like *Chlamydomonas,* anaerobic bacteria like *Clostridium*		Stored as metal hydride, used as H_2 (pollution).

* The listed plant species are fast growing and promising for biomass (wood) production to be used as energy source.

** This item does not represent an energy crop but is based on biomass of diverse origins.

† These species yield an inorganic gas (H_2), which is used to generate energy. Since they use solar energy to generate H_2, they are also regarded as energy crops.

APPENDIX LXXXIX

A Summary of the Different Features of Various Biofuels

Biofuel	*Substrate*	*Microorganism(s)*	*Status of production*	*Limiting factors*
Ethanol	1. Starch, sugar crops	1. *Bacillus licheniformis* (amylase activity) 2. *S. cerevisiae, Zymomonas* (sugar fermentation)	Billions of litres/yr (mostly in Brazil and USA)	1. Low productivity (Brazil) 2. High substrate cost (USA)
	2. Cellulosic wastes			
	(*a*) Enzyme hydrolysis	1. *Trichoderma reesei* (cellulase) 2. *S. cerevisiae* (hexose fermentaion) 3. Recombinant *E. coli* (pentose fermentation) 4. *Clostridium* sp., *Fusarium oxysporum* (consolidated processing)	Likely to enter commerical scale production; suited for energy crops	1. Low yields 2. Slow rate of production 3. Pretreatment needed
	(*b*) Acid hydrolysis	S. *cerevisiae, Zymomonas* (for fermentation)	Likely to enter commercial production; comparable to enzymatic process; suited for waste materials	1. Low yields 2. High acid recycling costs
	(*c*) From synthesis gas	*Clostridium ljungdahlii*	Preliminary stages of development	Mass transfer limitations in bioreactor
Methane	Farm and human wastes; municipal solid wastes, effluents from food and dairy industries, etc.	A group of anaerobic microorganisms	Widely used	1. Slow rates 2. Economically unattractive as transport fuel
Butanol	Soluble carbohydrates	*Clostridium acetobutylicum, C. beijernickii*	Commercial production possible in near future for use as an additive in gasoline	1. Low product tolerance 2. High product cost
Hydrogen	Sunlight and water	*Chlamydomonas reinhardtii C. moewusii*	Long-term research and development needed	Efficiency declines with high light intensities
	Sugars and fatty acids (from starch, cellulose)	Anaerobic bacteria like *Clostridium*	—	—
Biodiesel	Sunlight and CO_2	*Monoraphidium minutum, Cyclotella crypticum,* Euphorbian plants, *Copaifera* tree, etc.	Long-term research and development required	Lack of a genetic transformation system.

APPENDIX XC

A Brief Summary of the Major Types of Wastes and Pollutants Generated by Various Human Activities. This List is Only Illustrative and Definitely not Comprehensive

Human activity	*Wastes*	*Pollutants*		
		Air	*Surface water*	*Soil/ground water*
Manufacturing				
1. Chemical industry	Chemical refuse (solid/liquid)	Volatile organic compounds, SO_x*, NO_x*	Organic and inorganic compounds, heavy metals, cyanides	Organic and inorganic compunds, heavy metals, cyanides
2. Oil refinery	Waste water	Volatile hydrocarbons, SO_x*, NO_x*, aerosols, etc.	Oil, acids, heavy metals, phenolics, etc.	Oil, acids, phenolics, etc.
3. Fertilizer industry	Contaminated gypsum	SO_x*, NO_x*, NH_3	Inorganic chemicals	Inorganic chemicals
Energy production	Fly ash, heavy metals, radioactive waste, etc.	CO, CO_2, SO_x, NO_x, aerosols, water vapour	Heat, coal residues, fly ash, etc.	Fly ash, coal residues
Agriculture and dairy				
1. Agriculture	Crop residues, pesticides, plastics	Pesticides	Pesticides, NO_3^-, PO_4^{3-}	Pesticides, NO_3^-, PO_4^{3-}
2. Dairy	Animal refuse, feed residues	NH_3^-, CH_4	NO_3^-, PO_4^{3-} (from manure)	NO_3^-, PO_4^{3-} (from manure), feed residues
Transport	Scrapped vehicles, used up oil, greese, etc.	CO_2, CO, SO_x, NO_x, volatile hydrocarbons, aerosols, lead	Oil products	Oil products
House-building and domestic				
1. House-building	Building and demolition refuse : wood, metals asbestos, fly ash, etc	CO_2, CO, SO_x, NO_x, heavy metals, volatile organic compounds, etc.	NO_3^-, PO_4^{3-}, O_2^- binding compounds	Metals, wood, fly ash, etc.
2. Domestic	Sewage, garbage, scrapped utensils, appliances, etc.	CO_2, CO, SO_x, NO_x, C.F.C.**, CH_4	Percolation water, NO_3^-, PO_4^{3-}	Solid refuse, percolation water

*SO_x, NO_x, different oxides of S and N, respectively.
** CFC, chlorofluorohydrocarbons.

APPENDIX XCI

A List of Pullants Included in the 'Black List' by European Economic Community (ECC)

Category	Compounds/Materials
1.	Heavy metals, metalloides and containing them.
2.	Halogenated organic compounds.
3.	Organophosphates.
4.	Organic stannous compounds.
5.	Oil and hydrocarbons from crude oil, which are persistent in nature.
6.	Other persistent and hazardous organic compounds.
7.	Cyanides.
8.	Asbestos.

APPENDIX XCII

Accumulation of Metals by Some Plants

Plant	Metal	Concentration (mg kg^{-1} shoot weight) of metal
Thlaspi caerulenscens	Cd	1,800
Ipomoea alpina	Cu	12,300
Haumanisatrum robertis	Co	10,200
T. rotundifolium	Pb	8,200
Macadamia neurophylla	Mn	51,000
Psychotria douarrei	Ni	47,000
Sebertia acuminata	Ni	25% by weight of dried sap
T. caerulenscens	Zn	51,600

APPENDIX XCIII

The Maximum Permissible Limits of Some of the Parameters of Water Quality for Water Intended for Human Consumption [UK Water Supply (Water Quality) Regulations, 1989]

Parameter	*Maximum concentration/value*	*Parameter*	*Maximum concentration/value*
Part A		Chromium (μg/l)	50
Colour units	20	Mercury (μg/l)	1
Turbidity units	4	Lead (μg/l)	50
Odour (dilution number)	3 at 25°C	Nickel (μg/l)	50
Taste (dilution number)	3 at 25°C	Pesticides, total (μg/l)	0.5
pH value	9.5	Polycyclic aromatic hydrocarbons, total (μg/l)	0.2
Temperature	25°C	**Part C**	
Sulphate (mg/l)	250	Total coliforms	0/100 ml
Magnesium (mg/l)	50	Faecal coliforms	0/100 ml
Sodium (mg/l)	150	Faecal streptococci	0/100 ml
Potassium (mg/l)	12	Sulphite reducing clostridia	≤1/100 ml
Dry residues (mg/l)	1,500	**Part D**	
Nitrate (mg/l)	50	Cloride (mg/l)	400
Nitrite (mg/l)	0.1	Calcium (mg/l)	250
Ammonium (mg/l)	0.5	Substances extractable in chloroform (mg/l dry residue)	1
Dissolved or emulsified hydrocarbons (μg/l)	10	Boron (μg/l)	2,000
Phenols (μg/l)	0.5	Barium (μg/l)	1,000
Surfactants (μg/l)	200	**Part E**	
Part B		Total hardness (mg Ca/l)	60
Arsenic (μg/l)	50	Alkalinity (mg HCO_3/l)	30
Cyanide (μg/l)	50		

APPENDIX XCIV

A List of Selected Communicable Diseases Spread through Contaminated Food/Water

Disease	*Spread through*
Amoebiosis	Contamination of food/water by human excreta.
Cholera	Contamination of food/water by human faeces.
Diarrhoea	Contamination of food/water by human excreta.
Typhoid	Contamination of food/water with human, rats, pests or poultry excreta.
Hepatitis (except B)	Contamination of food/water by human excreta.

APPENDIX XCV

The Potential Biohazards from Process of Manufacture in Biotechnology Industries

Sl. No.	*Operation*	*Hazard*
1.	Raw material weighing, mixing etc.	Allergic dust or aerosols.
2.	Bioreactor fermentation.	Aerosols from the reactor, spillage, effluent contamination of gases.
3.	Biomass separation by centrifugation, filtration.	Aerosols, spillage, leakage.
4.	Product purification.	Aerosols, spillage.
5.	Product blending, filtration, drying, packaging.	Aerosols, dust, spillage.
6.	Effluent sterilization, disposal.	Discharge of untreated effluent.

APPENDIX XCVI

A List of Selected Examples of Non-infectious Illnesses Associated with Production Processes in Biotechnology Industries

Sl. No.	***Product/Process***	***Non-infectious illness***
1.	Antibiotics	Cardiovascular disorders, condidiasis, etc.
2.	Brewing	Dermatitis, malt fever.
3.	Citric acid	Asthma, bronchitis.
4.	Enzymes	Asthma, dermatitis, conjunctivitis.
5.	Endotoxin	Flu symptoms.
6.	Fungal fermentation	Asthma, bronchitis.
7.	Single cell protein	Allergic, asthma, dermatitis.
8.	Steroids	Feminization of males, hypertension, increased body weight

APPENDIX XCVII

Allergenic and Toxic Effects of Some Compounds that Confer Disease and/or Insect Resistance (based on Franckoberaspach and Keller, 1997)

Compound	*Role in plant defence*	*Toxic effects*	*Allergenicity*
Alkaloids[1]	Insect resistance	Toxicity problems[1]	—
β-1, 3-glucanases	Fungus resistance	—	—
Cry protein	Insect resistance	Most likely non-toxic (toxicity not reported)	—
Lectins	Involved in fungus and insect resistance	Weight loss and hyper-growth of small intestine in rats	Allergenic
Phytoalexins[2]	Fungus and insect resistance	Toxicity problems[2]	—
Proteinase inhibitors	Insect resistance	Pancreas enlargement, hyperplasia and adenoma	Allergenic
Thionins	Antifunal	Toxic on intravenous injection; nontoxic orally (insufficient data)	—
Virus coat protein	Virus resistance (transgenic)	Most likely nontoxic (toxicity not reported)	—

1. A potato variety derived from a cross with *Solanum chalcoense* had upto 650 mg/kg of glycoalkaloids (normal varieties have only 20–150 mg/kg of glycoalkaloids). It had to be with drawn from the market due to acute toxicity to humans.
2. A conventionally developed insect resistance variety of celery had 8-fold higher psoralen (a phytoalexin) content. Psoralen is known to be toxic, mutagenic and carcinogenic.

APPENDIX XCVIII

Dates and Days to Remember

Date	*Day*
28th February	National Science Day
21st March	World Forest Day
7th April	World Health Day
22nd April	Earth Day
31st May	Anti tobacco Day
5th June	World Environmental Day
11th July	World Population Day
16th September	Ozone Day
1-7th October	World Life Week
3rd October	World Nature Day
16th October	World Food Day
24th October	United Nations Day
19th November–18th December	National Environment Awareness Month

APPENDIX XCIX

A List of Important Journals in Genetics, Cytogenetics Plant Breeding and Biotechnology

S.No.	Name of Journal	Standard abbreviation	Publisher
1.	Acta Cytologia	Acta Cytol.	Science Printers and Publishers St. Louis, Missouri
2.	Advances in Agronomy	Adv. Agron.	Academic Press, N.Y.
3.	Advances in Applied Microbiology	Adv. Appl. Microbiol.	Academic Press, N.Y.
4.	Advances in Biological and Medical Physics	Adv. Biol. Med. Phys.	Academic Press, N.Y.
5.	Advances in Cell and Molecular Biology	Adv. Cell Mol. Biol.	Academic Press, N.Y.
6.	Advances in Cell Biology	Adv. Cell Biol.	Appleton-Century-Crofts.
7.	Advances in Genetics	Adv. Genet.	Academic Press, N.Y.
8.	Advances in Human Genetics	Adv. Human Genet.	Plenum Publishing Co.
9.	Advances in Morphogenesis	Adv. Morphogen.	Academic Press, N.Y.
10.	Advances in Radiation Biology	Adv. Radiat. Biol.	Academic Press, N.Y.
11.	Agri-Hortique Genetica	—	Plant Breeding Insitutute, Sweden
12.	Agronomy Journal (Formerly, Journal of the American Society of Agronomy)	Agron. J.	American Society of Agronomy, U.S.A.
13.	American Journal of Human Genetics	Am. J. Human Genet.	University of Chicago Press, Chicago
14.	American Journal of Medical Genetics	Am. J. Human Genet.	Alan R Liss Inc.
15.	Animal Breeding Abstracts	—	Commonwealth Agricultural Bureau
16.	Animal Cell Biotechnology	Animal Cell Biotech.	Academic Press, N.Y.
17.	Animal Genetics	Animal Genet.	Blackwell Scientific Publishers Ltd.
18.	Annals of Botany	Ann. Bot.	Academic Press, U.K.
19.	Annals of Human Genetics	Ann. Human Genet.	Cambridge University Press, U.K.
20.	Annual Review of Biochemistry	Ann. Rev. Biochem.	Annual Reviews Inc.
21.	Annual Review of Cell Biology	Ann. Rev. Cell Biol.	Annual Reviews Inc.
22.	Annual Review of Genetics	Ann. Rev. Genet.	Annual Reviews Inc.
23.	Annual Review of Microbiology	Ann. Rev. Microbiol.	Annual Reviews Inc.
24.	Australian Journal of Agricultural Research	Aust. J. Agric. Res.	Commonwealth Scientific and Industrial Research Organisation (CSIRO). Australia.
25.	Australian Journal of Biological Sciences	Aust. J. Biol. Sci.	CSIRO, Australia.
26.	Barley Newsletter	Barley Newslett.	Dr. D.R. Metcalfe, Canada Agriculture Research Station, 25-Dafue Road, Winnipeg 19, Manitoba, Canada
27.	Behaviour Genetics	Behav. Genet.	Plenum Publishing Co.
28.	Biochemical Genetics	Biochem. Genet.	Plenum Publishing Co.
29.	Biochemistry and Cell Biology	Biochem. Cell Biol.	National Research Council of Canada
30.	Biology of Cell	—	Elsevier, Paris

31. Biomedical Ethics Review	Biomed. Ethics Rev.	Humana Press, New Jersey.
32. Biometrics	Biometrics	Biometrices, Suite 401, 1429 Duke Street, Alexandria, Virginia 22314
33. Biotechnology and Bioengineering	Biotech. Bioengg.	John Wiley and Sons, N.Y.
34. Biotechnology and Genetic-Engineering News	Biotech. Genet. Engg. News	Intercept Ltd., England
35. Botanical Review	Bot. Rev.	New York Botanical Gardens, N.Y.
36. Canadian Journal of Genetics and Cytology (Superceded by Genome)	Can. J. Genet. Cytol.	Canadian Society of Genetics and Cytology
37. Canadian Journal of Microbiology	Can. J. Microbiol.	National Research Council of Canada
38. Caryologia	Caryologia	Journal of Cytology, Firenze, Italy
39. Cell	Cell	Cell Press, Cambridge
40. Cellular and Molecular Biology	Cell Mol. Biol.	Pergamon Press
41. Chromosome Today	—	Plenum Publishing Co.
42. Chromosoma	Chromosoma	Springer-Verlag, Berlin, Germany
43. Crop Science	Crop Sci.	Crop Science Society of America, Wisconsin
44. Current Genetics	Curr. Genet.	Springer-Verlag, Berlin, Germany
45. Current Science	Curr. Sci.	Current Science Association, Indian Academy of Science, Bangalore.
46. Cytogenetics (Supereceded by Cytogenetics and Cell Genetics)	—	Cytogenetics and Cell Genetics, S. Karger-AG.
47. Cytologia (Tokyo)	Cytologia	Botanical Society of Japan, Tokyo, Japan.
48. Developmental and Cell Biology	Develop. Cell Biol.	Cambridge University Press.
49. Developmental Biology	Develop. Biol.	Academic Press
50. Developmental Genetics	Develop Genet.	Allan R. Liss. Inc.
51. Egyptian Journal of Genetics and Cytology	Egyptian J. Genet. Cytol.	Egyptian Society of Genetics, Alexandria, Egypt.
52. Euphytica	Euphytica	Kluwer Academic Publishers, Wageningen, The Netherlands
53. Evolution	Evolution	Society of the Study of Evolution, University of Kansas, Kansas
54. Genetica	Genetica	Kluwer Academic Publishers
55. Genetica Agraria	Genet. Agrar.	Institute Sperimantale per la Cereaticoltura, Rome, Italy.
56. Genetic Engineering	Genet. Engg.	Academic Press, N.Y.
57. Genetic Engineering Principles and Methods	—	Plenum Press
58. Genetics	Genetics	Genetics, Baltimore, Maryland
59. Genetik	Genetik	Gustav Fischer Varlag.
60. Genome	Genome	National Research Council of Canada
61. Genomics	Genomics	Academic Press.
62. Hereditas	Hereditas	J.D. Tornquists Bokhandel, A.B. Landskrona, Sweden.
63. Heridity	Heridity	Longman Group Ltd.

S.No.	Name of Journal	Standard abbreviation	Publisher
64.	Indian Journal of Agricultural Sciences	Indian J. Agric. Sci.	Indian Council of Agricultural Research, New Delhi, India.
65.	Indian Journal of Biochemistry and Biophysics	Indian J. Biochem. Biophys.	CSIR, New Delhi, India.
66.	Indian Journal of Experimental Biology	Indian J. Expl. Biol.	CSIR, New Delhi
67.	Indian Journal of Genetics and Plant Breeding	Indian. J. Genet.	Indian Society of Genetics and Plant Breeding, New Delhi, India
68.	Japanese Journal of Breeding	Jap. J. Breed	Japanese Society of Breeding, Tokyo, Japan.
69.	Japanese Journal of Genetics	Jap. J. Genet.	Japan Publications Trading Co.
70.	Japanese Journal of Microbiology	Jap. J. Microbiol.	Japan Bacteriologists and Virologists, Shinamachi, Shinjuku.
71.	Journal of Agricultural Research	J. Agric. Res.	US Deptt. of Agriculture, Washington
72.	Journal of Agricultural Sciences	J. Agric. Sci.	Cambridge University Press.
73.	Journal of Animal Breeding and Genetics	J. Animal Breed. Genet.	Paul Parsey Scientific Publishers, New York
74.	Journal of Cytology and Genetics	J. Cytol. Genet.	Deptt. of Botany, Bangalore University, Bangalore, India.
75.	Journal of Experimental Biology	J. Expt. Biol.	Company of Biologist Ltd.
76.	Journal of Genetics	J. Genet.	Indian Academy of Sciences, Bangalore, India
77.	Journal of Heredity	J. Heredity	Oxford University Press
78.	Journal of Oilseeds Research	J. Oilseeds Res.	Indian Society of Oilseeds Research, DOR, Hyderabad
79.	Maize Genetics Corporation Newsletter	Maize Genet. Corp. Newslett.	Indiana University, Bloomington, Indiana
80.	Molecular and General Genetics	Mol. Gen. Genet.	Springer-Verlag, Berlin, Germany.
81.	Mutation Research	Mutation Res.	Elsevier/North Holland.
82.	Nature	Nature	Nature Publishing Group, England
83.	Nature Biotechnology	Nature Biotech.	Nature Publishing Group, England
84.	New Scientist	—	—
85.	Nucleic Acid Research	Nucleic Acid Res.	Oxford University Press.
86.	Pisum Newsletter	Pisum Newslett.	Weibullsholm Plant Breeding Institute, Landskrona, Sweden.
87.	Plant Breeding	Plant Breed.	Blackwell Berlin, Germany
88.	Plant Breeding Abstracts	Plant Breed. Aastr.	Commonwealth Agricultural Bureau
89.	Plant Breeding Review	Plant Breed. Rev.	—
90.	Plant Cell Reports	Plant Cell Rep.	Springer-Verlag, Berlin, Germany.
91.	Plant Cell, Tissue and Organ Culture	Plant Cell Tissue Organ Cult.	Kluwer Academy Publishers. Dordrecht, The Netherlands
92.	Plant Molecular Biology	Plant Mol. Biol.	Kluwer Academy Publishers.
93.	Plasmid	Plasmid	Academic Press, N.Y.

94.	Protoplasma	Protoplasma	Springer-Verlag.
95.	Radiation Botany	Radiation Bot.	Pergamon Press.
96.	Science	Science	American Association for the Advancement of Science, Washington
97.	Scientific Agriculture	Sci. Agric.	Agricultural Institute of Canada, Ottawa, Ontario, Canada.
98.	Scientific American	Sci. Amer.	New York
99.	Theoretical and Applied Genetics	Theor. Appl. Genet.	Springer-Verlag.
100.	Trends in Biotechnology	Trends Biotech.	Elsevier-North Holland.
101.	Trends in Genetics	Trends Genet.	Elsevier/North Holland.
102.	Wheat Newsletter	Wheat Newlett.	Dr. E.G. Heyne, Agronomy Department Kansas State University, Kansas

REFERENCES

Anonymous. 1993. *Biosafety in Microbiological and Biochemical Laboratories.* 3rd ed. U.S. DHHS. Public Health Survice, Centres for Disease Control and Prevention, Atlanta, Georgia and NIH, Bethesda, Maryland.

Anonymous. *NIH Guidelines for Recombinant DNA Technology Research.* National Institute of Health, USA.

Atman, A. 1999. Plant biotechnology in the 21st century : the challenges a head. Electronic J. Biotech. **2** : 51-55.

Babu, R., Nair, S.K., Prasanna, B.M. and Gupta, H.S. 2004. Integrating marker-assisted selection in crop breeding—perspects and challenges. Curr. Sci. **87** : 607-619.

Baenzinger, S.P., Kleese, R.A. and Barnes, R.F. (eds) 1993. *Intellectual Property Rights : Protection of Plant Materials.* Executive Summary and Work Group Reports. CSSA Publication No. 21, Crop Science Society of America, Wisconsin, Madison.

Baldwin, T.O., Raushel, F.M. and Scott, A.I. (eds). 1991. *Chemical Aspects of Enzyme Biotechnology– Fundamentals.* Plenum Press, New York.

Balkwill, F.R. 1989. *Cytokines in Cancer Therapy.* Oxford University Press, Oxford.

Berlin, J. 1997. Secondary products from plant cell cultures. *In* H. Kleinkauf and H. von Dohren (eds) *Products of Secondary Metabolism.* Vol. 7 of the series of Biotechnology. VCH, Weinheim, Germany.

Bhojwani, S.S. (ed.) 1990. *Plant Tissue Culture : Applications* and *Limitations.* Elsevier, Amsterdam.

Bhojwani, S.S. and Razdan, M.K. 1996. *Plant Tissue Culture : Theory and Practice,* a Revised Edition. Elsevier, Amsterdam.

Brinster, R.L. 1993. Stem cells and transgenic mice in the study of development. Int J. Dev. Biol. **37** : 89–99.

Brown, T.A. 1995. *Gene Cloning, An Introduction.* 3rd edn. Chapman and Hall, London.

Bu'lock, J.D. and Kristiansen, B. (eds). 1987. *Basic Biotechnology.* Academic Press, New York.

Carter, J.E. and Langridge, W.H.R. 2002. Plant-based vaccines for protection against infections and autoimmune diseases. Crit. Rev. Plant Sci. **21** : 93-109.

Casida, Jr. L.E. 1966. *Industrial Microbiology* (Reprinted in 1991). Wiley Eastern Ltd. New Delhi.

Chaplin, M. F. and Bucke, C. 1990. *Enzyme Technology.* Cambridge University Press, Cambridge.

Chawla, H.S. 2002. *Introduction to Plant Biotechnology.* 2nd ed. Oxford & IBH Publ. Co. Pvt. Ltd., New Delhi.

Chen, T.T. and Powers, D.A. 1990. Transgenic fish. Trends Biotechnol. **8** : 209-217.

Chopra, V.L. 1993. Biotechnological tools for conserving biodiversity Indian Farming **43(7)** : 13-16.

Christensen, H. 1989. *Sanitary Land Filling, Process, Technology and Environmental Impact.* Academic Press, London.

Collins, C.R. and Lyne, P.M. 1976. *Microbiological Methods.* 4th ed. Butterworths, London.

Cunningham, S.D. and Ow, D.W. 1996. Promises and prospects of phytoremediation. Plant Physiol. **110** : 715-719.

DBT 1994. *The Indian Recombinant DNA Safety Guidelines and Regulations.* DBT, New Delhi.

Demain, A.L. and Solomon, N.A. (eds.) 1986. *Industrial Microbiology and Biotechnology.* American Society for Microbiology. Washington, D.L.

Forster, C.F. and Wase, D.A.J (eds) *Environmental Biotechnology*. Ellis Horwood.

Franck-Oberaspach, S.L. and Keller, B. 1997. Consequence of classical and biotechnological resistance breeding for food toxicology and allergenicity. Plant Breed. **116** : 1-17.

Freshney, R.I. 1987. *Culture of Animal Cells : A Manual of Basic Techniques*, 2nd ed. Alan R. Liss, New York.

Ganguli, P. 1998. *Gearing up for patents*—The Indian Scenario. Universities Press, Hyderabad.

Ganguli, P. 1998. Patenting innovations : New demands in emerging contexts. Curr. Sci. **75** : 433-439.

Gaskell, Georg and coworker 1999. Worlds Apart ? The reception of genetically modified foods in Europe and the US. Science **285** : 384-387.

Ghosh, P.K. 1997. Transgenic plants and biosafety concerns in India. Curr. Sci. **72** : 172-179.

Gilpin, A. 1994. *Environmental Impact Assesment.* Cambridge University press, Cambridge.

Goding, J.W. 1993. *Monoclonal Antibodies : Principles and Practice.* 3rd ed. Academic Press, New York.

Golub, E.S. 1987. *Immunology, A synthesis.* Sinaver Associates, Inc. Publishers, Sunderland, Massachusetts.

Gregoriadis, G. 1989. *Targetting of Drugs : Implications in Medicines.* Wiley, New York.

Hansen, E. 1977. Production of recombinant antigens in plants for animal and human immunization— a review. Braz. J. Genetics. **20** : 703-711.

Haslberger, Alexander G. 2000. Monitoring and labelling for genetically modified products. Science **287** : 431-432.

Hobson, P.N. and Whately, A.D. 1993. *Anaerobic Digestion, Modern Theory and Practice.* Elsevier, London.

Hogan, B., Constantini, F. and Lacy, E. 1994. *Manipulating the Mouse Embryo : A Laboratory Manual.* Cold Spring Harbour Laboratory, Cold Spring Harbour, New York.

Hubbell, B. J. and Welsh, R. 1998. Transgenic crops : Engineering a more sustainable agriculture ? Agriculture Human values **15** : 43-56.

Jentschke, G. and Godbold, D.L. 2000. Metal toxicity and ectomycorrhizas. Physiol. Plant. **109** : 107-116.

Keayla, B.K. 2000. Protection of Plant Varieties and Farmers Rights Bill, 1999 : Some critical issues. J. Intellectual Property Rights **5** : 251-255.

Kharatyan, S.G. 1978. Microbes as food for humans. Ann. Rev. Microbial. **32** : 301-307.

Klasson, K.T., Ackerson, M.D., Clausen, E.C. and Gaddy, J.L. 1992. Bioconversion of synthesis gas into liquid or gaseous fuels. Enzyme Microb. Technol. **4** : 602-608.

Kumar, S., Kumar, S., Singh, M. and Rai, M. 2003. Marker aided selection for disease resistance in vegetable crops. Veg. Sci. 31(1) : 10-20.

Leach, C.K and Van Dam-Mieras, M.C.E. (eds). 1994. *Biotechnological Innovations in Energy and Environmental Management*. Butter-worth-Heinemann Ltd, Oxford.

Lesser, W. (ed). 1989. *Animal Patents : The Legal Economic and Social Issues.* Stockton Press, New York.

Lynd, L.R., Cushman, J.H., Nichols, R.J. and Wyman, C.E. 1991. Fuel ethanol from cellolosic biomass. Science **251** : 1318-1323.

Malik, V.S. and Saroha, M.K. 1999. Marker gene controversy in transgenic plants. J. Plant Biochem. Biotechnol. **8** : 1-13.

Mann, Charles C. 1997. Reseeding the green revolution. Science **277** : 1038-1043.

Messeguer, J. 2003. Gene flow assessment in transgenic plants. Plant Cell Tiss. Organ Cult. **73** : 201-212.

Meyers, R.A. (ed) 1995. *Molecular Biology and Biotechnology : A Comprehensive Desk Reference.* VCH Publishers, New York.

Mulligan, R.C. 1993. The basic science of gene therapy. Science **260** : 926-932.

National Research Council 2000. *Genetically Modified Pest-protected plants : Science and Regulation.* Washington, D.C. : National Academy of Science.

Old, R.W. and Primrose, S.B. 2001. *Principles of Gene Manipulation, An Introduction to Genetic Engineering.* 2nd ed. Blackwell Scientific Publications, London.

Ortiz, R. 1998. Critical role of plant biotechnology for genetic improvement of food crops : Perspectives for the next millennium. Electronic J. Biotech. **1** : 1-8.

Paarlberg, Robert 2000. Genetically modified crops in developing countries : promise or peril ? Environment **42** : 19-27.

Pental, D. 2003. Transgenics for productive and sustainable agriculture : Some considerations for the development of a policy framework. Curr. Sci. **84** : 413-424.

Pinkert, C.A. 1994. *Transgenic Animal Technology : A Laboratory Handbook.* Academic Press, San Diego, C.A.

Primrose, S.B. and Twyman, R.M. 2003. *Principles of Genome Analysis and Genomics.* Blackwell publishing Co., Oxford.

Purdon, P.W. 1990. *Environment Health.* Academic Press, London.

Rashidi, H.H. and Buchler, L. K. 2000. *Bioinformatics Basics : Applications in Biological Science and Medicine.* CRC Press, London.

Sensen, C.W. (ed) 2002. *Essentials of Genomics and Bioinformatics.* Wiley-VCH Verlay GmbH, Weinheim.

Serageldin, Ismael, 1999. Biotechnology and food security in the 21 century. Science **285** : 387-389.

Sharma, R., Khanna, V.K. and Bisht, B. 2009. Bt-cotton and its current status in India. Indian Farmer Digest 17-20.

Singh, B.D. 2003. *Genetics.* Kalyani Publishers, Ludhiana.

Singh, B.D. 2005. *Plant Breeding : Principles and Methods.* 7th edn. Kalyani Publishers, Ludhiana

Singh, B.D. 2006. *Plant Biotechnology.* Kalyani Publishers, Ludhiana.

Singh, B.D. 2008. *Biotechnology : Expanding Horizons.* Kalyani Publishers, Ludhiana.

Singh, M., Chakraborty, S., Kumar, S. and Kalloo, G. 2000. Genetic engineering for insect resistance in vegetable crops. Veg. Sci. 27 : 105-116.

Stryer, L. 1988. *Biochemistry.* 3rd ed. Freeman, New York.

TeBeest, D.O. 1996. Biological control of weeds with plant pathogens and microbial pesticides. Adv. Agron. **56** : 115.

Thompson, P.B. 1997. *Food Biotechnology in Ethical Perspective.* Blackie Academic & Professional, London.

Thompson, P.B. 2003. Value judgements and risk comparisons. The case of genetically engineered crop : Plant Physiol. **132** : 10-16.

Trevan, M.D. 1980. *Immobilized Enzymes : An Introduction and Applications in Biotechnology* John Wiley & Sons, New York.

Vasil, I.K. and Thorpe, T.A. 1994. *Plant Cell and Tissue Culture.* Kluwer Academic Publishers, Dordrecht, Boston, London.

Willadsen, S.M. 1989. Cloning of ship and cow embryos. Genome **31** : 956-962.

Wilmut, I., Schnieke, A.E., McWhir, J., Kind, A.J. and Campbell, K.H.S. 1997. Viable offspring derived from fatal and adult mammalian cells. Nature **385** : 810-813.

Winnacker, Ernst-L. 1987. *From Genes to Clones, Introduction to Gene Technology* (translated by M. Ibelgaufts). VCH Verlagsggescellschaft mbH, Weinheim (FRG).

Winter, P. and Kahl, G. 1995. Molecular marker technologies for plant improvement. World J. Microbiol. Biotech. **11** : 438-448.

Wright, Richard T. and Nebbel, Bernard J. 2002. *Environmental Science : Towards a Sustainable Future.* Printice-Hall of India Private Limited, New Delhi.

Ye, Xudong and coworkers 2000. Engineering the provitamin A (β-carotene) biosynthetic pathway into (carotenoid-free) endosperm. Science **287** : 303-305.

Zhong, J.J., Yu, J.T. and Yoshida, T. 1995. Recent advances in plant cell cultures in bioreactors. World J. Microbiol. Biotech. **11** : 461-467.

●●●